T0178295

Lecture Notes in Artificial Intelligence 13612

Subseries of Lecture Notes in Computer Science

Series Editors

Randy Goebel
University of Alberta, Edmonton, Canada

Wolfgang Wahlster
DFKI, Berlin, Germany

Zhi-Hua Zhou
Nanjing University, Nanjing, China

Founding Editor

Jörg Siekmann
DFKI and Saarland University, Saarbrücken, Germany

More information about this subseries at https://link.springer.com/bookseries/1244

Obdulia Pichardo Lagunas ·
Juan Martínez-Miranda ·
Bella Martínez Seis (Eds.)

Advances in Computational Intelligence

21st Mexican International Conference
on Artificial Intelligence, MICAI 2022
Monterrey, Mexico, October 24–29, 2022
Proceedings, Part I

Springer

Editors
Obdulia Pichardo Lagunas 🆔
Instituto Politécnico Nacional
Mexico, Mexico

Juan Martínez-Miranda 🆔
Centro de Investigación Científica y de
Educación Superior de Ensenada
Ensenada, Baja California, Mexico

Bella Martínez Seis 🆔
Instituto Politécnico Nacional
Mexico, Mexico

ISSN 0302-9743 ISSN 1611-3349 (electronic)
Lecture Notes in Artificial Intelligence
ISBN 978-3-031-19492-4 ISBN 978-3-031-19493-1 (eBook)
https://doi.org/10.1007/978-3-031-19493-1

LNCS Sublibrary: SL7 – Artificial Intelligence

This Springer imprint is published by the registered company Springer Nature Switzerland AG
The registered company address is: Gewerbestrasse 11, 6330 Cham, Switzerland

Preface

The Mexican International Conference on Artificial Intelligence (MICAI) is a yearly international conference series that has been organized by the Mexican Society for Artificial Intelligence (SMIA) since 2000. MICAI is a major international artificial intelligence (AI) forum and the main event in the academic life of the country's growing AI community.

MICAI conferences publish high-quality papers in all areas of AI and its applications. The proceedings of the previous MICAI events have been published by Springer in its Lecture Notes in Artificial Intelligence (LNAI) series (volumes 1793, 2313, 2972, 3789, 4293, 4827, 5317, 5845, 6437, 6438, 7094, 7095, 7629, 7630, 8265, 8266, 8856, 8857, 9413, 9414, 10061, 10062, 10632, 10633, 11288, 11289, 11835, 12468, 12469, 13067, and 13068). Since its foundation in 2000, the conference has both grown in popularity and improved in quality.

The proceedings of MICAI 2022 are published in two volumes. The first volume, Advances in Computational Intelligence (Part I), contains 34 papers structured into three sections:

- Machine and Deep Learning
- Image Processing and Pattern Recognition
- Evolutionary and Metaheuristic Algorithms

The second volume, Advances in Computational Intelligence (Part II), contains 29 papers structured into two sections:

- Natural Language Processing
- Intelligent Applications and Robotics

The two-volume set will be of interest to researchers in all fields of artificial intelligence, students specializing in related topics, and the general public interested in recent developments in AI.

The conference received for evaluation 137 submissions from authors in 20 countries: Belgium, Bolivia, Brazil, Colombia, Cuba, Ecuador, France, Ireland, Japan, Kazakhstan, Mexico, Morocco, The Netherlands, Pakistan, Peru, Russia, Serbia, Spain, the UK and the USA. From these submissions, 63 papers were selected for publication in these two volumes after a peer-reviewing process carried out by the international Program Committee, with each paper receiving a minimum of 2 reviews. The acceptance rate was 46%.

The international Program Committee consisted of 112 experts from 14 countries: Brazil, China, Colombia, France, Iran, Ireland, Japan, Kazakhstan, Malaysia, Mexico, Pakistan, Portugal, Russia, and the UK.

Three workshops were held jointly with the conference:

- WILE 2022: 15th Workshop on Intelligent Learning Environments
- HIS 2022: 15th Workshop of Hybrid Intelligent Systems
- CIAPP 2022: 4th Workshop on New Trends in Computational Intelligence and Applications

The authors of the following papers included in this volume received the Best Paper Awards based on the papers' overall quality, significance, and originality of the reported results:

- "Diachronic Neural Network Predictor of Word Animacy" by Vladimir Bochkarev, Andrey Achkeev, Anna Shevlyakova, and Stanislav Khristoforov, Russia
- "A Novel Hybrid Endoscopic Dataset for Evaluating Machine Learning-based Photometric Image Enhancement Models" by Carlos Axel García Vega, Ricardo Abel Espinosa Loera, Gilberto Ochoa Ruiz, Thomas Bazin, Luis Eduardo Falcón Morales, Dominique Lamarque, and Christian Daul, Mexico/France
- "Towards an interpretable model for automatic classification of endoscopy images" by Rogelio García-Aguirre, Luis Torres-Treviño, Eva María Navarro-López, and José Alberto González-González, Mexico/UK

We want to thank all the people involved in the organization of this conference: the authors of the papers published in these two volumes – it is their research work that gives value to the proceedings, the reviewers for their great effort spent on reviewing the submissions, the Track Chairs for their hard work, and the Program and Organizing Committee members.

We are grateful to all the executive members at Tecnológico de Monterrey: David Garza Salazar, President; Juan Pablo Murra Lascurain, Rector General; Guillermo Torre Amione, Vice President of Research; Neil Hernández Gress, Director of Research; Mario Adrián Flores Castro, Vice President of North Region; Manuel Zertuche Guerra, Dean of Engineering; and Luis Ricardo Salgado Garza, Director of the Computer Science Department, for the invaluable support to MICAI and providing the infrastructure for the keynote talks, tutorials, and workshops.

We are also grateful to the personnel of Tecnológico de Monterrey for their warm hospitality and hard work, as well as for their active participation in the organization of this conference. We greatly appreciate the generous sponsorship provided by the Monterrey government via the Tourism Office.

We deeply grateful to the conference staff and to all members of the Local Organizing Committee headed by José Carlos Ortiz Bayliss. We gratefully acknowledge the support received from the following project: FI-NEXT, Europe – CONACYT Project 274451.

The entire submission, reviewing, and selection process, as well as preparation of the proceedings, was supported by the EasyChair system (www.easychair.org). Last but not least, we are grateful to Springer for their patience and help in the preparation of these volumes.

October 2022

Obdulia Pichardo Lagunas
Juan Martínez-Miranda
Bella Martínez Seis

Conference Organization

MICAI 2022 was organized by the Mexican Society for Artificial Intelligence (SMIA, Sociedad Mexicana de Inteligencia Artificial) in collaboration with the Tecnológico de Monterrey.

The MICAI series website is www.MICAI.org. The website of the Mexican Society for Artificial Intelligence, SMIA, is www.SMIA.mx. Contact options and additional information can be found on these websites.

Conference Committee

General Chair

Hiram Calvo — Instituto Politécnico Nacional, Mexico

Program Chairs

Obdulia Pichardo Lagunas — Instituto Politécnico Nacional, Mexico

Juan Martínez-Miranda — Centro de Investigación Cienífica y de Educación Superior de Ensenada, Mexico

Bella Martínez Seis — Instituto Politécnico Nacional, Mexico

Workshop Chair

Noé Alejandro Castro-Sánchez — Centro Nacional de Investigación y Desarrollo Tecnológico, Mexico

Tutorials Chair

Roberto Antonio Vázquez Espinoza de los Monteros — Universidad La Salle, Mexico

Doctoral Consortium Chairs

Miguel González Mendoza — Tecnológico de Monterrey, Mexico

Francisco Javier Cantú Ortiz — Tecnológico de Monterrey, Mexico

Keynote Talks Chair

Sabino Miranda-Jiménez — Centro de Investigación e Innovación en Tecnologías de la Información y Comunicación, Mexico

Publication Chair

Hiram Ponce   Universidad Panamericana, Mexico

Financial Chairs

Hiram Calvo   Instituto Politécnico Nacional, Mexico
Lourdes Martínez-Villaseñor   Universidad Panamericana, Mexico

Grant Chair

Félix A. Castro Espinoza   Universidad Autónoma del Estado de Hidalgo,
                                     Mexico

Local Organizing Committee

José Carlos Ortiz Bayliss   Tecnológico de Monterrey, Mexico
Luis Ricardo Salgado Garza   Tecnológico de Monterrey, Mexico
Héctor Gibrán Ceballos Cancino   Tecnológico de Monterrey, Mexico
Ivan Mauricio Amaya Contreras   Tecnológico de Monterrey, Mexico
Neil Hernández Gress   Tecnológico de Monterrey, Mexico
Joanna Alvarado Uribe   Tecnológico de Monterrey, Mexico
Luis Alberto Muñoz Ubando   Tecnológico de Monterrey, Mexico
Miguel González Mendoza   Tecnológico de Monterrey, Mexico
Sergio Camacho León   Tecnológico de Monterrey, Mexico
Laura Hervert Escobar   Tecnológico de Monterrey, Mexico
Gilberto Ochoa Ruiz   Tecnológico de Monterrey, Mexico
Francisco Javier Cantú Ortiz   Tecnológico de Monterrey, Mexico

Track Chairs

Natural Language Processing

Grigori Sidorov   Instituto Politécnico Nacional, Mexico
Sabino Miranda-Jiménez   Centro de Investigación e Innovación en
                                     Tecnologías de la Información y
                                     Comunicación, Mexico

Machine Learning

Alexander Gelbukh   Instituto Politécnico Nacional, Mexico
Navonil Majumder   Singapore University of Technology and Design,
                                     Singapore

Deep Learning

Hiram Ponce   Universidad Panamericana, Mexico

Evolutionary and Metaheuristic Algorithms

Roberto Antonio Vázquez   Universidad La Salle, Mexico
  Espinoza de los Monteros

Soft Computing

Miguel González Mendoza   Tecnológico de Monterrey, Mexico
Félix A. Castro Espinoza   Universidad Autónoma del Estado de Hidalgo,
                                     Mexico

Image Processing and Pattern Recognition

Lourdes Martínez-Villaseñor   Universidad Panamericana, Mexico

Robotics

Gilberto Ochoa Ruiz   Tecnológico de Monterrey, Mexico

Intelligent Applications and Social Network Analysis

Iris Iddaly Méndez Gurrola   Universidad Autónoma de Ciudad Juárez, Mexico

Other Artificial Intelligence Approaches

Nestor Velasco Bermeo   University College Dublin, Ireland
Gustavo Arroyo Figueroa   Instituto Nacional de Electricidad y Energías
                                     Limpias, Mexico
David Eduardo Pinto Avendaño   Benemérita Universidad Autónoma de Puebla,
                                     Mexico

Program Committee

Iskander Akhmetov   Institute of Information and Computational
                                     Technologies, Kazakhstan
José David Alanís Urquieta   Universidad Tecnológica de Puebla, Mexico
Giner Alor Hernandez   Instituto Tecnologico de Orizaba, Mexico
Joanna Alvarado-Uribe   Tecnológico de Monterrey, Mexico
Miguel Alvarez Carmona   Centro de Investigación Cienífica y de Educación
                                     Superior de Ensenada, Mexico
Maaz Amjad   Instituto Politécnico Nacional, Mexico
Gustavo Arroyo Figueroa   Instituto Nacional de Electricidad y Energías
                                     Limpias, Mexico

Ignacio Arroyo-Fernández	Universidad Tecnológica de la Mixteca, Mexico
Ramon Barraza	Universidad Autonoma de Ciudad Juarez, Mexico
Ari Yair Barrera-Animas	Tecnológico de Monterrey, Mexico
Ildar Batyrshin	Instituto Politecnico Nacional, Mexico
Gemma Bel-Enguix	Universidad Nacional Autónoma de México, Mexico
Vadim Borisov	National Research University, Russia
Monica Borunda	Instituto Nacional de Electricidad y Energías Limpias, Mexico
Alexander Bozhenyuk	Southern Federal University, Russia
Ramon F. Brena	Tecnológico de Monterrey, Mexico
Davide Buscaldi	Université Paris 13, France
Sabur Butt	Instituto Politécnico Nacional, Mexico
Ruben Carino-Escobar	Instituto Nacional de Rehabilitación, Mexico
Heydy Castillejos	Universidad Autónoma del Estado de Hidalgo, Mexico
Felix Castro Espinoza	Universidad Autónoma del Estado de Hidalgo, Mexico
Hector Ceballos	Tecnológico de Monterrey, Mexico
Jaime Cerda Jacobo	Universidad Michoacana de San Nicolás de Hidalgo, Mexico
Haruna Chiroma	Federal College of Education (Technical) Gombe, Malaysia
Elisabetta Crescio	Tecnológico de Monterrey, Mexico
Laura Cruz	Instituto Tecnológico de Ciudad Madero, Mexico
Nareli Cruz Cortés	Instituto Politécnico Nacional, Mexico
Jorge De La Calleja	Universidad Politécnica de Puebla, Mexico
Omar Arturo Domínguez-Ramírez	Universidad Autónoma del Estado de Hidalgo, Mexico
Andrés Espinal	Universidad de Guanajuato, Mexico
Karina Figueroa	Universidad Michoacana de San Nicolás de Hidalgo, Mexico
Denis Filatov	Sceptica Scientific Ltd, UK
Dora-Luz Flores	Universidad Autónoma de Baja California, Mexico
Sofia N. Galicia-Haro	Universidad Nacional Autónoma de México, Mexico
Vicente Garcia	Universidad Autónoma de Ciudad Juárez, Mexico
Claudia Gomez	Instituto Tecnológico de Ciudad Madero, Mexico
Pedro Pablo Gonzalez	Universidad Autónoma Metropolitana, Mexico
Miguel Gonzalez-Mendoza	Tecnológico de Monterrey, Mexico
Gabriel Gonzalez-Serna	Centro Nacional de Investigación y Desarrollo Tecnológico, Mexico

Alicia Morales-Reyes	Instituto Nacional de Astrofísica, Óptica y Electrónica, Mexico
Masaki Murata	Tottori University, Japan
Nikita Murzintcev	Institute of Geographical Sciences and Natural Resources Research, China
Antonio Neme	Universidad Nacional Autónoma de Mexico, Mexico
César Núñez	Instituto Politécnico Nacional, Mexico
Gilberto Ochoa-Ruiz	Tecnológico de Monterrey, Mexico
C. Alberto Ochoa-Zezatti	Universidad Autónoma de Ciudad Juárez, Mexico
Juan Carlos Olivares Rojas	Instituto Tecnológico de Morelia, Mexico
José Luis Oliveira	University of Aveiro, Portugal
Jesús Patricio Ordaz Oliver	Universidad Autónoma del Estado de Hidalgo, Mexico
José Carlos Ortiz-Bayliss	Tecnológico de Monterrey, Mexico
Ismael Osuna-Galán	Universidad Politécnica de Chiapas, Mexico
Abigail Pallares-Calvo	Instituto Politécnico Nacional, Mexico
Obed Pérez Cortés	Universidad Autónoma del Estado de Hidalgo, Mexico
Humberto Pérez-Espinosa	Centro de Investigación Científica y de Educación Superior de Ensenada, Mexico
Obdulia Pichardo-Lagunas	Instituto Politécnico Nacional, Mexico
Garibaldi Pineda García	University of Sussex, UK
David Pinto	Benemérita Universidad Autónoma de Puebla, Mexico
Hiram Ponce Espinosa	Universidad Panamericana, Mexico
José Federico Ramírez Cruz	Instituto Tecnológico de Apizaco, Mexico
Tania Aglaé Ramírez Del Real	Universidad Politécnica de Aguascalientes, Mexico
Jorge Reyes	Universidad Autónoma de Yucatán, Mexico
Elva Lilia Reynoso Jardón	Universidad Autónoma de Ciudad Juárez, Mexico
Katya Rodriguez-Vazquez	Universidad Nacional Autónoma de México, Mexico
Alberto Rosales	Instituto Politécnico Nacional, Mexico
Horacio Rostro Gonzalez	Universidad de Guanajuato, Mexico
Angel Sanchez	Universidad de Veracruz, Mexico
Luis Humberto Sánchez Medel	Instituto Tecnológico de Orizaba, Mexico
Eddy Sánchez-Delacruz	Instituto Tecnológico Superior de Misantla, Mexico
Alejandro Santiago	Instituto Politécnico Nacional, Mexico
Grigori Sidorov	Instituto Politécnico Nacional, Mexico
Juan Humberto Sossa Azuela	Instituto Politécnico Nacional, Mexico
Ramon Soto de la Cruz	Universidad de Sonora, Mexico

Antonio Tamayo	Universidad de Antioquia, Colombia
Eric S. Tellez	Centro de Investigación e Innovación en Tecnologías de la Información y Comunicación, Mexico
David Tinoco Varela	Universidad Nacional Autónoma de México, Mexico
Nasim Tohidi	K. N. Toosi University of Technology, Iran
Aurora Torres	Universidad Autónoma de Aguascalientes, Mexico
Diego Uribe	Instituto Tecnológico de la Laguna, Mexico
Genoveva Vargas Solar	Laboratoire d'Informatique en Image et Systèmes d'Information, France
Roberto Antonio Vázquez Espinoza	Universidad Lasalle, Mexico
Nestor Velasco Bermeo	University College Dublin, Ireland
Luis M. Vilches-Blázquez	Instituto Politécnico Nacional, Mexico
Juan Villegas-Cortez	Universidad Autónoma Metropolitana, Mexico
Yenny Villuendas-Rey	Instituto Politécnico Nacional, Mexico
Saúl Zapotecas Martínez	Instituto Nacional de Astrofísica, Óptica y Electrónica, Mexico

Additional Reviewers

Rogelio Florencia
Daniel Flores Araiza
Ivan Reyes-Amezcua
Mirna Patricia Ponce Flores
J. David Terán-Villanueva
Alejandro Humberto Garcia Ruiz
Francisco López Ramos
Nelson Rangel-Valdez
Patricia Sánchez

Ricardo Espinosa Loera
Francisco Lopez-Tiro
Marco Sotelo-Figueroa
Francisco López-Orozco
Jesus German Ortiz Barajas
Carlos Aguilar
Juan Vásquez
Valery Solovyev

Contents – Part I

Evolutionary and Metaheuristic Algorithms

Contents – Part II

Intelligent Applications and Robotics

Machine and Deep Learning

Skipped Nonsynaptic Backpropagation for Interval-valued Long-term Cognitive Networks

Mabel Frias[1,5]([✉]), Gonzalo Nápoles[2], Yaima Filiberto[3], Rafael Bello[4], and Koen Vanhoof[1]

[1] Faculty of Business Economics, Universiteit Hasselt, Hasselt, Belgium
{mabel.friasdominguez,koen.vanhoof}@uhasselt.be
[2] Tilburg University, Tilburg, The Netherlands
g.r.napoles@uvt.nl
[3] AMV Solutions, Vigo, Spain
yaima.filiberto@amvsoluciones.com
[4] Department of Computer Science, Universidad Central de las Villas, Santa Clara, Cuba
rbellop@uclv.edu.cu
[5] Department of Computer Science, Universidad de Camaguey, Camaguey, Cuba
mabel.frias@reduc.edu.cu

Abstract. The recently published Interval-valued Long-term Cognitive Networks have shown promising results when reasoning under uncertainty conditions. In these recurrent neural networks, the interval weights are learned using a nonsynaptic backpropagation learning algorithm. Similar to traditional propagation-based algorithms, this variant might suffer from vanishing/exploding gradient issues. This paper proposes three skipped learning variants that do not use the backpropagation process to deliver the error signal to intermediate abstract layers (iterations in the recurrent neural network). The numerical simulations using 35 synthetic datasets confirm that the skipped variants work as well as the nonsynaptic backpropagation algorithm.

Keywords: Interval-valued Long-term Cognitive Networks · Interval sets · Nonsynaptic learning

1 Introduction

In the last years, several neural reasoning models based on Fuzzy Cognitive Maps (FCMs) [8] have been proposed. The need for models having improved approximation capabilities was concluded in the theoretical analysis presented by Concepción et al. [3]. Short-Term Cognitive Networks (STCNs) [14] is one of these models that attained superior predictive power by removing the constraint that weights should be confined to $[-1, 1]$ interval.

O. Pichardo Lagunas et al. (Eds.): MICAI 2022, LNAI 13612, pp. 3–14, 2022.
https://doi.org/10.1007/978-3-031-19493-1_1

Despite the improvements compared with traditional FCM models, STCNs often struggle to establish long-term dependencies. Long-term Cognitive Networks (LTCNs) [13] tried to overcome this issue by using a long-term reasoning mechanism. In principle, LTCNs allow learning longer dependencies with the aid of a nonsynaptic backpropagation learning algorithm.

The low simulation errors of LTCNs and their ability to retain the network interpretability have motivated the inclusion of mechanisms to deal with the uncertainty that may be present in the knowledge provided by human experts. The Long-term Grey Cognitive Networks (LTGCNs) [12] emerged as a partial solution to this issue. Even when the domain experts can express the weights using interval grey numbers in this model, the reasoning and learning processes are performed after whitening the interval grey numbers. In other words, neither the reasoning nor the learning steps fully handle the uncertainty. In contrast, the Interval-valued Long-term Cognitive Networks (IVLTCNs) [5] deal with complex systems involving uncertainty through a structure expressing the activation values and weights as interval grey numbers. The model neither imposes restrictions on the weights nor performs a whitenization process. A nonsynaptic backpropagation (IV-NSBP) is used to adjust the learnable parameters considering the uncertainty in the network without affecting the model's performance and retaining the knowledge provided by experts.

Unfortunately, the IV-NSBP method might suffer from vanishing/exploding gradient issues, a difficult task when training recurrent neural networks [2]. This paper presents three skipped IV-NSBP learning algorithms that attempt to circumvent these issues. The skipped variants modify the IV-NSBP algorithm by using different weights during the forward pass and backward pass in the training phase. Moreover, only two parameters associated with the generalized sigmoid transfer function are adjusted. It should be stated that our nonsynaptic versions are based on the algorithms presented in [11]. The simulation results show that by performing a skipping operation, we can bring the error signal directly from the output layer to any intermediate iteration (hidden abstract layer) without the need for the backpropagation process.

The outline of this paper is as follows. Section 2 briefly describes the IVLTCN model and the original IV-NSBP learning algorithm, while Sect. 3 introduces the skipped IV-NSBP variants proposed in this paper. In Sect. 4, the numerical simulations using synthetic datasets and the ensuing discussion of results are presented. Section 5 concludes the paper.

2   Interval-valued Long-term Cognitive Networks

The recently proposed IVLTCN model [5] is a recurrent neural network to deal with uncertainty evidenced with interval grey numbers. In this knowledge-based reasoning system, weights and the neuron's activation values are expressed as interval-valued grey numbers. Each problem variable is mapped into a grey neural concept, thus explicit hidden neurons are not allowed. The iterative reasoning process of the IVLTCN model is formalized below:

$$a_i^{\pm(t+1)}(k) = f_i^{\pm(t+1)}\left(\sum_{j=1}^{M} w_{ji}^{\pm} a_j^{\pm(t)}(k)\right) \tag{1}$$

where

$$f_i^{\pm(t)}(x) = L_i^{\pm} + \frac{U_i^{\pm} - L_i^{\pm}}{1 + e^{-\lambda_i^{\pm(t)}(x - h_i^{\pm(t)})}} \tag{2}$$

stands for the grey transfer function associated with the i-th neuron in the t-th iteration, M is the number of grey neurons, and $a_i^{\pm(t+1)}(k)$ represents the grey activation value for a given initial condition k. Moreover, $w_{ji}^{\pm}$ is the grey weight connecting two neurons, while $\lambda_i^{\pm(t)}$ and $h_i^{\pm(t)}$ are the parameters of the grey sigmoid function. The $\lambda_i^{\pm(t)}$ parameter is the function slope and $h_i^{\pm(t)}$ stand for the sigmoid offset. These parameters will be adjusted during the nonsynaptic learning phase, similar to a standard backpropagation algorithm [16] [15].

The parameters $L_i^{\pm}$ and $U_i^{\pm}$ are two white numbers that denote the lower and upper limits for the activation value of each neuron. These parameters are not optimized during the learning phase. Instead, they should be configured by experts taking into account the problem domain.

The IVLTCN model takes from LTCNs model [13] the structure and learning algorithm, and from the Grey System Theory (GST) [4] the grey arithmetic operations to perform the neural reasoning process. According to GST, an interval grey number can be denoted as $a^{\pm} \in [a^-, a^+] \mid a^- \leqslant a^+$ where (a^+) is the upper limit and (a^-) is the lower limit [17]. If the grey number $a^{\pm}$ only has an upper limit, then it is denoted by $a^{\pm} \in (-\infty, a^+]$. If the grey number only has a lower limit, then it is denoted by $a^{\pm} \in [a^-, +\infty)$. If both limits are unknown, then $a^{\pm} \in (-\infty, +\infty)$ is a black number. Finally, it is said that the number is white if both limits have the same value [10], that is to say, $a^- = a^+$.

Let $a^{\pm}$ and $b^{\pm}$ be two interval grey numbers. The arithmetic operations for these numbers are formalized as follows:

$$a^{\pm} + b^{\pm} \in [a^- + b^-, a^+ + b^+] \tag{3}$$

$$a^{\pm} - b^{\pm} \in [a^- - b^+, a^+ - b^-] \tag{4}$$

$$a^{\pm} \times b^{\pm} \in [\min\{a^- \times b^-, a^+ \times b^+, a^- \times b^+, a^+ \times b^-\}, \\ \max\{a^- \times b^-, a^+ \times b^+, a^- \times b^+, a^+ \times b^-\}] \tag{5}$$

$$\frac{a^{\pm}}{b^{\pm}} \in [\min\{\frac{a^-}{b^-}, \frac{a^+}{b^+}, \frac{a^-}{b^+}, \frac{a^+}{b^-}\}, \max\{\frac{a^-}{b^-}, \frac{a^+}{b^+}, \frac{a^-}{b^+}, \frac{a^+}{b^-}\}] \\ \mid b^-, b^+ \neq 0 \tag{6}$$

$$(a^{\pm})^x \in [\min\{(a^-)^x, (a^+)^x\}, \max\{(a^-)^x, (a^+)^x\}] \\ = [(a^-)^x, (a^+)^x]. \tag{7}$$

Next, it will be describe the IV-NSBP learning algorithm [5], which is devoted to fine-tuning $\lambda_i^{\pm(t)}$ and $h_i^{\pm(t)}$ in Eq. (2). The first step in that regard is to formalize the error function as follows:

$$\mathcal{E}^\pm = \sum_{i=1}^{M} \frac{(y_i^\pm(k) - a_i^{\pm(t)})^2}{2} \tag{8}$$

where $y_i^\pm(k)$ is the value of the i-th variable for the k-th instance.

After computing $\partial\mathcal{E}^\pm/\partial a_i^{\pm(t)}(k)$ (see details in [5]), the partial derivative of the global error with respect to the target parameters can be calculated. Let $\Theta_i^{\pm(t)} = \{\lambda_i^{\pm(t)}, h_i^{\pm(t)}\}$ denote the set of grey parameters to be adjusted by the i-th neuron in the t-th iteration. The partial derivative of the global error with respect to the target parameters are computed as follows:

$$\frac{\partial\mathcal{E}^\pm}{\partial\theta_i^{\pm(t)} \in \Theta_i^{\pm(t)}} = \frac{\partial\mathcal{E}^\pm}{\partial a_i^{\pm(t)}(k)} \times \frac{\partial a_i^{\pm(t)}(k)}{\partial\theta_i^{\pm(t)} \in \Theta_i^{\pm(t)}}, \tag{9}$$

such that

$$\frac{\partial a_i^{\pm(t)}}{\partial h_i^{\pm(t)}} = \frac{-(U_i^\pm - L_i^\pm)\Gamma_i^{\pm(t)}\lambda_i^{\pm(t)}}{(1 + \Gamma_j^{\pm(t)})^2} \tag{10}$$

$$\frac{\partial a_i^{\pm(t)}}{\partial\lambda_i^{\pm(t)}} = \frac{(U_i^\pm - L_i^\pm)\Gamma_i^{\pm(t)}(\bar{a}_i^{\pm(t)} - h_i^{\pm(t)})}{(1 + \Gamma_j^{\pm(t)})^2}. \tag{11}$$

Equation (12) update the sigmoid function parameters associated to each neural processing entity in the t-th abstract layer. The momentum is represented by β and η is the learning rates,

$$\nabla\theta_i^{\pm(t)} \in \Theta_i^{\pm(t)} = \beta\left(\nabla\theta_i^{\pm(t)} \in \Theta_i^{\pm(t)}\right) - \eta \times \frac{\partial\mathcal{E}^\pm}{\partial\theta_i^{\pm(t)} \in \Theta_i^{\pm(t)}}. \tag{12}$$

The parameters' update was done using grey arithmetic operations instead of the standard vector-wise operations. This is required because the gradient vector is composed of grey numbers.

3   Skipped Nonsynaptic Backpropagation

In this section, we modify three versions of the nonsynaptic learning variants: Random Nonsynaptic Backpropagation (R-NSBP), Skipped Nonsynaptic Backpropagation (S-NSBP), and Random-Skipped Nonsynaptic Backpropagation (RS-NSBP) published in [11]. Those variants emerged because the NSBP backpropagation learning algorithm could fail when dealing with very long dependencies since the error signal reaching the first abstract layers might be weak [11]. Therefore, their authors proposed three strategies to modify the NSBP's backward step and prevent the network from stopping its learning. The nonsynaptic learning variants are based on the idea that employing the same weights during the forward and backward passes is not necessary to train a recurrent neural network. The results reported in [9] and [1] support this idea. The difference among the variants is given by the approach used to compute the partial derivatives of the error for the activation values of the abstract hidden neurons. This research proposed three versions that bring the advantage of being prepared to work in uncertain environments. Besides, the inference process in these new learning algorithms is done without a whitenization process in any way, and the learnable parameters to be optimized are just two; $\lambda_i^{\pm(t)}$ and $h_i^{\pm(t)}$.

3.1 Interval-value Random NSBP Algorithm, IVR-NSBP

Our first version is based on the Random NSBP (R-NSBP) introduced at [11] where the weight matrix in the backward pass is replaced with a matrix comprised of normally distributed random numbers. Equations (13) and (14) shows how to compute partial derivative of the total error with respect to the neuron's activation value in the current iteration, for the R-NSBP and the method proposed in this subsection IVR-NSBP;

$$\frac{\partial \mathcal{E}}{\partial a_i^{(t)}} = \sum_{j=1}^{M} \frac{\partial \mathcal{E}}{\partial a_j^{(t+1)}} \times \frac{\partial a_j^{(t+1)}}{\partial \bar{a}_j^{(t+1)}} \times \bar{w}_{ij}. \tag{13}$$

$$\frac{\partial \mathcal{E}^{\pm}}{\partial a_i^{\pm(t)}} = \sum_{j=1}^{M} \frac{\partial \mathcal{E}^{\pm}}{\partial a_j^{\pm(t+1)}} \times \frac{\partial a_j^{\pm(t+1)}}{\partial \bar{a}_j^{\pm(t+1)}} \times \bar{w}_{ij}^{\pm}. \tag{14}$$

where $\bar{w}_{ij}^{\pm}$ is the Gaussian random number generated with the following probability distribution function:

$$f(x|\mu_{ij}^{\pm}, \sigma^2) = \frac{1}{\sqrt{2\pi\sigma^2}} * e^{-\frac{(x-\mu_{ij}^{\pm})^2}{2\sigma^2}} \tag{15}$$

where $\mu_{ij}^{\pm} = \bar{w}_{ij}^{\pm}$ denotes the mean and $\sigma^2 = 0.2$ represents the variance. The random weights can be forced to share the same sign as the weights defined during the network construction step. On the other hand, weights in the forward pass and the nonsynaptic parameters are employed as indicated in the original NSBP learning algorithm.

3.2 Interval-value Skipped NSBP Algorithm, IVS-NSBP

The second proposal is a method named Interval-value Skipped NSBP algorithm (IVS-NSBP), as its predecessor S-NSBP [11] uses deep learning channel to deliver the error signal directly to the current abstract hidden layer. The partial derivative of the global error concerning the neuron's output in the contemporary abstract layer can be computed by the Eq. (16) in the method S-NSBP and by Eq. (17) in IVS-NSBP.

$$\frac{\partial \mathcal{E}}{\partial a_i^{(t)}} = \sum_{j=1}^{M} -(y_j(k) - a_j^{(T)}) \times w_{ij}. \tag{16}$$

$$\frac{\partial \mathcal{E}^{\pm}}{\partial a_i^{\pm(t)}} = \sum_{j=1}^{M} -(y_j^{\pm}(k) - a_j^{\pm(T)}) \times w_{ij}^{\pm}. \qquad (17)$$

One of the points in favor of this variant is that the skipping operations reduce the algorithm's computational border since the effort of computing the error signal does not escalate with the number of IVLTCN iterations.

3.3 Interval-value Random-Skipped NSBP Algorithm, IVRS-NSBP

The Interval-value Random-Skipped NSBP algorithm (IVRS-NSBP) is a method that allows skipping operations while use random Gaussian numbers with mean $\mu_{ij}^{\pm} = w_{ij}^{\pm}$ and $\sigma^2 = 0.2$. The IVRS-NSBP is based on the RS-NSBP [11]. A slight variance was adopted to avoid weight in the deep learning channel being too different from those used during the forward pass. This idea is formalizes by the Eq. (18) in the method RS-NSBP and Eq. (19) for IVRS-NSBP.

$$\frac{\partial \mathcal{E}}{\partial a_i^{(t)}} = \sum_{j=1}^{M} -(y_j(k) - a_j^{(T)}) \times \bar{w}_{ij} \qquad (18)$$

$$\frac{\partial \mathcal{E}^{\pm}}{\partial a_i^{\pm(t)}} = \sum_{j=1}^{M} -(y_j^{\pm}(k) - a_j^{\pm(T)}) \times \bar{w}_{ij}^{\pm} \qquad (19)$$

In essence, the three variants are different from the ones proposed at [11] because now the map can handle a higher level of uncertainty due to perform of the inference process being in a range of grey numbers and without any whitenization process. Also, just two learnable parameters associated with the generalized sigmoid transfer function are adjusted.

4 Numerical Simulations

This section presents an experimental study to evaluate the performance of the proposed nonsynaptic learning algorithms (IVR-NSBP, IVS-NSBP and IVRS-NSBP). To the simulations, it was used 35 synthetic datasets taken from the UCI machine learning repository[1] with a number of attributes that ranges from 3 to 22, and the number of instances goes from 106 to 625. The datasets have been modified as indicated [11] and [5] to simulate uncertainty environments.

Equation (20) shows how to estimate white weights from the numeric features in a dataset comprised of K instances,

$$w_{ji} = \frac{K \sum_k x_i(k)x_j(k) - \sum_k x_i(k) \sum_k x_j(k)}{K(\sum_k x_j(k)^2) - (\sum_k x_j(k))^2} \qquad (20)$$

where $x_i(k)$ is the white value of the i-th variable for the k-th instance. As a second step, it can be transform them into grey weights such that $w_{ji}^{\pm} = [w_{ji} - \xi, w_{ji} + \xi]$, where $\xi \leq 0$ is the uncertainty threshold.

---

[1] http://www.ics.uci.edu/~mlearn/MLRepository.html.

4.1   Effect of Uncertainty Level on the Internal Size

The first experiment analyzes the relationship between the uncertainty added to the data and the size of the grey intervals produced by grey neurons (for all neurons in each iteration steps). The following equation is used to compute the average size of the prediction intervals in an IVLTCN model,

$$S(\mathcal{N}(k)) = \frac{1}{TM} \sum_{t=1}^{T} \sum_{i=1}^{M} |a_i^{+(t)}(k) - a_i^{-(t)}(k)| \tag{21}$$

where $\mathcal{N}(k)$ represent the IVLTCN model using the k-th initial activation vector (intance), $a_i^{-(t)}(k)$ and $a_i^{+(t)}(k)$ denote the rigtht and left activation value of the i-th neuron in the current iteration, respectively.

Figure 1 shows the average interval size values across the 35 grey datasets. As we can observe in these simulations, there is a proportional relationship between the size of intervals and the amount of uncertainty (defined by the threshold parameter used to build the grey weights).

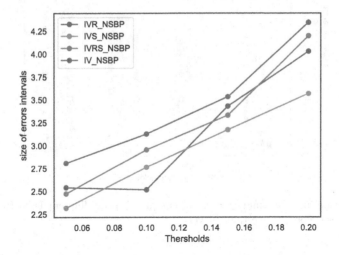

Fig. 1. Average interval size for different uncertainty levels.

Another interesting observation is that the intervals determined by the proposed nonsynaptic learning variants are smaller than those obtained by the original IV-NSBP algorithm. However, this does not imply that these learning algorithms produce more accurate models.

4.2   Assessing the Prediction Accuracy

In this subsection, it is compare the IV-NSBP learning algorithms in terms of the Grey Mean Squared Error ($MSE^{\pm}$). This performance metric is defined in terms of grey numbers and formalized as follows:

$$MSE^{\pm}(X,Y) = \frac{1}{MK} \sum_{x \in X, y \in Y} \sum_{i=1}^{M} (a_i^{\pm(T)}(x) - y_i^{\pm})^2 \tag{22}$$

where X represents the set of predicted intervals and Y is the set of original intervals, $a_i^{\pm(T)}(x)$ denotes the response of the i-th neural concept in the last iteration (i.e., the abstract output layer) for the corrupted pattern $x \in X$. Moreover, T is the number of iterations and can be equal to the maximum number of variables to be predicted in a pattern.

The configuration of the stochastic descendent gradient is as follows: momentum is set to 0.8, the learning rate is set to 0.004, and the number of epochs is set to 200. Figure 2 illustrates the median $MSE^{\pm}$ by each variant.

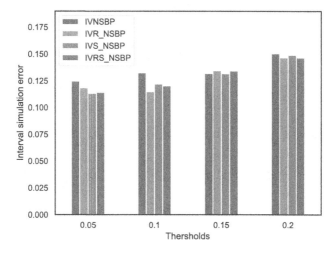

Fig. 2. Average interval simulation errors computed using different IVNSBP learning algorithms for different uncertainty levels.

The simulation results in Fig. 2 show a slight increase in the simulation errors as the uncertainty (thresholds) increases. These numbers do not reach high values because they do not exceed 0.15. It was verified the directly proportional relationship between the uncertainty and the $MSE^{\pm}$ values.

The authors in [11] found that the methods implementing the skipping operation performed slightly better than the NSBP algorithm. The best MSE values computed by each one of those variants are as follows: NSBP $= 0.0569$, R-NSBP $= 0.0582$, S-NSBP $= 0.0558$ and RS-NSBP $= 0.0556$.

Following this line of experimental study, Fig. 3 shows the lowest simulation error computed by each nonsynaptic learning variant: (a) IV-NSBP, (b) IVR-NSBP, (c) IVS-NSBP, and (d) IVRS-NSBP for different uncertainty level. The $MSE^{\pm}$ calculated with the variants proposed in this paper are as good and sometimes better (threshold $= 0.05$) than those obtained in the previous variants. Only when $\xi \geq 0.20$, we can observe a tendency for the error intervals to increase, which is to be expected.

As we can see in Fig. 3, the IVS-NSBP learning algorithm yields the best results. Another interesting conclusion is that the $MSE^{\pm}$ values obtained for uncertainty levels of 0.05 and 0.10 are lower than those obtained by the nonsynaptic learning variants proposed in [11].

Friedman test was used [6] to determine whether the performance differences are statistically significant or not. The p-values are 2.15E$-$01, 3.23E$-$01, 8.73E$-$01 and 3.42E$-$02, respectively, for a confidence interval is 95%. The Wilcoxon signed-rank test is used to perform pairwise comparisons. The p-values for the four uncertainty levels are displayed in Tables 1, 2, 3 and 4, using the IV-NSBP algorithm as the control method. Besides, we report the p-values computed by the Holm post-hoc procedure [7], the negative ranks (R^-), the positive ranks (R^+), and whether the null hypothesis H_0 is rejected or not.

Table 1. Pairwise analysis for $\xi = 0.05$

Algorithm	p-value	R^-	R^+	Holm	H_0
IVR-NSBP	1.36E$-$01	13	22	2.72E$-$01	Fail to reject
IVS-NSBP	4.92E$-$01	16	19	4.92E$-$01	Fail to reject
IVRS-NSBP	7.97E$-$02	11	24	2.39E$-$01	Fail to reject

Table 2. Pairwise analysis for $\xi = 0.10$

Algorithm	p-value	R^-	R^+	Holm	H_0
IVR-NSBP	5.74E$-$02	14	21	1.72E$-$01	Fail to reject
IVS-NSBP	6.58E$-$01	15	20	6.58E$-$01	Fail to reject
IVRS-NSBP	2.52E$-$01	16	19	5.03E$-$01	Fail to reject

Tables 1, 2, 3 and 4 show that there are no significant differences between the algorithms. However, the rankings indicate that, as the uncertainty increases, the IVS-NSBP method performs slightly better than the other learning algorithms. This result agrees with the conclusions in [11], thus verifying that backpropagating the error signal through the inner (abstract) layers is an expendable operation to deliver the error to the first hidden layer.

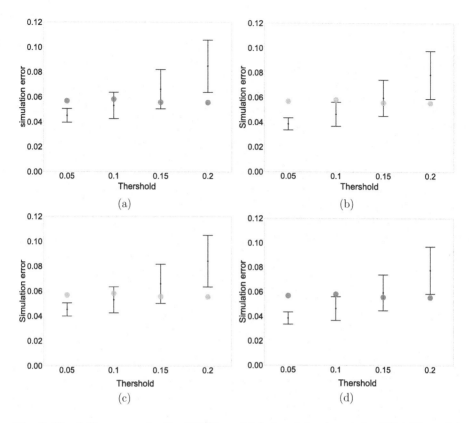

Fig. 3. Simulation errors for the LTCN model (colored dots) and the IVLTCN model (intervals) for different uncertainty levels. The learning algorithms are (a) IV-NSBP, (b) IVR-NSBP, (c) IVS-NSBP, and (d) IVRS- NSBP.

Table 3. Pairwise analysis for $\xi = 0.15$

Algorithm	p-value	R^-	R^+	Holm	H_0
IVR-NSBP	8.06E−01	16	19	1.00E+00	Fail to reject
IVS-NSBP	6.58E−01	14	21	1.00E+00	Fail to reject
IVRS-NSBP	8.83E−01	20	15	1.00E+00	Fail to reject

Table 4. Pairwise analysis for $\xi = 0.20$

Algorithm	p-value	R^-	R^+	Holm	H_0
IVR-NSBP	5.53E−02	14	21	1.11E−01	Fail to reject
IVS-NSBP	2.18E−02	9	26	6.55E−02	Fail to reject
IVRS-NSBP	6.42E−02	15	20	1.11E−01	Fail to reject

5   Conclusions

This paper presented three learning algorithm variants for training the IVLTCN model, which operates with interval numbers. The median of the errors computed by these three variants (IVR-NSBP, IVS-NSBP, and IVRS-NSBP) does not exceed 0.15. Therefore, the proposals have an effectiveness of more than 85% of the cases in uncertain environments. In the comparative analysis between the best results of the predecessor models and our proposals, it is observed that the performance of the new variants was similar or slightly better. In other words, the simulation errors were as low as those obtained by the predecessor models and sometimes lower. It is worth highlighting that this result has a more significant impact because it was achieved in uncertainty environments (less information in the datasets) which shows that the new variants are as powerful as their predecessors. More importantly, the experiments confirmed that backpropagating the error signal through the abstract layers described by interval weights is not needed to train the network effectively.

It would be interesting to complement this research with new experimental studies such as the determination of the dispersion of $\lambda_i^{\pm(t)}$ and $h_i^{\pm(t)}$, parameters adjusted during the Nonsynaptic Backpropagation algorithms and considered key parameters on the algorithm's approximation ability. Also the model could be applied in real case studies, for example, in analyzing the incidence of features that determine the level of service at intersections without traffic lights. Usually, these studies are very tedious because of the field and cabinet work needed to collect the accurate values of the main factors. So getting a tool that handles data sets with uncertainty and allows valid conclusions to be drawn will shorten the measurement times of the variables and can form the basis for more in-depth traffic studies, with the same reliability as traditional procedures and incredible speed.

References

1. Baldi, P., Sadowski, P., Lu, Z.: Learning in the machine: random backpropagation and the deep learning channel. Artif. Intell. **260**, 1–35 (2018). https://doi.org/10.1016/j.artint.2018.03.003, https://www.sciencedirect.com/science/article/pii/S0004370218300985
2. Bengio, Y., Simard, P., Frasconi, P.: Learning long-term dependencies with gradient descent is difficult. IEEE Trans. Neural Netw. **5**(2), 157–166 (1994). https://doi.org/10.1109/72.279181
3. Concepción, L., Nápoles, G., Falcon, R., Vanhoof, K., Bello Perez, R.: Unveiling the dynamic behavior of fuzzy cognitive maps. IEEE Trans. Fuzzy Syst. **29**(5), 1252–1261 (2021). https://doi.org/10.1109/TFUZZ.2020.2973853
4. Deng, J.: Introduction to grey system theory. Grey Syst. **1**(1), 1–24 (1989)
5. Frias, M., Nápoles, G., Vanhoof, K., Filiberto, Y., Bello, R.: Nonsynaptic backpropagation learning of interval-valued long-term cognitive networks. In: 2021 International Joint Conference on Neural Networks (IJCNN), pp. 1–9 (2021). https://doi.org/10.1109/IJCNN52387.2021.9533586

6. Friedman, M.: The use of ranks to avoid the assumption of normality implicit in the analysis of variance. J. Am. Stat. Assoc. **32**(200), 675–701 (1937)

7. Holm, S.: A simple sequentially rejective multiple test procedure. Scand. J. Stat. **6**, 65–70 (1979)

8. Kosko, B.: Fuzzy cognitive maps. Int. J. Man-Mach. Stud. **24**(1), 65–75 (1986)

9. Lillicrap, T., Cownden, D., Tweed, D., Akerman, C.: Random synaptic feedback weights support error backpropagation for deep learning. Nat. Commun. **7**, 13276 (2016). https://doi.org/10.1038/ncomms13276

10. Liu, S., Forrest, J.: Grey Information: Theory and Practical Applications. Springer, London (2006). https://doi.org/10.1007/1-84628-342-6

11. Nápoles, G., Grau, I., Concepción, L., Salgueiro, Y.: On the performance of the nonsynaptic backpropagation for training long-term cognitive networks. In: 11th International Conference of Pattern Recognition Systems (ICPRS 2021), vol. 2021, pp. 25–30 (2021). https://doi.org/10.1049/icp.2021.1434

12. Nápoles, G., Salmeron, J., Vanhoof, K.: Construction and supervised learning of long-term grey cognitive networks. IEEE Trans. Cybern. (2019). https://doi.org/10.1109/TCYB.2019.2913960

13. Nápoles, G., Vanhoenshoven, F., Falcon, R., Vanhoof, K.: Nonsynaptic error backpropagation in long-term cognitive networks. IEEE Trans. Neural Netw. Learn. Syst. (2019). https://doi.org/10.1109/TNNLS.2019.2910555

14. Nápoles, G., Vanhoenshoven, F., Vanhoof, K.: Short-term cognitive networks, flexible reasoning and nonsynaptic learning. Neural Netw. (2019). https://doi.org/10.1016/j.neunet.2019.03.012

15. Rumelhart, D.E., Hinton, G.E., Williams, R.J.: Learning representations by backpropagating errors. In: Neurocomputing: Foundations of Research, pp. 696–699. MIT Press, Cambridge (1988)

16. Werbos, P.J.: Beyond regression: new tools for prediction and analysis in the behavioral sciences. Ph.D. thesis, Harvard University (1974)

17. Yang, Y., John, R.: Grey sets and greyness. Inf. Sci. **185**, 249–264 (2012). https://doi.org/10.1016/j.ins.2011.09.029

Cross-target Stance Classification
as Domain Adaptation

Matheus Camasmie Pavan◉ and Ivandré Paraboni(✉)◉

University of São Paulo, São Paulo, Brazil
{matheus.pavan,ivandre}@usp.br

Abstract. As in many NLP tasks, stance classification - the computational task of inferring attitudes towards a given target topic from text - often relies on supervised methods and annotated corpora. However, given the costs associated with corpus annotation, and the need to provide stance labels for every target of interest, cross-target methods (that is, the use of an existing corpus of stance towards a particular target to classify stance towards a different, previously unseen target), are of great interest. Based on these observations, in the present work we address the issue of cross-target stance classification with the aid of an existing domain adaptation method based on BERT in combination with adversarial learning and knowledge distillation, and which has been shown to be successful in the related tasks of cross-domain sentiment analysis and cross-domain author profiling. To this end, we envisage a number of experiments to compare cross-target stance classification between target pairs with different degrees of semantic relatedness, and examine how much loss is observed from single-target to cross-target stance classification settings, and attempt to identify possible ways forward.

Keywords: Natural language processing · Stance classification · Cross-target stance · Domain adaptation

1 Introduction

Stance classification [1, 10] is the computational task of inferring attitudes (e.g., for/against) towards a particular target (e.g., an individual, a piece of legislation etc.) that may or may not be explicitly mentioned in the text. For instance, 'killing animals is unacceptable' may represent a stance in favour of veganism, or against a particular individual who kills animals etc. The task bears some resemblance to sentiment analysis, but stance (for/against) and sentiment (positive/negative) do not necessarily correlate [1].

Stance classifier models are usually built by making use of supervised machine learning methods that rely upon labelled training data. As in other text classification tasks of this kind, best results are usually observed in *single-target*

Supported by the University of São Paulo.

settings, that is, when both train and test documents discuss the same topic of interest. Thus, for instance, single-target stance classification would normally consist of building a classifier from stances in favour and against, e.g., a target president, and would subsequently use the model to classify previously unseen stances towards the same individual.

From a machine learning perspective, single-target settings will arguably obtain optimal results but, in many practical situations, training data about the intended target may be simply unavailable. In these cases, a possible alternative to (often costly) corpus annotation is to consider a *cross-target* setting, that is, building a model from data about a certain target for which a labelled corpus happens to be available (e.g., stances towards president A), and then using it to classify stances towards a different target (e.g., president B, or presumably even a more semantically-distant target, such as a political activist, a country, a product etc.)

If compared to single-target settings, cross-target settings may of course convey a certain degree of accuracy loss, but the appeal of circumventing the need for corpus annotation (for every possible topic of interest) remains strong in the field [3,4,7,12,25,26].

Of particular interest to the present work, [18] has introduced a domain adaptation method based on pre-trained BERT language models [6] in combination with adversarial learning and knowledge distillation [9] called BERT-AAD. The method has been shown to obtain positive results in cross-domain sentiment analysis and, more recently, also in cross-domain author profiling [5], that is, the task of predicting an author's demographics (e.g., gender, age, personality etc.) based on text that he/she has written [20–22]. However, it remains unclear whether this method may also be useful for stance classification, which is arguably closer to a text inference task [1].

To shed light on this issue, the present work extends previous studies in cross-domain sentiment analysis and author profiling by applying BERT-AAD [18], possibly for the first time, to stance classification. To this end, we introduce a novel multi-topic corpus of tweets labelled with stance information in the Portuguese language, and we envisage a number of experiments to compare cross-target stance classification between target pairs with different degrees of semantic relatedness. In doing so, our main objective is to examine how much loss is observed from single-target to cross-target stance classification settings, and to identify possible ways forward.

2   Background

Existing work in stance classification has grown considerable as a result of the SemEval-2016 shared task 6 [13], which introduced supervised (task A) and unsupervised (task B) challenges, and an accompanying dataset labelled with stance information (for, against, and none) towards five topics (Atheism, Climate Change, Feminist Movement, Hillary Clinton, and Abortion Legalisation.) An additional, unlabelled topic (Donald Trump) was taken as test data for task B which, although not particularly focused on cross-target stance classification, was modelled in this way by some of the participant systems that attempted to circumvent the lack of labelled test data (about Donald Trump) by using data about the other targets. Section 2.1 describes some of these studies, and more recent approaches to cross-target stance classification. Section 2.2 focuses on the cross-domain sentiment analysis method in [18] that will be taken as the basis for the present work.

2.1 Cross-target Stance Classification

The work in [4] presents a cross-target stance classification approach that uses a feature extraction method based on auto-encoders. To this end, the encoder takes as an input a bag-of-words representation of the 50k most frequent words in the corpus, performs dimensionality reduction and then recreates the original embeddings. Stance classification proper (using Hillary Clinton train data and Donald Trump test data from Semeval-2016 task B) is performed by using logistic regression.

The work in [24] was also a participant system at SemEval-2016 task B, introducing a cross-target stance classification approach based on support vector machines (SVMs) and a range of lexical and syntactic features. First, the model identifies whether the input text conveys any stance at all and, if so, determines its polarity (for/against) by measuring the similarity between a test instance (about Trump) and other topics.

The work in [7] introduces a similar two-step model to classify stance in texts. The first step consists of detecting subjectivity, i.e., whether the text contains any stance at all. The second step, applicable only to non-neutral texts, predicts stance polarity. Classification is performed with the aid of SVMs and engineered features (e.g., sentiment, word and char n-grams, presence of target keywords in the text, among others). The models used for cross-target stance detection are trained using all available data from other topics in the SemEval-2016 corpus, and are shown to outperform previous participant systems in task B.

The work in [25] presents a deep neural network with attention mechanism for cross-target stance classification. The model architecture consists of two bidirectional LSTM networks (BiLSTMs) to encode the contextual information in the input sentence and target, an attention mechanism to focus on common aspects shared by source and target domains, and the final prediction layer. The model outperforms the best participant systems from previous SemEval-2016.

The work in [8] approaches the cross-target stance detection task by introducing a recurring neural network based on LSTM cells with a double attention mechanism (called 'target' attention and 'target towards' attention, respectively.) The model consists of a hierarchical architecture in which the first level encodes words, and the second level encodes the relevance of each sentence in the text. First level outputs are individually fed into a pooling layer and then to the second level. The model outperforms a number of existing baseline systems applied to the SemEval-2016 Task B data.

The work in [26] introduces a cross-target stance classification model comprising two main components, namely, a semantic-emotion graph (SE-graph) and a graph convolution network. The SE-graph component encodes semantics-related and emotion-related lexicons and incorporates external knowledge at the word and concept levels. Graph nodes represent either a word or an emotion tag, and edges represent the co-occurrence of two nodes. The convolution network encodes the graph structure to generate a representation of the connections between words or emotion tags. These two components are used in a knowledge-aware memory unit (KAMU) that extends a BiLSTM model and encodes the sentence, and which uses a second BiLSTM network to encode topic information. Results suggest that the model obtains SOTA accuracy for most target topics from the SemEval-2016 corpus.

The work in [2] addressed the cross-target stance detection task from a zero-shot perspective, that is, without training examples about any particular target. The work introduces a dataset called VAST and a model to perform zero-shot stance detection called Topic-Grouped Attention (TGA). This consists of a contextual conditional embedding layer followed by topic-grouped attention using generalised representations, and a feed-forward network. The conditional embedding layer is composed by two encoders that use BERT to generate representations for both topic and text. The TGA module uses scaled dot-product attention to compute the importance of each topic token.

Based on the same dataset and also focused on zero-shot settings to address the cross-target stance detection task, the work in [3] introduces TOAD (TOpic-ADversarial network). This consists of four main components. First, there is a topic-oriented document encoder, which encodes both text and topic using BiLSTM and Attention mechanisms. The second component, called topic-invariant transformation, performs domain adaptation to generate topic-invariant representations without removing stance cues. The third component is a stance classifier consisting of a two-layer feed-forward network. Finally, the fourth component is a topic discriminator, which predicts the topic of the input sentence. This module is used alongside topic-invariant transformation to train the domain adaptation model.

Finally, in [12] a neural model based on a knowledge graph and BERT is used to address the cross-target stance classification. The architecture is composed of a BERT encoder to generate both topic and text representations, and which is followed by a knowledge graph encoding with a form of Graph Convolution Network (GCN). The graph is taken to represent common sense knowledge, in which nodes represent concepts found in the document and the edges represent the relations between them.

2.2   Domain Adaptation Using BERT

The work in [18] introduces a domain adaptation method called BERT-AAD, which combines BERT pre-trained models and adversarial discriminative domain adaptation (ADDA) [23] for cross-domain sentiment analysis.

ADDA consists of mapping source and target domains into a space of shared features as an adversarial framework (comprising discriminative modelling, untied weight sharing, and GAN-based loss) as a means to transfers knowledge from a larger (teacher) model to a smaller (student) one.

Given the logits predictions z^S and z^T made by a student and teacher models, and a degree of knowledge transfer t, knowledge distillation (KD) seeks to minimise the following objective function [9,18]:

$$t^2 \; x \sum_k -softmax(z_k^T/t) \; x \; log(softmax(z_k^S/t)) \tag{1}$$

The combination of ADDA and KD (named as AAD in [18]) is motivated by the observation that, in the case of BERT, using ADDA alone would amount to random classification due to the overly large number of model parameters. The combined BERT-AAD approach, by contrasts, operates as a regularisation method that preserves the knowledge acquired from the source domain, and enables the output model to adapt to the target domain without overfitting.

3 Materials and Method

BERT-AAD [18] has been shown to obtain results that are close to in-domain classification in both cross-domain sentiment analysis and also in cross-domain author age and gender classification [5]. In the present work, we will extend these studies by turning to the issue of cross-target stance classification. More specifically, we envisage a number of experiments intended to investigate to which extent BERT-AAD is suitable for cross-target stance classification, and how its results compare to those observed in single-target settings. We notice, however, that since cross-target settings are unlikely to outperform the single-target settings, the focus of the present work is on minimising the accuracy loss observed from single- to cross-target settings in a novel multi-target stance corpus.

3.1 Corpus

Although a number of data sets for stance classification in our language of interest - Portuguese - have been developed in previous work [16,17,19], these do not focus on cross-target settings. For that reason, we created a novel corpus of Portuguese Twitter data labelled with binary (for/against) stance information towards six targets that are popular topics of hyperpartisan discourse on Brazilian social media.

The corpus, hereby called UstanceBR r1, is organised in three polarised topic categories, each of them comprising a target generally favoured by more conservative individuals, and another target of more liberal leaning as follows.

- Presidents: Bolsonaro, Lula
- Covid-19: Hydroxychloroquine, Sinovac vaccine

Table 1. Corpus descriptive statistics.

Target	Against	For	Overall (A+F)	Words	Avg words
Bolsonaro	5,603	4,119	9,722	233,799	24.05
Lula	4,601	3,814	8,415	213,684	25.39
Hydroxychloroquine	4,007	4,018	8,025	228,617	28.49
Sinovac	4,061	3,945	8,006	227,310	28.39
Church	3,553	3,600	7,153	172,530	24.12
Globo TV	3,451	2,698	6,149	110,586	17.98
Overall	25,276	22,194	47,470	1,186,526	25.00

– Institutions: Church, Globo TV network

Table 1 presents the descriptive statistics for the six datasets.

The three target pairs were chosen so as to represent different degrees of similarity for the purpose of cross-target stance classification. The Presidents target pair is arguably the more closely related of the three, at least in the sense that many of the arguments used for/against one particular president tend to be applicable to another as well. For instance, 'X proposed a bad economic plan' works equally well as a stance against any president X. By contrast, the two Covid-19-related targets are only moderately close (e.g., 'X is a well-known Malaria medicine' is only applicable to Hydroxychloroquine), and the Institutions target pair is arguably the least related of the three. Arguments used for/against church (e.g., social work, freedom of expression etc.) are generally distinct from those that would be applicable to a TV network (e.g., editorial standards, broadcast quality etc.)

3.2   Classifier Models

We consider a number of cross-target stance classifiers that take as an input a dataset from a train domain (e.g., Bolsonaro) and attempt to perform stance classification on a different test domain. In doing so, rather than attempting every possible combination of target pairs, we shall focus on cross-target learning between more closely related targets (e.g., Bolsonaro-Lula) for brevity.

Our main approach, hereby called *CT.AAD*, is a straightforward adaptation of the AAD sentiment analysis method in [18] to stance classification. This consists of a BERT model that has been fine-tuned to the underlying (stance classification) task, and subsequently combined with the adversarial adaptation with distillation method discussed in Sect. 2.2.

As baseline alternatives to *CT.AAD*, we will consider a general architecture that leverages a BERT pre-trained language model as a token embedding generator with no fine-tuning. More specifically, we concatenate the last four layers of the language model - making a 3072-dimension vector - to represent each input token. This representation is taken as an input to a LSTM network with multi-head self-attention, and followed by a dense layer activated by a softmax function to generate the final class predictions.

By varying the way in which train and test data are used in our experiments, the general LSTM architecture gives rise to three baseline systems of interest. These are summarised as follows.

Single-target uses train and test data about the same target, and is intended as our main (and strongest) baseline system.

CT.Base uses train data from each individual source domain and test data from a different (target) domain, and it is intended to represent a standard LSTM-BERT approach to cross-target stance classification.

Finally, *CT.Replace* is a cross-target strategy similar to *CT.Base*, but in which keywords describing the source target (e.g., Lula) were replaced by their counterparts (e.g., Bolsonaro) in the target domain before actual training. Thus, for instance, given the task of classifying a stance towards Lula using training data about Bolsonaro, a source sentence as in 'I'm outraged after Bolsonaro's speech' would be converted into 'I'm outraged after Lula's speech', the underlying assumption being that replacements of this kind may narrow the gap between source and target domains, at least when these are sufficiently close (as it may be the case of our Presidents dataset), but perhaps less so in the case of more distant pairs (e.g., church and TV network.)

4   Results

Table 2 summarises single- and cross-target stance classification F1 results for the six text targets under consideration. The best cross-target strategy for each target is highlighted, and the bottom line shows the F1 loss observed between *Single-target* and the best cross-target results. Recall that cross-target models were built using only their counterpart target as training data. For instance, Bolsonaro cross-target stance classification uses data from the Lula dataset, and vice-versa.

Table 2. Single-target (top row) versus best cross-target (CT rows) stance classification F1 results.

Strategy	Presidents		Covid-19		Institutions	
	Bolsonaro	Lula	Hydroxy	Sinovac	Globo TV	Church
Single-target (ST)	0.83	0.83	0.83	0.84	0.86	0.85
CT.Base	0.59	0.57	0.47	0.47	0.69	**0.77**
CT.Replace	0.59	0.57	**0.58**	**0.62**	0.27	0.30
CT.AAD	**0.62**	**0.59**	0.41	0.35	**0.79**	0.76
(ST - CT.AAD) loss	0.21	0.24	0.25	0.22	0.07	0.08

As expected, results from Table 2 show that none of the cross-target alternatives are able to outperform *Single-target* classification. Moreover, we notice that

CT.AAD outperforms the other cross-target alternatives in only three tasks, and it performs particularly poorly in the intermediate, partially related Covid-19 target pair.

Interestingly, however, F1 losses from *Single-target* to *CT.AAD* are generally similar for the first two target pairs (i.e., within the -0.21 to -0.25 range), whereas for the third pair (Institutions) *CT.AAD* results are much closer to *Single-target*. This may in principle seem counter-intuitive as the Institutions target pair is arguably the least semantically related of the three and, as a result, less knowledge transfer should be expected between these two targets if compared to, say, the Presidents target pair. One possible explanation for this outcome may be related to the observation that the two more closely-related target pairs (Presidents and Covid-19) are also more polarised in the sense that being for/against one president or medicine often means the opposite if considering the second president or medicine. For instance, an argument in favour of a given president will almost always represent an argument against his political opponent. Thus, we hypothesise that topic polarisation, which is arguably less pronounced in the Institutions target pair, may have hindered the present domain adaptation methods to a certain extent, although more research on this issue is clearly needed. For the use of polarised political information in stance classification, we refer to, e.g., [11].

5   Final Remarks

The present work has addressed the issue of cross-target stance classification by introducing a novel stance corpus in the Portuguese language, and by investigating the use of an existing sentiment analysis domain adaptation method based on BERT in combination with adversarial learning and knowledge distillation. Our experiments compared cross-target stance classification between target pairs with different degrees of semantic relatedness, and examined how much loss is observed from single-target to cross-target stance classification settings.

Our current findings suggest that the use of the domain adaptation method for cross-target stance classification is partially successful, but results vary considerably depending on which target pair is considered. Perhaps surprisingly, best results were not those obtained by the more closely related target pairs (e.g., presidents), which suggests that other variables play a role in cross-target learning. Among these, topic polarisation (i.e., when being in favour of target A implies being against target B) may have limited the opportunities for knowledge transfer. A more detailed study along these lines is left as future work. We notice also that the present task may benefit from pronoun resolution [14,15], which is also left as future work.

The present dataset - called UstanceBR r1 - is freely available for research purposes[1].

---

[1] https://drive.google.com/drive/folders/1Mj22A9jCeaTcyp7FX9RLHJjMQ-II5bQ2?usp=sharing.

Acknowledgements. This work has been supported by the University of São Paulo.

References

1. Aldayel, A., Magdy, W.: Stance detection on social media: state of the art and trends. Inf. Process. Manage. **58**(4), 102597 (2021). https://doi.org/10.1016/j.ipm.2021.102597

2. Allaway, E., McKeown, K.: Zero-shot stance detection: a dataset and model using generalized topic representations. In: Proceedings of the 2020 Conference on Empirical Methods in Natural Language Processing (EMNLP), pp. 8913–8931. Association for Computational Linguistics, November 2020. https://doi.org/10.18653/v1/2020.emnlp-main.717, https://aclanthology.org/2020.emnlp-main.717

3. Allaway, E., Srikanth, M., McKeown, K.: Adversarial learning for zero-shot stance detection on social media. In: Proceedings of the 2021 Conference of the North American Chapter of the Association for Computational Linguistics: Human Language Technologies, pp. 4756–4767. Association for Computational Linguistics, June 2021. https://doi.org/10.18653/v1/2021.naacl-main.379, https://aclanthology.org/2021.naacl-main.379

4. Augenstein, I., Vlachos, A., Bontcheva, K.: USFD at SemEval-2016 task 6: Any-target stance detection on twitter with autoencoders. In: Proceedings of the 10th International Workshop on Semantic Evaluation (SemEval-2016), San Diego, California, pp. 389–393. Association for Computational Linguistics, June 2016. https://doi.org/10.18653/v1/S16-1063

5. Delmondes Neto, J.P., Paraboni, I.: Multi-source BERT stack ensemble for cross-domain author profiling. Expert Systems pp. - (2021). https://doi.org/10.1111/EXSY.12869

6. Devlin, J., Chang, M., Lee, K., Toutanova, K.: BERT: pre-training of deep bidirectional transformers for language understanding. In: Burstein, J., Doran, C., Solorio, T. (eds.) Proceedings of the 2019 Conference of the North American Chapter of the Association for Computational Linguistics: Human Language Technologies, NAACL-HLT 2019, Minneapolis, MN, USA, June 2–7, 2019, Volume 1 (Long and Short Papers), pp. 4171–4186. Association for Computational Linguistics (2019)

7. Dey, K., Shrivastava, R., Kaushik, S.: Twitter stance detection - a subjectivity and sentiment polarity inspired two-phase approach. In: IEEE International Conference on Data Mining Workshops, ICDMW, vol. 2017-November, pp. 365–372 (2017). https://doi.org/10.1109/ICDMW.2017.53

8. Gao, W., Yang, Y., Liu, Y.: Stance detection with target and target towards attention. In: Proceedings - 9th IEEE International Conference on Big Knowledge, ICBK 2018, pp. 432–439 (2018). https://doi.org/10.1109/ICBK.2018.00064

9. Hinton, G., Vinyals, O., Dean, J.: Distilling the knowledge in a neural network. In: NIPS Deep Learning and Representation Learning Workshop (2015)

10. Kucuk, D., Can, F.: Stance detection: a survey. ACM Comput. Surv. **53**(1), 1–37 (2020). https://doi.org/10.1145/3369026

11. Lai, M., Hernández Farías, D.I., Patti, V., Rosso, P.: Friends and enemies of clinton and trump: using context for detecting stance in political tweets. In: Sidorov, G., Herrera-Alcántara, O. (eds.) MICAI 2016. LNCS (LNAI), vol. 10061, pp. 155–168. Springer, Cham (2017). https://doi.org/10.1007/978-3-319-62434-1_13

12. Liu, R., Lin, Z., Tan, Y., Wang, W.: Enhancing zero-shot and few-shot stance detection with commonsense knowledge graph. In: Findings of the Association for Computational Linguistics: ACL-IJCNLP 2021, pp. 3152–3157. Association for Computational Linguistics, August 2021. https://doi.org/10.18653/v1/2021. findings-acl.278, https://aclanthology.org/2021.findings-acl.278

13. Mohammad, S., Kiritchenko, S., Sobhani, P., Zhu, X., Cherry, C.: SemEval-2016 task 6: Detecting stance in tweets. In: Proceedings of the 10th International Workshop on Semantic Evaluation (SemEval-2016), San Diego, California, pp. 31–41. Association for Computational Linguistics, June 2016. https://doi.org/10.18653/ v1/S16-1003

14. Paraboni, I.: Uma arquitetura para a resolução de referências pronominais possessivas no processamento de textos em língua portuguesa. Master's thesis, PUCRS, Porto Alegre (1997)

15. Paraboni, I., de Lima, V.L.S.: Possessive pronominal anaphor resolution in Portuguese written texts. In: Proceedings of the 17th international conference on Computational linguistics-Volume 2, pp. 1010–1014. Association for Computational Linguistics (1998)

16. Pavan, M.C., et al.: Morality classification in natural language text. IEEE Trans. Affective Comput. (2020). https://doi.org/10.1109/TAFFC.2020.3034050

17. Pavan, M.C., dos Santos, W.R., Paraboni, I.: Twitter moral stance classification using long short-term memory networks. In: Cerri, R., Prati, R.C. (eds.) BRACIS 2020. LNCS (LNAI), vol. 12319, pp. 636–647. Springer, Cham (2020). https://doi. org/10.1007/978-3-030-61377-8_45

18. Ryu, M., Lee, K.: Knowledge distillation for BERT unsupervised domain adaptation. CoRR abs/2010.11478 (2020). https://arxiv.org/abs/2010.11478

19. dos Santos, W.R., Paraboni, I.: Moral stance recognition and polarity classification from twitter and elicited text. In: Recents Advances in Natural Language Processing (RANLP-2019), pp. 1069–1075. INCOMA Ltd., Varna, Bulgaria (2019). https://doi.org/10.26615/978-954-452-056-4_123

20. dos Santos, W.R., Ramos, R.M.S., Paraboni, I.: Computational personality recognition from facebook text: psycholinguistic features, words and facets. New Rev. Hypermedia Multimedia 25(4), 268–287 (2019). https://doi.org/10.1080/ 13614568.2020.1722761

21. Silva, B.B.C., Paraboni, I.: Learning personality traits from Facebook text. IEEE Lat. Am. Trans. 16(4), 1256–1262 (2018). https://doi.org/10.1109/TLA.2018. 8362165

22. da Silva, B.B.C., Paraboni, I.: Personality recognition from facebook text. In: Villavicencio, A., Moreira, V., Abad, A., Caseli, H., Gamallo, P., Ramisch, C., Gonçalo Oliveira, H., Paetzold, G.H. (eds.) PROPOR 2018. LNCS (LNAI), vol. 11122, pp. 107–114. Springer, Cham (2018). https://doi.org/10.1007/978-3-319-99722-3_11

23. Tzeng, E., Hoffman, J., Saenko, K., Darrell, T.: Adversarial discriminative domain adaptation. In: 2017 IEEE Conference on Computer Vision and Pattern Recognition (CVPR), pp. 2962–2971 (2017). https://doi.org/10.1109/CVPR.2017.316

24. Wojatzki, M., Zesch, T.: ltl.uni-due at SemEval-2016 task 6: Stance detection in social media using stacked classifiers. In: Proceedings of the 10th International Workshop on Semantic Evaluation (SemEval-2016), San Diego, California, pp. 428–433. Association for Computational Linguistics, June 2016. https://doi.org/ 10.18653/v1/S16-1069

25. Xu, C., Paris, C., Nepal, S., Sparks, R.: Cross-target stance classification with self-attention networks. In: Proceedings of the 56th Annual Meeting of the Association for Computational Linguistics (Volume 2: Short Papers), pp. 778–783, Melbourne, Australia. Association for Computational Linguistics, July 2018
26. Zhang, B., Yang, M., Li, X., Ye, Y., Xu, X., Dai, K.: Enhancing cross-target stance detection with transferable semantic-emotion knowledge. In: Proceedings of the 58th Annual Meeting of the Association for Computational Linguistics, pp. 3188–3197. Association for Computational Linguistics, July 2020. https://doi.org/10.18653/v1/2020.acl-main.291

Impact of Loss Function in Deep Learning Methods for Accurate Retinal Vessel Segmentation

Daniela Herrera[1(✉)], Gilberto Ochoa-Ruiz[1,2], Miguel Gonzalez-Mendoza[1],
Christian Stephan-Otto[3], and Christian Mata[3,4]

[1] Tecnologico de Monterrey, School of Engineering and Sciences, Monterrey, Mexico
danielahmo98@gmail.com
[2] Tecnologico de Monterrey, Institute of Advanced Materials for Sustainable Manufacturing,
Monterrey, Mexico
[3] Pediatric Computational Imaging Research Group, Hospital Sant Joan de Déu,
Esplugues de Llobregat, Barcelona, Spain
[4] Research Centre for Biomedical Engineering (CREB), Barcelona East School of Engineering
Universitat Politècnica de Catalunya, 08019 Barcelona, Spain

Abstract. The retinal vessel network studied through fundus images contributes to the diagnosis of multiple diseases not only found in the eye. The segmentation of this system may help the specialized task of analyzing these images by assisting in the quantification of morphological characteristics. Due to its relevance, several Deep Learning-based architectures have been tested for tackling this problem automatically. However, the impact of loss function selection on the segmentation of the intricate retinal blood vessel system hasn't been systematically evaluated. In this work, we present the comparison of the loss functions Binary Cross Entropy, Dice, Tversky, and Combo loss using the deep learning architectures (i.e. U-Net, Attention U-Net, and Nested UNet) with the DRIVE dataset. Their performance is assessed using four metrics: the AUC, the mean squared error, the dice score, and the Hausdorff distance. The models were trained with the same number of parameters and epochs. Using dice score and AUC, the best combination was SA-UNet with Combo loss, which had an average of 0.9442 and 0.809 respectively. The best average of Hausdorff distance and mean square error were obtained using the Nested U-Net with the Dice loss function, which had an average of 6.32 and 0.0241 respectively. The results showed that there is a significant difference in the selection of loss function.

Keywords: Segmentation · Retinal vessels · Deep learning · Loss functions

1 Introduction

Analyzing eye fundus images is relevant for the identification of not only eye diseases but also systemic diseases, since the retina is susceptible to changes in the blood circulation in the brain [2]. The study of retinal vessel structure is conducted through non-invasive techniques. In particular, the characterization and segmentation of retinal

ⓒ The Author(s), under exclusive license to Springer Nature Switzerland AG 2022
O. Pichardo Lagunas et al. (Eds.): MICAI 2022, LNAI 13612, pp. 26–37, 2022.
https://doi.org/10.1007/978-3-031-19493-1_3

images are relevant for evaluating and assisting in the identification of cardiovascular diseases, hypertension, strokes, and retinopathies [12]. Diabetic retinopathy is present in 80% to 85% of the patients who have had diabetes for more than 10 years [15] and the gold standard for detecting it is through fundus imaging [10].

The examination of the images obtained by this means and the assessment of morphological changes in this structure is a specialized and operator-dependent task. As a consequence of the process of projecting the 3-D semi-transparent retinal tissue into a 2-D imaging plane [2], the evaluation of the image faces various challenges. Quantification of the structure analysis of the vessels (i.e., symmetry, width, length), to understand the pathological changes produced, is made through image processing and segmentation of the vessels [6]. Manual segmentation of these vessels is a time-consuming and subjective task and therefore tools for automating this process are necessary to aid in the diagnostic process. Even though the images obtained have a high resolution, the contrast of the background and the blood vessels are similar to each other, making the task of segmentation and identification difficult [3].

The segmentation of the retinal vascular network has been addressed using deep learning with several architectures. There are multiple works based on the U-Net structure: SA-UNet [6], Attention-UNet [13], Generative Adversarial Networks [16], among others. Attention modules have been added to the principal architectures since this mechanism tells the optimization process in which features to put more focus during the CNN weight updates [19], which may help in the segmentation of intricate patterns such as the vessel network.

Besides the variety of architectures that exist for segmentation, the learning algorithm is instigated by the loss function, which should be selected depending on the objective [7]. For evaluating segmentation results, there also exist multiple metrics that need to be selected considering the purpose and sensitivity of each one. The impact in the segmentation and evaluation of the quality by choosing loss functions and metrics is a challenge in deep learning segmentation applications.

In this paper, we explore recent architectural strides (i.e., U-Net, Attention U-Net, SA-UNet, and Nested U-Nets) for segmentation to evaluate their performance in the segmentation of retinal irrigation structures. Although comparisons have been made between the performance of architectures in retinal vessel segmentation [9, 16], the effect of loss function selection and its impact on the evaluation metric hasn't been reported in the literature to the best of our knowledge.

To conduct our experiments, we used the Digital Retinal Images for Vessel Extraction (DRIVE) [17] dataset and we explored several modern deep learning-based segmentation methods. The four deep learning-based models were trained in similar conditions with four loss functions, four metrics were used for assessing the results. The pipeline of the experiments is shown in Fig. 1. In this study, we compare the loss function using different metrics with four models that are U-Net structure-based, some of them also present attention modules.

The rest of this paper is organized as follows. In Sect. 2, we discuss previous studies related to segmentation and specialized works in retinal vessel segmentation. Section 3 contains the description of the dataset, loss functions, metrics, and experimentation details. The results are presented in Sect. 4. The conclusion and future work are presented in the Sect. 6.

2 State of the Art

The segmentation of retinal vessel structures aims to identify and distinguish the retina's vasculature from other anatomical structures that form the background of the image [1]. Although there have been improvements and developments in these tasks in recent years, robust segmentation still faces challenges such as the small number of available datasets for training, most of them having 50 images at most. Misclassification of vessels as background is related to the high imbalance problem found in these images, as typically only 10% are classified as vessels [9].

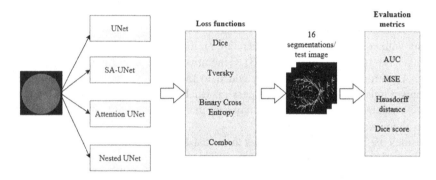

Fig. 1. Pipeline for our experiments. Four models were trained using four loss functions, giving a result of 16 images for each test image. The results were assessed using four segmentation metrics.

The segmentation methods that have been used for these type of images can be grouped into three groups, based on the classification dine by Abdulsahib et al. [1]. In the first group, there are the rule-based methods, which were the first approaches used for this problem. These methods are fully unsupervised, meaning that they don't require any annotations. The second group includes machine learning (ML) techniques, which are usually supervised methods; the feature extraction of the fundus image is done manually. Lastly, we consider separately a sub-group from ML techniques, which are the Deep Learning methods, due to their large impact and variety of architectures for segmentation. In such approaches, the biggest advantage is that the features from the images are automatically extracted and combined [4]. This last group is the focus of this study.

2.1 Rule-Based Methods

A filtering approach is the kernel-based methods, which are constructed on the basis of the retinal vessel's intensity distribution. These methods are capable of detecting the boundaries of vessels [1]. There are examples of this method applied to retinal vessel segmentation [8]. The vessel tracking method uses seed points to detect vessel ridges. However, such methods require a high level of pre-processing to enhance the sizes and orientation of the vessels. Another conventionally used method are the mathematical morphological operations, which are associated with the shapes found in the features of an image instead of the intensities in the pixels [1]. The advantage of these methods is that they don't require any form of labeling. However, their performance does not usually surpass the supervised methods [4].

2.2   Machine Learning Methods

ML-based methods require a manual extraction of local descriptors from the images that are then followed by a classifier. They have shown a better performance than the conventional methods previously mentioned [5]. An example of these algorithms is the k-nearest neighbors classifier (KNN) where the features obtained from the DRIVE dataset are classified [17]. There are also examples of super vector machine (SVM) classifiers, an example is a semi-supervised approach using fully and weakly labeled [20]. The limitations of these methods are that due to the lack of automatic feature extraction, they lack the capability of generalization [4].

2.3   Deep Learning Methods

Since the emergence of Convolutional Neural Networks (CNN) multiple architectures have been developed and applied to segmentation and other tasks related to computer vision. Their success in outperforming previous methods stems from the capability of such architectures to automatically learn features from raw data [5].

There exist multiple types of CNN architectures. In this work, we will focus on deep learning architectures created specifically for medical image segmentation, as it is the case of U-Net [14] and its variants. The architecture has convolutional layers and is formed by a encoder that does the down sampling of the image using a max pooling. Then, the feature maps are up sampled in the decoder. Both stages of the architecture are communicated through skip connections to solve the degradation problem in deep neural networks. This architecture outperformed previous methods for multiple types of medical images. Due to its relevance in segmentation, this model is the base for the deep learning models selected in this study.

From the U-Net architecture, there are multiple variants derived from it. An example is the Nested U-Net or U-Net ++ [21]. This model is also formed by an encoder and a decoder network. The difference is that the skip connections are formed of a series of nested dense convolutional blocks. The number of convolutional layers in the skip connection depends on the pyramid levels.

Variations in the segmentation architectures have been created by incorporating attention modules [6, 13, 19]. These modules help focus on the important features and ignore the rest by improving the representation of interest and helping where to center [19]. An example of the integration of an attention gate is the Attention U-Net [13]. The module is located at each level of the skip connections, filtering the features and allowing the coefficients to be local, improving the performance against the global gating.

Another example of attention modules applied to a U-Net is the Spatial Attention U-Net (SA-UNet) [6], which uses a spatial attention module located between the encoder a the decoder. Additionally, this architecture adds dropout convolutional blocks.

Although the segmentation of retinal vessels has improved through the development of deep learning-based architectures, there is still a lack of comparative studies on how the decision of a metric, loss function, and model affects the segmentation. Therefore, in this work we compare them to understand how it affects the behavior of the segmented vessels, which can be thin, intricate, and with similar contrast to the background.

3   Data and Methods

The technical contribution of this work is the evaluation of the impact of four loss functions with four metrics on the retinal vessel segmentation using U-Net, SA-UNet, Attention U-Net, and Nested U-Net architectures. The experiments comprise a total of 16 segmentation comparisons. These experiments are summarized in Fig. 1. The methodology followed is detailed in the following section.

3.1   Dataset

The images used in this work come from a retinal vessel segmentation dataset: the Digital Retinal Images for Vessel Extraction (DRIVE) [17] dataset. It contains 40 images, of which 7 are abnormal pathology cases. We use the version with data augmentation that includes random rotation, Gaussian noise, color jittering, and flips (horizontal, vertical, and diagonal) from the SA-UNet paper [6]. This increased the number of training images from 20 to 256 images. An example of the DRIVE dataset is the shown in Fig. 2; there is the fundus image and the binary ground truth with the labels of the blood vessels.

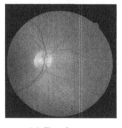   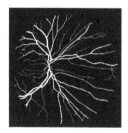

(a) Test image   (b) Ground truth

Fig. 2. Sample images for the DRIVE dataset [17].

3.2 Segmentation Metrics

To evaluate the quality of the segmentation, there are numerous metrics that can be used depending on the data and the segmentation task [18]. For the first part of our experiments (loss function comparison), we used the following metrics: the Dice coefficient, the area under the ROC curve (AUC), means square error, and Hausdorff distance (HD).

The Dice coefficient computes the pair-wise overlap between the segmentation and ground truth divided by the common pixels between them:

$$\text{DICE} = \frac{2|\text{Segmenation} \cap \text{Ground Truth}|}{|\text{Segmenation}| + |\text{Ground Truth}|} \tag{1}$$

The Receiver Operating Characteristic (ROC) curve is the plot of the true positive rate (TPR) and the false positive rate (FPR). The area under the curve (AUC) was designed as a measure of accuracy. In the case of retinal vessels, segmentation evaluates the accurately classified as background and vessels. The mean square error (MSE) averages the difference between the ground truth and the predicted pixel. The Hausdorff distance is a spatial-based metric measured in voxel size, which quantifies the distance between the ground truth and the segmentation.

3.3 Loss Functions

The loss functions help us in the mathematical representation of our segmentation objectives in deep learning to make it more accurate and faster [7]. In this sense, it is expected that different loss functions will yield different segmentation results. Therefore, four loss functions were evaluated for this study: Dice, Tversky, Binary Cross Entropy, and Combo loss.

The Dice loss function is based on the dice coefficient explained in the previous section (Eq. 1), which minimizes the similarity between the ground truth and the segmentation results. The Tversky loss is based on the Dice loss and achieves a better balance between precision and recall, emphasizing the false negatives, by reshaping the dice loss [11]. The Binary Cross Entropy loss measures the dissimilarity between two probability distributions. The Combo loss is a weighted summation between the Dice loss and a variation of the cross-entropy; this brings together the advantages from both losses [7].

3.4 Deep Learning Architectures

We tested four deep learning architectures for our experiments, comparing various loss functions and multiple metrics, as described above. The selected models are all based on the U-Net based architecture, originally proposed by Ronneberger et al. [14], this model is considered for the comparison. We selected the Spatial Attention U-Net (SA-UNet) proposed by Guo et al. [6]. This architecture adds a spatial attention module between the encoder and decoder. It also integrates dropout convolutional blocks for reducing the overfitting Attention UNet proposed by Oktay et al. [13] was also selected; it adds an Attention Gate between the union of the skip connection and the decoder. The UNet++ is a nested UNet architecture where the encoder and decoder are connected through a series of nested dense convolutional blocks [21] is the last model selected.

3.5   Training

The four models were trained using equal parameters and circumstances. The SA-UNet model was trained using an implementation from the authors made in Keras [6]. The Nested UNet implementation PyTorch made by its authors was used [21], they also made an implementation for U-Net and Attention U-Net in PyTorch which was also used. The code implementation was taken from the official github cite found in the papers cited. The models were trained for 100 epochs, the weights that had the best validation score were the ones saved. The training was done using the Nvidia DGX workstation, two GPUs were used for each model except for Nested U-Nets where four GPUs were needed. The batch size was 4 and a learning rate was 0.001.

4   Results

In previous works, there were limitations presented in the segmentation of retinal blood vessels due to the class imbalance, similar contrast between vessels and background, and limited labeled datasets. The impact of loss function selection and metrics hasn't

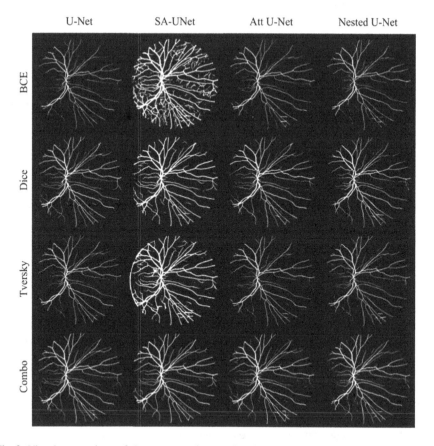

Fig. 3. Visual comparison of the segmentation results obtained by the U-Net, Attention U-Net, SA-UNet, and Nested UNet models using four loss functions (i.e., BCE, Dice, Tversky and Combo, respectively)

been compared using multiple models. Throughout experiments, we expect to understand the influence of this selection on the quality of the segmentation of the vessel structure.

The 16 segmentations results can be seen in Fig. 3. The figure shows the same test image for the multiple combinations. The original images showed in Fig. 2a with their respective ground truth. The combination results are shown with different loss functions (i.e. BCE, Dice, Tversky, and Combo, respectively) and models (i.e. U-Net, SA-UNet, Attention U-Net, and Nested U-Net) respectively.

A summary of the quantitative results of the models, employing the four discussed loss functions and the performance of the model under the four discussed metrics of the experiments is shown in Table 1. The table displays the average metric for each experiment. The symbol ↑ represents that the metric is better when is bigger, while a ↓ symbol means that is better when is close to 0. The numbers in bold indicate the loss function that had the best performance for each metric. We can see that although they were trained for the same number of epochs, the metrics differ depending on the loss function. For the discussion that follows, the models are going to be first analyzed individually, then against each other and finally, the loss functions performance is studied.

Table 1. Results using multiple loss functions and metrics (average) for U-Net based architectures.

Loss function	AUC ↑	MSE ↓	Hausdorff distance ↓	Dice score ↑	AUC ↑	MSE ↓	Hausdorff distance ↓	Dice score ↑
	U-Net				SA-UNet			
Dice	**0.9387**	**0.0250**	**6.4304**	0.7667	0.9431	0.0565	9.3039	0.7327
Tversky	0.9117	0.0260	6.5534	0.6776	**0.9442**	0.0692	10.1913	0.6951
BCE	0.8911	0.0286	6.7546	0.6276	0.9197	0.1339	21.0970	0.5470
Combo	0.9373	0.0259	6.4871	0.7668	0.9335	**0.0355**	7.9129	**0.809**
	Attention U-Net				Nested U-Net			
Dice	**0.9392**	**0.0251**	6.4251	0.7695	0.9318	**0.0242**	**6.3211**	0.7345
Tversky	0.9094	0.0261	6.5723	0.6708	0.8917	0.0279	6.7341	0.6434
BCE	0.9047	0.264	6.522	0.6470	0.8863	0.0288	6.7185	0.6212
Combo	0.9391	0.0259	**6.4342**	**0.7731**	**0.9344**	0.0251	6.4174	**0.7659**

If we would base the performance on only one metric, we could ignore the overall performance. For the U-Net model, which is the base architecture, the best average score for AUC, MSE, and HD had it the dice loss function. For the case of the Dice Score, the dice and combo loss had similar performance with a difference of 0.0001. In this case, if we had only used the dice score for evaluating the results, we could have concluded that the best performance had it the combo loss (see Fig. 3).

For the SA-UNet in the case of AUC, the loss function that had the best performance was the Tversky loss. However, looking at the other metrics, the Combo loss had the best performance for the rest of the metrics of interest.

For the segmentations obtained in this model, we can observe (Fig. 3) that for BCE loss there is the presence of noise and in the Tversky loss the limit of the fundus and the black background is also segmented. These details may be associated with a need of more epochs of training.

5   Discussion

The performance of the Attention U-Net had the best results for the dice loss function using the AUC and MSE, while using the HD and dice score, the best one was performed by the combo loss. By observing the segmentations (Fig. 3) the one that segmented most fine vessels was the combo loss.

The Nested UNet presented the best performance with the dice loss function with the metrics that need to be minimized (HD and MSE). The combo loss obtained better results for the metrics that need to be maximized (AUC and dice score). This model was the one that required the most computational resources (4 GPUs instead of 2).

For comparing the segmentation results against models (UNet, SA-UNet, Attention UNet, and Nested UNets), the outcomes were evaluated using the Dice score ↑. The summary of the results can be seen in the boxplots from Fig. 4, where the distribution of the dice score for each loss function and model is shown. The SA-UNet is the one that had the best dice score results by using the combo loss since it had the highest average and the most compact results, meaning that they are less variable.

The model that had the worst performance using the dice score is also the SA-UNet, but using the BCE function. If we consider the average of the rest of the metrics in Table 1 (AUC, MSE, and HD) we may have different results. The highest average for AUC was also obtained by the SA-UNet using the Tversky loss. The smallest HD and MSE average were obtained by the Nested UNets using the dice loss.

In the performance comparison by loss functions in the dice score, it is observed in the boxplot (Fig. 4) that the combo and dice loss results (dark and light blue) have the highest and most compact results, its average is above 0.7. The average of the dice score for the binary cross entropy loss (orange) was above 0.6, except in the case of the SA-UNet. For the case of the Tversky loss function, the average is also above 0.6 for the four models. Considering only averages from other metrics, the performance of the binary cross entropy loss didn't have the highest average in any of the cases.

To determine whether the results between each type of loss function were significantly different, a post-hoc Tukey test was performed using an alpha of 0.05, between the segmentation dice score results of the four architectures. The test does a pairwise mean comparison between the loss functions. The results are shown in a graph (Fig. 5). This test helps us determine whether the loss function selection indeed is significantly different.

The graph (Fig. 5) shows the dice score mean differences between the loss function and has a confidence interval of 95%. The dotted line represents 0 difference between them. The loss functions that had the greatest difference were the Tversky and the Combo loss. Of the six comparisons, the only ones that were not significantly different were the Dice and Combo loss function comparison. This may be associated with the fact that the Combo loss also uses the dice score in its formula.

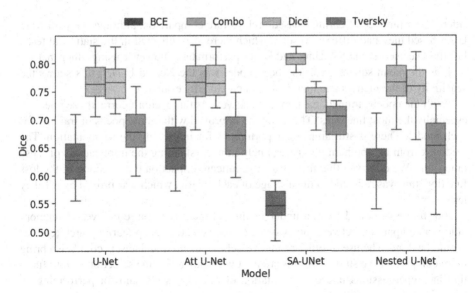

Fig. 4. Results from Deep Learning based architectures dice score comparison

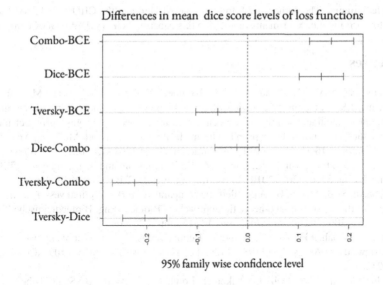

Fig. 5. Results of Tukey post-hoc statistical tests for the segmentation results against dice score for each loss function.

6   Conclusion and Future Work

Considering the overall performance of the metrics, the best loss function was the Combo. The conclusion could have been different if it had only been determined by one metric. Therefore, the combination of the loss function and metric needs to be considered. For the Deep Learning-based architecture comparison, although they all were UNet based they had different results, which were also reflected in the statistical tests. For the Dice score, the SA-Unet had better performance, however using other metrics such as the mean square error, the best model was the Nested U-Net, this shows the sensitivity of the metrics and how it should be globally evaluated.

With the epochs trained, each model had vessels that weren't correctly segmented, especially the most fine ones. This could be improved with more epochs of training for each model. There is still areas of opportunities for improving the segmentation. The feedback from an ophthalmologist can help in understanding the implications of these omissions. We observed that there was a significant impact on the selection of the loss function, this was reflected in the average of each metric, which was proved by a Tukey test.

For future work and a better understanding of the impact on retinal vessel segmentation, a comparison between other types of segmentation deep learning architectures should be done. The use of other retinal vessels segmentation datasets could also bring more comprehensive studies. In this study, it was shown that the selection of loss function has repercussions in the segmentation of retinal vessels, and for performing an intrinsic evaluation multiple metrics should be considered.

Acknowledgments. The authors wish to thank the AI Hub and the CIIOT at ITESM for their support for carrying the experiments reported in this paper in their NVIDIA's DGX computer.

References

1. Abdulsahib, A.A., Mahmoud, M.A., Mohammed, M.A., Rasheed, H.H., Mostafa, S.A., Maashi, M.S.: Comprehensive review of retinal blood vessel segmentation and classification techniques: intelligent solutions for green computing in medical images, current challenges, open issues, and knowledge gaps in fundus medical images. Network Modeling Anal. Health Inf. Bioinform. **10**(1), 1–32 (2021). https://doi.org/10.1007/s13721-021-00294-7

2. Abramoff, M.D., Garvin, M.K., Sonka, M.: Retinal imaging and image analysis. IEEE Rev. Biomed. Eng. **3**, 169–208 (2010). https://doi.org/10.1109/RBME.2010.2084567

3. Çetinkaya, M.B., Duran, H.: A detailed and comparative work for retinal vessel segmentation based on the most effective heuristic approaches. Biomed. Eng./Biomedizinische Technik **66**(2), 181–200 (2021). https://doi.org/10.1515/bmt-2020-0089

4. Chen, C., Chuah, J.H., Ali, R., Wang, Y.: Retinal vessel segmentation using deep learning: A review. IEEE Access **9**, 111985–112004 (2021). https://doi.org/10.1109/ACCESS.2021.3102176

5. Galdran, A., Anjos, A., Dolz, J., Chakor, H., Lombaert, H., Ayed, I.B.: State-of-the-art retinal vessel segmentation with minimalistic models. Sci. Rep. **12**(1), 6174 (2022). https://doi.org/10.1038/s41598-022-09675-y

6. Guo, C., Szemenyei, M., Yi, Y., Wang, W., Chen, B., Fan, C.: Sa-unet: Spatial attention u-net for retinal vessel segmentation. ArXiv abs/2004.03696 (2020)

7. Jadon, S.: A survey of loss functions for semantic segmentation. In: 2020 IEEE Conference on Computational Intelligence in Bioinformatics and Computational Biology (CIBCB), pp. 1–7. IEEE, October 2020. https://doi.org/10.1109/CIBCB48159.2020.9277638

8. Kar, S.S., Maity, S.P.: Blood vessel extraction and optic disc removal using curvelet transform and kernel fuzzy c-means. Comput. Biol. Med. **70**, 174–189 (2016). https://doi.org/10.1016/j.compbiomed.2015.12.018

9. Khanal, A., Estrada, R.: Dynamic deep networks for retinal vessel segmentation. Front. Comput. Sci. **2**, 35 (2020). https://doi.org/10.3389/fcomp.2020.00035

10. Kumari, S., Venkatesh, P., Tandon, N., Chawla, R., Takkar, B., Kumar, A.: Selfie fundus imaging for diabetic retinopathy screening. Eye (2021). https://doi.org/10.1038/s41433-021-01804-7

11. Ma, J., Chen, J., Ng, M., Huang, R., Li, Y., Li, C., Yang, X., Martel, A.L.: Loss odyssey in medical image segmentation. Med. Image Anal. **71**, 102035 (2021). https://doi.org/10.1016/j.media.2021.102035

12. Miri, M., Amini, Z., Rabbani, H., Kafieh, R.: A comprehensive study of retinal vessel classification methods in fundus images. J. Med. Sig. Sens. **7**(2), 59–70 (2017)

13. Oktay, O., et al.: Attention u-net: learning where to look for the pancreas (2018). https://doi.org/10.48550/ARXIV.1804.03999

14. Ronneberger, O., Fischer, P., Brox, T.: U-Net: convolutional networks for biomedical image segmentation. In: Navab, N., Hornegger, J., Wells, W.M., Frangi, A.F. (eds.) MICCAI 2015. LNCS, vol. 9351, pp. 234–241. Springer, Cham (2015). https://doi.org/10.1007/978-3-319-24574-4_28

15. Sisodia, D.S., Nair, S., Khobragade, P.: Diabetic retinal fundus images: preprocessing and feature extraction for early detection of diabetic retinopathy. Biomed. Pharmacol. J. **10**(2), 615–626 (2017)

16. Son, J., Park, S.J., Jung, K.-H.: Towards accurate segmentation of retinal vessels and the optic disc in fundoscopic images with generative adversarial networks. J. Digit. Imaging **32**(3), 499–512 (2018). https://doi.org/10.1007/s10278-018-0126-3

17. Staal, J., Abramoff, M., Niemeijer, M., Viergever, M., van Ginneken, B.: Ridge-based vessel segmentation in color images of the retina. IEEE Trans. Med. Imaging **23**(4), 501–509 (2004). https://doi.org/10.1109/TMI.2004.825627

18. Taha, A.A., Hanbury, A.: Metrics for evaluating 3d medical image segmentation: analysis, selection, and tool. vol. 15, p. 29, December 2015. https://doi.org/10.1186/s12880-015-0068-x

19. Woo, S., Park, J., Lee, J.-Y., Kweon, I.S.: CBAM: convolutional block attention module. In: Ferrari, V., Hebert, M., Sminchisescu, C., Weiss, Y. (eds.) ECCV 2018. LNCS, vol. 11211, pp. 3–19. Springer, Cham (2018). https://doi.org/10.1007/978-3-030-01234-2_1

20. You, X., Peng, Q., Yuan, Y., Cheung, Y.m., Lei, J.: Segmentation of retinal blood vessels using the radial projection and semi-supervised approach. Pattern Recogn. **44**(10–11), 2314–2324 (2011). https://doi.org/10.1016/j.patcog.2011.01.007

21. Zhou, Z., Rahman Siddiquee, M.M., Tajbakhsh, N., Liang, J.: UNet++: a nested u-net architecture for medical image segmentation. In: Stoyanov, D., Taylor, Z., Carneiro, G., Syeda-Mahmood, T., Martel, A., Maier-Hein, L., Tavares, J.M.R.S., Bradley, A., Papa, J.P., Belagiannis, V., Nascimento, J.C., Lu, Z., Conjeti, S., Moradi, M., Greenspan, H., Madabhushi, A. (eds.) DLMIA/ML-CDS -2018. LNCS, vol. 11045, pp. 3–11. Springer, Cham (2018). https://doi.org/10.1007/978-3-030-00889-5_1

Embedded Implementation
of the Hypersphere Neural Network
for Energy Consumption Monitoring

Jesús Alfredo García-Limón[1], Juan Pablo Serrano Rubio[1(✉)],
Rafael Herrera-Guzmán[2], Luz Maria Rodriguez-Vidal[1],
and Cesar Manuel Hernández-Mendoza[1]

[1] Tecnológico Nacional de México/ITS de Irapuato (ITESI), Carretera Irapuato -
Silao Km 12.5, Col. El Copal, Irapuato, Guanajuato, Mexico
juan.sr@irapuato.tecnm.mx
[2] Center for Research in Mathematics (CIMAT-Mérida), Carretera Sierra Papacal -
Chuburná Puerto Km 5, 97302 Sierra Papacal, Yucatán, Mexico
rherrera@cimat.mx
https://irapuato.tecnm.mx, https://www.cimat.mx/

Abstract. The combination of the Internet of Things and Machine
Learning has promoted the development of new technological approaches
such as Edge Computing and Tiny Machine Learning. The contribution
of this paper is the implementation of the Hypersphere Neural Network
using the NodeMCU board and the Esp8266 microcontroller for energy
consumption monitoring. The energy consumption monitoring consists
of recognising the device operating with an IoT device. We use our IoT
device for evaluating the performance of the embedded implementation
of the Hypersphere Neural Network. The implementation of the Hypersphere Neural Network is carried out from the geometric algebra and
conformal geometric algebra viewpoints. The idea behind the design and
implementation of the Hypersphere Neural Network is to estimate hyperspheres which produce non-linear decision boundaries and separate the
pattern classes. Our approach achieves 99.7% and 99.4% of classification
success rate for training and validation stages respectively using a simple
Hypersphere Neural Network topology.

Keywords: Energy consumption · Geometric algebra · Tiny machine
learning

1 Introduction

The Internet of Things (IoT) is a technological paradigm which is changing
our life style. Nowadays, IoT devices have capabilities to readily transmit and
receive data from anywhere in the world at any time [1]. The large amount of

O. Pichardo Lagunas et al. (Eds.): MICAI 2022, LNAI 13612, pp. 38–51, 2022.
https://doi.org/10.1007/978-3-031-19493-1_4

data collected by IoT devices through sensors has enabled a wide number of applications in industry, business, cities, offices and houses [2,3].

The number of IoT devices connected to the cloud is growing at an amazing rate, and by the end of 2025 it is expected to be greater than 50 billion [4,5]. Therefore, a very high volume of data is being stored, processed and analysed in the cloud. Currently, IoT devices present several problems related to bandwidth issues [6]. Recently, scientists have developed new technological paradigms such as the Edge computing and Tiny Machine Learning (TinyML), which incorporate efficient implementations of algorithms in the IoT devices to process the collected data [6,7]. These technological paradigms have incorporated artificial intelligence to recognise patterns and enable IoT devices to control certain variables through actuators [8]. The combination of technological paradigms provides reduction of latency and bandwidth use as well as smart task automation [4,6].

Recently, the IoT and machine learning paradigms have prompted the development of a wide number of applications for the intelligent automation of tasks in industries and homes [3,9]. It is estimated that these IoT solutions can mitigate significantly the effects of the climate change crisis, since it is possible to monitor several variables related to the efficient use of resources, such as energy and water. The contribution of this paper is the monitoring in real time the energy consumption of appliances using an embedded implementation of a Hypersphere Neural Network (HNN) in a programmable smart IoT device.

The implementation of the HNN is carried out in two stages: one offline and one online. The first (offline) stage consists of training the HNN using the energy consumption patterns in order to recognise which type of appliance is operating as well as some consumption patterns. The main issue of this stage is to determine a simple topology for an efficient implementation in the Esp8266 microcontroller of the IoT device. The second (online) stage is the implementation of the HNN in the microcontroller of the smart IoT device using conformal geometric algebra calculations [10,11]. The conformal geometric algebra provides us with a better geometric understanding to obtain the HNN topology and perform simple calculations to implement a non-linear associator to estimate the hyperspheres. Recently, geometric algebra and conformal geometric algebra have prompted the development of new artificial neural network models which can operate with non-linear associators and produce nonlinear decision boundaries using hyperconics for classification tasks and function approximation [12–14].

The rest of the paper is organized in five sections. In Sect. 2, we provide an overview of conformal geometric algebra and the inner product to recognise when a point is inside or outside hypersphere. In Sect. 3, we give a detailed implementation of the HNN. In Sect. 4, we describe the IoT architecture for an energy consumption monitoring system. In Sect. 5, we describe the experiments and discuss our results. Finally, conclusions and future work are discussed in Sect. 6.

2   Geometric Algebra

The heart of geometric algebra is the geometric product, which is defined as the sum of the inner and outer products of vectors. The geometric product of two vectors $a, b \in \mathbb{R}^n$ is defined by:

$$ab = a \bullet b + a \wedge b. \tag{1}$$

The symbol $\bullet$ denotes the inner/scalar product [11]. The outer product is the operation denoted by the symbol $\wedge$. The properties of the outer product are: antisymmetry, scaling, distributivity and associativity. The product $a \wedge b$ is called a bivector. The bivector $a \wedge b$ can be visualized as the parallelogram formed by a and b. The orientation of $b \wedge a$ will be the opposite to that of $a \wedge b$, due to the antisymmetry property. Therefore, the outer product is not commutative. The outer product is generalizable in higher dimensions, since it is associative. For instance, the outer product $(a \wedge b) \wedge c$ gives a trivector which can be visualized as a parallelepiped. In particular, the outer product of k linearly independent vectors is called a $k - blade$ and can be written as:

$$A_{<k>} = a_1 \wedge a_2 \wedge ...a_k =: \bigwedge_{i=1}^{k} a_i. \tag{2}$$

The grade $< k >$ of a blade is simply the number of vectors included in the outer product. A k-vector is a finite linear combination of k-blades. The set of all k-vectors is a vector space denoted by $\bigwedge^k \mathbb{R}^n$, of dimension $\binom{n}{k} = \frac{n!}{(n-k)!k!}$. If $\{e_1, ..., e_n\} \subset \mathbb{R}^n$ is an orthonormal basis for $\mathbb{R}^n$, then the set of k-blades

$$\{e_{i1} \wedge ... \wedge e_{ik} \mid i_{i1}, ..., i_k \in \{1, ..., n\} \text{ and } i_1 < i_2 < ... < i_k\} \tag{3}$$

forms a vector space basis for $\bigwedge^k \mathbb{R}^n$. The geometric algebra $Cl_n = Cl(\mathbb{R}^n)$ is the space of all linear combinations of blades of arbitrary grade, so that

$$Cl_n = \overset{0}{\bigwedge} \mathbb{R}^n \oplus \overset{1}{\bigwedge} \mathbb{R}^n \oplus \overset{2}{\bigwedge} \mathbb{R}^n \oplus ... \oplus \overset{n}{\bigwedge} \mathbb{R}^n, \tag{4}$$

where $\bigwedge^0 \mathbb{R}^n = \mathbb{R}$, $\bigwedge^1 \mathbb{R}^n = \mathbb{R}^n$. Thus, the dimension of the Geometric Algebra $Cl(\mathbb{R}^n)$ is

$$\sum_{k=0}^{n} \binom{n}{k} = 2^n. \tag{5}$$

A vector space basis of the Geometric Algebra Cl_n is given by the union of all the bases of the multivector spaces of every grade. The element $I = e_1 \wedge ... \wedge e_n$ is called the pseudoscalar. For example, the Geometric Algebra Cl of 3-dimensional space $\mathbb{R}^3$ has $2^3 = 8$ basis blades.

$$\underbrace{1}_{scalar}, \underbrace{e_1, e_2, e_3}_{vectors}, \underbrace{e_1 \wedge e_2, e_2 \wedge e_3, e_3 \wedge e_1}_{bivectores}, \underbrace{e_1 \wedge e_2 \wedge e_3 \equiv I}_{trivector}. \tag{6}$$

2.1   Conformal Geometric Algebra

The conformal model provides a way to deal with Euclidean Geometry in a higher dimensional space. Let $e_0, e_1, ..., e_n, e_\infty$ be a basis of $\mathbb{R}^{n+2}$. We will consider the Euclidean points $x = x_1 e_1 + x_2 e_2 +, ..., x_n e_n \in \mathbb{R}^n$ to be mapped to points in $\mathbb{R}^{n+1,1}$ according into the following conformal transformation:

$$\mathbb{P}(x) = (x_1 e_1 + x_2 e_2 + ... + x_n e_n) + \frac{1}{2}x^2 e_\infty + e_0, \tag{7}$$

where $\mathbb{R}^{n+1,1}$ is a $(n + 2)$-dimensional real vector space that includes the Euclidean space $\mathbb{R}^n$ and has two more independent directions generated by two basic vectors e_0 and e_∞ [11]. Furthermore, it is endowed with a scalar product of vectors satisfying: $e_i \bullet e_j = 1$, for $i = j$, $e_i \bullet e_j = 0$, for $i \neq j$, $e_i \bullet e_\infty = 0$, for $i = 1, ..., n$, $e_i \bullet e_0 = 0$, for $i = 1, ..., n$, $e_\infty \bullet e_0 = $ -1, and $e_\infty^2 = e_0^2 = 0$. Note that the Euclidean points $x \in \mathbb{R}^n$ are now mapped into points of the null cone in $\mathbb{R}^{n+1,1}$. The vectors e_0 and e_∞ represent the origin and a point at infinity respectively. The number x^2 is:

$$x^2 = \sum_{i=1}^{n} x_i^2. \tag{8}$$

A hypersphere in $\mathbb{R}^n$ is determined by its center $c \in \mathbb{R}^n$ and its radius $r \in \mathbb{R}$. Its conformal representation is the point:

$$\mathbb{S}(c, r) = \mathbb{P}(c) - \frac{1}{2}r^2 e_\infty. \tag{9}$$

The representation of the sphere s in *Outer Product Null Space* notation (OPNS) in $\mathbb{R}^n$, can be written with the help of $n + 1$ conformal points that lie on it.

$$s^* = \bigwedge_{i=1}^{n+1} \mathbb{P}(x_i). \tag{10}$$

A hyper-plane Θ in $\mathbb{R}^n$ is represented by:

$$\Theta(n, \delta) = n + \delta e_\infty, \tag{11}$$

where n is the normal vector to the hyper-plane in $\mathbb{R}^n$ and $\delta > 0$ is its oriented distance (with respect to n) to the origin. A hyper-plane in $\mathbb{R}^n$ can be defined by n points belonging to it, thus, in the conformal model is represented by the outer product of the n image conformal points plus the vector e_∞.

$$\Theta^* = \left(\bigwedge_{i=1}^{n} P_i \right) + e_\infty. \tag{12}$$

Point Inside or Outside a Hypersphere

The inner product between a point $\mathbb{P}(\mathbf{x})$ and a hypersphere $\mathbb{S}(\mathbf{c}, \rho)$ can be used to decide whether a point is inside or outside of the hypersphere,

$$
\begin{aligned}
\mathbb{S}(\mathbf{c}, r) \bullet \mathbb{P}(\mathbf{x}) &= \sum_{i=1}^{n}(c_i)(x_i) - \frac{1}{2}\left(\mathbf{c}^2 - r^2\right) - \frac{1}{2}\left(\sum_{i=1}^{n}(x_i e_i)^2\right) \\
&= \sum_{i=1}^{n}(c_i)(x_i) - \frac{1}{2}\left(\mathbf{c}^2\right) - \frac{1}{2}\left(r^2\right) - \frac{1}{2}\left(\mathbf{x}^2\right) \\
&= \frac{1}{2}(r^2) - \frac{1}{2}\left(\mathbf{c}^2 - 2\sum_{i=1}^{n}(c_i)(x_i) - \mathbf{x}^2\right) \\
&= \frac{1}{2}(r^2) - \frac{1}{2}(\mathbf{c} - \mathbf{x})^2 \\
&= \frac{1}{2}\left(r^2 - (\mathbf{c} - \mathbf{x})^2\right)
\end{aligned}
\tag{13}
$$

where

$$
\mathbb{S}(\mathbf{c}, r) = \underbrace{\left(\underbrace{\sum_{i=1}^{n} c_i e_i}_{\mathbf{c}} + \frac{1}{2}\underbrace{\left(\sum_{i=1}^{n}(c_i e_i)^2 - r^2\right)}_{\mathbf{c}^2} e_\infty + e_0\right)}_{\mathbb{S}(\mathbf{c},r)}
\tag{14}
$$

$$
\mathbb{P}(\mathbf{x}) = \underbrace{\left(\underbrace{\sum_{i=1}^{n} x_i e_i}_{\mathbf{x}} + \frac{1}{2}\underbrace{\sum_{i=1}^{n}(x_i e_i)^2}_{\mathbf{x}^2} e_\infty + e_0\right)}_{\mathbb{P}(\mathbf{x})}
\tag{15}
$$

The sign of the result indicates the location of the point $\mathbf{x}$ with respect to the hypersphere:

- $\mathbb{P}(\mathbf{x}) \bullet \mathbb{S}(\mathbf{c}, r) = 0$: $\mathbf{x}$ is on the hypersphere,
- $\text{Sign}(\mathbb{P}(\mathbf{x}) \bullet \mathbb{S}(\mathbf{c}, r)) > 0$: $\mathbf{x}$ is inside the hypersphere,
- $\text{Sign}(\mathbb{P}(\mathbf{x}) \bullet \mathbb{S}(\mathbf{c}, r)) < 0$: $\mathbf{x}$ is outside the hypersphere.

Figure 1 illustrates how the scalar product in the conformal space can be used to identify when a point is inside or outside a hypersphere.

3   Hypersphere Neural Network Topology

The Hypersphere Neural Network (HNN) includes the Hypersphere Neuron (HN) which produces spherical decision boundaries for classification of classes as is presented in Fig. 1. Therefore the computation complexity is similar to the traditional neuron that estimates hyperplanes. In total, the number of parameters for the HNN is given as follows:

$$\alpha = \underbrace{n_h(n+2)}_{\beta_1} + \underbrace{n_o(n_h+1)}_{\beta_2}, \tag{16}$$

where n_h is the number of neurons in the hidden layer, n_o is the number of neurons in the output layer, n is the dimension of the input, β_1 is the number of parameters in the hidden layer and β_2 is the number of parameters in the output layer. In terms of conformal geometric algebra, the output o_i of the HN for the i-th neuron in the hidden layer and output layer is computed using the sigmoid function G

$$G(x) = \frac{1}{1 + exp(-\lambda x)}$$

as follows

$$o_i = \frac{1}{1 + exp(-\lambda[\mathbb{S}(\mathbf{c}, r) \bullet \mathbb{P}(\mathbf{x})])} \tag{17}$$

in order to recognize when a input $\mathbb{P}(\mathbf{x})$ (conformal point) is inside our outside a hypersphere $\mathbb{S}(\mathbf{c}, r)$.

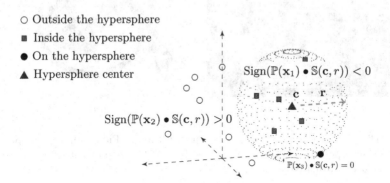

Fig. 1. Decision region produced by the Hyperspherical Neuron (HN).

The parameter λ represents the slope of the sigmoid function. The number computed in Eq. (17) can be positive or negative, depending on the relative position of the input with respect to hypersphere. Figure 6 shows the topology of the HNN. The input signals $\mathbf{x} = [x_1, x_2, x_3, ...x_q]$ are propagated through the network from left to right. The input vector $\mathbf{x}$ is mapped to conformal space. The symbols $o_1, ..., o_k, ..., o_p$ denote the output vector $\mathbf{o}$ from the hidden layer to the output layer. The output scalar of the output layer is described by $\mathbf{y} = y_1, ..., y_q$.

4 IoT Architecture for Energy Consumption Monitoring

The proposal of this paper is based on the NodeMCU board and Arduino. The board is mainly used for the IoT and provides important advantages for the development of smart IoT devices since it is an open-source firmware and development kit [15]. In addition, the low-cost of the NodeMCU has increased its popularity for developing IoT devices in a wide number of applications. The NodeMCU board provides all the features of the Esp8266 microchip. The Esp8266 has a WiFi connection at 2.4 GHz, with a protocol 802.11 b/g/n. It has 4 MB of flash memory, 80 MHz of the system clock, 80 kB of RAM. NodeMCU operates with 3.3 V [16].

Figure 2 presents the IoT device which is used to collect the energy consumption data. The Hypersphere Neural Network is implemented in this IoT device. Figure 3 presents an overview of the IoT architecture of the proposal. The advantages of the IoT platform is the use of open source frameworks such as Hypertext Preprocesor (PHP), MySQL database and Hypertext Markup Language (HTML). In [3], the IoT platform and the design of the IoT device was presented. The platform allows us to control the IoT device remotely either using a smartphone (Android App) or using a personal computer (Web Application).

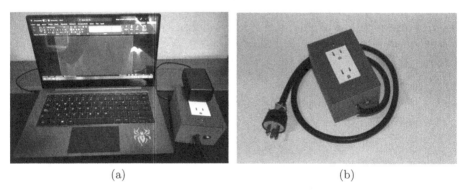

(a)   (b)

Fig. 2. IoT Device for energy consumption monitoring. a) Figure on left side presents the IoT device operating with a computer laptop. b) Figure on right side presents the IoT device used in this paper.

The project was divided in two stages: a) On-line stage and b) Off-line stage. Figure 4 shows the steps to perform both stages. The Off-line stage was developed in MATLAB. In this stage, we collect the energy consumption data and the feature vectors are selected to be used to train the HNN. The values of a feature vector are obtained by the next equations:

$$E = \sum_{i=1}^{N} y_i^2, \tag{18}$$

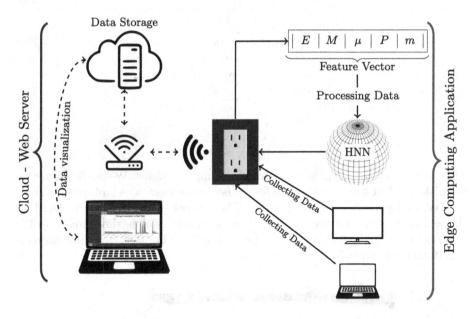

Fig. 3. An overview of the IoT architecture.

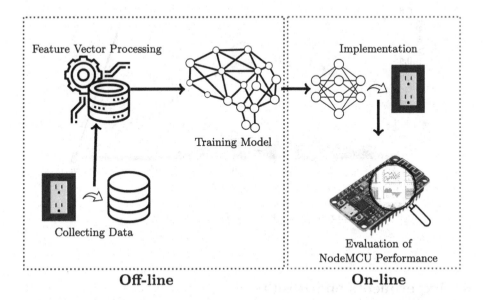

Fig. 4. Implementation of the embedded implementation of the HNN.

$$M = y_{\left[\frac{N}{2}\right]}, \tag{19}$$

$$\mu = \frac{1}{N} \sum_{i=0}^{N} y_i, \tag{20}$$

$$P = \frac{1}{N} \sum_{i=1}^{N} y_i^2, \tag{21}$$

$$m = \frac{1}{N} \sum_{i=1}^{N-1} \left(\frac{y_{i+1} - y_i}{t_{i+1} - t_i} \right), \tag{22}$$

where $\overline{y} = y_1, y_2, y_3, ..., y_n$, is the energy consumption signal. We use 30 values to calculate the features. We evaluate four classes of devices: a) a laptop computer, b) a tv, c) a projector and d) a fridge. The dataset is available in [17,18]. For the sake of convenience, the feature vectors are normalised in the domain $(0, 1)$. Figure 5 presents the feature vectors for each class. Note that, the dimension of each feature vector is 5.

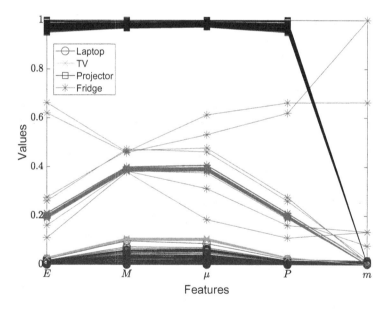

Fig. 5. Four classes of feature vectors.

5   Experiments and Results

We use the Spherical Evolutionary Algorithm (SEA) for training the HNN [19]. The goal of the training is to find the vector (or parameters) that determines an optimal approximation to the target outputs. The parameters are encoded in a vector that represents a solution as in Fig. 6, which shows a topology diagram of the HNN and the form to encode the vector of parameters of the neural network model for its implementation in NodeMCU board.

The experimental setup is the following:

- the dimension of the input patterns is 5;
- the parameters of the HNN were initialised in the domain $[-1, +1]$;
- the number of neurons in the hidden layer was varied from 1 to 6;
- the population for the evolutionary algorithm is set to 30 individuals;
- the stop criteria of the training occurs when the evolutionary algorithm reaches an error of $1e^{-4}$ or 30000 fitness function evaluations (FFEs);
- the objective function is based on the mean square error (MSE).

We use 300 input feature vectors for the training of the HNN. The classification task consists of recognising the appliance or device which is operating. The dataset is balanced according to number of classes. We use 75 input features for each class. Table 1 presents the results of the HNN over 30 independent runs for recognising the class of device which is operating with the IoT device. For each independent run, the input patterns are randomly selected to set the data training set and validation set. Note that for one neuron in the hidden layer, the HNN does not obtain competitive results for the classification task. However, we select a topology with two neurons in the hidden layer since it achieves a good classification rate for the training and validation stages. In addition its implementation requires a low number of parameters (11 parameters) which can be computed in the NodeMCU board.

5.1 NodeMCU Performance

Online-stage consist of implementing the topology of HNN with two neuron in the hidden layer in the NodeMCU. The implementation of the HNN is carried out with Arduino. The performance of the board is obtained using the ESP8266WiFi library. This library contains multiple functions for obtaining several parameters such as free memory and CPU frequency. The execution time (microseconds, milliseconds or seconds) is obtained using micros function. The micros() function returns the number of microseconds which is the time it takes to execute the program. The feature vectors are calculated in real time as well as the classification of classes using the HNN.

Due to the hardware computing power, we are careful with the implementation of the HNN. The memory is the main limitation, because the board has only 80 kB of RAM memory, this memory is for global and local variables. The algorithms are implemented using the dynamic memory approach. The implementation of this proposal consumes approximately 50% of the RAM memory. Table 2 shows the execution time and used memory for the classification process using HNN.

According to Table 2, the classification of feature vectors is performed in 1 s overall. At the end of each phase of classification process, the memory is erased in order to free up memory space and avoid a memory overflow error.

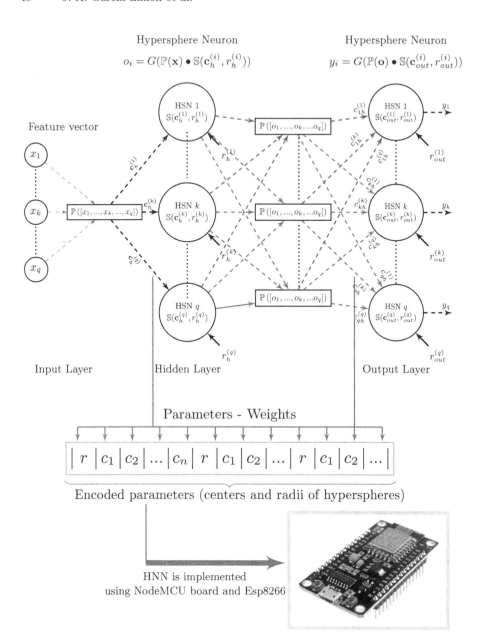

Fig. 6. Hypersphere neural network topology, encoded parameters of neural network model for its implementation in NodeMCU board.

Table 1. Results of training HNN with different topologies

Topology Average of Number of Generations $\alpha = n_h(n+2)+n_o(n_h+1)$		MSE Training	Validation
$5-1-2$ 1000 $\alpha = 11$	Mean	$6.7803e-01$	$6.6713e-01$
	Median	$6.7773e-01$	$6.6240e-01$
	Standard Deviation	$1.6271e-02$	$7.5115e-02$
	Min	$6.4868e-01$	$4.9739e-01$
	Max	$7.1265e-01$	$8.2233e-01$
	Classification Rate	24.9867%	25.0000%
$5-2-2$ 913 $\alpha = 20$	Mean	$8.1045e-03$	$2.0411e-02$
	Median	$8.0910e-04$	$7.1176e-04$
	Standard Deviation	$1.4035e-02$	$4.3083e-02$
	Min	$7.3124e-05$	$1.2739e-07$
	Max	$4.8381e-02$	$1.6001e-01$
	Classification Rate	99.7067%	99.4000%
$5-3-2$ 927 $\alpha = 29$	Mean	$6.0612e-03$	$2.0138e-02$
	Median	$8.6611e-04$	$1.4670e-03$
	Standard Deviation	$8.5903e-03$	$4.6482e-02$
	Min	$3.5789e-05$	$3.8859e-17$
	Max	$3.5630e-02$	$1.9003e-01$
	Classification Rate	99.7733%	99.4000%
$5-4-2$ 937 $\alpha = 38$	Mean	$5.6213e-03$	$2.5034e-02$
	Median	$2.3429e-03$	$2.3048e-03$
	Standard Deviation	$7.6705e-03$	$4.6842e-02$
	Min	$6.6380e-05$	$1.0019e-05$
	Max	$3.2969e-02$	$1.6067e-01$
	Classification Rate	99.7733%	99.3333%
$5-5-2$ 934 $\alpha = 47$	Mean	$3.6645e-03$	$1.1437e-02$
	Median	$5.9240e-04$	$1.2887e-03$
	Standard Deviation	$5.0322e-03$	$2.8705e-02$
	Min	$5.4979e-05$	$2.1070e-05$
	Max	$1.8664e-02$	$1.4313e-01$
	Classification Rate	99.8133%	99.4667%
$5-6-2$ 940 $\alpha = 56$	Mean	$5.8423e-03$	$2.0315e-02$
	Median	$1.1646e-03$	$1.5817e-03$
	Standard Deviation	$1.2901e-02$	$3.8192e-02$
	Min	$5.2692e-05$	$1.5683e-05$
	Max	$7.0273e-02$	$1.6210e-01$
	Classification Rate	99.6000%	99.2000%

Table 2. Required execution time and use of memory of the NodeMCU for the energy consumption monitoring.

Phases for classification process	Execution time *seconds*	NodeMCU memory
Data collection process	$1.0072e+00$	$45.7633\ \%$
Calculation of the features Vector	$9.8333e-04$	$45.7633\ \%$
Pre-processing of feature vectors	$9.1250e-05$	$45.9684\ \%$
Classification task with HNN	$5.8825e-04$	$45.9684\ \%$
Total	$1.0089e+00$	

6   Conclusions

The implementation of the HNN for energy consumption monitoring has been presented in this paper. The implementation of HNN is based on a non-linear associator whose design is obtained from geometric algebra and conformal geometric algebra approaches. The implementation is carried out into two stages: a) Off-line and b) On-line. The training of the HNN is performed using an evolutionary algorithm. The HNN is implemented in the Esp8266 microcontroller for energy consumption monitoring after the off-line stage. Our approach achieves competitive results, obtaining on average 99.7% and 99.4% classification rates for training and validation respectively using a simple topology. Our approach presents a good performance using only two neurons in the hidden layer. Therefore, we implement the HNN using only 20 parameters to recognise the device operating in our IoT device. Our embedded implementation approach in the NodeMCU board presents a good performance for processing the data in real time. On average, only 45.7% of the board's memory is used. The recognition of devices operating in the IoT device is performed in seconds.

Acknowledgments. The authors would like to thank the Science and Technology Council of Mexico, CONACyT, for its financial support during this research through the project CB-2015/256126 and the SNI Research Assistant Grant 156381. The second author would like to thank the Tecnológico Nacional de México/ITS de Irapuato for its support.

References

1. Bertha Mazon-Olivo, A.P.: Internet of things: state-of-the-art, computing paradigms and reference architectures. IEEE Lat. Am. Trans. **20**, 49–63 (2022)
2. López-Alfaro, G.A., et al.: Mobile robot for object detection using an iot system. In: 2020 IEEE International Autumn Meeting on Power, Electronics and Computing (ROPEC), vol. 4, pp. 1–6 (2020)
3. López-Alfaro, G.A., et al.: Smart iot device for energy consumption monitoring in real time. In: 2021 IEEE International Autumn Meeting on Power, Electronics and Computing (ROPEC), vol. 5, pp. 1–6 (2021)
4. Mohamed, K.S.: The era of internet of things: towards a smart world. In: The Era of Internet of Things, pp. 1–19. Springer, Cham (2019). https://doi.org/10.1007/978-3-030-18133-8_1
5. Pan, J., McElhannon, J.: Future edge cloud and edge computing for internet of things applications. IEEE Internet Things J. **5**, 439–449 (2018)
6. Cao, J., Zhang, Q., Shi, W.: Edge Computing: A Primer. Springer Briefs in Computer Science. Springer International Publishing (2018)
7. Zhang, C.: Intelligent internet of things service based on artificial intelligence technology. In: 2021 IEEE 2nd International Conference on Big Data, Artificial Intelligence and Internet of Things Engineering (ICBAIE), pp. 731–734 (2021)
8. Su, W., Li, L., Liu, F., He, M., Liang, X.: Ai on the edge: a comprehensive review. Artificial Intelligence Review, 1–59 (2022)

9. Mendoza, C.M.H., Rubio, J.P.S., Carillo, A.O.M., Vidal, L.M.R., Guzmán, R.H.: Sistema iot para el cuidado de plantas ornamentales. Revista de Investigación en Tecnologías de la Información **10**, 15–30 (2022)

10. Melnyk, P., Felsberg, M., Wadenbäck, M.: Embed me if you can: a geometric perceptron. In: Proceedings of the IEEE/CVF International Conference on Computer Vision, pp. 1276–1284 (2021)

11. Dorst, L., Fontijne, D., Mann, S.: Geometric algebra for computer science: an object-oriented approach to geometry. Elsevier (2010)

12. Serrano-Rubio, J.P., Hernández-Aguirre, A., Herrera-Guzmán, R.: Hyperconic multilayer perceptron. Neural Process. Lett. **45**, 29–58 (2017)

13. Murrieta-Dueñas, R., Serrano-Rubio, J., López-Ramírez, V., Segovia-Dominguez, I., Cortez-González, J.: Prediction of microbial growth via the hyperconic neural network approach. Chemical Engineering Research and Design (2022)

14. Serrano-Rubio, J.P., Herrera-Guzmán, R., Hernández-Aguirre, A.: Hyperconic multilayer perceptron for function approximation. In: IECON 2015–41st Annual Conference of the IEEE Industrial Electronics Society, pp. 004702–004707 (2015)

15. Team, N.: Nodemcu-an opensource firmware based on esp8266 wifi-soc (2014). https://www.nodemcu.com

16. Systems, E.: Esp8266 overview (2022). https://www.espressif.com/en/products

17. Serrano-Rubio, J., García-Limón, J.A.: Edcube: Energy consumption dataset. https://sites.google.com/cimat.mx/jpsr/projects/machine-learning-for-edge-computing/edcube (2022) [Web (accessed August 26, 2022)]

18. García-Limón, J.A., Serrano-Rubio, J.: Edcube: energy consumption dataset (2022). https://sites.google.com/view/limon-alfredo/projects/hnn. Accessed 26 Aug 2022

19. Serrano-Rubio, J.P., Hernandez-Aguirre, A., Herrera-Guzman, R.: An evolutionary algorithm using spherical inversions. Soft. Comput. **22**, 1993–2014 (2018)

MACFE: A Meta-learning and Causality Based Feature Engineering Framework

Ivan Reyes-Amezcua[1(✉)], Daniel Flores-Araiza[2], Gilberto Ochoa-Ruiz[2],
Andres Mendez-Vazquez[1], and Eduardo Rodriguez-Tello[3]

[1] Department of Computer Science, CINVESTAV, Guadalajara, Mexico
ivan.reyes@cinvestav.mx
[2] Tecnológico de Monterrey, School of Engineering and Sciences, Monterrey, Mexico
[3] Cinvestav - Tamaulipas, Km. 5.5 Carretera Victoria - Soto La Marina,
87130 Victoria, Tamaulipas, Mexico

Abstract. Feature engineering has become one of the most important steps to improving model prediction performance, and producing quality datasets. However, this process requires non-trivial domain knowledge which involves a time-consuming task. Thereby, automating such processes has become an active area of research and interest in industrial applications. In this paper, a novel method, called Meta-learning and Causality Based Feature Engineering (MACFE), is proposed; our method is based on the use of meta-learning, feature distribution encoding, and causality feature selection. In MACFE, meta-learning is used to find the best transformations, then the search is accelerated by pre-selecting "original" features given their causal relevance. Experimental evaluations on popular classification datasets show that MACFE can improve the prediction performance across eight classifiers, outperforms the current state-of-the-art methods on average by at least 6.54%, and obtains an improvement of 2.71% over the best previous works.

Keywords: Automated feature engineering · Automated machine learning · Causal feature selection

1 Introduction

Extracting features from raw data and transforming them into formats that are appropriate for Machine Learning (ML) models is what is known as feature engineering [12]. This task is usually carried out by a data scientist with good domain knowledge and the data sources of the task at hand [19,21,33]. Generally, feature engineering entails the daunting manual labor of designing, selecting, and evaluating features where even a great intuition is needed [6,18]. This is due to the fact that the performance of most machine learning algorithms heavily relies on the training data quality. These type of datasets usually consists of a large collection of different formats that need to be curated to be exploited by machine

O. Pichardo Lagunas et al. (Eds.): MICAI 2022, LNAI 13612, pp. 52–65, 2022.
https://doi.org/10.1007/978-3-031-19493-1_5

learning algorithms [6]. Therefore, by using feature engineering, we can select and obtain novel features from the raw data that would better represent the problem.

However, most of the existing automated feature engineering proposals perform this task by applying the *expansion-reduction* method [17], which is the process of trying a predefined set of transformation functions applied to raw features. Then, those transformed features are selected based on the improvement of model performance or some evaluation metric [21]. However, *expansion-reduction* leads to an exponential growth in the space of constructed features, which is known as the *feature explosion* problem [5]. In addition, extracting novel features without a proper and systematic method can lead to an unnecessary increase in the dimensionality of the data, and hence a poor performance in the learning process of the model [3]. Thus, the *curse of dimensionality* arises [20], which is the potential of high-dimensional data to be more complicated to process than low-dimensional data [8].

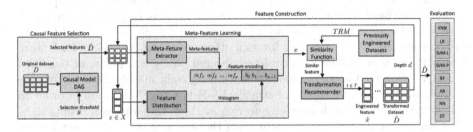

Fig. 1. The framework of our method. MACFE extracts meta-features from dataset D and a frequency table for each feature $x \in X$. Then, an encoding e is generated by the meta-features and feature distribution. Next, we search for the most similar encoding on the Transformation Recommendation Matrix (TRM) in order to recommend a useful transformation from it. The transformed dataset $\hat{D}$ is built from the constructed novel features and the original ones selected by the Directed Acyclic Graph (DAG) causal model.

It is crucial to realize that there are dozens of types of machine learning models, and each has its peculiarities and needs [19]. For instance, some models neither work with highly correlated features nor with highly multi-collinearity. Additionally, other models have trouble dealing with missing, noisy, or irrelevant features. Furthermore, since data and models are so diverse, it is difficult to generalize the practice of feature engineering across projects [33]. Thus, finding a proper process to treat data agnostically from a specific learning algorithm can help to choose transformations that better suit the learning process. To tackle this issue, a possibility is to incorporate only the generated features that have more appropriate knowledge about the data. For this, we present MACFE, a novel meta-learning and causality approach for automated feature engineering for classification problems using tabular data. The main contributions of this paper are briefly described as follows:

- We present a causality-based method for feature selection on the original dataset. For this, we use the mean magnitude effect of the features on the target to rank and select a subset of them.
- We propose a novel meta-learning generation for unary, binary, and high-order features based on non-linear transformations. This approach addresses the feature explosion problem by only searching for feature transformations that were found useful in past experiences.

In order to evaluate the proposed method, we designed a series of experiments on fourteen popular public classification datasets with relatively small dimensions to evaluate the feature generation and selection performance of MACFE. The results are obtained from eight machine learning models: Logistic Regression *(LR)*, K-Nearest Neighbors *(KNN)*, Lineal Support Vector Machine *(SVC-L)*, Polynomial Support Vector Machine *(SVC-P)*, Random Forest *(RF)*, AdaBoost *(AB)*, Multi-layer Perceptron *(MLP)* and Decision Tree *(DT)*. As illustrated in Fig. 1, our approach is divided into three phases. In the first one, the feature selection is carried out by using a Structural Causal Model (SCM) [22] for choosing the most promising features. Then, we move to a meta-learning phase (the second one), where meta-features are extracted from datasets and feature distributions to create encodings for each attribute. Then, we lookup for feature transformation on similar previously engineered datasets. Finally, in the third phase, we evaluate the engineered features among eight machine learning models and obtain the mean accuracy of stratified 5-Fold Cross Validation in order to assess the quality of the feature engineering method. Experimental results show that our proposal is effective in surpassing the scores of state-of-the-art feature engineering methods by achieving a mean accuracy of 81.83% across the fourteen testing datasets and the eight machine learning models evaluated.

The rest of this paper is organized as follows. In Sect. 2, we review the state of the art in automated feature engineering. In Sect. 3, we elaborate on the need for automated methods like ours. In Sect. 4, we introduce our proposed method MACFE, whereas Sect. 5, we show in detail our evaluation results, and finally, in Sect. 6 the conclusions drawn in this research work are given.

2   Related Work

In recent years, many automated feature engineering methods have been proposed using different methodologies. For instance, Data Science Machine (DSM) [14] is an automated feature engineering approach for structured and relational data. DSM proposed a Deep Feature Synthesis (DFS) method, which searches for relations and transformations across features in databases. They include a depth hyper-parameter d for setting the maximum composition, which recursively enumerates all possible transformations. In addition, DSM generates a large novel feature space, which is reduced by using Singular Value Decomposition (SVD) based feature selection. However, DSM is only suitable for relational data and it could take high computational times due to all the transformation functions used for processing all the original feature sets.

The data-driven approach presented in FCTree [9], creates novel features from sequential transformations of the original space by employing decision trees and then selecting the best features with the aid of information gain. The method in [25], known as the TFC framework, presents an iterative feature generation algorithm. The method applies feature transformation across all the features, and then it selects the best features based on information gain. Nevertheless, the generated feature space grows in a combinatorial way, leading to feature explosion. AutoFeat [13] and AutoLearn [16] are also data-driven methods. They can generate large transformations of features, selecting useful features by using regularized regression models for each pair of features. However, these methods require training a regression model, which can be time-consuming. Also, they both suffer from the feature explosion problem. Label based Regression (LbR) [30] is another method for generating novel features by using Ridge Regression and Kernel Ridge Regression. This method selects features based on the Distance Correlation Coefficient and the Maximum Information Coefficient (MIC) for each feature pair, which leads to discriminate features that are useful in combination with others.

2.1   Meta-learning for Feature Engineering

Recently, meta-learning has been proposed as a means of improving the quality of the generated features [21]. Meta-data can be simply defined as data about data [31]. For this work, meta-features are used to characterize and identify features with attributes in the context of meta-learning [1,4,10,28]. Some examples of meta-features are: a) *General*, such as the number of samples, features or classes, etc. b) *Statistical* like standard deviation, correlation coefficients, etc. c) *Information-theoretic* such as entropy, mutual information, noise ratio, etc. d) *Model-based* describes some characteristics of models such as Decision Trees, Bayesian Networks, SVMs, etc.

ExploreKit [15] is an example of a method that uses meta-learning for ranking and selecting the most promising generated features. ExploreKit does this by applying all possible transformations on features, suffering from the feature explosion problem. Furthermore, Learning Feature Engineering (LFE) is an approach that also uses meta-learning for recommending useful features for classification problems. The transformation recommender in LFE is based on the construction of a meta-feature vector based on the feature values associated with a class label. However, LFE can recommend only unary and binary transformations, lacking high-order transformations.

2.2   Causality Feature Selection

Classical feature selection approaches to leverage the correlations between features and class variables but lack taking advantage of the causal relationships between them. In contrast, knowing the causal relationship implies the underlying mechanism of a dataset [32], and thus causal variables are expected to be persistent across different settings or environments.

Hence, basing the feature engineering on relevant causally related features to the class of interest ideally should provide a more rich and robust output of engineered features. Consequently, if we work only with causally related variables to the target variable, independently of the type of relationship, it should be possible to be learned by an ML model, which additionally implies it facilitates, at some level, the efficacy of applying feature engineering to causally related variables.

3   Problem Definition

Let $D = \{X, Y\}$ be a dataset of input-output pairs, X a collection of n features $\{x_1, x_2, ..., x_n\}$, and m labels $Y = \{y_1, ..., y_m\}$. A machine learning algorithm L (e.g. SVM, Logistic Regression, or Random Forest), and an evaluation metric E (e.g. accuracy, F1-score).

We refer to a transformation $t \in T$ as a function $t(x)$ that takes a feature as an argument, and maps it to a transformed feature output $\hat{x} \in X'$. Where T is our set of transformations $\{t_1, t_2, ..., t_k\}$ that can be unary or binary, depending on the number of given arguments. Here, a high-order transformation is a composition of unary and binary transformations. Over each feature it is possible to define a series of non-linear transformations, $t_i : x_i \to \hat{x}_i$ that allow to extract as much intra and inter information from the "original" data. The goal of feature engineering is thus to transform X into X' by applying T such that X' maximizes the evaluation metric E of a machine learning algorithm L. The search for new transformed features and their combinations grows exponentially, and the feature explosion problem arises. MACFE, our proposed feature engineering approach, was devised to help mitigate this problem by employing meta-features to guide the search for transformations on features.

3.1   Meta-learning and Meta-features

A formal definition of meta-features was proposed in [28], in which meta-features are a set of q values extracted from a dataset D by a function f.

$$f(D) = \sigma(\mu(D, h_\mu), h_\sigma), \tag{1}$$

where $f : D \mapsto \mathbb{R}^q$ is the extraction of q values from dataset D, $\mu : D \mapsto \mathbb{R}^{q'}$ is a characterization measure, $\sigma : \mathbb{R}^{q'} \mapsto \mathbb{R}^q$ can be a summarization function such as: mean, minimum, maximum, etc. Moreover, h_μ and h_σ are hyperparameters for μ and σ, respectively. Thus, the function f is built by measuring some characteristic from D by μ, and a summarizing function defined by σ.

Here, meta-features describe features using meta-data. An example is the mean or median, as they are features that provide extra information about the underlying data distribution. In particular, the core of this work is meta-learning applied to the identification of data through meta-features.

4   Proposed Approach

In the following sections, we describe the dataset preprocessing along with the construction of the meta-feature vector and encodings for features. Also, we present the training of our method including the Meta-learning and Causal Selection phases.

4.1   Datasets

Preprocessing. MACFE is guided by meta-feature learning based on past experience to create novel features. Our method is trained with M random datasets $D_{train} = \{D_1, D_2, ..., D_M\}$ collected from Open ML [29], which have a structured format and a classification task related to the data. First, the preprocessing and cleaning of data are performed for each dataset by removing non-numerical features and imputing missing values with the feature mean. Next, a meta-feature *extractor* is used to obtain meta-data about the datasets. Let mf be a meta-feature vector composed by the main characteristics of a given dataset $D_i \in D_{train}$. Thus, a meta-feature vector for a dataset D_i is defined as:

$$mf = [mf_1, mf_2, ..., mf_p], \tag{2}$$

where each mf_i is a meta-feature value extracted from the data, and p is the size of the extracted meta-features.

However, describing datasets by mapping their main characteristics can be a challenging task. A full set of estimators and metrics can be extracted from a dataset, e.g., the number of classes or instances in a dataset can be a meta-feature value from such a dataset. For this, we use the approach of [24] to perform the automatic meta-feature extraction process. The extraction of meta-features is divided into five categories proposed by Rivolli *et al.* [28]: simple or general, statistical, information-theoretic and model-based, and landmarking. In order to automate the process of extracting meta-features from datasets, we use the framework Meta-feature Extractor (MFE) [1] for each training datasets $D_i \in D_{train}$, which implements the standard meta-feature extraction described above.

Next, we treat each feature $x \in D_i$ as follows:

1. We create a frequency table with a fixed number of *buckets* or *bins* b, for each feature x
2. A range r is calculated on the feature values given by the *upper* and *lower* bounds of the feature.
3. We generate s disjoint sets or bins b with uniform width w. Thus, each bin range b_i is a bucket in which values that are in the bin range lie. Each b_i range starts with the lower bound of x *plus* i times the width w, and ends with the lower bound of x *plus* $i + 1$ times the width w.
4. Finally, each frequency table or histogram is normalized in the range [0,1].

Thus, we obtain an encoding $e \in \mathbb{R}^{1 \times \eta}$ for each feature $x \in D_i$, composed by the meta-feature vector mf of the dataset and the feature distribution as follows:

$$e = [mf_1, mf_2, \ldots, mf_p, b_0, b_1, \ldots b_{s-1}] \tag{3}$$

4.2 Model Training

Meta-learning Phase. The meta-learning phase is described as follows. The unary, binary, and scaling feature transformations $t \in T$ are applied to the original features X. Then, an evaluation is performed on both original features and the generated features $t(X)$. For this, we use the Maximal Information Coefficient (MIC) [27], which measures the strength of the linear or non-linear relationships between two variables. MIC generates values between 0 and 1, where 0 means statistical independence and 1 stands for a noiseless statistical relationship between variables. Thus, we get the set of selected transformations T_{sel} for each original feature in $x \in X$ with the maximum score as follows:

$$T_{sel} = \underset{t \in T}{\arg\max} \; g_t \Big(MIC(t(x)) - MIC(x) \Big). \tag{4}$$

Finally, the selected transformations $t \in T_{sel}$ are stored in the Transformation Recommendation Matrix (TRM) for each $x \in D_{train}$ represented by its corresponding encoding e. Thus, TRM is represented as follows (Fig. 2).

$$TRM = \begin{bmatrix} e_{1,1} & e_{1,2} & \cdots & e_{1,\eta} & t_1 \\ \vdots & \vdots & \ddots & \vdots & \vdots \\ e_{N,1} & e_{N,2} & \cdots & e_{N,\eta} & t_N \end{bmatrix}$$

Fig. 2. TRM Matrix, where the ith row in the matrix is the feature $x \in D_{train}$, and the jth column is the encoding value of e (Eq. 3). N is the size of all the features in D_{train}, and η is the size of encoding e composed by the meta-feature vector mf (Eq. 2) and feature histogram. The last column stands for the transformations $t \in T$ with the resulting highest MIC score for the given features (Eq. 4).

In Algorithm 1 the training procedure to learn the most appropriated unary T_{un} and binary T_{bin} transformations is presented. This process is done for each feature in a given dataset D. Similarly, high-order transformations are built by combining several unary or binary transformations one after the other (Algorithm 2).

Algorithm 1. Training TRM

Input: Structured Dataset D
Output: TRM
$D = \text{preprocess}(D)$
for each $x_i \in D$ do
  $e_i = \text{encode\_feature}(x_i)$
  for each $t \in T_{un}$ do
    $\hat{x}_i = t(x_i)$
    $s.\text{append}(MIC(\hat{x}_i) - MIC(x_i))$
  end for
  $t_{top} = \text{argmax}(s)$
  $TRM.\text{append}(e_i, t_{top})$
  for each $x_j \in D | j > i$ do
    $e_j = \text{encode\_feature}(x_j)$
    for each $t \in T_{bin}$ do
      $\hat{x}_{i,j} = t(x_i, x_j)$
      $s_i = MIC(\hat{x}_{i,j}) - MIC(x_i)$
      $s_j = MIC(\hat{x}_{i,j}) - MIC(x_j)$
      if $s_i > 0$ and $s_j > 0$ then
        $TRM.\text{append}(e_i, e_j, t)$
      end if
    end for
  end for
end for

Algorithm 2. Data Transformation

Input: D, d, s
Output: $\hat{D}$
$\hat{D} = \text{preprocess}(D)$
$\hat{D} = \text{causal\_selection}(\hat{D}, s)$
for 1 to d do
  for each $x_i \in \hat{D}$ do
    $e_i = \text{encode\_feature}(x_i)$
    $t_{un} = \text{Similarity}(TRM, e_i)$
    $\hat{x}_i = t_{un}(x_i)$
    $\hat{D}.\text{append}(\hat{x}_i)$
    for each $x_j \in \hat{D}$, $x_i \neq x_j$ do
      $e_j = \text{encode\_feature}(x_j)$
      $t_{bin} = \text{Similarity}(TRM, e_i, e_j)$
      $\hat{x_{i,j}} = t_{bin}(x_i, x_j)$
      $\hat{D}.\text{append}(\hat{x_{i,j}})$
    end for
  end for
end for
$e_{\hat{D}} = \text{encode\_dataset}(\hat{D})$
$t_{scaler} = \text{Similarity}(TRM, e_{\hat{D}})$
$\hat{D} = t_{scaler}(\hat{D})$

The order value of the transformation function is related to the number of times a feature is processed by a transformation, e.g., an input feature x_1 is given as an argument of the *log* function, so $f_1(x_1) = log(x_1)$. Then, the resulting feature is combined with another feature x_2, lets say a multiplication, thus, $f_2(f_1(x_1), x_2) = mult(log(x_1), x_2)$. Finally, the output feature is given to the unary function *square*. Thus, the final transformed feature $\hat{x}$ has an order of 3, and can be seen as follows:

$$\hat{x} = f_3(f_2(f_1(x_1), x_2)) = square(mult(log(x_1), x_2))) \qquad (5)$$

Hence, we look for the underlying information about data through the extraction of more complex features. This gives us the capability of creating novel features from raw features that apparently do not have any predictive power, but in combination with high-order functions can have suitable predictive power for some machine learning models.

Causal Feature Selection Phase. Once the TRM is trained, MACFE is ready to recommend useful transformations for new datasets and features. For this, we start selecting the most promising original features, a causality-based feature selection is performed on the features. A DAG Classifier is trained to discover a causal graph from data. For this, we use the implementation of CausalNex [2]. This graph underlies the causal relationship between features and a target variable. The mean identified causal magnitude effect of the features on the target is used to rank the features. Then, a given threshold hyperparameter s determines the top k selected features. The resulting subset of selected features are processed to obtain an encoding e (Eq. 3).

Then, for a given feature encoding e, we search for a transformation in TRM by retrieving the most similar feature encoding using the *cosine distance* as a similarity measure. We benefit from this measure for ranking the most similar feature-vectors in the range 1.0 for identical feature-vectors and 0.0 for orthogonal feature-vectors [26]. Next, the most similar feature transformation is applied to the feature. The process is followed by the binary transformations and iterating over the features in the dataset (Algorithm 2). Furthermore, a depth d hyper-parameter is set to look for the maximum transformation order across *unary* and *binary* functions. Lastly, for the *Scaling transformations* we refer to those transformations on features that change the scale on a standard range. Many machine learning algorithms struggle to find patterns in data when features are not on the same scale. For this, having scaled features can help gradient descent to converge faster towards a minimum.

We scale features as follows. For a given feature $x \in X$, the following scaling functions can be applied. *Normalization*, also called *Min-Max Scaler*, is a method that scales each feature value to the range [0,1]. *Standardization*, this method scales each feature value so that the mean is 0 and the standard deviation is 1. *Robust Scaler*, this scaler is useful when the input feature has a lot of *outliers*. The Robust Scaling is done by calculating the median (50th percentile), and also the 25th and 75th percentiles. Then, each feature value is subtracted from the median, and divided by the Interquartile Range (IQR). In order to learn and recommend which scaler is appropriate for a given dataset, we follow a series of data testings. First, we test the features to know the proportion of outliers. If this proportion is larger than a certain threshold γ, then a Robust Scaler is applied to the features. Secondly, if the data follows a normal distribution, then we use a Standard Scaler. In particular, we use a *Shapiro-Wilk* test [11] to evaluate the normality of data. Then, if the test value is greater than 0.05 we consider the data is normally distributed. Finally, if none of the above tests is true about the data, then we use a Min-Max Scaler on the features. The resulting scaling method is saved in TRM according to the dataset encoding.

5   Experimental Results

For the evaluation of MACFE, first, we describe the evaluation details, such as the case study datasets and learning algorithms. Next, we briefly describe each of the implementation details of the classifiers and evaluation methods. Finally, a comparison with previous work is done and a discussion is presented by analyzing the characteristics of datasets and algorithms where MACFE is convenient.

5.1 Evaluation Details

Table 1. Statistics of 14 case study datasets

ID	Dataset	Source	Labels	Features	Instances
1	*Pima Diabetes*	UCI ML	2	8	768
2	*Sonar*	UCI ML	2	60	208
3	*Ionosphere*	UCI ML	2	34	351
4	*Haberman*	UCI ML	2	3	306
5	*Fertility*	UCI ML	2	9	100
6	*Wine*	UCI ML	3	13	178
7	*E.coli*	UCI ML	8	7	336
8	*Abalone*	UCI ML	29	7	4177
9	*Dermatology*	UCI ML	4	34	366
10	*Libras*	UCI ML	15	90	360
11	*Optical*	UCI ML	10	64	5620
12	*Waveform*	OpenML	3	21	5000
13	*Fourier*	OpenML	10	76	2000
14	*Pixel*	OpenML	10	240	2000

The evaluation of MACFE as an automated feature engineering method is performed on a set of fourteen classification datasets and eight machine learning algorithms commonly cited in the literature [15,16,30]. These datasets are from different areas, such as medical, physical, life, and computer science. In addition, these datasets are publicly available in the UCI ML Repository [7] and OpenML Repository [29]. The main statistics of these datasets are shown in Table 1.

5.2 Implementation Details

For our experiments, we tested the following learning algorithms: Logistic Regression *(LR)*, K-Nearest Neighbors *(KNN)*, Linear Support Vector Machine *(SVC-L)*, Polynomial Support Vector Machine *(SVC-P)* and Random Forest *(RF)*, AdaBoost *(AB)*, Multi-layer Perceptron *(MLP)* and Decision Tree *(DT)*. The scoring method for the evaluations is the mean accuracy of stratified 5-Fold Cross Validation on each dataset. Same as the state-of-the-art methodology for scoring. Each algorithm is used with scikit-learn [23] default parameters. This is because our objective is to enhance the accuracy of a model by improving the data through our automated feature engineering process, MACFE.

5.3 Comparison with Previous Works

The comparison of our proposal takes into account the same scenario conditions of the results presented in recent feature engineering proposals such as TFC [25], FCTree [9], ExploreKit [15], AutoLearn [16] and LbR [30]. In Table 2 are shown

Table 2. Mean accuracy results in 5-fold cross validation among original datasets (ORIG) and consulted state-of-the-art (TFC [25], FCTree [9], ExploreKit [15], AutoLearn (AL) [16], LbR [30]) and MACFE (ours). The best performing approach is shown in bold, each dataset is shown with its corresponding ID from Table 1.

D. ID	CLF	ORIG	TFC [25]	FCT [9]	EK [15]	AL [16]	LbR [30]	MACFE
1	KNN	71.48	72.42	73.52	73.6	68.36	72.13	**75.12**
	LR	76.55	75.92	76.52	73.9	74.99	71.86	**77.47**
	SVM-L	65.23	62.71	72.52	73.7	74.85	75.22	**77.34**
	SVM-P	64.89	65.71	70.52	72.6	76.32	**78.32**	78.12
	RF	75.37	72.42	73.52	74.0	73.05	72.47	**78.12**
	AB	74.34	74.08	74.08	74.3	72.52	73.01	**76.29**
	NN	64.32	64.12	64.22	67.3	72.39	72.50	**77.86**
	DT	**72.38**	70.23	70.46	70.9	71.05	71.12	71.74
2	KNN	78.35	81.48	82.70	82.4	83.19	**83.33**	81.27
	LR	77.42	78.12	78.72	78.7	79.00	**90.47**	86.05
	SVM-L	73.54	74.54	75.75	76.1	77.30	**90.47**	86.06
	SVM-P	53.36	58.41	66.44	33.6	81.71	80.95	**86.57**
	RF	73.55	81.00	82.54	47.4	77.87	76.19	**85.62**
	AB	80.74	80.00	81.04	54.0	78.83	**85.71**	83.69
	NN	80.30	81.07	82.00	82.4	84.09	85.71	**88.03**
	DT	75.01	74.23	74.52	75.0			**75.53**
3	KNN	84.31	84.66	84.87	86.0	83.46	**92.95**	89.74
	LR	87.44	87.26	87.39	87.7	87.95	**95.77**	93.44
	SVM-L	87.44	86.71	87.78	88.0	84.30	90.14	**92.58**
	SVM-P	64.10	70.16	71.45	72.6	74.63	78.87	**93.72**
	RF	93.15	91.65	93.16	94.0	92.30	91.54	**95.44**
	AB	92.02	90.94	90.12	90.3	92.43	90.14	**94.01**
	NN	93.14	92.45	92.13	93.6	92.29	**97.18**	92.58
	DT	88.32	87.12	88.04	88.1	88.59	88.73	**94.87**
4	KNN	71.89	70.00	71.28	72.3	68.68	70.36	**76.14**
	LR	74.19	72.07	73.96	74.5	76.16	**76.50**	74.51
	SVM-L	74.18	73.97	74.18	75.4	75.82	**76.01**	73.53
	SVM-P	74.18	73.98	74.81	75.1	**75.52**	75.52	74.51
	RF	68.63	68.91	69.07	70.0	65.34	70.17	**72.22**
	AB	70.25	71.19	71.57	72.2	69.93	**73.05**	71.89
	NN	73.19	69.02	71.19	72.2	70.91	75.02	**76.13**
	DT	66.65	66.09	66.79	67.2	66.34	67.74	**73.86**
5	KNN	85.00	86.00	86.00	87.0	87.00	88.00	**88.95**
	LR	88.00	88.00	89.00	88.0	87.00	88.00	**89.95**
	SVM-L	85.00	87.00	88.00	87.0	87.00	87.00	**89.95**
	SVM-P	88.00	87.00	88.00	88.0	88.00	88.00	**88.89**
	RF	82.00	87.00	87.00	**90.0**	84.00	88.00	89.89
	AB	79.00	83.00	84.00	83.0	79.00	85.00	**87.84**
	NN	88.00	88.00	88.00	88.0	85.00	88.00	**90.00**
	DT	80.00	84.00	84.00	85.0	85.00	**88.00**	87.89
6	KNN	67.93	74.89	79.93	83.4	93.84	95.49	**97.22**
	LR	95.52	96.89	97.24	95.1	98.30	**99.44**	98.87
	SVM-L	83.03	88.14	88.14	90.94	90.8	**98.87**	98.32
	SVM-P	96.65	96.68	96.65	92.1	92.68	94.74	**99.43**
	RF	96.07	96.68	97.12	90.0	97.20	**98.89**	97.19
	AB	85.82	88.12	**91.23**	62.8	84.71	83.03	89.27
	NN	42.73	46.23	49.56	64.6	97.19	**98.87**	98.32
	DT	91.57	91.79	92.01	92.5	93.22	93.37	**95.49**
7	KNN	86.59	**88.42**	87.56	88.4	84.82	85.39	87.81
	LR	75.88	78.23	79.24	82.8	87.19	87.19	**87.73**
	SVM-L	85.71	85.71	85.71	86.3	86.30	86.80	**88.87**
	SVM-P	56.54	59.32	62.14	72.3	80.33	81.59	**93.72**
	RF	82.73	83.46	83.76	85.1	86.59	84.80	**95.44**
	AB	62.47	63.54	64.37	65.8	65.75	63.06	**93.44**
	NN	78.28	80.37	81.97	83.7	86.90	86.89	**92.30**
	DT	79.74	76.32	77.67	80.3	76.40	82.11	**94.87**
8	KNN	**23.27**	21.64	22.60	23.1	22.71	21.69	22.62
	LR	24.61	23.69	23.60	24.8	26.50	25.25	**26.84**
	SVM-L	25.71	25.64	25.72	25.7	26.07	25.23	**26.57**
	SVM-P	19.46	17.64	22.12	21.4	23.77	23.98	**26.33**
	RF	22.91	18.78	23.02	23.2	22.21	24.15	**25.52**
	AB	20.61	19.10	19.97	21.1	20.61	21.01	**21.45**
	NN	25.53	26.32	26.41	27.1	27.81	26.40	**28.27**
	DT	19.27	19.00	19.13	19.3	19.41	19.42	**20.13**
9	KNN	89.11	90.46	92.89	91.0	96.09	96.66	**97.82**
	LR	97.21	97.97	97.97	97.6	**98.61**	97.77	97.81
	SVM-L	97.21	96.02	96.27	96.3	96.92	**98.32**	97.54
	SVM-P	94.41	94.00	94.12	92.0	93.56	**98.04**	95.90
	RF	96.92	96.45	96.61	95.5	95.81	98.04	**98.09**
	AB	54.13	57.12	61.00	57.3	54.96	54.13	**75.67**
	NN	98.04	97.13	97.22	97.7	**98.22**	97.77	98.09
	DT	95.24	95.06	94.96	95.4	94.68	96.08	**96.45**
10	KNN	70.00	71.00	71.18	73.7	69.44	70.27	**75.28**
	LR	60.27	64.68	67.12	71.7	70.00	68.88	**79.72**
	SVM-L	68.61	69.88	70.83	70.4	67.22	68.61	**82.22**
	SVM-P	2.22	36.68	47.97	47.8	49.44	50.13	**85.83**
	RF	71.94	72.12	73.07	77.6	70.22	72.50	**86.11**
	AB	8.05	10.12	13.11	16.9	**18.05**	14.57	15.28
	NN	71.66	72.35	74.24	75.7	78.33	**85.56**	83.06
	DT	62.50	62.64	63.12	63.7	65.55	65.27	**73.06**
11	KNN	98.77	97.20	98.02	98.0	97.03	**99.03**	98.74
	LR	96.49	96.40	96.40	97.0	95.83	94.82	**97.88**
	SVM-L	94.89	94.12	95.17	95.1	94.01	94.71	**98.49**
	SVM-P	99.09	99.03	99.03	99.1	96.20	**99.21**	99.06
	RF	96.38	96.36	96.91	97.3	96.57	92.68	**98.26**
	AB	68.65	67.62	68.35	69.7	73.78	**75.46**	68.17
	NN	98.02	95.62	95.37	96.5	96.93	96.77	**98.33**
	DT	89.90	88.00	88.46	90.4	90.41	87.42	**91.10**
12	KNN	**82.48**	81.28	82.00	82.1	81.14	81.54	81.44
	LR	86.58	86.72	**87.18**	86.9	85.12	87.14	86.90
	SVM-L	86.90	84.54	86.23	86.9	84.40	**87.18**	86.66
	SVM-P	81.70	81.62	82.54	80.4	85.42	**86.18**	83.84
	RF	82.10	81.45	82.04	82.1	81.12	80.90	**86.12**
	AB	83.62	82.54	82.84	83.0	**83.78**	83.04	83.34
	NN	85.84	82.31	3.10	84.7	83.72	83.94	**86.26**
	DT	75.04	72.46	73.00	73.2	73.06	76.60	**78.72**
13	KNN	83.85	82.17	83.82	**84.0**	83.55	82.17	82.85
	LR	79.45	79.97	80.00	82.2	83.15	**84.03**	82.20
	SVM-L	81.45	81.15	82.86	82.5	83.05	83.05	**84.40**
	SVM-P	8.70	42.25	57.97	66.7	82.30	81.10	**85.10**
	RF	79.90	78.90	79.16	80.8	79.31	81.85	**84.45**
	AB	48.65	46.66	49.29	50.0	**50.40**	48.65	43.75
	NN	81.90	82.34	83.12	83.4	85.50	**86.90**	83.40
	DT	74.00	74.00	74.00	74.1	74.35	74.50	**75.40**
14	KNN	97.75	**98.12**	97.23	98.0	97.95	97.45	97.75
	LR	94.35	94.22	94.28	95.5	95.75	94.95	**96.75**
	SVM-L	92.90	92.57	93.26	94.3	94.27	93.45	**97.70**
	SVM-P	98.35	98.22	**98.66**	98.7	97.25	98.66	98.10
	RF	95.50	94.26	95.12	96.5	94.20	95.50	**97.60**
	AB	54.05	54.00	54.86	55.3	54.60	55.60	**65.10**
	NN	97.15	97.15	97.15	97.2	97.15	**97.90**	97.20
	DT	87.30	86.12	86.78	86.6	87.65	87.90	**88.55**

the scores achieved by our proposal compared against the scores obtained by other approaches in the state-of-the-art. The best scores are shown in bold, each dataset is represented by its ID defined in Table 1. The improvement among algorithms and datasets is notable: as shown in Fig. 3 we achieve an average accuracy of 81.83% across all tested datasets and classifiers, outperforming TFC, FCT, ExploreKit, AutoLearn (AL), LbR, by 6.54%, 5.99%, 5.63%, 3.95%, and 2.71%, respectively.

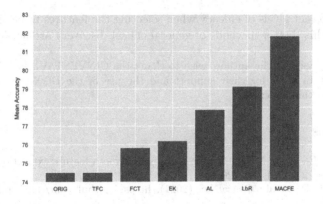

Fig. 3. Mean accuracy of state-of-the-art methods and MACFE (ours) across fourteen case study datasets and eight machine learning models.

5.4 Discussion

The transformation recommendation procedure of this method is agnostic of the learning algorithm. But, some transformations can be more appropriate for a certain algorithm. Therefore, MACFE achieves 100% of efficacy in terms of improving at least one model for each dataset. The depth hyperparameter d of MACFE can generate different orders of complex features to improve the model performance. A high value in d can result in too complex novel features, thus the algorithm cannot learn from the data. In contrast, a small value of the hyperparameter s can lead to a small subset of the original features, thus not finding good relationships between features. Hence, it is recommended a grid search to find the optimal values of hyperparameters.

6   Conclusions and Future Work

In this paper, we presented a causality-based feature selection to reduce the feature space search for feature transformations. Also, a meta-learning-based method for automated feature construction, on which the number of transformations executed on features depends on the number of useful transformations found on historical past similar features. In particular, this method has the capability of constructing novel features from raw data that are informative and useful for a learning algorithm. Hence, MACFE can automatically create features by applying selected transformations to the data, either unary, binary, or high-order, instead of applying all possible combinations of those. Hence, the feature explosion problem is minimized. However, MACFE has a fixed set of unary, binary, and scaling transformations. In future work, we intend to increase this set by adding more transformation functions, leading to the construction of more informative features from raw features. In addition, the causal selection of features could be improved, since it is applied equally to all datasets but different datasets can be expected to satisfy different causal assumptions, which produces different levels of efficacy when selecting the features to be engineered. To improve this, better methods of general causal discovery are needed.

Acknowledgments. The authors wish to thank the CINVESTAV, the AI Hub, and the CIIOT at ITESM, for their support and the use of the DGX for running the experiments in this paper.

References

1. Alcobaça, E., et al.: MFE: towards reproducible meta-feature extraction. J. Mach. Learn. Res. **21**(111), 1–5 (2020)
2. Beaumont, P., et al.: CausalNex (2021). https://github.com/quantumblacklabs/causalnex
3. Blumer, A., Ehrenfeucht, A., Haussler, D., Warmuth, M.K.: Learnability and the Vapnik-Chervonenkis dimension. J. ACM (JACM) **36**(4), 929–965 (1989)
4. Brazdil, P., Carrier, C.G., Soares, C., Vilalta, R.: Metalearning: Applications to Data Mining. Springer, Heidelberg (2008). https://doi.org/10.1007/978-3-540-73263-1
5. Chen, X., et al.: Neural feature search: a neural architecture for automated feature engineering. In: 2019 IEEE International Conference on Data Mining (ICDM), pp. 71–80. IEEE (2019)
6. Domingos, P.: A few useful things to know about machine learning. Commun. ACM **55**(10), 78–87 (2012)
7. Dua, D., Graff, C.: UCI machine learning repository (2017). http://archive.ics.uci.edu/ml
8. Duda, R.O., Hart, P.E., et al.: Pattern Classification. Wiley (2006)
9. Fan, W., et al.: Generalized and heuristic-free feature construction for improved accuracy. In: Proceedings of the 2010 SIAM International Conference on Data Mining, pp. 629–640. SIAM (2010)
10. Filchenkov, A., Pendryak, A.: Datasets meta-feature description for recommending feature selection algorithm. In: 2015 Artificial Intelligence and Natural Language and Information Extraction, Social Media and Web Search FRUCT Conference (AINL-ISMW FRUCT), pp. 11–18. IEEE (2015)
11. Hanusz, Z., Tarasinska, J., Zielinski, W.: Shapiro-Wilk test with known mean. REVSTAT-Stat. J. **14**(1), 89–100 (2016)
12. Heaton, J.: An empirical analysis of feature engineering for predictive modeling. In: SoutheastCon 2016, pp. 1–6. IEEE (2016)
13. Horn, F., Pack, R., Rieger, M.: The `autofeat` Python library for automated feature engineering and selection. In: Cellier, P., Driessens, K. (eds.) ECML PKDD 2019. CCIS, vol. 1167, pp. 111–120. Springer, Cham (2020). https://doi.org/10.1007/978-3-030-43823-4_10
14. Kanter, J.M., Veeramachaneni, K.: Deep feature synthesis: towards automating data science endeavors. In: 2015 IEEE International Conference on Data Science and Advanced Analytics (DSAA), pp. 1–10. IEEE (2015)
15. Katz, G., Shin, E.C.R., Song, D.: ExploreKit: automatic feature generation and selection. In: 2016 IEEE 16th International Conference on Data Mining (ICDM), pp. 979–984. IEEE (2016)
16. Kaul, A., Maheshwary, S., Pudi, V.: AutoLearn-automated feature generation and selection. In: 2017 IEEE International Conference on Data Mining (ICDM), pp. 217–226. IEEE (2017)

17. Khurana, U., Samulowitz, H., Turaga, D.: Feature engineering for predictive modeling using reinforcement learning. In: Proceedings of the AAAI Conference on Artificial Intelligence, vol. 32 (2018)
18. Khurana, U., Turaga, D., Samulowitz, H., Parthasrathy, S.: Cognito: automated feature engineering for supervised learning. In: 2016 IEEE 16th International Conference on Data Mining Workshops (ICDMW), pp. 1304–1307. IEEE (2016)
19. Kuhn, M., Johnson, K.: Feature Engineering and Selection: A Practical Approach for Predictive Models. CRC Press, Boca Raton (2019)
20. Kuo, F.Y., Sloan, I.H.: Lifting the curse of dimensionality. Not. AMS **52**(11), 1320–1328 (2005)
21. Nargesian, F., Samulowitz, H., Khurana, U., Khalil, E.B., Turaga, D.S.: Learning feature engineering for classification. In: IJCAI, pp. 2529–2535 (2017)
22. Pearl, J.: Causality: Models, Reasoning and Inference, 2nd edn. Cambridge University Press, Cambridge (2009)
23. Pedregosa, F., et al.: Scikit-learn: machine learning in Python. J. Mach. Learn. Res. **12**, 2825–2830 (2011)
24. Pinto, F., Soares, C., Mendes-Moreira, J.: Towards automatic generation of metafeatures. In: Bailey, J., Khan, L., Washio, T., Dobbie, G., Huang, J.Z., Wang, R. (eds.) PAKDD 2016. LNCS (LNAI), vol. 9651, pp. 215–226. Springer, Cham (2016). https://doi.org/10.1007/978-3-319-31753-3_18
25. Piramuthu, S., Sikora, R.T.: Iterative feature construction for improving inductive learning algorithms. Expert Syst. Appl. **36**(2), 3401–3406 (2009)
26. Qian, G., Sural, S., Gu, Y., Pramanik, S.: Similarity between Euclidean and cosine angle distance for nearest neighbor queries. In: Proceedings of the 2004 ACM Symposium on Applied, pp. 1232–1237 (2004)
27. Reshef, D.N., et al.: Detecting novel associations in large data sets. Science **334**(6062), 1518–1524 (2011)
28. Rivolli, A., Garcia, L.P., Soares, C., Vanschoren, J., de Carvalho, A.C.: Towards reproducible empirical research in meta-learning. arXiv preprint arXiv:1808.10406, pp. 32–52 (2018)
29. Vanschoren, J., Van Rijn, J.N., Bischl, B., Torgo, L.: OpenML: networked science in machine learning. ACM SIGKDD Explor. Newsl. **15**(2), 49–60 (2014)
30. Wang, M., Ding, Z., Pan, M.: LbR: a new regression architecture for automated feature engineering. In: 2020 International Conference on Data Mining Workshops (ICDMW), pp. 432–439. IEEE (2020)
31. Witten, I.H., Frank, E., Hall, M.A., Pal, C.J.: Practical Machine Learning Tools and Techniques. Morgan Kaufmann **578**, 1 (2005)
32. Yu, K., et al.: Causality-based feature selection: methods and evaluations. ACM Comput. Surv. (CSUR) **53**(5), 1–36 (2020)
33. Zheng, A., Casari, A.: Feature Engineering for Machine Learning: Principles and Techniques for Data Scientists. O'Reilly Media, Inc. (2018)

Time Series Forecasting with Quantum Machine Learning Architectures

Mayra Alejandra Rivera-Ruiz[1(✉)] ⓘ, Andres Mendez-Vazquez[1],
and José Mauricio López-Romero[2] ⓘ

[1] CINVESTAV Unidad Guadalajara, Av. del Bosque 1145, colonia el Bajío, C.P, 45019 Zapopan, Jalisco, Mexico
{mayra.rivera,andres.mendez}@cinvestav.mx
[2] CINVESTAV Unidad Querétaro, Libramiento Norponiente 2000, Fracc. Real de Juriquilla, C.P, 76230 Santiago de Querétaro, Querétaro, México
jm.lopez@cinvestav.mx

Abstract. Time series forecasting has been a topic of special interest due to its applications in Finance, Physics, Environmental Sciences and many other fields. In this article, we propose two classical-quantum hybrid architectures for time series forecasting with a multilayered structure inspired by the multilayer perceptron (MLP): a Quantum Neural Network (QNN) and a Hybrid-Quantum Neural Network (HQNN). These architectures incorporate quantum variational circuits with specific encoding schemes and the optimization is carried out by a classical computer. The performance of the proposed hybrid models is evaluated in four forecasting problems: Mackey-Glass time series and USD-to-euro currency exchange rate forecasting (univariate time series) as well as Lorenz attractor and prediction of the Box-Jenkins (Gas Furnace) time series (multivariate time series). The experiments were conducted by using the built-in Pennylane simulator lighting.qubit and Pytorch. Finally, these architectures, compared to the MLP, CNN and LSTM show a competitive performance with a similar number of trainable parameters.

Keywords: Quantum machine learning · Time series forecasting · Quantum neural networks

1 Introduction

A time series is a series of data ordered in time. There are two types of time series: multivariate time series and univariate time series [4]. The former involves multiple dependent variables whereas in the latter there is only one dependent variable. Time series forecasting aims to find the dependency between the past values and the future values of the time series. Time series has been an active research topic and can be found in areas of special interest such as economy, finance, and physical sciences [6,23].

O. Pichardo Lagunas et al. (Eds.): MICAI 2022, LNAI 13612, pp. 66–82, 2022.
https://doi.org/10.1007/978-3-031-19493-1_6

In the last few years, machine learning has become quite popular in a wide range of areas including time series forecasting. Specifically, there have been many attempts to use Artificial Neural Networks (ANNs) as an alternative to traditional statistical methods due to the fact that they are universal function approximators [31]. Additionally, Machine Learning models have been compared to traditional statistical methods, showing that neural networks are generally more accurate, and in specific situations, they improve significantly the accuracy of time series data prediction [9,15,18]. Specifically, Recurrent Neural Networks (RNNs) are widely used to solve time series forecasting due to their success in modeling sequential data [14]. Long Short-Term Memory Networks (LSTM) aim to solve the vanishing gradient problem of standard RNNs and are capable of learning long-term dependencies, which makes them very efficient for time series forecasting [10]. Quantum versions of RNNs and LSTM are proposed in [5,11]. On the other hand, a Convolutional Neural Network (CNN) is a class of ANN mainly used for computer vision and image processing tasks. Recently, CNNs have been applied for time series forecasting with very promising results [3,24,30]. A quantum version of CNN is introduced in [13] and has been applied in image classification [2,17,27].

On the other hand, Quantum Computing promises improvements in solving complex problems that the most powerful supercomputers cannot solve. Thus, Quantum Machine Learning (QML) has emerged as a tool to find patterns in data [8,16]. Specifically, Variational Quantum Circuits (VQCs) have emerged as a quantum counterpart of Neural Networks [21]. VQCs have begun to be used as a possible alternative to Deep Learning and are known in the literature as Quantum Neural Network or Quantum Circuit Learning (QCL). In this framework entangling operations are used to create multilayered structures, similar to Deep Learning. Furthermore, QCL is a classical-quantum hybrid algorithm that can perform supervised learning tasks [21]. In QCL, the output is computed by a quantum circuit whereas the update of parameters is performed by a classical computer. Since quantum circuits admit a universal model [7], quantum hybrid architectures become attractive for time series forecasting.

Classical models inspired by quantum computing have been proposed for predicting chaotic time series produced by a Lorentz system with competitive results when compared with classical neural networks [28,29]. On the other hand, quantum models have been proposed and evaluated with univariate time series showing to be on par with existing classical models [19,25,26]. In [19] stock prices using a quantum reservoir computer are predicted. Models based on a quantum optimization algorithm are proposed in [25,26]. In [26] a new neutrosophic set based time series forecasting model is presented, where a quantum optimization algorithm is used to improve the accuracy. The model is verified and validated with datasets of the university enrollment of Alabama (USA), Taiwan futures exchange (TAIFEX) index and Taiwan Stock Exchange Corporation (TSEC) weighted index. In [25] a fuzzy-quantum time series forecasting model (FQTSFM) is introduced. The FQTSFM is tested with three different datasets, namely the daily average temperatures of Taipei, TAIFEX index and

TSEC weighted index. Otherwise, QML is applied for finance in [12], where a parameterized quantum circuit (PQC) is used for forecasting time series signals with simulated quantum forward propagation.

In this paper the contribution is threefold:

– A Quantum Neural Network (QNN) for time series forecasting that consists of a multilayered VQC is proposed, where the number of qubits is set according to the size of the regressor vector.
– A Hybrid-Quantum Neural Network (HQNN) for time series forecasting is presented, where two or more dressed quantum circuits (quantum circuits sandwiched between two classical layers) are concatenated in order to construct a multilayered architecture.
– The range of applicability of previous quantum models [19,25,26] is extended by including not only univariate but also multivariate time series forecasting.

From the variety of experiments performed in this work, it is possible to conclude that these hybrid models show a competitive performance when compared to MLP, CNN and LSTM in univariate and multivariate time series forecasting.

The rest of the paper is organized as follows. The basics of quantum computing are covered in Sect. 2. In Sect. 3, the problem to be solved is established. The proposed architectures are formalized in Sect. 4. The experimental setups and results are presented in Sect. 5. Finally, the conclusions are presented in Sect. 6.

2   Preliminaries

We begin by introducing basic concepts of quantum computing before presenting our contribution. In this section we use the notation introduced in [20].

2.1   The Qubit

The qubit is the basic unit of information in quantum computing. A qubit is a two-state quantum mechanical system. This means that while a classical bit can be 0 or 1, a qubit can also exist in what we call a superposition state, which is a linear combination of the states $|0\rangle$ and $|1\rangle$. This property is the main difference between the bit and the qubit [22]. Mathematically, we can represent a qubit as a two-dimensional complex vector in which the basis vectors are the allowed states $|0\rangle$ and $|1\rangle$. These vectors are given by $|0\rangle = \binom{1}{0}$ and $|1\rangle = \binom{0}{1}$. Then a superposition state is written as

$$|\Psi\rangle = \alpha |0\rangle + \beta |1\rangle, \tag{1}$$

where α and β are complex numbers that satisfy the normalization condition: $|\alpha|^2 + |\beta|^2 = 1$. We can construct multi-qubit states through the tensor product. For example, the state $|01\rangle = |0\rangle \otimes |1\rangle$ represents a two-qubit system where the first and second qubit are in the state $|0\rangle$ and $|1\rangle$, respectively.

The state of the qubits could be modified through unitary operations (quantum gates) to perform a computation. Quantum circuits are used for this purpose. The final state of a quantum circuit is the measurement of the qubits in a given basis.

2.2   Quantum Circuits

A quantum circuit is a model of quantum computation that consists of a sequence of quantum operations (quantum gates) applied to quantum data (multi-qubit states). A quantum gate is a unitary operator which can be described as a unitary matrix. Then, if we have a set of unitary operators $\{U_i\}_{i=1}^{k}$, we can mathematically represent the state $|\Psi\rangle$ prepared by the quantum circuit as

$$|\Psi\rangle = \prod_{i=1}^{k} U_i \, |0\rangle^{\otimes n}, \qquad (2)$$

where $|0\rangle^{\otimes n}$ is an initial n-qubit state. The graphical representation of Eq. 2 is shown in Fig. 1.

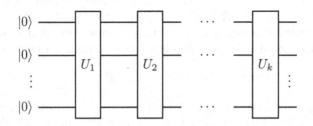

Fig. 1. Graphical depiction of the quantum circuit of $\prod_{i=1}^{k} U_i \, |0\rangle^{\otimes n}$

The quantum gates can act on one (single-qubit gate) or several qubits (multiple-qubit gates). The quantum NOT gate can be represented with the Pauli-X matrix. The NOT operator acts on a single qubit, and it is equivalent to a NOT classical gate. Hence, we have: $U_{NOT} |0\rangle = |1\rangle$ and $U_{NOT} |1\rangle = |0\rangle$. Since the other Pauli matrices are unitary, they are also used as single-qubit gates. The action of the Pauli Y and Z gates is a rotation around the Y-axis and Z-axis respectively of the Bloch sphere by π radians. Quantum gates can also be parametrised. The main parametrised gates are the Pauli rotations: $R_x = e^{-i\frac{\theta}{2}X}$, $R_y = e^{-i\frac{\theta}{2}Y}$ and $R_z = e^{-i\frac{\theta}{2}Z}$, which rotate the Bloch vector about the x, y and z axes by an angle θ.

The quantum gate that allows us to create superposition states is known as Hadamard gate. It acts on a single qubit and maps the basis states $\{|0\rangle, |1\rangle\}$ into the superposition states $\left\{\frac{|0\rangle+|1\rangle}{\sqrt{2}}, \frac{|0\rangle+|1\rangle}{\sqrt{2}}\right\}$. Another important quantum gate is the CNOT gate and acts on a qubit in the following way: $|a, b\rangle \rightarrow |a, b \oplus a\rangle$.

Mathematically serial operations are represented by a matrix product starting with the first operation on the left followed by subsequent operations moving to the right. On the other hand, when quantum operations are performed in parallel, we need to compute the tensor product.

2.3   Variational Quantum Circuits

A Variational Quantum Circuit (VQC) is a quantum circuit with adjustable parameters which are optimized in a classical computer. VQCs can be used as a quantum version of classical feed-forward neural networks [1,21].

A VQC consists of three parts:

- **Embedding circuit:** The classical data $\mathbf{x} = (x_1, ..., x_N)$ is encoded into a quantum state by applying a $\mathbf{x}$-parameterized unitary operator $U_{in}(\mathbf{x})$ to an initial quantum state $|0\rangle^{\otimes n}$:

$$\mathcal{E} : \mathbf{x} \to |\Psi_{in}(\mathbf{x})\rangle = U_{in}(\mathbf{x}) |0\rangle^{\otimes n}. \tag{3}$$

In other words, $\mathcal{E}$ maps the classical input from a classical vector space to a Hilbert space. A common choice of $U_{in}(\mathbf{x})$ is to apply a Pauli rotation gate (e.g., a Pauli-Y rotation gate), for each input feature in $\mathbf{x}$ as follows: $U_{in}(\mathbf{x}) = R_y(x_1) \otimes \cdots \otimes R_y(x_N) = \otimes_{i=1}^{N} R_y(x_i)$.

- **Parameterized circuit**: A parameterized circuit of depth q is equivalent to the hidden layers of the ANNs and is a concatenation of quantum layers:

$$\mathcal{U} = \mathcal{L}_q \circ \cdots \mathcal{L}_2 \circ \mathcal{L}_1, \tag{4}$$

where $\mathcal{U}$ is a unitary operator. A quantum layer $\mathcal{L}$ consists of single-qubit operations followed by entangling operations (multi-qubit operations).

- **Measurement:** To obtain the output vector $\mathbf{y}$, the expectation values of the n observables $\hat{\mathbf{y}} = [\hat{y}_1, ..., \hat{y}_n]$ are measured. The observable $\hat{y}_i$ is a tensor product of n operators as follows:

$$\hat{y}_1 = B \otimes I \otimes I ... \otimes I$$
$$\hat{y}_2 = I \otimes B \otimes I ... \otimes I$$
$$\vdots$$
$$\hat{y}_n = I \otimes I \otimes I ... \otimes B$$

where I is the identity operator and B is a Hermitian operator that could be different for each observable. Usually, B is chosen as the Pauli-Z operator. This operation is defined as a measurement layer:

$$\mathcal{M} : |\Psi_{out}\rangle \to \mathbf{y} = \langle \Psi_{out}| \hat{\mathbf{y}} |\Psi_{out}\rangle, \tag{5}$$

where $|\Psi_{out}\rangle$ is the transformed qubit state. $\mathcal{M}$ is a map from a quantum state to a classical vector.

Finally, the full quantum network is given by

$$Q = \mathcal{M} \circ \mathcal{U} \circ \mathcal{E}. \tag{6}$$

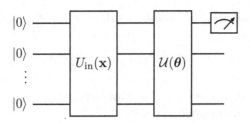

Fig. 2. Illustration of a variational quantum circuit. The input $\mathbf{x}$ is encoded into a quantum state by the embedding circuit. $\mathcal{U}(\boldsymbol{\theta})$ is the parameterized circuit with the trainable parameters $\boldsymbol{\theta}$ of the network. A quantum measurement is made on the first qubit.

3 Problem Statement

A time series is a sequence of observations of the values that one (univariate time series) or more variables (multivariate time series) take over time, where the time interval between observations is constant. For a time series of size N, the main problem is to predict $x(t + \Delta t)$ based on the input:

$$\mathbf{x} = (x(t + \Delta t - P), ..., x(t + \Delta t - 2), x(t + \Delta t - 1)), \tag{7}$$

where $P < N$. In other words, the objective is to predict $x(t + \Delta t)$ using P past values building the forecasting model $\hat{x}(t + \Delta t) = f(\mathbf{x})$. This problem can be approached as a supervised learning problem.

The supervised learning scheme applied to time series will have as input the regressor vector $\mathbf{x}$ given by Eq. 7 and the corresponding teacher data will be given by the future values $x(t + \Delta t)$.

4 Quantum Machine Learning Architectures for Time Series Forecasting

In this section, the two proposed architectures for time series forecasting are described.

4.1 Quantum Neural Network

As we mentioned earlier, one way to construct a quantum counterpart of neural networks is in terms of VQCs. A general structure of a VQC is shown in Fig. 2. Thus, the output is obtained from a quantum device (quantum circuit) whereas the optimization of parameters $\boldsymbol{\theta}$ is performed by a classical device (classical computer). To this end, the regressor vector $\mathbf{x}$ is encoded into a quantum state as in Eq. 3, where the number of qubits n is equal to the P past values.

Thus, selecting the Pauli-Y rotation gate, the input quantum state can be expressed as:

$$|\Psi_{\text{in}}(\mathbf{x})\rangle = \bigotimes_{j=1}^{n} R_Y(\pi\mathbf{x}_j)|0\rangle^{\otimes n}. \tag{8}$$

The output state $|\Psi_{\text{out}}(\mathbf{x}, \boldsymbol{\theta})\rangle$ can be obtained by applying a $\boldsymbol{\theta}$-parametrized unitary $\mathcal{U}(\boldsymbol{\theta})$ to the input quantum state:

$$|\Psi_{\text{out}}(\mathbf{x}, \boldsymbol{\theta})\rangle = \mathcal{U}(\boldsymbol{\theta})|\Psi_{\text{in}}(\mathbf{x})\rangle. \tag{9}$$

The $\boldsymbol{\theta}$-parametrized unitary $\mathcal{U}(\boldsymbol{\theta})$ consists of l layers. The k-th layer is chosen to be

$$\mathcal{L}^{(k)}(\theta_k) = U_{\text{ent}} \bigotimes_{j=1}^{n} R_Z(\theta_{j,k}^Z)R_Y(\theta_{j,k}^Y)R_X(\theta_{j,k}^X), \tag{10}$$

where the entangling gate U_{ent} is composed of CNOT gates. Consequently, $\mathcal{U}(\boldsymbol{\theta})$ can be expressed in compact form as follows:

$$\mathcal{U}(\boldsymbol{\theta}) = \mathcal{L}^{(D)}(\theta_D)\mathcal{L}^{(D-1)}(\theta_{D-1})\cdots\mathcal{L}^{(2)}(\theta_2)\mathcal{L}^{(1)}(\theta_1). \tag{11}$$

The proposed VQC is shown in Fig. 3.

Then, in the simplest case of one-step-ahead forecasting models, the estimated output $\hat{x}(t + \Delta t)$ can be expressed as the following expectation value:

$$\hat{x}(t + \Delta t) = \langle \Psi_{\text{out}}|B|\Psi_{\text{out}}\rangle, \tag{12}$$

were B is some chosen observable. The loss function L corresponds to the conventional squared loss

$$L = ||\, x(t + \Delta t) - \hat{x}(t + \Delta t)\, ||^2, \tag{13}$$

due to the fact that time series forecasting is approached as a regression problem.

4.2   Hybrid Quantum Neural Network

In the previous subsection, we used a VQC as a model for time series forecasting with a multilayered structure. However, one of its limitations is that the number of features depend on the number of qubits, contrary to classical feed-forward neural networks, where we can freely choose the number of features of each layer. One way of overcoming this constraint is by sandwiching the VQC between two classical layers as shown in Fig. 4. This solution is formalized by introducing the concept of Dressed Quantum Circuit (DQC) [20]. The general form of a DQC is given by:

$$\tilde{Q}_{n_{\text{in}} \rightarrow n_{\text{out}}} = L_{n_q \rightarrow n_{\text{out}}} \circ Q_{n_q \rightarrow n_q} \circ L_{n_{\text{in}} \rightarrow n_q}, \tag{14}$$

where $L_{n \rightarrow n'}$ is a classical layer with n input and n' output variables. $Q_{n_q \rightarrow n_q}$ is the quantum circuit given by Eq. (6). The classical layer $L_{n_q \rightarrow n_{\text{out}}}$ is responsible of the pre-processing of the inputs of the VQC whereas $L_{n_{\text{in}} \rightarrow n_q}$ performs the

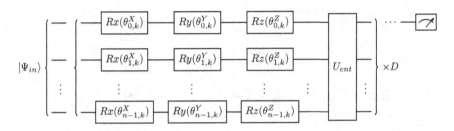

Fig. 3. VQC used for the proposed model. $|\Psi_{in}\rangle$ is the input state prepared by the input gate $U_{in}(\mathbf{x})$. D denotes the depth of the circuit. The U_{ent} gate is composed of CNOT gates.

post-processing of the outputs of the VQC [20]. Since both classical layers contain trainable parameters, the pre-processing of inputs and the post-processing of outputs of the VQC are optimized during the training process. The main advantage of a DQC is that n_{in} and n_{out} (the number of input and output variables) are independent of the number of qubits of the VQC.

Inspired by the Classical Deep Neural Networks we propose a multilayered hybrid classical-quantum neural network (HQNN):

$$\mathrm{HQNN} = \tilde{Q}_{n_{d-1}\to n_d} \circ \cdots \tilde{Q}_{n_1\to n_2} \circ \tilde{Q}_{n_0\to n_1}, \tag{15}$$

where d denotes the depth of the HQNN.

In this work, a two-layer HQNN is applied to time series forecasting:

$$\mathrm{HQNN} = \tilde{Q}_{n_1\to n_2} \circ \tilde{Q}_{n_0\to n_1}, \tag{16}$$

where n_0 is equal to the number of variables of the regressor vector. In the case of one-step ahead forecasting $n_2 = 1$. We use the same structure for the DQC of each layer. Then, the encoding and variational layers of the l-th layer of the HQNN are given by:

$$\mathcal{E}_l(\mathbf{x}) = \bigotimes_{j=1}^{n} R_Y\left(\tanh\left(x_{j,l}\right)\right)|0\rangle^{\otimes n}, \tag{17}$$

$$\mathcal{U}_l\left(\boldsymbol{\theta}\right) : |x\rangle \longrightarrow |y\rangle = U_{\mathrm{ent}} \bigotimes_{j=1}^{n} R_Z(\theta_{j,l}^Z)R_Y(\theta_{j,l}^Y)R_X(\theta_{j,l}^X), \tag{18}$$

where U_{ent} is composed of CNOT gates. In the measurement layer we take the expectation value of the Pauli-Z operator of each qubit.

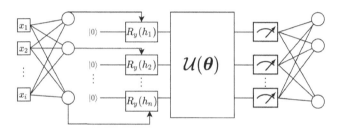

Fig. 4. Illustration of a dressed quantum circuit. It is built with a VQC between two classical layers. The k-th output from the classical pre-processing layer is denoted by h_k.

5   Results and Discussion

In this section, we evaluate the performance of the proposed quantum machine learning architectures by applying the models to four standard problems: Mackey-Glass time series, Lorenz attractor, prediction of the Box-Jenkins time series and USD-to-euro currency exchange rate forecasting.

The experiments performed in this research are conducted by using the built-in Pennylane simulator lighting.qubit and Pytorch. Additionally, for the purpose of a fair comparison, the same optimizers, learning rates and number of epochs (100 for all cases) are applied to the MLP, CNN, LSTM and the proposed models. In addition, the time series data is scaled within the range $[0, 1]$ using the min-max normalization formula.

The SGD optimizer is used in the Lorenz attractor problem with a learning rate of 0.001. In the case of Mackey-Glass and USD-to-euro currency exchange, the Adam Optimizer is used with a learning rate of 0.001. In the case of the Box-Jenkins problem, the Adam Optimizer is used with a learning rate of 0.0005.

The depth of the QNN and the number of qubits used in the HQNN are equal to 5 and 3 in the Mackey-Glass time series problem, 7 and 4 for the Lorenz attractor, 10 and 2 in the Box-Jenkins time series and finally, 4 and 3 in the USD to Euro currency exchange rate forecasting.

The CNN model consists of a 1D convolutional layer and two fully connected layers. After the 1D convolutional layer, a 1D max-pooling layer is applied. The ReLU activation function is used in the convolutional layer and the first fully-connected layer. In the case of the Lorenz attractor problem, the number of output channels of the convolutional layer and the number of units in the first fully connected layer is equal to 8 and 16, respectively, and in the rest of the time series datasets, equal to 4 and 8. The LSTM model has a hidden state size equal to 5 in the Lorenz attractor problem and equal to 3 in the rest of the time series datasets.

The performance results of the proposed models in terms of RMSE, MAE and MAPE are summarized in Tables 1, 2, 3 and 4.

Mackey-Glass Time Series. Mackey-Glass time series data are derived from the following differential equation:

$$\dot{x} = \frac{\alpha x(t - \tau)}{1 + x^{\gamma}(t - \tau)} - \beta x(t), \tag{19}$$

where τ is the time-delay parameter. When $\tau \geqslant 17$ Eq. (19) shows the chaotic phenomenon. To obtain its numerical solution, the Runge-Kutta method is applied with the initial condition $x(0) = 1.2$ and integration step equal to 0.1. The parameters α, β and γ are equal to 0.2, 0.1 and 10, respectively. We use 1000 simulation data points to build our model, which are described as follows:

$$[x(t - 18), x(t - 12), x(t - 6), x(t); x(t + 6)], \tag{20}$$

where $t = 19, 20, ..., 1017, 1018$. The first 500 points are selected as the training data and the rest as the testing data. The vector $\mathbf{x} = (x(t - 18), x(t - 12), x(t - 6), x(t))$ is selected as the input vector and the last variable $x(t + 6)$ as the output variable of the model. Figures 5a and 6a show the comparison between the original and forecasted outputs of both models QNN as well as HQNN for the training and validation phases. Additionally, the Fig. 7a shows the MSE loss curves of the HQNN, QNN, MLP, CNN and LSTM. When comparing the QNN and MLP, the QNN shows a superior performance. We can observe an improvement of about 34% in RMSE, 33% in MAE, and 33% in MAPE. On the other hand, the MLP shows a better performance than the HQNN, improving the RMSE, MAE and MAPE by approximately 3%, 12% and 1%, respectively. Additionally, the QNN outperforms the LSTM. We can observe an improvement of about 27% in RMSE, 18% in MAE and 20% in MAPE.

Table 1. Comparison results among the proposed models, MLP, CNN and LSTM for Mackey-Glass time series prediction.

Network	Parameters	RMSE	MAE	MAPE
QNN	60	0.01360	0.0114	0.01319
HQNN	68	0.02117	0.01726	0.01992
MLP (4,5,6,1)	68	0.02047	0.01697	0.01963
CNN	65	0.04586	0.03419	0.04159
LSTM	76	0.01866	0.01395	0.01659

Lorenz Time Series. The Lorenz equations are given by

$$\dot{x} = \sigma(y - x),$$
$$\dot{y} = -y - zx + \rho x,$$
$$\dot{z} = -\beta z + xy. \tag{21}$$

Let $\sigma = 10$, $\rho = 28$ and $\beta = 8/3$. We get its numerical solutions by using the Euler method to obtain the time series dataset by taking the initial conditions:

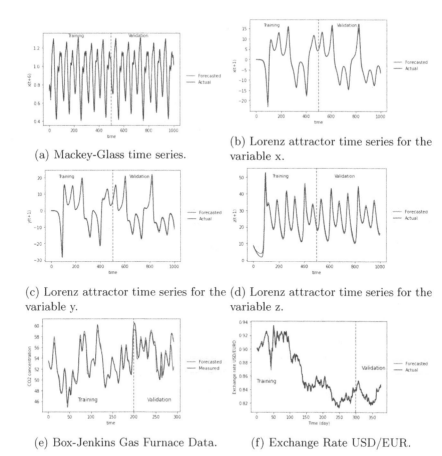

(a) Mackey-Glass time series.

(b) Lorenz attractor time series for the variable x.

(c) Lorenz attractor time series for the variable y.

(d) Lorenz attractor time series for the variable z.

(e) Box-Jenkins Gas Furnace Data.

(f) Exchange Rate USD/EUR.

Fig. 5. Actual and forecasted outputs using the QNN.

$x(0) = 0$, $y(0) = -0.01$ and $z(0) = 9$. The vector $\mathbf{x} = [x(t), y(t), z(t)]$ is chosen as the input vector and the three variables $x(t + 1), y(t + 1), z(t + 1)$ are the output variables, where $t = 1, ..., 1000$. The first 500 points are used during the training phase and the rest in the testing phase.

For the QNN we use a different unitary input gate:

$$U_{\text{in}} = \bigotimes_{j=0}^{n-1} R_Y(\cos^{-1}(\mathbf{x}_j^2)) R_Z(\sin^{-1}(\mathbf{x}_j)). \tag{22}$$

To get the output variables, we take the following expectation values:

$$\begin{aligned}
\hat{x}(t + 1) &= \langle \Psi_{out} | X \otimes I \otimes I | \Psi_{out} \rangle, \\
\hat{y}(t + 1) &= \langle \Psi_{out} | I \otimes Y \otimes I | \Psi_{out} \rangle, \\
\hat{z}(t + 1) &= \langle \Psi_{out} | I \otimes I \otimes Z | \Psi_{out} \rangle.
\end{aligned} \tag{23}$$

Figures 5b–5d and 6b–6d show the comparison between the original and forecasted outputs of both models QNN as well as HQNN for $x(t+1)$, $y(t+1)$ and $z(t+1)$ in the training and validation phases. In addition, the Fig. 7b shows the MSE loss curves of the HQNN, QNN, MLP, CNN and LSTM. When comparing the QNN, HQNN and MLP, the HQNN shows the worst performance when predicting $y(t+1)$ and $z(t+1)$ despite the fact that this model has more trainable parameters. When forecasting $x(t+1)$ the HQNN slightly outperformed the MLP, improving the RMSE and MAE by about 7% and 3%, respectively. On the other hand, when forecasting $x(t+1)$, the QNN noticeably outperformed the MLP. We can observe an improvement of approximately 97% in RMSE, 75% in MAE, and 77% in MAPE. Similarly, for $y(t+1)$, the QNN outperformed the MLP, improving the RMSE, MAE and MAPE by about 51%, 52% and 81%, respectively. However, when predicting $z(t+1)$, the MLP is superior to the QNN, improving the RMSE by around 14%, the MAE by about 27% and the MAPE by approximately 26%. Additionally, the QNN outperformed the CNN in predicting $x(t+1)$, $y(t+1)$ and $z(t+1)$. When comparing the QNN and the LSTM, the QNN shows a superior performance in predicting $x(t+1)$ and $y(t+1)$. However, when predicting $z(t+1)$, the LSTM is superior to the QNN, improving the RMSE by around 5%, the MAE by about 15% and the MAPE by approximately 28%.

Box-Jenkins Gas Furnace Data. The Box-Jenkins gas furnace time series is widely used in the literature. To obtain this times series, the carbon dioxide concentration (CO_2) is measured in the gases product of a combustion process of a methane-air mixture. Every 9 s a record is taken by keeping the gas flow rate constant and methane rate changing randomly. Thus, in this work, the following prediction model is chosen:

$$[\nu(t-4), y(t-1); y(t)] \qquad t = 5, ..., 296 \tag{24}$$

where $\nu(t)$ is the methane gas flow, and $y(t)$ is the CO_2 concentration in the output gases. The first 200 points are selected as the training data, and the rest as the testing data.

The comparison between the measured and forecasted outputs for the training and validation phases is shown in Figs. 5e and 6e. Furthermore, the Fig. 7c shows the MSE loss curves of the HQNN, QNN, MLP, CNN and LSTM. We can observe that the HQNN model provided better results than the QNN and MLP. The HQNN outperformed the MLP by approximately 8% in RMSE and 4% in both MAE as well as MAPE. Similarly, the HQNN is superior to the QNN, improving the RMSE by approximately 57% and the MAE and MAPE by about 51%. In addition, the HQNN outperformed the CNN, improving the RMSE by approximately 13% and the MAE and MAPE by about 12%. However, the LSTM slightly outperformed the HQNN, improving the MAE by approximately 8% and the RMSE and MAPE by about 7%.

Table 2. Comparison results among the proposed models, MLP, CNN and LSTM for the Lorenz attractor.

Network	Parameters	RMSE	MAE	MAPE
QNN	63	0.065382	0.37843	0.12376
		0.91871	0.65624	0.13911
		1.10889	0.94987	0.04039
HQNN	194	1.9695	1.44324	0.55534
		3.16348	2.24749	1.12748
		2.25607	1.72386	0.07503
MLP (3,12,9,3)	195	2.11768	1.48587	0.52687
		1.87211	1.35788	0.72274
		0.9579	0.69229	0.02976
CNN	227	2.04956	1.44207	0.40423
		2.71476	2.10219	0.85086
		2.48987	1.62512	0.0626
LSTM	178	1.95701	1.53737	0.52913
		3.22944	2.13337	1.18607
		1.05513	0.81134	0.02923

Exchange Rate USD/EUR. The data about exchange rate USD/EUR are retrieved from the site http://fx.sauder.ubc.ca/data.html. Data are gathered for the period from 01/01/2020 until 08/07/2021 with daily step. We use 376 simulation data points to build the model:

$$[x(t-4), x(t-3), x(t-2), x(t-1), x(t); x(t+1)], \tag{25}$$

where $t = 5, ..., 380$. The first 300 data points are used in the training phase and the remaining data in the testing phase.

Figures 5f and 6f show the comparison between the original and forecasted outputs of both models QNN as well as HQNN for the training and validation phases. Additionally, the Fig. 7d shows the MSE loss curves of the HQNN, QNN, MLP, CNN and LSTM. When comparing the QNN, HQNN and MLP, the QNN shows the best performance of the three models. The QNN outperformed the MLP. We can observe an improvement of around 39% in RMSE, MAE, and MAPE. Similarly, the HQNN shows a better performance than the MLP, improving the RMSE by about 35% and both MAE as well as MAPE by approximately 36%. In addition, both the QNN and the HQNN outperformed the CNN and LSTM models. When comparing the QNN and CNN, the QNN showed an improvement of approximately 23% in RMSE and 22% in MAE as well as MAPE.

Table 3. Comparison results among the proposed models, MLP, CNN and LSTM for Box Jenkins time series prediction.

Network	Parameters	RMSE	MAE	MAPE
QNN	60	1.62488	0.97698	0.01733
HQNN	58	0.69741	0.47627	0.00851
MLP (2,6,5,1)	59	0.75594	0.49578	0.00885
CNN	65	0.80361	0.54213	0.00968
LSTM	76	0.64989	0.43938	0.00788

Table 4. Comparison results among the proposed models, MLP, CNN and LSTM for USD-to-euro currency exchange rate forecasting.

Network	Parameters	RMSE	MAE	MAPE
QNN	60	0.00281	0.00215	0.00258
HQNN	64	0.00298	0.00224	0.00269
MLP (5,6,3,1)	61	0.00458	0.00352	0.00422
CNN	65	0.00364	0.00274	0.0033
LSTM	76	0.00432	0.00323	0.00388

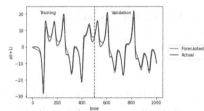

(a) Mackey-Glass time series.

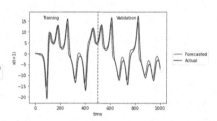

(b) Lorenz attractor time series for the variable x.

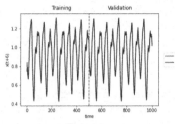

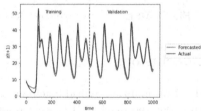

(c) Lorenz attractor time series for the variable y.

(d) Lorenz attractor time series for the variable z.

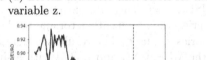

(e) Box-Jenkins Gas Furnace Data.

(f) Exchange Rate USD/EUR.

Fig. 6. Actual and forecasted outputs using the HQNN.

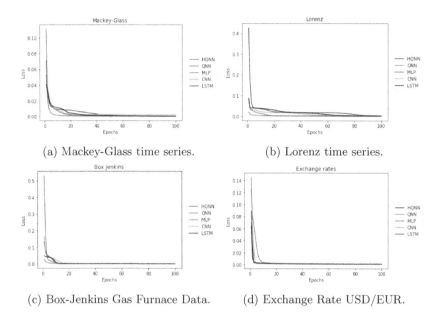

(a) Mackey-Glass time series.   (b) Lorenz time series.

(c) Box-Jenkins Gas Furnace Data.   (d) Exchange Rate USD/EUR.

Fig. 7. MSE loss curves of the HQNN, QNN, MLP, CNN and LSTM.

6   Conclusions

Two classical-quantum hybrid machine learning architectures with a multilayered structure inspired by the MLP are proposed. In order to evaluate the prediction performance of the models, two univariate time series, Mackey-Glass time series and USD-to-euro currency exchange rate forecasting, as well as two multivariate time series, the Lorenz attractor and prediction of the Box-Jenkins (Gas Furnace) time series are used. The results are competitive compared with those obtained with the MLP, CNN and LSTM with a similar number of trainable parameters, opening the possibility of further exploring how to improve classical models by incorporating quantum computing elements. Additionally, we established a strategy to use quantum architectures in time series forecasting. Future work would focus on exploring more complex hybrid quantum-classical architectures with different embedding circuits and their application to real-world time series data.

Acknowledgment. The authors wish to thank CINVESTAV for the financial support for the realization of this work.

References

1. Abbas, A., Sutter, D., Zoufal, C., Lucchi, A., Figalli, A., Woerner, S.: The power of quantum neural networks. Nat. Comput. Sci. **1**(6), 403–409 (2021)
2. Alam, M., Kundu, S., Topaloglu, R.O., Ghosh, S.: Quantum-classical hybrid machine learning for image classification (ICCAD special session paper). In: 2021 IEEE/ACM International Conference On Computer Aided Design (ICCAD), pp. 1–7. IEEE (2021)
3. Amarasinghe, K., Marino, D.L., Manic, M.: Deep neural networks for energy load forecasting. In: 2017 IEEE 26th International Symposium on Industrial Electronics (ISIE), pp. 1483–1488. IEEE (2017)
4. Barba Maggi, L.M.: Multiscale Forecasting Models. Springer, Cham (2018). https://doi.org/10.1007/978-3-319-94992-5
5. Bausch, J.: Recurrent quantum neural networks. Adv. Neural. Inf. Process. Syst. **33**, 1368–1379 (2020)
6. Bhardwaj, S., Chandrasekhar, E., Padiyar, P., Gadre, V.M.: A comparative study of wavelet-based ANN and classical techniques for geophysical time-series forecasting. Comput. Geosci. **138**, 104461 (2020). https://doi.org/10.1016/j.cageo.2020.104461
7. Biamonte, J.: Universal variational quantum computation. Phys. Rev. A **103**, L030401 (2021). https://doi.org/10.1103/PhysRevA.103.L030401
8. Biamonte, J., Wittek, P., Pancotti, N., Rebentrost, P., Wiebe, N., Lloyd, S.: Quantum machine learning. Nature **549**(7671), 195–202 (2017)
9. Chakraborty, K., Mehrotra, K., Mohan, C.K., Ranka, S.: Forecasting the behavior of multivariate time series using neural networks. Neural Netw. **5**(6), 961–970 (1992)
10. Chandra, R., Goyal, S., Gupta, R.: Evaluation of deep learning models for multistep ahead time series prediction. IEEE Access, 1–1 (2021). https://doi.org/10.1109/ACCESS.2021.3085085
11. Chen, S.Y.C., Yoo, S., Fang, Y.L.L.: Quantum long short-term memory. In: ICASSP 2022–2022 IEEE International Conference on Acoustics, Speech and Signal Processing (ICASSP), pp. 8622–8626. IEEE (2022)
12. Emmanoulopoulos, D., Dimoska, S.: Quantum machine learning in finance: time series forecasting. arXiv preprint arXiv:2202.00599 (2022)
13. Henderson, M., Shakya, S., Pradhan, S., Cook, T.: Quanvolutional neural networks: powering image recognition with quantum circuits. Quantum Mach. Intell. **2**(1), 1–9 (2020). https://doi.org/10.1007/s42484-020-00012-y
14. Hewamalage, H., Bergmeir, C., Bandara, K.: Recurrent neural networks for time series forecasting: current status and future directions. Int. J. Forecast. **37**(1), 388–427 (2021)
15. Hill, T., O'Connor, M., Remus, W.: Neural network models for time series forecasts. Manage. Sci. **42**(7), 1082–1092 (1996)
16. Huang, H.Y., et al.: Power of data in quantum machine learning. Nat. Commun. **12**(1), 1–9 (2021)
17. Hur, T., Kim, L., Park, D.K.: Quantum convolutional neural network for classical data classification. Quant. Mach. Intell. **4**(1), 1–18 (2022)
18. Kolarik, T., Rudorfer, G.: Time series forecasting using neural networks. ACM Sigapl. Apl. Quote Quad **25**(1), 86–94 (1994)
19. Kutvonen, A., Fujii, K., Sagawa, T.: Optimizing a quantum reservoir computer for time series prediction. Sci. Rep. **10**(1), 1–7 (2020)

20. Mari, A., Bromley, T.R., Izaac, J., Schuld, M., Killoran, N.: Transfer learning in hybrid classical-quantum neural networks. Quantum **4**, 340 (2020). https://doi.org/10.22331/q-2020-10-09-340
21. Mitarai, K., Negoro, M., Kitagawa, M., Fujii, K.: Quantum circuit learning. Phys. Rev. A **98**, 032309 (2018). https://doi.org/10.1103/PhysRevA.98.032309
22. Nielsen, M.A., Chuang, I.: Quantum computation and quantum information (2002)
23. Sezer, O.B., Gudelek, M.U., Ozbayoglu, A.M.: Financial time series forecasting with deep learning: a systematic literature review: 2005–2019. Appl. Soft Comput. **90**, 106181 (2020). https://doi.org/10.1016/j.asoc.2020.106181
24. Shi, X., Chen, Z., Wang, H., Yeung, D.Y., Wong, W.K., Woo, W.C.: Convolutional lstm network: a machine learning approach for precipitation nowcasting. In: Advances in Neural Information Processing Systems, vol. 28 (2015)
25. Singh, P.: Fqtsfm: A fuzzy-quantum time series forecasting model. Information Sciences 566, 57–79 (2021). https://doi.org/10.1016/j.ins.2021.02.024, https://www.sciencedirect.com/science/article/pii/S0020025521001663
26. Singh, P., Huang, Y.P.: A new hybrid time series forecasting model based on the neutrosophic set and quantum optimization algorithm. Comput. Ind. **111**, 121–139 (2019). https://doi.org/10.1016/j.compind.2019.06.004, https://www.sciencedirect.com/science/article/pii/S0166361518309072
27. Sridevi, S., Kanimozhi, T., Issac, K., Sudha, M.: Quanvolution neural network to recognize arrhythmia from 2D scaleogram features of ECG signals. In: 2022 International Conference on Innovative Trends in Information Technology (ICITIIT), pp. 1–5. IEEE (2022)
28. Teguri, T., Isokawa, T., Matsui, N., Nishimura, H., Kamiura, N.: Time series prediction by quaternionic qubit neural network. In: 2020 International Joint Conference on Neural Networks (IJCNN), pp. 1–6. IEEE (2020)
29. Ueguchi, T., Matsui, N., Isokawa, T.: Chaotic time series prediction by qubit neural network with complex-valued representation. In: 2016 55th Annual Conference of the Society of Instrument and Control Engineers of Japan (SICE), pp. 1353–1358. IEEE (2016)
30. Wang, H.Z., Li, G.Q., Wang, G.B., Peng, J.C., Jiang, H., Liu, Y.T.: Deep learning based ensemble approach for probabilistic wind power forecasting. Appl. Energy **188**, 56–70 (2017)
31. Zhang, G., Patuwo, B.E., Hu, M.Y.: Forecasting with artificial neural networks: the state of the art. Int. J. Forecast. **14**(1), 35–62 (1998)

Explainable Model of Credit Risk Assessment Based on Convolutional Neural Networks

Carlos Cardenas-Ruiz[✉], Andres Mendez-Vazquez, and Luis M. Ramirez-Solis

Department of Computer Science, CINVESTAV - Guadalajara, Zapopan, Mexico
carlos.cardenasruiz@cinvestav.mx

Abstract. Credit Risk Assessment estimates the probability of loss due to a borrower's failure to repay a loan or credit. Therefore, one of the principal challenges of financial institutions is to lower the losses generated by leading financial resources to possible default clients. Current models for Credit Risk Assessment used by the industry are based on Logistic regression (LR), thanks to their operational efficiency and interpretability. However, Deep Learning (DL) Algorithms have become more attractive than conventional Machine Learning due to their best general accuracy. However, Models for Credit Risk Assessment based on DL have a problem because their complexity makes them difficult for humans to interpret. Additionally, international regulations for financial institutions require that models be interpretable. In this work, we propose the use of a model based on Convolutional Neural Networks (CNN) and SHapley Additive exPlanations (SHAP) to generate a more accurate and explainable model than LR models. In order to demonstrate its efficacy, we use four datasets commonly used to benchmark classification algorithms for credit scoring. The results show that the method proposed is more accurate than LR for large datasets (more than 5900 samples), with an improvement in accuracy up to 12.3%.

Keywords: Credit risk assessment · DeepInsight · Explainability · CNN

1 Introduction

Even though Logistic Regression (LR) is one of the most common algorithms used in the financial industry [4], different studies have demonstrated that it is not the most accurate estimation for credit risk classification. A reference to this is two benchmarking studies published by Baesen [2,3] that demonstrate that for the category of individual classifier, Deep Learners are more accurate than LR.

Despite better accuracy of Deep Learners, Financial Institutions use LR for credit scoring due to their Operational efficiency (simplicity), and Interpretability (transparency) in predictions [11]. These two points, and statistical accuracy

© The Author(s), under exclusive license to Springer Nature Switzerland AG 2022
O. Pichardo Lagunas et al. (Eds.): MICAI 2022, LNAI 13612, pp. 83–96, 2022.
https://doi.org/10.1007/978-3-031-19493-1_7

form part of the five key characteristics of a successful credit risk mode defined for Baesen [4], shown in Table 1. However, due to the complex nature of Deep Learners, they are considered as Black Box Model(BBM), which refers to complex models that are not straightforwardly interpretable by humans [25], making them unviable for the use of financial institutions due to International regulations [7]. However, the application of interpretability methods permits us to give transparency to DL models.

In this work, we propose an explainable Deep Learning model based on a 2D Convolutional Neural Network (CNN) for credit risk classification. The use of CNN for credit risk is not new. However, Our approach uses DeepInsight [31], a methodology proposed by Alok Sharma et al., to transform tabular data into a 2D representation as input for CNN. The classification accuracy of the DeepInsight combined with CNN showed a better performance than Decision Tree (DT), LR, and RF for large datasets (more than 5900 samples), as shown in the results of our paper. Additionally, the use of SHapley Additive exPlanations (SHAP) to explain the model's prediction gives us an explainable and more accurate model than the LR model for credit risk classification.

Table 1. Key characteristics of successful credit risk model [4]

Characteristic	Description
Statistical accuracy	Refers to the power of prediction of a model to generalize well and avoid overfitting to the historical data.
Interpretability	A model needs to be interpretable. In other words, the model gives enough information to an expert to understand why the model takes those decisions.
Operational efficiency	This point refers to the time needed for the model to evaluate whether a customer is a defaulter. Operational efficiency also includes the following tasks: - Collection and preprocessing of data - Evaluation of the model - monitor and back-test - Reestimate
Economical cost	Developing and implementing models have a cost for the organizations. The total cost of all tasks and resources needed is the economical cost of the model. The cost of tasks mentioned in the operational efficiency plus cost of resources like: - Software cost - Human and Computing resources
Regulatory compliance	A model construction needs to comply with all applicable regulations and legislation. Basel, for example, specifies what information can or cannot be used. Other regulations like privacy and/or discrimination should be respected

The rest of the paper is organized as follows. In Sect. 2 we present the motivation for this work, while Sect. 3 discusses the state of the art of Credit risk assessment. In Sect. 4 we introduce the proposed method and in Sect. 5 we provide details about the implementation and experiments made in order to obtain the best model, as well as the comparison with previous models. Finally, in Sect. 6 we summarize our work and discuss some perspectives for future work.

2   Motivation

Why is credit risk so important? First, it is a matter of common knowledge that any economy, no matter how advanced, cannot develop in the absence of credit [5]. On other hand, a relaxed credit policy can become the core of a global financial crisis like 2007–2009.

The credit cycle begins with credit being easily accessible to customers, and they can borrow and spend more. In the same way, enterprises can borrow and make more significant investments. More consumption and investment create jobs and lead to income and profit growth. However, all economic expansion induced by credit ends when critical economic sectors become incapable of paying off their debts [17]. When the credit cycle is broken, there is a strong possibility of crisis (Fig. 1).

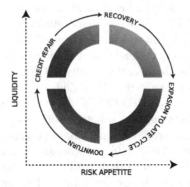

Fig. 1. Credit cycle [15]

The production of accurate credit risk tools for financial institutions allows them to make better decisions about granting credits. A reasonable administration of credit is an essential part of the growth of almost all economies. Economic growth is the most powerful instrument for reducing poverty and improving the quality of people's life. Growth can generate virtuous circles of prosperity and opportunity [12]. In conclusion, the research of credit risk topics profoundly impacts the world and people's lives.

3   Related Work

Durand [13] gave the bases for statistical credit risk scoring about 80 years ago. Nowadays, thanks to the evolution of statistical classification techniques, computational power, and easy access to sizable and reliable data, financial institutions use the statistical approach for credit risk management [4]. Many different classification models have been developed to address the credit scoring problem during the past few decades. Logistic Regression [6] and Random Forest [4] are the most widely-used model for credit scoring. However, more sophisticated machine learning techniques like Support Vector Machine (SVM) and Artificial Neural Networks (ANN) are also widely applied to credit scoring. Furthermore, ensemble methods that combine the advantage of various single classifiers get good scores like HCES-Bag with the best score in benchmark scoring published by Lessmann and Baesens [3].

Different empirical studies have compared the performance of different classification models for credit scoring. For example, West [33] compares ANN against traditional machine learning techniques. The result showed that ANN has better performance than LR. On the other hand, Cuicui et al. designed a Deep Belief Network (DBN) for credit classification and compared it against SVM, LR, and Multilayer Perceptron on the credit default swaps dataset [23]. The result showed that DBN yields the best performance.

Convolutional Neural Network (CNN) is a representative technique in DL; it first appeared in the work of Yann Lecun et al., designed to handle the variability of data in 2D shape [19]. The impressive achievements of CNN in different areas, including but not limited to Natural Language Processing (NLP) and Computer Vision, attract the attention of industry and academia [21]. Moreover, in the last few years, attracted by the classification ability of CNN, some studies have begun to apply CNN to managing credit risk. Bing Zhu, Wenchuan Yang, and Huaxuan Wang propose a model named "Relief-CCN" [37] that combines CNN and Relief algorithm. The results demonstrate a better performance against LR and RF with the dataset from a Chinese consumer finance company. On the other hand, Xolani Dastale and Turga Gelik [10] propose another CNN model for credit scoring getting better performance than traditional Machine learning methods. However, the last two models change the tabular data into a 2D representation for the CNN input discretizing the data and generating a representation with only ones or zeros in the values with possible data loss.

4   Proposed Approach

Credit risk classification is a data mining problem, thinking about this, we propose a process based on CRoss-Industry Standard Process for Data Mining (CRISP-DM) which is a process model for data mining [9]. Our proposal is a modification in the last step, called implementation on CRISP-DM, and changed by Interpretability where the generation of local and global explanations are generated, as shown in Fig. 2.

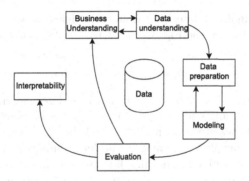

Fig. 2. Proposed model phases based on CRISP-DM

However, all the steps of CRISP-DM are essential, we will focus on the steps of Data preparation (especially on the task of Format data), Modeling, and an extra step called Interpretability defined for us after the evaluation step where we make the explanations of the generated mode.

4.1   Data Preparation

Format data [9] is part of the data preparation phase, which refers to all activities needed to transform the initial raw data into the data used as input for Machine Learning algorithms. The data used for financial institutions are generally in tabular [4] form (data displayed in columns or tables). However, The proposed 2D CCN requires image data representation.

DeepInsight [31] transforms the tabular data with a sequence of steps. First, it generates a feature vector transposing the dataset. Second, it maps each feature into a 2D space using t-SNE. Third, for efficiency, DeepInsight finds the small rectangle area that covers all points to be horizontal framed. Fourth, based on the dimensions of the final image defined for the user DeepInsight make a process of framing and mapping each feature. Finally, each instance is represented using the general feature image generated in the last step modifying the values of each

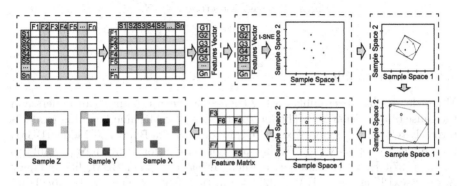

Fig. 3. Illustration of the DeepInsight [31] methodology to transform a feature vector to image pixels.

feature for the normalized value of the instance features values, which can be seen as a greyscale image; the Fig. 3 shows the transformation process.

4.2   Modeling

Convolutional Neural Network is one of the most used deep learning architectures for image processing [36]. The basic structure of CNN is shown in Fig. 4. There are two particular types of layers in CNN called the convolutional layer and the pooling layer. The convolutional layer is the basic building block of CNN [26]. It contains a set of learnable filters that slide over the image to extract features. The pooling layer reduces the spatial size representation and the number of parameters giving more efficiency and control overfitting.

Convolutional neural networks differ from traditional neural networks by replacing general matrix multiplication with convolutional, reducing the weights in the network, and allowing the import of an image directly. Additionally, The convolution layer has several main features, two of which are local perception and parameter sharing. Local perception refers to the high relevance of image parts that are close compared to the low relevance of the distant parts [35]. On the other hand, parameter sharing learn one set of parameters throughout the whole process instead of learning different parameter sets at each location [37]. These features help to improve the efficiency of the network.

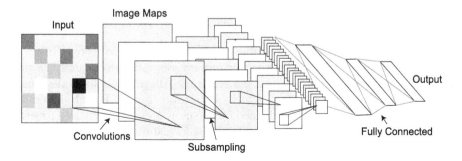

Fig. 4. The basic structure of CNN.

4.3   Interpretability

Miller defines interpretability as the degree to which a human can understand the cause of a decision [24]. The interpretability of a Machine Learning model is inversely related to its complexity. CCN is considered a Black Box Model (BBM) that refers to complex models that are not straightforwardly interpretable to humans [27]. However, different methods exist to explain BBM, like SHapley Additive exPlanations (SHAP) [22] used in this paper to generate the local and global explanations.

SHAP was proposed by Lundberg and Lee is a unified approach to interpreting model predictions. SHAP is a method to explain individual predictions based on the calculation of Shapley Values [22]. However, SHAP can give us a global explanation of a model based on the average of absolute Shapley values per feature of a random subset of dataset samples.

Shapley Values (SV) proposed by Shapley is a method based on coalitional game theory (or cooperative game theory) [30]. SV explains a prediction assuming that each feature value of a sample is a "player" in a game where the prediction is the goal. In other words, SV is the average marginal contribution of a feature value across all possible coalitions.

A linear model prediction is an explainable model because we can see how a feature affects the prediction.

$$\hat{f}(x) = \beta_0 + \sum_{j=1}^{p} \beta_j x_j$$

where x is the instance that we want to calculate the contributions. Each x_j is a feature value, with $j = 1, \ldots, p$. β_j is the weight of feature j.

The contribution ϕ_j of the j-th feature on the prediction $\hat{f}$ is:

$$\phi_j\left(\hat{f}\right) = \beta_j x_j - E\left(\beta_j X_j\right) = \beta_j x_j - \beta_j E\left(X_j\right)$$

The mean effect of feature j is $E\left(\beta_j X_j\right)$, and the contribution of j-th feature is the difference between the feature effect minus the average effect. If we sum all the contributions, we get the following result:

$$\sum_{j=1}^{p} \phi_j\left(\hat{f}\right) = \sum_{j=1}^{p} \beta_j x_j - E\left(\beta_j X_j\right)$$

$$= \left(\beta_0 + \sum_{j=1}^{p} \beta_j x_j\right) - \left(\beta_0 + \sum_{j=1}^{p} E\left(\beta_j X_j\right)\right)$$

$$= \hat{f}(x) - E\left(\hat{f}(X)\right)$$

The result is the predicted value for the instance x minus the average predicted value. To do the same to different models other than linear is necessary to compute feature contribution for a single prediction.

To get the Shapley value of a feature value, we need to calculate the contribution made to the result, weighted and summed over all combinations [25]. Then, the Shapley value is defined via a value function for players contained in set S:

$$\phi_j \left(val\right) = \sum_{S \subseteq \{x_1,...,x_p\} \backslash \{x_j\}} \frac{|S|! \left(p - |S| - 1\right)!}{p!} \left(val \left(S \cup \{x_j\}\right) - val \left(S\right)\right) \quad (1)$$

where S is a subset of model features, p is the number of features and x is the vector of feature values. The result is the contribution of feature j for all feature coalitions.

The exact solution to get the Shapley value requires the evaluation of all coalitions of feature values with and without the $j-th$ feature. However, the exact solution becomes problematic for more than a few features because the number of possible coalitions exponentially increases with each added feature. Therefore, Strumbelj et al. (2014) [32] propose an approximation with the use of Monte-Carlo sampling:

$$\hat{\phi}_j = \frac{1}{M} \sum_{m=1}^{M} \left(\hat{f} \left(x_{+j}^m\right) - \hat{f} \left(x_{-j}^m\right)\right)$$

where $\hat{f} \left(x_{+j}^m\right)$ is the prediction for the instance x, with a random number of feature values taken from another instance z taken a random, except for the value of feature j, the $\hat{f} \left(x_{-j}^m\right)$ is equal to $\hat{f} \left(x_{+j}^m\right)$, with the difference that the value of j feature is taken from z. The procedure to approximate the Shapley value is explained next:

Algorithm 1 Shapley value approximation

Input: Instance of interest x, data matrix X, feature index j, ML model f, and the number of iterations M.

Output: Shapley value of j-th feature

  for 1 to M **do**

    Get random instance z from matrix X

    Generate a random permutation o of features

    Order the instance x: $x_o = \left(x_{(1)}, ..., x_{(j)}, ..., x_p\right)$

    Order the instance z: $z_o = \left(z_{(1)}, ..., z_{(j)}, ..., z_p\right)$

    Generate two new instances

$$x_{+j} = \left(x_{(1)}, ..., x_{(j-1)}, x_{(j)}, z_{(j+1)}, ..., z_{(p)}\right)$$
$$x_{-j} = \left(x_{(1)}, ..., x_{(j-1)}, z_{(j)}, z_{(j+1)}, ..., z_{(p)}\right)$$

    Compute MC: $\phi_j^m = \hat{f} \left(x_{+j}\right) - \hat{f} \left(x_{-j}\right)$

  end for

  return the Shapley value as the average: $\phi_j \left(x\right) = \frac{1}{M} \sum_{m=1}^{M} \phi_j^m$

SHAP uses Shapley values to make explanations of BBM. However, SHAP proposes different kernel-based estimation approaches for Shapley values inspired by local surrogate models. KernelSHAP [22] is a model-agnostic based on LIME and Shapley values. On the other hand, TreeSHAP and DeepSHAP are model-specific, the first is an efficient estimation approach for tree-based models and the second for Deep learning models.

SHAP Feature Importance (FI) is one of the global interpretations based on aggregations of Shapley values. SHAP FI order features importance based on the absolute value of Shapley values per feature across the data [25]:

$$I_j = \frac{1}{n} \sum_{i=1}^{n} \left| \phi_j^{(i)} \right|$$

After, SHAP order features by decreasing importance. For example, Fig. 5 shows the SHAP FI for a pre-trained CNN for the lending club dataset.

After training the CNN models and judging their performances, we use SHAP to generate local and global explanations of the model. For example, SHAP can generate local explanations of tabular data and images but not the same for the global explanation of images. Additionally, explanations of images are given for the SHAP values of pixels based on the predictions of the trained model, which is not easy to understand for humans an example is shown in Fig. 6. Nevertheless, thanks to DeepInsight, we have the mapping between each pixel and feature. It allows us to return SHAP values to tabular form that generates more interpretable local and global explanations (Fig. 7).

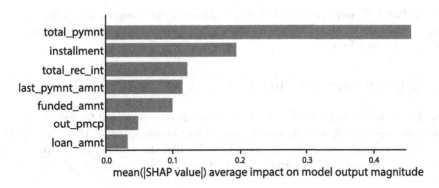

Fig. 5. SHAP Global explanation of first eight important features measured as the mean absolute Shapley values for Lending club dataset

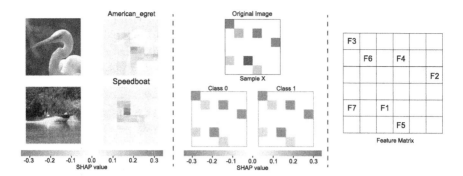

Fig. 6. (left) Example of SHAP local explanation for a Multi-class ResNet50 on ImageNet [29]. (middle) Example of SHAP local explanation of credit image generated from tabular data transformed using DeepInsight. (right) Example of feature matrix generated using DeepInsight.

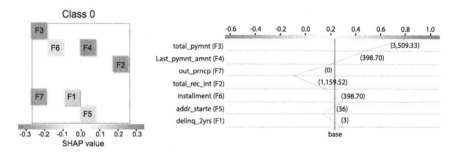

Fig. 7. (left) Example of SHAP local explanation for DeepInsight credit image. (right) Example of SHAP local explanation for DeepInsight credit image after conversion to tabular form.

5   Experimental Results

The datasets used in this thesis is about four datasets provided for financial and academic institutions widely used in research of credit scoring. All the datasets are different in almost all their characteristics like the number of samples and features. A resume of the characteristics of the dataset are shown in Table 2:

Table 2. Datasets

	Datasets			
	Australian [28]	German [18]	HMEQ [4]	LC 2007–2014 [20]
# Samples	690	1,000	5,960	466,285
# non default	307	700	4,771	415,317
# default	383	300	1,189	50,968
# features	14	20	13	75
Categorical	8	13	2	22
Continuous	6	7	11	53

Since the data contained in the four datasets may contain redundant features that can increase computation and affect the performance, for numerical and categorical features, we use ANOVA and Chi-Squared, respectively [8]. Additionally, when features with high correlation exist, SHAP generates redundant local and global explanations with features with the same SHAP values. Then eliminating high correlated features is need it.

For each dataset, we use cross-validation with ten stratified folds. The training set was used to find the optimal parameter of the CNN model. The metrics of the test set were used to assess the performance of the CNN model. Table 3 shows the optimal architecture of our CNN model for Australian, German, HMEQ, and Lending club datasets, respectively.

To compare the performance of our model, we use different studies that use the same datasets. Additionally, we train base models with LR and RF to compare the results. For each dataset, we calculate Accuracy and Area Under the Receiver Operating Characteristics (AUROC). Accuracy is not the best metric for the evaluation of models of credit risk classification. However, many studies only use Accuracy for evaluation. Therefore, Table 4 compares the Accuracy against each model and dataset. On the other hand, a better metric than Accuracy for credit risk classification is AUROC; in Table 5, we compare the AUROC for the different studies containing this information and our results.

Table 3. CNN Architecture: Parameters and architectures of the CNN model in (a) Australian dataset epochs = 500, (b) German dataset epochs = 50, (c) HMEQ dataset epochs = 1000, and (d) Lending club dataset epochs = 50. Legend: Conv (Convolutional Layer), PL (Pooling Layer), FC (Fully Connected Layer).

Layer	Parameters and Architecture	Layer	Parameters and Architecture
Input	Input shape: k=8, d=8, c=1	Input	Input shape: k=20, d=20, c=1
Conv1	Fil: 64, Kernel: 3x3, Str=1,Pad=1	Conv1	Fil:128, Kernel: 3x3, Str=1,Pad=1
PL1	type: max, size 2x2	PL1	type: max, size 2x2
Conv2	Fil:128, Kernel: 3x3, Str=1, Pad=1	Conv2	Fil:256, Kernel: 3x3, Str=1,Pad=1
PL2	type: max, size 2x2	PL2	type: max, size 2x2
FC1	neurons:128	FC1	neurons:128
FC2	neurons: 2, activation: softmax	FC2	neurons:64
Act. F.	ReLU	FC3	neurons: 2, activation: softmax
		Act. F.	ReLU

a		b	
Layer	Parameters and Architecture	Layer	Parameters and Architecture
Input	Input shape: k=8, d=8, c=1	Input	Input shape: k=20, d=20, c=1
Conv1	Fil: 64, Kernel: 3x3, Str=1,Pad=1	Conv1	Fil:128, Kernel: 3x3, Str=1,Pad=1
PL1	type: max, size 2x2	PL1	type: max, size 2x2
Conv2	Fil:128, Kernel: 3x3, Str=1, Pad=1	Conv2	Fil:256, Kernel: 3x3, Str=1,Pad=1
PL2	type: max, size 2x2	PL2	type: max, size 2x2
FC1	neurons:128	FC1	neurons:128
FC2	neurons: 2, activation: softmax	FC2	neurons: 2, activation: softmax
Act. F.	ReLU	Act. F.	ReLU

c		d	

Table 4. Accuracy comparison against datasets and models

Source	Year	Algorithm	Australian	German	HMEQ	LC 2007–2014
[16]	2016	MLP	0.860	0.750	–	–
[1]	2016	ENSEMBLE	0.880	0.780	–	–
[34]	2017	ENSEMBLE	0.880	0.770	–	–
[14]	2018	ENSEMBLE	**0.930**	0.860	–	–
[10]	2021	CNN	0.880	**0.950**	0.820	–
Base	2022	LR	0.871	0.761	0.803	0.945
Base	2022	RF	0.869	0.771	0.810	0.874
Our	2022	CNN-DeepInsight	0.844	0.734	**0.926**	**0.991**

Table 5. AUROC comparison against datasets and models

Source	Year	Algorithm	Australian	German	HMEQ	LC 2007-2014
[1]	2016	ENSEMBLE	**0.940**	0.802	–	–
[10]	2021	CNN	0.800	**0.960**	0.830	–
Base	2022	LR	0.931	0.790	0.631	0.952
Base	2022	RF	0.870	0.803	0.872	0.937
Our	2022	CNN-DeepInsight	0.897	0.738	**0.907**	**0.995**

6 Conclusions

In this paper, tabular datasets were converted into images using DeepInsight. The images were used to train 2D CNN. The performance of the trained CNN was compared with literature results and base models trained by us using LR and RF for reference. We found that the trained CNN performed better than the literature results, and our base models based on LR and RF when the dataset size was greater than 5,900 samples, getting results that surpassed the Accuracy and AUROC of the second-best model with up to 0.106 and 0.046, respectively.

Additionally, thanks to the mapping generated for DeepInsight when the images were created, we can return SHAP values based on predictions of trained models to the tabular form, allowing us to generate local and global explanations.

Acknowledgments. This work was carried out with the support of CONACYT and the Centro de Investigacion y de Estudios Avanzados del Instituto Politecnico Nacional.

References

1. Ala'Raj, M., Abbod, M.F.: Classifiers consensus system approach for credit scoring. Knowledge-Based Systems **104**, 89–105 (2016). https://doi.org/10.1016/j.knosys.2016.04.013

2. Baesens, B., Gestel, T.V., Viaene, S., Stepanova, M., Suykens, J., Vanthienen, J.: Benchmarking state-of-the-art classification algorithms for credit scoring. J. Oper. Res. Soc. **54**(6), 627–635 (2003)
3. Baesens, B., Lessmann, S., Seow, H.V., Thomas, L.C.: Benchmarking state-of-the-art classification algorithms for credit scoring: An update of research. Eur. J. Oper. Res. **247**(1), 124–136 (2015). https://doi.org/10.1016/j.ejor.2015.05.030
4. Baesens, B., Rosch, D.: Credit Risk Analytics, vol. 1 (2016)
5. Banu, I.M.: The impact of credit on economic growth in the global crisis context. Procedia Econ. Fin. **6**(February 2007), 25–30 (2013). https://doi.org/10.1016/s2212-5671(13)00109-3
6. Bensic, M., Sarlija, N., Zekic-Susac, M.: Modelling small-business credit scoring by using logistic regression, neural networks and decision trees. Intell. Syst. Account. Finan. Manage. **13**(3), 133–150 (2005). https://doi.org/10.1002/ISAF.261,https://onlinelibrary.wiley.com/doi/full/10.1002/isaf.261, https://onlinelibrary.wiley.com/doi/abs/10.1002/isaf.261https://onlinelibrary.wiley.com/doi/10.1002/isaf.261
7. BIS: Basel iii: International regulatory framework for banks (12 2017). https://www.bis.org/bcbs/basel3.htm
8. Brownlee, J.: Data Preparation for Machine Learning (2020). https://doi.org/10.1109/ICIMCIS51567.2020.9354273
9. Chapman, P., et al.: Crisp-dm 1.0 (2000)
10. Dastile, X., Celik, T.: Making deep learning-based predictions for credit scoring explainable. IEEE Access **9**, 50426–50440 (2021). https://doi.org/10.1109/ACCESS.2021.3068854
11. Dastile, X., Celik, T., Potsane, M.: Statistical and machine learning models in credit scoring: a systematic literature survey. Appl. Soft Comput. J. **91**, 106263 (2020). https://doi.org/10.1016/j.asoc.2020.106263, https://doi.org/10.1016/j.asoc.2020.106263
12. DFID: Growth Building Jobs and Prosperity in Developing Counttries. Departement for International Development pp. 1–25 (2007). https://www.oecd.org/derec/unitedkingdom/40700982.pdf
13. Durand, D.: Risk elements in consumer instalment financing 8 (1941)
14. Edla, D.R., Tripathi, D., Cheruku, R., Kuppili, V.: An efficient multi-layer ensemble framework with BPSOGSA-based feature selection for credit scoring data analysis. Arabian J. Sci. Eng. **43**(12), 6909–6928 (2017). https://doi.org/10.1007/S13369-017-2905-4, https://link.springer.com/article/10.1007/s13369-017-2905-4
15. Fahey, T.: Unlocking the credit cycle (2019). https://info.loomissayles.com/unlocking-the-credit-cycle
16. Ha, V.S., Nguyen, H.N.: Credit scoring with a feature selection approach based deep learning. MATEC Web Conf. **54** (2016). https://doi.org/10.1051/matecconf/20165405004
17. Hayes, A.: Credit Cycle (2021). https://www.investopedia.com/terms/c/credit-cycle.asp
18. Hofmann, H.: UCI Machine Learning Repository: Statlog (German Credit Data) Data Set. https://archive.ics.uci.edu/ml/datasets/statlog+(german+credit+data)
19. LeCun, Y., Bottou, L., Bengio, Y., Haffner, P.: Gradient-based learning applied to document recognition. Proc. IEEE **86**(11), 2278–2323 (1998). https://doi.org/10.1109/5.726791
20. Lending-club: loan data 2007 2014 Kaggle. https://www.kaggle.com/datasets/devanshi23/loan-data-2007-2014

21. Li, Z., Liu, F., Yang, W., Peng, S., Zhou, J.: A survey of convolutional neural networks: analysis, applications, and prospects. IEEE Trans. Neural Networks Learn. Syst. 1–21 (2021). https://doi.org/10.1109/TNNLS.2021.3084827

22. Lundberg, S.M., Lee, S.I.: A Unified Approach to Interpreting Model Predictions. Advances in Neural Information Processing Systems 2017-Decem, 4766–4775 (2017). https://doi.org/10.48550/arxiv.1705.07874, https://arxiv.org/abs/1705.07874v2

23. Luo, C., Wu, D., Wu, D.: A deep learning approach for credit scoring using credit default swaps. Eng. Appl. Artif. Intell. **65**, 465–470 (2017). https://doi.org/10.1016/J.ENGAPPAI.2016.12.002

24. Miller, T.: Explanation in artificial intelligence: insights from the social sciences. Artif. Intell. **267**, 1–38 (2019). https://doi.org/10.1016/J.ARTINT.2018.07.007

25. Molnar, C.: Interpretable Machine Learning (2021)

26. Montagnon, E., et al.: Deep learning workflow in radiology: a primer. Insights into Imaging **11**(1), 1–15 (2020). https://doi.org/10.1186/S13244-019-0832-5/TABLES/2, https://insightsimaging.springeropen.com/articles/10.1186/s13244-019-0832-5

27. Petch, J., Di, S., Nelson, W.: Opening the black box: the promise and limitations of explainable machine learning in cardiology. Can. J. Cardiol. **38**(2), 204–213 (2022). https://doi.org/10.1016/J.CJCA.2021.09.004

28. Quinlan: UCI Machine Learning Repository: Statlog (Australian Credit Approval) Data Set. https://archive.ics.uci.edu/ml/datasets/statlog+(australian+credit+approval)

29. Shap: Explain ResNet50 ImageNet classification using Partition explainer - SHAP latest documentation. https://shap.readthedocs.io

30. Shapley, L.S.: Contributions to the Theory of Games (1953)

31. Sharma, A., Vans, E., Shigemizu, D., Boroevich, K.A., Tsunoda, T.: DeepInsight: a methodology to transform a non-image data to an image for convolution neural network architecture. Sci. Rep. **9**(1), 1–7 (2019). https://doi.org/10.1038/s41598-019-47765-6

32. Štrumbelj, E., Kononenko, I.: Explaining prediction models and individual predictions with feature contributions. Knowl. Inf. Syst. **41**(3), 647–665 (2014). https://doi.org/10.1007/S10115-013-0679-X/TABLES/4, https://link.springer.com/article/10.1007/s10115-013-0679-x

33. West, D.: Neural network credit scoring models. Comput. Oper. Res. **27**(11–12), 1131–1152 (2000). https://doi.org/10.1016/S0305-0548(99)00149-5

34. Xia, Y., Liu, C., Li, Y.Y., Liu, N.: A boosted decision tree approach using Bayesian hyper-parameter optimization for credit scoring. Expert Syst. Appl. **78**, 225–241 (2017). https://doi.org/10.1016/J.ESWA.2017.02.017

35. Yang, J., Li, J.: Application of deep convolution neural network. In: 2016 13th International Computer Conference on Wavelet Active Media Technology and Information Processing, ICCWAMTIP 2017 2018-February, 229–232, October 2017. https://doi.org/10.1109/ICCWAMTIP.2017.8301485

36. Zhang, S., Wu, Y., Men, C., He, H., Liang, K.: Research on OpenCL optimization for FPGA deep learning application. PLoS ONE **14**(10), e0222984 (2019). https://doi.org/10.1371/JOURNAL.PONE.0222984,https://journals.plos.org/plosone/article?id=10.1371/journal.pone.0222984

37. Zhu, B., Yang, W., Wang, H., Yuan, Y.: A hybrid deep learning model for consumer credit scoring. In: 2018 International Conference on Artificial Intelligence and Big Data, ICAIBD 2018 pp. 205–208, June 2018. https://doi.org/10.1109/ICAIBD.2018.8396195

Reinforcement Learning with Success Induced Task Prioritization

Maria Nesterova[1], Alexey Skrynnik[1,2,3], and Aleksandr Panov[2,3(✉)]

[1] Moscow Institute of Physics and Technology, Moscow, Russia
nesterova.mi@phystech.edu
[2] AIRI, Moscow, Russia
panov.ai@mipt.ru
[3] Federal Research Center "Computer Science and Control" of the Russian Academy of Sciences, Moscow, Russia

Abstract. Many challenging reinforcement learning (RL) problems require designing a distribution of tasks that can be applied to train effective policies. This distribution of tasks can be specified by the curriculum. A curriculum is meant to improve the results of learning and accelerate it. We introduce Success Induced Task Prioritization (SITP), a framework for automatic curriculum learning, where a task sequence is created based on the success rate of each task. In this setting, each task is an algorithmically created environment instance with a unique configuration. The algorithm selects the order of tasks that provide the fastest learning for agents. The probability of selecting any of the tasks for the next stage of learning is determined by evaluating its performance score in previous stages. Experiments were carried out in the Partially Observable Grid Environment for Multiple Agents (POGEMA) and Procgen benchmark. We demonstrate that SITP matches or surpasses the results of other curriculum design methods. Our method can be implemented with handful of minor modifications to any standard RL framework and provides useful prioritization with minimal computational overhead.

Keywords: Reinforcement learning · Curriculum learning ·
Multi-agent reinforcement learning · Multi-agent pathfinding · Deep learning

1 Introduction

In numerous complex Reinforcement Learning (RL) problems, the agent must master a number of tasks. That number of tasks may be explicitly defined by the environment authors or may be implicit. E.g. in case then the environment is procedurally generated, and the agent is given only a few world instances in which it can learn. The proper order can, on the one hand, speed up the agent's learning process, and on the other hand, prevent him from catastrophic forgetting. Training using task sequencing order is called curriculum learning [1]. More formally, the curriculum learning is a method of optimization of the order in which experience is accumulated by the agent, so as to improve performance or training speed on a set of final tasks.

O. Pichardo Lagunas et al. (Eds.): MICAI 2022, LNAI 13612, pp. 97–107, 2022.
https://doi.org/10.1007/978-3-031-19493-1_8

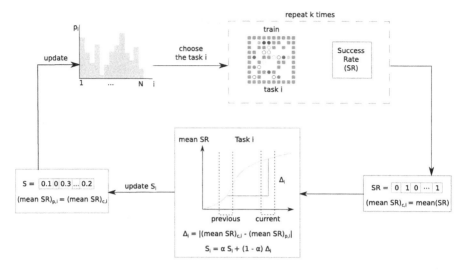

Fig. 1. Overview of SITP method. The probability of selecting task i depends on how much earlier the mean Success Rate (SR) increased after training on task i, k times.

There are many ways of creating a curriculum. One of the possible ways of constructing a curriculum is to arrange the tasks by difficulty. The second option is to choose a sequence of tasks according to a certain distribution, using additional information received during training [2,3]. The third option is to create a teacher, whose goal is to gradually increase the complexity of the tasks, while the teacher itself learns to create them [4]. For example, the teacher can generate obstacles on the map [5]. It is also possible to create an implicit curriculum based on competition or interaction between agents [2,3].

In this paper, we introduce Success Induced Task Prioritization (SITP)[1], illustrated in Fig. 1, a new method for task sequencing. The main concept for this method is a binary metric, Success Rate (SR), which shows whether the task was completed on the episode or not. During training, the method updates scores estimating each task's learning potential, basing on mean SR for this task. Then this method selects the next training task from a distribution derived from a normalization procedure over these task scores. Our method also does not apply any external, predefined ordering of tasks by difficulty or other criteria, but instead derives task scores dynamically during training based on SR. It is assumed that tasks which get the highest rate of selection are the ones on which the agents learn the fastest, or that those tasks are the hardest to complete.

We consider the SITP method in the application for the Multi-agent Pathfinding (MAPF) problem, which is based on POGEMA environment [6]. The MAPF problem is that several agents must go from their starting positions to the goals without colliding with obstacles or other agents. In this problem domain, SR is defined as an indicator of whether all agents have reached

---

[1] Our code is available at https://github.com/cds-mipt/sitp.

their goals or not. We argue that such simple information is enough to improve learning results. Moreover, we provide additional experiments with a well-known Procgen benchmark [7], showing the applicability of the SITP approach to a wide class of RL problems.

The rest of the paper is organized as follows. Section 2 provides a brief overview of related works. Section 3 describes the background behind RL. Section 4 introduces SITP method. Section 5 is devoted for experimental study of presented method and comparison with other approaches. In the conclusion we discuss obtained results.

2   Related Work

The central problem of creating a curriculum is the definition of a sequence of tasks or the generation of tasks automatically (without human intervention). Several papers address the last one, showing that it is possible to generate a curriculum automatically by confronting several agents [1,8]. A similar idea assumes the sequential interaction of two agents [9], where one sets the task, and the other solves it.

Separately, one can consider the methods that create the curriculum for a set of already known tasks. The Prioritized Level Replay (PLR) [2] provides a curriculum scheme automatically using additional information collected during training. The main idea is to define a priority for each task using some scoring scheme. The authors propose to accumulate L1 General Advantage Estimation (GAE) during training for each task and sample new ones based on that scores. This score shows whether it is promising to train on this task in the future. On the other hand, the Teacher-Student Curriculum Learning (TSCL) [3] provides several ways to estimate the prospects of a task using the learning progress curve. Despite the method's conceptual simplicity, there may be difficulties with the formation of a set of tasks or the choice of a metric for that tasks.

The tasks could be created in process of training an additional agent, as in the self-play algorithm [9]. This algorithm is focused on two kinds of environments: reversible environments and environments that can be reset. An automatic learning program is created based on the interaction of two agents: Alice and Bob. Alice will "propose" the task by doing a sequence of actions and then Bob must undo or repeat them, respectively. Authors argue that this way of creating a training program is effective in different types of environments.

3   Background

The reinforcement learning problem is to train an agent (or several agents) how to act in a certain environment so as to maximize some scalar reward signal. The process of interaction between the agent and the environment is modeled by the partially observable Markov decision process (POMDP), which is a variant of the (plain) Markov decision process (MDP). Partially Observable Markov Decision Process (POMDP) is a tuple $\langle \mathcal{S}, A, O, \mathcal{T}, p, r, \mathcal{I}, p_o, \gamma \rangle$, where: $\mathcal{S}$ – set of states of the environment, A – set of available actions, O – set of observations, $T : S \times A \to S$ – transition function, $p(s'|s, a)$ – probability of transition to state s' from state s under the action a, $r : S \times A \to \mathbb{R}$ – reward function, $\mathcal{I} : S \to O$ – observation function, $p_o(o|s', a)$ – probability to get observation o if the state transitioned to s' under the action a, $\gamma \in [0, 1]$ – discount factor. At each timestep t, the agent chooses its action a_t based on the policy $\pi(a|s) : A \times S \to [0, 1]$ and receives the reward r_t. The goal of the agent is to learn an optimal policy π^*, which maximizes the expected return.

In this paper we apply the Proximal Policy Optimization (PPO) [10] algorithm to find that policy. PPO has proven itself as a highly robust approach for many tasks, including multi-agent scenarios [11], large-scale training [12], and even fine-tuning other policies [13]. PPO is a variation of advantage actor-critic, which leans on clipping in the objective function to penalize the new policy for getting far from the old one.

4   Success Induced Task Prioritization

In this section, we present Success Induced Task Prioritization (SITP), an algorithm for selecting the next task for learning by prioritizing tasks basing on previous learning results. SITP assumes that a finite set of N tasks $T = [T_1, \ldots, T_N]$ is defined in the environment. A task is an algorithmically created environment instance with unique configuration. Task configuration is a broad term, several instances of the environment, united by one common property, can be located inside the same task. We assume that if the agent learns tasks in a certain order, then this will contribute to improve results of learning and accelerate it.

A curriculum C is a directed acyclic graph that establishes a partial order in which tasks should be trained [1]. Linear sequence is the simplest and most common structure for a curriculum. A curriculum can be created online, where the task order is determined dynamically based on the agent's learning progress.

An important feature of our algorithm is the application of the success rate (SR). SR is a binary score that is utilized to measure the success of training on a single episode. There are several ways to set the metric. For example, if the environment has a specific goal that the agent must achieve, then SR $= 1$ if this goal is achieved, 0 otherwise. If there is no specific goal, then SR can be determined using the reward for the episode (in case the reward is bigger than a certain threshold, then SR $= 1$, otherwise 0). The concept of a mean SR is introduced to evaluate the effectiveness of an agent. Mean SR shows the percentage of successfully completed episodes.

We assume that with proper task sequencing the speed of learning and success rate could be increased. The target task is the task on which mean SR is meant to improve. In cases where more than one task is being considered to be the target task, the curriculum is supposed to improve the mean SR of all of them. All of the methods described below are meant to be used for multiple target tasks.

Assume, N tasks $T = [T_1, \ldots, T_N]$ and number of iterations M of the algorithm are given. Let T_i be a task, S_i a score, obtained as a result of training on this task, p_i a probability of the task being selected on the next training iteration:

$$p_i = \frac{\exp(S_i)}{\sum\limits_{j=1}^{N} \exp(S_j)}, \quad i = \overline{1, N}. \qquad (1)$$

In such a way, probability distribution $p = [p_1, \ldots, p_N]$ is constructed. It gives priority to tasks depending on scores $S = [S_1, \ldots, S_N]$. Initially the tasks are sequenced with equal probability. General idea of our method illustrated in Fig. 1 and specified in Algorithm 1.

Algorithm 1: Training loop with SITP

Input : Tasks T, N – number of tasks
Initialize agents learning algorithm
Initialize probability distribution $p \leftarrow [\frac{1}{N}, \ldots, \frac{1}{N}]$
Initialize scores S
for $t = 1, \ldots, M$ **do**
    Choose task T_i based on p
    Train agents using task T_i based on the evaluation method and
      observe *score*
    Update score $S[i] \leftarrow score$
    Update probability distribution p
end

Depending on the way of evaluating S, different variations of an algorithm are possible. SITP is based on the idea that if one of the tasks increases mean SR more than others, then this task is better to be leaning on. We presume that on such task SR will keep increasing. In the same manner, forgetting of the task is taken into account. If mean SR is decreasing on a certain task, then this task should be run again. In such a way, evaluation of S_i depends on the absolute value of mean SR's change. The bigger the effect on mean SR from the T_i task, the bigger the chance of it being selected. Thus, at first the task T_i is selected, basing on probability distribution p. Then the agents learn and S_i scores for T_i tasks are evaluated. Agents train for k episodes on the selected task T_i, get a SR for each episode, and then mean SR is calculated. SR^i_{old}- mean SR of previous learning stage on T_i task. Initially SR^i_{old} equals 0. The mean SR changes during the training of agents by $\Delta_i = |SR^i_{new} - SR^i_{old}|$. A moving average also should be used for smoothing out short-term fluctuations. The final score is calculated:

$$S_i = \alpha S_i + (1 - \alpha)|SR^i_{new} - SR^i_{old}|,$$

where α is smoothing coefficient. Additionally, a condition is established that if SR^i_{new} exceeds a certain threshold max_SR, then it is considered that agents are good enough at solving this problem and it should be chosen less frequently.

This is controlled by the *min_score* number. The procedure for constructing the estimate S_i is shown in Algorithm 2.

Algorithm 2: Task sampling estimation using SITP

Input : T_i – selected task, k – number of episodes, SR^i_{old} – mean SR for the previous stage, *max_SR* – the maximum mean SR, when this mean SR is reached, then the task should be selected less frequently, *min_score* – the number by which the task is selected less frequently, α – smoothing coefficient.

Output: Score S_i for T_i, SR^i_{old}

Initialize SR for k episodes $C \leftarrow [0, \ldots, 0]$

if *first stage for T_i* **then**
  | Initialize $SR^i_{old} \leftarrow 0$
end

for $\tau = 1, \ldots, k$ **do**
  | Train agents using task T_i and observe SR score
  | $C[\tau] \leftarrow SR$
end

$SR^i_{new} \leftarrow \mathbf{mean}(C)$

$S_i \leftarrow \alpha S_i + (1 - \alpha)|SR^i_{new} - SR^i_{old}|$

$SR^i_{old} \leftarrow SR^i_{new}$

if $SR^i_{new} > max\_SR$ **then**
  | $S_i \leftarrow min\_score$
end

---

5   Experiments

In this section, we present an empirical evaluation of SITP approach. First, we describe the POGEMA environment and show a motivational example with a simple experiment with two tasks. For that experiment, we provide a comparison with the TSCL algorithm and a baseline (uniform sampling of the tasks). Second, we present the results on a number of complex multi-agent pathfinding maps. Finally, we evaluate our approach using Procgen-Benchmark, comparing it with the state-of-the-art curriculum learning technique – PLR.

5.1   Motivational Experiment in POGEMA Environment

The POGEMA environment [6] is a framework for simulating multi-agent pathfinding problems in partially observable scenarios. Consider n homogeneous agents, navigating the shared map. The task of each agent is to reach the given goal position (grid cell) from the start point in less than m steps. The environment allows both to create maps procedurally and to add existing ones. The environment is multi-agent, thus we consider that the episode ended successfully only in the case when each agent reached its goal. We will refer to this metric as Cooperative Success Rate (CSR).

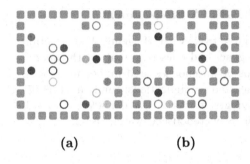

(a)   **(b)**

Fig. 2. Easy **(a)** – easy (obstacle density 5%) and **(b)** hard (obstacle density 30%) Pogema configuration for 8 × 8 map.

Even a single task in this domain combines many maps of the same distribution. An example task is a set of maps with size 8 × 8, 16 agents, and random positions of obstacles with density 30%, start and goal points. We compare SITP with TSCL [3], where the scoring function will take into account the slope of the CSR curve. We use a PPO implementation from Sample Factory paper [14]. The hyperparameters were tuned ones on procedurally generated maps without curriculum learning. We use the same network architecture as in [15,16].

The first experiment was based on two small tasks, the difference between which was in the complexity of the maps (different density of obstacles). The tasks are shown in Fig. 2. The results are summarized in Fig. 3. They show that this method quickly learns using the easy task and then selects mostly only the difficult one. SITP outperforms other methods of selecting training levels (TSCL and baseline) in terms of general mean CSR.

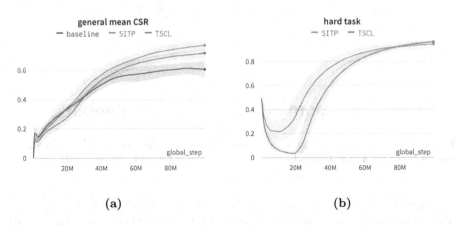

(a)   **(b)**

Fig. 3. The first experiment is trained on two tasks: easy (8 × 8 map, 8 agents, density 5%) and hard (8 × 8 map, 8 agents, density 30%). **(a)** General mean CSR of each method. **(b)** Percentage of learning on a hard task. The baseline usage of that map is 0.5, since maps are sampled uniformly. The results are averaged over 10 runs. The shaded area denotes standard deviation.

5.2   Large-Scale Experiment in POGEMA Environment

The second experiment was held on ten large tasks with 64 agents. Tasks contain maps of different formats: procedurally generated ones (e.g. maps with random obstacles), maps from videogames, maps of warehouses, and indoor maps (e.g. rooms). We select two procedurally generated configurations: random-64-64-05, random-64-64-3, and 8 maps from MovingAI dataset [17]: den009d, den204d, den308d, den312d, den998d , room-64-64-8, warehouse-1, warehouse-2.

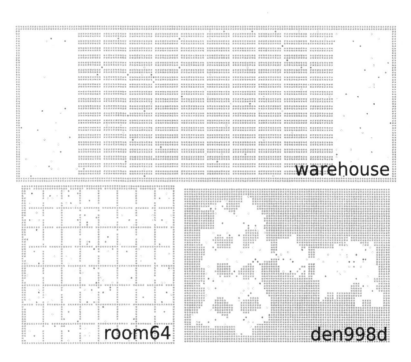

Fig. 4. Example of three tasks with a fixed obstacle position and with a random position of the start and goal points.

Figure 4 shows three examples of the maps: *warehouse* is a room where the obstacles are of the same shape and the distance between them is one cell, *room64* are 64 rooms of size 7×7 with at least one exit, *den998d* is a map of a house with obstacles from the videogame. The agent's goal point is generated in such a way so that the agent could always reach it from its starting point (ignoring possible collisions with other agents). Figure 5 shows the superiority of learning results SITP compared to baseline and better results than the TSCL approach. Note that SITP gives a significant increase in mean CSR on hard maps, while mean CSR on easy maps for SITP and baseline are comparable.

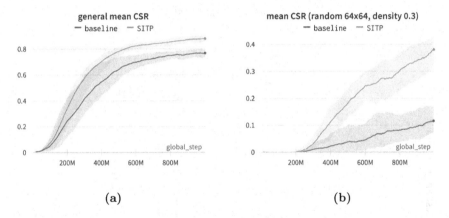

(a)   (b)

Fig. 5. Training agents on 10 tasks. **(a)** General mean CSR of SITP and baseline. **(b)** Mean CSR for the most difficult procedurally generated task (64×64 map, density 30%). The results are averaged over 6 runs. The shaded area denotes standard deviation.

5.3   Procgen Benchmark

We train and test SITP on 4 environments in the Procgen Benchmark at simple difficulty levels and make direct comparisons with PLR [2], in which the probability of choosing a task is formed using L1 GAE collected along the last trajectory τ sampled on that level. The learning potential of a task is calculated using the scoring function based on the GAE magnitude (L1 value loss): $score = \frac{1}{T} \sum_{t=0}^{T} |R_t - V_t|$. We reproduce experiments settings from PLR paper and train the agent for $25M$ total steps on 200 fixed levels, using PPO implementation from that paper. We measure episodic test returns for each game throughout the training.

For environments in the Procgen Benchmark, SR is specified by a fixed threshold SR_{min} depending on the total reward per episode such that if $reward > SR_{min}$ then $SR = 1$, otherwise $SR = 0$. SR_{min} is manually selected based on the following rule: the threshold must be greater than the maximum mean episode return per training for baseline, or approximately equal to the maximum mean episode return per training for PLR.

In contrast to multi-agent experiments (for which every episode was a new configuration), for Procgen environment we compare agents using evaluation on the test tasks. The results are summarized in Fig. 6. The fixed threshold was chosen (using expert knowledge) as follows: bigfish ($SR_{min} = 10$), leaper ($SR_{min} = 8$), plunder ($SR_{min} = 12$), miner ($SR_{min} = 10$). We show that SITP, based on the SR, achieves comparable training results with PLR approach. At the same time, PLR higly depends on the implementation of algorithm, and requires additional computations for algorithms differ from Advantage Actor-Critic family.

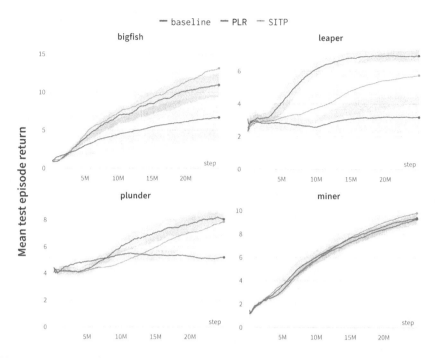

Fig. 6. Mean episodic test returns over 10 runs of each method for four environments (bigfish, plunder, leaper and miner). The shaded area denotes standard deviation.

6   Conclusion

In the paper, we investigated the problem of automated curriculum generation for reinforcement learning and introduced Success Induced Task Prioritization (SITP) algorithm, that estimates the learning potential on a task using Success Rate (SR). The SITP can be easily integrated into environments for which a success rate metric is already defined. But also we demonstrated that the SR score can be used in any kind of environments where the reward function is dense and more complicated.

We showed that SITP improves the efficiency of task sampling in the POGEMA and Procgen Benchmark environments. SITP shows comparable results with the leading curriculum learning methods: TSCL and PLR. Our method does not directly interact with the agent's learning algorithm, it only needs information about the SR after each episode. The future directions of the research includes experiments with other environments. i.e. robotic tasks.

References

1. Narvekar, S., Peng, B., Leonetti, M., Sinapov, J., Taylor, M.E., Stone, P.: Curriculum learning for reinforcement learning domains: a framework and survey. J. Mach. Learn. Res. **21**, 181:1-181:50 (2020)

2. Jiang, M., Grefenstette, E., Rocktäschel, T.: Prioritized level replay. In: International Conference on Machine Learning, pages 4940–4950. PMLR (2021)
3. Matiisen, T., Oliver, A., Cohen, T., Schulman, J.: Teacher-student curriculum learning. IEEE Trans. Neural Networks Learn. Syst. **31**(9), 3732–3740 (2019)
4. Chen, J., et al.: Variational automatic curriculum learning for sparse-reward cooperative multi-agent problems. Advances in Neural Information Processing Systems, vol. 34 (2021)
5. Dennis, M., et al.: Emergent complexity and zero-shot transfer via unsupervised environment design. Adv. Neural. Inf. Process. Syst. **33**, 13049–13061 (2020)
6. Skrynnik, A., Andreychuk, A., Yakovlev, K., Panov, A.: POGEMA: partially observable grid environment for multiple agents. In: ICAPS 2022 Planning and Reinforcement Learning Workshop (2022)
7. Cobbe, K., Hesse, C., Hilton, J., Schulman, J.: Leveraging procedural generation to benchmark reinforcement learning. In International Conference on Machine Learning, pp. 2048–2056. PMLR (2020)
8. Baker, B.,. Emergent tool use from multi-agent autocurricula. In: International Conference on Learning Representations (2019)
9. Sukhbaatar, S., Lin, Z., Kostrikov, I., Synnaeve, G., Szlam, A., Fergus, R.: Intrinsic motivation and automatic curricula via asymmetric self-play. In 6th International Conference on Learning Representations, ICLR 2018, Vancouver, BC, Canada, April 30 - May 3, 2018, Conference Track Proceedings. OpenReview.net (2018)
10. Schulman, J., Wolski, F., Dhariwal, P., Radford, A., Klimov, O.: Proximal policy optimization algorithms. arXiv preprint arXiv:1707.06347 (2017)
11. de Witt, C.S., et al.: Is independent learning all you need in the starcraft multi-agent challenge? arXiv preprint arXiv:2011.09533 (2020)
12. Berner, C., et al.: Dota 2 with large scale deep reinforcement learning. arXiv preprint arXiv:1912.06680 (2019)
13. Baker, B., et al.: Video pretraining (vpt): learning to act by watching unlabeled online videos. arXiv preprint arXiv:2206.11795 (2022)
14. Petrenko, A., Huang, Z., Kumar, T., Sukhatme, G., Koltun, V.: Sample factory: egocentric 3d control from pixels at 100000 fps with asynchronous reinforcement learning. In: International Conference on Machine Learning, pp. 7652–7662. PMLR (2020)
15. Skrynnik, A., Andreychuk, A., Yakovlev, K., Panov, A.: Pathfinding in stochastic environments: learning vs planning. PeerJ Comput. Sci. **8**, e1056 (2022)
16. Skrynnik, A., Yakovleva, A., Davydov, V., Yakovlev, K., Panov, A.I.: Hybrid policy learning for multi-agent pathfinding. IEEE Access **9**, 126034–126047 (2021)
17. Sturtevant, N.: Benchmarks for grid-based pathfinding. Trans. Comput. Intell. AI Games **4**(2), 144–148 (2012)

Cooperative Chaotic Exploration with UAVs Combining Pheromone Dispersion and Hopfield Chaotic Neural Network

Jonathan Daniel Díaz-Muñoz, Israel Cruz-Vega$^{(\boxtimes)}$, and Esteban Tlelo-Cuatle

Electronics Department, Instituto Nacional de Astrofísica, Óptica y Electrónica (INAOE), Luis Enrique Erro No.1, Tonantzintla 72840, Puebla, Mexico
{jdiazm,icruzv,etlelo}@inaoep.mx
https://www.inaoep.mx

Abstract. Currently, Unmanned Aerial Vehicles (UAVs) or Drones have been presented as new tools for terrain exploration in multiple applications and objectives. UAV exploration has challenges in how the vehicle scans the environment, which must be fast, safe, and complete. This paper presents some mobility models previously developed for chaotic exploration with multiple UAVs, called cooperative exploration. The main mobility model uses pheromone dispersion based on the Ant Colony Optimization (ACO) algorithm. In addition, we propose some modifications to these models by introducing the Hopfield Chaotic Neural Network dynamics to generate the chaotic behavior and improve the area coverage performance. Likewise, we present simulation results exploring an area size of 50 m × 50 m with 2 UAVs.

Keywords: Neural network · Chaotic · Drones · UAV · Exploration · Coverage

1 Introduction

The way to explore the terrain is essential to ensure that it is completely covered in the shortest possible time and without jeopardizing the security of the explorer or the environment. Other features vary according to the application or the objective of the exploration task, such as a complete, autonomous, and unpredictable exploration. There are various techniques and methodologies to meet these or other characteristics, and a particular approach is to take advantage of the properties of dynamic systems with chaotic behavior used in various applications such as cryptography, communications, random number generators, and activation functions in neural networks, among others. These applications have proven that chaotic systems are unpredictable, random, and sensitive. Taking advantage of these properties can benefit the exploration process and help meet the objectives of that task.

O. Pichardo Lagunas et al. (Eds.): MICAI 2022, LNAI 13612, pp. 108–122, 2022.
https://doi.org/10.1007/978-3-031-19493-1_9

With the development of technologies and robotics, there are more and more new tools for multiple applications related to terrain exploration and autonomous robots. The primary investigations of these applications are focused on military [6,18]. Industrial, [19,23]. Civil subjects [3,16]. And search and rescue in natural disasters [20], exploration and reconnaissance of remote environments [12,14], etc. In particular, UAVs can travel at relatively high speed and explore an area in less time than mobile robots. Most of these have cameras, sensors, and communication systems that provide essential environmental information. These characteristics improve performance in many applications [18]. However, UAVs have a reduced flight time depending on their battery, they cannot carry huge loads, and the flight depends on weather conditions. Recent research addresses these issues and decides whether to optimize cost, time, distance, or energy.

Maximizing the coverage area in an application with UAVs depends on how to explore the terrain. The main characteristics are that the exploration is complete, autonomous, and unpredictable. This unpredictability is an essential feature in applications such as surveillance, patrol, and search. Furthermore, it is an intrinsic characteristic of chaotic systems, which are very sensitive to initial conditions and used in applications requiring unpredictable and random behavior. These characteristics are necessary for terrain exploration tasks [18,25].

This paper presents some previously developed mobility models for cooperative exploration with UAVs. These mobility models are Random Walk Mobility Model (RWMM), Chaotic Rössler Mobility Model (CROMM), and Chaotic Ant Colony Optimization for Coverage (CACOC) Mobility Model. We propose to modify the dynamic system of the mobility models by changing the probability distribution in the actions of the UAVs. This modification consists of introducing the Hopfield Chaotic Neural Network model to replace the Rössler chaotic system and seek to improve the performance in the coverage of the explored area. We present simulation results of an area size of $50m \times 50m$ with 2 UAVs, we program the mobility models in Python, and the dynamics of the UAVs trajectories are simulated in the CoppeliaSim Simulator.

This document is organized as follows: Sect. 2 presents some investigations related to chaotic exploration. Section 3 describes the mobility models used for the exploration. Section 4 describes the metrics used to evaluate the results. Section 5 shows the simulation results. Finally, Sect. 6 summarizes the conclusions and future work.

2   Related Work

The authors of [9] start their research looking for chaotic behavior in a mobile robot. To achieve this behavior, they extend the equations of the mobile robot model by integrating Arnold's chaotic equation. Making the mobile robot have chaotic movements to explore an environment. In [2] they used this method to integrate chaotic behavior, where the authors propose a cooperation scheme between multiple mobile robots with chaotic behavior for cooperative exploration of an environment. This N-robot scheme is composed of a master robot that integrates the Chen and Lorenz chaotic systems in discrete-time, and the other robots are synchronized to the master using an Extended Kalman Filter to estimate the chaotic motion.

Continuing with the work of [2], the authors of [8] use the same cooperation scheme between multiple mobile robots. However, in this work, the authors modify the synchronization process, which consists of extending the mathematical model of the mobile robot again and adding the error dynamics between the master and slave systems. As in [2], one robot fulfills the master function, and the rest will be the slave systems synchronized to the chaotic behavior of the master robot.

Another chaotic exploration approach is proposed in [24] and [25], where the authors use a two-scrolls chaotic system and a logistic map as the source for a Pseudo-Random Bit Generator (PRBG). In this PRBG, the time series of the chaotic system is threshold encoded to obtain a bit sequence. The values of these bits are actions for the mobile robot (forward, right, left, standstill). Notably, in [25], the authors propose to use a PRBG for each wheel of the mobile robot. Each PRBG has different initial conditions and parameters, i.e., different bit sequences are generated for the two independent wheels of the robot.

Based on the method proposed in [9], the authors of [10] propose to use the Chua multi-scroll chaotic oscillator integrated with the model of a mobile robot, making the robot angle depend on the chaotic states of the oscillator, which can vary the number of scrolls and improve scanning performance. However, a disadvantage of these schemes is that the explorer can concentrate its trajectories around a point of oscillation, a higher number of scrolls improves this behavior, but it can considerably increase the computational load of the system.

The previous papers do not use drones or UAVs as explorers. However, the mentioned techniques could be applied to UAVs for terrain exploration. On the other hand, some research focuses on using UAVs as explorers, e.g., in [13] and [14], the authors study various mobility models to operate unmanned aerial vehicles (UAVs) as a swarm system that scouts a given area. In these mobility models, the classic random walks (Random Walk), a mobility model based on the Rössler system (CROMM), and the mobility model based on the Ant Colony Optimization algorithm (ACO) combined with chaotic dynamics of the Rössler system. This algorithm is called CACOC (Chaotic Ant Colony Optimization for Coverage). Subsequently, the authors continue their investigation in [15] by plating a colony of 10 UAVs to explore an area with the CACOC mobility model.

The CACOC mobility algorithm is based on an evolutionary algorithm (ACO) in which several parameters affect its performance, so in [17], the authors face the problem of parameterizing and optimizing 3 of the CACOC mobility model parameters, improving performance depending on the area or number of UAVs in the swarm. The parameters defined in this article are the number of pheromones left by each vehicle (τ_a), the pheromone radius (τ_r), and the maximum detection distance of pheromones (τ_d). These parameters are optimized using a Genetic Algorithm (GA) and two Cooperative Coevolutionary Genetic Algorithms (CCGA). In the GA, they design the value of the operators and propose the fitness function to maximize the area explored by the UAV. The first CCGA is a configuration of an independent GA for each UAV, where each GA focuses on optimizing the parameters of its UAV. The second CCGA has a shared population that randomly samples individuals from the previous GA populations.

Similarly, in [18], the authors use the Cooperative Coevolutionary Genetic Algorithms (CCGA) optimization scheme proposed in [17] to optimize the CROMM mobility model. In this paper, they propose to have explorers of different types, Unmanned Aerial Vehicles (UAV), Unmanned Ground Vehicles (UGV), and Unmanned Marine Vehicles (UMV) to have a multi-swarm with the mobility model called CROMM-MS. Some vehicles act as predators and others as prey, and both are optimized to improve vehicle parameters, the search capacity of predators, and the evasion capacity of prey. In addition, the authors modify the optimization algorithm by adding a population called "Hall of Fame" that contains the best individuals. From there, 30 are randomly taken, and the current individual is evaluated against these 30 opponents. After each generation, the "Hall of Fame" is updated with the best individual.

In [7], the authors return to the Pseudo-Random Bit Generators (PRBG) approach to obtain the chaotic movements of a UAV exploring a terrain. There they propose a chaotic map generating a time series encoded with 4 bits in each iteration, 3 bits are instructions for the UAV (up, up-right, right, down-right, down, down-left, left, and up-left), the instructions that leave the work area are discarded, and the UAV waits for a new instruction.

3   UAV Mobility Models

Several mobility models for terrain exploration with UAVs like those mentioned in the previous section have different advantages and disadvantages. This section describes the mobility models used in this paper.

Random Walk Mobility Model (RWMM). The RWMM is introduced in [5]. It is based on a Markov process, in which the following explorer action depends on the previous action and a random value between 0 and 1, called ρ. Table 1 shows the probability of an action, where the turns are 45° relative to the current direction of the UAV, and Algorithm 1 describes the mobility model based on Random Walk.

Table 1. Action table for the RWMM [5]

Last action	Probability of action		
	Turn left	*Ahead*	*Turn right*
Ahead	10%	80%	10%
Turn left	70%	30%	0%
Turn right	0%	30%	70%

Algorithm 1. RWMM.

```
1:  Initialize UAV
2:  Initialize parameters for RWMM
3:  current_state = "Ahead"
4:  loop
5:      ρ = random()
6:      current_state = action(ρ, current_state) {See Table 1}
7:      move according to current_state
8:  end loop
```

Chaotic Rössler Mobility Model (CROMM). For the CROMM mobility model, the authors in [14] propose a methodology to use the dynamics of chaotic systems. This methodology consists of the value of the action probability ρ obtained from the chaotic system, specifically from the first-return map or Poincaré map (ρ_n). In this case, the authors use the Rössler chaotic system described by (1), Fig. 1a shows the chaotic attractor of this system. The first-return map (Fig. 1b) is constructed from the normalized points that cross the Poincaré section (2).

$$\begin{aligned}
\dot{x} &= -y - z \\
\dot{y} &= x + ay \\
\dot{z} &= b + z(x - c)
\end{aligned} \tag{1}$$

where x, y, and z are the states, and a, b and c are the system's parameters.

$$P_n = \{(y_n, z_n) \mid x_n = 0, \dot{x}_n > 0\} \tag{2}$$

Finally, with the action probability value (Fig. 1b), the next movement of the UAV is established according to the Algorithm 2, which describes the Chaotic Rössler system mobility model (CROMM).

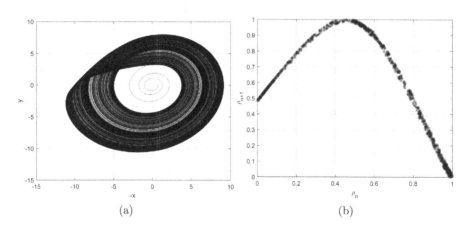

(a)   (b)

Fig. 1. Simulation results of the Rössler system using fourth-order Runge-Kutta with step size $\Delta t = 0.1$, initial conditions $x_0 = -0.75$, $y_0 = z_0 = 0$, and parameters $a = 0.1775, b = 0.215, c = 5.995$. (1a) Chaotic attractor $(y, -x)$. (1b) First-return map of the chaotic attractor with Poincaré section (2).

Algorithm 2. CROMM.

```
1: Initialize UAV
2: Initialize parameters for CROMM
3: current_state = "Ahead"
4: Evaluate Rössler's system and obtain the first-return map
5: Calculate ρ_n from first-return map
6: loop
7:     ρ = next value of ρ_n
8:     if ρ < 1/3 then
9:         current_state = "Turn right"
10:    else if 1/3 ≤ ρ < 2/3 then
11:        current_state = "Turn left"
12:    else
13:        current_state = "Ahead"
14:    end if
15:    move according to current_state
16: end loop
```

Chaotic Ant Colony Optimization for Coverage (CACOC) Mobility Model. The CACOC mobility model proposed in [13] and [14] is based on the concept of pheromone dispersion used by the ACO and applied in one of the mobility models proposed in [5]. This dispersion consists of the UAV leaving a finite amount of pheromones in its trajectory. In addition, the UAV detects these pheromones. The probability of action is affected according to the number of pheromones detected to avoid going to previously visited points, i.e., pheromones indicate recently visited points. However, the pheromones evaporate overtime when the maximum pheromones are deposited. Algorithm 3 describes

Algorithm 3. CACOC.

```
1: Initialize UAV
2: Initialize parameters for CACOC
3: current_state = "Ahead"
4: Evaluate Rössler's system and obtain the first-return map
5: Calculate ρ_n from first-return map
6: loop
7:     ρ = next value of ρ_n
8:     if total_ph = 0 then
9:         current_state = CROMM
10:    else
11:        if ρ < P_R then
12:            current_state = "Turn right"
13:        else if P_R ≤ ρ < P_R + P_L then
14:            current_state = "Turn left"
15:        else
16:            current_state = "Ahead"
17:        end if
18:    end if
19:    move according to current_state
20: end loop
```

the CACOC mobility model, the probability of action (P_R, P_L, and P_A) according to the number of pheromones detected in the three directions of movement (*right*, *left*, and *ahead*), and the total number of pheromones detected (*total* = *right* + *left* + *ahead*). Thus, the direction with more pheromones detected has a lower probability of the following action. On the other hand, if the UAV does not detect pheromones, the action is given by the Algorithm 2 CROMM.

Chaotic Hopfield Mobility Model (CHOMM) and Chaotic Hopfield Ant Colony Optimization for Coverage (CHACOC) Mobility Model. The methodology proposed in [14] for the CROMM mobility model can be used with other dynamical systems that provide a different probability distribution from the first-return map or from a different encoding of the time series of the chaotic system. We test a Neural Network model proposed by Hopfield in [4] and used for image encryption in [21] and [1]. The Hopfield Chaotic Neuron Network is described by (3), the chaotic attractor of this system is shown in Fig. 2a and its respective first-return map in Fig. 2b constructed from the normalized points that cross the Poincare section (6).

$$
\begin{aligned}
\dot{x} &= -x + W_{1,1}f(x) + W_{1,2}f(y) + W_{1,3}f(z) \\
\dot{y} &= -y + W_{2,1}f(x) + W_{2,2}f(y) + W_{2,3}f(z) \\
\dot{z} &= -z + W_{3,1}f(x) + W_{3,2}f(y) + W_{3,3}f(z)
\end{aligned}
\tag{3}
$$

where x, y, and z are the neuronal states, $f(\bullet)$ is the neuronal activation function (4), and W is the neural connection weight matrix (5).

$$
\begin{aligned}
f(x) &= \tanh(x) \\
f(y) &= \tanh(y) \\
f(z) &= \tanh(z)
\end{aligned}
\tag{4}
$$

$$
W = \begin{pmatrix} 2 & -1.2 & 0 \\ 1.9997 & 1.71 & 1.15 \\ -4.75 & 0 & 1.1 \end{pmatrix}
\tag{5}
$$

$$
P_n = \{(y_n, z_n) \mid x_n = 0.2, \dot{x}_n > 0\}
\tag{6}
$$

In the case of the CHOMM, the next movement of the UAV is established according to Table 2 and the probability distribution ρ_n of Fig. 2b. Also, the turns are 45° relative to the current direction of the UAV. Algorithm 4 describes the Chaotic Hopfield Mobility Model (CHOMM).

In the case of CHACOC, we used the pheromone dispersion methodology combined with the Hopfield Chaotic Neural Network (3) and the probability distribution of Fig. 2b. Table 3 shows the probability of action according to the number of pheromones detected in the three directions of movement (*right*, *left*, and *ahead*), where P_R, P_L, and P_A are the probability of action in the three directions. Again, if the UAV does not detect pheromones, the action is given by the Algorithm 4 CHOMM. Algorithm 5 describes the CHACOC mobility model.

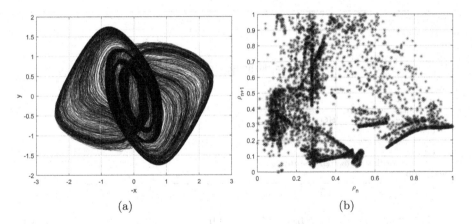

(a)   (b)

Fig. 2. Simulation results of the Hopfield system using fourth-order Runge-Kutta with step size $\Delta t = 0.565$, initial conditions $x_0 = 0.2$, $y_0 = -0.2929$, and $z_0 = -3.4720$. (2a) Chaotic attractor $(y, -x)$. (2b) First-return map of the chaotic attractor with Poincaré section (6).

Table 2. Action table for the CHOMM

Turn right	Turn left	Ahead
if $\rho_n < 1/3$	if $1/3 \leq \rho_n < 2/3$	if $2/3 \leq \rho_n$

Algorithm 4. CHOMM.

1: Initialize UAV
2: Initialize parameters for CHOMM
3: $current\_state$ = "Ahead"
4: Evaluate Hopfield's system and obtain the first-return map
5: Calculate ρ_n from first-return map
6: **loop**
7:     ρ = next value of ρ_n
8:     $current\_state$ = action(ρ) {See Table 2}
9:     move according to $current\_state$
10: **end loop**

Table 3. Action table for the CHACOC

Turn right	Turn left	Ahead
$P_R = \frac{total-right}{2 \times total}$	$P_L = \frac{total-left}{2 \times total}$	$P_A = \frac{total-ahead}{2 \times total}$
if $\rho_n < P_R$	if $P_R \leq \rho_n < P_R + P_L$	if $P_R + P_L \leq \rho_n$

4   Metrics

The primary metric used is **the coverage rate** of the explored area. This metric quantifies the percentage of the area that was explored by the UAVs, indicating the performance of the exploration and is given by (7), where %C is the coverage rate, N_{cell} is the total number of cells in the area (the area is divided into

---

Algorithm 5. CHACOC.

1: Initialize UAV
2: Initialize parameters for CHACOC
3: $current\_state$ = "Ahead"
4: Evaluate Hopfield's system and obtain the first-return map
5: Calculate ρ_n from first-return map
6: **loop**
7:       ρ = next value of ρ_n
8:       **if** $total_{ph}$ = 0 **then**
9:           $current\_state$ = CHOMM {See Table 2}
10:      **else**
11:          $current\_state$ = action(ρ,P_R,P_L,P_A) {See Table 3}
12:      **end if**
13:      move according to $current\_state$
14: **end loop**

$1\,\mathrm{m} \times 1\,\mathrm{m}$ cells, i.e., 2500 cells), $cell(i)$ is an array that stores 1 if cell i was scanned and 0 if it was not.

$$\%C = \frac{1}{N_{cell}} \sum_{i=1}^{N_{cell}} I(i),$$
$$I(i) = \begin{cases} 1 & if\ i\ is\ covered \\ 0 & if\ i\ is\ not\ covered \end{cases} \tag{7}$$

In addition, **coverage fairness** is used to quantify whether the cells are scanned equally and regularly. Ideally, the scanning of each cell has a uniform probability distribution. Fairness is calculated as the standard deviation of the number of times each cell is scanned and is given by (8), i.e., a lower fairness value indicates better performance than a higher value.

$$fairness = \sqrt{\frac{1}{N_{cell}} \sum_{i=1}^{N_{cell}} |\mathrm{n}_{\exp}(\mathrm{i}) - \mathrm{u}_{\exp}|^2} \tag{8}$$

where N_{cell} is the total number of cells in the area, $n_{exp}(i)$ is the number of times cell i is scanned, and u_{exp} is the mean of n_{exp}. Finally, since the mobility models are executed several times, some tests are made, such as the mean and the standard deviation of the results.

Furthermore, we use the Lyapunov exponents and the Kaplan-Yorke fractal dimension to quantify the chaos of the systems and observe the difference between them. Lyapunov exponents are asymptotic measures that characterize the contraction or growth rate of small perturbations on the solutions of a dynamical system, providing a quantitative measure of the sensitivity of a system to small changes in its initial conditions [22]. A positive Lyapunov exponent means an expansion characteristic of the dynamical system. This characteristic indicates the system's sensitivity to the variation of the initial conditions, i.e., a positive Lyapunov exponent indicates the presence of chaos in dynamical systems [11]. On the other hand, the dimension of an attractor is the lower bound on the number of state variables needed to describe the steady-state behavior of a dynamic system. Non-chaotic systems have an integer dimension, but chaotic systems have a non-integer or fractal dimension. The Kaplan-Yorke fractal dimension (9) calculates the dimension of a chaotic attractor from the Lyapunov exponents [11].

$$D_{KY} = j + \frac{\lambda_1 + \cdots + \lambda_j}{|\lambda_{j+1}|} \tag{9}$$

5   Results

The simulation tests correspond to an area size of $50m \times 50m$ with 2 UAVs. Each mobility model is executed ten times with 10000 steps or actions, and the chaotic systems have the initial conditions ($\epsilon + 0.01(\#UAV)$), where ϵ is a random seed between -0.5 and 0.5, and $\#UAV$ is 1 for the first UAV and 2 for the second, ensuring that in each execution the trajectories are different. Mobility models are programmed in Python and send the instructions to the CoppeliaSim Simulator (Fig. 3), where the dynamics of the UAVs are simulated with a scanning speed of $1m/s$, and to avoid a collision, the UAVs fly at a different height. In addition, the pheromone-based mobility models (CACOC and CHACOC) are executed with the parameters parameterized in [17], i.e., $\tau_a = 74$, $\tau_r = 1.5$, and $\tau_d = 4$. We use the TISEAN Software to evaluate the Lyapunov exponents and the Kaplan-Yorke fractal dimension of the time series of chaotic systems (series of 200000 points). Table 4 shows the results of both metrics, and both chaotic systems have a Kaplan-Yorke dimension with similar and non-integer values indicating the presence of chaos. In the case of the Lyapunov exponents, both systems have positive exponents. However, the Hopfield Chaotic Neural Network has a higher exponent, i.e., it is more sensitive to changes in the initial conditions. This sensitivity makes the trajectories have a more significant

Fig. 3. CoppeliaSim Simulator screenshot of the 2 UAVs.

Table 4. Results of the Lyapunov exponents and Kaplan-Yorke dimension.

Chaotic system	Lyapunov exponents			Kaplan-Yorke dimension
Rössler	$6.727013e-3$	$1.742690e-5$	$-1.090885e-1$	2.061825
Hopfield	$64.14496e-3$	$-5.019493e-2$	$-2.639096e-1$	2.052859

variation in each execution. Figure 4a shows the results of the percentage of coverage of the explored area. There it is observed that the mobility model based on the dispersion of pheromones with the Hopfield system (CHACOC) has a better performance in the exploration than the other models, followed by the CHOMM and CACOC models. So the change in the action probability distribution significantly influences the exploration performance. Table 5 shows the results of the tests (mean and standard deviation) of the coverage rate. There it is observed that the mobility models that use the Hopfield Chaotic Neural Network have better results, even without using the dispersion of pheromones.

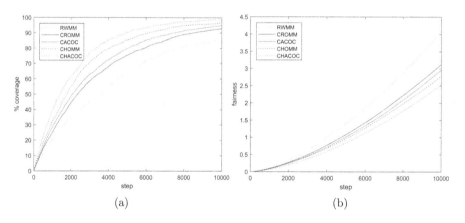

(a)   (b)

Fig. 4. Results of the different mobility models. (4a) Coverage results. (4b) Fairness results.

The performance improvement is also evidenced in the number of times that the UAVs visit a point, quantified with fairness Fig. 4b. There it is observed that with the CHACOC the UAVs pass more uniformly through each of the points visited and proportionally a smaller number of times through the same point.

In Fig. 5, the trajectories of the UAVs are observed during four stages of the exploration with the CHACOC mobility model. In the initial stage (1000 steps), the UAVs have traveled about 40% of the area, and it is observed that the trajectories cross little. In the second stage (4000 steps), the coverage exceeds 80%, and the trajectories are more overlapping. Finally, in the following two stages (7000 and 10000 steps), the coverage is greater than 95%, and the unexplored area is low.

Table 5. Results of the tests of the different mobility models.

Mobility model	Test Value		
	Mean (%)	Std	Value Max (%)
RWMM	85.8533	0.04875	89.40
CROMM	92.8400	0.00667	93.76
CACOC	95.0267	0.00435	95.64
CHOMM	96.5733	0.00603	97.20
CHACOC	98.9333	0.00132	99.12

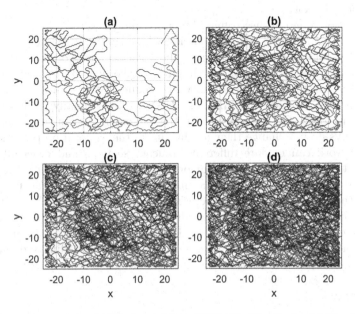

Fig. 5. Trajectory results (UAV #1: red line, UAV #2: blue line) with the CHACOC in different number of steps. *(a)*: 1000 steps, *(b)*: 4000 steps, *(c)*: 7000 steps, *(d)*: 10000 steps. (Color figure online)

6 Conclusions

All the mobility models used provide a percentage of successful coverage and exceed 90%, except the RWMM. However, changing the action probability distribution with the Hopfield Chaotic Neural Network improves scanning performance, even without pheromone dispersion. This improvement is because the first-return map points reflect the chaotic behavior of the system and do not have an even distribution as in the map of the CROMM and CACOC models. Hence, the importance of selecting the Poincaré section is evident to obtain different distributions of probability of action.

The dispersion of pheromones has a more significant influence on the fairness of the coverage and the variability of exploration between executions. These results are reflected in Fig. 4b and Table 5, where the standard deviation between each execution is lower for CACOC and CHACOC models. These results reflect run-to-run reliability when using pheromone dispersion and reduce the uncertainty that the scan will complete if the initial system conditions change.

An essential factor is that the computational effort is reduced when using the Hopfield Chaotic Neural Network since to obtain the 10000 steps of the trajectories, 625000 points of the time series must be calculated for the mobility models with the Rössler system and 125000 for mobility models with the Hopfield Chaotic Neural Network, i.e., a reduction of 80%. This reduction could be increased if the Poincaré section is modified or if another encoding represents the chaotic behavior.

A limitation found in these types of mobility models is that the movements of the UAVs are limited to a couple of angles, which can mean sudden movements that increase energy consumption, and the UAVs cannot complete the exploration due to battery depletion, which is one of the biggest challenges of these systems. This problem can be addressed by reducing the scan angles or introducing control strategies that allow the UAV to be optimally guided through chaotic trajectories. On the other hand, the exploration is not in 3 dimensions, and the UAVs do not change their height during the exploration process.

Future work can explore different Poincaré sections and especially other encodings to represent chaotic behavior instead of the first-return map. It is essential to add 3-dimensional displacement to the exploration and modify the height of the UAVs since this characteristic is an advantage in the exploration processes. It is also necessary to add an obstacle avoidance system to achieve this. On the other hand, reduce the angles of action of the UAVs or implement control strategies to improve the system's efficiency by avoiding sudden movements. These implementations are necessary and have several challenges.

References

1. Díaz-Muñoz, J.D., Cruz-Vega, I., Tlelo-Cuautle, E., Ramírez Cortés, J.M., de Jesús Rangel-Magdaleno, J.: Kalman observers in estimating the states of chaotic neurons for image encryption under MQTT for IoT protocol. Eur. Phys. J. Spec. Top., 1–18 (2021). https://doi.org/10.1140/epjs/s11734-021-00319-2
2. Fallahi, K., Leung, H.: A cooperative mobile robot task assignment and coverage planning based on chaos synchronization. Int. J. Bifurcat. Chaos **20**(01), 161–176 (2010). https://doi.org/10.1142/S021812741002548X
3. Gao, X., Li, K., Wang, Y., Men, G., Zhou, D., Kikuchi, K.: A floor cleaning robot using Swedish wheels. In: 2007 IEEE International Conference on Robotics and Biomimetics (ROBIO), pp. 2069–2073. Sanya, China (2007). https://doi.org/10.1109/ROBIO.2007.4522487
4. Hopfield, J.J.: Neural networks and physical systems with emergent collective computational abilities. Proc. Natl. Acad. Sci. **79**(8), 2554–2558 (1982). https://doi.org/10.1073/pnas.79.8.2554
5. Kuiper, E., Nadjm-Tehrani, S.: Mobility models for UAV group reconnaissance applications. In: 2006 International Conference on Wireless and Mobile Communications (ICWMC'06), vol. Computer Science, pp. 33–39. IEEE, Bucharest, Romania (2006). https://doi.org/10.1109/ICWMC.2006.63

6. Marsland, S., Nehmzow, U., Shapiro, J.: On-line novelty detection for autonomous mobile robots. Robot. Auton. Syst. **51**(2–3), 191–206 (2005). https://doi.org/10.1016/j.robot.2004.10.006

7. Moysis, L., Rajagopal, K., Tutueva, A.V., Volos, C., Teka, B., Butusov, D.N.: chaotic path planning for 3D area coverage using a pseudo-random bit generator from a 1D chaotic map. Mathematics **9**(15), 1821 (2021). https://doi.org/10.3390/math9151821

8. Mukhopadhyay, S., Leung, H.: Cluster synchronization of predator prey robots. In: 2013 IEEE International Conference on Systems, Man, and Cybernetics, pp. 2753–2758. IEEE, Manchester, UK (2013). https://doi.org/10.1109/SMC.2013.470

9. Nakamura, Y., Sekiguchi, A.: The chaotic mobile robot. IEEE Trans. Robot. Autom. **17**(6), 898–904 (2001). https://doi.org/10.1109/70.976022

10. Nasr, S., Mekki, H., Bouallegue, K.: A multi-scroll chaotic system for a higher coverage path planning of a mobile robot using flatness controller. Chaos, Solitons Fractals **118**, 366–375 (2019). https://doi.org/10.1016/j.chaos.2018.12.002

11. Parker, T.S., Chua, L.: Practical Numerical Algorithms for Chaotic Systems. Springer-Verlag, New York (1989). https://doi.org/10.1007/978-1-4612-3486-9

12. Pinto, J., et al.: To boldly dive where no one has gone before: experiments in coordinated robotic ocean exploration. In: Siciliano, B., Laschi, C., Khatib, O. (eds.) ISER 2020. SPAR, vol. 19, pp. 472–487. Springer, Cham (2021). https://doi.org/10.1007/978-3-030-71151-1_42

13. Rosalie, M., Danoy, G., Chaumette, S., Bouvry, P.: From random process to chaotic behavior in swarms of UAVs. In: Proceedings of the 6th ACM Symposium on Development and Analysis of Intelligent Vehicular Networks and Applications, pp. 9–15. DIVANet 2016, Association for Computing Machinery, Malta, Malta (2016). https://doi.org/10.1145/2989275.2989281

14. Rosalie, M., Danoy, G., Chaumette, S., Bouvry, P.: Chaos-enhanced mobility models for multilevel swarms of UAVs. Swarm Evol. Comput. **41**, 36–48 (2018). https://doi.org/10.1016/j.swevo.2018.01.002

15. Rosalie, M., et al.: Area exploration with a swarm of UAVs combining deterministic chaotic ant colony mobility with position MPC. In: 2017 International Conference on Unmanned Aircraft Systems (ICUAS), pp. 1392–1397. Miami, FL (2017). https://doi.org/10.1109/ICUAS.2017.7991418

16. Samarakoon, S.M.B.P., Muthugala, M.A.V.J., Le Vu, A., Elara, M.R.: hTetro-Infi: a reconfigurable floor cleaning robot with infinite morphologies. IEEE Access **8**, 69816–69828 (2020). https://doi.org/10.1109/ACCESS.2020.2986838

17. Stolfi, D.H., Brust, M.R., Danoy, G., Bouvry, P.: A cooperative coevolutionary approach to maximise surveillance coverage of UAV swarms. In: 2020 IEEE 17th Annual Consumer Communications Networking Conference (CCNC), pp. 528–535. Las Vegas, NV, USA (2020). https://doi.org/10.1109/CCNC46108.2020.9045643

18. Stolfi, D.H., Brust, M.R., Danoy, G., Bouvry, P.: UAV-UGV-UMV multi-swarms for cooperative surveillance. Front. Robot. AI **8**, 616950 (2021). https://doi.org/10.3389/frobt.2021.616950

19. Suh, J.H., Lee, Y.J., Lee, K.S.: Object-transportation control of cooperative AGV systems based on virtual-passivity decentralized control algorithm. J. Mech. Sci. Technol. **19**(9), 1720–1730 (2005). https://doi.org/10.1007/BF02984184

20. Tadokoro, S. (ed.): Rescue Robotics: DDT Project on Robots and Systems for Urban Search and Rescue, 1st edn. Springer-Verlag, London (2009). https://doi.org/10.1007/978-1-84882-474-4

21. Tlelo-Cuautle, E., et al.: Chaotic image encryption using Hopfield and Hindmarsh-Rose neurons implemented on FPGA. Sensors **20**(5), 1326 (2020). https://doi.org/10.3390/s20051326

22. Tlelo-Cuautle, E., Pano-Azucena, A.D., Carbajal-Gomez, V.H., Sanchez-Sanchez, M.: Experimental realization of a multiscroll chaotic oscillator with optimal maximum lyapunov exponent. Sci. World J. 2014 (2014). https://doi.org/10.1155/2014/303614

23. Viloria, D.R., Solano-Charris, E.L., Muñoz-Villamizar, A., Montoya-Torres, J.R.: Unmanned aerial vehicles/drones in vehicle routing problems: a literature review. Int. Trans. Oper. Res. **28**(4), 1626–1657 (2021). https://doi.org/10.1111/itor.12783

24. Volos, C.K., Kyprianidis, I.M., Stouboulos, I.N.: A chaotic path planning generator for autonomous mobile robots. Robot. Auton. Syst. **60**(4), 651–656 (2012). https://doi.org/10.1016/j.robot.2012.01.001

25. Volos, C.K., Kyprianidis, I.M., Stouboulos, I.N.: Experimental investigation on coverage performance of a chaotic autonomous mobile robot. Robot. Auton. Syst. **61**(12), 1314–1322 (2013). https://doi.org/10.1016/j.robot.2013.08.004

Machine Learning-Based Decision Making in Evolutionary Multiobjective Clustering

Aarón Leonardo Sánchez-Martínez[1] , Mario Garza-Fabre[1]([⊠]) ,
Ricardo Landa[1] , and Edwin Aldana-Bobadilla[1,2]

[1] Center for Research and Advanced Studies, Cinvestav Campus Tamaulipas,
87130 Ciudad Victoria, Tamaulipas, Mexico
{aaron.sanchez,mario.garza,ricardo.landa,edwyn.aldana}@cinvestav.mx
[2] National Council of Science and Technology of Mexico, Conacyt,
Mexico City, Mexico
https://www.tamps.cinvestav.mx

Abstract. Clustering is an important optimization problem which is at
the core of many data mining and machine learning applications. Evolutionary multiobjective clustering algorithms optimize multiple partition
quality criteria simultaneously, producing a set of trade-off solutions in
a single execution. How can a final solution be selected from this set
of candidate trade-offs? Decision making is concerned with such a task,
acknowledging that obtaining a single solution may represent the ulti-
mate goal in practice. Given the limitations of current techniques, we
explore a novel approach to decision making: tackling this task as a
supervised learning problem. Our approach attempts to learn from the
decision-making process in example (training) problems, with the aim of
later applying the learned model to lead the identification of final solutions in new applications. In this paper, we present preliminary results
on the evaluation of this proposal. Our experiments include comparisons
with respect to a set of decision-making approaches from the literature
and consider a collection of synthetic clustering problems with diverse
characteristics. The results obtained are promising, highlighting the relevance of devising alternative decision-making strategies, the effectiveness
of our proposal, and motivating further research on this matter.

Keywords: Decision making · Clustering · Multiobjective
optimization · Evolutionary algorithms · Evolutionary multiobjective
clustering

1 Introduction

The *clustering* task is concerned with finding the best possible partitioning for a
given group of elements. The resulting subgroups, called *clusters*, are expected to
reflect the similarity between these elements, bringing together those with similar

O. Pichardo Lagunas et al. (Eds.): MICAI 2022, LNAI 13612, pp. 123–137, 2022.
https://doi.org/10.1007/978-3-031-19493-1_10

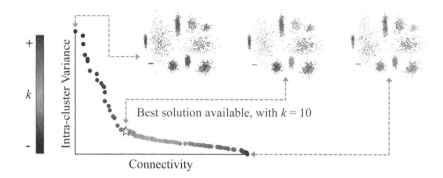

Fig. 1. Example PFA produced by algorithm Δ-MOCK [8].

characteristics and at the same time separating those which are less alike. From this definition it is possible to highlight the intrinsic multiobjective nature of this optimization problem, a nature which was recognized since the pioneering work of Delattre and Hansen [6]. It was not until more recently, however, when the first applications of *evolutionary multiobjective algorithms* in this particular context were reported [2,9–11], that the multiobjective approach to clustering popularized, motivating numerous research efforts [1,18].

Evolutionary multiobjective algorithms allow us to fully exploit the benefits of a multiobjective formulation of the clustering problem. They are able to optimize multiple, complementary criteria to evaluate partition quality simultaneously. This is particularly relevant, as individual criteria often lack the ability to capture all desirable aspects of a solution and their effectiveness is problem-dependent (*i.e.*, it depends on the compatibility of the criterion with the specific characteristics of the data under consideration). A multiobjective formulation thus provides us with a more flexible definition of solution quality, offering an increased robustness against changing problem characteristics. Moreover, due to their population-based optimization strategy, evolutionary multiobjective algorithms are capable of approximating the *Pareto front*, generating a set of trade-off (mutually *nondominated*) solutions within a single algorithm execution.

To illustrate this, consider the *Pareto front approximation* (PFA) shown in Fig. 1, which was obtained using the recently proposed algorithm Δ-MOCK [8]. This algorithm uses two specific clustering criteria as objective functions (both to be minimized): *intra-cluster variance* (VAR), which favors the homogeneity or compactness of the clusters; and *connectivity* (CNN), which promotes that neighboring elements are grouped together regardless of how similar they are. These criteria are in conflict with each other, not only because of the contrary (but equally important) goals they pursue, but also because of the opposing biases they exert with respect to the number of clusters, k: improving VAR tends to increase k, whereas improving CNN has the opposite effect, as can be seen from the figure. Hence, the simultaneous optimization of VAR and CNN produces a set of candidate partitions, representing different trade-offs between these criteria and exhibiting a potentially diverse range of values for k.

Having access to such a variety of potential solutions can certainly be useful. As Fig. 1 exemplifies, frequently the correct partitioning of the data is closely resembled by one of the trade-offs in the PFA, a solution which may be difficult to discover through the (single-objective) optimization of the individual criteria. Furthermore, the value of k is commonly unknown in advance, emphasizing the relevance of obtaining a range of choices regarding this parameter. Nevertheless, in a practical scenario, the delivery of a single, final solution is usually required. *Decision making* (DM) is the last step in the *evolutionary multiobjective clustering* (EMC) process, concerned with the identification of such a final solution from the initially produced PFA (it is noteworthy that DM is not particular to the clustering domain, but rather it extends to the broader area of multiobjective optimization). Despite its importance, no conclusive approach exists to automate DM (in the EMC context), as we analyze in the next section.

In this paper, we explore an alternative approach to DM: *machine learning-based decision making* (MLDM). It tackles DM as a learning problem, training a model based on examples and later exploiting it to guide DM in new scenarios. Our preliminary evaluation of this proposal considers a diverse collection of datasets and comparisons against several DM methods from the literature.

This paper is structured as follows. First, Sect. 2 reviews the relevant literature, discussing limitations of current DM approaches. Then, Sect. 3 introduces our MLDM strategy. Section 4 presents our experiments and results. Finally, Sect. 5 concludes and discusses directions for future work.

2   Related Work

Three categories of DM methods can be distinguished in the EMC literature. The first category follows a conceptually simple approach: using an additional criterion as a tiebreaker. That is, a criterion different from those used as objectives is considered to discriminate between the otherwise incomparable members of the PFA. The *Silhouette index* is a popular choice, appearing as the DM criterion in several studies [3,7,13,16]. Other alternatives include the *Davies-Bouldin, SD, Dunn, S_Dbw, $\mathcal{I}$,* and *Calinski-Harabasz* indices, which have been used for DM purposes by different authors [2,7,14,20]. Despite the simplicity of this approach, the use of a single criterion to guide DM entails the same disadvantage of single-objective clustering (as discussed in Sect. 1): the effectiveness of the criterion chosen will be problem-dependent. In view of this, some authors have considered criteria combinations; for example, a linear combination of the Calinski-Harabasz, Davies-Bouldin, and Silhouette indices was explored recently [25]. However, it might be difficult (and, once again, problem-dependent) to find the right balance (weighting) between the criteria being combined.

The second category includes strategies that focus on the shape of the PFA. These strategies adhere to a common assumption in multiobjective optimization: that the *knee* regions of the Pareto front offer the most promising trade-offs and may correspond to the preferences of a decision maker [5]. A clear representative of this category is algorithm MOCK [9] (predecessor of Δ-MOCK [8], discussed earlier). MOCK's strategy identifies the PFA member that maximizes the distance to some control fronts (generated by clustering random data), which is assumed to be at a knee of the PFA and picked as the final solution. Other approaches have been presented as less computationally demanding alternatives to MOCK's strategy. For example, it has been proposed to simply select the solution with the lowest sum of objective values [23], assuming minimization. Another proposal reduces the cardinality of the PFA and then selects the most knee-like solution by inspecting the angles defined by neighboring PFA members [15]. Unfortunately, though, these assumptions regarding the regions of the PFA that should be favored, which are reasonable in the general area of multiobjective optimization, do not necessarily hold in the more specific case of EMC. If one of the objectives contributes significantly more (it is more compatible) than others to solving the problem, the best solution choices are expected to be near the corresponding extreme of the PFA rather than at central, trade-off regions.

Instead of selecting a solution from the PFA, methods in the last category generate a partition anew, representing a consensus among PFA members. In [19], for instance, the authors employ three different *ensemble clustering* techniques (proposed in [24]) to integrate the nondominated solutions obtained by their EMC method. One of them, the *meta-clustering algorithm* [24], has also been used to generate a final solution in the context of MOCK [21]. An interesting approach combines a consensus strategy with the use of a classifier [17]. First, part of the elements are assigned to clusters whenever an agreement is observed for the majority of PFA members. Such initial clusters are used to train a classifier, which then helps define the cluster assignment of the remaining elements. The ensemble techniques reported in [12] have recently been exploited to generate a range of consensus partitions from those in the PFA, where a final decision is made by means of additional clustering criteria (methods in the first category) [25]. For some of the above consensus-based strategies, it is unclear if they can be used to integrate partitions with varying values of k (as in the PFAs considered here). However, the main limitation of the methods in this category is the assumption that all PFA members are equally reliable. As discussed before, some of the optimization criteria may become incompatible when dealing with specific problems; consequently, considering solutions that excel for such incompatible criteria may be equivalent to including noise in the final consensus.

The above discussion exhibits the complexity of DM under the peculiarities of EMC. Limitations derived from inherent assumptions of existing methods have prevented the development of a definitive approach to tackle this challenge, highlighting the need for exploring alternative solution methodologies.

3   Machine Learning-Based Decision Making

The approach proposed in this paper is based on the core idea of considering DM as a supervised learning problem, in this way letting the learning mechanism to capture the complexities of this task as a means to address the limitations of current techniques. As can be seen later from the results, this framework is promising, providing competitive results in a wide range of datasets.

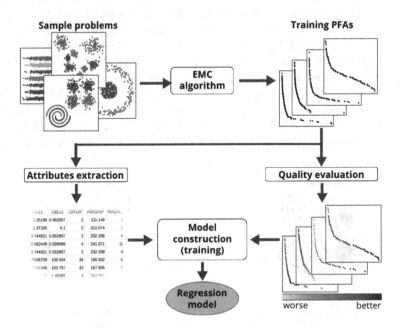

Fig. 2. Learning stage of MLDM.

3.1 Description of the Proposed Decision-Making Strategy

As a supervised learning technique, the aim of MLDM is to build a model from several DM example cases, so the model can be further applied to cases with unknown settings, in order to identify the best partition available in a PFA.

It is necessary to perform a *learning stage* first, following the steps depicted in Fig. 2. The outcome of this stage is a regression model, which will be used at a subsequent stage to predict the quality of each partition in a given PFA (as we explain later). The input is a set of sample problems, datasets with a known cluster structure, to make supervised learning possible. Each problem is fed into an EMC algorithm, which will produce PFAs. Given the stochastic nature of these algorithms, several runs are required so we will end up with several PFAs per dataset, which will serve the purposes of training the predictive model.

It is possible to assess the quality of the partitions in the PFAs by using an indicator which compares them to the (known) correct solution. Such an indicator is an *external clustering criterion*. The value of this indicator is then considered as the response variable of the model. Now, regarding the explanatory variables required for training, a set of attributes are extracted for each partition, so the model can predict partition quality based on those attributes.

The complementary part of MLDM, illustrated in Fig. 3, is the *application stage*. Here, a new problem with unknown correct partition (as in a real-world scenario) is presented, to which the EMC method is applied to obtain a PFA. Each candidate partition in the PFA needs to be characterized by the same set of attributes adopted during training. Attributes are used by the regression model for quality prediction, information which will enable the discrimination among PFA members. Thus, model predictions are effectively used to break ties: candidates in the PFA are the best trade-offs obtained by the EMC method, but they are also equally good (*i.e.*, they are nondominated with respect to each other). DM actually takes place in the last step, when the partition with the best quality, as estimated by the regression model, is selected as the final solution.

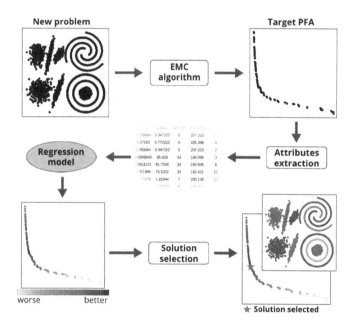

Fig. 3. Application stage of MLDM.

3.2 Definition of Main Design Components

In the previous description of our proposal there are several components mentioned, not as particular instances, but as generic mechanisms instead. This is indeed the case, MLDM is proposed as a generic framework that can be implemented with a variety of algorithmic choices, for example, to adapt it to a particular context, specifications of the user, or limitations of the infrastructure.

However, in order to perform the experiments and validate our proposal, such choices are made in this paper trying to reflect the current state-of-the-art, by selecting representative approaches. Our specific choices are listed below:

1. *EMC algorithm.* The algorithm chosen is Δ-MOCK [8], firstly because it is a more recent variant of MOCK [9], which is a representative algorithm, but also because it adopts the same (or equivalent) optimization criteria as several other algorithms from the literature, namely, VAR and CNN.
2. *Attribute extraction.* There are no precedents in the literature, to the best of our knowledge, of choosing a set of attributes to characterize different partitions in a PFA obtained by an EMC method. An important share of the effort in this work was invested in selecting a diverse set of attributes, so the PFAs can be properly characterized and relevant information is provided to the model. Our selection of attributes is further discussed in Sect. 3.3.
3. *Partition quality criterion.* This component is necessary for assessing the quality of candidate partitions. The *adjusted Rand index* (ARI) indicator [22] has been chosen. ARI allows us to compare how similar a candidate solution is with respect to the correct partition of the data, mapping this similarity to a value between 0 and 1. A greater value means more similar partitions. By using this indicator as the response variable, and the set of attributes as the explanatory variables, it is possible to proceed with the modeling.
4. *Supervised learning approach.* The approach used for constructing the model is *random forest* [4], mainly because it is practical and robust, specially in high-dimensional settings and scenarios with mixed-type attributes (scenario considered here), with successful applications in a wide variety of domains.

3.3   Characterization of Pareto Front Approximations

To train the regression model, it is imperative to define a set of attributes to characterize the solutions in the PFA, so that the model can learn to associate these attributes with the adopted measure of solution quality. We use a total of 55 attributes in this study. Due to space restrictions, a description of each of these attributes is not included in this paper, but below we summarize the five categories defined to organize them and provide some examples:

1. *Attributes describing PFA members individually.* The 11 attributes in this category consider aspects of the PFA members at the individual level. Examples of these attributes include the objective values of a given solution, the specific sub-range of the x-axis and y-axis where it locates, and its distance with respect to the *ideal* and *nadir* points (as approximated by the PFA).
2. *Attributes describing the partition that PFA members represent.* Each point in the PFA encodes a clustering solution. The four attributes in this category refer to aspects of such solution: the value of k and the quality of the partition, as measured by the Silhouette, Davies-Bouldin, and Dunn indices.
3. *Attributes depending on other PFA members.* This category includes a total of 16 attributes, which describe a given PFA member in relation to other

candidate members of the PFA. Some of the attributes in this category are: whether or not the PFA member is a vertex of the convex hull of the PFA, the specific contribution of the PFA member to the hypervolume indicator, and the angle that forms with respect to neighboring PFA members.

4. *Attributes describing the PFA as a whole.* This category encompasses 22 attributes that refer to global aspects of the PFA, such as: the cardinality of the PFA, the computed value for the hypervolume indicator, and the area, perimeter and total number of vertices of convex hull of the PFA.

5. *Attributes describing the clustering problem.* This last category involves only two attributes, both referring to the specific clustering problem (dataset) under consideration: its size (number of elements) and dimensionality.

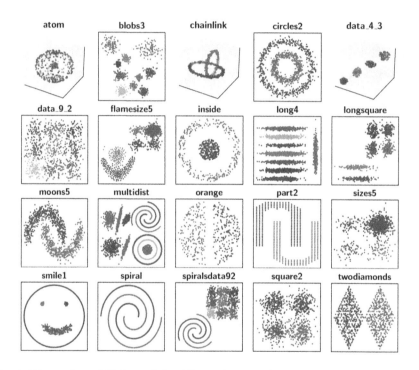

Fig. 4. Illustration of 20 (out of the 40) synthetic problems used in our experiments.

4   Experiments and Results

In this section, we present the results of our preliminary evaluation of the proposed MLDM technique. First, our experimental conditions are described in Sect. 4.1, including the clustering problems, reference approaches, and performance assessment measures considered. Then, Sects. 4.2 and 4.3 present the results for separate experiments considering scenarios of different difficulty.

4.1   Evaluation Setup

We consider 40 clustering problems, some of them illustrated in Fig. 4. All these problems are synthetic and low-dimensional, which allows us to draw conclusions that relate performance to the observable characteristics of the data. The size of each dataset (N) and the correct value of k is provided in Tables 1 and 2.

Four reference DM approaches from the EMC literature are included in our evaluation. The first three are clustering criteria commonly used for decision-making purposes (see Sect. 2): the Silhouette (SIL), Davies-Bouldin (DB), and Dunn (DUNN) indices. The remaining method is that implemented by MOCK, based on the identification of the knee of the PFA. In addition, the best and worst solutions available in the PFA are considered as baselines (denoted BEST and WORST), which represent upper and lower bounds on performance.

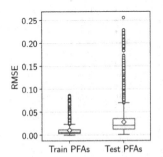 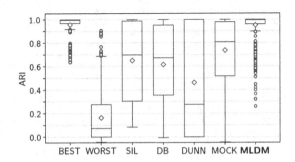

Fig. 5. Results for Scenario 1 are shown in terms of prediction performance, RMSE measure (left), and in terms of decision-making performance, ARI measure (right).

Two performance measures are used. The first one is the *root-mean-square error* (RMSE), which we use to assess prediction performance, *i.e.*, to quantify the differences between the quality values predicted by the regression model and the real (measured) quality of the solutions in the PFA. To assess DM performance, we focus on the quality of the final solutions selected by the methods evaluated, as given by the ARI indicator. Whereas RMSE is to be minimized, ARI is to be maximized. Finally, we use the *Mann-Whitney U test*, considering a significance level of $\alpha = 0.05$ and *Bonferroni correction*, to determine the statistical significance of the differences observed between the methods compared.

4.2   Scenario 1: Unknown PFAs for Known Problems

The first scenario considers the selection of final solutions from new (previously unseen) PFAs. However, other example PFAs, independently produced for the same clustering problems, were included in the training set and may present similar characteristics to the ones reserved for testing (these conditions make this scenario less difficult when compared to that considered in Sect. 4.3). We generated 40 independent PFAs for each of our 40 synthetic problems. The first

20 PFAs were included in the training set, and the other 20 to the testing set. Thus, both of these sets contain 800 PFAs, each including approximately 100 solution samples. We performed 20 repetitions of the full process of training (including cross-validated hyperparameter tuning) and testing in order to compute relevant statistics. A summary of the results obtained is presented in Fig. 5, whilst detailed results for the individual problems are provided in Table 1.

Table 1. Results for Scenario 1, presented separately for the 40 datasets and evaluated in terms of the median ARI of the final solutions selected. The best result for each problem is highlighted. Results for references SIL, DB, DUNN, and MOCK are marked • whenever a statistically significant difference is observed with respect to MLDM.

Dataset	N	k	BEST	WORST	SIL	DB	DUNN	MOCK	MLDM
atom	800	2	1.000	0.524	0.545 •	**1.000**	**1.000**	0.563 •	**1.000**
blobs1	1000	5	1.000	0.522	0.997	0.532 •	0.614 •	**1.000**	0.999
blobs2	1000	5	0.990	0.374	0.975 •	0.662 •	0.374 •	**0.990**	**0.990**
blobs3	1000	10	0.996	0.047	**0.996**	0.750 •	0.808 •	0.808 •	**0.996**
chainlink	1000	2	1.000	0.085	0.145 •	0.687 •	**1.000**	0.253 •	**1.000**
circles1	1000	2	1.000	0.070	0.189 •	**1.000**	**1.000**	0.671 •	**1.000**
circles2	1000	2	0.695	0.000	0.145 •	0.327 •	0.000 •	0.623 •	**0.695**
data_4_3	400	4	1.000	0.255	**1.000**	0.580 •	**1.000**	**1.000**	**1.000**
data_5_2	250	5	0.914	0.000	**0.914**	0.204 •	0.000 •	**0.914**	**0.914**
data_6_2	300	6	1.000	0.332	**1.000**	0.725 •	**1.000**	0.983 •	**1.000**
data_9_2	900	9	0.735	0.000	**0.731** •	0.144 •	0.000 •	0.720	0.714
flame	240	2	0.967	0.000	0.485 •	0.950 •	0.000 •	0.696 •	**0.967**
flamesize5	1240	6	0.963	0.000	0.489 •	0.209 •	0.000 •	0.489 •	**0.956**
fourty	1000	40	1.000	0.880	**1.000**	0.880 •	**1.000**	0.926 •	**1.000**
inside	600	2	1.000	0.093	0.587 •	**1.000**	**1.000**	0.590 •	**1.000**
long1	1000	2	1.000	0.107	0.375 •	**1.000**	**1.000**	0.514 •	**1.000**
long2	1000	2	1.000	0.100	0.292 •	**1.000**	**1.000**	0.687 •	**1.000**
long4	4000	8	0.960	0.000	0.589 •	0.837 •	0.000 •	0.485 •	**0.944**
longsquare	900	6	0.995	0.275	0.275 •	0.567 •	0.275 •	0.332 •	**0.992**
moons3	1000	2	0.996	0.000	0.191 •	0.854 •	0.000 •	0.303 •	**0.992**
moons5	1000	2	0.984	0.000	0.338 •	**0.984**	0.000 •	0.340 •	**0.984**
multidist	3012	11	0.745	0.398	0.603 •	0.398 •	0.398 •	0.447 •	**0.713**
orange	400	2	1.000	0.079	**1.000**	**1.000**	**1.000**	0.796 •	**1.000**
part2	417	2	1.000	0.168	0.296 •	**1.000**	**1.000**	0.783 •	**1.000**
r15	600	15	0.991	0.264	**0.991**	0.706 •	0.264 •	**0.991**	0.989
sizes1	1000	4	0.958	0.000	**0.958**	0.239 •	0.000 •	**0.958**	**0.958**
sizes3	1000	4	0.974	0.000	**0.974** •	0.001 •	0.000 •	**0.974**	0.973
sizes5	1000	4	0.965	0.000	**0.956**	0.113 •	0.000 •	0.954	0.954
smile1	1000	4	1.000	0.671	0.740 •	**1.000**	**1.000**	0.831 •	**1.000**
spiral	1000	2	1.000	0.105	0.106 •	0.532 •	**1.000**	0.830 •	**1.000**
spiralsdata52	562	8	0.728	0.000	0.277 •	0.649 •	0.000 •	0.277 •	**0.704**
spiralsdata92	1212	12	0.694	0.000	0.106 •	0.601 •	0.000 •	0.106 •	**0.673**
spiralsizes5	2000	6	0.986	0.000	0.685 •	0.780 •	0.000 •	0.780 •	**0.985**
spiralsquare	1500	6	0.999	0.261	0.290 •	0.641 •	0.800 •	0.894 •	**0.998**
square1	1000	4	0.976	0.000	**0.976**	0.489 •	0.000 •	**0.976**	**0.976**
square2	1000	4	0.906	0.000	**0.901**	0.462 •	0.000 •	**0.901**	**0.901**
triangle1	1000	4	1.000	0.271	**1.000**	0.299 •	**1.000**	0.982 •	**1.000**
triangle2	1000	4	0.980	0.000	**0.980**	0.244 •	0.000 •	**0.980**	**0.980**
twenty	1000	20	1.000	0.702	**1.000**	0.708 •	**1.000**	**1.000**	**1.000**
twodiamonds	800	2	0.998	0.000	**0.998**	0.250 •	0.000 •	0.995	0.995
Overall			0.995	0.073	0.697 •	0.674 •	0.275 •	0.808 •	**0.993**

Focusing first on prediction performance (left side of Fig. 5), we can see that, as expected, our method obtains higher RMSE values when predicting the quality of solutions in the testing PFAs (in comparison to those obtained for the training PFAs, which are shown as a reference). The RMSE values scored are still very low in the majority of the cases, being this a satisfactory result.

Turning our attention to the most important aspect of this evaluation, decision-making performance (right side of Fig. 5 and Table 1), we can confirm the suitability of the proposed MLDM strategy. MLDM is seen to outperform methods SIL, DB, DUNN, and MOCK, with statistically significant differences observed for most of the problems considered. It is possible to note that MLDM identifies high-quality final solutions, which report comparable ARI values to those of the best solutions available in the PFA (as indicated by baseline BEST).

4.3   Scenario 2: PFAs for Completely Unknown Problems

The second scenario also tests the ability of MLDM to select final solutions from completely unknown PFAs. In this case, however, no example PFAs are included in the training set for the specific problems used for testing (representing therefore a more difficult scenario than the one considered before). For each of our 40 datasets, we computed 20 PFAs independently. In contrast to the previous experiment, only 39 of these problems were used for training the model at any given time, whereas the remaining problem was reserved for testing purposes (resulting in 780 and 20 PFAs in the train and test sets, respectively, each containing around 100 solutions). We repeated the training and testing process so that each problem was considered exactly once for testing. As before, we ran each of these experiment configurations 20 times to compute relevant statistics. The results of these experiments are reported in Fig. 6 and Table 2.

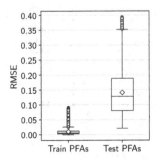 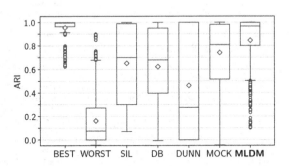

Fig. 6. Results for Scenario 2 are shown in terms of prediction performance, RMSE measure (left), and in terms of decision-making performance, ARI measure (right).

Figure 6 (left side) reveals that the more challenging conditions of this scenario caused a decrease in MLDM's prediction performance. This is evidenced by the higher RMSE values scored for testing PFAs in comparison to those obtained during the previous experiment. Although this has certainly affected decision-making performance, as interpreted from the lower ARI values obtained with respect to the previous scenario (right side of the figure), the model's predictions are still sufficiently informative so as to allow MLDM to achieve highly competitive results, outperforming (in average) all four contestant methods.

Analyzing the results of Table 2, it is possible to identify three problems for which our method reports a notably low performance (namely, circles2, data_9_2, and spiralsdata92). Besides the fact that these problems are challenging on their own (see the lower ARI values of baseline BEST for these particular problems), it might be the case that their specific characteristics are not well represented in the training set, which would evidently lead to a low performance of MLDM (supervised learning approaches depend on the availability of

Table 2. Results for Scenario 2, presented separately for the 40 datasets and evaluated in terms of the median ARI of the final solutions selected. The best result for each problem is highlighted. Results for references SIL, DB, DUNN and MOCK are marked • whenever a statistically significant difference is observed with respect to MLDM.

Dataset	N	k	BEST	WORST	SIL	DB	DUNN	MOCK	MLDM
atom	800	2	1.000	0.528	0.548 •	**1.000**	**1.000**	0.563 •	**1.000**
blobs1	1000	5	1.000	0.503	0.997 •	0.526 •	0.614 •	**1.000** •	0.963
blobs2	1000	5	0.990	0.374	0.975 •	0.590 •	0.374 •	**0.990** •	0.985
blobs3	1000	10	0.996	0.047	**0.996** •	0.787 •	0.808 •	0.808 •	0.984
chainlink	1000	2	1.000	0.086	0.144 •	0.687 •	**1.000**	0.256 •	**1.000**
circles1	1000	2	1.000	0.070	0.173 •	**1.000** •	**1.000** •	0.697	0.697
circles2	1000	2	0.692	0.000	0.136 •	0.327 •	0.000 •	**0.624** •	0.160
data_4_3	400	4	1.000	0.246	**1.000**	0.507 •	**1.000**	**1.000**	**1.000**
data_5_2	250	5	0.914	0.000	**0.914** •	0.204 •	0.000 •	**0.914** •	0.447
data_6_2	300	6	1.000	0.320	**1.000** •	0.750 •	**1.000** •	**1.000** •	0.967
data_9_2	900	9	0.747	0.000	**0.737** •	0.144 •	0.000 •	0.735 •	0.145
flame	240	2	0.967	0.000	0.479	**0.950** •	0.000 •	0.489	0.484
flamesize5	1240	6	0.963	0.000	0.489 •	0.487 •	0.000 •	0.489 •	**0.815**
fourty	1000	40	1.000	0.891	**1.000** •	0.891 •	**1.000** •	0.926 •	0.999
inside	600	2	1.000	0.094	0.577 •	**1.000**	**1.000**	0.589 •	**1.000**
long1	1000	2	1.000	0.104	0.375 •	**1.000**	**1.000**	0.516 •	**1.000**
long2	1000	2	1.000	0.099	0.291 •	**1.000**	**1.000**	0.686 •	**1.000**
long4	4000	8	0.953	0.000	0.589 •	**0.817**	0.000 •	0.485 •	**0.817**
longsquare	900	6	0.995	0.275	0.275 •	0.567 •	0.275 •	0.332 •	**0.870**
moons3	1000	2	0.996	0.000	0.209 •	0.854 •	0.000 •	**0.996**	0.988
moons5	1000	2	0.984	0.000	0.334 •	0.782 •	0.000 •	0.339 •	**0.960**
multidist	3012	11	0.715	0.398	0.600 •	0.398 •	0.398 •	0.447 •	**0.634**
orange	400	2	1.000	0.081	**1.000** •	**1.000** •	**1.000** •	0.796 •	0.995
part2	417	2	1.000	0.155	0.290 •	**1.000**	**1.000**	0.783 •	**1.000**
r15	600	15	0.991	0.264	**0.991** •	0.697 •	0.264 •	**0.991** •	0.862
sizes1	1000	4	0.958	0.000	0.958	0.000 •	0.000 •	**0.958**	**0.958**
sizes3	1000	4	0.974	0.000	**0.974** •	0.176 •	0.000 •	**0.974** •	0.971
sizes5	1000	4	0.967	0.000	**0.960** •	0.125 •	0.000 •	0.950 •	0.953
smile1	1000	4	1.000	0.677	0.739 •	**1.000** •	**1.000** •	0.812 •	0.999
spiral	1000	2	1.000	0.097	0.101 •	0.532 •	**1.000** •	0.829 •	0.998
spiralsdata52	562	8	0.720	0.000	0.277 •	**0.649** •	0.000 •	0.277 •	0.617
spiralsdata92	1212	12	0.701	0.000	0.106 •	**0.584** •	0.000 •	0.106 •	0.101
spiralsizes5	2000	6	0.986	0.000	0.687 •	0.785 •	0.000 •	0.780 •	**0.981**
spiralsquare	1500	6	0.999	0.260	0.291 •	0.644 •	0.800	**0.894** •	0.800
square1	1000	4	0.976	0.000	**0.976**	0.489 •	0.000 •	**0.976**	**0.976**
square2	1000	4	0.911	0.000	**0.910**	0.453 •	0.000 •	**0.910**	0.909
triangle1	1000	4	1.000	0.272	**1.000** •	0.325 •	**1.000** •	0.982 •	0.889
triangle2	1000	4	0.980	0.000	0.979 •	0.246 •	0.000 •	**0.980** •	0.967
twenty	1000	20	1.000	0.706	**1.000** •	0.716 •	**1.000** •	**1.000** •	0.987
twodiamonds	800	2	0.995	0.000	**0.995** •	0.242 •	0.000 •	**0.995** •	0.975
Overall			0.995	0.074	0.699 •	0.679 •	0.275 •	0.808 •	**0.967**

representative training samples). Due to their inherent limitations under particular conditions, as discussed earlier in Sect. 2, approaches SIL, DB, DUNN, and MOCK score competitive results in many cases but notably fail in many others (which is evidenced also by the wide distribution of ARI values these approaches show in Fig. 6). In general, MLDM exhibits an increased robustness against the variety of characteristics that our collection of datasets involves.

5   Concluding Remarks

Decision making (DM) is a challenging task in the particular context of evolutionary multiobjective clustering (EMC). Given the limitations of exiting DM techniques, we have explored an alternative approach to carry out this task. In particular, we have demonstrated that DM can be address as a learning problem, in such a way that knowledge available regarding the DM process on some example problems can be exploited to accomplish this task in new scenarios.

Our proposal, machine learning-based decision making (MLDM), was evaluated and compared with respect to several references from the literature, considering distinct experimental conditions and a collection of problems with diverse characteristics. The preliminary results reported in this paper are encouraging: MLDM has consistently exhibited a superior performance in comparison with the adopted references. More importantly, our proposal has shown a better robustness against changing problem features, highlighting the suitability of the learning-based approach to capture the complexities of the DM process.

The findings of this study motivate future research efforts, which will mainly focus on the improvement of the proposed technique. Potential improvements may arise from the analysis of the set of attributes used for the characterization of the approximation solution sets. Such an analysis should consider the identification of possible redundancies, the potential impacts of dimensionality reduction, as well as the definition of new attributes which can contribute to capture more precisely the peculiarities of DM in the EMC domain.

References

1. Abu Khurma, R., Aljarah, I.: A review of multiobjective evolutionary algorithms for data clustering problems. In: Aljarah, I., Faris, H., Mirjalili, S. (eds.) Evolutionary Data Clustering: Algorithms and Applications. AIS, pp. 177–199. Springer, Singapore (2021). https://doi.org/10.1007/978-981-33-4191-3_8
2. Bandyopadhyay, S., Maulik, U., Mukhopadhyay, A.: Multiobjective genetic clustering for pixel classification in remote sensing imagery. IEEE Trans. Geosci. Remote Sens. 45(5), 1506–1511 (2007). https://doi.org/10.1109/TGRS.2007.892604
3. Bandyopadhyay, S., Mukhopadhyay, A., Maulik, U.: An improved algorithm for clustering gene expression data. Bioinformatics 23(21), 2859 (2007)
4. Breiman, L.: Random forests. Mach. Learn. 45(1), 5–32 (2001)
5. Deb, K., Gupta, S.: Understanding knee points in bicriteria problems and their implications as preferred solution principles. Eng. Optim. 43(11), 1175–1204 (2011). https://doi.org/10.1080/0305215X.2010.548863

6. Delattre, M., Hansen, P.: Bicriterion cluster analysis. IEEE Trans. Pattern Anal. Mach. Intell. **PAMI-2**(4), 277–291 (1980). https://doi.org/10.1109/TPAMI.1980. 4767027
7. Garcia-Piquer, A., Sancho-Asensio, A., Fornells, A., Golobardes, E., Corral, G., Teixidó-Navarro, F.: Toward high performance solution retrieval in multiobjective clustering. Inf. Sci. **320**, 12–25 (2015). https://doi.org/10.1016/j.ins.2015.04.041
8. Garza-Fabre, M., Handl, J., Knowles, J.: An improved and more scalable evolutionary approach to multiobjective clustering. IEEE Trans. Evol. Comput. **22**(4), 515–535 (2018). https://doi.org/10.1109/TEVC.2017.2726341
9. Handl, J., Knowles, J.: An evolutionary approach to multiobjective clustering. IEEE Trans. Evol. Comput. **11**(1), 56–76 (2007). https://doi.org/10.1109/TEVC. 2006.877146
10. Handl, J., Knowles, J.: Evolutionary multiobjective clustering. In: Yao, X., et al. (eds.) PPSN 2004. LNCS, vol. 3242, pp. 1081–1091. Springer, Heidelberg (2004). https://doi.org/10.1007/978-3-540-30217-9_109
11. Handl, J., Knowles, J.: Exploiting the trade-off — the benefits of multiple objectives in data clustering. In: Coello Coello, C.A., Hernández Aguirre, A., Zitzler, E. (eds.) EMO 2005. LNCS, vol. 3410, pp. 547–560. Springer, Heidelberg (2005). https://doi.org/10.1007/978-3-540-31880-4_38
12. Huang, D., Wang, C.D., Lai, J.H.: Locally weighted ensemble clustering. IEEE Trans. Cybernet. **48**, 1460–1473 (2018). https://doi.org/10.1109/TCYB.2017. 2702343
13. José-García, A., Handl, J., Gómez-Flores, W., Garza-Fabre, M.: An evolutionary many-objective approach to multiview clustering using feature and relational data. Appl. Soft Comput. **108**, 107425 (2021). https://doi.org/10.1016/j.asoc.2021. 107425
14. Liu, Y., Özyer, T., Barker, K.: Integrating multi-objective genetic algorithm and validity analysis for locating and ranking alternative clustering. Informatica (Slovenia) **29**, 33–40 (2005)
15. Matake, N., Hiroyasu, T., Miki, M., Senda, T.: Multiobjective clustering with automatic k-determination for large-scale data. In: Proceedings of the 9th Annual Conference on Genetic and Evolutionary Computation, pp. 861–868, GECCO 2007. Association for Computing Machinery, London (2007). https://doi.org/10.1145/ 1276958.1277126
16. Maulik, U., Bandyopadhyay, S., Mukhopadhyay, A.: Multiobjective Genetic Algorithm-Based Fuzzy Clustering, pp. 89–121. Springer, Heidelberg (2011). https://doi.org/10.1007/978-3-642-16615-0_5
17. Mukhopadhyay, A., Maulik, U., Bandyopadhyay, S.: Multiobjective genetic algorithm-based fuzzy clustering of categorical attributes. IEEE Trans. Evol. Comput. **13**(5), 991–1005 (2009)
18. Mukhopadhyay, A., Maulik, U., Bandyopadhyay, S.: A survey of multiobjective evolutionary clustering. ACM Comput. Surv. **47**(4), 61:1–61:46 (2015). https:// doi.org/10.1145/2742642
19. Mukhopadhyay, A., Maulik, U., Bandyopadhyay, S.: Multiobjective genetic clustering with ensemble among pareto front solutions: application to MRI brain image segmentation. In: 2009 Seventh International Conference on Advances in Pattern Recognition, pp. 236–239 (2009). https://doi.org/10.1109/ICAPR.2009.51
20. Özyer, T., Liu, Y., Alhajj, R., Barker, K.: Multi-objective genetic algorithm based clustering approach and its application to gene expression data. In: Yakhno, T. (ed.) ADVIS 2004. LNCS, vol. 3261, pp. 451–461. Springer, Heidelberg (2004). https://doi.org/10.1007/978-3-540-30198-1_46

21. Qian, X., Zhang, X., Jiao, L., Ma, W.: Unsupervised texture image segmentation using multiobjective evolutionary clustering ensemble algorithm. In: IEEE Congress on Evolutionary Computation, pp. 3561–3567 (2008). https://doi.org/10.1109/CEC.2008.4631279

22. Rand, W.M.: Objective criteria for the evaluation of clustering methods. J. Am. Stat. Assoc. **66**(336), 846–850 (1971)

23. Shirakawa, S., Nagao, T.: Evolutionary image segmentation based on multiobjective clustering. In: IEEE Congress on Evolutionary Computation, pp. 2466–2473 (2009). https://doi.org/10.1109/CEC.2009.4983250

24. Strehl, A., Ghosh, J.: Cluster ensembles - a knowledge reuse framework for combining multiple partitions. J. Mach. Learn. Res. **3**, 583–617 (2003). https://doi.org/10.1162/153244303321897735

25. Zhu, S., Xu, L., Goodman, E.D.: Evolutionary multi-objective automatic clustering enhanced with quality metrics and ensemble strategy. Knowl.-Based Syst. **188**, 105018 (2020). https://doi.org/10.1016/J.KNOSYS.2019.105018

RBF Neural Network Based on FT-Windows for Auto-Tunning PID Controller

O. F. Garcia Castro[1], L. E. Ramos Velasco[1]([✉]), M. A. Vega Navarrete[1],
R. Garcia Rodriguez[1], C. R. Domínguez Mayorga[1], E. Escamilla Hernández[2],
and L. N. Oliva Moreno[3]

[1] Postgraduate Program of Aerospace Engineering, Metropolitan Polytechnic
University of Hidalgo, Mexico City, Mexico
{213220003,lramos,mvega,rogarcia,cdominguez}@upmh.edu.mx
[2] ESIME Culhuacan, National Polytechnic Institute, Mexico City, Mexico
eescamillah@ipn.mx
[3] UPIIH Hidalgo, National Polytechnic Institute, Hidalgo, Mexico
loliva@ipn.mx

Abstract. The weighted function windows are used in many areas as signal analysis and application systems. In addition, the weighted functions are broad uses in filter design where different windows allow to choose different filter characteristics. The most common individual window types are rectangular, Hanning, Flat Top, and Keiser-Bessel. This paper presents the Flat-Top Windows (FTW) applied to control systems where the FTW are used as activation functions on a radial basis neural network (RBF). Contrary to the "traditional" FT weighted function windows, where time windows limit the information, this paper proposes new ones that, including new parameters, allow translation and dilation of the window. Additionally, these new parameters are updated using a gradient descent algorithm. The new FTW is applied to the Quanser helicopter control where the RBF neural network is used for: a) the input-output identification of the system and b) auto-tuning PID controllers. Numerical simulation results are presented to show the system's performance under different conditions.

Keywords: FT windows · RBF neural network · Autotuning PID controller · Helicopter model

1 Introduction

Technology advance has produced that any real-world signal to be processed digitally in many ways. Thus, from analyzing a few signals earlier to massive and simultaneous datasets today, the signal converted methods to digital form are fundamentals. One way used is to split into discrete blocks continuous signals, which allows analyzing each one separately. So, to study each discrete block, the community of signal processing has proposed many functions called windows

O. Pichardo Lagunas et al. (Eds.): MICAI 2022, LNAI 13612, pp. 138–149, 2022.
https://doi.org/10.1007/978-3-031-19493-1_11

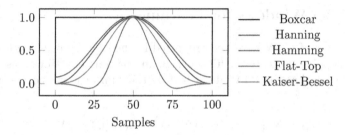

Fig. 1. Some windows functions

function as rectangular, Hanning, Flat Top, and Keiser-Bessel [1,2]. The windows function can be defined as a mathematical expression with zero value outside the chosen interval, see Fig. 1. The windows function is defined as: a) the frequency characteristic of a window is a continuous spectrum, b) the main lobe centered at each frequency component of the time-domain signal, and c) several side lobes approaching zero. One of the significant applications of the windows functions is to minimize the undesirable effects related to spectral leakage. Recently, Reljin [3] has presented the new windows functions, called Extremely Flat-Top, where the main lobe and high side-lobe attenuation were generated. Moreover, the new windows functions exhibit faster decaying side lobes than parent windows. Finally, the efficiency of windows in the high-accuracy harmonic analysis was demonstrated through computer simulations in [2].

Advances in the last years on machine learning [4–8], particularly in Deep Learning, non-traditional activation functions have been proposed as Rectified Linear Units, ReLU, Exponential Linear Unit, ELU, Scaled Exponential Linear Unit, SELU, Gaussian Error Linear Unit, GELU, and Inverse Square Root Linear Unit ISRLU. Unlike traditional literature, this paper focuses on studying the performance of the Flap-Top Window (FTW) as a part of the neural network applied to control systems. As a first evaluation, awaiting test for machine learning algorithms, the proposed FTW are used as an activation function with two new parameters that allow translation and dilation of the signal, which is responsible for improving the non-linear mapping. Specifically, FTW is applied to control the 2 DOF Quanser helicopter model. Assuming that the model system is unknown, an auto-tuning FTW-IIR PID control scheme is proposed. The RBF neural network, with an infinite impulse response filter (IIR), is used simultaneously to tunning the PID feedback gains and the input-output identification. In addition, a gradient descent algorithm to update the parameters of the neural network is used. Finally, numerical simulations on LabVIEW 2013 to control the pitch and yaw axes of the Quanser helicopter are presented. To the best author's knowledge, this is the first time that any windows functions are applied as part of the neural network to control a dynamic system.

The paper is organized as follows: in Sect. 2 brief background on Flat Top Windows is presented, and in Sect. 3 the FTW-IIR PID algorithm is applied on the 2DOF helicopter. Next, numerical simulation results are shown in Sect. 4. Finally, some conclusions are given in the Sect. 5.

2 Flat-Top Windows for Learning

Different classes of FTW have been reported in the signal processing literature, where some applications are the filter design and parameter estimations, to mention a few, [1,2]. Let the FTW described by the sum of weighted cosine terms as [2,3]:

$$\psi(\lambda) = \sum_{j=0}^{Q} (-1)^j a_j \cos\left(2\frac{\pi}{\Lambda} j\lambda\right), \quad \lambda = 0, 1, ..., \Lambda - 1. \tag{1}$$

where the weighting coefficients in Eq (1) are normalized according to

$$\sum_{j=0}^{Q} a_j = 1. \tag{2}$$

In this paper we are employed a FTW given in [3], but we modify it in its argument by adding the time parameter $\tau(k, q, s) = (k - q)/s$ where k is related to the instant at which the operation is performed, q and s represent the translate and the dilation of the windows, respectively. Such that Eq (1) can be re-written as

$$\psi(\tau) = \sum_{j=0}^{Q} a_j \cos(Gj\tau) \tag{3}$$

where a_j and G represent constant coefficients given by the designer. The Eq (3) will be called "mother" FTW. Behind this change, the goal is to provide capacities of translation and dilation to the FT windows useful for many applications as control systems. Thus, representing Eq (3) as a linear combination of its translations and dilations, it is possible to define a set of new windows, called "daughters" FTW, as

$$\psi_i(\tau_i) = \text{FT}(\tau_i) = \sum_{j=0}^{Q} a_j \cos(Gj\tau_i), \quad \tau_i(k, q_i, s_i) = \frac{k - q_i}{s_i} \tag{4}$$

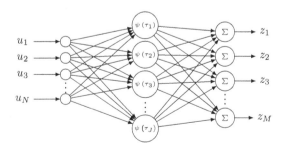

Fig. 2. RBF artificial neural network where FT windows are the activation function

As in previous work [9,10] for each value of i a new window is generated that serves as an activation function in a neural network RBF, see Fig. 2. That is, each activation function is defined as a finite series of cosines weighted by a coefficient a_j given by the designer such that it satisfies condition of the Eq (2). Finally, in this paper the parameters q and s, refer to the translation and dilation, respectively; are adjusted according to the task by the gradient descent algorithm.

3   Applied FTW for Control Quanser Helicopter

The FTW-IIR PID control scheme is composed of four blocks: $i)$ The plant block, which consists of a 2 DOF helicopter model, represented by linear differential equations, $ii)$ Identification block (FTW-IIR), the input-output identification of the helicopter is carried out, $iii)$ the feedback auto-tuning block, and $iv)$ discrete PID controllers evaluation block, see Fig. 3. Now a detailed description of each of the blocks is presented.

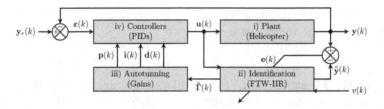

Fig. 3. FTW-IIR PID control scheme for the 2 DOF Quanser helicopter.

i) Plant (helicopter). The dynamics that describes the behavior of the helicopter model is given by two coupled transfer functions, [11]:

$$H_{\theta\theta}(s) = \frac{y_\theta(s)}{V_\theta(s)} = \frac{2.361}{s^2 + 9.26s}, \qquad H_{\phi\theta}(s) = \frac{y_\phi(s)}{V_\theta(s)} = \frac{0.2402}{s^2 + 3.487} \qquad (5)$$

$$H_{\theta\phi}(s) = \frac{y_\theta(s)}{V_\phi(s)} = \frac{0.07871}{s^2 + 9.26s}, \qquad H_{\phi\phi}(s) = \frac{y_\phi(s)}{V_\phi(s)} = \frac{0.7895}{s^2 + 3.487} \qquad (6)$$

where y_θ and y_ϕ are the model outputs for each axis of motion, while V_θ and V_ϕ are the voltages for the motors of each axis. The physical model, the free body diagram and the coupling of the model are shown in Fig. 4.

Additionally, the helicopter has a block where the electrical interpretation of the control signal is performed $\mathbf{u} = [u_\theta, u_\phi]^T$, that is, the mechanical-electrical relationship that is given by the following expressions

$$V_\theta = 0.4899u_\theta - 0.7387u_\phi, \quad V_\phi = 0.0793u_\phi - 0.7387u_\theta. \qquad (7)$$

where u_θ and u_ϕ are the signals from each PID controller. Some helicopter parameters are shown in Table 1.

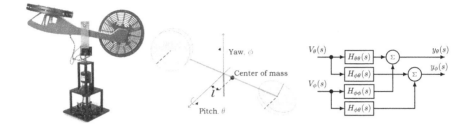

Fig. 4. Models and diagrams of the 2 DOF Quanser helicopter

Table 1. Parameters of the 2 DOF Quanser helicopter [11]

Parameters	Definition	Value
K_{pp}	Torque constant of yaw propeller	0.2040 N N m/V
K_{py}	Torque constant yaw propeller acting on pitch axis	0.0068 N N m/V
K_{yy}	Torque constant from yaw propeller on yaw axis	0.0720 N N m/V
K_{yp}	Torque constant pitch propeller acting on yaw axis	0.0219 N N m/V
V_θ	Voltage at pitch motor	±24 V
V_ϕ	Voltage at yaw motor	±15 V

ii) FTW-IIR Identification. In this block, the input-output dynamics of the system are identified and its structure is composed of a radial-based neural network [12] whose activation functions are FTW, see Fig. 5. Similarly, in Fig. 6 is shown the internal configuration of the infinite impulse response filter (IIR), where $\hat{y}_\theta$ and $\hat{y}_\phi$ are the positions of the helicopter. It should be noted that these filters "prune" the neurons that have little contribution to the identification process, and with it, an input-output structure is obtained [10].

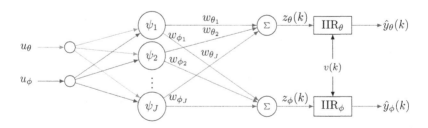

Fig. 5. FTW neural network diagram with IIR filters

From Fig. 5, the output of the FTW-IIR $\hat{\mathbf{y}}(k) = [\hat{y}_\theta, \hat{y}_\phi,]^\mathrm{T}$ is defined as

$$\hat{\mathbf{y}}(k) = \hat{\boldsymbol{\Gamma}}(k) + \mathbf{D}\hat{\mathbf{Y}}(k)\mathbf{v}(k) \tag{8}$$

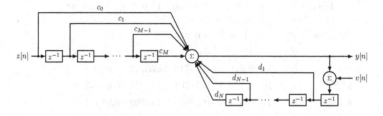

Fig. 6. Structure of the IIR filter where M and N represent the number of feed-forward coefficients and feedback coefficients, respectively.

where $\mathbf{v}(k) = [v(k), v(k)]^{\mathrm{T}}$ is the persistent excitation signal of the filters, the matrices $\hat{\mathbf{Y}}, \mathbf{D} \in \mathbb{R}^{2 \times N}$ are given as

$$\hat{\mathbf{Y}}(k) = \begin{bmatrix} \hat{y}_\theta(k-1) \; \hat{y}_\theta(k-2) \; \cdots \; \hat{y}_\theta(k-N) \\ \hat{y}_\phi(k-1) \; \hat{y}_\phi(k-2) \; \cdots \; \hat{y}_\phi(k-N) \end{bmatrix}, \quad \mathbf{D} = \begin{bmatrix} d_{\theta 1}, d_{\theta 2}, \cdots, d_{\theta N} \\ d_{\phi 1}, d_{\phi 2}, \cdots, d_{\phi N} \end{bmatrix}. \quad (9)$$

The matrices $\hat{\mathbf{Y}}, \mathbf{D}$ are used to store the positions estimated in previous calculations and the feed-forward coefficients for the IIR filters. The parameter $\hat{\boldsymbol{\varGamma}}(k)$ is obtained with

$$\hat{\boldsymbol{\varGamma}}(k) = [\hat{\varGamma}_\theta, \; \hat{\varGamma}_\phi]^{\mathrm{T}} = \mathbf{C}\mathbf{z}(k) \quad (10)$$

where the output of the neural network $\mathbf{z}(k)$ is given by

$$\mathbf{z}(k) = \mathbf{u}^{\mathrm{T}}(k)\mathbf{W}(k)\boldsymbol{\psi}^{\mathrm{T}}(k) \quad (11)$$

with $\mathbf{u} = [u_\theta, u_\phi]^{\mathrm{T}}$ is the control signal, $\mathbf{q} = [q_1, q_2, \cdots, q_J]^{\mathrm{T}}$ is the translation parameter, $\mathbf{s} = [s_1, s_2, \cdots, s_J]^{\mathrm{T}}$ is the dilation parameter, $\boldsymbol{\psi} = [\psi_1, \psi_2, \cdots, \psi_J]^{\mathrm{T}}$ with ψ_1 the daughter FTW, while the matrices of the synaptic weights $\mathbf{W} \in \mathbb{R}^{2 \times J}$ and the feedback coefficients $\mathbf{C} \in \mathbb{R}^{2 \times M}$ are defined as:

$$\mathbf{W} = \begin{bmatrix} w_{\theta 1}, w_{\theta 2}, \cdots, w_{\theta J} \\ w_{\phi 1}, w_{\phi 2}, \cdots, w_{\phi J} \end{bmatrix}, \quad \mathbf{C} = \begin{bmatrix} c_{\theta 0}, c_{\theta 1}, \cdots, c_{\theta M} \\ c_{\phi 0}, c_{\phi 1}, \cdots, c_{\phi M} \end{bmatrix}. \quad (12)$$

Based on the Eq (4), the i-th "daughter" FTW and its the derivative, choosen $Q = 5$, are given as

$$\psi_i(\tau_i) = \mathrm{FT}_i^f(k, \tau) = \sum_{j=0}^{5} a_j \cos(Gj\tau) \quad (13)$$

$$\frac{\partial \psi_i(\tau_i)}{\partial \tau_i} = d\mathrm{FT}_i^f(k, \tau_i) = \sum_{j=1}^{5} -Gj a_j \sin(Gj\tau_i). \quad (14)$$

where $i = 1, 2, ..., j$, j is the number of "daughters" FTW or the number of neurons in the network, f represents one of the member FT family, the value G is defined by the designer, and the values a_j are taken from Table 2. For further details on the methodology to select the parameters a_j, see [2].

Table 2. Coefficients Describing Flat-Top Windows.

Window	Window Coefficients					
	a_0	a_1	a_2	a_3	a_4	a_5
FT[1]	0.13996	0.27964	0.26715	0.20212	0.09288	0.01824
FT[2]	0.18810	0.36923	0.28701	0.13076	0.02487	0
FT[3]	0.20142	0.39291	0.28504	0.10708	0.01352	0
FT[4]	0.20978	0.40753	0.28117	0.09247	0.00904	0
FT[5]	0.21375	0.41424	0.27860	0.08592	0.00746	0

The parameters update equation is defined as

$$\boldsymbol{\lambda}(k+1) = \boldsymbol{\lambda}(k) + \mu_\lambda \Delta\boldsymbol{\lambda}(k), \quad \Delta\boldsymbol{\lambda}(k) = -\frac{\partial \mathbf{E}}{\partial \boldsymbol{\lambda}(k)} \tag{15}$$

where $\boldsymbol{\lambda}$ can be any of the parameters $\mathbf{C}$, $\mathbf{D}$, $\mathbf{W}$, $\mathbf{q}$ y $\mathbf{s}$, μ_λ learning rate, $\mathbf{E}(k) = \frac{1}{2}\sum_t [\mathbf{e}_t(k)]^2$ the cost function to minimize with $\mathbf{e}_t(k) = \mathbf{y}_t(k) - \hat{\mathbf{y}}_t(k)$ the estimation error, for $\mathbf{y}_t$ the output of the system and $\hat{\mathbf{y}}_t$ the estimated output of the neural network for $t = \theta, \phi$. Applying the gradient descent algorithm to minimize the cost function $\mathbf{E}(k)$, we have that $\Delta\boldsymbol{\lambda}(k) = -\partial\mathbf{E}/\partial\boldsymbol{\lambda}(k)$ for each parameters is defined as

$$\frac{\partial \mathbf{E}}{\partial \mathbf{W}(k)} = \mathbf{u}(k)\mathbf{e}^{\mathrm{T}}(k)\mathbf{C}(k)\boldsymbol{\psi}_a^{\mathrm{T}}(\tau) = U\mathbf{I}_e(\mathbf{C}\boldsymbol{\psi}_a)^{\mathrm{T}} \tag{16}$$

$$\frac{\partial \mathbf{E}}{\partial \mathbf{q}(k)} = -\mathbf{e}(k)\mathbf{u}(k)\mathbf{C}^{\mathrm{T}}(k)\boldsymbol{\psi}_b = U(\mathbf{I}_f(\mathbf{C}\boldsymbol{\psi}_b)^{\mathrm{T}}) \tag{17}$$

$$\frac{\partial \mathbf{E}}{\partial \mathbf{s}(k)} = \boldsymbol{\tau}\frac{\partial \mathbf{E}}{\partial \mathbf{q}(k)} = \frac{\partial \mathbf{E}}{\partial \mathbf{q}(k)} \odot \boldsymbol{\tau} \tag{18}$$

$$\frac{\partial \mathbf{E}}{\partial \mathbf{C}(k)} = -\mathbf{u}(k)\mathbf{e}^{\mathrm{T}}(k)\mathbf{z}(k-M) = U\mathbf{I}_e\mathbf{z}^{\mathrm{T}} \tag{19}$$

$$\frac{\partial \mathbf{E}}{\partial \mathbf{D}(k)} = -\mathbf{v}(k)\mathbf{e}^{\mathrm{T}}(k)\hat{\mathbf{y}}(k-N) = v\mathbf{I}_e(\hat{\mathbf{y}}\boldsymbol{\psi}_a)^{\mathrm{T}} \tag{20}$$

where $U = u_\theta(k) + u_\phi(k)$, $\mathbf{I}_e = \mathrm{diag}\{e_\theta(k), e_\phi(k)\}$, $\mathbf{I}_f = [e_\theta(k), e_\phi(k)]^{\mathrm{T}}$, $\boldsymbol{\tau} = [\tau_1, \tau_2, \cdots, \tau_J]$, and

$$\boldsymbol{\psi}_a = \begin{bmatrix} \psi_1(\tau_1) & \psi_2(\tau_2) & \cdots & \psi_J(\tau_J) \\ \psi_1(\tau_1-1) & \psi_2(\tau_2-1) & \cdots & \psi_J(\tau_J-1) \\ \vdots & & \ddots & \vdots \\ \psi_1(\tau_1-M) & \psi_2(\tau_2-M) & \cdots & \psi_J(\tau_J-M) \end{bmatrix}, \quad \boldsymbol{\psi}_b = \begin{bmatrix} \frac{\partial\psi_1(\tau_1)}{\partial s_1} & \cdots & \frac{\partial\psi_J(\tau_J)}{\partial s_J} \\ \frac{\partial\psi_1(\tau_1-1)}{\partial s_1} & \cdots & \frac{\partial\psi_J(\tau_J-1)}{\partial s_J} \\ \vdots & \ddots & \vdots \\ \frac{\partial\psi_1(\tau_1-M)}{\partial s_1} & \cdots & \frac{\partial\psi_J(\tau_J-M)}{\partial s_J} \end{bmatrix}. \tag{21}$$

For programming purposes, the third representation of each of the equations (16)-(20) was used, where $\odot$ represents the Hadamard operator[1]. The convergence identification proof is given in [14].

---

[1] Let the vectors $a, b, c \in \mathbb{R}^{n \times 1}$ where $c_x = a_x \cdot b_x$ with $x \in \{1, 2, ..., n\}$ [13].

iii) Auto Tuning of Proportional, Integral and Derivative Gains. This block is responsible for adjusting the gains of the controller $\mathbf{p}(k) = [p_\theta, p_\phi]^T$, $\mathbf{i}(k) = [i_\theta, i_\phi]^T$ y $\mathbf{d}(k) = [d_\theta, d_\phi]^T$, which is done as follows, respectively [10]

$$\mathbf{p}(k) = \mathbf{p}(k-1) + \boldsymbol{\mu}_p e(k)\hat{\boldsymbol{\Gamma}}(k)[\varepsilon(k) - \varepsilon(k-1)] \tag{22}$$

$$\mathbf{i}(k) = \mathbf{i}(k-1) + \boldsymbol{\mu}_i e(k)\hat{\boldsymbol{\Gamma}}(k)\varepsilon(k) \tag{23}$$

$$\mathbf{d}(k) = \mathbf{d}(k-1) + \boldsymbol{\mu}_d e(k)\hat{\boldsymbol{\Gamma}}(k)[\varepsilon(k) - 2\varepsilon(k-1) + \varepsilon(k-2)] \tag{24}$$

where $\boldsymbol{\mu}$ is the learning rate, $\hat{\boldsymbol{\Gamma}}(k)$ is the directive of the neural network given by (10), the signal $\varepsilon(k)$ is the tracking error which is defined as $\varepsilon(t) = y_r(t) - y(t)$ with $y_{ref}(t)$ as the reference signal and $y(t)$ as the output signal.

iv) PID Controllers. In this block, the control signal is generated $\mathbf{u}(k) = [u_\theta, u_\phi]^T$ which causes the output of the system to vary $\mathbf{y}(k)$ in order to approximate the reference signal $\mathbf{y}_r(k)$. This stage only needs the gains values $\mathbf{p}(k)$, $\mathbf{i}(k)$ y $\mathbf{d}(k)$ as well as the tracking error $\varepsilon(k)$. Then the control signal $\mathbf{u}$ in the instant $k+1$ is given by [10]:

$$\mathbf{u}(k+1) = \mathbf{u}(k) + \mathbf{p}(k)[\varepsilon(k) - \varepsilon(k-1)] + \mathbf{i}(k)[\varepsilon(k)]$$
$$+ \mathbf{d}(k)[\varepsilon(k) - 2\varepsilon(k-1) + \varepsilon(k-2)]. \tag{25}$$

4 Numerical Simulation Results

The numerical simulations were made using LabVIEW 2013. The simulation's goal is that the pitch y_θ and yaw y_ϕ angles of the Quanser helicopter follow the desired trajectories y_{r_θ} and y_{r_ϕ}, respectively, defined as

$$y_{r_\theta} = \begin{cases} 28\sin(\pi k/250), & 0 \le k < 2.5 \\ 30, & 2.5 \le k < 5.0 \\ -30, & 5.0 \le k < 7.5 \\ 12\sin(\pi k/250) + 4\sin(\pi k/320) + 8\sin(\pi k/100), & 7.5 \le k < 10 \end{cases} \tag{26}$$

and

$$y_{r_\phi} = \begin{cases} 120\sin(2\pi k/1000), & 0 \le k < 5 \\ 100\sin(2\pi k/1000) + 20\sin(2\pi k/100), & 5 \le k < 10 \end{cases}. \tag{27}$$

4.1 Classical PID

As a first step, a classical PID controller is implemented Figs. 7 and 8. Notice that classic PID control cannot adequately follow the desired trajectories, as shown in Fig. 7. Additionally, Fig. 8 shows how the control signals remain bounded.

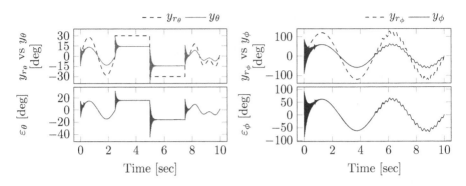

Fig. 7. Classical PID: Performances of y_θ Vs. y_{r_θ}, and y_ϕ vs. y_{r_ϕ}, respectively; and tracking errors ε_θ, ε_ϕ. The feedback gains used for pitch and yaw are $p = 10$, $i = 4$, $d = 5$, and $p = 10$, $i = 1.75$, $d = 7$, respectively.

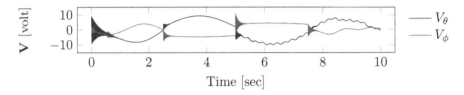

Fig. 8. Classical PID: Control signals V_θ and V_ϕ.

4.2   FTW-IIR PID

Firstly, a pre-training is performance to obtain the initial values of the neural network parameters, see Table 3.

Table 3. Proposed values for FTW-IIR PID controller

Parameter	Value	Parameter	Value	Parameter	Value
Neurons, J	3	μ_W	3.80×10^{-8}	μ_p	[1.00, 0.90]
Feed-back, M	3	μ_q	3.80×10^{-8}	μ_I	[0.80, 0.60]
Feed-forward, N	2	μ_s	3.80×10^{-8}	μ_d	[0.75, 0.80]
		μ_C	5.15×10^{-8}	$p(k)$	$[2.90 \times 10^{-2}, 9.04 \times 10^{-3}]$
		μ_D	5.90×10^{-5}	$i(k)$	$[1.58 \times 10^{-2}, 1.10 \times 10^{-2}]$
		$v(k)$	3.36×10^{-2}	$d(k)$	$[1.45 \times 10^{-2}, 5.50 \times 10^{-3}]$

In order to determine the best performance of each FT window a comparative tracking errors study is carried out using Root Mean Square Error, RMSE $= \sqrt{\frac{1}{T_k} \sum_{k=1}^{T_k} [\mathbf{e}_t(k)]^2}$, where T_k is the number of samples, see Table 4. Notice that the best performance is given by FT[1] for the yaw angle, while there is no noticeable difference between the RMSE obtained for the pitch axis.

Table 4. Comparative tracking errors using RMSE.

RMSE	Window FT[1]	FT[2]	FT[3]	FT[4]	FT[5]
Pitch, θ	3.89435	3.70977	3.70456	3.71065	3.75005
Yae, ϕ	5.23799	7.89246	7.83571	7.94127	7.21623

The numerical simulation results, using the FT[1] windows, is show in Fig. 9 considering that $\phi(0) = -30°$, $\phi(0) = -20°$. Notice that after few seconds the θ and ϕ angles follow rapidly the desired trajectories $y_{r\theta}$ y $y_{r\phi}$, respectively. Additionally, in Figs. 10 to 11 is show the behavior of the FTW-IIR PID parameters controller. As can be seen from Fig. 9, the tracking error ε_θ presents variations just at the moments when the desired trajectory $y_{r\theta}$ changes abruptly. However, in the case of the reference signal y_{r_ϕ}, which is smooth, the tracking error ε_ϕ does not present abrupt changes.

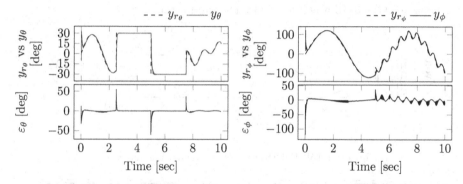

Fig. 9. FTW-IIR PID: Performances of y_θ Vs. $y_{r\theta}$, and y_ϕ vs. $y_{r\phi}$, respectively; and tracking errors ε_θ, ε_ϕ.

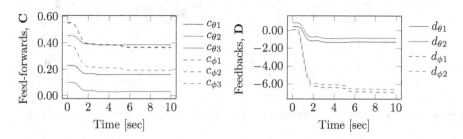

Fig. 10. IIR filter parameters: Feed-forward coefficients **C**, and feedback coefficients **D** for the pitch θ and yaw ϕ axes.

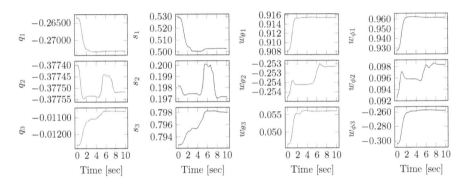

Fig. 11. Performance of the neuronal network parameters: dilation **q**, translation **s**, and synaptic weights **w** for the pitch θ and yaw ϕ angles.

The control signals performance is shown in Fig. 12. It is shown that the control signal $\mathbf{V}(k)$ is within the specified range for the motors shown in Table 1. In addition, the feedback gains performance for pitch and yaw in Fig. 13. Finally, the constant $G = 3/16$ was selected by trial and error.

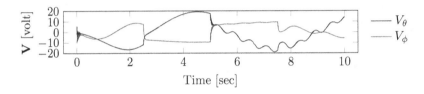

Fig. 12. FTW-IIR PID: Control signals $\boldsymbol{V}_\theta$ and $\boldsymbol{V}_\phi$.

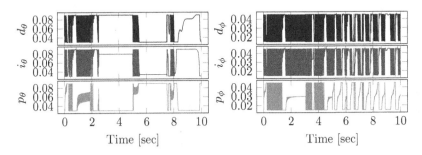

Fig. 13. PID feedback gains performance for the pitch θ and yaw ϕ axes, respectively.

5 Conclusions

The paper presents a Flat-Top Window (FTW) applied to control systems. Unlike the traditional use of the FTW in signal processing, the FTW has two parameters that allow the translation and dilation of the window. This paper uses the FTW as an RBF neural network activation function. Numerical simulation results are presented to control a 2 DOF Quanser Helicopter model.

Although the performance of the FTW as an activation function shows good performance, more studies are needed for complex systems such as non-linear systems or MIMO systems. Additionally, evaluating the FTW in the deep learning algorithms requires special studies.

References

1. Salvatore, L., Trotta, A.: Flat-top windows for PWM waveform processing via DFT. IEE Proc. B: Electr. Power Appl. **135**(6), 346–361 (1988)
2. Cortés, C.A., Mombello, E., Dib, R., Ratta, G.: A new class of flat-top windows for exposure assessment un magnetic field measurements. Signal Process., 2151–2164 (2007)
3. Reljin, I.S., Reljin, B.D., Papic, V.: Extremely flat-top windows for harmonic analysis. IEEE Trans. Instrum. Measur. **56**(3), 1025–1041 (2007)
4. Nguyen, A., Pham, K., Ngo, D., Ngo, T., Pham, L.: An analysis of state-of-the-art activation functions for supervised deep neural network. ICSSE, 215–220 (2021). https://doi.org/10.1109/ICSSE52999.2021.9538437
5. Zhao, Z., He, W., Yang, J., Li, Z.: Adaptive neural network control of an uncertain 2-DOF helicopter system with input backlash and output constraints. Neural Comput. Appl. (2022). https://doi.org/10.1007/s00521-022-07463-3
6. Zou, T., et al.: Adaptive neural network sliding mode control of a nonlinear two-degrees-of-freedom helicopter system. Asian J. Control, 199–205 (2022)
7. Yumuk, E., Copot, C., Ionescu, C.M.: A robust auto-tuning PID controller design based on S-shaped time domain response, vol. 1, pp. 525–530 (2022)
8. Kamenko, I., Čongradac, V., Kulić, F.: A novel fuzzy logic scheme for PID controller auto-tuning. Automatika **63**(2), 365–377 (2022)
9. Ramos-Velasco, L.E., Domínguez-Ramírez, O., Parra-Vega, V.: Wavenet fuzzy PID controller for nonlinear MIMO systems: experimental validation on a high-end haptic robotic interface. Appl. Soft Comput., 199–205 (2016)
10. Carrillo-Santos, C.A., Seck-Tuoh-Mora, J.C., Hernández-Romero, N., Ramos-Velasco, L.E.: WaveNet identification of dynamical systems by a modified PSO algorithm. Eng. Appl. Artif. Intell. **79**, 1–92 (2018)
11. Inc., Q.: User manual 2 DOF helicopter experiment, set up and configuration. Markham, Ontario (2012)
12. Haykin, S.: Neural Networks, a Comprehensive Foundation. Pearson Eduaction Inc, EUA (1999)
13. Deisenroth, M., Faisal, A., Ong, C.: Mathematics for Machine Learning. Cambridge University Press, USA (2020)
14. Díaz-López, F.A., Velasco, L.E.R., Ramírez, O.A.D., Parra-Vega, V.: Multiresolution WaveNet PID control for global regulation of robots, 1–6 (2013)

Pursuing the Deep-Learning-Based Classification of Exposed and Imagined Colors from EEG

Alejandro A. Torres-García$^{(\boxtimes)}$ (iD), Jesus S. García-Salinas(iD),
and Luis Villaseñor-Pineda(iD)

Biosignals Processing and Medical Computing Laboratory, Instituto Nacional de
Astrofísica Óptica y Electrónica, Luis Enrique Erro #1, Tonantzintla, Mexico
{alejandro.torres,jss.garcia,villasen}@ccc.inaoep.mx

Abstract. EEG-based brain-computer interfaces are systems aiming to integrate disabled people into their environments. Nevertheless, their control could not be intuitive or depend on an active external stimulator to generate the responses for interacting with it. Targeting the second issue, a novel paradigm is explored in this paper, which depends on a passive stimulus by measuring the EEG responses of a subject to the primary colors (red, green, and blue). Particularly, we assess if a compact and feature-extraction-independent deep learning method (EEGNet) can effectively learn from these EEG responses. Our outcomes outperformed previous works focused on a dataset composed of EEG signals belonging to 7 subjects while seeing and imagining three primary colors. The method reaches an accuracy of 45% for exposed colors, 43% for imagined colors, and 35% for the six classes. Last, the experiments suggest that EEGNet learned to discover patterns in the EEG signals recorded for imagined and exposed colors, and for the six classes, too.

Keywords: Deep learning-based classification · Color recognition · Imagined color recognition · EEGNet · Brain-Computer Interface (BCI)

1 Introduction

Currently, electroencephalography (EEG) offers a relatively low-cost and high-temporal resolution option for measuring the brain activity of a person compared to other techniques such as Functional near-infrared spectroscopy (fNIRS), functional magnetic resonance imaging (FMRI), magnetoencephalography (MEG) among others. This activity is used for different purposes, the most common ones are for clinical diagnostic and control of interfaces. Among the second ones lie the Brain-Computer interfaces, which are systems that exploit people's electrical brain activity to provide a new non-muscular channel to transmit messages and/or commands to the external world [1].

O. Pichardo Lagunas et al. (Eds.): MICAI 2022, LNAI 13612, pp. 150–160, 2022.
https://doi.org/10.1007/978-3-031-19493-1_12

The question about how to transmit the messages and commands with the EEG raises from the above-mentioned definition. This can be answered with the concept of neuroparadigm, being the most commonly used: the motor imagery, the p300 signals, and steady-state visual evoked potentials (SSVEPs). Despite all of them have interesting outcomes, the first one is not intuitive and few commands can be generated, whereas the second and third ones depend on an active external stimulator. In a P300 BCI, the stimulator system must help to produce the p300 peak about 300 ms after the appearance/flashing of the desired output. Whereas in SSVEP-based BCI, the stimulator system must blink all the commands but at different frequencies.

Aiming to avoid the use of an active stimulator and take advantage of passive stimulators already present in our daily life such as color-based cues (traffic lights, access door cues, etc.), recent works have analyzed the use of EEG responses to primary colors (a color-based BCI) as a novel neuroparadigm for BCI control. The outcomes got for these works are interesting but preliminary as it will be shown in Sect. 2.

As it is described in [2], color is a perceptual experience of a subject while seeing an object but not a characteristic of this. This experience depends on how the brain processes the information of light reflected from the object (having a different composition of wavelengths). Nevertheless, the color processing is fast enough to allow us to make decisions in real-life scenarios and it is a natural response to the environment without requiring any preparation such as motor imagery or an ad-hoc-stimulator like in P300 and SSVEPs-Based BCI, which would make it suitable for controlling a BCI. Based on this and the performances got for conventional algorithms (see Sect. 2), *we hypothesize that a deep learning algorithm, EEGNet, can discriminate between EEG responses to primary colors (red, green, and blue) exposure, reaching outcomes that outperform previous works.* Our hypothesis is based on the fact that EEGNet is an EEG-oriented deep learning method that has achieved outstanding outcomes in the most common neuroparadigms [3] used in BCI such as P300, error-related negativity responses (ERN), movement-related cortical potentials (MRCP), and sensory-motor rhythms (SMR).

The remaining sections are organized as follows. In Sect. 2, the related works are described. Later on, in Sect. 3 and Sect. 4 the main characteristics of the dataset and the deep-learning method analyzed are described. Then, in Sect. 5, the experiments and results are presented and discussed in detail. Finally, in Sect. 6, we show the paper's conclusions and present the future directions for improving the EEG-based color recognition.

2   Related Works

As far as we know, the first work that aimed to recognize the EEG responses to primary colors (red, green, and blue), and the imagination of these colors was described in [4]. They recorded an interesting dataset composed of the signals belonging to 7 subjects while seeing one of the primary colors at a time.

Due to its relevance for our research and comparison purposes, further details of this dataset will be provided in Sect. 3. As to the feature extraction and classification stages, the authors proposed a novel method based on Event-Related Spectral Perturbation (ERSP) and support vector machines (SVM). Unfortunately, the classification outcomes were over-estimated because global ERSPs were computed for each color, allowing the model to know information used in the training stage during the testing stage. In addition to that, a supervised stage of artifact removal was required, which resulted in a non-fully automated method for color classification.

Using a 14-channel Emotiv Epoc with a sampling rate 128 Hz, the EEG responses to the imaginations of 5 colors including primary ones were analyzed in [5]. The colors shown to 10 subjects were red, green, blue, yellow, and white. A method based on event-related potentials (ERP) along with artificial neural networks (ANN) was applied to the data. Even though the method got an average accuracy of about 65% for the 10 subjects, this only processed 10 epochs per color. Another interesting analysis based on a 30-channels fNIRS device was described in [6]. Also, this device had an optode configuration with 15 sources and 15 detectors. The three primary colors were exposed to 14 subjects (aged 22–34 years). For the classification stage, linear discriminant analysis (LDA) was applied to reach an accuracy of up to 74.07% for one of the subjects and an average of 55.29% for all subjects (using Peak-Skewness fts.). Unfortunately, fNIRS-based BCIs are still slower than EEG-based ones, which is explained by the changes in the oxygenated and deoxygenated hemoglobins (HbO and HbR) that can be measured with fNIRS.

Using the dataset recorded in [4], the works proposed in [7–9] got outstanding performances of about 90% when a binary classification between gray color and primary colors was considered. However, the works [7,10] also showed the difficulty of the effective recognition of the 3 primary colors from the EEG activity. The first one [7] got an average accuracy of 37% for 7 subjects after applying a strategy based on EMD-based features for feature extraction and random forest for classification. Whereas the second one [10] presented a comprehensive study of the feasibility of recognizing both exposed and imagined colors from EEG signals. Four classifiers (naive Bayes (NB), random forest (RF), SVM, and KNN) were trained with temporal and frequency features(based on discrete wavelet transform) and then tested for classifying the colors following three classification schemes: recognition of all the exposed and imagined colors (6 classes), classification of exposed and imagined colors (2 classes), and recognizing the three imagined colors and the three exposed colors by separate (3 classes). The average outcomes for the 7 subjects were 30.48% for the six classes (26.11% discarding alpha rhythms), 87.44% when imagined and exposed colors are treated as a binary problem (82.46% discarding alpha rhythms) and 37.64% for exposed colors and 35.9% (34.72% discarding alpha rhythms) for imagined colors.

In Table 1 is shown a summary of the related works on the exposed and imagined color recognition. We can observe that only typical machine learning has been studied. Also, the most works have attempted to classify EEG signals.

On the other hand, since the emerge of the first work in this area, many progress has done in the field of machine learning such as deep learning methods. Also, a more strict scheme of data management aiming to avoid any over-estimation of the outcomes is required. Besides, all the methods presented require of a feature extraction method. For these reasons, the question, if a novel compact deep learning method –EEGNet– can outperform the initial outcomes in the recognition of color-related tasks.

This method has the advantage of not relying on a separate feature extraction method and has shown good performances in other conventional BCI neuroparadigms [3].

Table 1. Summary of the related works for exposed and imagined color classification. Stage directions: Neuro - neurophysiological signal, chan - number of channels, fs - frequency sampling, and subj - number of subjects, R -red, G - green, B - blue, Y - yellow and W - white.

Work	Neuro	Chan (fs)	Subj	Epochs	Colors	Classification
Rasheed [2]	EEG	4 (256 Hz)	7	360	3 (R, G, B)	SVM (84–97% for exposed colors and 64–76% for imagined colors)[a]
Liu & Hong [6]	fNIRS	30 (1.81 Hz)	14	27	3 (R, G, B)	LDA (55.29%)
Yu & Sim [5]	EEG	14 (128 Hz)	10	50	5 (R,G,B,W,Y)	ANN (61.5% using only F4 for color imagination)
Åsley et al. [7]	EEG	4 (256 Hz)	7	180	3 (R, G, B)	RF (37% for exposed colors)
Torres-García & Molinas [10]	EEG	4 (256 Hz)	7	360	3 (R, G, B)	RF (37.64% for exposed colors) and SVM (35.9% for imaginated colors)

[a] Unfortunately, these outcomes were overestimated as described in this section.

3   Dataset

For our experiments, we will analyze and process the dataset recorded in [4]. This dataset is composed of the EEG signals belonging to 7 male subjects (aged 20–30) while they observed and imagined three colors (red, green, and blue). For recording the signals, a g.tec's g.MOBIlab+ portable device with frequency sampling 256 Hz. referenced to the right ear lobe and grounded at AFz was used. These signals come from the following four channels: P3, P4, O1, and O2.

Figure 1 shows an abstraction of the experimental protocol used to record the EEG signals. This process is repeated 30 times resulting in 60 epochs for each exposed color, and 60 epochs per imagined color. All epochs last 3 s (768 data points). Summing up, the dataset is composed of 180 epochs (instances) of the exposed colors and 180 epochs for imagined colors per subject. It is important to highlight that once the stimulator program randomly chose a color, this was then shown in full-screen mode. Further details about the experiment can be consulted in [4].

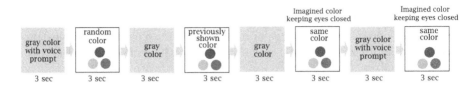

Fig. 1. Experiment protocol for recording the EEG signals (Adapted from [2]) (Color figure online)

3.1 Preprocessing

Although EEGNet usually does not require any preprocessing of the EEG signals, we applied an automatic strategy of artifact removal (proposed in [11]) based on independent component analysis (ICA) and the computing of the Hurst exponent. With this strategy, those independent components with Hurst exponents in the range 0.58–0.69 are discarded due to these are more likely to be related to eye blinks and heartbeats [11]. Later on, the EEG signals are reconstructed from the remaining components and those epochs with no useful components are gotten rid of the dataset. In this work, we applied ICA for computing for 4 independent components (equal to the number of channels).

4   EEGNet

Keeping in mind the assessment of our hypothesis, we will analyze the EEG-Net performance for the task of color recognition from EEG signals. EEGNet was proposed in [3], which is a compact convolutional neural network oriented to EEG-based BCI tasks, aiming to avoid the dependence between the kind of feature extraction method and the BCI neuroparadigm. Also, this deep learning method can be trained with small datasets and can produce features with neurophysiological interpretation (See [3]).

Briefly, the EEGNet inputs are the EEG signals without any transformation. Then frequency filters are learned by applying a temporal convolution. Later on, frequency-specific spatial filters are learned by applying a depthwise convolution and taking as inputs the feature maps individually computed as outputs in the previous stage. After that, a combination of depthwise convolution and pointwise convolution are grouped into a separable convolution looking for learning both a temporal summary of the feature maps individually and how to mix the feature maps optimally. The readers interested in more details about this method can consult [3].

5   Experiments and Results

For the next experiments, the dataset is organized in three ways to test our hypothesis, which looks at if a deep-learning-based classification method, EEG-Net, can learn from the EEG responses to color-related activities (color exposure and imagination of colors). Furthermore, accuracy is the measure selected for assessing EEGNet performance due to the dataset is balanced and will be obtained after 10-fold cross-validation for each subject.

On the other hand, all experiments were run in a server HP APOLLO 6500 10th gen, using 1 node with 84 cores (Intel(R) Xeon® Gold 6248 CPU @ 2.50 GHz), and 256 GB RAM. The GPU used for the DL algorithm was an NVIDIA Tesla V100 32 GB SXM2. Whereas, the relevant software was, OS Red Hat Enterprise Linux Server release 7.8, CUDA 10.2, and Python 3.7.6.

5.1   Classification of Exposed Colors

In the next experiment, we analyzed the epochs recorded during the exposure to the three primary colors, aiming to assess the feasibility of color recognition. This is the most relevant activity looking for implementing a color-based BCI. Because this task is more natural compared to the imagination of colors (keeping eyes closed). Besides, for EEGNet assessment, we used the 180 epochs regarding the color exposure responses (60 epochs per color) and the chance level is 33%.

Table 2. Percent accuracy and standard deviations obtained for EEGNet for recognition of the three exposed colors

Subject	EEGNet		SVM [10]	
	Acc	±std	Acc	±std
S1	45	12	35.52	11.1
S2	39	9	38.5	10.1
S3	52	13	45.56	8.2
S4	31	11	33.33	9.1
S5	57	9	43.33	7.8
S6	47	15	27.78	12
S7	44	10	39.44	9.2
Avg	45	11	37.64	9.6

The EEGNet results for classifying the 3 classes can be seen in Table 2. For almost all the subjects except S4, the method can find differences between the EEG responses to color exposures. The best outcomes were gotten for subjects S5 and S3 and the worst ones for S4 and S2. These results are consistent with [10] due to the subject S4 obtained the worst performances for 3 out of the four classifiers analyzed (except for Naive Bayes).

On the other hand, the global accuracy for the 7 subjects is also above the chance level but in this case for (3 classes), reaching an accuracy of 45%. This suggests that a deep-learning-based classification method makes color recognition from EEG signals feasible. Last, it is important to highlight that the EEGNet global performance (45%) outperforms previous works: 37.64% in [10] and 41% in [7][1].

5.2   Classification of Imagined Colors

In the next experiments, we also assessed the pertinence of recognizing the three imagined colors from EEG signals. Also, another motivation of this experimentation is to compare our results with one of the previous works ([10]). For the outcomes a set of 180 epochs were analyzed, 60 per imagined color. Which set the chance level at 33%.

The accuracies and the standard deviations are shown in Table 3. For all subjects, a global average accuracy of 43% was reached, which is slightly lower than the recognition of the exposed colors but is higher than the global accuracy of 35.9% got using SVM in [10].

Table 3. Percent accuracy and SDs obtained for EEGNet for recognition of the three imagined colors

Subject	EEGNet		SVM [10]	
	Acc	±std	Acc	±std
S1	54	12	31.11	8.8
S2	42	17	36.86	10.2
S3	39	17	36.11	9.9
S4	34	9	33.89	12.4
S5	44	9	37.78	13.3
S6	43	12	37.78	10.4
S7	45	13	37.78	9.7
Avg	43	13	35.9	11

Since the alpha rhythms are increased when a person keeps his/her eyes closed, we also evaluated if the outcomes could be reached because of this fact. Then, we applied a stop band filter at the alpha band (8–12 Hz) aiming to assess the impact of this rhythm on the outcomes. A relatively similar idea will be evaluated in Subsect. 5.3 due to color imagination is carried out keeping the eyes closed.

Table 4 shows the performances after alpha rhythms removal. Despite a decrement in the performance can be observed compared to the results in Table 3, this

---

[1] The individual accuracies for each subject were not available in this work.

is also higher than the previous work. Specifically, the global accuracies for EEG-Net and the previous work are 40% and 34.72% [10] (using NB), respectively.

Table 4. Percent accuracy and SDs obtained for EEGNet for recognition of the three imagined colors discarding alpha rhythms

Subject	EEGNet		NB [10]	
	Acc	±std	Acc	±std
S1	45	18	37.78	17.5
S2	48	14	35.82	16.4
S3	32	9	38.89	10.5
S4	37	8	30.56	8
S5	34	10	34.44	9
S6	42	11	32.78	7.6
S7	39	13	32.78	8.5
Avg	40	12	34.72	11.1

5.3   Simultaneous Classification of Imagined and Exposed Colors

This experiment aims to test if the deep-learning method chosen for this task, EEGNet, can simultaneously distinguish between the EEG responses to imagined and exposed colors. It means EEGNet must discover patterns for the six classes (red, green, blue, and their imaginations) and the chance level is 16%. In this section, we processed the whole dataset composed of 360 instances per subject having 60 epochs of each class.

EEGNet average accuracies and standard deviations are shown in Table 5. For all subjects, the average performances are above the chance level. Therefore, these outcomes suggest that there is a difference between each of the exposed and imagined colors that allows EEGNet to distinguish between the classes. Also, the average accuracy of 35% outperforms the previous work using RF [10] with an average accuracy of 30.48%.

Since the phenomenon described in Subsect. 5.2 related to eyes closed, a question arises about if the method takes advantage of the increase in alpha rhythms, or if these rhythms decrease the classification performances.

Table 6 shows the performances obtained by EEGNet. The accuracies are also above the chance level for 6 classes for all subjects. Furthermore, the global average accuracies for all subjects discarding or not the alpha rhythms are almost equal (see Table 5 and Table 6). Therefore, this suggests that the difference found is not related to the condition of eyes closed, which was carried out when colors were imagined. Furthermore, the average accuracy of 34% outperforms the previous work using SVM [10] whose average accuracy was 26.11%.

Table 5. Percent accuracy and standard deviations obtained for EEGNet for the simultaneous recognition of exposed and imagined colors (6 classes)

Subject	EEGNet		RF [10]	
	Acc	±std	Acc	±std
S1	38	13	30.12	7.8
S2	39	8	27.65	3.54
S3	39	10	37.78	5.27
S4	29	6	27.78	3.93
S5	31	7	30	4.1
S6	34	9	27.22	7.5
S7	39	9	32.78	9.15
Avg	35	9	30.48	5.9

Table 6. Percent accuracy and standard deviations obtained for EEGNet for the simultaneous recognition of exposed and imagined colors (6 classes) discarding alpha rhythms

Subject	EEGNet		SVM [10]	
	Acc	±std	Acc	±std
S1	33	7	23.44	8.93
S2	32	7	27.1	5.09
S3	32	5	28.89	7.2
S4	30	11	22.22	2.62
S5	32	5	32.22	8.9
S6	39	11	20.83	5.44
S7	39	9	28.06	7.11
Avg	34	8	26.11	6.47

6   Conclusions and Future Work

Throughout this paper, we analyzed if a deep-learning-based classification method (EEGNet) can distinguish between EEG responses to color-related tasks, which were the exposure to primary colors (red, green, and blue), imagined colors, and both simultaneously. We tested this hypothesis in the dataset collected in [2]. Our experimentation suggests that EEGNet can discover patterns in the EEG signals regardless of the kind of scheme of classification studied (See Tables 5, 2 and 3).

Another interesting finding was that the method throughput showed independence of the fact that alpha rhythms are increased when a person keeps his/her eyes closed (see Tables 6 and 4). Last happened when the epochs of imagined colors were recorded. For this reason, the classification of the six available classes (imagined and exposed colors) and the imagined colors were also analyzed with an additional stage of stop-band filtering discarding any effect of the alpha rhythms.

Using the dataset selected, EEGNet outperformed previous works in the classification of all the kinds of color-related tasks, reaching the following average accuracies for the 7 subjects: 45% for the 3 exposed colors, 43% (40% without alpha rhythms) for the imagined colors, and 35% (34% without alpha rhythms) for the recognition of the 3 exposed colors and their imaginations (6 classes at total). Furthermore, after applying sign tests[2] for all the tables shown, the method got statistically significant outcomes for the recognition of imagined colors ($Z = 2.2678$, $p < 0.024$, $\alpha = .05$) and the simultaneous classification of the six classes ($Z = 2.2678$, $p < 0.024$, $\alpha = .05$).

Although there are three classification tables in which the method did not show a statistically significant difference compared to previous work, the current algorithm has the advantage of being a method that does not depend on both the neuroparadigm and the feature extraction method. Therefore, this fact is agreed with previous outcomes obtained for EEGNet in other neuroparadigms [3] making it a suitable method for processing and analyzing novel neuroparadigms such as color recognition.

Despite the outstanding outcomes got in the present study, the problem of recognition of color-related tasks from EEG signals is still open, considering this is the core of an effective implementation of a color-based BCI. Accordingly, a tuning of EEGNet hyper-parameters along with a comprehensive study on its intermediate layers could be desirable targeting both an improvement in the classification performances and any clue that can help to bring light to the area of color-based BCI, respectively. Also, an optimal selection of the length and the beginning and end of the analysis window could help to improve the present results.

In future work, we could assess if the model can find any difference between the exposed color and its imagination. Also, we will extend our study to a larger dataset keeping in mind the augmentation of the number of subjects. Besides, an interesting question that arises is if a specific color can be identified when several of them are shown simultaneously.

Acknowledgment. This work was partially supported by the Consejo Nacional de Ciencia y Tecnología (CONACyT) from Mexico with a postdoctoral fellowship. The authors also thank CONACyT for the computer resources provided through the INAOE Supercomputing Laboratory's Deep Learning Platform for Language Technologies.

---

[2] This test was chosen because the data was not normally distributed and its distribution was not symmetric.

References

1. Wolpaw, J.R., Birbaumer, N., McFarland, D.J., Pfurtscheller, G., Vaughan, T.M.: Brain-computer interfaces for communication and control. Clin. Neurophysiol. **113**(6), 767–791 (2002)
2. Rasheed, S.: Recognition of primary colours in electroencephalograph signals using support vector machines. PhD thesis, Università degli Studi di Milano (2011)
3. Lawhern, V.J., Solon, A.J., Waytowich, N.R., Gordon, S.M., Hung, C.P., Lance, B.J.: Eegnet: a compact convolutional neural network for eeg-based brain-computer interfaces. J. Neural Eng. **15**(5), 056013 (2018)
4. Rasheed, S., Marini, D.: Classification of EEG signals produced by RGB colour stimuli. J. Biomed. Eng. Medical Imaging **2**(5), 56 (2015)
5. Yu, J.-H., Sim, K.-B.: Classification of color imagination using Emotiv EPOC and event-related potential in electroencephalogram. Optik **127**(20), 9711–9718 (2016)
6. Liu, X., Hong, K.-S.: Detection of primary RGB colors projected on a screen using fNIRS. J. Innovat. Opt. Health Sci. **10**(03), 1750006 (2017)
7. S. Åsly, L. A. Moctezuma, M. Gilde, and M. Molinas, "Towards EEG-based signals classification of RGB color-based stimuli," in 8th Graz Brain-Computer Interface Conference, p. In press, 2019
8. Torres-García, A.A., Moctezuma, L.A., Åsly, S., Molinas, M.: Discriminating between color exposure and idle state using EEG signals for BCI application. In: International Conference on e-Health and Bioengineering (EHB), vol. 2019. IEEE (2019) (In press)
9. Torres-García, A.A., Moctezuma, L.A., Molinas, M.: Assessing the impact of idle state type on the identification of RGB color exposure for BCI. In: Proceedings of the 13th International Joint Conference on Biomedical Engineering Systems and Technologies (Biostec), Valletta, Malta, pp. 24–26 (2020)
10. Torres-García, A.A., Molinas, M.: Analyzing the recognition of color exposure and imagined color from EEG signals. In: International Conference on BioInformatics and BioEngineering (BIBE), vol. 2019. IEEE (2019) (In press)
11. Vorobyov, S., Cichocki, A.: Blind noise reduction for multisensory signals using ICA and subspace filtering, with application to EEG analysis. Biol. Cybern. **86**(4), 293–303 (2002)

Data Stream Mining for Dynamic Student Modeling

María Yesenia Zavaleta-Sánchez$^{(\boxtimes)}$ and Edgard Benítez-Guerrero$^{(\boxtimes)}$

Facultad de Estadística e Informática, Universidad Veracruzana, Xalapa, Mexico
{yzavaleta,edbenitez}@uv.mx

Abstract. Data Stream Mining has become a research topic of greater interest in recent years. Its goal is to extract knowledge and hidden patterns from continuous data streams. In e-learning systems, a large amount of data is generated from the interaction of the student with the system in the form of data streams, which nature or distribution changes over time. Data Stream Mining techniques are able to incrementally analyze this kind of data, by creating models that adapt their structure on the fly. In this context, an interesting feature to model is the academic performance of students. In this paper, a methodology for dynamic student modeling using Data Stream Mining classifiers is proposed. For this, the Students' Academic Performance database, available on Kaggle, was used. Six Data Stream Mining classifiers were implemented in MOA. For the evaluation, the prequential error method, the Kappa statistic, and the execution time were used. The results obtained show that the Naive Bayes classifier generated the best results in terms of accuracy and execution times.

Keywords: Data stream · Data stream mining · Classification · Student profiling · Student modeling · Educational data mining

1 Introduction

Data Stream Mining (DSM) has become a research topic of greater interest in recent years. Its objective is to extract knowledge and hidden patterns from continuous data streams (data that are generated continuously over time) [17].

In recent decades, student modeling has attracted increased interest as a research topic. In online learning; for example, through e-learning systems (ELS) a large amount of data is generated in the form of continuous streams, from the interaction of the student with the ELS, over time that require to be analyzed on the fly so it becomes more challenging to create or personalized student models to predict student characteristics such as academic performance [9]. Particularly, a student model summarizes multiple characteristics of students, whether static (gender, place of birth, etc.) or dynamic (cognitive skills, emotions, etc.), drawn from various data sources to represent a profile [14].

Generally, educational data have been studied as stationary data using Educational Data Mining (EDM), which is a specific area of Data Mining (DM) techniques [22]. According to [10], EDM refers to the use of machine learning algorithms to model student behaviors so that predictive models can be used for monitoring, analysis, prediction, intervention, tutoring, personalization, feedback, adaptation, and recommendation purposes. For instance, EDM classification, regression, and clustering techniques are commonly used to model Students' Academic Performance (SAP).

The most popular technique for predicting SAP is classification [24]. The most commonly used classifiers include: Decision Tree (DT), Artificial Neural Networks (ANN), and Naive Bayes (NB) [1]. Recent studies have incorporated other techniques such as Recurrent Neural Network (RNN) [18]. However, given the dynamic nature of some characteristics that reflect student behavior, and can be continuously monitored and collected in the form of data streams through ELS, it is convenient to use other modeling techniques that reflect this behavior and allow for assessments of students on the fly [9,20].

In this paper, a methodology to model students dynamically by implementing DSM classifiers is proposed. The central idea is to classify students on the fly based on their academic performance, using as predictive variables characteristics of students that can be retrieved and monitored from ELS. For this, the SAP database, available in Kaggle, was used. Six DSM classifiers were implemented in MOA (Massive Online Analisys) framework: Naive Bayes, Hoeffding Tree, Hoeffding Adaptive Tree, OzaBag, OzaBagADWIN, and Adaptive Random Forest.

The outline of the study is organized as follows: In Sect. 2, a brief review of related work is presented. In Sect. 3, our proposed methodology for dynamic student modeling is discussed. Section 4 shows the experiments and results. Section 5 sets out the discussion. Finally, Sect. 6 summarizes conclusions and future work.

2 Related Work

In ELS, where educational content is provided, student activities and their interactions with the system such as reading, downloading or uploading material, participating in discussion forums, etc., are continuously monitored and collected through logs. These data streams form a valuable source of information about students' learning and behaviors, which could be used to optimize the learning process [23].

In the work [1], a model of prediction of SAP based on classification techniques is proposed considering characteristics of student behavior related to their interaction with an ELS called Kalboard 360. The authors used the ANN, NB, and DT classifiers. They obtained good classification results with behavioral features comparing with the results when removing behavioral features, they proved the strong relationship between student's academic achievement and the learner behavior in the classroom. The accuracy enhancement when using behavioral features obtained 28% with ANN, 22% with NB, and 6% with DT. Subsequently,

[2] performed a study similar to the previous one, but increasing the number of observations and the variables to be analyzed. In addition, they applied Bagging, Boosting, and Random Forest (RF) methods to improve the accuracy of classifiers. Their results showed that Boosting method outperform other ensembles methods. Using boosting, the accuracy of DT was improved from 75.8% to 77.7% and with NB model the accuracy increased from 67.7% to 72.2%.

Nevertheless, there are few works that address this research topic from a dynamic approach; for example, [20] presented a methodology to efficiently model students according to their behavior during a self-assessment process. Its approach formed and reviewed students' models on the fly, using three DSM classification techniques: HT, OzaBag, and Perceptron. In the results obtained, when the window size was 100 and the predicted classes were three, OzaBag was slightly more accurate (80%) than HT (79%) and Perceptron (70%). On the other hand, when the predicted classes were two, Perceptron achieved its highest accuracy (83%) compared to the HT (82%) and OzaBag which predicted with 82% of accuracy.

In [9], a case study on EDM is presented involving the application of RF and Adaptive Random Forest (ARF) classifiers. In the classification performance for the binary classification, RF was highly accurate, 90.5%. On the other hand, when considering the multiclass classification, the classification performance decrease and RF obtained 64.57% of accuracy. In its results demonstrated the effectiveness of the method to correctly classify student outcomes when processing educational data as data streams.

In the same way, the authors [16] focused their work on emotion recognition in e-learning using students' multimodal data streams, comparing several DSM classifiers for emotion recognition using multimodal physiological signal streams: NB, HT, OzaBag ML, OzaBag ADWIN ML, OzaBoost, OzaBoost ADWIN, SGD, and Perceptron. The HT achieved 66.8 % accuracy with an evaluation time of 7.44 s, but Oza Bag ADWIN ML obtained an accuracy of 66.9 %, in 36.88 s for the classification. From this, they conclude that HT was an effective one because it achieved significant with less evaluation time. But this was not significant enough for emotion recognition from multimodal physiological data streaming in e-Learning scenario.

According to the previous review, it is necessary to propose a methodology to classify students on the fly based on their academic performance, using features of students that can be retrieved and monitored from ELS.

3   Proposed Methodology

In traditional data mining, the data set can be read many times, runs with unlimited time and memory, and produces fairly accurate results. On the other hand, in DSM constraints, such as bounded memory, single pass, real-time response, and concept drift detection must be satisfied so that approximate results can be produced. Figure 1 shows the design of the proposed methodology for dynamic student modeling using DSM classifiers. The methodology includes five phases:

Data acquisition, preprocessing, DSM classification, evaluation, and student class characterization. The result of the inference provides the student's class based on their academic performance.

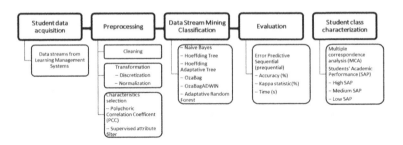

Fig. 1. Methodology for dynamic student modeling using DSM.

3.1   Overview

Getting started requires the acquisition of student data that can be automatically generated as a result of student interaction with ELS or other electronic platforms. Afterwards, a preprocessing of the data is carried out, this is cleaning, transformation and selection of characteristics with greater contribution to the classification process. Then the selected DSM classification algorithms are implemented that perform the incremental learning process, that is, instance by instance. Subsequently, classifiers are evaluated using the Predictive Sequential (prequential) error, the Kappa statistic, and the execution time of each classifier. Finally, the best classification model is chosen, the student's class is predicted based on their academic performance (low, medium, high) and their characteristics are described.

In this work, DSM classifiers are used under an incremental learning approach where the model gradually evolves to adapt to changes in incoming data and eliminates the effects of outdated data. We use different DSM classifiers described in [6]. Naive Bayes (NB) performs the classic Bayesian prediction while making a naive assumption that all inputs are independent. NB is a simple, low-cost computational classifier algorithm. Hoeffding Tree (HT) or Very Fast Decision Tree (VFDT) classifier, is an incremental decision tree induction algorithm that at any time is capable of learning from massive data streams, assuming that the examples of distribution generation do not change over time. Hoeffding Adaptive Tree (HAT), a new method that evolves from Hoeffding Window Tree, adaptively learns from data streams that change over time without the need for a fixed sliding window size [5].

OzaBag (OZB) proposed in [19], is an online incremental Bagging metaclassifier for data streams that simulates the process of sampling bootstrap replicates from training data in a data stream context. The probability that any individual example will be chosen for a replica is determined by a binomial distribution and tends to a Poisson distribution. OzaBagADWIN (OZBADW) [4], Bagging's incremental metaclassifier with ADWIN. ADWIN is a change detector and estimator that solves in a well-specified way the problem of tracking the average of a stream of bits or real-value numbers.

Adaptive Random Forest (ARF) is an adaptation of Random Forest (RF) that includes an effective resampling method in the configuration of streams and adaptive operators that can cope with different types of Concept drift, without further hyperparameter adjustments. Concept drift refers to the change in the relationships between input and output data over time [12].

4   Experiments and Results

The experiments were conducted on a DELL Laptop with 8 GB of RAM, Intel(R) Core (TM) i5-10300H CPU @ 2.50GHz. Weka was used for preprocessing (version 3.9.6) [13]. The data exploration and graphical analysis were done with R Project [21] (version 4.1.2). MOA Release 2021.07 was used for the implementation of the classifiers [7].

4.1   Data and Preprocessing

The SAP database described in [2] and available in en Kaggle was used [3]. Designed to predict SAP at the end of the semester in three classes (low, medium, high), see Table 1. According to [15] this dataset is widely used in EDM research, consisting of 480 student logs and 16 characteristics classified into: Demographic (N, G, PB, and RE), academic background (SID, GID, SCID, S, T, and SA), parental participation (PA and PSS), and student behavior in ELS (DG, VR, RH, and AV).

The data cleansing stage was not performed because the dataset has no missing data. In the transformation of the data, since the predictive variables have different types (categorical and numerical) and measurement scales (nominal, ordinal, and ratio), a discretization of the numerical variables (at 5 intervals) was performed in Weka using a filter not supervised by attributes.

Subsequently, two processes were used for the selection of characteristics: First, in R Project, Polychoric Correlation Coefficent (PCC) were obtained between each of the predictive variables (dichotomic or ordinal) and the Class. PCC is a technique that allows to estimate the correlation between pairs of ordinal variables or the interaction between dichotomic and ordinal variables, taking values between −1 and 1 [11].

As can be seen in the Table 2, the negative PCC between the SA and Class variables with a PCC=−0.86 stands out, which means that the absence of the student negatively affects the SAP. Similarly, VR (0.75), RH (0.71), AV (0.61), PASS (0.58), and RE (0.54) are positively highlighted with the Class variable. The first three are characteristics that reflect the students' behavior during interaction with the ELS Kalboard 360 and indicate that, as the students' level of interaction with ELS increases, their SAP level improves. It is also relevant to include variables on the participation of parents in the learning process.

Table 1. Student features and their types of data, categories or values.

Features	Code	Type of data	Categories or values
Nationality	N	Nominal	Egypt, Iran, Iraq, Jordan, KW, Lebanon, Lybia, Morocco, Palestine, SaudiArabia, Syria, Tunis, USA, Venezuela
Place of Birth	PB	Nominal	Egypt, Iran, Iraq, Jordan, KW, Lebanon, Lybia, Morocco, Palestine, SaudiArabia, Syria, Tunis, USA, Venezuela
Gender	G	Nominal	Female or male
Parent responsible	RE	Nominal	Father or mum
Educational Stages	SID	Ordinal	Lower level, middle school, and high school
Grade Levels	GID	Ordinal	G-02, G-04, G-05, G-06, G-07, G-08, G-09, G-10, G-11, G-12
Section ID	SCID	Nominal	A, B, C
Semester	S	Ordinal	First or second
Topic	T	Nominal	Arabic, Biology, Chemistry, English, French, Geology, History, IT, Math, Quran, Science, Spanish
Student Absence	SA	Ordinal	Above-7, Under-7
Answering Survey	PA	Nominal	Yes or not
School Satisfaction	PSS	Ordinal	Good, Bad
Discussion groups	DG	Numerical	0–100
Visited resources	VR	Numerical	0–100
Raised hand	RH	Numerical	0–100
View announcements	AV	Numerical	0–100
Class	Class	Ordinal	Lower (0–69), Medium (70–89), High (90–100)

Second, in Weka, a supervised attribute filter was applied that allows you to combine several search and evaluation methods. The parameters that Weka has defined by default were used (CfsSubsetEval-P1-E1, BestFirst-D1-N5), resulting in 7 relevant characteristics G, RE, SA, PAS, RH, VR, and AV. Six variables match with those previously identified as relevant. Therefore, it was decided to include only these variables for the study, excluding the Gender variable. Finally, for the classification process the variables VR, RH, and AV were taken on a continuous scale and their values were normalized in a range $[0, 1]$.

Table 2. PCC Predictor variables versus Class variable.

VR	RH	AV	PAS	RE	PSS	G	DG	S	SID	GID	SA
0.75	0.71	0.61	0.58	0.54	0.51	0.37	0.37	0.17	0.11	0.06	-0.87

4.2 Classification and Evaluation

Six DSM classifiers were used for the experiments. In the implementation of HT and HAT, Naive Bayes Adaptive (NBA) was employed as a prediction mechanism used in the sheets, and for the splits, the criterion of gain of information. For the metaclassifiers, it was selected as a basic classifier HT or VFDT. The values of the parameters defined by default in MOA were used. Tables 3 and 4 summarize the results of the average performance of the classification models, in terms of percentage accuracy, percentage of the Kappa statistic, and execution time in seconds. For the six classifiers, three sizes of sliding window were used ($w = 5$, $w = 10$, and $w = 20$). Moreover, two sample sizes were adapted to perform the prequential evaluation ($n = 1$ and $n = 10$).

As seen in Table 3, when the evaluation was performed for each instance ($n = 1$) and $w = 5$, ARF obtained the highest levels of accuracy (69.17%), but at a higher cost in terms of time (9.98 s). Followed by HAT with an accuracy of 68.33% with a shorter runtime (0.03 s). Likewise, with $w = 10$, ARF obtained the highest accuracy (68.81%) at a higher execution time than the others (9.78 s), followed by HAT accuracy (67.78 %) whose execution was carried out in a shorter time (0.03 s). In turn, when using $w = 20$, the results were similar in accuracy and time, ARF (68.43% and 9.82 s) followed by HAT (67.6% and 0.03 s). In contrast, OZB and OZBADW in all cases obtained the lowest performance in terms of accuracy. Another relevant result was that, regardless of the classifier used, as the size of the window increases, the percentage of accuracy decreases. Finally, the best results were obtained with ARF ($w = 5$).

Table 3. Results of the comparison of DSM classifiers, $n = 1$.

Parameters	Classifier	NB	HT	HAT	OZB	OZBADW	ARF
$w = 5$	Accuracy (%)	67.71	67.29	**68.33**	66.67	66.67	**69.17**
	Kappa (%)	44.79	43.79	44.97	42.53	42.52	44.14
	Time (s)	0.03	0.02	**0.02**	0.51	0.54	**9.98**
$w = 10$	Accuracy (%)	67.37	66.94	67.98	66.36	66.36	68.81
	Kappa (%)	47.08	46.09	47.31	44.89	44.89	47.49
	Time (s)	0.04	0.03	0.03	0.51	0.55	9.78
$w = 20$	Accuracy (%)	67.07	66.56	67.6	66.07	66.07	68.43
	Kappa (%)	46.95	45.73	47.15	44.65	44.65	47.64
	Time (s)	0.04	0.02	0.03	0.51	0.56	9.82

As seen in Table 4, when the evaluation was performed for ($n = 10$) and $w = 5$, NB get the highest levels of accuracy (70.83%) at a low cost in terms of time (0.02 s), followed by HT (70.42%), and HAT (70.42%), in both with equal execution time (0.02 s). On the other hand, when $w = 10$, the results changed, ARF obtained the highest accuracy (69.58%) with a longer execution time than the other classifiers (1.2 s), followed by HAT accuracy (68.75%) executed in a shorter time (0.02 s). Finally, when using $w = 20$ the results resemble the previous experiment in accuracy and time, ARF (69.58% and 1.14 s) followed by HAT (68.75% and 0 s). In contrast, OZB and OZBADW in all cases obtained the lowest performance in terms of accuracy. Furthermore, for the ARF classifier by increasing the window size from $w = 5$ to $w = 10$, the average percentage of accuracy obtained remained stable. In summary, in this experiment the best results were obtained in NB ($w = 5$).

Table 4. Results of the comparison of DSM classifiers, $n = 10$.

Parameters	Classifier	NB	HT	HAT	OZB	OZBADW	ARF
$w = 5$	Accuracy (%)	**70.83**	**70.42**	**70.42**	70	70	69.17
	Kappa (%)	49.97	47.89	46.25	45.09	45.09	43.58
	Time (s)	**0.02**	**0.02**	**0.02**	0.06	0.06	1.16
$w = 10$	Accuracy (%)	68.12	67.71	68.75	67.08	67.08	69.58
	Kappa (%)	46.26	45.15	46.76	43.92	43.92	47.39
	Time (s)	0	0.02	0.02	0.07	0.06	1.2
$w = 20$	Accuracy (%)	68.12	67.71	68.75	67.08	67.08	69.58
	Kappa (%)	46.26	45.15	46.76	43.92	43.92	47.39
	Time (s)	0	0.02	0	0.05	0.07	1.14

The evaluation method used was prequential that allows to monitor the evolution of the classifiers and evaluates the performance of the models by testing
each example and then using it to train in sequence. In addition, the Kappa
statistic measures the performance of stream classifiers by matching the prediction with the true class. A Kappa value equal to 1 means total agreement.

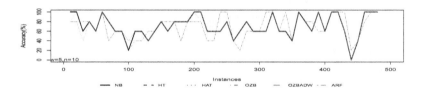

Fig. 2. Evolution of the accuracy measurement for DSM classifiers.

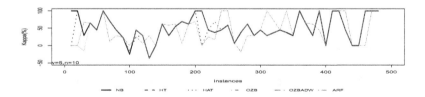

Fig. 3. Evolution of the Kappa statistic for DSM classifiers.

Figures 2, 3, and 4, show the evolution of the measurements obtained for the
classifiers under study ($n = 10, w = 5$). NB stood out with the best results in
terms of accuracy. As observed in Fig. 3, the evolution of the performance of
the classifiers was similar and variable, they had some coincidences in the low
accuracy when classifying certain instances.

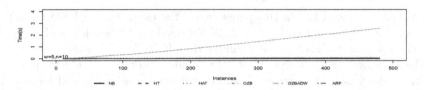

Fig. 4. Evolution of the execution time of DSM classifiers.

4.3 Student Class Characterization

Taking the predictions of NB ($w = 5$, $n = 10$), a visual representation of the dynamic modeling of the students was made. A Biplot was developed from Multiple correspondence analysis (MCA). Regarding the specific characteristics of the model and the three predicted classes, it was found that: High SAP (Class_Pred_H): Students are characterized by high levels of participation in ELS, that is, they frequently see advertisements, raise their hands, and visit resources ($AV, VR, RH > 66$); they have records of absences of less than 7 d, their tutor is their mother figure, who reflects a level of participation when answering surveys (Fig. 5, quadrant III). Medium SAP (Class_Pred_M): Students have average levels of participation, that is, they see ads, raise their hands, and visit resources in an interval of ($33 < AV, VR, RH \leq 66$) in ELS; they have records of absences of less than 7 d, their mother figure is their tutor, who reflects a level of participation in answering surveys (Fig. 5, quadrants I and II). Low SAP (Class_Pred_L): Students have low participation levels ($0 \leq AV, VR, RH \leq 33$), i.e. rarely see ads, raise their hands, and visit ELS resources; they have records of absences greater than 7 d, their tutor is their father figure, who does not reflect a level of participation by not answering surveys (Fig. 5, quadrant IV).

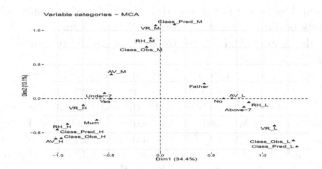

Fig. 5. Biplot of dynamic student modeling from NB ($w = 5$ and $n = 10$).

5   Discussion

Throughout this study we have found that the implementation of DSM classifiers can be used to model SAP when data are available that result from student interaction with an ELS. In this paper, when the evaluation of DSM classifiers was performed for $n = 1$ and $w = 5$, ARF obtained the highest levels of accuracy (69.17%), but at a higher cost in terms of time (9.98 s). Additionally, regardless of the classifier used, as the size of the window increases, the percentage of accuracy decreases. Otherwise, when the evaluation was performed for $n = 10$ and $w = 5$, NB get the highest levels of accuracy (70.83%) at a low cost in terms of time (0.02 s), followed by HT (70.42%), and HAT (70.42%), in both with equal execution time (0.02 s). For the ARF classifier by increasing the window size, the average percentage of accuracy obtained also increases slightly.

Compared to the work of [2], where they analyzed the same database, the proposal in this paper involves creating a model with a smaller number of predictive variables (parsimonious). With 6 features (SA, VR, RH, AV, PAS, RE), NB ($n = 10, w = 5$) obtained better results in terms of accuracy with 70.83% compared to its traditional NB model and Bagging NB. Although our values obtained from accuracy are not very high, they are encouraging as alternative ways can be sought to improve results.

In DSM one of the requirements is to work with large amounts of data [8]. In this study, we do not use a large database. However, we found that educational data coming from ELS can be modeled using DSM classification techniques to create student profiles. The advantage of using these incremental learning models is that they are able to make predictions on the fly, that is, they can be used to evaluate SAP during its course journey to detect in a timely manner underperforming students and provide timely support.

6   Conclusions and Future Work

Modeling student characteristics dynamically is a task that is of great interest to researchers and has a significant contribution to the educational field. In ELS a large amounts of data streams are generated that require analysis on the fly to identify students in critical circumstances that can be supported to improve their academic performance.

In this research work, a methodology to model students dynamically using DSM classifiers is proposed. Six classifiers were implemented: NB, HT, HAT, OZB, OZBADW, and ARF. According to the experiments performed, when the evaluation of the DSM classifiers was executed with $n = 1$, regardless of the size of the window (5,10,20), ARF obtained the highest levels of accuracy (69.17%) but at a higher cost in terms of time (9.98 s). On the other hand, when the evaluation was performed for $n = 10$ and the window size was 5, the best classifier to model SAP was NB ($n = 10, w = 5$) with 70.83% accuracy, 49.97% of the Kappa statistic and a time of 0.02 s.

Regarding the specific characteristics of the dynamic model it was found that: In High SAP, students frequently see advertisements, raise their hands, visit resources, they have records of absences of less than 7 d and, their tutor is their mother figure. In medium SAP students have average levels of participation, they see ads, raise their hands, and visit resources in an interval of $(33, 66]$ in

ELS and, their tutor is their mother figure too. In low SAP students rarely see ads, raise their hands, and visit ELS resources; they have records of absences greater than 7 d and, their tutor is their father figure.

Future work is intended to use other larger educational databases that have other dynamic variables that can be retrieved from different academic platforms or ELS to improve the accuracy levels of the classifiers, as well as to use other methods for modeling such as clustering of data streams.

References

1. Amrieh, E.A., Hamtini, T., Aljarah, I.: Preprocessing and analyzing educational data set using x-api for improving student's performance. In: 2015 IEEE Jordan conference on applied electrical engineering and computing technologies (AEECT), pp. 1–5. IEEE (2015)
2. Amrieh, E.A., Hamtini, T., Aljarah, I.: Mining educational data to predict student's academic performance using ensemble methods. Int. J. Database Theory Appli. 9(8), 119–136 (2016)
3. Amrieh, E.A., Hamtini, T., Aljarah, I.: Students' Academic Performance Dataset, Nov 2016. https://www.kaggle.com/datasets/aljarah/xAPI-Edu-Data
4. Bifet, A., Gavalda, R.: Learning from time-changing data with adaptive windowing. In: Proceedings of the 2007 SIAM International Conference on Data Mining, pp. 443–448. SIAM (2007)
5. Bifet, A., Gavaldà, R.: Adaptive learning from evolving data streams. In: Adams, N.M., Robardet, C., Siebes, A., Boulicaut, J.-F. (eds.) IDA 2009. LNCS, vol. 5772, pp. 249–260. Springer, Heidelberg (2009). https://doi.org/10.1007/978-3-642-03915-7_22
6. Bifet, A., Gavalda, R., Holmes, G., Pfahringer, B.: Machine learning for data streams: with practical examples in MOA. MIT press (2018)
7. Bifet, A., Gavaldà, R., Holmes, G., Pfahringer, B.: Machine Learning for Data Streams with Practical Examples in MOA. MIT Press (2018). https://moa.cms.waikato.ac.nz/book/
8. Bifet, A., Holmes, G., Pfahringer, B., Kirkby, R., Gavalda, R.: New ensemble methods for evolving data streams. In: Proceedings of the 15th ACM SIGKDD International Conference on Knowledge Discovery and Data Mining, pp. 139–148 (2009)
9. Casalino, G., Castellano, G., Mannavola, A., Vessio, G.: Educational stream data analysis: a case study. In: 2020 IEEE 20th Mediterranean Electrotechnical Conference (MELECON), pp. 232–237. IEEE (2020)
10. Chatti, M.A., et al.: Learning analytics: Challenges and future research directions. eleed 10(1) (2014)
11. Freiberg Hoffmann, A., Stover, J.B., De la Iglesia, G., Fernández Liporace, M.: Correlaciones policóricas y tetracóricas en estudios factoriales exploratorios y confirmatorios. Ciencias psicológicas 7(2), 151–164 (2013)
12. Gomes, H.M., et al.: Adaptive random forests for evolving data stream classification. Mach. Learn. 106(9), 1469–1495 (2017)
13. Hall, M., Frank, E., Holmes, G., Pfahringer, B., Reutemann, P., Witten, I.H.: The weka data mining software: an update. ACM SIGKDD Explorations Newsl 11(1), 10–18 (2009)

14. McCalla, G.I.: The central importance of student modelling to intelligent tutoring. In: New directions for intelligent tutoring systems, pp. 107–131. Springer (1992). https://doi.org/10.1007/978-3-642-77681-6_8

15. Mihaescu, M.C., Popescu, P.S.: Review on publicly available datasets for educational data mining. Wiley Interdis. Rev. Data Mining Knowl, Dis. **11**(3), e1403 (2021)

16. Nandi, A., Xhafa, F., Subirats, L., Fort, S.: A survey on multimodal data stream mining for e-learner's emotion recognition. In: 2020 International Conference on Omni-layer Intelligent Systems (COINS), pp. 1–6. IEEE (2020)

17. Nguyen, H.L., Woon, Y.K., Ng, W.K.: A survey on data stream clustering and classification. Knowl. Inf. Syst. **45**(3), 535–569 (2015)

18. Okubo, F., Yamashita, T., Shimada, A., Ogata, H.: A neural network approach for students' performance prediction. In: Proceedings of the Seventh International Learning Analytics & Knowledge Conference, pp. 598–599 (2017)

19. Oza, N.C., Russell, S.J.: Online bagging and boosting. In: International Workshop on Artificial Intelligence and Statistics, pp. 229–236. PMLR (2001)

20. Papamitsiou, Z., Economides, A.A.: Student modeling in real-time during self-assessment using stream mining techniques. In: 2017 IEEE 17th International Conference on advanced learning technologies (ICALT), pp. 286–290. IEEE (2017)

21. R Core Team: R: A Language and Environment for Statistical Computing. R Foundation for Statistical Computing, Vienna, Austria (2021). https://www.R-project.org/

22. Romero, C., Ventura, S.: Educational data mining and learning analytics: An updated survey. Wiley Interdis. Rev. Data Mining Knowl. Dis. **10**(3), e1355 (2020)

23. Romero, C., Ventura, S., García, E.: Data mining in course management systems: Moodle case study and tutorial. Comput. Educ. **51**(1), 368–384 (2008)

24. Salloum, S.A., Alshurideh, M., Elnagar, A., Shaalan, K.: Mining in educational data: review and future directions. In: Hassanien, A.-E., Azar, A.T., Gaber, T., Oliva, D., Tolba, F.M. (eds.) AICV 2020. AISC, vol. 1153, pp. 92–102. Springer, Cham (2020). https://doi.org/10.1007/978-3-030-44289-7_9

CESAMMO: Categorical Encoding by Statistical Applied Multivariable Modeling

Eric Valdez-Valenzuela[1]([✉]), Angel Kuri-Morales[2], and Helena Gomez-Adorno[3]

[1] Posgrado en Ciencia e Ingeniería de la Computación, Universidad Nacional Autónoma de México, Mexico City, Mexico
ericvaldez@comunidad.unam.mx
[2] Instituto Tecnológico Autónomo de México, Mexico City, Mexico
akuri@itam.mx
[3] Instituto de Investigaciones en Matemáticas Aplicadas y en Sistemas, Universidad Nacional Autónoma de México, Mexico City, Mexico
helena.gomez@iimas.unam.mx

Abstract. Categorical attributes are present in datasets used in machine learning (ML) tasks. Since most ML algorithms only accept numeric inputs, categorical instances must be converted to numbers. There are different encoding techniques to accomplish this task. During this conversion, it is important to preserve the underlying pattern in the dataset. Otherwise, there may be a loss of information that can negatively affect the performance of supervised learning algorithms. In this paper, we present an encoding technique based on finding those numbers or codes that preserve the relationship between the categorical attribute and the other variables of the dataset. We solved six supervised classification problems using the proposed technique with five different ML algorithms. Additionally, we compare the performance of the proposed technique with other ten encoding techniques. We found that the proposed technique outperforms the most commonly used encoding techniques for certain trained ML algorithms. On average, CESAMMO remained within the top 5 techniques in terms of performance of the 12 encoders tested.

Keywords: Categorical encoding · Machine learning · Data preprocessing

1 Introduction

Most machine learning (ML) algorithms require that all independent variables be numeric. There are, however, some exceptions. As mentioned in [1], algorithms for tree-based models and naive Bayes can naturally handle numeric or categorical inputs. Although these 2 models can directly handle categorical

O. Pichardo Lagunas et al. (Eds.): MICAI 2022, LNAI 13612, pp. 173–182, 2022.
https://doi.org/10.1007/978-3-031-19493-1_14

data in theory, during their implementation with the most used libraries (e.g. Scikit-learn, XGBoost), categorical instances need to be converted to a numeric value. Many techniques allow us to use categorical variables in ML algorithms. Choosing the proper technique does affect the model's performance.

Categorical encoding techniques can be classified into two groups: unsupervised or supervised. In the group of unsupervised techniques, the two most commonly used, due to their simplicity, are the following:

1) Ordinal or label encoding. Convert each unique category value (or instance) to an integer value. The use of this technique is appropriate when the categorical instances have a natural order (also named ordinal). For example, the variable "level of satisfaction" with instances: "Not at all Satisfied," "Partly Satisfied," "Satisfied," "More than Satisfied," "Very Satisfied," could be converted to an interval scale from 1 to 5. However, when the categorical variable does not have a natural order (also known as nominal, examples are: "country" and "marital status"), it is not recommended to use the ordinal encoder. As explained in [2], when applying ordinal encoding on nominal data, it can be expected to perform poorly because it introduces an artificial order among categorical variables. For example, when it is directly used in neural networks optimized with stochastic gradient descent, the larger label values will contribute more to gradients used to update weights. This does not make sense because the integer values are assigned arbitrarily to the categorical instances.

2) One-hot encoding. A categorical variable with k possible instances is encoded as a feature vector of length k. This technique suits better for nominal data and is relatively easy to implement. However, it does not capture similarities between distinct categorical values, since it assigns orthogonal vectors to each instance. According to [3], the disadvantages of this technique are: 1) It could be computationally inefficient, 2) It does not adapt to growing categories, 3) It is not feasible for anything other than linear models, and 4) It requires large-scale distributed optimization with huge datasets.

In the supervised group, the most used encoding techniques are target encoder [4] and catboost encoder [5]. These two techniques have been shown to outperform other encoding techniques [6–8], particularly when data contain high-cardinality categorical attributes. Nevertheless, all target-based techniques have the problem of target leakage: it uses information about the target. Because of such target leakage, models tend to overfit the training data, which results in unreliable validation and lower performances during the test stage. To overcome this drawback, these techniques require a regularization hyperparameter.

Regardless of the technique used, the main point in replacing categorical values with numbers is maintaining the data's underlying pattern. Otherwise, the risk of losing information can negatively affect the performance of ML algorithms. We denote Pattern Preserving Codes (PPCs) as those numerical values that keep the intrinsic relationship between the categorical attribute and the other variables in the data. For a clearer explanation, consider a set of $n-$dimensional tuples (say U) whose cardinality is m. Assume there are n unknown functions of $n-1$ variables each, which we denote with:

$$f_k(v_1, ..., v_{k-1}, v_k); k = 1, ..., n \tag{1}$$

Let us also assume that there is a method that allows us to approximate f_k (from the tuples) with F_k. Denote the resulting n functions of $n-1$ independent variables with F_i , thus

$$F_k \approx f_k(v_1, ..., v_{k-1}, v_k); k = 1, ..., n \tag{2}$$

The difference between f_k and F_k will be denoted with e_k such that, for attribute k and the m tuples in the dataset.

$$e_k = abs(f_{ki} - F_{ki}); i = 1, ..., m \tag{3}$$

The PPCs are the ones that minimize e_k for all k. This is so because only those codes which retain the relationships between variable k and the remaining $n-1$ variables AND do this for ALL variables in the ensemble will preserve the whole set of relations (i.e. patterns) present in the database.

There exist encoding techniques that attempt to find these PPCs. One of them is CENG: Categorical Encoding with Neural Networks and Genetic Algorithms [9]. However, this approach is computationally very costly and, to boost its efficiency, it ought to be tackled in ensembles of multiple CPUs.

To avoid the high computational costs associated with CENG, in [10] a new algorithm called CESAMO was designed. CESAMO stands for Categorical Encoding by Statistical Applied Modeling. It relies on statistical and numerical considerations making the application of neural networks and genetics algorithms unnecessary while achieving analogous results. CESAMO assigns PPCs to each and all the instances of every class (category) which will preserve the patterns present for a given dataset. Essentially, CESAMO samples multiple numerical codes randomly, these codes are evaluated in an approximation function, which yields an error. Those codes that produced the smallest error are the PPCs.

In this work, we propose a modification to the original CESAMO algorithm (which we shall call CESAMMO). It consists of finding those codes that take into consideration the relationship between the categorical attribute and all the other variables of the dataset. In other words, we make the algorithm multivariable. The details of this modification are explained in more detail in the general methodology section. We evaluate CESAMMO with 5 ML models in 6 classification problems. In addition, we compare its performance with 10 other encoding techniques.

The rest of the paper is organized as follows: In Sect. 2 we detail the implementation of the CESAMMO encoding technique. In Sect. 3 we present the experimental results obtained from the comparative framework. Finally, in Sect. 4 our conclusions are presented.

2 General Methodology

The main goal of this work is to measure the performance of the CESAMO and CESAMMO and to compare these results with other encoding techniques.

CESAMO implements a mathematical model (whose theoretical justification is given in what follows) considering high-order polynomial relations. It consists of a universal polynomial approximation:

$$y = c_0 + c_1 x + c_3 x^3 + c_5 x^5 + c_7 x^7 + c_9 x^9 + c_{11} x^{11} \tag{4}$$

The CESAMO algorithm samples candidate codes from the data. The codes that achieve the smallest error in the approximation function are considered to be the ones preserving the behavioral patterns embedded in the dataset (i.e. the PPCs). In order to do this CESAMO ought to solve two basic problems:

1. How to define the function which will preserve the patterns.
2. How to determine the number of codes to sample.

In [11] it was shown that any continuous function can be approximated with a linear combination of monomials which consists of a constant plus a set of terms of odd degree. The coefficients c in Eq. 4 may be found in several ways. The so-called Ascent Algorithm [12] was utilized in the original version of CESAMO but the gradient descent algorithm is an efficient alternative.

Regarding (b), it is known that, independently of the distribution of the errors, the distribution of the means of the errors will become Gaussian. Once the distribution becomes Gaussian, it has achieved statistical stability, in the sense that further sampling of the candidate codes will not significantly modify the characterization of the population. In essence, therefore, what CESAMO proposes is to sample enough codes to guarantee the statistical stability of the values calculated in the approximation function. The codes corresponding to the best approximation will be those inserted in the dataset. Furthermore, CESAMO relies on a double level sampling: only pairs of variables are considered in Eq. 4 and every pair is, in itself, sampling the multivariate space. Details of the original CESAMO algorithm can be reviewed at [10].

Since CESAMO performs bi-variate sampling identifying the codes that yield the smallest error as a function of one secondary (randomly selected) variable, only the relationship between the categorical attribute and the second variable is preserved in each and every sample. The random selection of the secondary variable results in the "double level" sampling alluded to above. To circumvent this possible loss of information, we proposed CESAMMO. In it, we assume that PPCs are those numerical codes that yield the least average error when evaluated in Eq. 4 with all the other variables present in the dataset. In Fig. 1 we show the flow chart of CESAMMO.

The CESAMMO algorithm can be summarized as:

1: Select a categorical attribute.
2: Randomly select possible candidate codes.
3: Randomly select a secondary variable.
4: Apply a polynomial approx. function between the cat. variable and the selected secondary variable, and store the resulting error in an array (A1).
5: Check if the size of array A1 is greater than 30. If true, proceed to step 6. Else: repeat step 3.

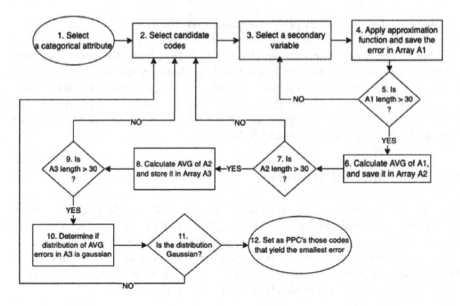

Fig. 1. Flowchart diagram of CESAMMO algorithm.

6: Calculate the average of array A1. Store the result in an array (A2).

7: Check if the size of array A2 is greater than 30. If true: proceed to step 8. Else: repeat step 2.

8: Calculate the average of array A2, and store it in an array (A3).

9: Check if the size of array A3 is greater than 30. If true: proceed to step 10. Else: repeat step 2.

10: Determine, via Chi-squared test [13], if the distribution of the errors' average in array A3 is Gaussian.

11: Check if the errors' avg. distribution is Gaussian. If true: proceed to step 12. else: repeat step 2.

12: The PPCs are those codes that yield the smallest errors.

The core modification of CESAMO may be found in steps 5, 6 and 7. We assume that by taking the average of the errors between the categorical attribute and all other variables in the training dataset, the PPCs will maintain the underlying pattern of the entire training dataset without appealing to the tacit double-level sampling considered above. This should, in principle, improve the performance of the ML models.

Regarding choosing a sample size of 30 in steps 5, 7, and 9, it is a rule of thumb based on the central limit theorem where sample distribution will approach normal distribution regardless of the population distribution as the sample size increases. This does not mean that 30 is a perfect size, but rather that it is the minimum needed for rendering normal sampling distributions of means independently of whether the sample itself is normal [14].

Once the modification to CESAMO has been implemented, the next step is to quantify its performance. For this purpose, we will use an available comparative framework of categorical encoding techniques [15]. This framework consists of six supervised classification problems taken from the Kaggle platform. In addition, it compares 10 categorical encoders with 5 ML algorithms. The categorical encoding techniques compared are Ordinal, One-Hot, Sum, Helmert, Backward Difference, Target, M-Estimate, Leave One Out, James Stein, and CatBoost. All of them are implemented with the Category Encoders library of Scikit- learn-contrib [16]. On the other hand, the classification problems were solved with the next ML algorithms: Logistic Regression, Gaussian Naïve-Bayes, Support Vector, Multilayer Perceptron, and XGBoost.

3   Experimental Results

We solved 6 classification problems with 5 distinct ML models. For each model, 12 different encoding techniques were implemented (including CESAMO and CESAMMO), and the accuracy of each combination Model-Encoder was measured. Accuracy was calculated by dividing the number of correct predictions by the total number of predictions. Tables 1, 2, 3, 4, 5, and 6 show the results obtained. The columns contain the following information:

- *Model*: The trained ML algorithm with which the problem was solved.
- *CESAMO Acc*: The accuracy that got CESAMO
- *CESAMMO Acc*: The accuracy that got CESAMMO
- *Encoder with the best acc*: contains the name of the encoding technique that got the highest accuracy.
- *Best Acc value*: the numerical value of the highest accuracy obtained by the best encoder.
- *Abs(CMMO, Best Enc.)*: shows the absolute difference between CESAMMO and the encoding technique with the highest accuracy.

To clarify the results, in Table 1, the first row could be read as: *"When solving the titanic problem, using the Naive-Bayes classifier, the CESAMO encoder got an accuracy of 0.7486. Likewise, the CESAMMO encoder yields an accuracy of 0.7795. On the other hand, the encoding technique that achieved the best accuracy for the Naïve-Bayes model was the Target encoder, with a value of 0.7968. Finally, the absolute difference between CESAMMO's accuracy and the best encoder was: 0.0173"*. The previous format applies to Tables 1, 2, 3, 4, 5, and 6.

Table 1. Results from the Titanic dataset.

Model	CESAMO acc.	CESAMMO acc.	Best encoder acc.	Best acc. value	Abs(CMMO, Best Enc.)
G. Naive Bayes	0.7486	**0.7795**	Target	0.7968	0.0173
Perceptron mult.	**0.8118**	0.8089	Backward diff.	0.8271	0.0182
Logistic reg.	**0.8174**	0.8146	Backward diff.	0.8215	0.0069
SVM	**0.8315**	0.8174	CESAMO	0.8315	0.0141
XGBoost	**0.8272**	0.823	Backward diff.	0.8283	0.0053

For the case of the 'Titanic' dataset, it can be observed in Table 1 that, for 4 of the 5 models, CESAMO's performance was better than CESAMMO's. Other than that, for the SVM model, CESAMO outperformed all other encoding techniques.

Table 2. Results from the Adult dataset.

Model	CESAMO acc.	CESAMMO acc.	Best encoder acc.	Best acc. value	Abs (CMMO, Best Enc.)
G. Naive Bayes	**0.806**	0.8035	James Stein	0.8336	0.0301
Perceptron mult.	**0.8522**	0.8521	James Stein	0.8589	0.0068
Logistic reg.	0.8329	**0.8353**	One-Hot	0.8528	0.0175
SVM	**0.8476**	0.8474	Target	0.8547	0.0073
XGBoost	**0.8655**	0.8634	Sum	0.8727	0.0093

In the case of the 'Adult' problem (Table 2), CESAMO and CESAMMO behave similarly (the difference was after the 3rd decimal).

Table 3. Results from the Credit dataset.

Model	CESAMO acc.	CESAMMO acc.	Best encoder acc.	Best acc. value	Abs(CMMO, Best Enc.)
G. Naive Bayes	**0.131**	0.1304	James Stein	0.1373	0.0069
Perceptron mult.	0.8778	**0.8814**	Leave one out	0.8914	0.01
Logistic reg.	0.915	**0.916**	Ordinal	0.9161	0.0001
SVM	0.9176	0.9176	CESAMMO	0.9176	0.0
XGBoost	0.9174	**0.9176**	Leave one out	0.9176	0.0

In the 'Credit' problem (Table 3), CESAMMO outperforms CESAMO in 2 models: the Multilayer Perceptron and the Logistic Regression. Moreover, CESAMMO got the highest performance given the SVM model.

Table 4. Results from the 'Employee' dataset.

Model	CESAMO acc.	CESAMMO acc.	Best encoder acc.	Best acc. value	Abs(CMMO, Best Enc.)
G. Naive Bayes	0.9395	**0.9418**	CESAMMO	0.9418	0.0
Perceptron mult.	0.9409	**0.9422**	Leave one out	0.9431	0.0009
Logistic reg.	0.9418	0.9418	Leave one out	0.9437	0.0019
SVM	0.9418	0.9418	CatBoost	0.944	0.0022
XGBoost	**0.9421**	0.9418	Ordinal	0.9455	0.0037

Similarly, for the 'Employee' dataset (Table 4), CESAMMO obtained a higher accuracy than CESAMO in two models: Gaussian Naive-Bayes and the Multilayer Perceptron. Furthermore, CESAMMO got the highest performance across all the other encoding techniques with the model G. Naive-Bayes.

Table 5. Results from the 'Car auction' dataset.

Model	CESAMO acc.	CESAMMO acc.	Best encoder acc.	Best acc. value	Abs(CMMO, Best Enc.)
G. Naive Bayes	**0.7045**	0.6951	MEstimate	0.8254	0.1303
Perceptron mult.	**0.8983**	0.8974	Ordinal	0.8989	0.0015
Logistic reg.	**0.8941**	0.8853	CatBoost	0.8952	0.0099
SVM	**0.898**	0.8949	Leave one out	0.8992	0.0043
XGBoost	**0.9**	0.8996	CESAMO	0.9	0.0004

In the 'Car auction' dataset (Table 5), there was not a significant difference between CESAMO and CESAMMO. However, CESAMO outperformed the other given encoders for the XGBoost model.

Table 6. Results from the 'Telco churn' dataset.

Model	CESAMO acc.	CESAMMO acc.	Best encoder acc	Best acc. value	Abs(CMMO, Best Enc.)
G. Naive Bayes	0.5582	**0.7219**	MEstimate	0.7378	0.0159
Perceptron mult.	**0.7886**	0.782	Backward diff.	0.7985	0.0165
Logistic reg.	0.7927	**0.798**	Backward diff.	0.8001	0.0021
SVM	**0.7897**	0.7961	Target	0.7993	0.0032
XGBoost	**0.8016**	0.7991	CESAMO	0.8016	0.0025

Finally, for the 'Telco churn' dataset, CESAMMO outperformed CESAMO in two models (the Gaussian Naive-Bayes and SVM). The highest accuracy obtained by the XGBoot model was given by CESAMO.

In the implementation of CESAMMO it was observed that, since it calculates the average of at least 30 errors for a single candidate code (which implies applying the approximation function), it increases the execution time of the algorithm compared to CESAMO. It is important to take this into account if the dataset has multiple categorical and high cardinality attributes.

4   Conclusions

In this paper, we evaluated two categorical encoders based on statistical applied modeling. The evaluation consisted of solving 6 classification problems, combining 5 ML algorithms with 12 encoding techniques (including CESAMO and CESAMMO), resulting in 60 model-encoder combinations. CESAMO and CESAMMO when applied to the Support Vector Machine and the XGBoost models, outperform other combinations.

It was expected that the multivariable consideration would improve the performance of CESAMO. However, there were problems for which CESAMMO was better than CESAMO. In all other cases, the opposite occurred. CESAMMO and CESAMO behaved similarly. One possible explanation is that a categorical attribute is not necessarily related to all the other variables in the dataset. Therefore, a possibly nonexistent relationship is being explored; it is more likely that a categorical attribute is related to a single variable in the entire dataset. Although this univariate relationship may be found in both versions, CESAMO achieves this more efficiently.

Making an average of the rating between all possible model-encoder combinations for the 6 solved classification problems, we found that both CESAMO and CESAMMO are, on average, among the 5 techniques with the highest performance out of the 12 encoding techniques tested. This is shown in Table 7. (consider that 1 is the best rating, and 12 the last place).

Table 7. Average rating of CESAMMO and CESAMO for the 6 classification problems

Problem	AVG ranking for CESAMMO (out of 12)	AVG ranking for CESAMO (out of 12)
Employee	2.6	3
Auction	3.6	3.4
Credit	3.8	4.8
Telco churn	3.8	4.2
Titanic	7.8	5.2
Adult	9.2	9.2
Overall ranking	5.1	4.9

Finally, as with most other challenges in ML, it is difficult to know a priori which will be the absolute best encoding technique for a particular problem. It is convenient to try out various types of encoders to find the absolute best for the problem to solve. Both CESAMO and CESAMMO represent good candidates to take into account.

References

1. Kuhn, M., Johnson, K.: Feature Engineering and Selection: A Practical Approach for Predictive Models. CRC Press, Boca Raton (2019)
2. Hancock, J.T., Khoshgoftaar, T.M.: Survey on categorical data for neural networks. J. Big Data **7**(1), 1–41 (2020)
3. Zheng, A., Casari, A.: Feature Engineering for Machine Learning: Principles and Techniques for Data Scientists. O'Reilly Media Inc., Boston (2018)
4. Micci-Barreca, D.: A preprocessing scheme for high-cardinality categorical attributes in classification and prediction problems. ACM SIGKDD Explor. Newsl. **3**(1), 27–32 (2001)
5. Prokhorenkova, L., et al.: CatBoost: unbiased boosting with categorical features. Adv. Neural Inf. Process. Syst. **31** (2018)
6. Pargent, F., et al.: Regularized target encoding outperforms traditional methods in supervised machine learning with high cardinality features. Comput. Stat., 1–22 (2022)

7. De La Bourdonnaye, F., Daniel, F.: Evaluating categorical encoding methods on a real credit card fraud detection database. arXiv preprint arXiv:2112.12024 (2021)
8. Seca, D., Mendes-Moreira, J.: Benchmark of encoders of nominal features for regression. In: Rocha, Á., Adeli, H., Dzemyda, G., Moreira, F., Ramalho Correia, A.M. (eds.) WorldCIST 2021. AISC, vol. 1365, pp. 146–155. Springer, Cham (2021). https://doi.org/10.1007/978-3-030-72657-7_14
9. Kuri-Morales, A.F.: Categorical encoding with neural networks and genetic algorithms. In: WSEAS Proceedings of the 6th International Conference on Applied Informatics and. Computing Theory, pp. 167–175 (2015)
10. Kuri-Morales, A.: Pattern discovery in mixed data bases. In: Martínez-Trinidad, J.F., Carrasco-Ochoa, J.A., Olvera-López, J.A., Sarkar, S. (eds.) MCPR 2018. LNCS, vol. 10880, pp. 178–188. Springer, Cham (2018). https://doi.org/10.1007/978-3-319-92198-3_18
11. Kuri-Morales, A., Cartas-Ayala, A.: Polynomial multivariate approximation with genetic algorithms. In: Sokolova, M., van Beek, P. (eds.) AI 2014. LNCS (LNAI), vol. 8436, pp. 307–312. Springer, Cham (2014). https://doi.org/10.1007/978-3-319-06483-3_30
12. Cheney, E.W.: Introduction to Approximation Theory. McGraw-Hill Book Company, New York (1966)
13. Rana, R., Singhal, R., et al.: Chi-square test and its application in hypothesis testing. J. Pract. Cardiovasc. Sci. 1(1), 69 (2015)
14. Cowles, M.: Statistics in Psychology: An Historical Perspective. Psychology Press, London (2005)
15. Valdez-Valenzuela, E., Kuri-Morales, A., Gomez-Adorno, H.: Measuring the effect of categorical encoders in machine learning tasks using synthetic data. In: Batyrshin, I., Gelbukh, A., Sidorov, G. (eds.) MICAI 2021. LNCS (LNAI), vol. 13067, pp. 92–107. Springer, Cham (2021). https://doi.org/10.1007/978-3-030-89817-5_7
16. McGinnis, W.D., et al.: Category encoders: a scikit-learn-contrib package of transformers for encoding categorical data. J. Open Source Softw. 3(21), 501 (2018)

Heart Failure Disease Prediction Using Machine Learning Models

Paola Tiburcio, Victor Guerrero, and Hiram Ponce[✉]

Facultad de Ingeniería, Universidad Panamericana, Augusto Rodin 498,
Ciudad de México 03920, Mexico
{0251987,0251983,hponce}@up.edu.mx

Abstract. Heart failure disease affects 26 million people worldwide and
it has a lower survival rate than breast or prostate cancer. An early
diagnostic of the disease is very important for prevention and possible
treatment. In this work, we propose using machine learning models to
predict the probability of developing a heart failure disease in a patient.
We compare two machine learning models over a public dataset of risk
factors and patients' clinical features. After a comparative analysis, we
find that a logistic regression model can predict 87% of the cases on
the data base. After that, we implement an easy web application for
heart failure disease prediction. We anticipate that applying this model
hospitals will be able to reduce their patient admission due to heart
failure disease and patients will be able to reduce their risk and avoid all
the implicit costs.

Keywords: Heart failure disease · Machine learning · Logistic
regression · Random forest · Prevention

1 Introduction

Heart failure is a condition in which the heart is unable to pump blood efficiently
to the entire body [7]. Although their symptoms are less serious than a heart
attack, it is still a life threatening disease. It is a worldwide disease that affects
approximately 26 million people with a lower survival rate than breast or prostate
cancer [7]. In addition, the majority of the patients admitted to the hospital
die within 5 years of admission. Even though heart failure is more common in
advanced age people, there are countries where this disease has been detected in
people that are 55 years or younger and it is predicted that the population with
this condition will increase in the next few years [7].

In the same way, there is an economic impact in the healthcare systems as
a consequence of this disease. In developed countries, heart failure represents
around 1% to 4% of the hospital's total admission [7]. However, these numbers

O. Pichardo Lagunas et al. (Eds.): MICAI 2022, LNAI 13612, pp. 183–191, 2022.
https://doi.org/10.1007/978-3-031-19493-1_15

are underestimated as heart failure may be recorded as a secondary diagnosis. The expense of caring for heart failure is around 1% to 3% of the total cost in North America, Western Europe, and Latin America [1]. This cost increases in some places, as there is usually a recurrence of heart failure and admission in less than a year [2].

Machine learning has been widely explored in the context of heart failure estimation. Literature reports different approaches based on a combination of predictors [1,6,8] and the stages of the disease [2]. As shown in the literature, it is hard to find an accurate model for predicting heart failure. Thus, it is important to try with different predictors or features and a combination of models to find more accurate solutions.

In this work, we propose a machine learning model to determine the probability that a person might develop heart failure in order to take preventive actions to reduce these probabilities and, at the same time, the costs implied by the treatment. For this, we use a public dataset of risk factors and the probability of developing heart failure. Two machine learning models were trained and validated. At last, the best model was implemented in an easy web application.

We consider that using machine learning techniques as predictive models will be useful to identify the patients that are more likely to develop heart failure based on different features such as chest pain type, cholesterol, age, sex, resting electrocardiogram results, chest pain during exercise, and increments in heart rate.

The rest of the paper is as follows. Section 2 describes the related work. Section 3 presents our proposal and Sect. 4 defines the experimentation setup. Section 5 presents the results and the application. Finally, Sect. 6 concludes the paper.

2   Related Work

There are several works related to heart failure prediction. In Rahimi et al. [8], the authors describe that the best approach to this problem requires a combination of several predictors using a multivariate model in order to improve the accuracy by using one single predictor. For this assessment, 64 models were analyzed, 43 predicted death, 10 predicted hospitalization, and 11 death or hospitalization. One of the main conclusions was that the models developed for death prediction were more accurate than the others. In general the median of features used in the evaluated models was less than 10. Another report, developed by Akshay et al. [2], focused on predicting the re-hospitalization of heart failure patients and not in propensity of developing heart failure. The authors mentioned that it is hard to assemble a model for this. There are physiological indicators, however, the patient quality of life is a very important predictor of the admission rate. In the same way, the phases from first admission, transition to home and readmission, make risk factors behave differently.

The approach, made by Lane et al. [6], is based on the prediction of sudden cardiac death. The work mentioned that an implantable cardioverter-defribillator is a very effective method of reducing mortality, however, it is a very expensive device. As there are more patients with this condition, the challenge is in identifying patients with heart failure with significant risk. Still, they are working on tests for better predictions. They conclude that prevention strategies are required and are being refined. In the work developed by Adler et al. [1], the authors describe a boosted decision tree algorithm to discriminate between high and low risk patients using demographic and physiological features like blood pressure, white blood cell count, platelets, etc. For this model age was not included in order to detect other silent predictors and also elderly people were excluded. It is a very good approach on using machine learning to predict heart failure.

In contrast with the literature, for our proposal, we use different descriptive features based on demographics, test results, and regular symptoms that are common in patients that suffer from heart failure disease. We use a logistic regression as a baseline and compare it with a random forest in order to look for the best accurate model. Finally, we developed a user friendly application that could be helpful in determining if a patient has a high or low probability to develop heart failure.

3   Description of the Proposal

3.1   Data

For this analysis we downloaded an open dataset from Kaggle [3]. This data set contains 918 observations from different patients and 11 clinical characteristics in order to see if they have heart disease or not. The risk factors obtained are the following:

- Age: age in years of the patient.
- Sex: sex of the patient.
- ChestPainType: chest pain type of the patient. The types are divided into Typical Angina, Atypical Angina, Non-Anginal Pain and Asymptomatic.
- RestingBP: resting blood pressure.
- Cholesterol: serum cholesterol level.
- FastingBS: fasting blood sugar. If it is > 120 mg/dl or otherwise.
- RestingECG: resting electrocardiogram results. If it is Normal, with ST-T wave abnormality or probable or definite left ventricular hypertrophy by Estes' criteria.
- MaxHR: maximum heart rate achieved. Between 60 and 202.
- ExerciseAngina: if there is an exercise-induced angina.
- Oldpeak: if there is an abnormality in the electrocardiogram.
- ST Slope: the slope of the peak exercise ST segment. The values are for: upsloping, Flat or downsloping.

3.2   Exploratory Data Analysis (EDA)

In order to get a better understanding of our data, we did an exploratory data analysis. First, we did a frequency analysis for the categorical variables grouped by our target variable HeartDisease to get better insight of the behavior of our data; second, for the numeric variables we did a descriptive analysis to look for the distribution and magnitude also we obtained the distribution plots; third, we did a two variable analysis through a pair plot (Fig. 1), to look for the relationship between the numeric variables and the target variable; last, we did a correlation analysis to look for those variables with a high relationship among them.

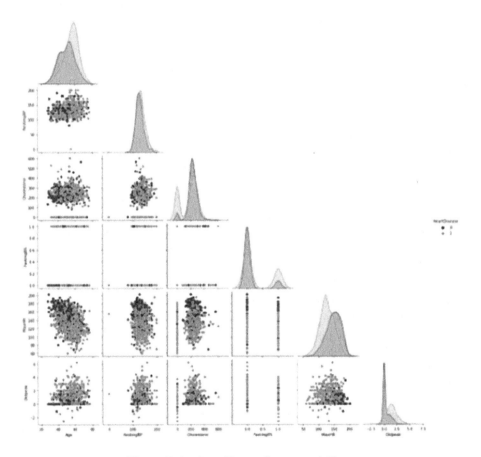

Fig. 1. Pair plot of heart disease variables.

3.3   Machine Learning Workflow

The machine learning workflow is shown on Fig. 2. It comprises of data collection, train-test split, data pre-processing, training the model, testing the model, model evaluation, and application implementation. Details are following.

ML WORKFLOW

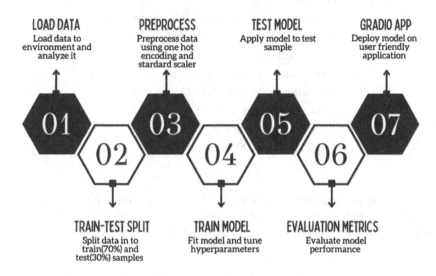

LOAD DATA
Load data to environment and analyze it

PREPROCESS
Preprocess data using one hot encoding and stardard scaler

TEST MODEL
Apply model to test sample

GRADIO APP
Deploy model on user friendly application

01   03   05   07

02   04   06

TRAIN-TEST SPLIT
Split data in to train(70%) and test(30%) samples

TRAIN MODEL
Fit model and tune hyperparameters

EVALUATION METRICS
Evaluate model performance

Fig. 2. Machine learning workflow adopted in this work.

Pre-processing Strategy. In the EDA there were no missing values detected and the target variable HeartDisease was found to be well balanced. However, one hot encoding is applied to the categorical variables: Sex, ChestPainType, RestingECG, ExerciseAngina, and ST Slope, also columns are renamed in order to maintain the interpretability of the variables. For the features MaxHR, Cholesterol, RestingBP and Age, we found different scales for the values, so the strategy is to do a standardization after splitting the data set into train and test samples.

Model Approach. We use logistic regression as the baseline model. Logistic regression [4] is a generalized linear model that is very simple for interpretation and because of that, it is widely used in different areas. In addition, we use a random forest classification model [5]. It is a very robust model that uses a bagging strategy for training, that allows to obtain a better performance during the training process. We decided to use these two models since they have a well-known performance on classification problems, they are easy to deploy, and they have good results without demanding too much computational resources. The implementation was done in Python.

Grid Search. In order to get the best models, the hyper-parameters were tuned using the grid search technique. The results are shown on Table 1.

Table 1. Hyper-parameter values used in grid search.

Logistic regression	
Solver	newton-cg, lbfgs, liblinear
Penalty	none, l1, elasticnet
Random Forest	
Criterion	gini, entropy, log loss
Bootstrap	True, False
Max depth	3, 6, 9, 12, 15, none
Max features	auto, sqrt, log2
N estimators	20, 40, 60, 80, 100

The best hyper-parameters for each model found are the following. For logistic regression: Solver–liblinear and Penalty–l1. For random forest: Criterion–entropy, Bootstrap–True, Max depth–12, Max features–auto, and N estimators–40.

4   Experimentation

In order to train and test our models, we split the data using 70% for training and 30% for testing. We implemented the stratified k-fold cross-validation with $k = 5$. The folds of the models are shown on Table 2.

Table 2. Cross validation fold results for best models

Model	Fold 1	Fold 2	Fold 3	Fold 4	Fold 5
Logistic regression	86.8%	84.2%	82.6%	86.3%	75.9%
Random forest	85.3%	83.1%	82.0%	84.1%	78.6%

We use the following evaluation metrics to compare both models: accuracy (1), precision (2), recall (3), and F1-score (4); where, TP, TN, FP, and FN represent true positive, true negative, false positive, and false negative, respectively.

$$Accuracy = \frac{TP + TN}{TP + TN + FP + FN} \tag{1}$$

$$Precision = \frac{TP}{TP + FP} \tag{2}$$

$$Recall = \frac{TP}{TP + FN} \tag{3}$$

$$F1 - score = \frac{2 * Precision * Recall}{Precision + Recall} = \frac{2 * TP}{2 * TP + FP + FN} \qquad (4)$$

5   Results and Discussion

The results of the performance for both models on train data are shown in Table 3, while the evaluation metrics on test data are summarized in Table 4. From the latter, it can be observed that random forest is slightly better than logistic regression in terms of accuracy (88%) and F1-score (89%); but contrasting the results from train and test data, random forest might be over-fitted. Thus, we consider logistic regression to be the best model found so far.

Table 3. Evaluation metrics for both models on train data.

Model	Accuracy	Precision	Recall	F1-score
Logistic regression	86%	86%	89%	88%
Random forest	100%	99%	100%	100%

Table 4. Evaluation metrics for both models on test data.

Model	Accuracy	Precision	Recall	F1-score
Logistic regression	87%	84%	93%	88%
Random forest	88%	84%	94%	89%

5.1   Application

In order to make the model accessible to people that are not familiar with code or machine learning, we developed an application using the Python library Gradio. Through a user friendly interface, it receives as inputs the patient's medical variables required by the model and returns whether the patient is prone to develop heart failure disease based on those inputs. The user friendly interface is as shown in Fig. 3. In this application, we implemented the logistic regression model as the core of the inference step. The web application can be public accessed here: https://huggingface.co/spaces/VictorMG/heart_failure.

5.2   Discussion

The main advantages of our proposed work comprise the analysis of two well-known machine learning models that were built and trained under grid search and cross validation techniques, making a fair comparison among them; some features are different from the literature; and also the implementation of an easy application that uses the best model found as the core of it. We also identify some

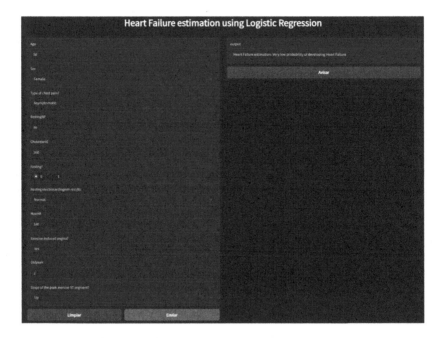

Fig. 3. User friendly application developed for the heart failure disease prediction.

limitations in our work, such as the number of machine learning models tested are limited; a more in-deep exploratory analysis of the features is required; and it might be ethnic bias under the data used. However, this work showed that machine learning techniques as predictive models might be useful to identify patients that are more likely to develop heart failures. This would be beneficial as a tool for prevention and acceleration of patient's treatment.

6   Conclusions

Based on a data set containing clinical features of many patients, the main objective of this work was to develop a prediction model to determine whether a person was prone to develop heart failure disease. Using machine learning techniques, we developed a logistic regression model, after prepossessing our data and after comparing the model results versus a random forest model. After a comparative analysis, we chose the logistic regression model as our final model. We also developed an application to make the model useful for any person who wishes to make a prediction based on the clinical features.

For future work, we would like to test the model on other populations in order to see if there is an ethnic bias, also to refine the model including a time variable that could give us an estimation of the time before a patient develops heart failure disease. Another implementation would be to include in the application the prevention instructions a patient must follow if the model predicts a high probability of developing heart failure disease, as well as, the estimated costs.

References

1. Adler, E., et al.: Improving risk prediction in heart failure using machine learning. Eur. J. Heart Fail. **22**(1), 139–147 (2020)
2. Akshay, S., Lynne, W.: Rehospitalization for heart failure. Circulation **126**(4), 501–506 (2012)
3. fedesoriano: Heart failure prediction dataset (2021). https://www.kaggle.com/fedesoriano/heart-failure-prediction
4. Hilbe, J.M.: Practical Guide to Logistic Regression. CRC Press (2015)
5. James, G., Witten, D., Hastie, T., Tibshirani, R.: An Introduction to Statistical Learning. STS, vol. 103. Springer, New York (2013). https://doi.org/10.1007/978-1-4614-7138-7
6. Lane, R., et al.: Prediction and prevention of sudden cardiac death in heart failure. Heart **91**(5), 674–680 (2005)
7. Ponikowski, P., et al.: Heart failure: preventing disease and death worldwide. ESC Heart Fail. **1**(1), 3–9 (2014)
8. Rahimi, K., et al.: Risk prediction in patients with heart failure. J. Am. Coll. Cardiol. HF **2**(2), 440–446 (2014)

Classification of Flood Warnings Applying a Convolutional Neural Network

Oscar-Alejandro García-Trujillo$^{(\boxtimes)}$, Luis Carlos Sandoval Herazo,
Eddy Sánchez-DelaCruz, and Raymundo González Moreno

National Tech, Misantla Campus, Misantla, Veracruz, Mexico
gtrujillo.oa@gmail.com

Abstract. The effects of climate change create climatic temporal imbalances that favor the development of hydrometeorological phenomena and cause socioeconomic damage when they occur. In the absence of Early Warning Systems and dedicated monitoring stations, the effectiveness of a Convolutional Neural Network model is tested to interpret and label dataset on the climatic conditions of the Misantla's river basin and its surroundings, regarding to the flood hazard level. Aiming to classify rainfall events in the region using dataset collected through 3 weather stations around the region: northern zone of Veracruz, Mexico, specifically the municipality of Misantla. Neural networks can maximize the use of dataset collected by weather stations, providing a safer environment in the event of floods, and having a positive effect on the preservation of human activity. The dataset provided allows to label data as 'GREEN', 'YELLOW' and 'RED' with more than 95% accuracy, performing better when working with a large number of validation data, but also shows a slowdown during the integration of larger training data sets.

Keywords: Convolutional Neural Network · Precipitation · Early warning system · Flood risk determination · Flood labeling

1 Introduction

The effects of climate change have caused an imbalance in climatic temporality, favouring the development of hydrometeorological phenomena, causing socio-economic havoc as they occur [4, 10]. In addition, technological developments make it possible to implement weather classification models to alert the population to possible disasters, such as floods [14].

The Misantla river basin, has been affected by the aforementioned imbalance, an example of which, was its overflow when it was affected by hurricane "Roxane" in October 1995, causing extensive damage to a population of approximately 8,000 inhabitants [4]. The lack of adequate monitoring of the variables that cause the river to overflow made it impossible to mitigate its impact on the city of Misantla. In the absence of an Early Warning System (EWS) and dedicated monitoring stations, the population is left at the mercy of inclement weather.

Therefore, the use of a model based on Convolutional Neural Networks (CNN) is explored, a model that is able to interpret and label the dataset on the climatic conditions

© The Author(s), under exclusive license to Springer Nature Switzerland AG 2022
O. Pichardo Lagunas et al. (Eds.): MICAI 2022, LNAI 13612, pp. 192–203, 2022.
https://doi.org/10.1007/978-3-031-19493-1_16

of the Misantla river basin and its surroundings, with respect to the present flood hazard level. This model functions as a EWS system supported by data from climate stations established at key points around the Misantla river basin.

The remainder of the article is divided as follows: in Sect. 2, information on different CNN applications in the field of flood prevention and weather forecasting can be seen. Section 3, contains the description of the dataset used, its processing and architecture 3.3 used to produce the results in Sect. 4 and their discussion 4.2. Finally, Sect. 5 presents conclusions and future work.

2   Related Work

This section describes related Convolutional Neural Network (CNN) work for weather forecasting, water body flow monitoring, flood warning and other elements. Larraondo et al. [13] demonstrate how CNNs can be used to interpret the output of Numerical Weather Prediction (NWP) automatically to generate local forecasts. aiming to prove that these models can capture part of the mental and intuitive process that human forecasters follow when interpreting numerical weather data.

Chen et al. [2] employ 3-Dimensional CNN and 2-Dimensional CNN as a method to better understand the spatial relationships of typhoon formation features. Fu et al. [6], apply a 1-Dimensional CNN in conjunction with Bi-directional Long Short-Term Memory in weather prediction because of the effectiveness of CNNs in extracting features and capturing short period connections between datasets.

Donahue et al [5], implement CNN as the basis of an Long-term Recurrent Convolutional Networks for its rapid progress on visual recognition problems, as well as its application to time-varying inputs and outputs.

Shi et al. [17], integrate convolutional layers in conjunction with an Fully Connected Long Short-Term Memory network to generate short-term precipitation forecasts as if it were a long-term spatio-temporal forecasting problem.

Zhang et al. [22], proposes deep architecture using a bidirectional 3-Dimensional CNN and Convolutional Long Short-Term Memory to transform video into a 2-D mapping of learning and classification features.

Han et al. [7], employs a CNN, converts the short-term forecasting problem into a binary classification problem and exploits the advantage of CNNs in its global pattern learning to demonstrate its superiority compared to other Machine Learning methods in short-term forecasting.

Pally, Jaku Rabinder Rakshit [16], developed a new python package called "FloodImageClassifier" including various CNNs architectures to classify and detect objects within the collected flood images, embeded in a smartly designed pipeline to train a large number of images and calculate flood water levels and inundation areas which can be used to identify flood depth, severity, and risk.

Nobuaki Kimura et al. [12], combine knowledge transfer and CNNs for time series flood predictions. Its application has a margin of error of less than 10 percent with respect to variation with water level.

Syed Kabir et al. [11] create a CNN model for fast real-time flood estimation and prediction, contrasting it with an Support Vector Machine model and showing the superiority of the former. Supported by data collected over a 10-year period (2005–2015).

Cho et al. [3] propose a model based on CNN classification to determine flood risk. This model is suggested as an initial study to determine time-optimal evacuation actions.

S. Smys et al. [18] through the use of Internet of Things (IoT) sensors that collect data and store it in the cloud, applies a CNN-based model that predicts the inflow of water into dams and lakes in order to prevent flash floods during rainfall events.

ChenChen et al. [1] offer a CNN deep learning-supported model for flood prediction in a watershed, with data collected over 10 years, via IoT devices.

Dostdar Hussain et al. [9] study a time series approach with CNN in the prediction of water flow in a river, comparing it with an Extreme Learning Machines (ELM) model.

Kou-Lin Hsu et al. [8] describe a system, which utilizes the computational strength and flexibility of an adaptive Artificial Neural Network model to estimate rainfall rates using infrared satellite imagery and ground-surface information.

Mhara [15], presents a two-layer CNN-based model, using 10 years of history for flood prediction in a catchment, considering temporal, geographical and trend characteristics. The model is intended to be used for water level monitoring through IoT and flood disaster prevention.

Zhang, C. et al. [21], offer the"Tiny-RainNet" model for short-term rainfall forecasting (nowcasting) in a period between 1 and 2 h, combining CNN and Bi-directional Long Short-Term Memory. The model takes into account the influence of spatiotemporal meteorological conditions, thus avoiding the cumulative error presented in conventional models.

WWang, Y. et al [19], apply two CNN-based models for flood susceptibility mapping that consider 13 flood triggers and demonstrates a higher accuracy of both models compared to an Support Vector Machine model. These models are intended to be used to assist in flood damage mitigation and management.

3   Methodology

3.1   Weather Stations

To collect weather data of Misantla municipality , in Veracruz, Mexico, three weather stations were deployed each in a specific location around Misantla. The deployment areas were selected considering principal points of rain runoff and the hydrological region "RH 27-Ae", where Misantla belongs.

The installed stations are three "ambient weather ws-2902a" liked to a wireless internet connection and powered by two AA batteries respectively, capable to gather indoor and outdoor data, creating each an online dataset available in https://ambientweather.net/ using the respective user and password to which the equipment is linked (Table 1).

3.2   Dataset

The dataset used, contains 10907 different inputs collected by the 3 weather stations over the past 2 years.

Table 1. Weather stations location table.

Station	Location	Coordinates
1	ITSM, Misantla, Veracruz, Mexico	725699N, 2207381E
2	Tenochtitlan, Veracruz, Mexico	718167N, 2191478E
3	Salvador Diaz Mirón, Veracruz, Mexico	723452N, 2187739E

Each input registered in the dataset is associated with a specific label regarding the flood warning that kind of record represents, "GREEN" labeled records mean "No risk of flood", "YELLOW" labeled records mean "Possible risk of flood" and "RED" labeled records mean "Imminent flood in the area". The dataset contains 3909 records labeled as "GREEN", 3501 records labeled as "YELLOW" and 3498 records labeled as "RED". Values in the dataset are used as listed in 2:

Table 2. Dataset data description

#	Value	Description
1	Simple date	Format "DD/MM/YYYY" is converted into integer values calculating the number of days between a given date and 1/1/1900.
2	Hour	Counts the whole hours passed in the current day.
3	Day	Registers the current day number.
4	Month	Registers the current month number.
5	Outdoor temperature	Logs air temperature in exteriors, expressed in degrees Celsius.
6	Hourly rain	Records millimeters of rain per hour, in the current hour.
7	Event rain	Tracks millimeters of rain between intervals lower than an hour. For instance, if 71 mm of rain are registered first and followed by 100 mm of rain in less than an hour, both are part of the same "Event Rain" interval.
8	Hourly rain	Records millimeters of rain per hour, in the current hour.
9	Daily rain	Counts millimeters of rain per day, in the current day, since midnight (00:00).
10	Weekly rain	Shows the amount of precipitation that has accumulated in the calendar week total, and resets on Sunday morning at midnight.
11	Monthly rain	Records millimeters of precipitation in the calendar month total, and resets on the first day of the Month.
12	Total rain	Is defined as the running total since station was powered up.
13	Outdoor humidity	Is the ratio of the current absolute humidity to the highest possible absolute humidity.
14	Solar radiation	Measures in Watts per square meter(W/m^2), radiant energy emitted by the sun from a nuclear fusion reaction that creates electromagnetic energy.
15	Label	Replaces titles like "GREEN", "YELLOW" and "RED" for numerical values 2, 0 and 1, respectively

The data cleansing process consists of the conversion of collected information into actionable numerical formats, converting values such as date, day, time and labels into standardized numerical values available for experimentation, in the dataset cleansing, incomplete records are erased, records that report "null" values due to the lack of data recorded by the weather stations, or periods in which the system reported data out of place because it was undergoing maintenance in an air-conditioned area.

For example, if the weather station required a battery change, or if a bird struck the weather station so hard it required fixing a sensor. The data collected during the maintenance hour reports null values in "Outdoor Temperature", "Outdoor Humidity" and "Solar Radiation", due to the lack of any listed field like the previous mentioned. The whole row is discarded.

Table 3. Dataset Sample

Simple date	Hour	Day	Month	Outdoor temperature (°C)	Hourly rain (mm/hr)	Event rain (mm)	Daily rain (mm)	Weekly rain (mm)	Monthly rain (mm)	Total rain (mm)	Outdoor humidity (%)	Solar radiation (W/m²)	Label
44706	23	24	5	24	0	0	0	1.8	60.7	278.2	81	0	GREEN
44705.81	19	24	5	25.5	0	0	0	1.8	60.7	278.2	84	21.6	GREEN
44705.8	19	24	5	25.8	0	0	0	1.8	60.7	278.2	84	30.3	GREEN
44705.8	19	24	5	25.8	0	0	0	1.8	60.7	278.2	84	38.2	GREEN
44690.63	15	9	5	33.7	2175	171	171	172.8	231.7	449.2	63	655.5	YELLOW
44690.63	15	9	5	33.5	2176	196	196	197.8	256.7	474.2	62	672.4	YELLOW
44690.63	15	9	5	33.5	2177	220	220	221.8	280.7	498.2	64	666.2	YELLOW
44650.75	18	30	3	28.3	0	265	265	266.8	325.7	543.2	54	22.9	RED
44650.75	17	30	3	28.4	0	266	266	267.8	326.7	544.2	52	26.4	RED
44650.74	17	30	3	28.5	0	257	257	258.8	317.7	535.2	52	29	RED

From the values registered in Table 3, flood predictions are heavily based on "Event Rain", "Outdoor Humidity" and "Outdoor Temperature" since the millimeters of water registered keep increasing in a rain event, the "Outdoor Temperature" marks how fast water can evaporate in the area and "Outdoor Humidity" establishes the water evaporation ratio. The other values in the dataset are provided to the machine in order to find a correlation between all the different values without evaluate them isolated.

3.3 CNN Architecture

A CNN usually takes a tensor of order 3 as input [20], the input dataset goes through a set of processing, called layers, which may be grouping, convolution or normalization, as well as fully connected or loss layers.

$$x^1 \longrightarrow \boxed{w^1} \longrightarrow x^2 \longrightarrow \cdots \longrightarrow x^{L-1} \longrightarrow \boxed{w^{L-1}} \longrightarrow x^L \longrightarrow \boxed{w^L} \longrightarrow z$$

Fig. 1. Abstract description of CNN structure

Figure 1 illustrates layer by layer how the dataset passes through a CNN, starting with the input layer x^1 for processing in the tensor w^1. The output of the first layer is x^2, which also acts as input for the processing of the second layer. This processing continues until all the layers of the CNN have been completed, providing an output in x^L. The last layer is a loss layer. Let us assume that t is the corresponding target value for the input x^1, then a cost or loss function can be used to measure the discrepancy between the forecast x^L of CNN and the target t.

In the conducted experiment, a Google Collab Instance was used with the following specs:

- GPU: Tesla P100-PCIE-16 GB
- CPU: Intel(R) Xeon(R) CPU @ 2.00 GHz
- Socket(s): 1
- Core(s) per socket: 1
- Thread(s) per core: 2
- L3 cache: 39424K
- RAM: 13 GB

– DISK SPACE: 100 GB Free Space

The algorithm was run using Python 3.6 including the following libraries:

– tensorflow
– numpy
– pandas
– sklearn

The CNN was fully connected, implementing a Sequential model, "sparse_categorical_crossentropy" as loss function, "Nadam" as Optimizer, initializing with an input layer of 13 values, 10 layers of linear rectification (ReLU) and an output layer of 3 values, training in sets of 600 entries at a time and 20 epochs. The number of convolutions is specified in Table 4:

Table 4. CNN layer data

Layer #	Convolutions	Activation
1	169	ReLU
2	169	ReLU
3	36	ReLU
4	49	ReLU
5	64	ReLU
6	64	ReLU
7	49	ReLU
8	36	ReLU
9	169	ReLU
10	169	ReLU

The experiment was conducted 3 times, each one dividing the current dataset in different proportions (Table 5):

Table 5. Dataset segmentation values

Experiment #	Train data %	Test data %
1	70	30
2	60	40
3	80	20

4   Experiments and Results

The aim of this experiment is to test different distributions of a dataset for a better classification of rainfall events in Misantla, Veracruz, using a dataset of weather data from strategically installed weather stations in the surrounding area. Assessing the effectiveness of CNN models taking part in the process of interpreting numerical climate data, similar to human interpretation.

4.1   Validation

The following are the results of experiments carried out with a data rate of: 60% training data and 40% test data (Figs. 2 and 3).

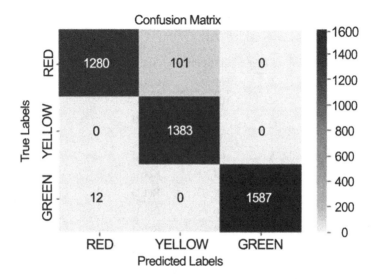

Fig. 2. Confusion matrix 60/40

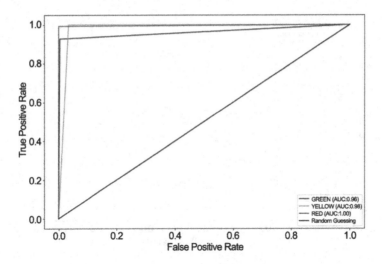

Fig. 3. ROC test 60/40

70% training data and 30% test data (Figs. 4 and 5).

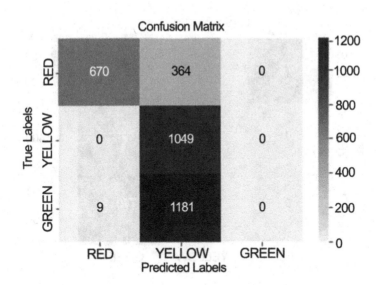

Fig. 4. Confusion matrix 70/30

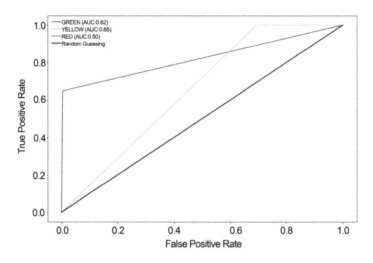

Fig. 5. ROC test 70/30

80% training data and 20% test data (Figs. 6 and 7).

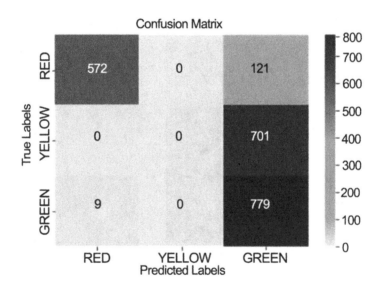

Fig. 6. Confusion matrix 80/20

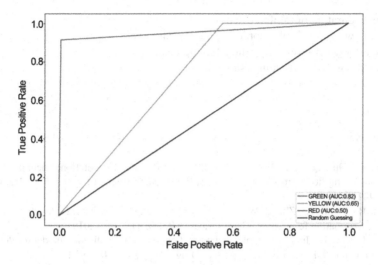

Fig. 7. ROC test 80/20

4.2   Discussion

The dataset provided performs better when working with a large number of validation data, but also shows a slowdown during the integration of larger training data sets.

It is understood that the system achieves adequate training and testing with a dataset ratio of 60/40 without disconnection between cells preparing it for a better integration with a validation subset, in contrast the number of labels mismatched increases in case of changing training and testing ratios. Furthermore, there is a difference in data accuracy between the three labels "GREEN", "YELLOW" and "RED", which seems to be related to the number of elements provided for each label, with the highest number of data provided by "GREEN" labeling, followed by "YELLOW" labeling and the lowest number by "RED" labeling.

Using Convolutional Neural Networks in a 'nowcasting' phenomenon as Flood forecasting, that is strongly dependent on recorded rainfall events, and real time monitoring allows to take advantage of variables that have little to negligible influence on its prediction and develop properly trained Early Warning Systems capable to use real-time inputs as a validation subset and keep track of possible incoming floods.

5   Conclusions and Future Work

Convolutional Neural networks are capable of monitor data collected by weather stations and identify inputs as possible flood warnings like a person could, removing the need of continuous human intervention, as well as the fast computing, prediction and response to flood warnings, providing a safe environment in the event of floods and having a positive effect on the preservation of human activity. Implementations of this nature offer opportunities for action in areas far from large cities or those that are in the process of development. Future applications include:

- – Estimate duration of rainfall events
- – Estimate water levels of recorded rainfall events
- – Estimating water levels of predicted rainfall events
- – Determining flood action intervals

References

1. Chen, C., Hui, Q., Xie, W., Wan, S., Zhou, Y., Pei, Q.: Convolutional neural networks for forecasting flood process in internet-of-things enabled smart city. Comput. Netw. **186**, 107744 (2021)
2. Chen, R., Wang, X., Zhang, W., Zhu, X., Li, A., Yang, C.: A hybrid cnn-lstm model for typhoon formation forecasting. GeoInformatica **23**(3), 375–396 (2019)
3. Cho, M., Kim, D., Jung, H.: Implementation of cnn-based classification model for flood risk determination. J. Korea Inst. Inf. Commun. Eng. **26**(3), 341–346 (2022)
4. CONAGUA: Análisis de las temporadas de huracanes de los años 2009, 2010 y 2011 en méxico. http://www.conagua.gob.mx/conagua07/publicaciones/publicaciones/cgsmn-2-12.pdf. Accessed June 2022
5. Donahue, J., et al.: Long-term recurrent convolutional networks for visual recognition and description. In: Proceedings of the IEEE Conference on Computer Vision and Pattern Recognition (CVPR) (2015)
6. Fu, Q., Niu, D., Zang, Z., Huang, J., Diao, L.: Multi-stations' weather prediction based on hybrid model using 1d cnn and bi-lstm. In: 2019 Chinese control conference (CCC), pp. 3771–3775. IEEE (2019)
7. Han, L., Sun, J., Zhang, W.: Convolutional neural network for convective storm nowcasting using 3-d doppler weather radar data. IEEE Trans. Geosci. Remote Sens. **58**(2), 1487–1495 (2019)
8. Hsu, K.L., Gao, X., Sorooshian, S., Gupta, H.V.: Precipitation estimation from remotely sensed information using artificial neural networks. J. Appl. Meteorol. **36**(9), 1176–1190 (1997)
9. Hussain, D., Hussain, T., Khan, A.A., Naqvi, S.A.A., Jamil, A.: A deep learning approach for hydrological time-series prediction: a case study of gilgit river basin. Earth Sci. Inf. **13**(3), 915–927 (2020)
10. INEGI: Características hidrográficas. méxico. https://www.inegi.org.mx/temas/hidrografia/. Accessed June 2022
11. Kabir, S., Patidar, S., Xia, X., Liang, Q., Neal, J., Pender, G.: A deep convolutional neural network model for rapid prediction of fluvial flood inundation. J. Hydrol. **590**, 125481 (2020)
12. Kimura, N., Yoshinaga, I., Sekijima, K., Azechi, I., Baba, D.: Convolutional neural network coupled with a transfer-learning approach for time-series flood predictions. Water **12**(1), 96 (2019)
13. Larraondo, P.R., Inza, I., Lozano, J.A.: Automating weather forecasts based on convolutional networks. In: Proceedings of the ICML Workshop on Deep Structured Prediction, PMLR, vol. 70 (2017)
14. Marín Vilca, D.G., Pineda Torres, I.A.: Modelo predictivo machine learning aplicado a análisis de datos hidrometeorológicos para un sat en represas (2019)
15. Mhara, M.A.O.A.: Complexity neural networks for estimating flood process in internet-of-things empowered smart city. Available at SSRN 3775433 (2021)

16. Pally, J.R.R.: Application of image processing and convolutional neural networks for flood image classification and semantic segmentation (2021)
17. Shi, X., Chen, Z., Wang, H., Yeung, D.Y., Wong, W.K., Woo, W.C.: Convolutional lstm network: a machine learning approach for precipitation nowcasting. Adv. Neural Inf. Process. Syst. **28**, 1–9 (2015)
18. Smys, S., Basar, A., Wang, H., et al.: CNN based flood management system with IoT sensors and cloud data. J. Artif. Intell. **2**(04), 194–200 (2020)
19. Wang, Y., Fang, Z., Hong, H., Peng, L.: Flood susceptibility mapping using convolutional neural network frameworks. J. Hydrol. **582**, 124482 (2020)
20. Wu, J.: Introduction to convolutional neural networks, vol. 5, no. 23, p. 495. National Key Lab for Novel Software Technology. Nanjing University, China (2017)
21. zhang, c., Wang, H., Zeng, J., Ma, L., Guan, L.: Tiny-rainnet: a deep cnn-bilstm model for short-term rainfall prediction (2019)
22. Zhang, L., Zhu, G., Shen, P., Song, J., Afaq Shah, S., Bennamoun, M.: Learning spatiotemporal features using 3d cnn and convolutional lstm for gesture recognition. In: Proceedings of the IEEE International Conference on Computer Vision Workshops, pp. 3120–3128 (2017)

Machine Learning Techniques in Credit Default Prediction

Emmanuel Malagon, Daniel Troncoso, Andres Rubio, and Hiram Ponce[✉]

Facultad de Ingeniería, Universidad Panamericana, Augusto Rodin 498,
Ciudad de México 03920, Mexico
{0241059,0252006,0252009,hponce}@up.edu.mx

Abstract. Digital transformation after the pandemic is a must if a company wants to survive in a highly competitive environment. Machine Learning (ML) applications are no strangers to Digital Transformations, and banks are looking for ways to improve efficiency by means of similar technologies. In this work, we propose a machine learning model for predicting the credit default using the LendingClub public dataset. The accepted loans include data ranging from 2007 to 2017. For this purpose, we implement support vector machines and logistic regression models. The results showed that support vector machines is a high accurate model (93%) for predicting the credit default.

Keywords: Credit default · Machine learning · Support vector classifier · Regression

1 Introduction

Today, we have witnessed the significant and rapid growth of machine learning, not only in banks, but in different industries ranging from streaming platforms to wholesale foods. Digital transformation after the pandemic is a must if a company wants to survive in a highly competitive environment. Machine Learning (ML) applications are no strangers to Digital Transformations, and banks are looking for ways to improve efficiency by means of similar technologies. With that being said, why is it important to spend some time revisiting credit default risk if banks are already doing it? Our world has changed after the pandemic and so did the banks. "The need to mitigate the risk of an increase in non-performing loans, due to COVID-19, calls for investments in automated credit decision-making that combined with the deployment of transactional behavioural data will allow for enhanced risk management and lead to improved credit decisions." [2]. This means, data automation is now a strategic target that will require jobs, resources and educated project proposals. Our motivation derives from the conjunction between the urgent need for automated decisions and talent needed to provide sufficient support.

Last but not least, there is a growing interest in fostering cooperation among policymakers to ease the constraints on collecting, storing and analysing big data.

O. Pichardo Lagunas et al. (Eds.): MICAI 2022, LNAI 13612, pp. 204–211, 2022.
https://doi.org/10.1007/978-3-031-19493-1_17

Numbers support the latter, "Central banks' interest in big data and machine learning has increased over the last years: around 80% of central banks discuss the topic of big data formally within their institution, up from 30% in 2015" [6].

In this work, we aim to predict if a certain user will default based on information provided for helping improving the loan methodology/pipeline. The data use in this work comes from a compilation of LendingClub records [1]. Then, the work follows an end-to-end path starting from pre-processing, feature engineering, modeling and evaluation through results given. Through a grid search method, we select the best configuration for both the support vector machines and the regression models. Our work, rather than focusing on what is the best option from collectively exhaustive testing, it shows a basic path to analyse credit default with ML.

The rest of the paper is as follows. Section 2 explores related works and research on credit risk in peer-to-peer lending. Then, Sect. 3 presents the methodology followed in the work. Section 4 shows the results. Lastly, Sect. 5 concludes the paper.

2 Related Work

As Osei Salomey, et al. [4] state in their work, there is a shortage of credit risk datasets, available to the public, this has been a big challenge in the domain of finance. A good way to tackle this problem is to share more resources to help researchers with their studies. We looked at well explained paper "Accuracies of some Learning or Scoring Models for Credit Risk Measurement" [4] in which the authors used techniques such as Multi-layer Perceptons and Convolutional Neural Networks. They used label encoders and metrics such as confusion matrix, accuracy and f1-score.

We found more complexities while studying credit default. As Mohammad Mubasil describes in his work "Credit Risk Analysis in Peer to Peer Lending Data set: Lending Club" [3], the market started to gain traction through the financial crisis of 2008 and as the economy improved so did the number of loans. The latter, means there is an exceptional time frame in credit default. Mubasil makes use of Decision Tree and Random Forest techniques.

3 Methodology

For our modeling of credit default, we consider two different ML techniques: (i) support vector machines (SVM) and (ii) logistic regression. Our methodology comprises five main steps: data pre-processing, feature extraction, feature selection, building models, and model evaluation, as shown in Fig. 1

3.1 Data Preparation

We use ten years of data, to somehow shadow the effect of 2008 crisis, from the Lending Club dataset [1]. The data goes from 2007 to 2017. It has around 100 thousand observations, 150 variables and one target column "loan-status".

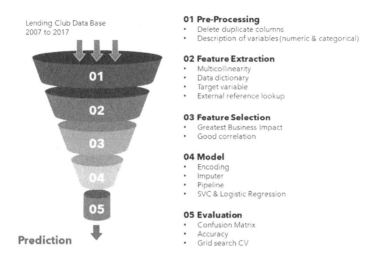

Lending Club Data Base
2007 to 2017

01

02

03

04

05

Prediction

01 Pre-Processing
- Delete duplicate columns
- Description of variables (numeric & categorical)

02 Feature Extraction
- Multicollinearity
- Data dictionary
- Target variable
- External reference lookup

03 Feature Selection
- Greatest Business Impact
- Good correlation

04 Model
- Encoding
- Imputer
- Pipeline
- SVC & Logistic Regression

05 Evaluation
- Confusion Matrix
- Accuracy
- Grid search CV

Fig. 1. Workflow for the credit default adapted from the Lending Club pipeline [1].

After downloading the data set, we found the first column was an index with no particular value, so we dropped the column in the first place. After that we looked at each column description to get a general idea of which variables are considered during the procedure the Club executed before lending money.

Then, we looked at the values of the target column, as shown in the excerpt of Table 1. In this case, the possible values of the loan status are shown in Table 2. Most of the observations fall in the Charge-Off and Fully-Paid classifications. The other options indicate the payment period is on-going so those status options are ignored in our analysis and data preparation. Then, we assigned 1 to those values containing "Charge-Off" and 0 to the "Fully Paid" loans.

Table 1. Examples of feature description, adapted from [1].

ID	Feature	Description
0	acc_now_delinq	Number of accounts borrower has
1	acc_open_past_24mths	Number of trades opened in past 24 months.
2	addr_state	The state provided by the borrower in the loan
3	all_util	Balance to credit limit on all trades
4	annual_inc	The self-reported annual income provided
		...
148	settlement_amount	The loan amount of the borrower to pay
149	settlement_percentage	Percentage payoff
150	settlement_term	Months to pay

Table 2. Target variable "Loan Status".

ID	Status code	Observations
1	Fully Paid	69,982
2	Charged Off	16,156
3	Current	12,726
4	Late 31 to 120 days	730
5	In Grace Period	264
6	Late 16 to 30	139
7	Default	3

With this, we proceeded to use the describe method in our data-set to get an idea of how numeric variables behave and the number of values the categorical variables have. Sometimes, columns have data contained in other columns, we deleted redundant sections from our input. We choose not only those variables with high correlation to our target, but also those variables that fundamentally made sense to the problem domain. Let's say we look closely at Home Ownership, FICO and Employment Tenure, those variables, although categorical, make a lot of sense to predict a possible default. A home owner that has a good FICO grade and a long employment history makes a good candidate for loans; we can infer they know how to manage payments versus their personal finance. This is why we included some of professional experience and the way banks work to better select the set of variables to work with. Finally, we ended up with a clean data-set of 10 features and 1 target, as shown in Table 3.

Table 3. Clean dataset.

ID	Column name	Data type
1	GEO	Category
2	Grade	Category
3	Home Ownership	Category
4	Initial List Status	Category
5	Purpose	Category
6	Term	Category
7	Verification	Category
8	Employment Length	Category
9	Last FICO range	CFloat
10	Total Recovered Principal	Float
11	Interest Rate	Float
Target	Charged Off	Category

We encoded the categorical variables using the one-hot encoding method. For the target variable, we use a binary encoding. After that, we standardized the numerical variables.

3.2   Building Models

We choose two models for our ML proposal, support vector machines and logistic regression.

Support Vector Machines (SVM). The goal of this model is to find a hyperplane in an N-dimensional space (N - the number of features) that neatly classifies the data points. To separate two classes of data points, there are many possible hyper-planes that could be chosen. A plane must be found that has the maximum margin, that is, the maximum distance between the data points of both classes. Maximizing the margin distance provides some reinforcement so that future data points can be classified with more confidence [7]. For our experimentation, we use a radial basis function kernel.

Logistic Regression. This model is a type of regression used to model situations where growth or decline accelerates rapidly at first and then slows down over time. Logistic regression is useful when you want to predict the presence or absence of a feature or outcome based on the values of a set of predictors. It is similar to a linear regression model, but it is adapted for models in which the dependent variable is dichotomous [5]. L2 regularization is used in our experimentation.

For training purposes, we split the data into 70% for training and 30% for testing. We used grid search for finding suitable hyper-parameters of the SVM. After that, a 5-fold cross validation technique was conducted in both models.

3.3   Model Evaluation

We evaluate the performance of the supervised models using four metrics: accuracy (1), precision (2), recall (3), and F1-score (4); where, TP are the true positive, TN are the true negative, FP are the false positive, and FN are the false negative.

$$accuracy = \frac{TP + TN}{TP + TN + FP + FN} \tag{1}$$

$$precision = \frac{TP}{TP + FP} \tag{2}$$

$$recall = \frac{TP}{TP + FN} \tag{3}$$

$$F\text{-}score = 2 \times \frac{precision \times recall}{precision + recall} \qquad (4)$$

Accuracy measures the total number of true positives in the whole testing data; precision is the ratio of the true positives and true negatives, and the total number of samples; recall is the ratio of true positives to all positives in the ground truth; and F1-score metric uses a combination of precision and recall. High F1-score means high precision as well as high recall.

4   Results and Discussion

We conducted the experiments described above. Table 4 and Table 5 summarize the results from both the SVM and the logistic regression models. Results reported are the mean values of the metrics.

Table 4. Performance of the SVM model.

Score	Precision	Recall	F-score	Support
Label 0	0.94	0.91	0.93	4861
Label 1	0.91	0.94	0.93	4833
Accuracy	–	–	0.93	9694
Macro avg	0.93	0.93	0.93	9694
Weighted avg	0.93	0.93	0.93	9694

Table 5. Performance of the logistic regression model.

Score	Precision	Recall	F-score	Support
Label 0	0.92	0.92	0.92	4861
Label 1	0.92	0.92	0.92	4833
Accuracy	–	–	0.92	9694
Macro avg	0.92	0.92	0.92	9694
Weighted avg	0.92	0.92	0.92	9694

The SVM model got an accuracy of 93%, while the logistic regression got an accuracy of 92%. Similar results were found in terms of the F-score. To validate the results, Fig. 2 and Fig. 3 show the confusion matrices of both models SVM and logistic regression, respectively.

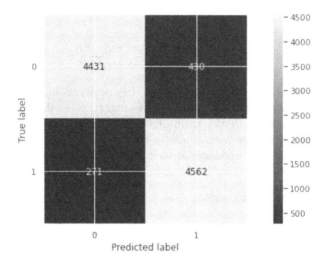

Fig. 2. Confusion matrix of the SVM model.

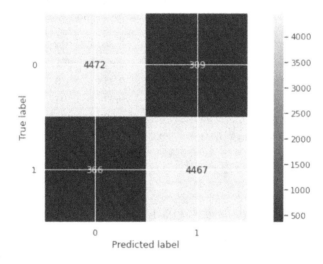

Fig. 3. Confusion matrix of the logistic regression model.

In this work, we consider SVM as the best model in terms of the F-score and the accuracy. The SVM model can predict the loan status as part of the credit risk measurement. In comparison with the state of the art, our work uses SVM for predicting the credit default, and not neural networks [4]. However, the current work is a preliminary workflow for predicting credit default. We consider there is room for more investigation before implementing it. For example, more robust experimentation is required and other features might be taken into account.

5   Conclusions

This work, we presented a machine learning model for predicting the credit default and helping improving the loan methodology/pipeline. For this, we adopted the ML workflow that comprises data pre-processing, feature extraction, feature selection, building models, and model evaluation steps.

In the end, our results showed good accuracy and acceptable confusion matrices. In this work, we only implemented SVM and logistic regression techniques, but using other alternatives could be of interest and then compare their performance amongst the models.

Finally, we highlight the importance of implementing ML in data analysis activities, because it helps make decisions in a more objective and customized way.

References

1. George, N.: All lending club loan data (2019). https://www.kaggle.com/datasets/wordsforthewise/lending-club
2. Giannaklis, I.: The five main imperatives for banks in a post-pandemic era (2021). https://www.worldfinance.com/banking/the-five-main-imperatives-for-banks-in-the-post-pandemic-era
3. Mohammad, M.: Credit risk analysis in peer to peer lending data set: Lending club. Digit. Commonds 1(1), 48 (2019). https://digitalcommons.bard.edu/cgi/viewcontent.cgi?article=1299&context=senproj_s2019
4. Osei, S.: Accuracies of some learning or scoring models for credit risk measurement. ResearchGate 1(1), 15 (2021). https://www.researchgate.net/publication/350067975_Accuracies_of_some_Learning_or_Scoring_Models_for_Credit_Risk_Measurement
5. Satchidananda, S., Simha, J.B.: Comparing Decision Trees with Logistic Regression for Credit Risk Analysis. International Institute of Information Technology, Bangalore (2006)
6. Sebastian, D.: Big data and machine learning in central banking. Working Papers 1(930), 26 (2021). https://www.bis.org/publ/work930.htm
7. Suthaharan, S.: Support vector machine. In: Machine Learning Models and Algorithms for Big Data Classification. ISIS, vol. 36, pp. 207–235. Springer, Boston, MA (2016). https://doi.org/10.1007/978-1-4899-7641-3_9

Convolutional and Dense ANN for Cloud Kinetics Forecasting Using Satellite Images

Mónica Borunda[1(✉)], Adrián Ramírez[2], Raul Garduno[3], Gerardo Ruiz[2],
Sergio Hernandez[2], and O. A. Jaramillo[4]

[1] Consejo Nacional de Ciencia y Tecnología, Mexico City, Mexico
mborundapa@conacyt.mx
[2] Facultad de Ciencias, Universidad Nacional Autónoma de México, Mexico City, Mexico
felos@ciencias.unam.mx, gruiz@unam.mx
[3] Instituto Nacional de Electricidad y Energías Limpias, Cuernavaca, Mexico
rgarduno@ineel.mx
[4] Instituto de Energías Renovables, Universidad Nacional Autónoma de México, Mexico City, Mexico
ojs@ier.unam.mx

Abstract. Intermittency of solar radiation over earth surface due to cloud presence poses a great challenge for power production at photovoltaic fields. Prediction of cloud kinetics may help to deal with variations of energy production and their compensation to satisfy electricity demand. Nowadays, there are huge amounts of satellite information available about clouds at most regions of the world. That information could be useful to characterize cloud kinetics and to calculate solar radiation ahead of time. In this paper, we propose two methods to predict cloud kinetics by using artificial neural networks (ANN) and satellite images. First method is mainly graphical and uses a convolutional ANN to predict the cloud satellite image at time k + 1 from the set of previous n cloud satellite images. Then, the cloud position vector, that represents the predicted image, is obtained. Second method is mainly numerical and uses a dense ANN to directly predict the cloud position vector at time k + 1 from the set of previous m position vectors of satellite images. The predicted cloud position vectors are compared to the real ones when the corresponding satellite image becomes available. Time series of predicted cloud position and velocity vectors are compared through the RMSE index to quantify the precision of predictions. We find that even though both methods offer a short-term forecasting with good accuracy, the method using dense ANN provides more accurate results though its performance should be checked under less simplified assumptions.

Keywords: Cloud kinetics · Convolutional ANN · Dense ANN · Satellite images · Kinetics forecasting · Cloud forecasting

1 Introduction

Solar energy is one of the most commonly available renewable energies that has found widespread use for electric power generation in all sorts of applications (i.e., industrial,

© The Author(s), under exclusive license to Springer Nature Switzerland AG 2022
O. Pichardo Lagunas et al. (Eds.): MICAI 2022, LNAI 13612, pp. 212–224, 2022.
https://doi.org/10.1007/978-3-031-19493-1_18

commercial, residential) in both urban and rural areas, connected to the electric grid or isolated from it, in large photovoltaic (PV) fields or just a few panels [1]. The amount of PV power generation is very sensitive to the atmosphere composition in the place where the panels are located. Solar radiation reaching the surface of PV panels varies continuously and randomly due to reflection, scattering, and absorption by air molecules, aerosols, clouds, and dust [2]. Clouds block most of direct radiation and constitute the major cause of intermittency of solar radiation, and therefore of uncontrolled increases or decreases of PV power generation [3].

The unavoidable intermittency of solar radiation poses great challenges to power generation such as: a) Maintaining electricity supply and system stability, b) Managing power generation cost effectively, and c) Lowering CO_2 emissions from nonrenewable sources [4]. Maintaining electricity supply during normal operation in the presence of intermittency affects reliability and flexibility of power system operation with loss of system inertia [5]. Achieving cost effectivity in the presence of intermittency may require flexible fuel-burning generation, importing electricity from other power systems, addition of electricity storage means, and variation of load demand patterns [6]. Dealing with lack of generation because of intermittency requires flexible operation of fossil-fueled generation, which will increase CO_2 emissions instead [7].

Knowledge of short-term variations of solar radiation at specific locations is essential for profitable, reliable, and sustainable operation of PV power plants of any size. The variability of solar PV power is mostly due to the instantaneous crossing of clouds across the PV power plant at timescales as short as 1, 5, or 10 min [8]. The effectiveness of solutions to compensate the effects of solar radiation intermittency on the power output of PV plants and on the operation of power systems largely depends on the accuracy of forecasting solar radiation. Even more, since cloudiness is the major cause of intermittency, predicting the behavior of solar radiation can be approached as a problem of predicting the movement of clouds [9, 10]. This relationship has inspired research projects about modeling and predicting solar radiation based on cloud behavior over specific areas of interest on earth's surface, e.g., the area around large PV plants. Many projects rely on cloud image processing as an appropriate way to find out the characteristics of cloud movement. Major approaches include processing geostation-ary satellite images [11, 12] and ground-based sky images [13].

Earliest attempts to analyze cloud motion from satellite images were done at the time the first geostationary operational environmental satellites (GOES) were launched [14, 15]. Calculation of cloud motion vectors (CMV) became an important asset of meteorological information at national fore-cast centers all around the globe. The Maximum Cross Correlation (MCC) method was developed to analytically determine CMV by application of the Fast Fourier Transform to determine the cross-correlation coefficients of cloud features (edges, bright, etc.) from a pair of consecutive pictures from geosynchronous satellites [16]. Additionally, to the fact that the MCC method is computationally intensive, it may produce many spurious velocity vectors. Nevertheless, thereafter numerous studies were carried out to improve calculation of CMV from displacements of cloud features observed in the infrared or visible band of satellite imagery [17].

The use of artificial neural networks (ANN) for solving image correspondence and object tracking problems is a more recent development [18, 19]. Later, the Hopfield neural network was applied for cloud tracking [20]. Since CMV are computed by extracting and tracking cloud features, enhanced feature extraction improved CMV computation performance. The deep convolutional neural network (CNN) [21] was proved able to extract and utilize image features effectively. Methods based on deep CNN were introduced to perform cloud detection [22], cloud classification [23] and satellite video processing [24] in more recent years. Despite deep CNN performed brilliantly with spatial data, it could not deal with temporal data [25], which is a major factor for cloud motion forecasting. Conversely, recurrent neural networks (RNN) are well suited to learn complex relationships in the time domain and have become the standard for time series forecasting [26]. Nevertheless, simple RNN are not able to backpropagate the error signal for long-term learning. To solve this problem, Long Short-Term Memory (LSTM) neural networks [27] were proposed. LSTM has become widely used in the solar power forecasting field [28, 29].

The research in this paper is concerned with the use of cloud kinetics (i.e., cloud position and velocity) to calculate solar radiation ahead of time to find out the variations of PV power generation due to solar intermittency caused by clouds crossing a specific area of earth surface. It takes advantage of the availability of satellite images at short timescales portraying the presence of clouds over the area of interest to calculate cloud kinetics, instead of deriving cloud velocity from an array of solar radiation measurements [30]. We introduce the definition of the position and velocity of cloud motion in terms of vectors in a Cartesian plane defined by a satellite image of the clouds in a specific area, and we explore two methods to predict cloud kinetics by using Artificial Neural Networks (ANNs). Section 2 provides the background of the techniques involved in this research including the processing of satellite images for cloud kinetics, the basis of convolutional and dense artificial neural networks for image and vector forecasting and, quantification of forecasting accuracy by means of forecasting errors and error indexes. Section 3 presents the results of cloud kinetics forecasting using both approaches, convolutional and dense ANNs. Prediction errors are calculated against the real images when they become available, and the prediction performance is obtained through the RMSE error index of the time series of cloud kinetics. Finally, in Sect. 4, a few meaningful conclusions are drawn, and future research work is pointed out.

2   Methodology

As mentioned before, this work aims to forecast cloud kinetics by using ANN and satellite images. In this section, we describe the methodology to achieve it. First, we describe the conversion of satellite images into pixeled images to be more easily used for forecasting. Second, we introduce the tools from Machine Learning, namely ANNs, to forecast cloud kinetics. Finally, we explain the calculation of forecasting errors and error indexes considering the real satellite images to quantify the performance of prediction.

2.1   Processing of Satellite Images for Cloud Kinetics

First step to forecast cloud kinetics is to process satellite images in order to detect clouds from the NOAA satellite image archive [31], *i.e.* separate cloudy from clear sky. In order to achieve this, GOES-R developed a Clear Sky Mask algorithm [32]. This algorithm determines the presence of clouds by converting a satellite image in the form of a binary cloud mask that identifies pixels as clear or cloudy sky as shown in Fig. 1. Figure 1a shows a satellite image in the infrared band 13, 10.3 µm, which is considered clean since it is less sensitive to water vapor. The binary cloud mask assigns to every pixel a one or zero, yellow or purple color, depending on the presence or absence of cloudiness, as shown in Fig. 1b. Thus, the binary cloud mask value *CMV* is a dimensionless quantity,

$$CMV = \begin{cases} 0 & clear\ sky \\ 1 & cloudy\ sky \end{cases}, \tag{1}$$

assigned to every pixel with approximately 2 km resolution.

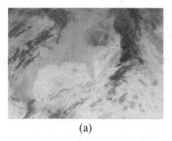
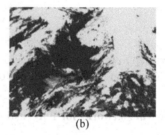

(a)   (b)

Fig. 1. Example of cloud detection in satellite images for an image in band 13, (a), and the resulting figure as generated by the GOES-R Clear Sky Mask algorithm, (b).

For the sake of simplicity, and to prove our methodology, we focus on a small image formed by 11×11 pixels which correspond to a surface of 22×22 km^2. An important step is to define the position of a cloud in the considered image. We define a representative position of a cloud in an image by the cloud centroid of the image. In this approximation, we consider that the cloud density is constant, and that the clouds scattered across the sky can be simplified by the corresponding projection on a 2D horizontal plane. We compute a center of mass for each image using the values provided by the cloud binary mask, *i.e.* a cloudy pixel gets a *CMV* as defined in Eq. (1). Then, we compute the clouds centroid for each image to calculate its kinetics. The cloud centroid for an image is defined by $\overline{C} = (C_x, C_y)$ and each component is computed as

$$C_x = \frac{\sum_{i=1}^{11}\sum_{j=1}^{11} CMV_{ij}\, i}{\sum_{i=1}^{11}\sum_{j=1}^{11} CMV_{ij}} \tag{2}$$

$$C_y = \frac{\sum_{j=1}^{11}\sum_{i=1}^{11} CMV_{ij}\, j}{\sum_{j=1}^{11}\sum_{i=1}^{11} CMV_{ij}} \tag{3}$$

where the indexes i and j correspond to the x and y coordinates respectively, and CMV_{ij} corresponds to the cloud mask value CVM at a pixel located at position (i, j) as shown in Fig. 2.

Fig. 2. Grid image example of an 11×11 pixel image. Yellow, purple, pixels correspond to cloud presence, absence, with a $CMV = 1$ or 0, respectively.

With this procedure we obtain a representative position of the cloud $\overline{C}$ for each image of our sequence, and by considering two adjacent images we can define a representative velocity of the clouds $\overline{V}$ at a given time k defined by

$$\overline{V}_t = \frac{\Delta \overline{C}}{\Delta T} = \frac{\overline{C}_k - \overline{C}_{k-1}}{5 \text{ min}} \tag{4}$$

Next step to forecast cloud kinetics is to use this information as inputs for Machine Learning tools and compare their performance.

2.2 Neural Networks for Forecasting

In the last years, several types of artificial neural networks (ANN) have been developed, which main inspiration is the brain's structure and functionality [33, 34]. For instance, some types of ANNs are built to use numerical data as input/output of the net, which we refer to as numerical-data approach. On the other hand, there are other kinds of ANNs designed to operate with images, which we refer to as image-data approach. As a first step towards the analysis of cloud kinetics using ANN, we use both approaches to forecast the cloud's centroid position and compare the goodness of the prediction as well as their advantages and disadvantages. In order to achieve this, and for the sake of simplicity, we use the simplest ANNs for the numerical-data and image-data approaches.

The simplest ANN is the so-called dense neural network (DNN) and it works with numerical-data set. It basically consists of linked layers of neurons, perceptrons, that map the input to the output data and its deepness is given by the number of hidden layers as shown in Fig. 3(a). A perceptron consists of a function that takes two inputs, multiplies them by a weight and a bias value and passes the result through an activation function to obtain the desired result. To obtain the best result the weight is adjusted by training the net using an algorithm. If the algorithm uses the input data to calculate the output, then it is called a feed-forward ANN, whereas if the training algorithm uses the output data to better adjust the weight and compute the final data it is called backpropagation ANN. The activation function of the model is very important since it provides the non-linear relation between inputs and outputs and is selected according to the data range. The main activation functions are the ReLu, Softmax, tanH and Sigmoid functions and are used according to the ANN application.

An ANN model that has been successfully used to deal with image-data sets is the Convolutional Neural Network (CNN) or ConvNet [35, 36]. The CNN main feature is the usage of a convolution process and is specifically designed to process data images. There are several types of CNNs and, depending on the application, each type is built with different layers being the convolutional layer the core building block. The input, which is an image, is represented by a tensor given by (number of inputs) × (input height) × (input width) × (input channels). When the image goes through a convolutional layer, it becomes a feature map given by (number of inputs) × (feature map height) × (feature map width) × (feature map channels). Thus, convolutional layers convolve the input and pass the result to the next layer. This kind of ANNs is ideal for data with a grid-like topology such as images. CNNs can contain other layers such as a pooling layer, that decreases the size of the convolved featured map, and/or a fully connected layer, with a similar architecture of a DNN. There are many types of CNNs and the layers contained in their architecture depend on the specific application. For the purposes of this preliminary work, we use a CNN formed only by convolutional layers as shown in Fig. 3b.

(a)   (b)

Fig. 3. Basic architectures of (a) dense neural network and (b) convolutional neural network.

In recent years, CNNs have been successfully used for image classification, object detection and image prediction. On the other hand, DNN have been widely used for numerical-data prediction. The CNN's inputs are mainly spatial data, such as images, of fixed size, while the DNN's input is a sequence of numerical data which size may vary. As mentioned, we use both approaches, numerical-data and image-data, for cloud kinetics forecasting. Our input data consists of a sequence of satellite images processed by the Clear Sky Mask algorithm every 5min as shown in Fig. 4. A centroid $\overline{C}\_i$ is computed for every image corresponding at time t according to Eqs. (2) and (3).

Then, in one approach, we use the sequential series of centroids, associated to the satellite images, as input of a DNN to predict the centroid of an image at a future time step, as shown in Fig. 5a. In the other approach, we use the graphical information, corresponding to the processed satellite images, as inputs to the CNN to forecast an image containing the cloud information at a future time step, as shown in Fig. 5b. Then, we compute the associated centroid position of the forecasted image to contrast it with the predicted centroid position of the numerical-data approach.

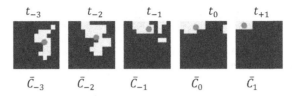

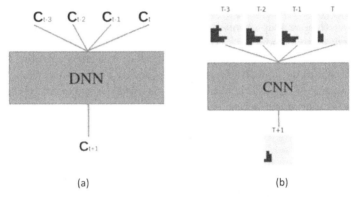

Fig. 4. Example of sequence of processed satellite images generated by Clear Sky Mask algorithm used as input data and their associated centroids.

Fig. 5. (a) Numerical-data and (b) image-data approaches for cloud kinetics forecasting using satellite images.

2.3 Forecasting Errors and Indexes

In order to quantify the accuracy prediction, we use forecasting errors and indexes. In general, for a given variable u, the prediction error at a given time $t = k\Delta T$, where ΔT is the sampling period, is defined as

$$err_u(t = k\Delta T) = u^{predicted}(t = k\Delta T) - u^{measured}(t = k\Delta T), \tag{5}$$

or simply

$$err_{u,k} = |u_k^p - u_k^m|, \tag{6}$$

where u_k^p and u_k^m are the k-th data of the predicted and measured values, respectively, of the variable u at $t = k\Delta T$ for $k = 1, 2, \ldots, K$. There are several used indexes to grade the goodness of a prediction such as Root Mean Square Error (RMSE), Mean Absolute Percentage Error (MAPE), Mean Absolute Error (MAE), etc.

In this work, we are interested in calculating the errors for the forecasted position of the cloud centroid and the related velocity. One common way to do this is by using the RMSE index [37, 38]. Let $\overline{C_k^p} = (C_{xk}^p, C_{yk}^p)$ and $\overline{C_k^m} = (C_{xk}^m, C_{yk}^m)$ be the predicted and measured position vectors, respectively, of the cloud's centroid in the (x, y) plane of the surface of the satellite image. The RMSE index for the forecasted centroids for the sequence of satellite images at times $k = 1, 2, ..., K$ is

$$RMSE_C = \sqrt{\frac{1}{K}\sum_{k=1}^{K}(C_{xk}^p - C_{xk}^m)^2 + (C_{yk}^p - C_{yk}^m)^2}. \tag{7}$$

Likewise, the RMSE for the forecasted velocity of the cloud centroid $\overline{V_k^p} = (V_{xk}^p, V_{yk}^p)$ is

$$RMSE_V = \sqrt{\frac{1}{K}\sum_{k=1}^{K}(V_{xk}^p - V_{xk}^m)^2 + (V_{yk}^p - V_{yk}^m)^2} \tag{8}$$

where $\overline{V_k^m} = (V_{xk}^m, V_{yk}^m)$ and $\overline{V_k^p} = (V_{xk}^p, V_{yk}^p)$ are the measured and predicted velocity vectors calculated from the measured and predicted centroids as defined in Eq. (4).

3   Results

3.1   Forecasting Cloud Kinetics

The training data set is composed of 8000 time series. The time series consist of 5 images, taken every 5 min, four for the inputs and one image for the output. The satellite images were taken in 625 locations at a latitude of 20.6 in Yucatan peninsula. We select these locations since they count with good solar resource, good cloudiness in the rainy season and a homogeneous topology, which provides a uniform environment to work with clouds. We consider the simplest dense and convolutional neural networks for the purpose of comparison analysis and program them ANNs in Python. Several architectures were explored providing similar results. Next, we describe the most successful we employ.

The dense neural network inputs are four vectors with components in the x-y plane corresponding to the cloud's centroid position at times $t_{n-3}, t_{n-2}, t_{n-1}, t_n$. The input layer consists of two neurons corresponding to the x and y coordinate of the centroid. The information goes through a flatten layer which converts the input set of four 2D vectors into an array of 8 components. It counts with 4 hidden layers as shown in Fig. 6a. The first three hidden layers have 15 neurons and the last one two neurons. Finally, the output layer infers the predicted vector of the cloud centroid's position at a future step in time t_{n+1}, namely 5 min ahead of time.

The convolutional neural network inputs are the four processed satellite images of 11×11 pixels. The CNN is built with 4 convolutional layers. The first three convolutional layers are built of 15 neurons, and the last one of 2 neurons. Finally, the output layer infers the predicted image of 11×11 pixels as shown in Fig. 6b.

A representative set of the evolution of cloud's centroids is shown in Fig. 7. In Fig. 7a we plot the cloud's centroid positions for the real values and the measured ones using the CNN and the DNN approaches. The horizontal plane represents the $x - y$ plane and the vertical axis corresponds to time. The blue line corresponds to the measured values and the orange and green lines correspond to the DNN and CNN respectively. Then, Fig. 7b corresponds to the evolution in the x direction, or projection in the $x - t$ plane, whereas Fig. 7c shows the dynamics in the y direction, *i.e.* in the $y - t$ plane.

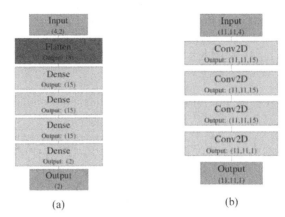

(a)   (b)

Fig. 6. Structure of forecasting ANNs. DNN and CNN are described in Fig. (a) and (b) respectively.

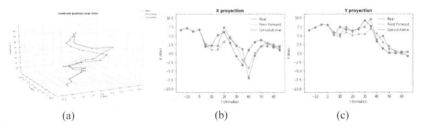

(a)   (b)   (c)

Fig. 7. Cloud centroids forecasting for one step of time ahead. (a) Evolution of cloud centroids positions in the x-y plane. Dynamics of the cloud centroids in the x and y planes are shown in figures (b) and (c) respectively.

As it is graphically shown, both approaches provide similar outcomes resulting in a good forecasting for one step ahead of time, namely 5 min ahead of time. In order to obtain a measure of the goodness of the forecasting with both techniques we compute the errors and indexes in the next subsection.

3.2 Performance Evaluation of Forecasting

In this section, we compute the forecasting error for the centroids position in each direction using Eq. (6). Prediction errors in every direction are shown in Table 1. As noted, both approaches provide very similar results, being the numerical-data approach, or the DNN, the one with smallest error.

Moreover, in Table 2, we compute the RMSE index for the cloud centroids positions, according to Eq. (7), to quantify the goodness of the accuracy prediction in both approaches. Once again, the numerical-data approach, DNNs, provide a smaller error index than the image-data approach, CNNs.

Cloud centroids velocities were also calculated using Eq. (4) in order to obtain the cloud kinetics. The RMSE index for the forecasted velocities were also computed using

Table 1. Prediction errors in the x and y components of the clouds' centroid position for each forecasting approach.

	Numerical-data approach	Image-data approach
$x-$ direction [km]	1.09	1.18
$y-$ direction [km]	1.19	1.21

Eq. (8) and shown in Table 2. Once again, we notice that the numerical-data approach provides a smaller forecasting error.

Table 2. Prediction errors in the x and y components of the clouds' centroid, and their velocities, for each forecasting approach.

RMSE	Temporal approach	Spatial approach
Cloud centroids positions [km]	3.02	3.55
Cloud centroids velocities [km/h]	36.38	43.13

Therefore, our work shows that for cloud kinetics forecasting the simplified method of calculating a cloud centroid representative of the clouds in an image and then use a DNN to forecast the cloud position at short-term provides better accuracy results than using image-data together with CNN.

4 Discussion and Conclusion

With this work, we are undertaking the development of simple, yet effective, methodologies based on Artificial Intelligence and aerospace techniques to predict cloud kinetics as a first attempt to deal with the intermittency of solar energy to compensate for electricity production. In general, the problem of weather prediction, including cloud kinetics, is very complex and clever simplifications should be made to arrive to practical and valuable solutions. In this work, we use two widely available ANN to process satellite images. On the one hand, CNN are used to directly process satellite pictures of large areas of earth surface, where clouds can be easily identified. In this method digitized land images are inputs to the CNN, which produces a new image with the prediction of the evolving cloud. Then, cloud kinetics are calculated to compare against those of the actual image. On the other hand, DNN are used to directly predict cloud kinetics from cloud kinetics numerical inputs. Then, the predicted cloud kinetics are compared against the actual cloud kinetics. Prediction errors and indexes are calculated for both approaches to quantify the prediction performance of both methodologies.

Intuitively, one would expect that an image-data approach for image forecasting would provide a more accurate result than a numerical-data approach, since the graphical method's input, which is an image, contains more information. However, it seems that for the purposes of this preliminary work, calculating the center of mass, centroid, of the cloudiness in the image, and forecasting it, provides the necessary information to obtain a good result. In order to reinforce this conclusion, one must consider using bigger images with more pixels. On the other hand, this conclusion may not be any more valid if the forecasting horizon becomes larger. So far, this result is valid for 11×11 pixel images for 5 min ahead forecasting. It would be interesting to find out the maximum size of the image and the maximum forecasting horizon for which this result still holds. Moreover, the fact that the numerical approach provides better results than the graphical one with less computer power is an advantage that should be consider as a bonus.

As future work, more classes of ANN should be used. An ad hoc one is the Recurrent Neural Network (RNN) which relies on feedback from its inputs and outputs to improve its outputs [39], they are considered to have "memory". One type of RNN which is very promising for these problems is the Long Short-Term Memory (LSTM) [40], which we are currently working with it.

Another method to solve the problem could be with finite element analysis, but we consider that the preliminary results found for the proposed numerical-data approach are promising for cloud kinetics forecasting.

This paper is product of a research project to forecast solar radiation using satellite images from the Collage Space Program of the National Autonomous University of Mexico. Future work includes the improvement of the forecast of the clouds position and their velocity to predict solar radiation [41]. In order to improve this work, we can use correction techniques for the parallax effect in the satellite vision and the computation of the clouds shadow position on earth surface [42] since this information is extremely important to precisely estimate PV power generation for a given surface and to anticipate intermittency and take action to diminish its effects. Therefore, one should rescue that the image-based approach yields good results in the right track to estimate PV power generation. Besides, a pixelated cloud image always determines unique cloud position and velocity vectors, but the inverse is not true.

Acknowledgments. This work arises from the project "Predicción del recurso solar usando imágenes satelitales para impulsar el desarrollo sostenible en comunidades aisladas con energía asequible y no contaminante" approved in the Proyecto Espacial Universitario (PEU) from UNAM. The authors wish to thank the PEU program for their support in the elaboration and publication of this work. M.B. also thanks CONACYT for her "Investigadora por México Research Position" with ID 71557.

References

1. National Renewable Energy Laboratory (NREL), Renewable Energy: An Overview. Energy Efficiency and Renewable Energy Clearinghouse. DOE/GO-102001-1102, FS175 (2001)
2. Dumka, U.C., Kosmopoulos, P.G., Ningombam, S.S., Masoom, A.: Impact of aerosol and cloud on the solar energy potential over the central gangetic Himalayan Region. Remote Sens. **13**, 3248 (2021)
3. Engeland, K., Borga, M., Creutin, J.-D., François, B., Ramos, M.-H., Vidal, J.-P.: Space-time variability of climate variables and intermittent renewable electricity production – a review. Renew. Sustain. Energy Rev. **79**, 600–617 (2017)

4. Goater, A.: Intermittent electricity generation. Parliamentary Office of Science and Technology. POSTnote, 464, May 2014
5. Denholm, P., Mai, T., Kenyon, R.W., Kroposki, B., O'Malley, M.: Inertia and the power grid: a guide without the spin. National Renewable Energy Laboratory. Technical report NREL/TP-6A20-73856 (2020)
6. Gowrisankaran, G., Reynolds, S.S., Samano, M.: Intermittency and the value of renewable energy. NBER Working Paper No. 17086 (2011)
7. Bandyopadhyay, R., Ferrero, V., Tan, X.: Coordinated operations of flexible coal and renewable energy power plants: challenges and opportunities. UNECE Energy Series No. 52 (2017)
8. McCormick, P.G., Suehrcke, H.: The effect of intermittent solar radiation on the performance of PV systems. Sol. Energy **171**, 667–674 (2018)
9. Hoff, T.E., Perez, R.: Modeling PV fleet output variability. Sol. Energy **86**(8), 2177–2189 (2012)
10. Lave, M., Kleissl, J.: Cloud speed impact on solar variability scaling - application to the wavelet variability model. Sol. Energy **91**, 11–21 (2013)
11. Escrig, H., et al.: Cloud detection, classification and motion estimation using geostationary satellite imagery for cloud cover forecast. Energy **55**, 853–859 (2013)
12. Peng, Z., Yoo, S., Yu, D., Huang, D.: Solar irradiance forecast system based on geostationary satellite. In: 2013 IEEE International Conference on Smart Grid Communications, pp. 708–713 (2013)
13. Pfister, G., McKenzie, R.L., Liley, J.B., Thomas, A., Forgan, B.W., Long, C.N.: Cloud coverage based on all-sky imaging and its impact on surface solar irradiance. J. Appl. Meteorol. **42**(10), 1421–1434 (2003)
14. Fujita, T.: Outline of a technique for precise rectification of satellite cloud photographs. The University of Chicago. Department of Geophysical Sciences. Mesoscale Research Project Paper 3 (1961)
15. Fujita, T.: Present status of cloud velocity computations from ATS-1 and ATS-3. COSPAR Space Res. **9**, 557–570 (1968)
16. Leese, J.A., Novak, C.H., Clark, B.B.: An automated technique for obtaining cloud motion from geosynchronous satellite data using cross correlation. J. Appl. Meteorol. Climatol. **10**(1), 118–132 (1971)
17. Zavialov, P.O., Grigorieva, J.V., Moller, O.O., Kostianoy, A.G., Gregoire, M.: Continuity preserving modified maximum cross-correlation technique. J. Geophys. Res. **107**(C10), 24-1–24-10 (2002)
18. Nasrabadi, N.M., Choo, C.Y.: Hopfield network for stereo vision correspondence. IEEE Trans. Neural Netw. **3**, 5–13 (1992)
19. Chang, J.Y., Lee, S.W., Horng, M.F.: Image sequence correspondence via a Hopfield neural network. Opt. Eng. **32**, 1531–1538 (1993)
20. Côté, S., Tatnall, A.R.L.: A neural network-based method for tracking features from satellite images. Int. J. Remote Sens. **16**, 3695–3701 (1995)
21. Lecun, Y., Bengio, Y.: Convolutional networks for images, speech, and time series. In: The Handbook of Brain Theory and Neural Networks, vol. 3361, pp. 255–258. MIT Press (1995)
22. Shi, M., Xie, F., Zi, Y., Yin, J.: Cloud detection of remote sensing images by deep learning. In: Proceedings of the IEEE International Geoscience and Remote Sensing Symposium, Beijing, China, pp. 701–704 (2016)
23. Ye, L., Cao, Z., Xiao, Y.: Deep cloud: ground-based cloud image categorization using deep convolutional features. IEEE Trans. Geosci. Remote Sens. **55**, 5729–5740 (2017)
24. Xu, F., Hu, C., Li, J., Plaza, A., Datcu, M.: Special focus on deep learning in remote sensing image processing. Sci. China Inf. Sci. **63**, 140300 (2020)

25. Wang, H., Klaser, A., Schmid, C., Liu, C.L.: Action recognition by dense trajectories. In: Proceedings of the IEEE Conference on Computer Vision and Pattern Recognition, USA, pp. 20–25 (2011)
26. Hewamalage, H., Bergmeir, C., Bandara, K.: Recurrent neural networks for time series forecasting: current status and future directions. Int. J. Forecast. **37**(1), 388–427 (2021)
27. Bengio, Y., Simard, P., Frasconi, P.: Learning long-term dependencies with gradient descent is difficult. IEEE Trans. Neural Netw. **5**, 157–166 (1994)
28. Srivastava, S., Lessmann, S.: A comparative study of LSTM neural networks in forecasting day-ahead global horizontal irradiance with satellite data. Sol. Energy **162**, 232–247 (2018)
29. Michael, N.E., Mishra, M., Hasan, S., Al-Durra, A.: Short-term solar power predicting model based on multi-step CNN stacked LSTM technique. Energies **15**, 2150 (2022)
30. https://www.ospo.noaa.gov/Products/imagery/archive.html
31. https://www.star.nesdis.noaa.gov/goesr/product_cp_clearskymask.php
32. Michalski, R.S., Carbonell, J.G., Mitchell, T.M.: Machine Learning: An Artificial Intelligence Approach. Springer, Heidelberg (2013)
33. Dupond, S.: A thorough review on the current advance of neural network structures. Annu. Rev. Control. **14**, 200–230 (2019)
34. Valueva, M.V., Nagornov, N.N., Lyakhov, P.A., Valuev, G.V., Chervyakov, N.I.: Application of the residue number system to reduce hardware costs of the convolutional neural network implementation. Math. Comput. Simul. **177**, 232–243 (2020)
35. Zhang, W.: Shift-invariant pattern recognition neural network and its optical architecture. In: Proceeding of Annual Conference of the Japan Society of Applied Physics (1988)
36. Misra, P., Enge, P.: Global Positioning System. Signals, Measurements and Performance. Ganga-Jamuna Press, Massachusetts (2001)
37. Diggelen, F.: GNSS accuracy: lies, damn lies, and statistics. GPS World **18**(1), 26–32 (2007)
38. Williams, R.J., Hinton, G.E., Rumelhart, D.E.: Learning representations by back-propagating errors. Nature **323**, 533–536 (1986)
39. Hochreiter, S., Schmidhuber, J.: Long short-term memory. Neural Comput. **9**(8), 1735–1780 (1997)
40. Ramírez, A., Borunda, M.: A first approach to the estimation of solar radiation using satellite images and convolutional neural networks in Mexico. Res. Comput. Sci. (2021)
41. Bieliński, T.: A parallax shift effect correction based on cloud height for geostationary satellites and radar observations. Remote Sens. **12**(3), 365 (2020)
42. Miller, S.D., Rogers, M.A., Haynes, J.M., Sengupta, M., Heidinger, A.K.: Short-term solar irradiance forecasting via satellite/model coupling. Sol. Energy **168**, 102–117 (2018)

The Role of the Number of Examples in Convolutional Neural Networks with Hebbian Learning

Fernando Aguilar-Canto[✉] and Hiram Calvo

Laboratorio de Ciencias Cognitivas Computacionales, Centro de Investigación en Computación, Instituto PolitÉcnico Nacional, Mexico, USA
{faguilarc2021,hcalvo}@cic.ipn.mx

Abstract. Both synaptic plasticity rules (the so-called Hebbian rules) and Convolutional Neural Networks are based on or inspired by well-established models of Computational Neuroscience about mammal vision. There are some theoretical advantages associated with these frameworks, including online learning in Hebbian Learning. In the case of Convolutional Neural Networks, such advantages have been translated into remarkable results in image classification in the last decade. Nevertheless, such success is not shared in Hebbian Learning. In this paper, we explore the hypothesis of the necessity of a wider dataset for the classification of mono-instantiated objects, this is, objects that can be represented in a single cluster in the feature space. By using 15 mono-instantiated classes, the Adam optimizer reaches the maximum accuracy with fewer examples but using more epochs. In comparison, Hebbian rule BCM demands more examples but keeps using real-time learning. This result is a positive answer to the principal hypothesis and enlights how Hebbian learning can find a niche in the mainstream of Deep Learning.

1 Introduction

Research conducted in the last century about vision neurobiology has allowed us to understand how this process occurs at a computational level, which eventually has led to the formulation of models of artificial neural networks with great capacities to reach high accuracy in the classification of large image datasets (Krizhevsky et al. 2012), which supposes an empirical confirmation about the validity of the development.

At this structural level, the work of Hubel and Wiesel (1962,1959) revealed the existence of neurons in the Primary Visual Cortex that process even more complex stimuli, inducing the idea of hierarchical and localist processing, which finally led to the so-called Hierarchical Model of vision (Van Essen and Maunsell 1983; Riesenhuber and Poggio 1999), which have received experimental confirmation about how visual pattern recognition emerges from Primary Visual Cortex (V1) to the Infratemporal Cortex, where complex patterns such as faces are recognized (Desimone et al. 1984; Rolls 1984).

O. Pichardo Lagunas et al. (Eds.): MICAI 2022, LNAI 13612, pp. 225–238, 2022.
https://doi.org/10.1007/978-3-031-19493-1_19

Recent evidence has questioned the hierarchical nature of visual information processing (Herzog and Clarke 2014), however, this model leaded to the formulation of the Neocognitron (Fukushima 1988), and some of these ideas appeared in the proposal of Convolutional Neural Networks (ConvNets) (LeCun et al. 1998), which could manage to achieve groundbreaking results in vision-related tasks (Krizhevsky et al. 2012; He et al. 2015), and despite the formulation of Vision Transformers, there is still the state-of-art solution in tasks with high-resolution images (Han et al. 2022).

Since the paper of LeCun et al. (1998), ConvNets use gradient-based parameter optimization and backpropagation. Nevertheless, some authors are skeptical of the idea of backpropagation in the brain (Tavanaei et al. 2019) while others assert that a similar process happens in the brain (Lillicrap et al. 2020). Instead of gradient-based learning, empirical evidence supports Hebbian learning.

The Hebbian rule was first formulated in 1949, but it did not receive experimental evidence until the 1960 decade, with the discovery of Long-Term Potentiation (Lømo 1966; Bliss and Lømo 1973). Since then, new mathematical formulations have been proposed such as the Oja rule (Oja 1982), the Bienenstock-Cooper-Munro (BCM) rule (Bienenstock et al. 1982) and the Spiking Time-Dependent Plasticity (STPD) rules Markram et al. (1997).

The Hebbian-based rules have been implemented in artificial neural networks, especially in Spiking Neural Networks (see Related work). However, the neural networks with Hebbian learning have not shown better results than traditional optimization schemes, except in simplified cases such as in Aguilar Canto and Brito-Loeza (2021), which are hard to scale to a higher number of variables. In the same paper, the authors propose several reasons why a more biologically inspired model does not reach or surpass the accuracy of the gradient-based approaches, including the following points:

1. The models of synaptic plasticity are insufficient.
2. Backpropagation and gradient ascent are consistent with biology.
3. The model of neural activity is too simple.
4. Other factors such as evolution play a bigger role.
5. The tested neural architecture is inappropriate.

In this work, we considered an additional factor: the human brain receives a great quantity of data to operate. For example, instead of receiving a single image of a specific object, it uses several close representations of the same object from different angles due to the movement of the head, body, and the object itself. In this manner, it receives many frames of the object instead of a single image. Therefore, it suggests that Hebbian learning demands larger datasets to reach a comparable performance with the gradient-based optimizers.

This paper structurates as follows: Sect. 2 is devoted to Related work; in Sect. 3 we present the Methodology and the corresponding empirical design; finally Results and Conclusions are presented in Sects. 4 and 5, respectively.

2 Related Work

The implementation of Hebbian Learning in artificial neural networks is not recent (see for example Wallis (1996) or even the Perceptron Learning Rule (Rosenblatt 1958) can be somehow considered part of the Hebbian Learning). However, not only until recent years have some authors started to consider applying Hebbian rules in Convolutional Networks or similar approaches, probably as a consequence of the hype of Deep Learning. We can classify the proposal into three clusters:

1. Spiking Neural Networks (SNNs) with convolutional layers or similar.
2. Conventional networks with hybrid learning.
3. Conventional networks with Hebbian Learning.

Subsection 2.1 is devoted to points 1 and so on. By "conventional networks" we will refer to the Non-Spiking Neural Networks. In Table 1, we present a summary of the State-of-Art.

Table 1. Summary of the recent proposals related to Hebbian-based rules in Vision-related tasks.

SNNs	Conventional networks	
	Hybrid	Pure Hebb
STDP: Cao et al. (2015); Kheradpisheh et al. (2018); Liu and Yue (2016); Kheradpisheh et al. (2018).	Adaptative Hebbian Learning: Wadhwa and Madhow (2016)	Non-convolutional: Keck et al. (2012); Holca-Lamarre et al. (2017)
Pre-defined kernels: Kheradpisheh et al. (2018); Masquelier and Thorpe (2007); Tavanaei et al. (2019); Zhao et al. (2014)	SVM final layer: layer:Wadhwa and Madhow (2016); Bahroun et al. (2017); Bahroun and Soltoggio (2017)	
Trainable kernels: Tavanaei et al. (2016 2018)	Competitive Hebbian Learning: Lagani et al. (2021a,2021b,2021c 2022)	
Hybrid approach: Panda and Roy (2016)	Transfer Learning: Magotra and Kim (2019), (2020), (2021)	
BCM: Huang et al. (2021)	Online Learning: Bahroun et al. (2017); Bahroun and Soltoggio (2017); Aguilar Canto (2020)	
	Neuromodulation: Magotra and Kim (2021); Miconi et al. (2018); Miconi (2021); Pogodin et al. (2021)	Neuromodulation: Holca-Lamarre et al. (2017)

2.1 Spiking Neural Networks with Hebbian Learning and Similar Approaches

Spiking Neural Networks are a more biologically inspired model of artificial neural networks, and thus, most authors of this approach attempt to use biologically plausible learning rules, which include Hebbian Learning, or even combined methods such as backpropagation with Hebbian rules (Burbank 2015). As a consequence, the usage of synaptic plasticity rules is more diverse than in conventional networks. Nevertheless, despite these advantages, conventional networks still show better results for most tasks, even if this gap has been shortening in recent years (Tavanaei et al. 2019).

In the case of STDP, there are some implementations in SNNs such as in Cao et al. (2015); Kheradpisheh et al. (2018) or SNNs with a hierarchical model of vision (Liu and Yue 2016). In some cases, the convolutional kernels are directly designed instead of being trainable, which is the case of operators such as the Difference of Gaussians in the first layer (Kheradpisheh et al. 2016 2018; Masquelier and Thorpe 2007; Tavanaei et al. 2019; Zhao et al. 2014). Likewise, there are spiking networks with trainable parameters in convolutional layers (Tavanaei et al. 2016 2018). In some particular cases, SNNs have achieved similar accuracy than in conventional approaches, which is the case of the work of Panda and Roy (2016), although it depends on backpropagation. Outside STPD, other learning rules such as BCM have been implemented, such as in neuromorphic hardware with memristors (Huang et al. 2021).

2.2   Conventional Networks with Hybrid Learning

The usage of non-spiking convolutional networks with Hebbian learning first appeared in papers such as Wadhwa and Madhow (2016), where the authors implement Adaptative and Discriminative Hebbian Learning with a final classification with Support Vector Machines (SVM). Since then, several articles appeared with Hebbian Learning in convolutional layers with a final SVM classification or a combination of gradient-based optimizers with Hebbian learning. The first case is represented by (Bahroun et al. 2017; Bahroun and Soltoggio 2017), where the authors used a hierarchical model similar to the ConvNets.

In the case of networks with Hebbian Learning and gradient-based optimizers, Amato et al. (2019) implemented Competitive Hebbian Learning with Stochastic Gradient Descent in different layers, reaching better results when Hebbian Learning is implemented in final or initial layers. In the same line, appeared articles such as Lagani et al. (2021b) or Lagani et al. (2021a 2022), with the usage of soft-Winner-Takes-All algorithm and Hebbian Principal Component Analysis. Competitive Hebbian Learning is implemented in Lagani et al. (2021c)

In Magotra and Kim (2019), the authors propose the usage of transfer learning with the gradient-based methods, but it does not consider online learning such as in (Bahroun et al. 2017; Bahroun and Soltoggio 2017). Following this line, appeared papers such as Magotra and Kim (2020) and Magotra and Kim (2021), which incorporates a model of neuromodulation by dopamine. Another model of neuromodulation is the *backpropamina* (Miconi et al. 2018 2020). Another proposal for incorporating Hebbian learning in ConvNets is given by Pogodin et al. (2021).

In the previous proposals, we have presents different recent advances related to Hebbian learning in Convolutional-like networks. The starting point of this research corresponds to the paper of Aguilar Canto (2020). Previously, we have mentioned the possibility of combining Hebbian Learning with gradient-based optimizers (Amato et al. 2019), applying Transfer Learning of gradient-based methods (Magotra and Kim 2019), and implementing online learning (Bahroun et al. 2017; Bahroun and Soltoggio 2017). Amato et al. (2019) suggests using Hebbian Learning in final or initial layers and gradient descent in intermediate layers. Despite biological plausibility inducing us to consider Hebbian Learning, there are other computational advantages of the Hebbian approach. One of the most important of these advantages is the online learning property, shared in most Hebbian rules, which is commonly lost when gradient-based optimizers are introduced.

One solution for the problem of balancing online learning with acceptable evaluation metrics relies on using pre-trained convolutional layers with backpropagation and using the last classification layer as re-trainable, in a Transfer Learning scheme. In this manner, since convolutional layers are already pre-trained, new categories can be added training the last layer with Hebbian Learning. One advantage of this process consists in keeping the online learning property while reaching similar accuracy to gradient-based approaches.

Even when Hebbian Learning is not mentioned, Yeo et al. (2020) used a similar framework by implementing the pre-trained convolutional network DeepLab v2 to perform semantic segmentation and use the feature vectors to classify them by using an algorithm to the Basic Hebb Rule.

2.3 Conventional Networks with Pure Hebbian Learning

Neural networks with exclusively Hebbian Learning are scarce, although some slight changes can turn previous solutions into a purely Hebbian Learning implementation, such as substituting the SVM layer with Hebbian Learning. In the case of non-convolutional architectures, there are some proposals such as the work of Keck et al. (2012) and in particular, Holca-Lamarre et al. (2017), where used dopamine and acetylcholine models to reduce the classification error, which is achieved.

2.4 Difference of This Proposal with Previous Works

In the Related work, we review two types of neural networks used in the literature: SNNs and conventional. In the first case, STDP is generally implemented whereas in the conventional networks is more common to see Adaptative or Competitive Hebbian Learning, while STDP or BCM rules are less used.

Conventional networks can still be used as biologically inspired models, since their output can be represented as a continuous version of the spiking activity, following the firing rate model example Dayan and Abbott (2001). In comparison, there still exists a gap between the spiking and conventional approach to neural networks. In 2016, for instance, Panda and Roy (2016) (a spiking proposal with backpropagation) achieved 99.1 % of classification accuracy in MNIST whereas Wadhwa and Madhow (2016) (a non-spiking approach with Hebbian Learning) reached 99.3 %. Even though this difference might not be updated or significant, it represents an example of how conventional approaches might still be useful.

As stated, the introduction of Hebbian rules such as BCM is scarce. In addition, there are a few examples where Hebbian Learning can reach the metrics of gradient-based optimizers. This knowledge gap in the state-of-art must be filled, or at least, explain what might be needed to reach or surpass the extant solutions. In this paper, we studied the role of the number of examples in a flexible custom dataset to allow the addition of data points to test the hypothesis about what might be the problems related to Hebbian Learning.

3   Methodology

As established previously, this work is based on the preliminary paper of Aguilar Canto (2020) as starting point to evaluate Hebbian Learning in Convolutional Neural Networks. In Aguilar-Canto and Calvo (2022), the authors observed some of the usages of BCM learning advantages over other plasticity rules, including the lack of necessity of using balanced data. We will describe the experimental design in this section and the theoretical foundations of the implemented algorithms.

3.1   BCM Learning Rule

A common computational problem observed in Basic Hebb and Covariance learning rules relies on the unbounded growth of the weights. If these weights are not regulated, it can lead to undesired and biased results. In addition, there is strong evidence that "weights" in biological neural networks are bounded (Dayan and Abbott 2001). In 1982, two solutions appeared: Oja (1982) rule and Bienenstock-Cooper-Munro or BCM learning rule (Bienenstock et al. 1982). The first rule adds a dynamic penalizer to the weight growth. On the other hand, the BCM rule introduces a dynamical threshold θ which determines if the synaptic activity would be depressive or potentiative. Mathematically, it is formulated with the coupled differential equations (1)-(2):

$$\tau_w \frac{d\mathbf{w}}{dt} = y\mathbf{x}(y - \theta_y), \tag{1}$$

$$\tau_\theta \frac{d\theta_y}{dt} = y^2 - \theta_y, \tag{2}$$

where $\frac{1}{\tau_w}$ is the learning rate, y is the activity of the post-synaptic neuron, $\mathbf{x}$ represents the vector of activity of pre-synaptic neurons, $\mathbf{w}$ is the weight vector, θ_y is the threshold of the neuron with activity y, whereas τ_θ is a constant that regulates the weight change.

3.2 Empirical Design

The principal hypothesis of this paper is the following:

(1) BCM (Hebbian) learning rule requires more data to reach gradient-based optimizers' accuracy in mono-instantiated. image classification.

The term "mono-instantiated" refers to the class of objects that can be represented in a single cluster in the feature space. In human vision, mono-instantiated objects do not appear in two visually different shapes. Since ConvNets are computational models of vision, two objects with different shapes are probably represented in different clusters in the feature space.

For example, the blue cotton facemasks and KN95 white facemasks are visually different image clusters and might be represented in different places in the feature space. To check this idea, we can visualize the first three entries of the feature vectors, which is the output of the penultimate layer of a ConvNet (Xception in this case, with an output of 2048 variables). Figure 1 depicts four classes, two of them are two instances of the same class of facemasks. We can observe that the class of blue facemasks and KN95 are grouped in different clusters.

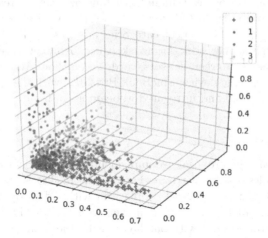

Fig. 1. Depiction of three variables of the feature vectors extracted for images of 4 classes. 2 of the classes (labels 0 and 1) represent two instances of images of facemasks. Classes 2 and 3 represent other objects. The axis represents the values of the variables of the feature vectors.

As anticipated, to verify the hypothesis, we used the proposed architecture in Aguilar Canto (2020), which is a pre-trained convolutional neural network to perform feature extraction and a final Hebbian classification layer (Fig. 2). Following the results of the paper, we used the pre-trained network Xception (Chollet 2017).

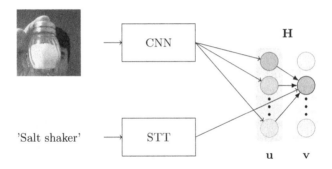

Fig. 2. Schematic representation of the architecture used in Aguilar Canto (2020) and adapted to this task. A convolutional neural network (CNN) performs feature extraction and outputs the vector $\mathbf{u}$, whereas a supervised layer $\mathbf{v}$ implements Hebbian Learning and receives inputs of a Speech-to-Text system as labels.

The training design in this case differed from offline datasets. In these experiments, we presented an object to the webcam and the labels by voice (using the Apple's default Speech-to-Text). While voice recognition is not part of the presented problem, it provides a human-machine interface in real-time. Instead of one processed frame by introduced label, we use five frames to increase the available data. A total of 15 object categories are presented, which are the following: banana, salt shaker, sock, facemask, sauce, oximeter, case, thermometer, hat, medicine, glasses, marker, scissors, card, and a shoe. All experiments were implemented in a specific device: MacBook Pro 2012, with the operative system MacOS Catalina 10.15.6 and intregated webcam as an input.

3.3   Evaluation

In order to evaluate the proposal, we implemented the metric accuracy by using 225 testing examples equally distributed among the 15 classes. All feature vectors were stored to perform a principal comparison with Adam optimizer (Kingma and Ba 2015), one of the most used in neural networks. This optimizer was included in a neural network with one layer, using the same architecture as the Hebbian layer. Finally, we evaluated the execution time with other optimizers.

4   Results

BCM learning rule required a total of 450 examples to achieve 100 % of accuracy in the testing set (see Fig. 3). In comparison, Adam required 225 images to achieve a perfect classification accuracy. This represents an empirical confirmation of hypothesis (1).

On the other hand, this empirical design only considered a few classes. It would be undesired to need an intractable number of cases for larger datasets, for instance, 1000 categories such as Imagenet. Figure 4 depicts the number of

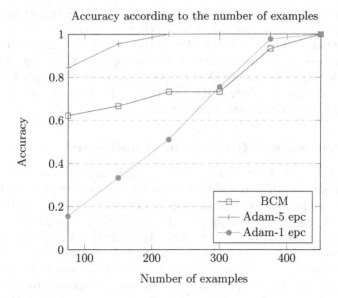

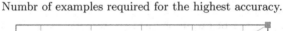

Fig. 3. Accuracy improvement according to the provided number of examples. The red line stands for the accuracy of the Adam optimizer with five epochs, the green line represents the accuracy of Adam with one epoch, whereas the blue line stands for the accuracy of the BCM learning rule. (Color figure online)

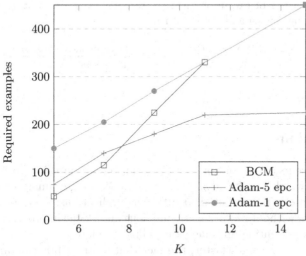

Fig. 4. Number of examples required to achieve 100 % of accuracy by the number of classes (K). The red line stands for Adam with 5 epochs, the green line represents Adam with a single epoch, whereas the blue line stands for the BCM learning rule. (Color figure online)

examples needed to reach the maximum accuracy in the testing set according to the number of classes. In the case of BCM, the distribution of the data points is linear (Rainbow test, $p = 0.3447310$), therefore, the complexity of the number of examples needed by the number of classes might be linear. By using linear regression, we estimate $41.58784X - 156.92568$ as the best fit line (X represents the number of classes). Thus, in the case of $X = 1000$ classes, we can estimate 41431 as the number of required examples.

4.1   Comparison with Gradient-Based Optimizers

Even though the database used is relatively small and we only focus on mono-instantiated images, this work contributes evidence about the importance of the number of examples for the correct usage of Hebbian rules such as BCM. In this case, the results are directly compared with gradient-based optimizers, which are the most widely used in neural networks. Since all the selected optimizers were able to classify all the samples in the testing set, we perform the comparison with the execution time to verify that the usage of Hebbian learning is indeed more efficient. The tested optimizers were Adam, RMSprop, Stochastic Gradient Descent, Nesterov Adam, Follow The Regularized Leader (McMahan et al. 2013), Adadelta, Adagrad, and Adamax. Table 2 summarizes the comparison in execution time with common gradient-based optimizers. As we can see, the BCM learning rule is about 2 million times more efficient than all gradient-based optimizers.

Table 2. Comparison of execution time (in seconds) with different gradient-based optimizers using one epoch and the BCM rule.

BCM	Adam	RMSprop	SGD	NAdam	FTRL	Adadelta	Adagrad	Adamax
9.536×10^{-7}	1.704	1.742	3.166	2.678	2.129	3.685	2.107	3.852

5   Conclusions

This paper presents an evaluation of a Convolutional Neural Network with Hebbian Learning, which has the advantage of online learning of image classification. Such advantage can be exploited in different applications, such as the case of transfer learning without requiring any previous knowledge in programming since it only requires presenting an image and telling the label.

Despite Adam converges faster, the fact that a larger but tractable dataset allows BCM to reach the accuracy of Adam is, in general terms, a hopeful indicator, since BCM can perform real-time learning, without demanding to store data. In addition, a time-based comparison yields a much better scenario for Hebbian-based rules. Moreover, we estimated that the distribution of required examples to reach the highest accuracy by the number of classes is linear. Therefore, it is possible to escalate the addition of new classes. For instance, we estimate that for 1000 classes we will demand 41431 examples. Nevertheless, although these estimations are helpful, with a higher number of classes transfer learning might not work at all, even with gradient-based optimizers.

Finally, the training procedure differs from the usual scheme of data collection and learning with the dataset. In the Hebbian case, the learning process begins with data collection instead of using a fixed dataset, as implemented in Aguilar Canto (2020). This study suggests that better results can be achieved with Hebbian learning if the learning procedure is online. One explanation of this observation is that in this online process, the experimenter shows the appropriate examples to maximize data diversity and reduce classification errors. While it can introduce a bias, it seems that the experimenter plays a role in the learning process. If this procedure is more closely related to the learning process that humans experiment with, it might also be useful for machines.

5.1 Further Research

For now, we have presented a relatively small and somehow ideal case by presenting mono-instantiated classes. For multi-instantiated classes, since it presents multiple clusters, it seems convenient to add another layer of unsupervised classification, which can be performed with Hebbian rules (such as the Kohonen self-organizing maps). However, training an additional layer might demand even more data, although such data might not be labeled. Moreover, other ideas such as the inclusion of neurotransmitters models can help to reduce the number of required resources in terms of time and number of examples.

References

Aguilar Canto, F., Brito-Loeza, C.: El potencial del aprendizaje hebbiano en la clasificación supervisada. Boletín de la Sociedad Mexicana de Computación Científica y sus Aplicaciones (2021)

Aguilar-Canto, F., Calvo, H.: A hebbian approach to non-spatial prelinguistic reasoning. Brain Sci. **12**(2), 281 (2022)

Aguilar Canto, F.J.: Convolutional neural networks with hebbian-based rules in online transfer learning. In: Martínez-Villaseñor, L., Herrera-Alcántara, O., Ponce, H., Castro-Espinoza, F.A. (eds.) MICAI 2020. LNCS (LNAI), vol. 12468, pp. 35–49. Springer, Cham (2020). https://doi.org/10.1007/978-3-030-60884-2_3

Amato, G., Carrara, F., Falchi, F., Gennaro, C., Lagani, G.: Hebbian learning meets deep convolutional neural networks. In: Ricci, E., Rota Bulò, S., Snoek, C., Lanz, O., Messelodi, S., Sebe, N. (eds.) ICIAP 2019. LNCS, vol. 11751, pp. 324–334. Springer, Cham (2019). https://doi.org/10.1007/978-3-030-30642-7_29

Bahroun, Y., Hunsicker, E., Soltoggio, A.: Building efficient deep hebbian networks for image classification tasks. In: Lintas, A., Rovetta, S., Verschure, P.F.M.J., Villa, A.E.P. (eds.) ICANN 2017. LNCS, vol. 10613, pp. 364–372. Springer, Cham (2017). https://doi.org/10.1007/978-3-319-68600-4_42

Bahroun, Y., Soltoggio, A.: Online representation learning with single and multi-layer hebbian networks for image classification. In: Lintas, A., Rovetta, S., Verschure, P.F.M.J., Villa, A.E.P. (eds.) ICANN 2017. LNCS, vol. 10613, pp. 354–363. Springer, Cham (2017). https://doi.org/10.1007/978-3-319-68600-4_41

Bienenstock, E.L., Cooper, L.N., Munro, P.W.: Theory for the development of neuron selectivity: orientation specificity and binocular interaction in visual cortex. J. Neurosci. **2**(1), 32–48 (1982)

Bliss, T.V., Lømo, T.: Long-lasting potentiation of synaptic transmission in the dentate area of the anaesthetized rabbit following stimulation of the perforant path. J. Physiol. **232**(2), 331–356 (1973)

Burbank, K.S.: Mirrored STDP implements autoencoder learning in a network of spiking neurons. PLoS Comput. Biol. **11**(12), e1004566 (2015)

Cao, Y., Chen, Y., Khosla, D.: Spiking deep convolutional neural networks for energy-efficient object recognition. Int. J. Comput. Vision **113**(1), 54–66 (2015)

Chollet, F.: Xception: deep learning with depthwise separable convolutions. In Proceedings of the IEEE Conference on Computer Vision and Pattern Recognition, pp. 1251–1258 (2017)

Dayan, P., Abbott, L.F.: Theoretical neuroscience: computational and mathematical modeling of neural systems (2001)

Desimone, R., Albright, T.D., Gross, C.G., Bruce, C.: Stimulus-selective properties of inferior temporal neurons in the macaque. J. Neurosci. **4**(8), 2051–2062 (1984)

Fukushima, K.: Neocognitron: a hierarchical neural network capable of visual pattern recognition. Neural Netw. **1**(2), 119–130 (1988)

Han, K., et al.: A survey on vision transformer. In: IEEE Transactions on Pattern Analysis and Machine Intelligence (2022)

He, K., Zhang, X., Ren, S., and Sun, J.: Delving deep into rectifiers: Surpassing human-level performance on imageNet classification. In: Proceedings of the IEEE international conference on computer vision, pp. 1026–1034 (2015)

Herzog, M.H., Clarke, A.M.: Why vision is not both hierarchical and feedforward. Front. Comput. Neurosci. **8**, 135 (2014)

Holca-Lamarre, R., Lücke, J., Obermayer, K.: Models of acetylcholine and dopamine signals differentially improve neural representations. Front. Comput. Neurosci. **11**, 54 (2017)

Huang, Y., Liu, J., Harkin, J., McDaid, L., Luo, Y.: An memristor-based synapse implementation using BCM learning rule. Neurocomputing **423**, 336–342 (2021)

Keck, C., Savin, C., Lücke, J.: Feedforward inhibition and synaptic scaling-two sides of the same coin? PLoS Comput. Biol. **8**(3), e1002432 (2012)

Kheradpisheh, S.R., Ganjtabesh, M., Masquelier, T.: Bio-inspired unsupervised learning of visual features leads to robust invariant object recognition. Neurocomputing **205**, 382–392 (2016)

Kheradpisheh, S.R., Ganjtabesh, M., Thorpe, S.J., Masquelier, T.: STDP-based spiking deep convolutional neural networks for object recognition. Neural Netw. **99**, 56–67 (2018)

Kingma, D.P., Ba, J.: Adam: a method for stochastic optimization. In 3rd International Conference for Learning Representations, San Diego (2015)

Krizhevsky, A., Sutskever, I., Hinton, G.E.: Imagenet classification with deep convolutional neural networks. In: Advances in Neural Information Processing Systems 25 (2012)

Lagani, G., Falchi, F., Gennaro, C., Amato, G.: Evaluating hebbian learning in a semi-supervised setting. In: LOD 2021. LNCS, vol. 13164, pp. 365–379. Springer, cham (2021). https://doi.org/10.1007/978-3-030-95470-3_28

Lagani, G., Falchi, F., Gennaro, C., Amato, G.: Hebbian semi-supervised learning in a sample efficiency setting. Neural Netw. **143**, 719–731 (2021)

Lagani, G., Falchi, F., Gennaro, C., Amato, G.: Training convolutional neural networks with competitive hebbian learning approaches. In: LOD 2021. LNCS, vol. 13163, pp. 25–40. Springer, cham (2021). https://doi.org/10.1007/978-3-030-95467-3_2

Lagani, G., Falchi, F., Gennaro, C., Amato, G.: Comparing the performance of hebbian against backpropagation learning using convolutional neural networks. In: Neural Computing and Applications, pp. 1–17 (2022)

LeCun, Y., Bottou, L., Bengio, Y., Haffner, P.: Gradient-based learning applied to document recognition. Proc. IEEE **86**(11), 2278–2324 (1998)

Lillicrap, T.P., Santoro, A., Marris, L., Akerman, C.J., Hinton, G.: Backpropagation and the brain. Nat. Rev. Neurosci. **21**(6), 335–346 (2020)

Liu, D., Yue, S.: Visual pattern recognition using unsupervised spike timing dependent plasticity learning. In 2016 International Joint Conference on Neural Networks (IJCNN), pp. 285–292. IEEE (2016)

Lømo, T.: Frequency potentiation of excitatory synaptic activity in dentate area of hippocampal formation. In: Acta Physiologica Scandinavica, p. 128. Blackwell Science Ltd. Po. Box 88, Osney Mead, Oxford Ox2 0ne, Oxon, England (1966)

Magotra, A., Kim, J.: Transfer learning for image classification using hebbian plasticity principles. In: Proceedings of the 2019 3rd International Conference on Computer Science and Artificial Intelligence, pp. 233–238 (2019)

Magotra, A., Kim, J.: Improvement of heterogeneous transfer learning efficiency by using hebbian learning principle. Appl. Sci. **10**(16), 5631 (2020)

Magotra, A., Kim, J.: Neuromodulated dopamine plastic networks for heterogeneous transfer learning with hebbian principle. Symmetry **13**(8), 1344 (2021)

Markram, H., Lübke, J., Frotscher, M., Sakmann, B.: Regulation of synaptic efficacy by coincidence of postsynaptic aps and EPSPs. Science **275**(5297), 213–215 (1997)

Masquelier, T., Thorpe, S.J.: Unsupervised learning of visual features through spike timing dependent plasticity. PLoS Comput. Biol. **3**(2), e31 (2007)

McMahan, H.B., et al.: Ad click prediction: a view from the trenches. In: Proceedings of the 19th ACM SIGKDD international conference on Knowledge discovery and data mining, pp. 1222–1230 (2013)

Miconi, T.: Hebbian learning with gradientes: hebbian convolutional neural networks with modern deep learning frameworks. arXiv preprint arXiv:2107.01729

Miconi, T., Rawal, A., Clune, J., Stanley, K.O.: Backpropamine: training self-modifying neural networks with differentiable neuromodulated plasticity. arXiv preprint arXiv:2002.10585

Miconi, T., Stanley, K., Clune, J.: Differentiable plasticity: training plastic neural networks with backpropagation. In: International Conference on Machine Learning, pp. 3559–3568. PMLR (2018)

Oja, E.: A simplified neuron model as a principal component analyzer. J. Math. Biol. **15**(3), 267–273 (1982)

Panda, P., Roy, K.: Unsupervised regenerative learning of hierarchical features in spiking deep networks for object recognition. In: 2016 International Joint Conference on Neural Networks (IJCNN), pp. 299–306. IEEE (2016)

Pogodin, R., Mehta, Y., Lillicrap, T., Latham, P.: Towards biologically plausible convolutional networks. In: Advances in Neural Information Processing Systems 34 (2021)

Riesenhuber, M., Poggio, T.: Hierarchical models of object recognition in cortex. Nat. Neurosci. **2**(11), 1019–1025 (1999)

Rolls, E.: Neurons in the cortex of the temporal lobe and in the amygdala of the monkey with responses selective for faces. Hum. Neurobiol. **3**(4), 209–222 (1984)

Rosenblatt, F.: The perceptron: a probabilistic model for information storage and organization in the brain. Psychol. Rev. **65**(6), 386 (1958)

Tavanaei, A., Ghodrati, M., Kheradpisheh, S.R., Masquelier, T., Maida, A.: Deep learning in spiking neural networks. Neural Netw. **111**, 47–63 (2019)

Tavanaei, A., Masquelier, T., Maida, A.: Representation learning using event-based STDP. Neural Netw. **105**, 294–303 (2018)

Tavanaei, A., Masquelier, T., Maida, A.S.: Acquisition of visual features through probabilistic spike-timing-dependent plasticity. In: 2016 International Joint Conference on Neural Networks (IJCNN), pp. 307–314. IEEE (2016)

Van Essen, D.C., Maunsell, J.H.: Hierarchical organization and functional streams in the visual cortex. Trends Neurosci. **6**, 370–375 (1983)

Wadhwa, A., Madhow, U.: Bottom-up deep learning using the hebbian principle (2016)

Wallis, G.: Using spatio-temporal correlations to learn invariant object recognition. Neural Netw. **9**(9), 1513–1519 (1996)

Yeo, W.-H., Heo, Y.-J., Choi, Y.-J., Kim, B.-G.: Place classification algorithm based on semantic segmented objects. Appl. Sci. **10**(24), 9069 (2020)

Zhao, B., Ding, R., Chen, S., Linares-Barranco, B., Tang, H.: Feedforward categorization on AER motion events using cortex-like features in a spiking neural network. IEEE Trans. Neural Netw. Learn. Syst. **26**(9), 1963–1978 (2014)

Hubel, D.H., Wiesel, T.N.: Receptive fields of single neurones in the cat's striate cortex. J. Physiol. **148**(3), 574 (1959). Wiley-Blackwell

Hubel, D.H., Wiesel, T.N.: Receptive fields, binocular interaction and functional architecture in the cat's visual cortex. J. Physiol. **160**(1), 106 (1962). Wiley-Blackwell

Image Processing and Pattern Recognition

Vision-Based Gesture Recognition for Smart Light Switching

Hiram Olivera-García⬥, Jorge Cervantes-Ojeda⬥,
and María C. Gómez-Fuentes(✉) ⬥

Universidad Autónoma Metropolitana, Vasco de Quiroga 4871, 05348 México City, Mexico
hiram.oligar@gmail.com, {jcervantes,mgomez}@cua.uam.mx

Abstract. Detecting human gestures is important in many areas for humans. The creation of new technologies and methods to simplify the creation of such sensors is important for their rapid and cheap implementation in new applications. We used a Convolutional Neural Network for the visual recognition of a hand or a wand signal and tested it by switching on/off a normal lamp. By taking the difference between two contiguous images from a single video file and processing them to get one filtered image as the CNN input, we simplified the collection of samples to train the neural network. In this way, the images can be small enough to considerably speed up the system throughput. We added a redundancy layer to increase the robustness of the system to confusing signals and obtained 100% accuracy. We also achieved good system performance under different lighting conditions without specifically training the neural network for this.

Keywords: Smart switch · Static gesture detector · CNN for computer vision

1 Introduction

The fact that nowadays the human interaction with some devices can occur in various ways makes it possible for disabled people to operate these devices too. Here we explain how, through a Convolutional Neural Network (CNN), we achieved an efficient gesture recognition system to switch on/off a normal lamp without the need to talk, touch or using a cell phone and without the need of an internet connection.

The so-called *smart lights* have as their main feature that they can be controlled remotely, for instance, with a motion sensor. Magic lights have, additionally, advanced features like controlling brightness, color, temperature, timer and more. Smart lights can be controlled from a cell phone app, by touching them, with a clap or with voice. However, there are people who are hearing impaired, who can't communicate orally or people who can't clap their hands for some reason and those who have difficulty for moving or for handling a cell phone.

Inclusion of disabled people is a current trend. With our proposed solution, the user can switch on/off a normal lamp with a hand (or some other body part) signal or with some object (a wand for instance), which offers an alternative to people unable to use the other options. Furthermore, our solution can be used by anyone else too.

O. Pichardo Lagunas et al. (Eds.): MICAI 2022, LNAI 13612, pp. 241–248, 2022.
https://doi.org/10.1007/978-3-031-19493-1_20

The main contributions of this work are: the simplified method we use to train the CNN, the high throughput of the resulting system, its perfect effectiveness and its very high efficiency.

The structure of the paper is as follows. In Sect. 2 we mention recent works related to gesture recognition in the computer vision area. In Sect. 3 we describe the applied methodology for gesture recognition and lamp switch control. Section 4 has the results, and Sect. 5 has our conclusions.

2 Background

Gesture recognition techniques can be divided into vision-based and sensor-based techniques. Different kinds of gesture recognition systems are applied to many real applications that use human-machine interface [1]. CNNs are one of the most widely used deep learning architectures in computer vision [2]. Image classification is the basis for computer vision tasks such as localization, detection and segmentation. These tasks have many applications in practice. Convolutional layers in CNNs are used to extract the image features and, once extracted and passed through a pooling (subsampling) layer, a Fully Connected Feed Forward Network is fed to obtain the desired outputs [2, 3].

Within the computer vision area, gesture recognition is an important research area in HCI systems [4, 5]. Vision-based hand gesture recognition systems are widely used in communication through hand sign language [4, 5, 6, 7] and other human-computer interaction systems, like the one reviewed in [8].

Gesture recognition systems can also be divided into static or dynamic. With static recognition, only one input image is required to be processed, while dynamic recognition requires processing image sequences and more complex gesture recognition approaches. Hence, static recognition has a lower computational cost [7]. Here we use a CNN for the recognition of a hand signal or a wand signal to switch on/off a normal lamp. With our approach, we perform a semi-static gesture recognition by taking two images from a video stream and process them to get one reduced image as the CNN input. With this, we simplified the acquisition to training data for the CNN. In addition, the processed image that we get can be small enough to improve the system performance.

3 Applied Methodology for Gesture Recognition and Lamp on/off Control

We used a camera as a gesture sensor. We feed the CNN input with processed camera images, and the CNN output was connected to a normal lamp through a USB device. This configuration is shown in Fig. 1.

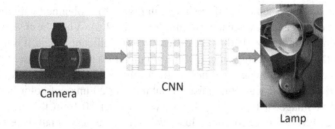

Fig. 1. System configuration overview

3.1 Actuator

We used a single bulb table lamp with its own switch. We cut the cable of the lamp and connected it with a USB relay that can be controlled from the computer. The lamp switch was kept in the on position since the current flow is controlled by the relay.

3.2 The Sensor and Image Processing

Images were obtained with a digital camera. We obtained the camera information and process it with the OpenCV library for Python. An image is represented as a matrix of pixels. Each pixel of an image is represented as a three-dimensional array: horizontal, vertical and color brightness for green, red and blue.

If we used all the information provided by the camera to train the CNN, we would have over-fitting, which would cause the system to fail with slight conditions changes such as background, brightness or moving the camera. So, in order to avoid over-fitting and to obtain information that is easier to process for the CNN, we simplified the camera images with the procedure described below and illustrated in Fig. 2.

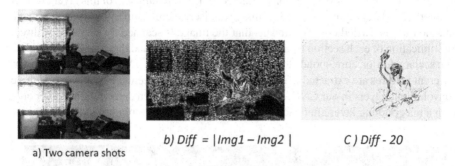

a) Two camera shots

b) Diff = | Img1 – Img2 |

C) Diff - 20

Fig. 2. Image processing

- The first step of the image processing is to take two images with a small-time difference between the shots, as it is shown in Fig. 2. a).

- For the second step, each pixel of the image in Fig. 2. b) is obtained with the absolute value of the difference between the two images in Fig. 2. a). When the absolute value of this difference is large (>20), then the difference is significant, that is, it is information indicating that there was movement, while small values represent noise. In Fig. 2. b) it can be seen that there is a lot of noise, that is, unwanted additional information.
- In the third step, we discard the noise by subtracting 20 units of color brightness to each pixel in image of Fig. 2. b), that is, we subtract 20 from the green level, 20 from the red level and 20 from the blue level. Thus, the very small differences were converted into gray tones (negative numbers become numbers close to 255, the highest brightness) and we obtained an image that only shows the significant differences, as it is shown in Fig. 2. c).

With this procedure there is no need to have a high-resolution image to detect significant information so we were able to reduce the image size to a 360×180 pixel matrix, which sped up both its processing and the CNN training.

3.3 Controller: Convolutional Neural Network

The CNN operates on a computer which has the lamp connected via USB. The matrix of the image, processed according to the procedure of Sect. 3.1, is the input of the CNN.

As it can be seen in Fig. 1, the CNN has two mutually exclusive outputs: (*a*) turn the lamp on/off and (*b*) do nothing. A positive signal in output (*a*) indicates a trigger action (turn on/off the light), and a positive signal in output (b) means that there should be no trigger action. With two outputs we get a more robust training because a positive signal in the output (a) must be reinforced with a negative signal in output (*b*) and vice versa.

Convolutional Neural Network Configuration
The convolutional layer of a CNN is the one that takes the most computational effort. It has a set of feature maps with neurons arranged in it. The parameters of this layer are a set of filters [2]. By applying filters to an image, a discrete convolution between the image and the filter is carried out. This means that the image is scanned by sections. A direct multiplication of each section by a matrix (the filter) is made and these results are added. The scalar addition corresponds to a pixel of the filtered image. With each applied filter, different features are extracted from the image. As it can be seen in Fig. 3, we used three convolutional layers in our CNN. We applied 30 filters on each convolutional layer and, with a max pooling layer after each convolutional layer, the resolution of the 30 filtered

```
model = models.Sequential()
model.add(layers.Conv2D(30, (3, 3), activation='relu', input_shape=(180, 320, 3)))
model.add(layers.MaxPooling2D((2, 2)))
model.add(layers.Conv2D(30, (3, 3), activation='relu'))
model.add(layers.MaxPooling2D((2, 2)))
model.add(layers.Conv2D(30, (3, 3), activation='relu'))
model.add(layers.MaxPooling2D((2, 2)))
model.add(layers.Flatten())
model.add(layers.Dense(10, activation='relu'))
model.add(layers.Dense(2, activation='softmax'))
```

Fig. 3. CNN configuration with tensorflow.

images was reduced (see Fig. 4). After that, with the flattening layer, we obtained the input vector to a fully connected Feed Forward Neural Network of two layers with two outputs, one for the positive detection signals and one for the negative ones.

```
Model: "sequential"

Layer (type)                 Output Shape              Param #
=================================================================
conv2d (Conv2D)              (None, 178, 318, 30)      840

max_pooling2d (MaxPooling2D) (None, 89, 159, 30)       0

conv2d_1 (Conv2D)            (None, 87, 157, 30)       8130

max_pooling2d_1 (MaxPooling2 (None, 43, 78, 30)        0

conv2d_2 (Conv2D)            (None, 41, 76, 30)        8130

max_pooling2d_2 (MaxPooling2 (None, 20, 38, 30)        0

flatten (Flatten)            (None, 22800)             0

dense (Dense)                (None, 10)                228010

dense_1 (Dense)              (None, 2)                 22
=================================================================
Total params: 245,132
Trainable params: 245,132
Non-trainable params: 0
```

Fig. 4. CNN layer dimensions and their number of parameter in tensorflow.

Supervised Training

The CNN learns from two sets of training images, one of the sets contains the images that must be detected as positive signals to turn on/off the light while the other is a set of images with negative signals. The training images were obtained from two videos, one with the subject moving around the room while giving a positive signal and another one in which the subject does not make any signal. This conditioned the CNN to operate mainly with the distances from the person to the camera with which it was trained, but it can also be trained to work with different distances.

We ran 6 training iterations (epochs) of the Adam optimizer with the parameters recommended by [9] 50 times back to back, randomizing starting points every time and choosing the best resulting configuration. Training and validation accuracies during the training process can be seen in Fig. 5.

Implementation Details

The experiments were performed on a single PC with Windows 10 Pro 21H1, an AMD Ryzen 7 1700 8 core CPU @ 3.50 GHz, 16 GB in RAM, and an NVIDIA GeForce GTX 1660 SUPER GPU with 1408 CUDA cores and 6 GB of GDDR6 RAM. The architectures were implemented in Keras [10] with Tensorflow 1.14.0 [11] as a backend called from the Python 3.9.4 interpreter.

Additional Processing at the Controller

To increase the robustness of the system, which is the effectiveness that the user experiences, a controller was introduced that records the last 10 network outputs. As shown in

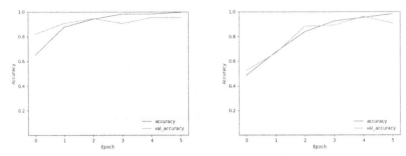

Fig. 5. Neural network effectiveness during the training process (two different cases). It shows training accuracy and validation accuracy.

Fig. 6 a), 1 means a positive signal, that is, an indication to turn the light on/off. If few positive signals are registered, then they are ignored and the on/off action will only be performed when 6 or more positive signals out of the 10 are registered as shown in Fig. 6 b). This allows the system to be robust against confusing signals and inter-signal noise. After a successful detection of a trigger, a 2 s idle time is forced to prevent consecutive triggers with a single gesture.

```
[0, 0, 0, 0, 0, 0, 0, 0, 0, 0]: -
[0, 0, 0, 0, 0, 0, 0, 0, 0, 0]: -
[0, 0, 0, 0, 0, 0, 0, 0, 0, 0]: -
[0, 0, 0, 0, 0, 0, 0, 0, 0, 0]: -
[0, 0, 0, 0, 0, 0, 1, 1, 0, 0]: -        [0, 0, 0, 0, 0, 0, 0, 0, 0, 0]: -
[0, 0, 0, 0, 0, 0, 1, 1, 0, 0]: -        [0, 0, 0, 0, 0, 0, 0, 0, 0, 1]: -
[0, 0, 0, 0, 0, 1, 1, 0, 0, 0]: -        [0, 0, 0, 0, 0, 0, 0, 0, 1, 1]: -
[0, 0, 0, 1, 1, 0, 0, 0, 0, 0]: -        [0, 0, 0, 0, 0, 0, 0, 1, 1, 1]: -
[0, 0, 1, 1, 0, 0, 0, 0, 0, 0]: -        [0, 0, 0, 0, 0, 0, 1, 1, 1, 1]: -
[0, 1, 1, 0, 0, 0, 0, 0, 0, 0]: -        [0, 0, 0, 0, 0, 1, 1, 1, 1, 1]: -
[1, 1, 0, 0, 0, 0, 0, 0, 0, 0]: -        [0, 0, 0, 0, 1, 1, 1, 1, 1, 1]: Toggle Lights
```

a) Only two positives   b) Six positives

Fig. 6. Necessary conditions to toggle the switch. There must be at least 6 positive signal detections in the last 10 outputs.

4   Results

The user can control a lamp by a pointing signal, either with a hand, or an object such as a wand. This allows users with different abilities to use the system.

As it is shown in Fig. 7, the system is resilient to confusing signals. In Fig. 7 a) the lamp turns on with a clear signal, while in Fig. 7 b) the lamp does not change state with a confusing signal.

Fig. 7. The system is robust to confusing signals.

In images of Fig. 8 it is shown that the change in the lamp state can be triggered by a hand or a wand signal (if trained accordingly).

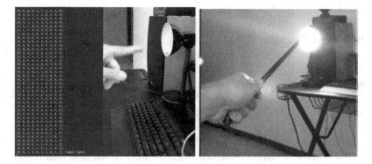

Fig. 8. The change in the lamp state can be triggered by a hand or a wand signal.

The accuracy obtained while training was 97.8% but it improved to 100% when the additional processing at the controller was used. For a classification system to be considered to work in real time, it should return a response in less than 300 ms after the execution of the gesture finishes [12]. The neural network can produce 30 outputs per second. To collect at least 6 positive outputs, it takes 0.2 s.

5 Conclusions

CNNs can solve very complex problems due to their high generalization capabilities, this makes them very useful for performing image recognition tasks. Taking advantage of the ability of a CNN to detect gestures, we used a digital camera, a CNN and a relay with usb connection to control a normal lamp.

We implemented a system that works with very small images (360 × 180) and obtained real-time processing with high recognition precision.

"A typical disadvantage of traditional static gesture recognition methods is that they are not robust to the recognition performance under complex background and lighting conditions" [6]. With our approach, the non-moving background almost vanishes after the images are processed and it is also clearly separated from the true signal, which filters out different lighting conditions as well. Even at night and with the light off the system works well.

Another obtained advantage is that the low resolution of the images processed as in Sect. 3.1, allows our CNN to work well with different users, since it does not take into account the face features or the person's complexion.

Machine learning systems can be applied to intelligently automate simple home functions, resulting in improved accessibility of these functions. With our developed system we a user can turn a lamp on and off without having to activate a switch, and without using the voice, clapping or a cell phone. This results especially favorable for disabled people.

The next step will be to use an Arduino device instead of a computer and extend it to control different accessories, appliances and even some parts of a house such as doors and windows. Another extension is to include multiple gestures detection.

References

1. Chen, R.C., Dewi, C., Zhang, W.W., Liu, J.M., Huang, S.W.: Integrating gesture control board and image recognition for gesture recognition based on deep learning. Int. J. Appl. Sci. Eng. **17**(3), 237–248 (2020)
2. Aloysius, N., Geetha M.: A review on deep convolutional neural networks. In: 2017 International Conference on Communication and Signal Processing (ICCSP), pp. 0588–0592 (2017) https://doi.org/10.1109/ICCSP.2017.8286426
3. Rawat, W., Wang, Z.: Deep convolutional neural networks for image classification: a comprehensive review. Neural Comput. **29**(9), 2352–2449 (2017)
4. Areeb, Q.M., Maryam, M.N., Alroobaea, R., Anwer, F.: Helping hearing-impaired in emergency situations: a deep learning-based approach. IEEE Access **10**, 8502–8517 (2022)
5. Chakraborty, B.K., Sarma, D., Bhuyan, M.K., MacDorman, K.F.: Review of constraints on vision-based gesture recognition for human–computer interaction. IET Comput. Vision **12**(1), 3–15 (2018)
6. Xie, B., He, X., Li, Y.: RGB-D static gesture recognition based on convolutional neural network. J. Eng. **2018**(16), 1515–1520 (2018)
7. Pinto, R.F., Borges, C.D.B., Almeida, A.M.A., Paula, I.C.: Static hand gesture recognition based on convolutional neural networks. J. Electr. Comput. Eng. **2019**, 1–12 (2019)
8. Oudah, M., Al-Naji, A., Chahl, J.. Hand gesture recognition based on computer vision: a review of techniques. J. Imaging **6**(8), 73 (2020)
9. Kingma, D.P., Ba, J.: Adam: a method for stochastic optimization. In: 3rd International Conference on Learning Representations (ICLR), San Diego, USA (2015)
10. Chollet, F., et al.: Keras (2015). https://github.com/fchollet/keras
11. Abadi M.: TensorFlow: large-scale machine learning on heterogeneous systems (2015). https://www.tensorflow.org/
12. Benalcázar, M.E., Motoche, C., Zea, J.A., Jaramillo, A.G., Anchundia, C.E., Zambrano, P., Pérez, M.: Real-time hand gesture recognition using the MYO armband and muscle activity detection. In: 2017 IEEE Second Ecuador Technical Chapters Meeting (ETCM), pp. 1–6. IEEE, October 2017

On the Generalization Capabilities of FSL Methods Through Domain Adaptation: A Case Study in Endoscopic Kidney Stone Image Classification

Mauricio Mendez-Ruiz[1], Francisco Lopez-Tiro[1,5(✉)], Daniel Flores-Araiza[1],
Jonathan El-Beze[3], Gilberto Ochoa-Ruiz[1,2], Miguel Gonzalez-Mendoza[1],
Jacques Hubert[3], Andres Mendez-Vazquez[4], and Christian Daul[5]

[1] School of Engineering and Sciences, Tecnologico de Monterrey, Monterrey, Mexico
a01799045@tec.mx
[2] Institute of Advanced Materials for Sustainable Manufacturing, Tecnologico de
Monterrey, Monterrey, Mexico
[3] CHU Nancy, Service d'urologie de Brabois, 54511 Nancy, France
[4] Centro de Investigación y de Estudios Avanzados del Instituto Politécnico
Nacional, Mexico City, Mexico
[5] CRAN (UMR 7039), Université de Lorraine and CNRS, 2 avenue de la Forêt de
Haye, 54518 Vandœuvre-lès-Nancy Cedex, France

Abstract. Deep learning has shown great promise in diverse areas
of computer vision, such as image classification, object detection and
semantic segmentation, among many others. However, as it has been
repeatedly demonstrated, deep learning methods trained on a dataset
do not generalize well to datasets from other domains or even to similar
datasets, due to data distribution shifts. In this work, we propose the use
of a meta-learning based few-shot learning approach to alleviate these
problems. In order to demonstrate its efficacy, we use two datasets of
kidney stones samples acquired with different endoscopes and different
acquisition conditions. The results show how such methods are indeed
capable of handling domain-shifts by attaining an accuracy of 74.38%
and 88.52% in the 5-way 5-shot and 5-way 20-shot settings respectively.
Instead, in the same dataset, traditional Deep Learning (DL) methods
attain only an cross-domain accuracy of 45%.

Keywords: Deep learning · Computer vision · Kidney stones

1 Introduction

Progresses made in Artificial Intelligence (AI) in recent years have shown outstanding results that compare or surpass human capabilities in a set of problems such as natural language processing, smart agriculture, object recognition,

healthcare and medical applications, among others. Such AI-based models have been possible due to the existence of large scale labeled datasets enabling the extraction of profound knowledge about the data. However, it has been demonstrated that if the same models are deployed in slightly different operating conditions (i.e., medical imaging applications) such AI methods are in fact very fragile and exhibit very poor generalization properties [21].

These variations in performance stem from changes in acquisition devices and/or the operating conditions in clinical settings, which can hamper the adoption of AI-based CAD tools in many applications. To make matters worse, most DL methods in the state of the art still require humongous amounts of data to be trained, which is not realistic in most of the medical application domains. Therefore, in recent years, the meta-learning and Few-Shot Learning (FSL) paradigms have emerged as a means to cope with this training data scarcity problem and furthermore, to make models more capable of generalization with less computing effort and incremental learning capabilities [12].

In this work, we propose a novel meta learning-based Few-Shot Learning approach for image classification to assess the generalization of a trained model in two different kidney stones datasets. Our method is based on the following two core ideas: i) The use of a pre-trained model that learns representations through self-supervised learning can enhance the features generalization and ii) a meta-learning stage can be used to further fine-tune the model for specific domains in order to improve its performance. The advantage of our method is that, compared to other DL approaches to classify kidney stones, it can better generalize to other data distributions and obtain good results without the need of manual data augmentation. In order to validate our proposal, we make use of two datasets of kidney stones acquired using endoscopes of two different vendors and of different technical characteristics and under different acquisition conditions (in-vivo, ex-vivo). As illustrated in Fig. 1 our approach is divided in three stages. First, in the pre-training phase, we use a self-supervised model for the embedding network. Then, we proceed to a meta-learning stage, where we fine-tune our model. Lastly, we evaluate the model with the two kidney stones datasets and obtain the corresponding metrics and features visualization, which are of great help to better assess the generalization capabilities of the model.

The rest of the paper is organized as follows. In Sect. 2 we present the medical motivation for this work, while Sect. 3 discusses the state of the art of FSL. In Sect. 4 we introduce the proposed method and in Sect. 5 we provide details about the implementation and experiments done to find the best model, as well as the comparison with previous models.

2   Medical Context and Motivation

In recent years, there has been an increased interest in the recognition of kidney stones morphologies (i.e. crystalline type) for speeding the diagnosis and treatment processes. The traditional (ex-vivo) approach, known in the medical field as morpho-constitutional analysis (MCA [5,7]), relies on an inspection of

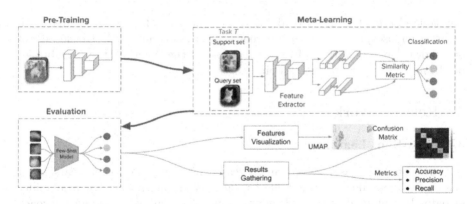

Fig. 1. The proposed model is divided into three stages: pre-training, meta-learning and evaluation.

the surface and section views of the images under the microscope, followed by a SPIR analysis to determine their biochemical composition (i.e. stone type). This analysis is essential as it provides very important information about the lithogenesis (i.e. cause of formation) of the stone, but modern extraction techniques increasingly rely on a technique for pulverizing the stone. This technique, known as dusting, leads to a destruction of the morphological information of the sample or even an alteration of its biochemical composition [10] used for diagnosis.

Therefore, specialists have sought solutions in the form of image classification methods for categorizing kidney stone samples, first using ex-vivo images corpuses [1,16] and later tackling the problem of endoscopy stone recognition (ESR) [13,14]. Although the results have been encouraging (up to 98% average precision for pure stones), some of the methodological choices make the results far from conclusive as more complete studies are needed.

First, the majority of ML-based ESR methods make use of very small datasets and rely heavily on patch sampling [1,13], which might introduce bias towards certain classes (i.e. data leakage). Furthermore, most datasets reported in the literature contain only a small fraction of the 21 identified classes of kidney stones (up to 6 classes) which might yield overly optimistic results. Another aspect is that most of the existing methods have been tested on images acquired using one or at most two endoscopes types from the same hospital, which can lead to problems such as shortcut learning, or simply the samples might not be representative enough of the underlying distribution. This leads to a problem increasingly reported in the literature: models trained with data from certain acquisition devices or under certain imaging circumstances do not generalize well to data from a different distribution [20].

In order to address some of the issues mentioned above, in this work we explore recent developments in the DL field, namely FSL and meta-learning strategies that are promising areas of research for training models with few samples and capable of better generalization capabilities. For validating our approach we make use of two very distinct kidney stones datasets, containing data from the same classes, but different distributions (i.e., the data was acquired with different endoscopes and under different acquisition conditions). To the best of our knowledge, our work is of the firsts to assess the generalization capabilities of ML models applied on endoscopic images.

3   Related Work

3.1   Few-Shot Learning

Research on FSL has received an increased attention on recent years, as it has continuously demonstrated good results on problems with low availability of data. Recent models for FSL adopt a meta-learning strategy, an approach that seeks to learn discriminant features across tasks, later adapting the model to new tasks. FSL approaches can be categorized into two main branches: 1) metric-learning based, and 2) optimization based. The goal of metric-learning approaches is to learn a similarity metric expected to generalize across different tasks. There are baseline methods which have achieved important milestones for FSL, such as Prototypical Networks [17] and Matching Networks [19]. Optimization based approaches make use of a base-learner and a meta-learner, where the meta-learner's parameters are optimized by gradual learning across tasks to promote a faster learning of the base-learner for each specific task. The Model-Agnostic Meta-Learning (MAML) approach [8] was the first one to use this strategy to parameter initialization, such that the base learner can rapidly generalize from an initial guess of parameters.

3.2   Cross-Domain FSL

Domain adaptation refers to the transfer of knowledge from one or multiple source domains to a target domain with a different data distribution. Several approaches have been proposed to address this issue, but most of these methods operate in situations where the training and test sets contain the same classes.

For cross-domain FSL, where base and novel classes come from different domains, this can introduce non-desirable variations in the performance of the models. In [3], the authors made an analysis of different meta-learning methods in the cross-domain setting. They proposed a cross-domain scenario which trains on miniImageNet dataset and test with CUB dataset images. Further on, the authors established a challenging benchmark consisting of images of diverse types with an increasing dissimilarity degree to natural images and with various levels of perspective distortion, semantic content and color depth. They also evaluated the performance of existing meta-learning methods on this benchmark. These recent works show how the cross-domain paradigm is able to enhance the results of the base models in disjoint distributions, making cross-domain approaches one of the corner stones of FSL research.

3.3 Kidney Stones Classification

Different approaches have been proposed to deal with the classification of kidney stones from still images, acquired through different means. For instance, authors in [16] made use of ex-vivo images to train a Random Forest classifier, which exploits histograms of RGB colours and local binary patterns. As a continuation of this work, they trained a DL method base on a Siamese CNN [18] using the same dataset. Although such methods showed the potential of image-based recognition of kidney stones, the proposed models obtained a moderate performance of 71% and 74% on mean accuracy, respectively. The authors in [1] improved these results by using a ResNet-101 and employing a data augmentation technique to leverage the small dataset. These previous methods have the limitation of being tested on ex-vivo images obtained in highly controlled acquisition conditions. For in-vivo images, authors in [14] used classical classifiers such as Random Forest and kNN ensemble models obtaining an improved accuracy of 85% over 3 kidney stone classes. Later on, [13] used CNN-based models to further improve their results, obtaining an accuracy of over 90% on precision and recall over 4 classes.

Although these kidney stone classification methods have yielded increasingly good performances, they pose certain problems. First, they all require a great deal of manual data augmentation work for creating several patches from the images to train DL models. Second, the training and evaluation has been made over those patches instead of the full images, which is not realistic in clinical settings. Third, all these previous methods have shown poor generalization capabilities, as they are trained with images from specific data acquisition conditions and fail to classify when using a different acquisition method.

4 Proposed Approach

FSL is a growing research field with the challenging problem of learning from limited data, while verifying the performance of the models on previously unseen classes. Additional to this, FSL methods are expected to generalize well to other data distributions. In this work, as shown in Fig. 1, we follow a two stages paradigm (pre-training and meta-learning) to train models capable of generalizing to a different data distribution to classify unseen kidney stones classes. In this approach, the model is first pre-trained on a large datasets of natural images (i.e., ImageNet) to obtain a good initial estimate of the model parameters. Then the model is fine-tuned using a meta-learning approach with increasingly similar datasets to the target domain. Finally, the model is tested with data coming from a completely new distribution to assess it generalization capabilities.

4.1 Datasets

Base Datasets. The miniImageNet dataset [19] is comprised of 100 classes with 600 images per class. This dataset is widely used in the FSL literature for image classification [17], following the same split proposed in [19] by sampling images of 64 classes for training, 16 classes for validation and 20 classes for testing. Caltech-UCSD Birds-200-2011 (CUB-200-2011) is an image dataset with more specialization in the categories, containing photos of 200 bird species.

Cross-Domain Datasets. For the cross-domain adaptation in FSL, we used the datasets suggested by [9], comprised of images from multiple domains (i.e., image modalities and acquisition conditions). The first dataset is CropDiseases, which contains 38 classes with images of plant leaves.

We split the dataset into 30 classes for training and 8 for validation. The second dataset is EuroSAT, which contains satellite images for land use and land cover classification. It is comprised of 10 classes that we split into 5 classes for training and 5 for validation. The third dataset is ISIC, containing skin diseases images for skin image analysis. It contains 7 categories, which we split by using 5 for training and 2 for testing.

Kidney Stones Datasets. We make use of two different kidney stones datasets, obtained using two different acquisition devices (i.e., endoscopes) and under divergent acquisition conditions and lighting environments: the first is comprised by in-vivo images, whilst the second was created by capturing images with an endoscope in ex-vivo conditions, see Fig. 2. For specific details of in-vivo and ex-vivo image acquisition conditions, see [7] and [6], respectively.

The in-vivo dataset includes 156 kidney stone images acquired in-vivo (i.e. during actual ureteroscopic interventions) and which were annotated by expert Dr. Vincent Estrade (an urologist involved in MCA) [7]. The dataset consists of 65 cross-section images and 91 surface images from the 4 classes of kidney stones with the highest incidence: uric acid (AU), brushite (BR), weddelite (WD) and whewellite (WW). Some images from this dataset are shown on Fig. 2a.

The ex-vivo dataset consists of 765 kidney stones images, with 318 corresponding to cross-section and 447 corresponding to surface images, from 6 of the kidney stones categories with higher incidence: uric acid (AU), brushite (BR), cystine (CYS), struvite (STR), weddelite (WD) and whewellite (WW) [6]. Figure 2b show examples of images from this dataset.

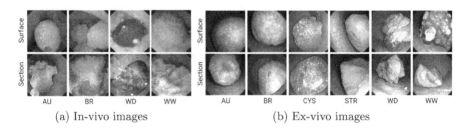

| (a) In-vivo images | (b) Ex-vivo images |

Fig. 2. Examples of kidney stone images from the (a) in-vivo and (b) ex-vivo datasets. The categories shown are, from left to right, uric acid (AU), brushite (BR), cystine (CYS), struvite (STR), weddelite (WD) and whewellite (WW). Surface images are on the top row and section images are on the bottom row.

4.2 Model Training and Design Choices

Pre-training Stage. The first approaches for FSL used a simple ConvNet backbone, made up of 4 convolutional blocks, as the feature extractor [17], leading to good results that supported the promising research of these methods. Current state-of-the-art models with high performance make use of a ResNet-12 [11] or a wide ResNet, outperforming other models which make use of deeper embedding networks.

This could stem from the fact that, as the tested models have access solely to a very small amount of training samples, deeper networks are more prone to overfitting in the supervised training setting. Therefore, an essential element for the meta-learning process is the initial embedding network. Several state-of-the-art methods [2,4] demonstrate that having a pre-trained network allows us to use a deeper backbone, thus greatly improving the performance of few-shot learning models.

Among the pre-training strategies for FSL available in the literature, a self-supervised learning (SSL) method [2] stands out, as it has demonstrated a good results in this task, outperforming other state-of-the-art models. We adopt this pre-training strategy, which allows us to use a large embedding network. The SSL stage works as follows: using the Augmented Multiscale Deep InfoMax (AMDIM) model, it optimizes the network by looking for mutual local and global features from different views of an instance, thus enhancing the feature's generalization for new tasks. This makes the trained network more transferable to different domains and data distributions.

Meta-learning Stage. After finding an appropriate initialization via SSL, we proceed with the meta-learning stage to learn to generalize across tasks. This stage is divided into two phases: Meta-training and meta-testing. A Few-Shot K-way C-shot image classification task is given K classes and C images per class. The task-specific dataset can be formulated as $D = \{D_{train}, D_{test}\}$, where $D_{train} = \{(X_i, y_i)\}_{i=1}^{N_{train}}$ denotes the classes reserved for the training phase and $D_{test} = \{(X_i, y_i)\}_{i=1}^{N_{test}}$ denotes the classes reserved for the testing phase. For each meta-train task T, K class labels are randomly chosen from D_{train} to form a support set and a query set. The support set, denoted by S, contains $K \times C$ samples (K-way C-shot) and the query set, denoted by Q, contains n number of randomly chosen samples from the K classes. The training phase uses an episodic mechanism, where each episode E is loaded with a new random task taken from the training data. For the meta-test, the model is tested with a new task T constructed with classes that weren't seen during the meta-train phase.

We follow a metric learning approach for the image classification component of our approach. Specifically, we implemented a prototypical networks [17] model by computing the prototypes c_k as the mean of embedded support samples for each class. For a class k, the prototype is represented by the centroid of the support embedding features, obtained as:

$$c_k = \frac{1}{|S_k|} \sum_{(x_i, y_i) \in S} f(x_i), \qquad (1)$$

The classification is performed by finding the nearest prototype for a given embedded query point. The Euclidean distance is chosen as the distance function to find the nearest class prototype. In the proposed method, we first apply SSL to pre-train the large embedding network, followed by a number of meta-learning iterations to fine-tune the model. The iterations are made by training and validating the model with different datasets, as a way to alleviate the domain shift preventing a successful classification of kidney stones.

The datasets used for meta-training were selected because they meet the requirement of decreasing its similarity with ImageNet based on three orthogonal criteria: i) Existence of perspective distortion, ii) the semantic content and iii) the color depth. The ImageNet dataset contains natural and colored images with perspective. The CropDisease dataset contains natural and colored images with perspective. Meanwhile, the EuroSAT dataset contains natural and colored images but without perspective. In contrast, the ISIC dataset contains medical and images with no perspective in color. We can place the kidney stones datasets used for this study within the spectrum of dissimilarity as ISIC, as they contain both medical and colored images with no perspective.

Therefore, the model gradually converges to a point in which more discriminating features are learned from the fine-tuning process. This domain-specific fine-tuning is done as follows: First, we meta-train the model with the base datasets (MiniImageNet and CUB-200); then we specialize the model domain by meta-training with the CropDisease, EuroSAT and ISIC datasets sequentially. After training and validating the model, we perform the meta-testing with the two kidney stone dataset separately. These datasets are not used in the meta-training phase, so we can evaluate the generalization capabilities of the proposed method.

5   Experimental Results

5.1   Implementation Details

For the training phase of our FSL model, we follow the same setting as other few-shot learning models [17] by learning across the 5-way 1-shot and 5-way 5-shot task settings and using 15 query samples for each class in the task. For the meta-training phase, we randomly sampled 100 tasks over 200 epochs. We validate each epoch with 500 randomly constructed tasks using the classes reserved for validation. For the testing phase, we randomly constructed 200 tasks which is enough for the little amount of data from the kidney stones datasets.

For the feature extraction backbone, we tested two different embedding networks, a ConvNet and an AmdimNet. Following the same approach as [17,19], the ConvNet is built using four layers of convolutional blocks. Each block is made up of a 3×3 convolution with 64 filters, followed by a batch normalization and a ReLU layer. The input images are resized to 84×84 and normalized. For this network, we do not apply a pre-training process due to the small scale of the model. In the meta-learning phase, we use the Adam Optimizer with an initial learning rate of 1×10^{-3} and a step size of 20. For the AmdimNet, we follow the same setup provided by [2] consisting of the pre-training stage and meta-learning stage. In the pre-train stage we use the Adam Optimizer with a learning rate of 0.0002 and an embedding dimension of 1536. We resize the unlabeled input images to a size of 128×128 pixels. In the meta-learning stage, the input images are resized to 84×84 pixels and we used the SGD as optimizer with an initial learning rate of 2×10^{-4}, a step size of 20 and weight decay of 0.0005.

5.2 Training Details

Our experiments were carried out in three main steps. In the first we performed quick tests to determine if the kidney stones classification was indeed a problem that few-shot learning could solve. We trained the base prototypical networks [17] on the 5-way 5-shot and 20-way 5-shot settings, and tested the models generalization on both kidney stones datasets. The results obtained in this step were promising, with models that generalized much better than previous deep learning methods. The second step was a round of experiments to find the best hyperparameters for the main model (AmdimNet). We tested a set of combinations for the optimizer, learning rate and step size, finding that the best combination was SGD optimizer with a learning rate of 0.0002 and step size of 20. Lastly, the third step was to carry out experiments to find the best performing model for the kidney stones classification. We explain the details below.

For the **pre-training** stage we trained two different embedding models: i) ImageNet900 (Img900) was trained using the SSL strategy from 900 classes of the ImageNet dataset (removing from ImageNet the 100 classes used in Mini-ImageNet) and ii) ImageNet1k (Img1k) is trained using self-supervised learning from the whole 1,000 classes of the ImageNet dataset without any label.

For the **meta-training** stage we adopted a domain-specific fine tuning to reduce the domain shifts between the source datasets and the target of kidney stones images. Since our testing phase is carried out with the kidney stones datasets, the base datasets were modified to only have training and validation classes in the following way. In MiniImageNet, we assign for training the classes previously used for training and validation, and for validation we use the classes previously used for testing, leading to a total of 80 classes for training and 20 for validation (Mini80). The same split is applied to the CUB dataset, in which we use 150 classes for training and 50 classes for validation (CUB150). We trained over 20 different models, splitting the experiments into 6 data configurations based on how the model would be trained. The meta-learning setting was either by incremental learning through different datasets or by meta-learning among all datasets at once.

Table 1 summarizes the experimental setup, comprised by the configurations just described above. The first three rows are models pre-trained with ImageNet900 and the last three configurations are models pre-trained with ImageNet 1k. For model 1, we sequentially meta-trained across Mini80, followed by

Table 1. Experimental setup with incrementally more similar datasets to the target domain.

	Pretrain	Mini80	CUB150	Crop-D	EuroSAT	ISIC	Details
		Meta-training					
1	ImageNet900	✓		✓	✓	✓	All datasets (except CUB) sequentially meta-trained
2	ImageNet900	✓	✓	✓	✓	✓	All datasets sequentially meta-trained
3	ImageNet900	✓	✓	✓	✓	✓	All datasets meta-trained at once
4	ImageNet1k		✓	✓	✓	✓	All datasets (except CUB) sequentially meta-trained
5	ImageNet1k		✓		✓	✓	All datasets sequentially meta-trained
6	ImageNet1k	✓	✓	✓	✓	✓	All datasets meta-trained at once

CropDiseases (Crop-D), then EuroSAT and lastly ISIC. The same applies for model 2, but adding CUB150 after meta-training with Mini80. For model 3, we tested the following 4 settings with the idea of learning from different datasets at once: i) Training the model first with Mini80, followed by a training with the rest of datasets, ii) training first with Mini80, followed by CUB150, and then the rest of datasets, iii) train with all datasets, except CUB150, at once, and iv) training with all the datasets at once. For the last 3 models in the Table 1, we repeated the same experiments but with the model pre-trained on ImageNet 1k and removing Mini80 from the datasets used in meta-training, since those would represent classes already seen in the pre-training stage.

5.3   Evaluation Results

In order to evaluate the generalization capabilities of the models trained using the various configurations in Table 1, the architectures were tested on the two kidney stones datasets described in Sect. 4.1.

Following the cross-domain setup described in [9], we conducted experiments by testing the proposed model across three main few-shot tasks (i.e., 5-way 5-shot, 5-way 20-shot and 5-way 50-shot). For the in-vivo dataset, we do not have enough images per class to test the 5-way 50-shot setting. Thus, the experiments with this setting are excluded for the in-vivo classification experiments.

Ablation Study Results. In order to assess how the various components of our proposed approach affect the generalization results of the generated model, we carried out several ablation studies, shown in Table 2. First, we validate

Table 2. Accuracy performance of the ablation studies on our method. *Mini80+CropDiseases, **Mini80+CUB+All, ***All (excluding CUB).

Model	In-vivo		Ex-vivo		
	5-shot	20-shot	5-shot	20-shot	50-shot
ProtoNet 5w5s	63.31	71.88	58.75	65.36	67.85
ProtoNet 20w5s	63.28	72.72	60.47	67.85	70.27
ImageNet 900	69.68	84.49	67.05	74.18	76.46
ImageNet 1k	70.26	84.25	66.75	74.36	77.01
ImageNet 1k-CUB-All	68.38	85.03	68.46	77.65	80.09
ImageNet 900*	70.61	84.53	69.45	77.72	79.87
ImageNet 900**	71.13	85.76	69.25	77.84	80.27
ImageNet 900***	**74.38**	**88.13**	**69.56**	**78.20**	**80.54**

the effectiveness of a traditional FSL approach to classify out of distribution datasets. Specifically, we trained the baseline prototypical networks [17] on the 5-way 5-shot and 20-way 5-shot settings. After testing both models, we obtained an accuracy performance of over 70% in ex-vivo and in-vivo images, and the models demonstrated an acceptable generalization as they do not exhibit an important loss of performance (around 2%–3%) when compared on the two kidney stones datasets.

Afterwards, we tested the performance yield by the models when only pre-training the models, to assess whether or not there is a gain in performance when applying the proposed meta-training strategy. After evaluating the effectiveness of two models (Img900 and Img1k), we found that the accuracy performance greatly increased (around 12% for the in-vivo dataset and around 7% for the ex-vivo dataset, using the Img900 and Img1k models, respectively). Nonetheless, a decrease in the generalization capabilities of the models can be observed, as there is a difference of around 8% in the results for both datasets. Finally, we tested the generalization performance after implementing the meta-learning strategies described in Sect. 4.2.

Through these experiments, we found out that there is indeed an improvement (an average of 4% for both datasets) over the model that was only pre-trained. The improvement on accuracy is not as large as for the ProtoNet and the pre-trained model. The difference in accuracy between the in-vivo and ex-vivo datasets is around 8%, which is the same difference using only pre-trained models. This means that our meta-learning approach was able to account for the domain-shift of the model, while maintaining its generalization capabilities.

The best meta-learning-based models are shown in the last row of Table 2. We can see that these models achieved a great performance improvement over the basic FSL models (values of 88.13% in the in-vivo dataset and 80.54% in the ex-vivo dataset). As we will see in the next subsection, these results are comparable with some of the shallow models in the literature [13,14] in terms

Table 3. Results comparison with previous work, the metrics in the ex-vivo model were obtained by feeding it samples used to train the in-vivo model.

Model	In-vivo			Ex-vivo		
	Precision	Recall	F-score	Precision	Recall	F-score
Random Forest	0.91	0.91	0.91	0.32	0.26	0.26
XGboost	0.96	0.96	0.96	0.48	0.24	0.36
AlexNet	0.92	0.92	0.92	0.49	0.42	0.45
VGG-19	0.94	0.92	0.93	0.47	0.45	0.45
Inception	0.97	0.98	0.98	0.51	0.45	0.45
ProtoNet	0.71	0.72	0.72	0.70	0.70	0.70
Ours	0.88	0.88	0.88	**0.82**	**0.81**	**0.81**

of performance, and still far below the results obtained by most deep learning models. Nonetheless, the results in generalization are far more superior. Also, while most models in the state of the art have been trained with thousands of image patches, the results discussed here make use of a few hundred images.

Comparison with Previous Works. To verify the effectiveness of our proposed method, we compare it with previous works in ESR using the same datasets presented in Sect. 4.1. In [13] several shallow ML methods and DL models were used to classify the images of the in-vivo dataset. We implemented some of these models and tested their generalization capabilities by trying to classify the same 4 classes of the in-vivo dataset but using the model trained on ex-vivo images. Even though the classes are the same, we obtained very poor results, showing that there is a large loss in performance (a decay of around 40% in accuracy) when the images come from another data distribution. This issue plagues all the methods equally, but it comes to show the fragility of the existing traditional DL models. Most of these problems can be partially fixed by using metric learning approaches. As it can be seen in Table 3, even the basic ProtoNet model [17] is more appropriate at generalizing with the same performance than the classical methods mentioned before.

Our method obtained a high performance in three metrics: precision, recall and F1-score. Compared with some of the classical machine learning methods (i.e., Random Forest, XGBoost), we obtained competitive results for the in-vivo and ex-vivo datasets. Moreover, we demonstrated that our method has much better generalization capabilities as our model exhibits a loss of 7% on accuracy, compared with the loss of over 40% from previous works.

5.4   Discussion

To have a better understanding of how our model is behaving, we visualize the features embeddings from the image samples from both kidney stones datasets using UMAP [15]. We can observe that in the feature space of the in-vivo

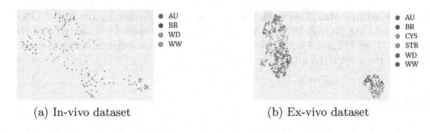

(a) In-vivo dataset   (b) Ex-vivo dataset

Fig. 3. UMAP feature visualization of the (a) in-vivo and (b) ex-vivo datasets. The visualizations can be used in tandem with the morpho-constitutional analysis proposed by Daudon [5] to understand the errors done by the models.

dataset (Fig. 3a), the WD class overlaps with BR and WW, something previously reported for traditional features in [13]. In the reduced manifold of the ex-vivo dataset (Fig. 3b), we can see that even some of the classes form distinct clusters, classes such as BR and STR tend to lie very close to each other (a similar trend also occurs in classification made by humans) and that overall, the overlap of the WW class is degrading the performance of the model for ex-vivo images. It may be the case that some classes follow a probability distribution, which would need other metric learning method to be used during the model training to alleviate this problem.

It must be emphasized the urologists make use of both surface and section images to perform the classification of a given kidney stones, using Daudon's morpho-constitutional analysis either under a microscope or with an endoscope [5]. The results for the shallow and DL models in Table 3 are for models trained in both types of images.

6   Conclusions

In this paper, we conducted a study on generalization capabilities of few-shot learning applied to two kidney stones classification. We were interested in evaluating the generalization capabilities of meta learning-based FSL methods in a scarce data regime (i.e. medical applications). For this purpose, we made use of two datasets with 4 overlapping but different data distributions: different acquisition conditions, (in-vivo and ex-vivo) and endoscope (type, brand, resolution). Where classical machine learning and deep learning models failed to generalize when trained on one dataset and tested on the other one, our few-shot learning method was able to obtain a high performance over of 80% in accuracy, recall and F1-score. The difference on accuracy from the evaluation of both datasets is of around 8% for our approach, which is much lower compared with the loss on performance from shallow machine and deep learning models. Although we obtained a performance lower than the previous work on the in-vivo dataset, it is still competitive and demonstrate much better generalization capabilities.

Acknowledgments. This work is part of a project finance by the SEP-CONACYT-ANUIES-ECOS NORD Project 315597. The authors wish to thank the AI Hub and the CIIOT at ITESM for their support for carrying the experiments reported in this paper in their NVIDIA's DGX computer.

References

1. Black, K.M., Law, H., Aldoukhi, A., Deng, J., Ghani, K.R.: Deep learning computer vision algorithm for detecting kidney stone composition. BJU Int. **125**(6), 920–924 (2020)
2. Chen, D., Chen, Y., Li, Y., Mao, F., He, Y., Xue, H.: Self-supervised learning for few-shot image classification. CoRR abs/1911.06045 (2019)
3. Chen, W., Liu, Y., Kira, Z., Wang, Y.F., Huang, J.: A closer look at few-shot classification. CoRR abs/1904.04232 (2019). http://arxiv.org/abs/1904.04232
4. Chen, Y., Wang, X., Liu, Z., Xu, H., Darrell, T.: A new meta-baseline for few-shot learning. CoRR abs/2003.04390 (2020)
5. Corrales, M., Doizi, S., Barghouthy, Y., Traxer, O., Daudon, M.: Classification of stones according to Michel Daudon: a narrative review. Eur. Urol. Focus **7**(1), 13–21 (2021)
6. El Beze, J., et al.: Evaluation and understanding of automated urolithiasis recognition methods. BJU Int. (2022)
7. Estrade, V., e al.: Toward improved endoscopic examination of urinary stones: a concordance study between endoscopic digital pictures vs. microscopy. Br. J. Urol. Int. (2020)
8. Finn, C., Abbeel, P., Levine, S.: Model-agnostic meta-learning for fast adaptation of deep networks. CoRR abs/1703.03400 (2017). http://arxiv.org/abs/1703.03400
9. Guo, Y., Codella, N.C.F., Karlinsky, L., Smith, J.R., Rosing, T., Feris, R.S.: A new benchmark for evaluation of cross-domain few-shot learning. CoRR abs/1912.07200 (2019). http://arxiv.org/abs/1912.07200
10. Keller, E.X., et al.: Fragments and dust after holmium laser lithotripsy with or without "Moses technology": how are they different? J. Biophotonics **12**(4), e201800227 (2019)
11. Li, H., Eigen, D., Dodge, S., Zeiler, M., Wang, X.: Finding task-relevant features for few-shot learning by category traversal. CoRR abs/1905.11116 (2019)
12. Liang, H., Zhang, Q., Dai, P., Lu, J.: Boosting the generalization capability in cross-domain few-shot learning via noise-enhanced supervised autoencoder (2021)
13. Lopez, F., et al.: Assessing deep learning methods for the identification of kidney stones in endoscopic images. In: 2021 43rd Annual International Conference of the IEEE Engineering in Medicine Biology Society (EMBC), pp. 1936–1939 (2021)
14. Martínez, A., et al.: Towards an automated classification method for ureteroscopic kidney stone images using ensemble learning. In: 2020 42nd Annual International Conference of the IEEE Engineering in Medicine Biology Society (EMBC), pp. 1936–1939 (2020)
15. McInnes, L., Healy, J., Melville, J.: UMAP: uniform manifold approximation and projection for dimension reduction. arXiv preprint arXiv:1802.03426 (2018)
16. Serrat, J., Lumbreras, F., Blanco, F., Valiente, M., López-Mesas, M.: myStone: a system for automatic kidney stone classification. Expert Syst. Appl. **89**, 41–51 (2017)

17. Snell, J., Swersky, K., Zemel, R.: Prototypical networks for few-shot learning. In: Guyon, I., et al. (eds.) Advances in Neural Information Processing Systems, vol. 30, pp. 4077–4087. Curran Associates, Inc. (2017). http://papers.nips.cc/paper/6996-prototypical-networks-for-few-shot-learning.pdf
18. Torrell-Amado, A., Serrat-Gual, J.: Metric learning for kidney stone classification. Universitat Autònoma de Barcelona. Escola d'Enginyeria (2018)
19. Vinyals, O., Blundell, C., Lillicrap, T., Kavukcuoglu, K., Wierstra, D.: Matching networks for one shot learning. In: Lee, D.D., Sugiyama, M., Luxburg, U.V., Guyon, I., Garnett, R. (eds.) Advances in Neural Information Processing Systems, vol. 29, pp. 3630–3638. Curran Associates, Inc. (2016). http://papers.nips.cc/paper/6385-matching-networks-for-one-shot-learning.pdf
20. Yao, L., Prosky, J., Covington, B., Lyman, K.: A strong baseline for domain adaptation and generalization in medical imaging. CoRR abs/1904.01638 (2019)
21. Zhang, L., et al.: Generalizing deep learning for medical image segmentation to unseen domains via deep stacked transformation. IEEE Trans. Med. Imaging 39(7), 2531–2540 (2020)

Best Paper Award

A Novel Hybrid Endoscopic Dataset for Evaluating Machine Learning-Based Photometric Image Enhancement Models

Axel García-Vega[1]([✉]), Ricardo Espinosa[3,4], Gilberto Ochoa-Ruiz[1,2], Thomas Bazin[5], Luis Falcón-Morales[1], Dominique Lamarque[5], and Christian Daul[4]

[1] School of Engineering and Sciences, Tecnologico de Monterrey, Monterrey, Nuevo León, Mexico
caaxgave@gmail.com
[2] ITESM, Institute of Advanced Materials for Sustainable Manufacturing, Monterrey, Mexico
[3] Facultad de Ingeniería, Universidad Panamericana, Josemaría Escrivá de Balaguer 101, 20290 Aguascalientes, Mexico
[4] Université de Lorraine and CNRS, CRAN UMR 7039, 2 avenue de la Forêt de Haye, 54518 Vandœuvre-Lés-Nancy Cedex, France
[5] Hôpital Ambroise Paré, 9 av. Charles de Gaulle, 92100 Boulogne-Billancourt, France

Abstract. Endoscopy is the most widely used medical technique for cancer and polyp detection inside hollow organs. However, images acquired by an endoscope are frequently affected by illumination artefacts due to the enlightenment source orientation. There exist two major issues when the endoscope's light source pose suddenly changes: overexposed and underexposed tissue areas are produced. These two scenarios can result in misdiagnosis due to the lack of information in the affected zones or hamper the performance of various computer vision methods (e.g., SLAM, structure from motion, optical flow) used during the non invasive examination. The aim of this work is two-fold: i) to introduce a new synthetically generated dataset generated by a generative adversarial techniques and ii) and to explore both shallow based and deep learning-based image-enhancement methods in overexposed and underexposed lighting conditions. Best quantitative results (i.e., metric based results), were obtained by the deep learning-based LMSPEC method, besides a running time around 7.6 fps.

Data available at: https://data.mendeley.com/datasets/3j3tmghw 33/1.

Keywords: Medical imaging · Image enhancement · Endoscopy

1 Introduction

1.1 Medical Context

Endoscopy is the most effective and common used examination tool to prevent colon cancer by screening for lesions. This technique is used to examine the

O. Pichardo Lagunas et al. (Eds.): MICAI 2022, LNAI 13612, pp. 267–281, 2022.
https://doi.org/10.1007/978-3-031-19493-1_22

human colon through a flexible tube called endoscope, while a camera attached at the tip gathers visual information in real-time. Additionally to the camera, a point light provides the lighting source during the surgery.

On the other hand, Minimally Invasive Surgery (MIS) is a type of endoscopic procedure that is increasingly becoming a mainstream medical procedure, over-taking traditional surgical operations and treatments. Such endoscopic interven-tion entails a less traumatic experience and less pain for the patient, quicker recovery after surgery and shortened hospital stays [9].

Both endoscopic examinations and MIS procedures require a great deal of expertise from the surgeon or specialist and demand complicated training and certifications. Despite of this, there is ample evidence in the literature that during the vast majority of endoscopic examinations, a great deal of regions of interest are missed [13], which poses a serious problem, as they might contain suspicious regions or other lesions such as polyps. Moreover, such issues make the inspection by the physician a strenuous and time consuming task. In general, these problems stem from how rapidly the lighting conditions in the endoscopic video can change from frame to frame (see Fig. 1). In fact, a highly non-linear illumination response produces endoscopic frames which are highly lit in some sections (overexposed) and poorly lit (underexposed) in other areas.

Additionally to affecting strongly the efficiency in the lesion detection by the doctor, the highly changing illumination conditions in endoscopic settings also hampers the performance of AI-based tools that are being increasingly developed for Computer-aided Detection (CADe) and Computer-aided Diagnosis (CADx) applications and in MIS and laparoscopy, among other areas of research, as we will discuss next.

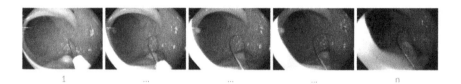

Fig. 1. Light condition changes in sequential video frames. Frame 1 shows a normal condition. Later frames show poor conditions while light points to the closest object.

1.2 Motivation for Our Proposal

In recent years computer vision (CV) has been playing significant role in endo-scopic explorations aided by novel deep learning (DL) techniques, which give computers the visual and temporal learning abilities to understand complex sur-gical procedures in hollow organs [9]. The integration of such techniques is cur-rently being investigated also for laparoscopy and MIS applications (i.e., such as instrument tracking, endoscopic view enhancement and suspicious lesion track-ing [9]). Among these applications, 3D reconstruction seems to be a promising solution for the poor depth perception which prevents the full-fledged adoption of the above-mentioned techniques in MIS and Robotic-assisted surgery (RAS).

However, as with other applications of computer vision in endoscopy, proper illumination conditions is an aspect of utmost importance for attaining a high performance in applications such a CADx and such reconstruction methods. In the latter case, the techniques traditionally employed for recovering 3D information, such as Simultaneous Localization and Mapping (SLAM) [7], Structure for Motion (SfM) and Optical Flow (OF) [15], work poorly on endoscopic images. This is due to strong photo-metric variations caused by moving light sources, moist surfaces, occlusions as well as reflections for surgical instruments that provoke underexposed and overexposed video frames [13].

As a matter of fact, 3D reconstruction techniques rest on the constraint of brightness constancy [15]. This constraint assumes that the values in intensity of the pixels remain constant or with a few variations, which usually holds in applications in natural imagery (i.e., photography) [1] or autonomous driving [8]. However, in endoscopic procedures, as Fig. 1 shows, the brightness constancy assumption does not hold due to the numerous illuminations variations when the camera and light move through the organs.

Therefore, the use of image enhancement techniques for pre-processing such images is a mandatory step to carry out a robust 3D reconstruction [18] and to develop reliable and robust CADe/CADx tools.

1.3   Contributions and Organization of the Article

Over the decades, multiple image enhancement techniques have been explored for illumination adaptation, exposure correction and high-dynamic-range tone mapping in several applications, to cite a few. Nevertheless, most of the proposed methods for exposure correction have been designed to deal either with low-light high-light settings separately, due to the different characteristics of these enhancing tasks in different areas. In enhancing endoscopic images, these methods have presented a general lack of robustness due to the fact that in endoscopy images both problems (under/over exposure) are present simultaneously.

Additionally, as we will discuss next, most of the machine learning based approaches to IE require large amounts of paired-data images (i.e., corrupted and non-corrupted ground truth images) for training and testing purposes. However, to the best of our knowledge, such a large database does not exist for testing image enhancement algorithms in endoscopic images.

Therefore, in order to mitigate the problems related to large variations in illumination in endoscopic interventions, in this paper we present novel synthetic dataset for testing and evaluating endoscopic image enhancement methods. In order to attain this goal, of our proposal consists of the following contributions:

- 1. We introduce a novel dataset containing synthetically generated over and under exposure frames, in tandem with their respective ground truth images. We believe that this dataset can serve as a cornerstone for testing well known IE methods and provide a baseline for future developments in ML for endoscopy and in DL-based image enhancement methods.

- 2. We perform a thorough evaluation of traditional and DL-based image enhancement (IE) methods in order to highlight the importance of the ground truth data and the scarcity of bidirectional (under/over exposure) methods.

The rest of this paper is organized as follows. In Sect. 3 we present the datasets from which the raw data was obtained, besides the methodology utilized for creating the synthetic dataset and both traditional and DL-based methods for enhancing the synthetic data. In Sect. 4 we provide a thorough description of the data preparation and training setup for our experiments. Also, we present a brief context about metrics implemented and their respective results. Finally, in Sect. 5, we give our conclusion and an ideas for future work.

2   State of the Art

Mainly, image enhancement consists of two main domains i) spatial domain that involves direct manipulation of pixels, and ii) frequency domain that involves Fourier transformation of the input image [22]. IE methods improve the perception of the image using spatial domain, frequency domain and a combination of both methods in order to output a modified image on its contrast, hue, or brightness.

These methods have been approached using either traditional or deep learning techniques. Some examples of the traditional methods group on the spatial domain are Histogram Equalization (HE) [19], Dehazing-based methods [17] and curve adjustment approaches [11]. Another category of image enhancement approaches are those based on Retinex theory, which decompose the images in reflection and illumination components [22]; examples of these methods are Single Scale Retinex (SSR) [16] and multi-scale Retinex (MSR) [16]. These methods suffer from a limitation in model capacity for the decomposition and it is difficult to implement successfully in endoscopy scenarios due to the challenging lighting changes.

Recently, deep learning based methods have been explored for achieving more accurate and real-time image enhancement procedures with successful results. However, most the works in the literature have been oriented to the low-light image enhancement such as deep-learning networks based on the Retinex assumption, which combines Retinex assumption with the Convolutional Neural Networks (CNN) [22].

Furthermore, although these methods have shown great promise in natural images, many of them cannot be directly applied to endoscopic images or videos. First of all, most of the existing methods can either enhance either under-or over-exposed images but not both. For instance, Deep UPE [20], or the work presented in [25,26] are examples of methods that can be applied successfully in under-exposed natural images, whereas just a few methods have been explored to correct both under-exposed and over-exposed images. Recently, Afifi et al.

[1] proposed a novel deep learning based technique to enhance images in both directions under- and over-exposure in a supervised manner.

Herein, we benchmark this technique against traditional methods in order to assess our real-synthetic paired dataset and highlight the need for reliable and standard datasets for future DL-based IE methods in endoscopic procedures. Nonetheless, another requirement for developing usable IE methods in endoscopy is related their inference time or latency. Most of the works found in the literature take several seconds to enhance a single image, hampering their use in real-time image processing applications such as video processing of underwater [12], X-ray imaging [14] and restoration in video endoscopy [9]. Endoscopy is an application area which requires dynamic and real-time image enhancement, which additionally needs to be accurate in the sense of not introducing any artifacts and we believe that the work presented in [1] can serve a launching pad to satisfy these requirements.

Figure 2 shows some examples of endoscopic video frames with some of these examples. These dramatic changes impede the development of robust computer vision methods for CADe and CADx among other tasks such as MIS or CIS (computer integrated surgery). Besides, it has been demonstrated that image enhancement pre-processing techniques can significantly boost the performance of 3D reconstruction pipelines using endoscopic images [26].

As detecting artifacts such as under and over exposed frames is so important for a variety of applications, and in other to improve the applicability of CADe and CADx application endoscopy, several datasets and challenges have been proposed [2,3]. The focus of these challenges has been to foster the development of real-time methods for detecting artefacts such as bubbles, instruments, blood or even some lesions, where under and overexposure play a major role, as they are typically discarded in many automated procedures. However, many computer vision algorithms such as SfM or SLAM require as many frames as possible for maximizing the quality of the obtained results and as such, discarding such frames is not an option and image enhancement is thus necessary.

An additional problem is that, to the best of our knowledge, datasets containing both pairs of ground truth (clean images) and corrupted images (with exposure errors) does not exist in for endoscopic imaging. This is in stark contrast to the more conventional/mainstream computational photography research field, in which several standard datasets have been proposed and are widely used for testing new algorithms and architectures [6,22].

Thus, in order to develop and test new image enhancement methods in endoscopy is necessary to develop and test such dataset from the ground up. The contribution of the work presented in herein is thus creation of such a novel real-synthetic paired dataset. For doing so, we leverage three existing endoscopic datasets and a Generative Adversarial Networks (GANs) approach for transferring under and over exposed over clean images. In this manner, we have both a reference image and a corrupted images over which reference-based metrics (i.e. SSIM) can be applied in order to assess the performance of newly developed enhancement methods.

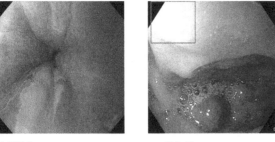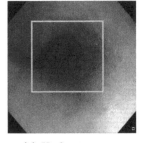

(a) Without exposure error.   (b) Overexposure.   (c) Underexposure.

Fig. 2. Example of endoscopic frames exhibiting the types of artefacts that we are interested on removing through image enhancement methods

3   Data and Methodology

3.1   Data

As briefly discussed above, the data for our experiments was obtained from three different sources, none of them containing enough information for doing image enhancement with deep learning-based methods, i.e., these are not datasets with paired frames for applying methods where we have access to the corresponding ground truth. The chosen datasets are: the EAD2020 Challenge dataset [2], EAD 2.0 from EndoCV2022 Challenge dataset [3] and the HyperKvasir dataset [5]. They were selected for our experiments as they contain single frames and also sequential frames from several hollow organs. Figure 2 shows examples of a normal frame (without exposure error) and two examples containing exposure problems that were extracted from the datasets.

EAD2020 Challenge Dataset. The Endoscopy Computer Vision Challenge (EndoCV2020) addressed two challenges both focused on finding novel methods for detection and segmentation in the endoscopic videos: Endoscopy Artifact Detection (EAD2020) and Endoscopy Disease Detection (EDD2020) [2] challenges. The goal of the EDD2020 sub-challenge was to develop methods for detecting and segmenting visible diseases. For this purpose, a full dataset comprised of images, annotations and masks was created from video frames and annotated by experts from various institutions. However, the nature of the challenge involves only classes related to diseases. On the other hand, EAD2020 challenge comprises a variety of endoscope positions, organs, disease/abnormality and image artefacts. All frames were annotated by experts with 8 different classes; in particular, two classes are of interest to our research: contrast and saturation artefacts. These classes denote what is well-known in photography as overexposure and underexposure errors but in specific areas on the image. From the 2531 images, only 770 frames were labeled with underexposure (contrast) and 249 with overexposure (saturation). Figure 2 shows two examples from the dataset containing these two kinds of artifacts.

EAD2.0 Dataset. Similarly to EAD2020 Challenge Dataset in Sect. 3.1, EAD2.0 Dataset [3] consists of multi-center and diverse population sub-datasets with tasks for detection and segmentation but focus on assessing generalizability of algorithms. This dataset contains more sequence/video data and multi-modality data from different centers. Particularly, the dataset consists of 24 sequences with 1106 video frames with multi-instance labels for training. However, unlike the EAD2020, EAD2.0 dataset was not labeled with any class related to underexposure errors. In Sect. 3.2 we will explain briefly the way we filtered out the dataset in order to have images with exposure errors.

HyperKvasir Datset. Borgli et al. in [5] presented the largest image and video dataset of the gastrointestinal tract available in literature with 110,079 images and 374 videos. The data was collected during real gastro- and colonoscopy examinations. The dataset is split into labeled images (10,662) and unlabeled images (99,417). Since this dataset had no a specific purpose, data was not annotated, and in fact the only labels that it contains are related to the organ type that the video frames comes from. In present work we only take the set of labeled images.

3.2   Methodology

Given a set of raw endoscopic frames collected from the three datasets previously mentioned, our pipeline aims to i) train an object detector to classify frames with and without exposure errors over unlabeled datasets (see Fig. 3a), ii) manually filter out non-informative frames, iii) train a GAN for creating synthetic frames with exposure errors (see Fig. 3b), and iv) quantitatively and qualitatively assess our dataset on various types of image enhancement methods: traditional algorithms based on histogram equalization, models based on Retinex theory and deep neural network architectures.

Data Preparation. We discarded non-informative frames. For instance, fully dark, bright or blurry images, were filtered out. After this process, we ended up with 7,064 images, 1049 from EAD2020, 654 from EAD2.0 and 5361 from HyperKvasir. As we mentioned before, the EAD2020 dataset already contains annotations about exposure errors of our concern, hence we trained a YOLOv4 object detector [4] with data from EAD2020 [2] and we obtained reliable results on detecting exposure errors. Finally, the model was applied to detect those instances in EAD2.0 [3] and HyperKvasir [5]. Therefore, as shown in Fig. 3, the object detector acts as a frame classifier, since it outputs frames without exposure errors, and with over and under exposure errors.

Image-to-Image Translation. Image-to-image translation is an application of GANs which manage to translate from one representation of an image to another, or rather it does style transfer. For instance, a scene may be rendered by a gray-scale image, RGB image or edge sketches [8].

One of the contributions of the present work is to use image-to-image translation [8] to take normal endoscopic frames and transfer to style with over- and underexposure. For implementing this task, we used the CycleGAN architecture [27] since the main problem to tackle is the lack of paired data, thus CycleGAN is a promising method for working with our unpaired data.

Image Enhancement. One of the concerns of this work has been to find image enhancement methods that perform the restoration of both types of exposure errors, since these problems are often found simultaneously in endoscopic examinations. Contrary to other methods in the literature, the model proposed by Afifi et al. [1]is capable of handling both problems in natural images with accurate

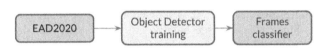

(a) Object detector for classifying frames.

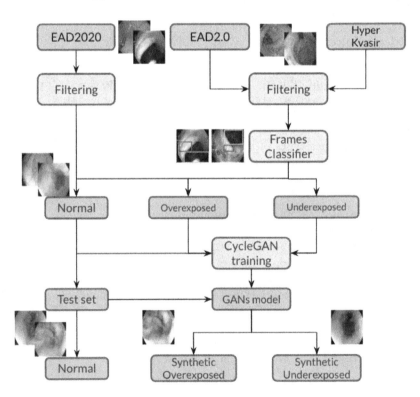

(b) Pipeline for creating our real-synthetic endoscopy dataset for IE.

Fig. 3. Overall pipeline of the methodology

results and with a very low latency and we will used as a baseline for comparison traditional image processing algorithms as well as for future developments.

The approach proposed by the authors, known as Learning Multi-Scale Photo Exposure Correction (LMSPEC) extracts random patches of three different sizes (128×128, 256×256 and 512×512) and decomposes each patch in four-level frequencies, i.e., it makes a Laplacian Pyramid (LP) of four levels. Then, each level of the resulting LP is utilized as input of a set of sequential U-Net-like sub-networks. For each patch, an L1 loss-based loss functions is proposed, aimed to store global color information besides detail information. A discriminator network is also for computing an adversarial loss aimed to preserve realism in the corrected patch. In this work, we implemented a quantitative and qualitative benchmark using i) traditional methods: RLBHE [28] and FHSABP [19] based on histogram equalization, and LIME [10] and DUAL [24] based on Retinex theory, and ii) DL-based method: LMSPEC [1].

3.3   Training Setup

All our models were trained and the experiments were executed on an NVIDIA DGX-1 system with eight Tesla V100 GPUs.

YOLOv4 Setup. Frames annotated by experts provided on the EAD2020 challenge [2] allowed us to train YOLOv4 object detector (for classifying frames without exposure errors, under- and over-exposed) with 90% for training and 10% for testing. For avoiding over-fitting, data augmentation techniques such as rotations, splits, blurry, and hue change, were applied. The hyper-parameters were set as follows: the number of classes were 2 (overexposure and underexposure), thus the number of filters on each convolutional layer was 30. The training steps was set to 6000 with an initial step decay learning rate of 0.01 and divided by factor of 10 at the 4,800 steps and 5,400 steps. The momentum was set as 0.9 and weight decay as 0.0005.

CycleGANs Setup. For the first experiment all frames with exposure errors, i.e., $1,296$ overexposed and $1,289$ underexposed, were taken as adversarial discriminators D_Y. On the other hand, the $4,478$ normal frames were split up into 65% for training and 35 %for testing. The hyper-parameters were set for both experiments as follows: 150 epochs, ADAM optimizer, learning rate of 0.0002, decay β_1 of 0.5, decay β_2 of 0.999, starting decay from epoch 100, cycle loss weight λ_{cyc} of 10 and identity loss weight λ_{id} of 5.

LMSPEC Setup. We perform the same split for manage both exposure errors, 70% for training, 27% for testing and 3% for validation. We only perform experiments on patches with dimensions 128×128 and 256×256. The hyper-parameters were setup for both experiments as follows: ADAM optimizer, decay rate β_1 of 0.9, decay β_2 of 0.999, a learning rate of 0.0001 for the generator and 0.00001 for the discriminator; for patches with dimension 128×128 we used a mini-batch size of 32, 40 epochs and at epoch 20 the learning rate was decayed by factor of 0.5. For patches with dimension 256×256 we used a mini-batch size of 8, 30 epochs and each 10 epochs the learning rate was decayed by the same factor; the adversarial loss was activated only for patches with dimensions 256×256 after 15 epochs.

3.4 Metrics

One of the drawbacks of implementing a framework like ours, which is based in GANs and synthetic datasets, is that there are not other works to compare against our results. Therefore, for evaluating our image enhancement results we make use of well-known of reference-based metrics, thus the need for a paired dataset with ground truth images. For instance, in [23] P. Welander et al. performed a perceptual study for evaluating the realism on the resulting synthetic images. Unlike them, herein we performed a perceptual study for evaluating the quality of the generated images. First of all, we use the Structure Similarity Index (SSIM) for filtering out similar frames, whereas the Main Square Error (MSE) on the gray-scale domain was used for filtering out very darkened/brightened frames, or for discarding frames without changes on light conditions after the GAN style transfer.

On the other hand, for evaluating our image enhancement experiments we implemented a statistical analysis, ground truth dependent evaluation. We used the Mean Squared Error (MSE) to evaluate the pixel-wise average squared errors in the image. We also make use of the Peak Signal-to-Noise Ratio (PSNR) and of Structural Similarity Index Metric (SSIM) [21] for evaluating quantitatively the quality of the enhanced images results.

4   Experiments and Results

We implemented three main experiments. i) we created a frames classifier by training and testing YOLOv4 object detector, ii) we created a paired real-synthetic dataset by training and testing CycleGANs, and iii) we utilized our dataset for exposure correction with traditional methods, and training and testing LMSPEC to highlight the importance of a paired data.

4.1 Results

After implementing the CycleGAN model, we obtained 1,564 frames for each type of exposure error. However, some frames were not useful or sufficiently informative, thus we carried out a statistical analyses based on the MSE and SSIM metrics which were used to establish boundaries that separate informative from non-informative frames. For our dataset, the range for the SSIM was between $0.6 \leq SSIM < 0.9$; on the other hand, the value of the MSE over gray-scale levels boundaries was $100 < MSE < 1,500$ for overexposure and

$100 < MSE < 750$ for underexposure errors. After this procedure, we finally obtained a dataset with 985 underexposed and 1,231 overexposed paired frames, that is both ground truth and corrupted images.

Table 1 reports the quantitative results of each method applied to our dataset, in which numbers in bold were the best results for each metric. As it can be inferred from the table, LMSPEC achieves a very competitive performance for both types of exposure errors in terms of noise removal and the preservation of the structure of the image.

Table 1. Results for full reference-based quality experiments.

Method	Overexposure			Underexposure			Inference time
	MSE↓	PSNR↑	SSIM↑	MSE↓	PSNR↑	SSIM↑	
LIME	0.048	8.566	0.597	0.054	17.331	0.699	44.0236
DUAL	0.043	0.907	0.726	0.053	20.012	0.708	30.9965
FHSABP	**0.036**	16.021	0.631	0.034	18.195	0.633	0.2953
RLBHE	0.051	19.425	0.746	0.055	21.053	0.723	0.2996
LMSPEC	**0.046**	**24.061**	**0.812**	**0.964**	**23.863**	**0.793**	**0.1316**

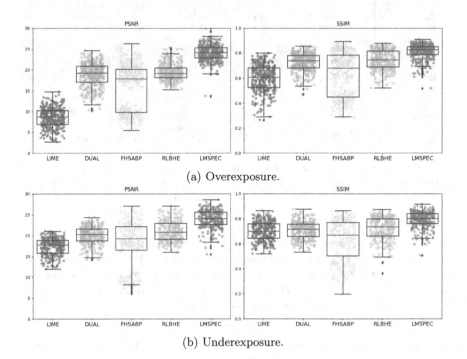

(a) Overexposure.

(b) Underexposure.

Fig. 4. Reference-based PSNR and SSIM evaluation results.

On the other hand, Fig. 4 shows distribution and density of the computed metrics (in the form of box and plots) obtained for every applied enhanced method. It turns out that LMSPEC got higher values for both compared metrics, and the results tend to be more robust as they show very low variance. Figure 5 shows qualitatively results of enhancement with all methods.

This qualitative comparison is very much required as by comparing methods in terms of MSE might suggest that the Retinex Theory-based DUAL method perform as well as LMSPEC. However, as it can be observed in Fig. 5, this is far from the truth, as a comparison between the 4th and 7th columns shows: DUAL is in general not able to remove overexposure artefacts, and in some cases it makes the problem worse.

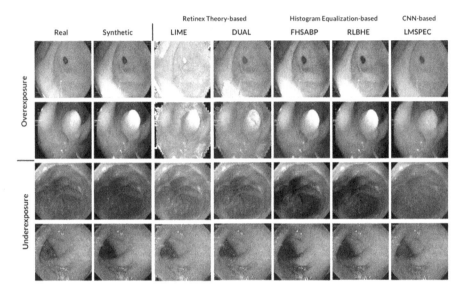

Fig. 5. Results of our methods: first column real images, second column GANs-made synthetic images with exposure error, and third column the image corrected. First pair of rows, we show two overexposed cases, and second pair underexposed cases.

Another advantage of LMSPEC over DUAL and other more traditional methods pertains the processing or inference time. As it can be observed in Table 1, more traditional methods require very long processing times (44 and 30 s in average for image for LIME and DUAL, respectively) whereas LMSPEC requires 0.13 s, attaining a very good performance (around $7.6 fps$).

Limitations. The implementation of GANs for creating the synthetic data with exposure errors implies stochastic results, therefore this methodology does not allow us to control the level of darkening or lightening on the output images, as well as the regions where these errors are induced.

5   Conclusion and Future Work

In this paper we have proposed a pipeline for generating a novel dataset which aim is to provide a baseline for comparing image enhancement methods. The dataset was built leveraging images from other publicly available datasets for finding suitable uncorrupted and under and over exposed images using an object detector. This intermediate dataset in the used for transferring the desired artifacts into the uncorrupted images, effectively enabling us to create a paired dataset that can be used for reference-based testing purposes. After a filtering process, this dataset was validated by expert endoscopists in our team.

However, some of the synthetic images still present drawbacks such as noise, color changes and other types distortions. We consider that a longer training, in tandem with a larger dataset or data augmentation techniques would alleviate this issue. Nonetheless, we demonstrate that this dataset is versatile enough for testing traditional and more advanced image enhancement methods such as LMSPEC. As our results suggest, this method has shown remarkable results, but further tests and improvements are necessary to make it useful for endoscopic settings. For instance, the model can introduce some artifacts in some images; this aspect needs to be properly characterized and taken into account for designing novel loss functions (i.e. perceptual loss) that preserve color and texture more effectively. Secondly, there are some areas of improvement in order to make this model to be able to run in real time (i.e., 24 FPS).

Acknowledgments. The authors wish to thank the AI Hub and the CIIOT at ITESM for their support for carrying the experiments reported in this paper in their NVIDIA's DGX computer. This work is part of a project financed by SEP-CONACYT-ANUIES-ECOS NORD Project 315597.

References

1. Afifi, M., Derpanis, K.G., Ommer, B., Brown, M.S.: Learning multi-scale photo exposure correction. In: Proceedings of the IEEE/CVF Conference on Computer Vision and Pattern Recognition, pp. 9157–9167 (2021)
2. Ali, S., et al.: A translational pathway of deep learning methods in gastrointestinal endoscopy. arXiv:2010.06034 (2020)
3. Ali, S., Ghatwary, N.: Endoscopic computer vision challenges 2.0. https://endocv2022.grand-challenge.org/
4. Bochkovskiy, A., Wang, C.Y., Liao, H.Y.M.: YOLOv4: optimal speed and accuracy of object detection. arXiv preprint arXiv:2004.10934 (2020)
5. Borgli, H., et al.: HyperKvasir, a comprehensive multi-class image and video dataset for gastrointestinal endoscopy. Sci. Data **7**, 1–14 (2020)
6. Bychkovsky, V., Paris, S., Chan, E., Durand, F.: Learning photographic global tonal adjustment with a database of input/output image pairs. In: The Twenty-Fourth IEEE Conference on Computer Vision and Pattern Recognition (2011)
7. Chen, L., Tang, W., John, N.W., Wan, T.R., Zhang, J.J.: SLAM-based dense surface reconstruction in monocular minimally invasive surgery and its application to augmented reality. Comput. Methods Programs Biomed. **158**, 135–146 (2018)

8. Elgendy, M.: Deep Learning for Vision Systems. Simon and Schuster (2020)
9. Fu, Z., et al.: The future of endoscopic navigation: a review of advanced endoscopic vision technology. IEEE Access **9**, 41144–41167 (2021)
10. Guo, X., Li, Y., Ling, H.: LIME: low-light image enhancement via illumination map estimation. IEEE Trans. Image Process. **26**(2), 982–993 (2016)
11. Huang, S.C., Cheng, F.C., Chiu, Y.S.: Efficient contrast enhancement using adaptive gamma correction with weighting distribution. IEEE Trans. Image Process. **22**(3), 1032–1041 (2012)
12. Li, C., et al.: An underwater image enhancement benchmark dataset and beyond. IEEE Trans. Image Process. **29**, 4376–4389 (2019)
13. Ma, R., Wang, R., Pizer, S., Rosenman, J., McGill, S.K., Frahm, J.-M.: Real-time 3D reconstruction of colonoscopic surfaces for determining missing regions. In: Shen, D., et al. (eds.) MICCAI 2019. LNCS, vol. 11768, pp. 573–582. Springer, Cham (2019). https://doi.org/10.1007/978-3-030-32254-0_64
14. Naidu, S., Parvatkar, P., Quadros, A., Kumar, K.C., Natekar, A., Aswale, S.: Medical image enhancement based on statistical and image processing techniques. Int. J. Eng. Res. Technol. **10**(5), 509–515 (2021)
15. Phan, T.B., Trinh, D.H., Wolf, D., Daul, C.: Optical flow-based structure-from-motion for the reconstruction of epithelial surfaces. Pattern Recogn. **105**, 107391 (2020)
16. Rahman, Z., Jobson, D.J., Woodell, G.A.: Multi-scale retinex for color image enhancement. In: Proceedings of 3rd IEEE International Conference on Image Processing, vol. 3, pp. 1003–1006. IEEE (1996)
17. Savelli, B., et al.: Illumination correction by dehazing for retinal vessel segmentation. In: 2017 IEEE 30th International Symposium on Computer-Based Medical Systems (CBMS), pp. 219–224. IEEE (2017)
18. Shao, S., et al.: Self-supervised monocular depth and ego-motion estimation in endoscopy: appearance flow to the rescue. Med. Image Anal. **77**, 102338 (2022)
19. Wang, C., Peng, J., Ye, Z.: Flattest histogram specification with accurate brightness preservation. IET Image Proc. **2**(5), 249–262 (2008)
20. Wang, R., Zhang, Q., Fu, C.W., Shen, X., Zheng, W.S., Jia, J.: Underexposed photo enhancement using deep illumination estimation. In: Proceedings of the IEEE/CVF Conference on Computer Vision and Pattern Recognition, pp. 6849–6857 (2019)
21. Wang, Z., Bovik, A.C., Sheikh, H.R., Simoncelli, E.P.: Image quality assessment: from error visibility to structural similarity. IEEE Trans. Image Process. **13**(4), 600–612 (2004)
22. Wei, C., Wang, W., Yang, W., Liu, J.: Deep retinex decomposition for low-light enhancement. CoRR (2018)
23. Welander, P., Karlsson, S., Eklund, A.: Generative adversarial networks for image-to-image translation on multi-contrast MR images-a comparison of CycleGAN and unit. arXiv preprint arXiv:1806.07777 (2018)
24. Zhang, Q., Nie, Y., Zheng, W.S.: Dual illumination estimation for robust exposure correction. In: Computer Graphics Forum, vol. 38, pp. 243–252 (2019)
25. Zhang, Y., Guo, X., Ma, J., Liu, W., Zhang, J.: Beyond brightening low-light images. Int. J. Comput. Vis. **129**(4), 1013–1037 (2021)
26. Zhang, Y., Wang, S., Ma, R., McGill, S.K., Rosenman, J.G., Pizer, S.M.: Lighting enhancement aids reconstruction of colonoscopic surfaces. In: Feragen, A., Sommer, S., Schnabel, J., Nielsen, M. (eds.) IPMI 2021. LNCS, vol. 12729, pp. 559–570. Springer, Cham (2021). https://doi.org/10.1007/978-3-030-78191-0_43

27. Zhu, J.Y., Park, T., Isola, P., Efros, A.A.: Unpaired image-to-image translation using cycle-consistent adversarial networks. In: Proceedings of the IEEE International Conference on Computer Vision, pp. 2223–2232 (2017)
28. Zuo, C., Chen, Q., Sui, X.: Range limited bi-histogram equalization for image contrast enhancement. Optik **124**(5), 425–431 (2013)

Comparison of Automatic Prostate Zones Segmentation Models in MRI Images Using U-net-like Architectures

Pablo Cesar Quihui-Rubio[1(✉)], Gilberto Ochoa-Ruiz[1,2],
Miguel Gonzalez-Mendoza[1], Gerardo Rodriguez-Hernandez[1],
and Christian Mata[3,4]

[1] School of Engineering and Sciences, Tecnologico de Monterrey, Monterrey, Mexico
A00820701@tec.mx
[2] Institute of Advanced Materials for Sustainable Manufacturing, Tecnologico de
Monterrey, Monterrey, Mexico
[3] Universitat Politècnica de Catalunya, 08019 Barcelona, Catalonia, Spain
[4] Pediatric Computational Imaging Research Group, Hospital Sant Joan de Déu,
Esplugues de Llobregat, 08950 Barcelona, Catalonia, Spain

Abstract. Prostate cancer is the second-most frequently diagnosed cancer and the sixth leading cause of cancer death in males worldwide. The main problem that specialists face during the diagnosis of prostate cancer is the localization of Regions of Interest (ROI) containing a tumor tissue. Currently, the segmentation of this ROI in most cases is carried out manually by expert doctors, but the procedure is plagued with low detection rates (of about 27–44%) or over-diagnosis in some patients. Therefore, several research works have tackled the challenge of automatically segmenting and extracting features of the ROI from magnetic resonance images, as this process can greatly facilitate many diagnostic and therapeutic applications. However, the lack of clear prostate boundaries, the heterogeneity inherent to the prostate tissue, and the variety of prostate shapes makes this process very difficult to automate.In this work, six deep learning models were trained and analyzed with a dataset of MRI images obtained from the Centre Hospitalaire de Dijon and Universitat Politecnica de Catalunya. We carried out a comparison of multiple deep learning models (i.e. U-Net, Attention U-Net, Dense-UNet, Attention Dense-UNet, R2U-Net, and Attention R2U-Net) using categorical cross-entropy loss function. The analysis was performed using three metrics commonly used for image segmentation: Dice score, Jaccard index, and mean squared error. The model that give us the best result segmenting all the zones was R2U-Net, which achieved 0.869, 0.782, and 0.00013 for Dice, Jaccard and mean squared error, respectively.

Keywords: Segmentation · Prostate cancer · Deep learning · Loss functions

1   Introduction

Prostate cancer (PCa) is the second leading cause of cancer deaths in the world and nowadays one of eight men are diagnosed with this disease in their lifetime [1]. There are some risk factors, such as the age above 50 years, family history, obesity, ethnicity that must be considered during the diagnosis process, and it is noteworthy that the survival rate for regional PCa is almost 100% when detected in early stages. In stark contrast, the survival rate when the cancer is spread to other parts of the body is of only 30% [2].

Magnetic Resonance Imaging (MRI) has been established as the best medical image tool for the detection, localization and staging of PCa, due to their high resolution, excellent spontaneous contrast of soft tissues, and the possibility of multi-planar and multi-parametric scanning [3]. Although MRI has been traditionally used for staging PCa, we will focus on PCa detection trough ROI segmented from MR images.

The use of image segmentation of MR images for PCa detection and characterisation can in fact help in determining the tissue volume, aiding as well in the localization the cancerous tissue in the ROI [4]. Thus, an accurate and consistent segmentation is crucial in PCa. Although prostate segmentation is a relatively old problem and some methods have been proposed in the past using conventional image processing pipelines, nowadays, the most common and traditional method to identify and delimit prostate gland and prostate regions of interest (central zone, peripheral zone, transition zone) is performed manually by radiologists [5].

This non-automated process has been proven to be time-consuming and, due to the subjectivity of the task and different interpretations from multiple specialists, it is highly operator dependant and difficult to reproduce [6]. Therefore, automating this process for the segmentation of prostate gland and regions of interest, in addition to saving time for radiologists, can be used as a learning tool for others and have consistency in contouring [7].

In recent years, the automatic segmentation of the prostate has been promoted with the use of deep learning techniques. These methods, called convolutional neural networks (CNNs) have generated results that outperform traditional methods due to their ability to learn complex features and perform an accurate classification of pixels, resulting in segmentation [8]. Several works have addressed the problem of prostate segmentation using deep learning, such is the case of the popular U-Net [9] model, which is the base of many recent works in literature: *MultiResU-Net* [10], *Dense-UNet* [11], *Attention U-Net* [12], among others. Although good results have been obtained by the authors of these models, there is a lack of datasets with enough information to segment the prostate and all of its ROI correctly.

In this paper, we explore six recent deep learning methods (i.e. U-Net, Attention U-Net, Dense-UNet, Attention Dense-UNet, Recurrent Residual Convolutional Neural Network based on U-Net (R2U-Net), and Attention R2U-Net architectures.) to segment the prostate and evaluate their performance in this task. Even though a comparison of metrics to evaluate the performance between these models have been performed in other works, most of them only evaluate between the whole prostate gland or two principal zones: CZ, and PZ.

The dataset we used to perform our experiments the Centre Hospitalaire de Dijon and consists of 16 patients, with a total of 205 images with their corresponding annotations that were validated by a collaboration of experts using a dedicated software tool [13]. The deep learning models studied and compared were trained in the same conditions, using categorical cross-entropy loss function and three metrics to measure their performance. In this work, we make a thorough comparison between six models, including five U-Net based models and original U-Net, using multiple loss functions and the same metrics for evaluation. The pipeline of our experiments is shown in Fig. 1.

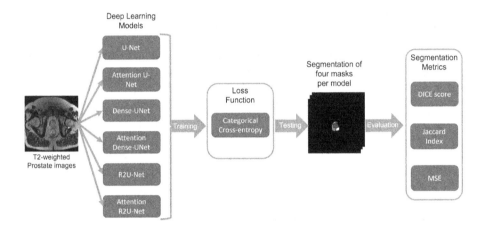

Fig. 1. Pipeline of experiments. Six models were trained with 16 patients (205 images) using categorical cross-entropy loss function. As a result, an image with four segmented zones was obtained for each test image on all models. The resulting images were evaluated using three segmentation metrics.

This paper has five sections including this introduction. Section 2 is divided in two subsections where we mentioned the motivation of doing this study, and also, discuss previous works related to prostate segmentation, focusing on deep learning methods. Section 3 is divided in four subsections, where we described the dataset, deep learning architectures, metrics, loss functions, and details for training and testing. In Sect. 4 the results of the experiments are discussed in detail. The conclusion and future work are in Sect. 5.

2   Motivation and State of the Art

2.1   Motivation for Segmenting Prostate Zones

In accordance with Sun et al. [14], analyzing multiparametric MRI (mpMRI) images is a technique used in patients with possible PCa, which can be performed before a transrectal ultrasound (TRUS) or after a negative TRUS. In the case of a potential cancerous tissue, it can also be analyzed by MRI guided biopsy or MRI-US guided biopsy, which both of them have shown higher accuracy than only using TRUS [14]. For patients who have been correctly diagnosed with PCa, morphology and localization are features that can be extracted from mpMRI images. An accurate localization of tumor can be carried out by mpMRI, chiefly those in anterior zone that TRUS may miss [15]. Also, mpMRI has shown a high accuracy defining tumor volume, which is a risk factor [14].

Therefore, segmentation of MRI images is crucial to define the prostate boundaries (including zones) and exclude other nearby organs that are not of interest at the moment [14]. As commented before, there are manual and automated methods to do it and the most common used is manual.

This manual method has several limitations that can affect in the analysis of PCa detection, such as time consumption, subjective results, variability, etc., and, for that reason, automated techniques are currently the main discussion in research [5].The difficulty in the segmentation process is due to the complex nature of medical images and the presence of non-linear features in most of them [16].

More precisely, the segmentation output can be affected by: intensity inhomogeneity, closeness in gray level of different soft tissue, partial volume effect, or presence of artifacts [16], which are not easy to fix or homogenize between acquisition or among patients and are highly operator dependant as well.

Another issue in image segmentation pertains validation fot the results by several specialists following a reproducible method. New automated methods have tried to overcome these limitations, and there are some examples such as U-net [9] network architecture which is dedicated to segment biomedical images, but it has some drawbacks [5].

2.2   Related Work

Machine Learning Methods. Several traditional methods in the literature for prostate zones segmentation have been proposed. They can be classified as atlas-based models, deformable models, and feature-based ML methods [17]. Atlas-based models consist in a collection of multiple images segmented manually by experts, which are used as a reference for new segmentation in images of other patients [17]. A study of Klein et al. [18] in 2007, proposed a model based in MR atlas images, they registered the target image in a non-rigidly way using a similarity measure, to use the same measure to select the best ones, and obtain the segmentation by averaging the selected deformed segmentation. They obtained a median Dice similarity coefficient (DSC) of 0.82 evaluating their model in 22 images [18].

Deformable models is another technique that has been used in the literature to get an accurate prostate segmentation, this models are based in mathematical, geometrical, and physical theories to constrain and guide a curve to delineate an object's border [19]. Liu et al. [20] in 200 proposed a deformable model using level set in MRI data, the model was tested in images from 10 patients and they obtained a DSC score of 0.81.

Another methods were introduced in order to get a more precise results of segmentation in medical devices such as: k-means clustering, thresholding, active contour methods, among others. Those techniques have shown good results in image segmentation. However, in the last years, the field of Deep Learning (DL) has growth exponentially in medical imaging, particularly in the segmentation process [21].

Deep Learning Based Methods. In medical imaging, deep-learning techniques have been improving the analysis, such as image segmentation, image registration, image fusion, image annotation, CADx, lesion detection, and microscopic image analysis [22]. In recent years, new DL models for image segmentation have been developed, specially focused on the biomedical area.

One of the best known models in the literature is U-Net, which is a CNN composed of a series of four convolution and max-pooling operations which reduce the dimension of the input image, followed by four convolution and up-sampling operations [9].

There are some works that use U-Net to get an automatic segmentation of the prostate. Zhu et al. [23] proposed a deeply-supervised CNN to segment the whole prostate gland, based on the structure of U-Net getting a mean DSC of 0.885. Also, Zabihollahy et al. [24] designed a model composed by two U-Net architectures to segment the prostate gland, as well as, its CZ and PZ in MRI T2-weighted images and ADC maps, obtaining a mean DSC score of 0.92, 0.91, 0.86, respectively. Also, Clark et al. [25] presented a new architecture based on U-Net and inception model to segment the prostate and transition zones using diffusion-weighted MR images, they obtained a mean DSC of 0.93 and 0.88, respectively. Rundo et al. [26] proposed a novel architecture called USE-Net, which incorporates Squeeze-and-Excitation into U-Net; they achieved a segmentation of the prostate zones outperforming most of the state-of-the-art results in peripheral zone segmentation. In another work, Runo et al. [27] analyzed some CNN models with datasets from different institutions using only T2-weighted MR images and concluded that U-Net outperforms other methods in the state of the art. More recently, Aldoj et al. [5] proposed a novel model based on U-Net and DenseNet and did a segmentation of prostate zones in 3D MR images with three variations of their architecture, they obtained a mean DSC for the whole gland, CZ, and PZ of 0.92, 0.89, and 0.78, respectively.

In 2018, Oktay et al. [12] proposed a novel attention gates to incorporate it into the existing U-Net model. The intention of using attention blocks is that, in an automatic way, the model learns to focus on the specific target structures, and ignore the rest of them on the image. In Attention U-Net model, the attention gates highlight the salient features from the skip connections between the encoder and decoder [12]. These attention gates modules have been implemented in other architectures such as Attention Dense-UNet [28], Spatial Attention U-Net [29], Attention R2U-Net, among others.

Although automatic prostate segmentation has improved during the last years, there is still work to do in segmentation of specific prostate zones such as CZ, PZ, and TZ. An accurate segmentation of these zones, as well as, of tumor (TUM) of different sizes and shapes, could lead in early detection of prostate cancer. Therefore in this work, we compared some models from the literature using categorical cross-entropy as loss function with a dataset of only T2-weighted images. We analyzed the segmentation of the prostate zones using different metrics to choose the best DL architecture.

3   Data and Methods

The technical contribution of this work is the evaluation of the impact of categorical cross-entropy as a loss function with three metrics on the prostate segmentation using U-Net, Attention U-Net, Recurrent Residual Convolutional Neural Network based on U-Net (R2U-Net), Attention R2U-Net, Dense-UNet, and Attention Dense-UNet architectures. A total of 6 segmentation processes with a maximum of four zones per image are compared in this work. A visual summary of the experiments carried out is shown in Fig. 1. In this section the data and methodology followed is described and explained.

3.1   Dataset

The dataset of images used in this work were provided by PhD. Christian Mata from UPC in Barcelona in collaboration with DIJON hospital in France. The examinations used in our study contained three-dimensional T2-weighted fast spin-echo (TR/TE/ETL: 3600 ms/143 ms/109, slice thickness: 1.25 mm) images acquired with sub-millimetric pixel resolution in an oblique axial plane. The institutional committee on human research approved the study, with a waiver for the requirement for written consent, because MRI was included in the workup procedure for all patients referred for brachytherapy or radiotherapy.

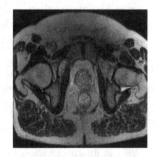   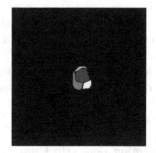

(a) Original T2-MRI prostate image   (b) Masks of prostate zones

Fig. 2. Sample image and mask of the dataset.

In addition to the images, a manual segmentation of each with four regions of interest (CZ, PZ, TZ, and TUMOR) was provided and this process was cautiously validated by multiple professional radiologists and experts using a dedicated software tool [13]. The format of the T2-weighted scans from the dataset are DICOM, with their correspondent annotations in format CSV of the prostate zones.

The ground truth masks were created from the CSV data files in a resolution of 256 × 256 pixels. Also, DICOM files were transformed to images of the same resolution after a data augmentation process was carried out. As is common with medical images, due to the difficulty of obtaining good images to work with them, a biomedical image augmentation algorithm [30] was performed. This process help us to increase the number of training images, and consisted of 16 geometrical transformations such as: rotations, zoom, translations, among others variations. At the end, the total number of images with their corresponding masks were 3485. An example from the dataset is shown in Fig. 2; in the image there is an original T2-MRI image of the prostate and the mask of the zones generated from the data file provided.

3.2   Deep Learning Architectures

As mentioned in Sect. 2, there are several deep learning architectures used for image segmentation in the literature. In this work, we focused on five models based in the U-Net architecture originally proposed by Ronnerberget et al. [9], and this one was also considered for comparison.

One of the architectures used in this work is Attention U-Net by Oktay et al. [12], which incorporates Attention Gates (AGs) into the standard U-Net architecture to highlight salient features that are passed through the skip connections. This is performed right before the concatenation operation to merge only relevant activations [12]. AGs progressively suppress feature responses in irrelevant background regions without the requirement to crop a regions of interest between networks [12].

Also, Dense-UNet proposed by Wu et al. [11] was selected for the comparison in this work, which consists of a network that combines the U-Net architecture with dense concatenation to reduce resolution loss. The network consists of a right side of the architecture with a dense downsampling path, and the left side with a dense upsampling path, also, it incorporates some skip connection channels to connect the paths.

Other model tested was R2U-Net presented by Zahangir et al. [31] consists of a recurrent residual convolutional neural network which has been demonstrated that outperforms classical U-Net due to the benefit of feature accumulation inside the model in training and testing processes, among other novel features proposed.

Attention Dense-Unet proposed by Li et al. [28], is an integration of Attention modules and the model Dense-UNet, and has been demonstrated in the literature to outperforms Dense-UNet, thus we decided to include it in the comparison. Finally, we did an integration of Attention U-Net [32] and R2U-Net [31] architectures called Attention R2U-Net to get a combination of the benefits of both models and compare the performance of the segmentation tasks.

3.3   Segmentation Metrics

There are several metrics used for image segmentation in the literature [33] and the selection of metrics for evaluation depends on the data and segmentation task. Therefore, the metrics we have selected to be used on this work aiming to get a robust comparison between the segmentation architectures and loss functions are Dice Similarity Coefficient (DSC), Jaccard Index (JAC), and Mean Square Error (MSE).

As are trying to segment multiple prostate zones, it is necessary to use the appropriate metrics, as mentioned by Taha et *al.* [33], the use of Jaccard index and DSC is appropriate in this case. The Jaccard Index, also known as Intersection Over Union (IOU), is a segmentation metric based on overlap and it is defined as the intersection between ground-truths and predictions divided by their union (see Eq. 1). DSC is the most used metric based for calculating the overlap between the ground-truth and predicted images divided by the common pixels between them, and it can be defined as shown in Eq. 2. The last metric is Mean Square Error (MSE), which averages the difference between the ground-truths and predicted segmentation.

$$JAC = \frac{|\text{Prediction} \cap \text{Ground Truth}|}{|\text{Prediction} \cup \text{Ground Truth}|} \tag{1}$$

$$DSC = \frac{2|\text{Prediction} \cap \text{Ground Truth}|}{|\text{Prediction}| + |\text{Ground Truth}|} \tag{2}$$

3.4   Loss Functions

The choice of a loss function is extremely important for any deep learning architecture, due to the fact that it guides the learning process of the algorithm. That is to say, it makes the algorithm to be more accurate, faster and reproducible during the training process. Also, a correct selection of loss function can reduce or mitigate the problem of overfitting in the model. Herein, we evaluated the models with Categorical Cross-Entropy (CCE), which is a common loss function used in multi-class segmentation, and it is designed to quantify the difference between two probability distributions [34].

3.5   Training

All the models in this work were trained using equal parameters and settings; the five tested models were implemented using Keras. The U-Net model was implemented using an adapted code for multiclass segmentation provided by Sha, Y. [35]. The implementation of Dense-UNet made by Wu et *al.* [11] was used in this work. For the Attention U-Net, R2U-Net, and Attention R2U-Net, the codes implementations were taken from a Github repository [36] and transformed to be used with Keras. Finally, Attention Dense-UNet architecture was designed combining Dense-UNet and Attention U-Net implementation.

The training process for each model was performed using 90% of images, 100 epochs, a batch size of 6, and a learning rate of 0.0001. All the training was done using a NVIDIA DGX workstation, using two V100 GPUs for each model. At the end, the trained weights were saved for future testing and prediction.

4 Results

As mentioned above, previous works in the literature have shown great promise in prostate segmentation. However, most of them have focused solely on specific zones. Segmenting the gland or only CZ and PZ, is a more common task due to its boundaries being more delimited than zones such as TZ and Tumor, where the size and shape presents more variability between patients and images. Therefore, comparing multiple deep learning architectures dedicated for medical image segmentation with a dataset with images and masks of all the zones of the prostate represents an interesting contribution.

In what follows, we will perform a comparison of the obtained results both quantitatively (through the selected metrics) and qualitatively (by comparing various sample images and their corresponding GT) to assess the performance of studied models.

Table 1. Results using multiple deep learning models and metrics (average) for Categorical Cross-Entropy Loss.

Model	Metrics		
	DSC ↑	JAC ↑	MSE ↓
U-Net	0.731	0.635	0.0021
Attention U-Net	0.839	0.741	0.0016
Dense-UNet	0.830	0.725	0.0018
Attention Dense-UNet	0.844	0.747	0.0016
R2U-Net	**0.869**	**0.782**	**0.0013**
Attention R2U-Net	0.864	0.775	0.0014

4.1 Quantitative Results

Table 1 shows a summary of the five models performance measured under the metrics mentioned before. A (↑) or lower (↓) symbol indicates whether these metrics have to be maximized or minimized for obtaining a better model, whereas the values correspond to the mean metric between the prostate zones and test images. The bold values represent the model that achieved the best metric score within all of them.

Although all the models analyzed in this work are U-Net based, with our dataset this base architecture had the worst results in metrics performance.

After incorporating attention modules to U-Net, the performance increased in 0.108, 0.106, and 0.05 for the DSC, JAC, and MSE metrics, respectively. On the other hand, Dense-UNet model achieved lower metric values before integrating attention gates. After integrating attention, the performance obtained by Attention Dense-UNet was the best.

Analyzing all the results in Table 1, it is can be inferred that R2U-Net is the model with the highest performance in Dice and Jaccard metrics (although a lowest value for MSE was obtained). The gain in performance between R2U-Net and the base U-Net model is around 13.8%, 14.7%, and 0.0008 for DSC, JAC, and MSE, respectively. Nonetheless, the architecture of R2U-Net with Attention modules obtained almost the same values in the test set, with a difference of only 0.004, 0.007 and 0.0001, respectively.

However, the two last models require more computational resources (and inference time). The difference in performance can be explained by the use of attention blocks, which requires extra parameters, possibly leading to overfitting. Nevertheless, due to the little discrepancy between the metrics in these two architectures, it could be difficult to notice the gap in a visual comparison with images. For comparing the segmentation performance of the models for each zone (CZ, PZ, TZ, and TUMOR), we selected the Jaccard Index metric ($\uparrow$) for evaluation due to the noticeable difference between the different classes. A summary of the results is shown in a box-plot (see Fig. 3), where each color represents a different model, and each point is the result of the Jaccard performance in a tested image.

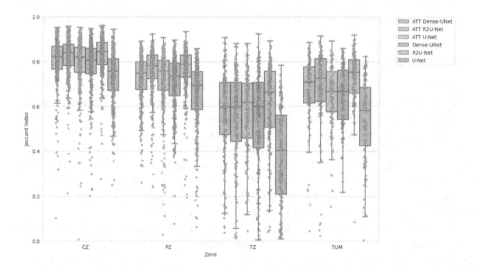

Fig. 3. Comparison of Jaccard Index per each class between Deep Learning Architectures. Each predicted segmentation is represented by a colored dot to visualize the variation in the results of the models.

As is shown in Fig. 3, the performance of the models varies according to the prostate zone segmented. The zone with the best Jaccard index, aside from the background, was the CZ, where all of the models performed similarly, with low variance between them. However, the best model was R2U-Net with a JAC value of 0.84, and the worst performance in this zone was U-Net base model.

For the segmentation of the peripheral zone, all the models behaved similarly, but they exhibited lower values for the metrics of interest in average. Although the other 2 zones were segmented with high values of JAC, it can be seen on Fig. 3 that the variance in this zone is higher than in CZ, yielding much lower values in some models such as U-Net and Dense-UNet. In this zone, the models with lower variance and higher mean score are R2U-Net and Attention R2U-Net with a mean JAC index of 0.763 and 0.751, respectively.

The Transition zone (TZ) was the one with worst segmentation performance of all the models, with high variances and an average JAC index below 0.57, achieved by the best architecture, R2U-Net. The variance and poor performance in this region can be explained by overall lack of ground truth masks of this zone in the training data, as well as the relatively small size of the zone compared to others. This zone is difficult to segment even for radiologists, so it is commonly taken as part of CZ or PZ. The above-mentioned problems could be solved by including more patients, with better delimited TZ masks to our dataset. Finally, the tumor was the last region analyzed, with less dispersion of points for all the models, but there was still variance for a few sample images. As in the previous zones, the best models for the tumor class were R2U-Net and Attention R2U-Net, with an average JAC index of 0.74 and 0.71, respectively. U-Net and Dense-UNet were the worst models; however, the implementation of attention modules improved the performance of those models by 11.6% and 39.3%, respectively.

4.2   Qualitative Results

Figure 4 presents a qualitative comparison for the tested models against the ground truth. We have selected three examples for assessing which models perform the best in different scenarios. The images were selected based on the JAC values obtained by R2U-Net (our best performing model) with the idea of showing the mos representative examples of the worst case image (first column), the image with the average JAC value in the dataset (center column) and the best segmented image in the entire test set (third column). The first row shows the input image, while the second depicts the GT mask, and each subsequent row displays the generated segmentation for each input image

As expected, the R2U-Net produces very good results for all the zones in a great share of the examples, but it struggles with the tumor zone and the transition zone, as the quantitative results suggested. Surprisingly, the U-Net model, which was the worst one, had acceptable results in images with only two or three zones to be segmented, as well as, Dense U-Net model.

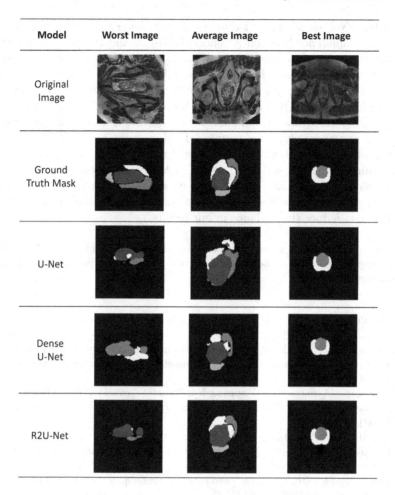

Fig. 4. Comparison of the worst, average and best images (obtained from R2U-Net) predicted by the worst, average, and best architectures analyzed in this work.

5   Conclusion and Future Work

After the analysis between all the models using the same conditions, the best architecture to segment prostate and its zones was R2U-Net. The segmentation of all the zones in any T2-weighted MR image is not easy, and in many cases there is not possible to delimit the boundaries of transition zone, even for experts.

This could be one of the reasons this zone is so difficult to segment for all the tested models. Even though all the models are U-Net based, there were differences in performance between them during segmentation tasks. The incorporation of attention gates in the U-Net and Dense-UNet architectures yielded better average metrics values, but this was not the case for Attention R2U-Net architecture. This could be due to the huge increase in the number of parameters in the A-R2U-Net model, which led to overfitting sooner that other models. Nevertheless, the difference between Attention R2U-Net and only R2U-Net metrics in average is not significant, but due to the resources and time consumption, we decided that the best model for training is R2U-Net.

It is well-known that the segmentation of prostate zones is a difficult task, even for radiologists, but it is possible to achieve good results using an automatic model with a verified dataset and the correct selection and implementation of a deep learning architecture for training. In this study, we concluded that the best option is R2U-Net, however there is still work to do in some zones such as TZ and Tumor, where it is desired to get higher dice score and Jaccard index. In order to achieve that, as a future work, we should train models with a larger dataset, as well as trying different loss functions focused on imbalanced datasets, which can also reduce the variance in our results.

Acknowledgments. The authors wish to thank the AI Hub and the CIIOT at ITESM for their support for carrying the experiments reported in this paper in their NVIDIA's DGX computer.

References

1. American Cancer Society. Key statistics for prostate cancer: Prostate cancer facts. https://www.cancer.org/cancer/prostate-cancer/about/key-statistics.html. Accessed 17 Oct 2021
2. AstraZeneca, A personalized approach in prostate cancer (2020). https://www.astrazeneca.com/our-therapy-areas/oncology/prostate-cancer.html. Accessed 17 Oct 2021
3. Chen, M., et al.: Prostate cancer detection: comparison of t2-weighted imaging, diffusion-weighted imaging, proton magnetic resonance spectroscopic imaging, and the three techniques combined. Acta Radiologica 49(5), 602–610 (2008)
4. Haralick, R., Shapiro, L.: Image segmentation techniques. Comput. Vision Graph. Image Process. 29(1), 100–132 (1985)
5. Aldoj, N., Biavati, F., Michallek, F., Stober, S., Dewey, M.: Automatic prostate and prostate zones segmentation of magnetic resonance images using densenet-like u-net. Sci. Rep. 10, 08 (2020)
6. Rasch, C.R.N., et al.: Human-computer interaction in radiotherapy target volume delineation: a prospective, multi-institutional comparison of user input devices. J. Digital Imaging 24(5), 794–803 (2011)
7. Mahapatra, D., Buhmann, J.-M.: Prostate mri segmentation using learned semantic knowledge and graph cuts. IEEE Trans. Biomed. Eng. 61(3), 756–764 (2014)
8. Elguindi, S., et al.: Deep learning-based auto-segmentation of targets and organs-at-risk for magnetic resonance imaging only planning of prostate radiotherapy. Phys. Imaging Radiat. Oncol. 12, 80–86 (2019)
9. Ronneberger, O., Fischer, P., Brox, T.: U-Net: convolutional networks for biomedical image segmentation. In: Navab, N., Hornegger, J., Wells, W.M., Frangi, A.F. (eds.) MICCAI 2015. LNCS, vol. 9351, pp. 234–241. Springer, Cham (2015). https://doi.org/10.1007/978-3-319-24574-4_28
10. Ibtehaz, N., Rahman, M.S.: Multiresunet: rethinking the u-net architecture for multimodal biomedical image segmentation. Neural Netw. 121, 74–87 (2020)

11. Yufeng, W., Jiachen, W., Jin, S., Cao, L., Jin, G.: Dense-u-net: dense encoder-decoder network for holographic imaging of 3D particle fields. Optics Commun. **493**, 126970 (2021)
12. Oktay, O., et al.: Attention u-net: learning where to look for the pancreas (2018)
13. Rodríguez, J., Ochoa-Ruiz, G., Mata, C.: A prostate mri segmentation tool based on active contour models using a gradient vector flow. Appl. Sci. **10**(18), 6163 (2020)
14. Sun, Y.: Multiparametric mri and radiomics in prostate cancer: a review. Aust. Phys. Eng. Sci. Med. **42**(1), 3–25 (2019)
15. Gupta, R., Kauffman, C., Polascik, T., Taneja, S., Rosenkrantz, A.: The state of prostate mri in 2013. Oncology (Williston Park) **27**(4), 262–70 (2013)
16. Sharma, N., Aggarwal, L.M.: Automated medical image segmentation techniques. J. Med. Phys./Assoc. Med. Phys. India **35**(1), 3 (2010)
17. Li, H., Lee, C.H., Chia, D., Lin, Z., Huang, W., Tan, C.H.: Machine learning in prostate MRI for prostate cancer: current status and future opportunities. Diagnostics **12**(2), 289 (2022)
18. Klein, S., van der Heide, U.A., Raaymakers, B.W., Kotte, A.N.T.J., Staring, M., Pluim, J.P.W.: Segmentation of the prostate in mr images by atlas matching. In: 2007 4th IEEE International Symposium on Biomedical Imaging: From Nano to Macro, pp. 1300–1303 (2007)
19. Reda, I., Elmogy, M., Aboulfotouh, A., Ismail, M., El-Baz, A., Keynton, R.: Prostate segmentation using deformable model-based methods. Biomed. Image Seg. Adv. Trends **293**, 15–40 (2016)
20. Liu, X., Haider, M.A., Yetik, I.S.: Unsupervised 3D prostate segmentation based on diffusion-weighted imaging mri using active contour models with a shape prior. In: JECE 2011 (2011)
21. Comelli, A., et al.: Deep learning-based methods for prostate segmentation in magnetic resonance imaging. Appl. Sci. **11**(2), 782 (2021)
22. Shen, D., Wu, G., Suk, H.-I.: Deep learning in medical image analysis. Ann. Rev. Biomed. Eng. **19**(1), 221–248 (2017). PMID: 28301734
23. Zhu, Q., Du, B., Turkbey, B., Choyke, P.L., Yan, P.: Deeply-supervised CNN for prostate segmentation. CoRR, abs/1703.07523 (2017)
24. Zabihollahy, F., Schieda, N., Jeyaraj, S.K., Ukwatta, E.: Automated segmentation of prostate zonal anatomy on t2-weighted (t2w) and apparent diffusion coefficient (adc) map mr images using u-nets. Med. Phys. **46**(7), 3078–3090 (2019)
25. Clark, T., Wong, A., Haider, M., Khalvati, F.: Fully deep convolutional neural networks for segmentation of the prostate gland in diffusion-weighted mr images, pp. 97–104 (2017)
26. Rundo, L., et al.: Use-net: incorporating squeeze-and-excitation blocks into u-net for prostate zonal segmentation of multi-institutional MRI datasets. CoRR, abs/1904.08254 (2019)
27. Rundo, L., et al.: Cnn-based prostate zonal segmentation on t2-weighted MR images: a cross-dataset study. CoRR, abs/1903.12571 (2019)
28. Li, S., Dong, M., Guangming, D., Xiaomin, M.: Attention dense-u-net for automatic breast mass segmentation in digital mammogram. IEEE Access **7**, 59037–59047 (2019)
29.) Guo, C., Szemenyei, M., Yi, Y., Wang, W., Chen, B., Fan, C.: Sa-unet: spatial attention u-net for retinal vessel segmentation. ArXiv, abs/2004.03696 (2020)
30. Bloice, M.D., Roth, P.M., Holzinger, A.: Biomedical image augmentation using Augmentor. Bioinformatics **35**(21), 4522–4524 (2019)

31. Alom, M.Z., Hasan, M., Yakopcic, C., Taha, T.M., Asari, V.K.: Recurrent residual convolutional neural network based on u-net (r2u-net) for medical image segmentation. CoRR, abs/1802.06955 (2018)
32. Oktay, O., et al.: Attention u-net: learning where to look for the pancreas. arXiv preprint arXiv:1804.03999 (2018)
33. Taha, A.-A., Hanbury, A.: Metrics for evaluating 3d medical image segmentation: analysis, selection, and tool. BMC Med. Imaging **15**(1), 1–28 (2015)
34. Yeung, M., Sala, E., Schönlieb, C.-B., Rundo, L.: Unified focal loss: generalising dice and cross entropy-based losses to handle class imbalanced medical image segmentation (2021)
35. Sha, Y.: Keras-unet-collection (2021). https://github.com/yingkaisha/keras-unet-collection
36. Hyun, L.J.: Pytorch implementation of u-net, r2u-net, attention u-net, attention r2u-net (2019). https://github.com/LeeJunHyun/Image_Segmentation

Towards an Interpretable Model for Automatic Classification of Endoscopy Images

Rogelio García-Aguirre[1]([✉]), Luis Torres-Treviño[1],
Eva María Navarro-López[2,3], and José Alberto González-González[4]

[1] Universidad Autónoma de Nuevo León, Facultad de Ingeniería Mecánica y Eléctrica, Ave. Universidad S/N, Cd. Universitaria,
N.L. CP 66455 San Nicolás de los Garza, Mexico
`Rogelio.garciag@uanl.edu.mx`
[2] School of Environment, Education and Development, University of Manchester, Oxford Road, Manchester M13 9PL, UK
[3] School of Engineering, Computing and Mathematical Sciences, Faculty of Science and Engineering, University of Wolverhampton, Alan Turing Building, Wulfruna Street, Wolverhampton WV1 1LY, UK
[4] Servicio de Gastroenterología, Facultad de Medicina, Hospital Universitario "Dr. José E. González", Universidad Autónoma de Nuevo León,
Monterrey N.L. CP 64700, Mexico

Abstract. Deep learning strategies have become the mainstream for computer-assisted diagnosis tools development since they outperform other machine learning techniques. However, these systems can not reach their full potential since the lack of understanding of their operation and questionable generalizability provokes mistrust from the users, limiting their application. In this paper, we generate a Convolutional Neural Network (CNN) using a genetic algorithm for hyperparameter optimization. Our CNN has state-of-the-art classification performance, delivering higher evaluation metrics than other recent papers that use AI models to classify images from the same dataset. We provide visual explanations of the classifications made by our model implementing Grad-CAM and analyze the behavior of our model on misclassifications using this technique.

Keywords: Interpretability · Convolutional Neural Networks · Endoscopy images

1 Introduction

We are living the third artificial intelligence (AI) boom [5,20]. Areas such as computer vision (CV) and natural language processing (NLP) have undergone

O. Pichardo Lagunas et al. (Eds.): MICAI 2022, LNAI 13612, pp. 297–307, 2022.
https://doi.org/10.1007/978-3-031-19493-1_24

considerable progress due to the deep learning (DL) schemes developed during the last decade. Referring to CV, Deep Neural Networks (DNN) have exceeded human performance in many applications [2], including medical image classification [1]. Nevertheless, DNNs are far from perfect. Numerous studies have stated their concerns about the relevance of the existing DL models in real-world applications. The focal limitations found for these systems are their interpretability scarcity [2,9,15,19] (often referred to as the"black box" condition [10,20,24]) and questionable generalizability [2,19,25,27].

In medicine, image-intensive specialties have benefitted from AI systems [14]. For the particular matter of endoscopy, numerous publications describe the current state of the applications and expectations of AI for this field [1,3,4,7,16]. Nevertheless, DL systems are usually unsuitable for clinical application due to the previously stated limitations of these systems (interpretability scarcity and questionable generalizability). As DL models become more and more present for critical applications (such as medicine), model interpretability has been suggested as a solution for the black box condition. Nevertheless, many papers lack a definition of interpretability [12]. For that matter, Lipton [12] stated that *interpretability is not a monolithic concept but reflects several distinct ideas.*

We take the following definition: the interpretability of an AI system refers to the possibility for a human to understand the relation between the system's predictions and the information used to make those predictions [21]. In that sense, for AI applications in medical image classification, the interpretability purpose is not to understand every part of an AI system but to have enough information for the assigned work [21]. Hence, the radiology field requires task-specific interpretability solutions with clinically oriented validations [21]. Following that idea, Reyes et al. [21] concluded that *saliency maps can be integrated easily into the radiology workflow because they work at the voxel level; hence, these visualization maps can be fused or merged with patient images and computer-generated results.*

In this work, we aim to explore the capabilities of the current AI tools to develop a system for automatic endoscopy image classification with the potential of having a clinical application. To that end, we construct an optimized Convolutional Neural Network (CNN) using a framework [6] based on genetic algorithms that perform hyperparameter optimization to increase the CNN classification performance as the model generalizability. Then, as an interpretability method, we apply the Grad-CAM technique [22] to the network to generate heat map-like images that aid the visualization of the relevant zones in the input images for the classification using the optimized CNN. We use the KVASIR dataset of endoscopy images to develop the optimized CNN and test the interpretability method. The classification performance of our optimized CNN is state-of-the-art, and the visualizations using the Grad-CAM technique can locate the regions relevant for the correct classifications.

2 Related Work

2.1 Classification of Endoscopy Images

Several studies are using AI to analyze endoscopic images. A great deal of these focuses on a specific gastrointestinal finding, such as polyp detection and segmentation (e.g., [23]), gastric cancer detection and diagnosis (e.g., [13]), diagnosis and detection of Helicobacter Pylori infection (e.g., [28]), among others. The publication in 2017 of the KVASIR dataset [18], consisting of 8000 images of different GI findings in images of upper endoscopy, made possible the development of a new generation of algorithms for endoscopic image classification. These studies aim to achieve a general classification of the different GI findings that can appear during endoscopy instead of concentrating on a particular suffering or symptom. For a detailed review of papers using AI to classify images of the gastrointestinal tract, refer to Jha et al. [9].

2.2 Interpretability

Interpretability is a critical research topic for AI due to the rise of DL approaches during the last years [21]. There are different kinds of interpretability methods, and this area is continually growing. Nevertheless, numerous interpretability methods have not yet reached the radiology AI systems [21].

In this paper, we focus on providing visual explanations (often refer as saliency maps), which is the typical form of explainability in medical image analysis [26]. Saliency maps are often gradient-based techniques [26], which foundation is the assumption that the magnitude of the gradients correlates with the contribution of voxels to a model's prediction [21]. For an overview of methods for interpretability of DL for medical image analysis, refer to van der Velden et al. [26].

3 Methods and Implementation

3.1 Dataset

For our approach development and evaluation, we used the KVASIR dataset [18], which consists of 8000 images of the gastrointestinal tract insides. This dataset includes anatomical landmarks, pathological findings, procedures, and normal findings. All the images in this dataset belong to one of the following classes: dyed lifted polyps, dyed resection margins, esophagitis, normal cecum, normal pylorus, normal z-line, polyps, and ulcerative colitis. We divided the dataset into three partitions: training, validation, and test. Each partition has 4800, 2000, and 1200 images, respectively.

3.2   Optimized CNN

We performed hyperparameter optimization on off-the-shelf CNNs based on the genetic algorithm presented in [6]. This approach automatically generates CNNs for image classification. The algorithm performs in parallel the training of the CNNs using gradient-based optimization and hyperparameter optimization with a genetic algorithm. The two optimization procedures have different optimization targets and use distinct partitions of the dataset to promote the generalizability of the resulting models. The hyperparameters of the resulted CNN are listed in Table 1.

Table 1. Hyperparameters of the resulting CNN using the approach described in [6].

Resulted hyperparameters								
a_γ	b_γ	c_γ	a_δ	b_δ	c_δ	Architecture	Loss function	Optimizer
0.0867	6.1762	0.5883	0.5547	2.9659	0.6659	ResNext-50 32 × 4d	Logit penalty	AdaMax

The hyperparameters a_γ, b_γ, and c_γ control the magnitude of the learning rate as a function of the training epoch and the total number of epochs. Similarly, a_δ, b_δ, and c_δ control the trainable layers of the CNN during training. The CNN architecture is the base CNN model. The loss function and optimizer are the hyperparameters used for the training using gradient-based optimization.

3.3   Grad-CAM

We used the Grad-CAM technique [22] to produce *visual explanations* of the classifications made by our CNN. This method is based on the fact that deeper layers in CNNs specialize in higher-level visual features and that convolutional layers maintain the spatial information of the input data [22].

Grad-CAM uses the gradients of the logit (of the class that is desired to know the Grad-CAM) with respect to the activations of the last convolutional layer [22]. Then, these gradients are global-average-pooled over the height and width [22]. These values function as weights that denote the importance of the feature maps in the last layer with respect to the given logit [22]. Then the linear combination of the weighted activations of the last layer is calculated. Finally, these values pass though a ReLU activation function to eliminate the negative values [22]. This is because the Grad-CAM focuses on elucidating the regions in the image that evoke a positive value for the given class's logit, and negative values of the weighted activations are assumed to represent regions in the input data that promote a positive value for the logits of other classes [22].

4   Results

4.1   Experimental Settings

The experiments were carried out using the following hardware specifications: AMD Ryzen 5 3400G CPU, one NVIDIA GeForce GTX 1660 Ti GPU, 16 GB

RAM, and 476 GB system memory. All the algorithms were implemented in Python 3.8.5, using the environment Spyder 4.1.5 and Pytorch 1.7.1 for the CNN modules and gradient-based optimization algorithms.

4.2 Optimized CNN Classification Performance

The Optimized CNN resulted of the implementation of the method described in Sect. 3.2 is a ResNext-50 32 × 4d. We evaluated the classification performance of the optimized CNN using the standar evaluation metrics: recall (REC), specificity ($SPEC$), accuracy (ACC), precision ($PREC$), Matthews correlation coefficient (MCC), and F_1 value ($F1$).

$$REC = \frac{TP}{TP + FN} \tag{1}$$

$$SPEC = \frac{TN}{TN + FP} \tag{2}$$

$$PREC = \frac{TP}{TP + FP} \tag{3}$$

$$ACC = \frac{TP + TN}{TP + FP + TN + FN} \tag{4}$$

$$MCC = \frac{(TP \times TN) - (FP \times FN)}{\sqrt{\rho}} \tag{5}$$

with $\rho = (TP + FN)(TN + FP)(TP + FP)(TN + FN)$

$$F1 = 2 \times \frac{PREC \times REC}{PREC + REC} \tag{6}$$

In the above, TP, TN, FP and, FN stand for *true positive, true negative, false positive* and, *false negative*, respectively. Table 2 shows the evaluation metrics of the optmized CNN using the three partitions of the dataset. Figure 1 shows the confusion matrix of the optimized CNN using the test partition. Figure 2 shows the evaluation metrics of the optimized CNN using the test partition as recommended in [25] to facilitate the visualization of the CNN classification performance.

Table 2. Evaluation metrics of the optimized CNN using the test set.

Data partition	ACC	REC	SPEC	PREC	F1	MCC
Train	0.9962	0.9850	0.9978	0.9850	0.9850	0.9828
Validation	0.9853	0.9415	0.9916	0.9415	0.9415	0.9331
Test	0.9860	0.9441	0.9920	0.9441	0.9442	0.9362

4.3 Visual Explanations Using Grad-CAM

Using the Grad-CAM technique and image processing, we generated heat map-like images to aid the visualization of the zones in the input images that evoke the CNN classification output. Figure 3 shows an example of the heat map-like images for a correctly classified image per class in the dataset.

We can also construct these heat map-like images to analyze the misclassification made by the optimized CNN. Figure 4 shows examples of misclassified images and compares the heat map-like of the input images for the output logitt of the wrong prediction and the output logit of the true class.

				Predicted class					
True class	147	3	0	0	0	0	0	0	**0**
	7	143	0	0	0	0	0	0	**1**
	0	0	128	0	1	21	0	0	**2**
	0	0	0	147	0	0	3	0	**3**
	0	0	1	0	149	0	0	0	**4**
	0	0	18	0	0	132	0	0	**5**
	0	0	0	4	3	0	141	2	**6**
	0	0	0	2	2	0	0	146	**7**
	0	**1**	**2**	**3**	**4**	**5**	**6**	**7**	

Fig. 1. Confusion matrix of the optimized CNN using the test partition. The classes' codes are: 0-dyed lifted polyps, 1-dyed resection margins, 2-esophagitis, 3-normal cecum, 4-normal pylorus, 5-normal z-line, 6-polyps, and 7-ulcerative colitis.

Fig. 2. Evaluation metrics of the optimized CNN using the test partition.

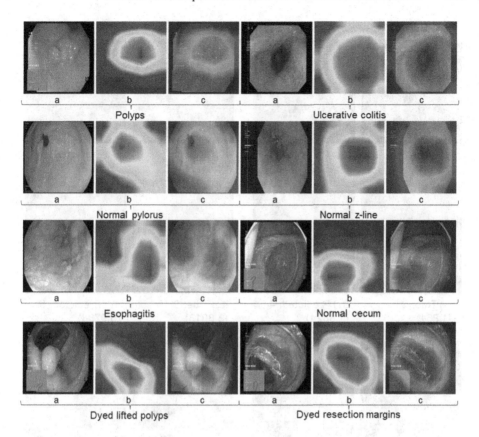

Fig. 3. Examples of every class correctly classified using the optimized CNN and its corresponding Grad-CAM: "a" correspons to the original image, "b" is the Grad-CAM rezied to match "a", and "c" is the superimpossed Grad-CAM "b" over "a".

5   Discussion and Conclusions

The classification performance of our optimized CNN is state-of-the-art. Table 3 shows the evaluation metrics of other recent papers using AI models to classify images of the same dataset.

The work presented by Hicks et al. [8] also used a CNN to classify the KVASIR dataset images and the Grad-CAM technique for visualization. The main difference between that paper and ours is the method used to develop the CNN. Hicks et al. [8] used a VGG-19 with no reported methodology to choose the other hyperparameters. Instead, we performed hyperparameter optimization based on genetic algorithms with the specific aim of improving the model classification performance and generalizability [6], taking into account that high classification performance is always desired, and the lack of generalization is currently one focal limitation for the adoption of these kind of systems into clinical practice.

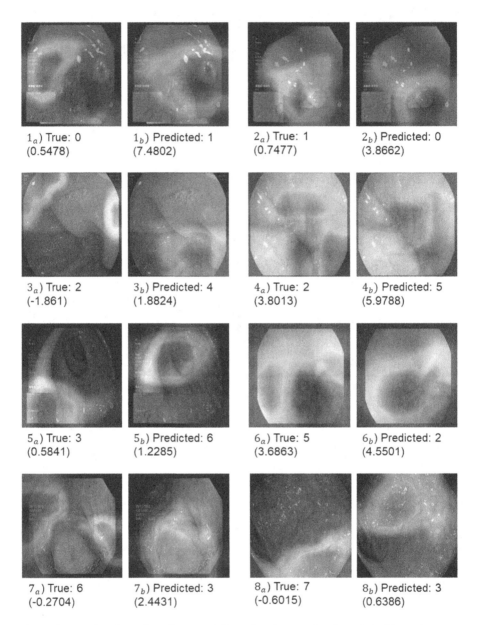

Fig. 4. Examples of misclassifications. The subscript a is for the original images superimposed with the Grad-CAM of the true class, and the subscript b is for the original images superimposed with the Grad-CAM of the predicted class. In parenthesis is the output logit for the given class. The classes' codes are: 0-dyed lifted polyps, 1-dyed resection margins, 2-esophagitis, 3-normal cecum, 4-normal pylorus, 5-normal z-line, 6-polyps, and 7-ulcerative colitis.

Table 3. Evaluation metrics of recent studies using the KVASIR dataset.

Study	Year	ACC	REC	SPEC	PREC	F1	MCC	FPS
Lafraxo et al. [11]	2020	0.9680	0.8770	—	0.874	0.876	—	—
Ozturk et al. [17]	2020	0.9790	0.9232	0.9910	0.9446	0.9264	—	—
Our optimized CNN	2022	0.9860	0.9441	0.9920	0.9441	0.9442	0.9362	35.5

Table 4. Evaluation metrics of studies that use a CNN to classify images of the KVASIR dataset and use a visualization technique for interpretability.

Study	Year	ACC	REC	SPEC	PREC	F1	MCC	FPS
Hicks et al. [8]	2018	0.9440	0.7980	0.7530	0.9680	0.7780	0.7780	—
Our optimized CNN	2022	0.9860	0.9441	0.9920	0.9441	0.9442	0.9362	35.5

Hicks et al. [8] used the visualizations generated with the Grad-CAM to find properties in the input images that were evoking misclassifications. Then, with this information, they used a preprocessing designed to correct the CNN behavior on the misclassified images, achieving a significant improvement in the CNN classification performance, proving that the visualizations generated using Grad-CAM can help understand both the areas in an image that evoke a specific classification and posible misbehaviors of the model. Table 4 provides a comparison of the highest evaluation metrics achieved by Hicks et al. [8] and ours.

From the confusion matrix of our optimized CNN (Fig. 1), we can observe that the majority of misclassification involve an anatomical landmark (normal z-line) and a pathological finding (esophagitis), and the misclassification examples shown in Fig. 4 illustrated that the CNN is focusing in different regions of the images for the classification of that two classes. Also, both classes have a positive logit in the examples of misclassification shown in Fig. 4. That means that the CNN determines that the image belongs to both classes, but the current operation mode of the CNN is to classify the image only in the class with the highest logit. Since the z-line is in the esophagus and the esophagitis is a pathology of it. It would be interesting to have a gastroenterologist assess if the misclassified images between these two classes, in fact, have both findings (esophagitis and normal z-line), as the positive logits suggest.

In this work, we used the existing techniques in the literature to develop a system for endoscopy image classification with interpretability criteria. Our optimized CNN has state-of-the-art classification performance, delivering higher evaluation metrics than other recent papers that use AI models to classify images from the same dataset. The visualizations constructed using the Grad-CAM provide information on the regions that evoke a given output logit. However, it is important to collaborate with physicians to fully understand the implications of the visualizations. In future work, we can explore other approaches, such as

Prototype-based interpretation to provide explanations by example or adopt a holistic approach, combining different forms of explanation.

References

1. Alagappan, M., Brown, J., Mori, Y., Berzin, T.: Artificial intelligence in gastrointestinal endoscopy: the future is almost here. World J. Gastrointest. Endosc. **10**, 239–249 (2018). https://doi.org/10.4253/wjge.v10.i10.239

2. Alzubaidi, L., et al.: Review of deep learning: concepts, CNN architectures, challenges, applications, future directions. J. Big Data **8**(1), 53 (2021). https://doi.org/10.1186/s40537-021-00444-8, https://journalofbigdata.springeropen.com/articles/10.1186/s40537-021-00444-8

3. Berzin, T., Parasa, S., Wallace, M., Gross, S., Repici, A., Sharma, P.: Position statement on priorities for artificial intelligence in gi endoscopy: a report by the asge task force. Gastrointest. Endosc. **92** (2020). https://doi.org/10.1016/j.gie.2020.06.035

4. Chahal, D., Byrne, M.: A primer on artificial intelligence and its application to endoscopy. Gastrointest. Endosc. **92** (2020). https://doi.org/10.1016/j.gie.2020.04.074

5. Fujita, H.: AI-based computer-aided diagnosis (AI-CAD): the latest review to read first. Radiol. Phys. Technol. **13**(1), 6–19 (2020). https://doi.org/10.1007/s12194-019-00552-4

6. García-Aguirre, R., et al.: Automatic generation of optimized convolutional neural networks for medical image classification using a genetic algorithm (2022). https://doi.org/10.2139/ssrn.4167905

7. Gross, S., Sharma, P., Pante, A.: Artificial intelligence in endoscopy. Gastrointest. Endosc. **91** (2019). https://doi.org/10.1016/j.gie.2019.12.018

8. Hicks, S., et al.: Dissecting deep neural networks for better medical image classification and classification understanding. In: 2018 IEEE 31st International Symposium on Computer-Based Medical Systems (CBMS), pp. 363–368 (2018). https://doi.org/10.1109/CBMS.2018.00070

9. Jha, D., et al.: A comprehensive analysis of classification methods in gastrointestinal endoscopy imaging. Med. Image Anal. **70**, 102007 (2021)

10. Kochhar, G.S., Carleton, N.M., Thakkar, S.: Assessing perspectives on artificial intelligence applications to gastroenterology. Gastrointest. Endosc. **93**(4), 971–975.e2 (2021). https://doi.org/10.1016/j.gie.2020.10.029

11. Lafraxo, S., El Ansari, M.: Gastronet: abnormalities recognition in gastrointestinal tract through endoscopic imagery using deep learning techniques. In: 2020 8th International Conference on Wireless Networks and Mobile Communications (WINCOM), pp. 1–5 (2020). https://doi.org/10.1109/WINCOM50532.2020.9272456

12. Lipton, Z.C.: The mythos of model interpretability (2016). https://arxiv.org/abs/1606.03490. https://doi.org/10.48550/ARXIV.1606.03490

13. Luo, H., et al.: Real-time artificial intelligence for detection of upper gastrointestinal cancer by endoscopy: a multicentre, case-control, diagnostic study. Lancet Oncol. **20** (2019). https://doi.org/10.1016/S1470-2045(19)30637-0

14. Maddox, T., Rumsfeld, J., Payne, P.: Questions for artificial intelligence in health care. JAMA **321** (2018). https://doi.org/10.1001/jama.2018.18932

15. Miotto, R., Wang, F., Wang, S., Jiang, X., Dudley, J.T.: Deep learning for health-care: review, opportunities and challenges. Brief. Bioinf. **19**(6), 1236–1246 (2018)
16. Mori, Y., et al.: Artificial intelligence and upper gastrointestinal endoscopy: current status and future perspective. Digest. Endosc. **31** (2018). https://doi.org/10.1111/den.13317
17. Öztürk, S., Özkaya, U.: Gastrointestinal tract classification using improved LSTM based CNN. Multimedia Tools Appl. **79**(39–40), 28825–28840 (2020). https://doi.org/10.1007/s11042-020-09468-3
18. Pogorelov, K., et al.: Kvasir: a multi-class image dataset for computer aided gastrointestinal disease detection. In: Proceedings of the 8th ACM on Multimedia Systems Conference, MMSys 2017, pp. 164–169. ACM, New York (2017). https://doi.org/10.1145/3083187.3083212
19. Prevedello, L., et al.: Challenges related to artificial intelligence research in medical imaging and the importance of image analysis competitions. Radiol. Artif. Intell. **1**, e180031 (2019). https://doi.org/10.1148/ryai.2019180031
20. Quinn, T.P., Jacobs, S., Senadeera, M., Le, V., Coghlan, S.: The three ghosts of medical ai: can the black-box present deliver? Artif. Intell. Med., 102158 (2021). https://doi.org/10.1016/j.artmed.2021.102158. https://www.sciencedirect.com/science/article/pii/S0933365721001512
21. Reyes, M., et al.: On the interpretability of artificial intelligence in radiology: challenges and opportunities. Radiol. Artif. Intell. **2**, e190043 (2020). https://doi.org/10.1148/ryai.2020190043
22. Selvaraju, R.R., Cogswell, M., Das, A., Vedantam, R., Parikh, D., Batra, D.: Grad-CAM: visual explanations from deep networks via gradient-based localization. Int. J. Comput. Vision **128**(2), 336–359 (2019). https://doi.org/10.1007/s11263-019-01228-7
23. Shin, Y., Balasingham, I.: Automatic polyp frame screening using patch based combined feature and dictionary learning. Comput. Med. Imaging Graph. **69**, 33–42 (2018). https://doi.org/10.1016/j.compmedimag.2018.08.001
24. Stead, W.W.: Clinical implications and challenges of artificial intelligence and deep learning. JAMA **320**(11), 1107–1108 (2018)
25. Thambawita, V., et al.: An extensive study on cross-dataset bias and evaluation metrics interpretation for machine learning applied to gastrointestinal tract abnormality classification. ACM Trans. Comput. Healthcare **1**(3) (2020). https://doi.org/10.1145/3386295
26. van der Velden, B.H., Kuijf, H.J., Gilhuijs, K.G., Viergever, M.A.: Explainable artificial intelligence (XAI) in deep learning-based medical image analysis. Med. Image Anal. **79**, 102470 (2022). https://doi.org/10.1016/j.media.2022.102470
27. Yao, A., Cheng, D., Pan, I., Kitamura, F.: Deep learning in neuroradiology: a systematic review of current algorithms and approaches for the new wave of imaging technology. Radiol. Artif. Intell. **2**, e190026 (2020). https://doi.org/10.1148/ryai.2020190026
28. Yasuda, T., et al.: Potential of automatic diagnosis system with linked color imaging for diagnosis of Helicobacter pylori infection. Digest. Endosc. **32**(3), 373–381 (2020). https://doi.org/10.1111/den.13509

Reversible Image Authentication Scheme with Tampering Reconstruction Based on Very Deep Super Resolution Network

G. Melendez-Melendez$^{(\boxtimes)}$ and Rene Cumplido

National Institute of Astrophysics, Optics and Electronics - INAOE, 72840 Puebla, Mexico
{melendez,rcumplido}@inaoep.mx

Abstract. Reversible image authentication (RIA) involves a data hiding process in which watermarks are imperceptibly embedded into an image to protect it against tampering attacks. If a marked image is not tampered, then watermarks can be erased from the marked image and the original cover image is obtained without distortion. Watermarks can be enhanced with recovery information for reconstruction of tampered image regions. However, due to embedding capacity limitations, recovery information must be strategically selected to obtain better image reconstruction quality. To address this issue, a very deep super resolution (VDSR) network is used in the reconstruction phase of the proposed scheme. Sparse signal representations of downscaled image blocks are obtained to apply compressed sensing theory and obtain the reference values used as recovery information. Experimental results indicate that our scheme outperforms previous state-of-the-art methods in terms of reconstructed images quality while reducing time complexity in sparse signal approximation phase as a result of dealing with downscaled image blocks.

Keywords: Very deep super resolution · Reversible data hiding · Tampering detection · Compressed sensing

1 Introduction

Information security applications have gained an increased attention in recent years as a result of new technology development and the Internet. Image authentication has become an essential tool for protecting digital image authenticity and integrity against manipulations. Different approaches such as digital signatures [8], perceptual hashing [12] or digital watermarking can be identified in the literature to address this issue. Among these approaches, digital watermarking techniques figure out by their potential capabilities [10]. First, watermarks travel into the cover media in which they are embedded, then, no additional information is transmitted or stored. Second, watermarks are imperceptible, thus, hidden information goes unnoticed by the attackers. Finally, watermarks can be

O. Pichardo Lagunas et al. (Eds.): MICAI 2022, LNAI 13612, pp. 308–326, 2022.
https://doi.org/10.1007/978-3-031-19493-1_25

designed to be distorted with minimal modifications, making them suitable for tampering detection and localization applications. However, most watermarking methods are irreversible. Consequently, embedded distortion remains in the marked image permanently.

Reversible image authentication methods address the above mentioned issues. RIA methods use reversible data hiding techniques [18] such as compression, histogram shifting modifications (HS) or prediction error expansion (PEE) to strategically incorporate watermarks into a cover image. After embedding process, a marked image is obtained. Then, when it is required, watermarks are extracted to authenticate the marked image content. However, if a marked image is not attacked, embedded watermarks can be eliminated from it to remove all introduced distortion, obtaining the corresponding original cover image.

Prior RIA works employ fragile watermarks to detect and localize tampering attacks. In [20], images blocks are marked with authentication codes (AC) obtained with a seeded pseudo-random number generator. Watermarks are embedded in every block by applying histogram shifting and predictive coding techniques. Tampering detection accuracy is improved in [22] by embedding similar AC into the coefficients of low frequency discrete wavelet transform (DWT). In [17], a RIA method is proposed to reduce detection errors when an equal image brightness modification is applied in marked images. Then, some block features are used to obtain their respective hash values and build the watermarks. In [30], a tampering detection improvement is achieved by selecting optimal block sizes to embed the AC generated with a hash function.

Recently, RIA schemes with reconstruction capabilities have been studied in the literature. Earlier works approximate the damaged image regions by storing recovery information in a third party service. In this way, two dual watermarking schemes were proposed in [14,27]. Short watermarks, created with AC, are embedded into the cover image while long watermarks with recovery information are registered into an intellectual property rights (IPR) database. The recovery information can be retrieved when authentication fails to approximate the tampered regions. However, using third party services could be unpractical in most applications. To address this issue, a RIA method with blind reconstruction is proposed in [13]. Compressed sensing theory is applied to obtain a reduced set of reference values, which are embedded into the same image for reconstruction purposes. In order to improve the reconstruction results, sparse signal modifications were analyzed in [21]. High frequency coefficients from discrete cosine transform (DCT) were omitted in sparse signal representations achieving better reconstruction results, specially when tampered areas were increased.

Although previous blind reconstruction methods have shown an acceptable performance, they still deal with large sparse signal representations. Consequently, reconstruction phase is not fully exploited. To overcome this issue, this work introduces a very deep super resolution [19] based RIA scheme. Watermarks are created with reference values obtained from downscaled image blocks using compressed sensing theory. In the reconstruction phase of the scheme, tampered blocks are approximated using the reference values extracted from untampered blocks to created a reconstructed dowscaled block. VDSR network is used to upscale each reconstructed block and create the reconstructed image. The obtained results indicate that the proposed scheme overcomes state-of-the-art methods when images are reconstructed in terms of two image quality metrics while runtime is significantly reduced as a result of reconstructing smaller sparse signal vectors.

The rest of this paper is organized as follows. Section 2 briefly explains two techniques used in the scheme: compressed sensing and VDSR network. Section 3 describes the proposed RIA scheme. Obtained results are drawn in Sect. 4. Finally, conclusions are presented in Sect. 5.

2   Preliminaries

2.1   Compressed Sensing

Compressed sensing (CS) is an innovative technique used to sample sparse signals at sub-Nyquist rates and then approximate or perfectly reconstruct them under certain conditions [5,11]. CS has recently attracted significant research interest due to its potential applications in digital signal processing [3,4] including image processing [16], medical imaging [23,24], video processing [25], wireless communications [9], etc.

One of the principal premises concerning CS theory is signal sparsity, as many signals can be concisely represented in a proper basis [6]. A signal $x \in \mathbb{R}^n$ is k-sparse when only k of its components are nonzero values, where $k \ll n$. CS allows the reconstruction of the sparse signal x from a reduced set of measurements denoted as $y \in \mathbb{R}^m$, with $m \ll n$, which are obtained by random projections. The measurements acquisition is performed with the help of a measurement matrix $\Phi \in \mathbb{R}^{m \times n}$, whose elements are independent and identically distributed (i.i.d) using a random distribution such as Gaussian, Bernoulli, etc. The reduced set of measurements is obtained with Eq. 1.

$$y = \Phi x \tag{1}$$

As $m \ll n$, the undetermined linear system of equations (1) contains more unknowns than equations and has an infinite number of solutions. However, reconstruction algorithms take advantage of signal sparsity to find an optimal solution to this problem. Basis pursuit (BP) [7] is a linear programming algorithm that formulates the problem as a convex optimization problem in which a signal $\tilde{x}$ is estimated by minimizing its ℓ_1-norm, subjected to $y = \Phi\tilde{x}$. Nevertheless, its computational cost and implementation complexity are high.

Orthogonal matching pursuit (OMP) is a much faster, easier to implement, and yet effective algorithm used to reconstruct sparse signals [26]. OMP is a greedy algorithm that iterates to look for those columns in Φ that participate in the measurements y. In each iteration, OMP picks a new active column of Φ based on the correlation with the current signal residuals and estimates the objective signal x by performing least squares method. Running OMP algorithm implies a computational complexity of $O(knm)$, which is in function of the sparse signal dimensions.

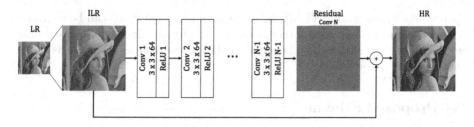

Fig. 1. VDSR network architecture.

2.2   VDSR Network

Single image super resolution (SISR) is an ill-posed problem in which a high resolution image is pretended to be approximated from one low resolution image [29]. Among a variety of proposed techniques, very deep super resolution network (VDSR) [19] is one of the most effective approaches as it achieves state-of-the-art performance, producing excellent quality images.

VDSR network approximates a high-resolution (HR) image from a given low-resolution (LR) image by cascading small filters many times in a deep network structure of 20 layers. Figure 1 illustrates the deep neural network architecture. First, input LR image is interpolated as ILR. Then, ILR image is passed N-1 times through convolution and ReLu layers followed by a N-th convolution layer to predict a residual image. Finally, the residual image is added to the ILR image to obtain a HR image. In every convolution layer, except the first and last ones, VDSR employs filters of size $3 \times 3 \times 64$. Then, image details are predicted as a residual image instead predicting the HR image directly.

For a given dataset with n sample pairs of interpolated and high-resolution images, denoted as $\{ILR^{(i)}, HR^{(i)}\}_{i=1}^{n}$, VDSR network aims to learn a model f to predict values $\hat{HR} = f(ILR)$, where $\hat{HR}$ is the approximation of the objective image HR. In this way, a residual image is obtained as $R = HR - ILR$. VDSR takes advantage of the similarity between ILR and HR images, as low frequency detail is preserved. Then, most residual image values are likely to be zero or near to zero. Consequently, VDSR minimizes the next loss function:

$$\frac{1}{2}\|R - f(ILR)\|^2 \tag{2}$$

where R is the residual target image, ILR is the interpolated low resolution image and f is the network prediction. The final super resolution result is obtained as:

$$\hat{HR} = f(ILR) + ILR \tag{3}$$

Finally, VDSR is trained by optimizing the the regression objective with mini-batch gradient descent based on backpropagation with momentum parameter set to 0.9.

The proposed scheme incorporates VDSR network in reconstruction phase to upscale recovered blocks corresponding to tampered image regions with good quality. By incorporating VDSR, smaller signal representations can be operated without compromising reconstructed images quality. Additionally, sparse signal approximations are performed faster as smaller sparse vectors are managed, alleviating OMP algorithm.

3   Proposed Scheme

This section details the proposed RIA scheme, which is divided in five stages. First two stages: watermark creation and watermark embedding, are used to protect images, see Fig. 2. The remaining three stages: watermark extraction, tampering detection and image reconstruction, are used to authenticate and repair the tampered images, see Fig. 3.

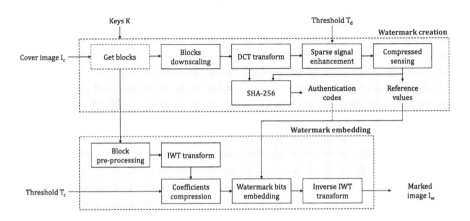

Fig. 2. Watermark creation and embedding phases.

3.1   Watermark Creation

The watermark creation phase receives a cover image I_c and constructs the watermarks required for authentication and reconstruction of tampered image regions. First, the cover image I_c of size $L_1 \times L_2$ is partitioned into 32×32 non-overlapping blocks. The total number of image pixels is $L = L_1 \times L_2$, then n_b blocks are obtained in this phase, where $n_b = L/1,024$. Every block B_k is downscaled by a scale factor of 0.5 using bicubic interpolation. In this way, the downscaled blocks are now of size 16×16. Next, each downscaled block $B_k^\downarrow$ is used as input to the DCT transform, obtaining the corresponding set of DCT coefficients with Eq. 4.

$$D_k = DCT(B_k^\downarrow - 128) \tag{4}$$

where $B_k^{\downarrow}$ is the kth downscaled block of pixels, D_k is the corresponding block of DCT coefficients and $1 \leq k \leq n_b$.

The obtained blocks are scrambled and divided into groups of size 16, then, a total number of $n_g = n_b/16$ groups are obtained. Next, a one-dimensional coefficients sequence C_g is created using the blocks of the same group. Each block D_k of size 16×16 is reshaped to a one dimensional array of size 256 and gathered with the arrays of the same group as

$$C_g = [D_{k_1}(1), ..., D_{k_1}(256), D_{k_2}(1), ...D_{k_2}(256), ...,$$
$$D_{k_{16}}(1), ..., D_{k_{16}}(256)]^T \tag{5}$$

Now, a threshold T_d is defined to omit some high-frequency DCT coefficients from C_g, using the following formula:

$$C_{gs}(i) = \begin{cases} 0, & \text{if } |C_g(i)| \leq T_d \\ C_g(i), & \text{if } |C_g(i)| > T_d \end{cases} \tag{6}$$

Threshold T_d modifies the signal sparsity level, i.e., when T_d is increased, more coefficients are omitted from C_g. Next, C_{gs} is permuted using a key K_1.

Compressed sensing is conducted to obtain a reduced set of measurements using a predefined measurement matrix $M \in \mathbb{R}^{800 \times 4,094}$, whose elements are pseudo-randomly generated as independent samples from a normal distribution with zero mean and variance one. In this work, M is obtained using the instruction $M = randn(800, 4096)$ in MATLAB software. Then, 800 references values per group are obtained using Eq. 7.

$$[r(1), r(2), ..., r(800)]^T = M \cdot C_{gs} \tag{7}$$

Next, each reference value is quantified using Eq. 8.

$$r' = \begin{cases} 127, & \text{if } r \geq g_{128} \\ u, & \text{if } g_u \leq r < g_{u+1} \\ -u - 1, & \text{if } -g_{u+1} \leq r < -g_u \\ -128, & \text{if } r < -g_{128} \end{cases} \tag{8}$$

where g_u is the monotonic function defined in [13, 21] as

$$g_u = u^2/90 + u/3, u = 0, 1, 2, ..., 128 \qquad (9)$$

When all reference values are quantified, a permutation is applied using a key K_2. Next, reference values are divided into n_b sets of size 50. As each quantified reference value can be represented using only 8 bits, each set is represented by a total of 400 bits.

A watermark W_k is created for each block B_k by appending a 10-bits authentication code to the previously computed reference values. Authentication bits are obtained with SHA-256 hash function using as input the binary pixel values of the block B_k, the position index of B_k in I_c and the corresponding set of binary quantified reference values. Finally, W_k is permuted using a key K_3.

3.2   Watermark Embedding

In this phase, each watermark W_k of 410 bits is embedded into the corresponding block B_k by adapting the reversible data hiding method proposed in [28]. Companding technique is applied to compress and expand larger IWT coefficients of high-frequency sub-bands, where watermark bits are embedded.

To avoid overflow/underflow problems B_k undergoes a block pre-processing phase in which grayscale values 0 and 1 are incremented by one unit meanwhile grayscale values 255 and 254 are decremented by one unit. Let B_{h_k} be the modified block corresponding to B_k, to preserve reversibility, a recovery sequence R_s is created by scanning B_{h_k}. We scan each B_{h_k} block from left to right and top to bottom, when grayscale values 2 or 253 are found, we compare the value in the same position of B_k, if values match, a bit 0 is appended to R_s, otherwise, a bit 1 is appended. This sequence is used in a block post-processing stage after watermark extraction to recover original grayscale values of the corresponding block B_k. Accordingly, R_s is embedded as control information of the scheme after all watermark bits are embedded.

Next, IWT is applied to the block B_{h_k} to obtain LL, LH, HL and HH sub-bands. High-frequency sub-bands (i.e., LH, HL and HH) are selected to embed the watermark bits as most of their coefficients are small in magnitude. Companding technique requires compression and expansion functions. Compression function is used to compress some large coefficients. Compression allows coefficients modification to incorporate watermark bits, thus every coefficient c of LH, HL and HH sub-bands is compressed using the following piecewise function:

$$\hat{c} = \begin{cases} c, & \text{if } |c| < T_c \\ sign(c) \cdot (\lfloor \frac{|c|-T_c}{2} \rfloor) + T_c, & \text{if } |c| \geq T_c \end{cases} \qquad (10)$$

where $\hat{c}$ is the compressed coefficient and T_c is a user predefined threshold. It can be inferred from above formula that when $|c| \geq T_c$, an error sequence e must be recorded and embedded as part of control information of the scheme. Original coefficients are recovered using Eqs. 11 and 12, respectively.

$$c_e = \begin{cases} \hat{c}, & \text{if } |\hat{c}| < T_c \\ sign(\hat{c}) \cdot (2|\hat{c}| - T_c), & \text{if } |\hat{c}| \geq T_c \end{cases} \tag{11}$$

$$c = c_e + e \tag{12}$$

Once all coefficients are compressed, every compressed coefficient $\hat{c}$ can be marked with one watermark bit $b \in \{0, 1\}$. Assuming that $\hat{c}$ is represented in binary form as $b_1b_2...b_l$, the watermark bit is appended after the least significant bit (LSB) of this representation, thus the marked coefficient is $\hat{c}_w = b_1b_2...b_lb$. A marked coefficient can be obtained using Eq. 13.

$$\hat{c}_w = 2\hat{c} + b \tag{13}$$

After all watermark bits are embedded, inverse IWT is applied to obtain the marked block B_{w_k}. This process is repeated for the n_b blocks and watermarks to obtain the marked image I_w.

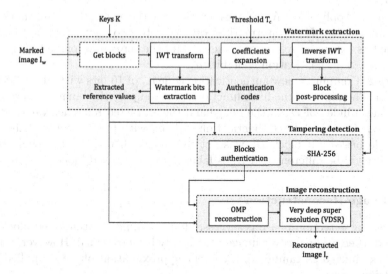

Fig. 3. Watermark extraction, tampering detection and image reconstruction phases.

3.3 Watermark Extraction

In the watermark extraction side, a marked image I'_w is received and the inverse process is applied to obtain the watermark bits and recover original image pixel values.

First, I'_w is divided into nonoverlapping blocks of size 32×32. Next, IWT is applied over B'_{w_k} to obtain the four IWT sub-bands. The corresponding watermark bits W'_k embedded in each block B'_{w_k} are extracted from the coefficients of high-frequency sub-bands, i.e., LH, HL and HH.

A bit b' is obtained from the LSB of each marked coefficient $\hat{c}'_w$, that is to say $b' = LSB(\hat{c}'_w)$. The compressed coefficient value is recovered using Eq. 14.

$$\hat{c}' = \frac{\hat{c}'_w - b'}{2} \tag{14}$$

After all bits are extracted, we obtain the watermark bits W'_k, recovery sequence R'_s and errors e'. Now, compressed coefficients are expanded using Eqs. 11 and 12. Next, inverse IWT is applied to obtain block pixels B'_{h_k}. Finally, original pixel values are recovered using R'_s to obtain B'_k.

3.4 Tampering Detection

Tampering attacks are detected by authenticating every block B'_k following the next steps.

Step 1: Apply the inverse permutation to the extracted watermark bits W'_k using the key K_3. Watermark is divided into two parts, first 400 bits are regarded as extracted reference values r'_e and the remaining part of 10 bits are the extracted authentication code bits a'_e.

Step 2: Compute a new authentication code a_n of 10 bits with SHA-256 hash function. The input to the hash function is made up by the binary values of B'_k, the position index of B'_k in the image and the extracted reference values r'_e.

Step 3: Compare the authentication code a_n with the extracted authentication code bits a'_e. If block B'_k was not tampered, then a_n and a'_e will match, otherwise will be different and B'_k is labeled as a tampered block.

3.5 Image Reconstruction

If tampering detection phase is successfully passed, i.e., no tampered blocks are detected, then original cover image has already been obtained. However, if there are blocks judged as tampered, a content approximation phase is applied as it is explained below.

First, the original value of each quantified reference value $\hat{r}_e$ extracted from intact blocks is estimated using Eq. 15.

$$r' = \begin{cases} 0.5(g_{\hat{r}_e} + g_{(\hat{r}_e+1)}), & \text{if } 0 \leq \hat{r}_e \leq 127 \\ 0.5(-g_{-\hat{r}_e} - g_{-\hat{r}_e-1}), & \text{if } -128 \leq \hat{r}_e \leq -1 \end{cases} \tag{15}$$

Estimated reference values r' are inversely permuted using the key K_2. Notice that reference values extracted from intact blocks of a corresponding group can be obtained as

$$[r(\lambda_1), r(\lambda_2), ..., r(\lambda_N)]^T = M^{(E)} \cdot C_{gs} \tag{16}$$

where $N \leq 800$ and $M^{(E)}$ is created using the rows of M corresponding to each $r(\lambda)$. Equation 16 can be rewritten as

$$[r(\lambda_1), r(\lambda_2), ..., r(\lambda_N)]^T = M^{(E,I)} \cdot C_{gsI} + M^{(E,T)} \cdot C_{gsT} \tag{17}$$

where C_{gsI} and C_{gsT} are the part of C_{gs} corresponding to the intact and tampered blocks respectively. $M^{(E,I)}$ and $M^{(E,T)}$ are the parts of $M^{(E)}$ created with the columns corresponding to C_{gsI} and C_{gsT}, respectively. By replacing $r(\lambda)$ with the estimated reference values $r'(\lambda)$, next equation is obtained

$$M^{(E,T)} \cdot C_{gsT} = [r'(\lambda_1), r'(\lambda_2), ..., r'(\lambda_N)]^T - M^{(E,I)} \cdot C_{gsI} \tag{18}$$

In Eq. 18, only the vector of coefficients C_{gsT} is unknown. Most of their coefficients are zero or near to zero, i.e., it is a sparse vector. Thus C_{gsT} can be reconstructed using a sparse signal reconstruction algorithm. We use the orthogonal matching pursuit (OMP) algorithm [26] to reconstruct the sparse signal.

Next, inverse permutation is applied over reconstructed vector C'_{gs} using K_1. After that, vectors are reshaped into blocks of size 16×16. Then, inverse DCT transformation is applied over the obtained block $B_k^{\downarrow'}$ and a constant value of 128 is added to every block value. Finally, the obtained block is upscaled by a scale factor of 2 with VDSR network to obtain an approximated block $B_k^{\uparrow'}$ of size 32×32. Once all tampered blocks are approximated, a reconstructed image I_r is obtained.

4   Experimental Results

In this section, we evaluate the performance of the proposed RIA scheme. All the experiments were carried out on a computer with an AMD Ryzen™ 9 3900X 12-Core CPU @ 3.8 GHz, 32 GB of RAM memory and a single NVIDIA RTX™ 3080 GPU, running Windows 11 64-bit operating system. The proposed scheme was implemented on MATLAB R2022a software, using the image processing, wavelet, parallel computing, deep learning, and statistics and machine learning toolboxes.

VDSR network was trained using 616 natural images of the IAPR TC-12 dataset [15]. Additionally, data augmentation was applied over the training data using rotation and reflection prepossessing. Images were divided into blocks of size 32×32 to obtain a total of $39,424$ sample pairs of interpolated and residual image blocks. The proposed watermark creation phase downscale the original blocks by a scale factor of 0.5, then, VDSR was trained with a single scale factor of 2, in such a way that each block is upscaled to its original dimensions.

The proposed scheme was evaluated using 135 grayscale benchmark images as in [21]. A total of 35 images were collected from the signal and image processing institute (SIPI) dataset [1] and the remaining images were obtained from break our watermarking system (BOWS-2) dataset [2]. Common tampering attacks were applied into the marked images to evaluate the scheme performance in terms of watermark imperceptibility, tampering detection accuracy and tampering reconstruction. PSNR and SSIM metrics were used to provide objective results about the similarity between the original images and the marked, tampered and reconstructed images, respectively.

Table 1. Marked images quality in terms of PSNR and SSIM.

Image	Airplane	Lena	Jellybeans	Bear	Snow	Sea	Mountain	House
PSNR	36.03	36.53	43.37	35.65	39.26	41.71	37.75	41.29
SSIM	0.97	0.96	0.99	0.95	0.97	0.98	0.96	0.98

4.1 Imperceptibility Results

Marked images quality depends on threshold T_c. When T_c is increased less coefficients are compressed, then, watermark bits produce considerable distortion in embedding process. On the other hand, when T_c is decreased, more coefficients are compressed, generating less distortion, however, recovery error sequence e is enlarged as more companding error must be hidden in order to preserve reversibility. For this reason, threshold T_c was established to the minimum value for which all watermark bits were successfully embedded into all images. In such manner, T_c was set to 15.

An image quality assessment was carried out to evaluate watermarks imperceptibility. PSNR and SSIM metrics are used to compare each original cover image I_c with its respective marked image I_w. A PSNR average of 39.33 dB $\pm$ 3.73 dB and a SSIM average of 0.97 $\pm$ 0.01 were obtained for the 135 test images. The obtained results indicate that the proposed scheme provides adequate watermark imperceptibility as a PSNR value over 35 dB implies an acceptable value. A comparison among original and marked images over *Airplane, Lena, Jellybeans, Bear, Mountain, Snow, Sea* and *House* images is provided in Fig. 4(a) and (b). When cover images are compared with their corresponding marked images, no visual degradation can be perceived, this is because all marked images achieved PSNR values above 35 dB. Table 1 specifies the obtained objective results in terms of PSNR and SSIM for the eight images.

Fig. 4. Tampering detection and reconstruction results. (a) Original cover images I_c. (b) Marked images I_w. (c) Tampered images I'_w attacked with copy-move, cut-paste and erase-fill attacks. (d) Authenticated images. (e) Reconstructed images I_r.

4.2   Tampering Detection and Reconstruction Results

Marked images were tested against tampering attacks, which are classified in three categories: copy-move, cut-paste and erase fill. Copy-move attack creates and integrates a new object in the image scene by cloning an existing object. Cut-paste attack adds a new object from an external image to the attacked image. Copy-move and cut-paste attacks are also known as splicing attack, new objects can undergo geometric transformations such as scaling or rotation. Erase-fill attack modifies an image scene by eliminating objects with the help of some image background or texture information. Attacked images are displayed in Fig. 4(c). Tampered images were attacked at 4.30, 12.5, 10.55, 8.59, 7.81, 2.34, 23.43 and 4.69%, respectively. Attacked images obtained PSNR values of 27.27, 25.21, 20.38, 23.04, 18.96, 38.22, 17.01 and 28.86 dB, correspondingly.

After marked images were tampered, authentication phase was applied for tampering detection purposes. Accuracy metric was used to evaluate tampering detection results. In the experiments, all blocks were correctly classified into tampered and non-tampered blocks, obtaining an accuracy value of 1. This is because the proposed scheme embeds 10-bit authentication codes, which mismatch the authentication bits extracted from tampered blocks with a probability of $1 - 2^{-10}$. Authenticated images revealing tampered image blocks are displayed in Fig. 4(d).

After damaged image regions are localized, each tampered block is approximated in the sparse signal reconstruction phase using OMP algorithm. Reference values retrieved from untampered blocks are used as input to the algorithm. Afterwards, for each tampered block a downscaled approximated block is produced. Finally, VDSR network is used to upscale the approximated blocks and build the recovered image I_r. Reconstructed images are listed in Fig. 4(e). It can be noticed that each reconstructed image I_r is almost identical to its corresponding original cover image I_c, even when more aggressive attacks are applied. Reconstructed images accomplished PNSR values of 43.12, 42.51, 41.82, 40.84, 44.68, 48.54, 33.99 and 46.24 dB, respectively. Based on the achieved results it can be inferred that the proposed scheme is able to restore damaged image regions with excellent quality.

4.3   Reconstruction Performance According to Signal Sparsity

In [21], it is stated that sparse signal enhancement can be applied to improve sparse signal approximations. Consequently, the proposed scheme was evaluated under modified sparse signal levels by testing various T_d values. Figure 5 illustrates the existing relationship between sparse signal representations and different T_d values over all test images. It can be observed that a small T_d value already impacts sparse signal levels. For example, when T_d is set to 10, an average of 84% $\pm$ 8% coefficients are set to zero value using Eq. 6. When T_d is increased, a larger number of coefficients are set to zero, enhancing sparse signal levels. Finally, when T_d is set to zero, original coefficients are preserved as no modifications are applied.

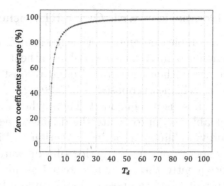

Fig. 5. Sparsity average results for different T_d values over all test images.

A reconstruction assessment was carried out by simulating several attacks over the 135 images. Images were tampered at different attack percentages, i.e., 5%, 12.5%, 25% and 50%. Watermarks were embedded using different T_d values. Each reconstructed image I_r was compared with its corresponding cover image I_c using PSNR and SSIM metrics. Figure 6 shows the obtained results in terms of PSNR (a) and SSIM (b) averages for the 135 test images. It can be observed that when images are attacked at 5% better reconstruction results can be achieved with a smaller T_d value. However, when the attacked area percentage is increased, a larger T_d value furnishes better reconstructed images. For example, when images were attacked at 50%, best reconstructed images were obtained with a T_d value set to 42, accomplishing a PSNR average of 31.80 $\pm$ 3.9 dB, which overcomes the PSNR average of reconstructed images with no coefficient modifications, i.e., 28.62 $\pm$ 4.5 dB.

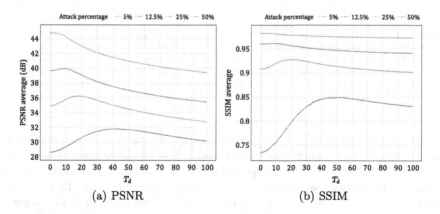

(a) PSNR   (b) SSIM

Fig. 6. Reconstruction results in terms of PSNR and SSIM averages for different T_d values.

4.4   Performance Comparison with Other RIA Schemes

This section provides a comparison among our scheme and relevant state-of-the art works. The comparison is limited to reversible authentication schemes that provide both, blind image authentication and blind reconstruction of damaged regions. In this concern, schemes proposed in [17,20,22,30] are discarded as a content approximation phase is not included. Then, when tampered regions are detected, they are not able to approximate the damaged regions. The schemes proposed in [14,27], provide blind tampering detection and include an approximation phase, which depends on the extraction of long watermarks stored into an IPR database. Consequently, these schemes are not totally blind. The schemes proposed in [13,21] provide blind tampering detection and blind reconstruction phases.

Table 2. Reconstruction comparison in terms of PSNR and SSIM values.

Image	Percentage	Tampered image PSNR (dB)	SSIM	Restored image [13] PSNR (dB)	SSIM	Restored image [21] $T_d = 20$ PSNR (dB)	SSIM	$T_d = 50$ PSNR (dB)	SSIM	Restored image proposed $T_d = 0$ PSNR(dB)	SSIM
Airplane	02.34%	33.06	0.97	36.95	0.99	40.66	0.99	40.46	0.99	42.68	0.99
	04.30%	27.27	0.96	35.04	0.97	37.57	0.98	37.73	0.98	43.12	0.99
	50.00%	5.98	0.48	21.97	0.62	22.91	0.66	23.91	0.70	25.57	0.74
Lena	03.91%	29.46	0.94	45.01	0.99	46.99	0.99	45.14	0.99	46.39	0.99
	12.50%	25.21	0.92	41.96	0.97	44.21	0.98	42.04	0.98	42.51	0.98
	50.00%	9.64	0.49	24.11	0.65	24.95	0.69	26.92	0.78	26.88	0.75
Jellybean	07.81%	21.01	0.96	40.37	0.97	44.67	0.98	43.07	0.98	45.09	0.98
	10.55%	20.38	0.95	36.64	0.96	38.84	0.97	38.97	0.97	41.82	0.98
	50.00%	6.29	0.49	34.89	0.89	36.95	0.93	36.26	0.91	36.12	0.92
Bear	08.59%	23.04	0.92	37.05	0.96	40.61	0.98	38.70	0.97	40.84	0.98
	15.63%	19.88	0.88	33.41	0.92	35.91	0.94	36.70	0.95	36.44	0.95
	50.00%	8.55	0.47	25.77	0.64	27.05	0.68	31.07	0.81	27.95	0.72
Snow	07.81%	18.96	0.93	43.53	0.98	43.66	0.98	43.00	0.97	44.68	0.98
	12.50%	20.69	0.94	35.19	0.94	36.60	0.96	36.46	0.96	39.93	0.97
	50.00%	6.99	0.48	29.74	0.76	31.34	0.82	35.10	0.92	32.88	0.86
Sea	02.34%	38.22	0.98	47.32	0.99	48.84	0.99	44.18	0.99	48.54	0.99
	06.64%	30.35	0.96	48.04	0.99	48.00	0.98	46.81	0.99	46.70	0.99
	50.00%	7.66	0.48	35.28	0.88	38.91	0.94	38.84	0.95	37.49	0.92
Mountain	07.81%	20.60	0.96	36.43	0.96	38.78	0.97	38.23	0.97	41.04	0.98
	23.43%	17.01	0.87	29.94	0.85	31.20	0.87	33.47	0.91	33.99	0.91
	50.00%	6.56	0.49	25.26	0.65	27.78	0.70	30.70	0.82	28.30	0.78
House	04.69%	26.86	0.97	46.67	0.99	48.51	0.99	43.71	0.99	46.24	0.99
	17.97%	20.33	0.91	38.72	0.96	40.59	0.97	39.47	0.96	40.20	0.97
	50.00%	7.45	0.49	33.02	0.87	33.22	0.85	37.22	0.93	34.79	0.88

A reconstruction comparison among [13,21] and our scheme is provided in Table 2. Several tampering attacks were applied over eight images. Our scheme was tested with a T_d value set to zero while [21] was tested with T_d values set to 20 and 50. It can be observed that our scheme clearly outperforms [13] achieving PSNR improvements of up to 8 dB. On the other hand, the proposed scheme overcomes [21] in most cases, obtaining an average improvement of 0.89 ± 1.86 dB when T_d is set to 20 and 0.92 ± 2.26 dB when T_d is set to 50. However, our reconstruction results can be improved for aggressive attacks by establishing a larger T_d value, as it was explained in previous experiments. To illustrate

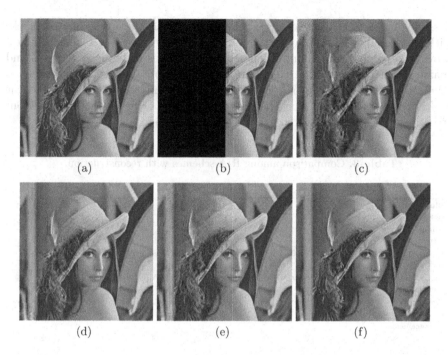

Fig. 7. Reconstruction results comparison for an aggressive attack in Lena image. (a) Original image. (b) Tampered image. (c) Reconstructed image [13]. (d) Reconstructed image [21] with $T_d = 50$. (e) Reconstructed image OMP+VDSR with $T_d = 0$ and (f) Reconstructed image OMP+VDSR with $T_d = 42$.

that, Fig. 7 provides a reconstruction comparison after *Lena* image was attacked at 50%, see Fig. 7(b). Figure 7(c) shows the reconstructed image obtained by [13], with a PSNR value of 24.11 dB. Figure 7(d) shows the reconstructed image obtained with [21], which was reported as the best reconstruction result produced with $T_d = 50$. A PSNR value of 26.92 dB. was obtained for this image. Figure 7(e), shows the reconstructed image obtained with the proposed scheme with no coefficient modifications, i.e., $T_d = 0$. The obtained PSNR was 26.88 dB, which already improves the result of [13] and has a similar result compared with [21]. However, when T_d is increased to 42, a better result is achieved, see Fig. 7(f), obtaining a PSNR value of 29.77 dB, which improves the results of [13] and [21]. According to Fig. 6(a) and (b) a similar behavior is presented over all test images.

The obtained results show that by downscaling image blocks in the watermark creation phase, better approximations can be achieved in reconstruction phase, even if no coefficients are modified. Notice that runtime is also improved as sparse signal representations are significantly reduced. For example, [13] and [21] employ sparse signal vectors of size 16, 384, a much larger number of signal coefficients compared with the 4, 096 coefficients used in the proposed scheme. As a result, OMP algorithm approximates a sparse signal in less time. This is possible due to VDSR network is employed to upscale the approximated blocks with good quality in the reconstruction phase of the proposed scheme. Table 3 provides a comparison among discussed RIA schemes in terms of features and sparse signal reconstruction time. An average computation time in seconds is reported over 100 reconstruction simulations of tampered images attacked at 50%. It can be observed that the proposed scheme achieves the lowest reconstruction time when compared against the other schemes.

Table 3. Comparison among RIA schemes with reconstruction.

	[27]	[14]	[13]	[21]	Proposed
Blind authentication	✓	✓	✓	✓	✓
Blind reconstruction	–	–	✓	✓	✓
Embedding technique	HS	PEE	PEE	Companding	Companding
Embedding domain	DWT	Spatial	Spatial	IWT	IWT
Watermarks	Short + Long	Short + Long	AC + Ref. values	AC + Ref. values	AC + Ref. values
Signal sparsity enhancement	–	–	–	✓	✓
Reconstruction strategy	CS	CS	CS	CS	CS + VDSR
Sparse signal size	–	–	$16,384$	$16,384$	$4,096$
Reconstruction time (s) Attacked area at 50%	–	–	7.20 ± 0.03	8.87 ± 0.20	2.56 ± 0.04

5   Conclusions

Tampering detection and reconstruction of tampered image-regions with good quality are complex tasks in reversible image authentication field, as reversibility requirement limits the amount of information that can be embedded into cover images to perform blind reconstruction. In this work, we introduce a reconstruction approach based on very deep super resolution network. In this way, watermarks are created by obtaining reference values from sparse signal representations of downscaled image blocks using compressed sensing. Watermarks are complemented with authentication codes for tampering detection purposes and embedded into IWT coefficients using companding technique. If the marked image is not attacked, then, all watermark bits can be deleted from the marked image and the original cover image is obtained. However, if the marked image is tampered, watermarks are extracted to detect damaged blocks and approximate their content using OMP algorithm. Finally, approximated blocks are upscale with VDSR network.

Several experiments were conducted over 135 images to validate the proposed scheme. The obtained results indicate that the proposed scheme not only achieves better reconstruction results, but also significantly reduces runtime as smaller sparse signal representations are approximated in the reconstruction phase compared with state-of-the-art methods.

Acknowledgments. This work was supported by the National Council of Science and Technology of Mexico (CONACYT) [grant number: 731618].

References

1. The USC-SIPI Image Database (1997). https://sipi.usc.edu/database/
2. Break Our Watermarking System 2nd Ed (2007). https://bows2.ec-lille.fr/
3. Abo-Zahhad, M.M., Hussein, A.I., Mohamed, A.M.: Compressive sensing algorithms for signal processing applications: a survey. Int. J. Commun. Network Syst. Sci. **8**(06), 197 (2015). https://doi.org/10.4236/ijcns.2015.86021'
4. Boche, H., Calderbank, R., Kutyniok, G., Vybíral, J.: Compressed Sensing and its Applications. Springer (2015). https://doi.org/10.1007/978-3-319-16042-9'
5. Candès, E.J.: Compressive sampling. In: Proceedings of the International Congress of Mathematicians, vol. 3, pp. 1433–1452, Madrid, Spain (2006)
6. Candès, E.J., Wakin, M.B.: An introduction to compressive sampling. IEEE Sign. Process. Mag. **25**(2), 21–30 (2008). https://doi.org/10.1109/MSP.2007.914731'
7. Chen, S., Donoho, D.: Basis pursuit. In: Proceedings of 1994 28th Asilomar Conference on Signals, Systems and Computers, vol. 1, pp. 41–44. IEEE (1994). https://doi.org/10.1109/ACSSC.1994.471413
8. Chennamma, H., Madhushree, B.: A comprehensive survey on image authentication for tamper detection with localization. Multimedia Tools Appl. 1–32 (2022). https://doi.org/10.1007/s11042-022-13312-1
9. Choi, J.W., Shim, B., Ding, Y., Rao, B., Kim, D.I.: Compressed sensing for wireless communications: useful tips and tricks. IEEE Commun. Surv. Tutor. **19**(3), 1527–1550 (2017). https://doi.org/10.1109/COMST.2017.2664421
10. Cox, I., Miller, M., Bloom, J., Fridrich, J., Kalker, T.: Digital Watermarking and Steganography. Morgan Kaufmann, Burlington (2007). https://doi.org/10.1016/B978-0-12-372585-1.X5001-3
11. Donoho, D.L.: Compressed sensing. IEEE Trans. Inf. Theory **52**(4), 1289–1306 (2006). https://doi.org/10.1109/TIT.2006.871582'
12. Du, L., Ho, A.T., Cong, R.: Perceptual hashing for image authentication: a survey. Signal Process. Image Commun. **81**, 115713 (2020). https://doi.org/10.1016/j.image.2019.115713
13. Gao, G., Cui, Z., Zhou, C.: Blind reversible authentication based on PEE and CS reconstruction. IEEE Signal Process. Lett. **25**(7), 1099–1103 (2018). https://doi.org/10.1109/LSP.2018.2844562
14. Gao, G., Cui, Z., Zhou, C., Yao, S., Xu, L.: Reversible authentication scheme based on prediction-error expansion with compound symbolic chaos. In: 2016 12th World Congress on Intelligent Control and Automation (WCICA), pp. 2169–2174. IEEE (2016). https://doi.org/10.1109/WCICA.2016.7578734
15. Grubinger, M., Clough, P., Müller, H., Deselaers, T.: The IAPR TC-12 benchmark: a new evaluation resource for visual information systems. In: International Workshop onto Image, vol. 2 (2006)

16. Gunasheela, S., Prasantha, H.: Compressed sensing for image compression: survey of algorithms. In: Emerging Research in Computing, Information, Communication and Applications, pp. 507–517. Springer (2019). https://doi.org/10.1007/978-981-13-6001-5_42

17. Hong, W., Chen, M., Chen, T.S.: An efficient reversible image authentication method using improved PVO and LSB substitution techniques. Signal Process. Image Commun. **58**, 111–122 (2017). https://doi.org/10.1016/j.image.2017.07.001

18. Khan, A., Siddiqa, A., Munib, S., Malik, S.A.: A recent survey of reversible watermarking techniques. Inf. Sci. **279**, 251–272 (2014). https://doi.org/10.1016/j.ins.2014.03.118

19. Kim, J., Lee, J.K., Lee, K.M.: Accurate image super-resolution using very deep convolutional networks. In: Proceedings of the IEEE Conference on Computer Vision and Pattern Recognition, pp. 1646–1654 (2016). https://doi.org/10.1109/CVPR.2016.182

20. Lo, C.C., Hu, Y.C.: A novel reversible image authentication scheme for digital images. Signal Process. **98**, 174–185 (2014). https://doi.org/10.1016/j.sigpro.2013.11.028

21. Melendez-Melendez, G., Cumplido, R.: Reversible image authentication scheme with blind content reconstruction based on compressed sensing. Eng. Sci. Technol. Int. J. **34**, 101080 (2022). https://doi.org/10.1016/j.jestch.2021.101080

22. Nguyen, T.S., Chang, C.C., Yang, X.Q.: A reversible image authentication scheme based on fragile watermarking in discrete wavelet transform domain. AEU-Int. J. Electron. Commun. **70**(8), 1055–1061 (2016). https://doi.org/10.1016/j.aeue.2016.05.003

23. Quan, T.M., Nguyen-Duc, T., Jeong, W.K.: Compressed sensing MRI reconstruction using a generative adversarial network with a cyclic loss. IEEE Trans. Med. Imaging **37**(6), 1488–1497 (2018). https://doi.org/10.1109/TMI.2018.2820120

24. Rahim, T., Novamizanti, L., Ramatryana, I.N.A., Shin, S.Y.: Compressed medical imaging based on average sparsity model and reweighted analysis of multiple basis pursuit. Comput. Med. Imaging Graph. **90**, 101927 (2021). https://doi.org/10.1016/j.compmedimag.2021.101927

25. Shi, W., Liu, S., Jiang, F., Zhao, D.: Video compressed sensing using a convolutional neural network. IEEE Trans. Circ. Syst. Video Technol. (2020). https://doi.org/10.1109/TCSVT.2020.2978703

26. Tropp, J.A., Gilbert, A.C.: Signal recovery from random measurements via orthogonal matching pursuit. IEEE Trans. Inf. Theory **53**(12), 4655–4666 (2007). https://doi.org/10.1109/TIT.2007.909108

27. Xiao, D., Deng, M., Zhu, X.: A reversible image authentication scheme based on compressive sensing. Multimedia Tools Appl. **74**(18), 7729–7752 (2015). https://doi.org/10.1007/s11042-014-2017-z

28. Xuan, G., Yang, C., Zhen, Y., Shi, Y.Q., Ni, Z.: Reversible data hiding using integer wavelet transform and companding technique. In: International Workshop on Digital Watermarking, pp. 115–124. Springer (2004). https://doi.org/10.1007/978-3-540-31805-7_10

29. Yang, W., Zhang, X., Tian, Y., Wang, W., Xue, J.H., Liao, Q.: Deep learning for single image super-resolution: a brief review. IEEE Trans. Multimedia **21**(12), 3106–3121 (2019), https://doi.org/10.1109/TMM.2019.2919431

30. Yao, H., Wei, H., Qin, C., Tang, Z.: A real-time reversible image authentication method using uniform embedding strategy. J. Real-Time Image Process. **17**(1), 41–54 (2020). https://doi.org/10.1007/s11554-019-00904-8

Improving Artifact Detection in Endoscopic Video Frames Using Deep Learning Techniques

Pedro E. Chavarrias-Solano[1(✉)], Mansoor Ali-Teevno[1], Gilberto Ochoa-Ruiz[1,2], and Sharib Ali[3]

[1] School of Engineering and Sciences, Tecnologico de Monterrey, Monterrey, Mexico
peterchavarrias@gmail.com
[2] Institute of Advanced Materials for Sustainable Manufacturing, Tecnologico de Monterrey, Monterrey, Mexico
[3] School of Computing, University of Leeds, Leeds, UK

Abstract. Colorectal cancer cases have been increasing at an alarming rate each year, imposing a healthcare burden worldwide. Multiple efforts have been made to treat this malignancy. However, early screening has been the most promising solution. Optical endoscopy is the primary diagnosis and treatment tool for these malignancies. Even though its success, the endoscopic process represents a challenge due to noisy data, a limited field of view and the presence of multiple artefacts. In this work, we present a comparison between two real-time deep learning frameworks trained to detect artefacts in endoscopic data. Both networks are trained using different data augmentation techniques to analyze their effect when the models are evaluated using data coming from a different distribution. We evaluated these models using the mean average precision (mAP) evaluation metric at a different intersection over union values. Both models outperformed state-of-the-art methods that were evaluated using the same dataset. Also, the use of data augmentation techniques showed an overall improvement in terms of mAP when compared to the case in which no augmentation was applied.

Keywords: Deep learning · Object detection · YOLO · YOLACT · Endoscopic artifact detection

1 Introduction

Colorectal cancer incidence has been increasing in the last years, imposing a healthcare burden globally. It represents the third most common type of cancer and the second most lethal one around the world [18]. Even though multiple efforts had been made to treat this pathology, early detection has been found

© The Author(s), under exclusive license to Springer Nature Switzerland AG 2022
O. Pichardo Lagunas et al. (Eds.): MICAI 2022, LNAI 13612, pp. 327–338, 2022.
https://doi.org/10.1007/978-3-031-19493-1_26

to be the most promising solution. Nowadays, optical endoscopy is the primary tool used for diagnosing and managing gastrointestinal (GI) malignancies [16]. This technique is based on the use of an endoscope, which is a flexible medical device that combines fiber-optics and charge-coupled devices for illumination and imaging of the interior of otherwise inaccessible sites [11].

The multiple applications and challenges of optical endoscopy has caught the attention of the research community, which has developed several methods to process and automatically analyze the video signal produced by the endoscopic camera [13] for various purposes. Some of the most outstanding applications have been focused on disease detection in real-time, e.g., polyp, ulcer, bleeding zones, or cancer.

This application is of particular interest within the research and medical community because an endoscopic procedure is tiring, time-consuming and subject to the experience of the clinician. Although these recent advances in endoscopic medical imaging have enable the access to high quality videos of the GI tract and could unleash a plethora of applications, many challenges still remain. For instance, during the endoscopic procedure, gastroenterologists need to move the endoscope around the GI track and to manipulate the folds of tissue in order to analyze a wider surface, in order to avoid missing important regions or suspicious lesions. To complicate matters further, issues like limited field-of-view, extreme lighting conditions, lack of depth information and difficulty in manipulating operating instruments demand strenuous amounts of effort from the surgeons, whereas the characteristics of the endoscopic interventions involve very complex dynamics which might produce undesired artefacts in the endoscopic videos [1].

Therefore, endoscopy as a field at large has seen an increased interest in applying artificial intelligence tools and methods for assisting in various CADe and CADx applications. In particular, given the rich visual information provided by the endoscope, has led to the development of a plethora of computer vision (CV) techniques, such as object detection and localisation or instance segmentation methods [17] specifically tailored to certain tasks such as disease detection and instrument tracking. These systems are expected to be a crucial component in tasks ranging from surgical navigation, skill analysis and complication prediction during surgeries, as well as other computer integrated surgery (CIS) applications [12]. Nonetheless, as mentioned above, such computer vision tools are often deployed in difficult operational scenarios in which the presence of bleeding, over or under exposed frames, smoke, reflection and other types of artifacts are oftentimes unavoidable [3]. The net effect of these issues increases the missed detection rates in endoscopic surveillance, limiting the overall robustness of CV algorithms, hampering the adoption of AI-based tools in this context [1]. Moreover, real-time deployment of such tools is of tremendous value and one of the major requirement for it to be applied in clinical settings.

In this regard, recent years have seen a significant increase in the number of CV contests geared towards endoscopy for different purposes. In particular, the Endoscopy Computer Vision Challenge (EndoCV) is a crowd-sourcing initiative launched to address some of the most pressing problems hampering the development of robust computer aided detection and diagnosis clinical endoscopy systems [1]. This challenge mainly focus on detecting multi-class artefacts and subtle precancerous precursors and cancer abnormalities [1] present in the endoscopic video signal.

Even though continuous efforts had been made to tackle this robustness challenge, we consider that still there is not a robust yet real-time object detector that would enable major computer vision applications in endoscopic video signals. Multiple approaches have been proposed to tackle the robustness challenge with the use of ensemble methods, however, these methods apply at least one two-stage model, increasing inference time [1,5]. In this paper, we perform a comparison between two real-time methods, YOLO and YOLACT, and we present a comparison between both of them.

The rest of this paper is organized as follows. Section 2 surveys recent study of state-of-the-art methods that have made use of the EAD datasets and discusses their limitations. Section 3 describes the EndoCV2020 challenge and the Endoscopy artefact detection sub-challenge 2020 dataset. In Sect. 4, we explain the methods used in this study. Section 5 includes the experimental design. In Sect. 6, we cover the obtained results. Finally, Sect. 7 recovers the conclusions generated by the authors.

2   Related Work

Object detectors can be classified into single-stage and multi-stage architectures. Single-stage methods, such as YOLO [15] or MobileNet [8], are faster than multi-stage detectors because they only require a single pass on the data and they also incorporate anchor boxes to detect multiple objects on the same image grid [1]. However, one drawback of one-stage detectors against multi-stage methods relies on the robustness of their detections. Multi-stage approaches use a region proposal networks to find regions of interest in which an object could probably be found and then apply a classifier to further refine the search in order to get the final outputs [1].

Several studies can be found in literature proposing multiple methods for the detection of artefacts in endoscopic images [1]. One proposal by Zhang & Xe, extended Faster R-CNN into a multi-stage cascade R-CNN framework combined with FPN which is intended to train bounding-box regressors that could improve the intersection over union between predictions and ground truth boxes [20]. Kirthika & Sargunam trained and evaluated YOLOv4 using the Endoscopy artifact detection dataset of 2019 and applying traditional data augmentation techniques, such as manual random flipping and stretching to increase the dataset size [10].

Some of the best performing methods in the Endoscopy artefact detection challenge of 2020 use an ensemble of multiple object detection architectures. An ensemble of Faster R-CNN (two-stage), Cascade R-CNN(two-stage), and RetinaNet(single-stage) with a class-agnostic NMS before the ensemble was presented on [14]. Another approach following an ensemble of three detectors: Faster

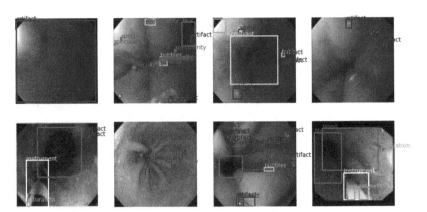

Fig. 1. Sample of artefacts. Eight sample images from EAD2020 with their corresponding ground truth bounding boxes: specularity (red), saturation (green), artifact (blue), blur (pink), contrast (yellow), bubbles (cyan), instrument (white), and blood (brown) (Color figure online)

R-CNN with ResNext101 + FPN, RetinaNet with ResNet101 + FPN, and Faster R-CNN with ResNext101 + DC5, was studied on [9]. An implementation using Hyper Task Cascade and Cascade R-CNN using ResNext1010 as the feature extractor with FPN for multi-scale feature representation was developed by Chen *et. al*, which also performed random flip, normalization and resizing of the images as data augmentation techniques [6]. All these methods were evaluated on non-publicly available testing data, as part of the official challenge.

The approach on [19], uses single-stage detector Efficient-Det with Efficient-Net backbone and proposes a pruning-based mechanism. In this work, the authors compared the intensity profiles of each predicted instance from the detection model with the pre-computed mean profile of that particular instance. Their experiments were conducted on the Endoscopy Artifact Detection 2020 dataset, using the single frame dataset for training and validation - 80% training and 20% validation - and the sequential frame as the testing set.

3   EndoCV2020 Challenge

The EndoCV challenge is a crowd-sourcing initiative that aims to address the main problems faced in clinical endoscopy. EndoCV2020 challenge consists of two sub-challenges: Endoscopy artefact detection and segmentation (EAD2020) and Endoscopy disease detection and segmentation (EDD2020). The datasets for both sub-challenges include multi-center, multi-modal, multi-organ, and multi-class artefacts. EAD2020 is an extended sub-challenge of the EAD2019, that includes both frame and sequence data with an addition of almost 1,000 frames and 41,832 annotations [1].

3.1 Endoscopy Artefact Detection

The EAD2020 sub-challenge consists of diverse endoscopic video frames collected from seven different institutions around the world, it includes three imaging modalities and five different human organs. Frames were annotated by clinical experts for detection of eight different artefact classes. These classes are named: specularity, saturation, artefacts, blur, contrast, bubbles, instrument and blood. Figure 1 shows five sample images with their corresponding ground truth bounding boxes with the following class-color label: specularity (red), saturation (green), artifact (blue), blur (pink), contrast (yellow), bubbles (cyan), instrument (white), and blood (brown).

This dataset is classified into two categories: single frames and sequence video data. Single frames data consist of 2,299 frames while sequence video data has 233 frames obtained from video recordings. A total of 2,532 frames with 31,069 bounding boxes were released for the detection task. The distribution of class occurrences is described in the graph chart found in Fig. 2. Specularity, artefact, and bubbles are the classes with higher occurrences; while blur, instrument and blood are the classes with less occurrences [1].

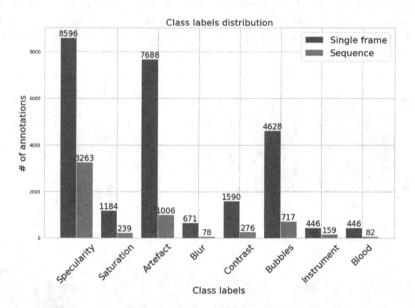

Fig. 2. Statistics of EAD2020. Class distribution of the Endoscopy Artefact Detection 2020 sub-challenge. Specularity, artefact, and bubbles are the more recurrent classes, while blood, instrument and blood are the less recurrent ones.

4 Methods

In this study, two real-time methods -YOLOv4 [2] and YOLACT [4]- are trained with the single frames dataset and evaluated over the sequence video dataset.

Both detectors are trained with three data augmentation techniques: *photometric*, *geometric* and *geophotometric*. The evaluation of such methods is performed in terms of mean average precision at different intersection over union thresholds.

YOLO is a unified single convolutional network that simultaneously predicts multiple bounding boxes and class probabilities for those boxes [15]. The authors frame object detection as a regression problem, which results in an extremely fast model. Figure 3 describes the building blocks of YOLOv4, in which the backbone, neck, and head of the detector are described. Its backbone consists of CSPDarknet53, which was defined as the feature extractor based on theoretical justification and numerous experiments. The backbone is followed by SPP and PANeth path-aggregation as the neck of the model, which were used for increasing the receptive field and aggregating parameters from different backbone levels. Its head is conformed by the head of YOLOv3 architecture [2].

This version of YOLO also apply Bag-of-freebies (BoF) and Bag-of-specials (BoS) for the backbone and the detector training stage. The Bag-of-freebies for the backbone includes certain techniques that boost the learning of the algorithm during the training stage, the authors include: CutMix and mosaic data augmentation, dropblock regularization, and class label smoothing techniques. Whereas, the Bag-of-specials for the backbone covers: Mish activation, cross-stage partial connections, and multi-input weighted residual connections. For

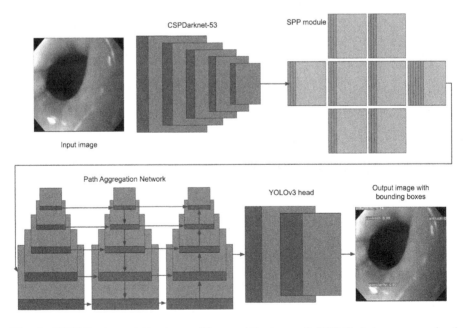

Fig. 3. YOLOv4 architecture. The architecture of YOLOv4 is composed of CSPDarknet-53 as the feature backbone, followed by SPP module and Path Aggregation Network as the neck of this architecture. The head of YOLOv3 conforms the dense network used for doing object detection.

the detector, the BoF uses: CIou-loss, CmBN, dropblock regularization, mosaic data augmentation, self-adversarial training, eliminate grid sensitivity, cosine annealing scheduler, optimal hyper-parameters,and random training shapes. The BoS in the detector applies: Mish activation, SPP-block, SAM-block, PAN path-aggregation block, and DIoU-NMS [2]. The main advantages of this method are speed, global reasoning considering the entire image to implicitly encode contextual information, and its ability to generalize representation of objects [2].

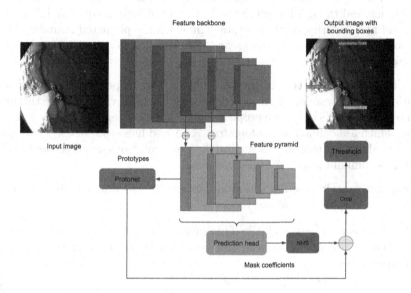

Fig. 4. YOLACT architecture. The building blocks of YOLACT are a feature back-bone - ResNet-50 -, a feature pyramid network, the prediction head and the NMS (non-maximum supression) module for the detection and generation of mask coefficients. Protonet modules is used for the generation of prototypes. Then, a linear combination of prototypes and mask coefficients undergoes a cropping process. Finally, a threshold is used for generating the final output

YOLACT is a simple, fully-convolution model for real-time instance segmentation that breaks this task into two parallel subtasks: generation of a set of prototype masks and prediction of per-instance mask coefficients. Instance masks are then produced by linearly combining the prototypes with the mask coefficients. Since this process does not depend on repooling - which means that it does not depend heavily on feature localization to produce masks - and proposes Fast NMS instead of standard NMS, it produces high-quality masks while keeping temporal stability [4]. Figure 4 shows a diagram of the building blocks conforming the architecture of YOLACT. The input image goes through the feature extractor, which for this study, ResNet-50 with FPN was selected. The authors modify the FPN by not producing P_2 and producing P_6 and P_7 as successive 3×3 stride 2 convolutional layers starting from P_5 and placing 3 anchors on each with the following aspect ratios: [1, 1/2, 2] [4]. The architecture then breaks up into two parallel tasks. The first branch, called protonet, is an FCN that predicts a set of prototype masks from the largest feature layers of FPN. The second branch generates mask coefficients by adding a third branch to the prediction head of the object detector, which closely follows the design of RetinaNet, in order to predict mask coefficients for each prototype. Unlike RetinaNet, the authors decide not to use focal loss, which was found not be viable in their situation. Finally, to produce instance masks, the results of the prototype branch and the mask coefficient branch are linearly combined, followed by a sigmoid non-linearity, a cropping stage in which the predicted bounding boxes are used to crop the output masks and a threshold-based decision to generate the final masks [4].

Data augmentation techniques are highly used to present the model with variations of the training data in order to increase the variability of the input training data. In this study, we propose three different categories of data augmentation, which are defined as *photometric* - blur and hue -, *geometric* - horizontal flip, vertical flip, horizontal and vertical flips, and rotations -, and *geophotometric* which is a combination of the previous ones.

Evaluation metrics used in this study include intersection over union, average precision and mean average precision.

– Intersection over union (IoU): This measure considers the area of overlap and the area of union between two bounding boxes to evaluate the overlap between them.

$$IoU = \frac{A \cap B}{A \cup B} \qquad (1)$$

This score ranges from 0 to 1, meaning no overlap and complete overlap, respectively. It is compared against a given threshold for determining whether or not a prediction is considered a true positive (TP) or a false positive (FP) [7].

– Average precision (AP): It is computed by calculating the area under the curve (AUC) of the precision-recall (PR) curve for each class at a given IoU. Retrieving the computations for precision and recall as [7]:

$$precision = \frac{TP}{TP + FP} \qquad (2)$$

$$recall = \frac{TP}{TP + FN} \qquad (3)$$

– Mean average precision (mAP): This metric computes the average of the AP calculated for all the classes based on different IoU thresholds [7].

$$mAP = \frac{1}{classes} \sum_{n=1}^{classes} AP_n \qquad (4)$$

5   Results

In this section, a brief description of the experimental setup is given, both quantitative and qualitative results are presented, and a comparison between them.

5.1   Experimental Setup

We implemented YOLOv4 and YOLACT using PyTorch on a single NVIDIA Tesla P100 GPU. Both methods were trained on the single frame dataset using different data augmentation techniques - original data, *photometric*, *geometric*, and *geophotometric* - and tested on sequential frames, as the out-of-sample test set. In the training process, we resized the images of the training data to 512×512. We trained YOLOv4 for 16,000 iterations with a batch size of 64, starting at an initial learning rate of 0.001, weight decay was set to 0.0005, and a momentum of 0.949. YOLACT method was trained for the same number of iterations with a batch size of 8, an initial learning rate of 0.001, weight decay of 0.0005, and momentum of 0.9.

Table 1. Quantitative results. Evaluation results of both methods, YOLOv4 and YOLACT, considering mAP_{25}, mAP_{50}, and mAP_{75} evaluation metrics. Evaluation results of other state-of-the-art methods in terms of mAP_{25} and mAP_{50}

Model	Data augmentation	mAP_{25}	mAP_{50}	mAP_{75}
EfficientDet-d0 [19]	None	30.67	20.93	–
EfficientDet-d0-NMS [19]	None	29.56	19.77	–
EfficientDet-d0-NMS-PDF [19]	None	31.69	19.98	–
YOLOv4	None	41.3	25.5	9.1
	Photometric	40.7	25.8	8.9
	Geometric	**45.1**	**27.6**	8.8
	Geophotometric	42.9	26.5	**10.1**
YOLACT	None	42.3	24.4	7.5
	Photometric	43.0	24.5	7.6
	Geometric	**44.9**	**26.8**	**9.9**
	Geophotometric	44.4	26.7	8.6

5.2   Quantitative Results

Both methods, YOLOv4 and YOLACT, are evaluated in terms of mean average precision using the sequential dataset. The mAP was evaluated at three different intersection over union thresholds: 25, 50, and 75. The evaluation results of both methods are concentrated in Table 1 in order to analyze which model achieves the best performance among them. Also, the results in terms of mAP_{25} and mAP_{50} of another state-of-the-art methods evaluated over the same sequential dataset are presented.

5.3 Qualitative Results

Figure 5, contains sample images with their corresponding ground truth bounding boxes and the predictions achieved by both methods, YOLOv4 and YOLACT. Based on these results, YOLACT is less likely to predict small object instances, e.g. specularities. Also, none of the proposed methods of this study show a good performance for detecting bubbles, which are also small objects and are one of the less recurrent classes found in the training set.

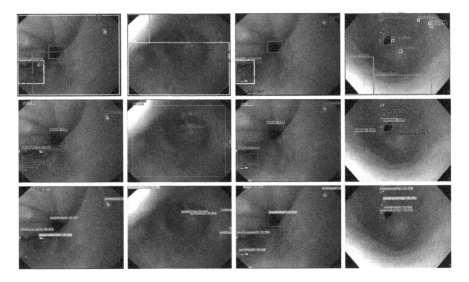

Fig. 5. Qualitative results. First row contains sample images with their corresponding ground truth bounding boxes. Second row corresponds to the predictions done by YOLOv4 detector. Third row shows the predictions done by YOLACT.

5.4 Comparative Results

Based on our experiments, the data augmentation technique that generates a higher mAP is *geometric* data augmentation. This technique increases mAP_{25} and mAP_{50} of the YOLOv4 model by 3.8% and 2.1%, respectively, when compared to the model trained with the original data without augmentation. The YOLACT model shows an increase in mAP_{25}, mAP_{50}, and mAP_{75} of 2.6%, 2.4%, and 2.4%, respectively, when compared against the model trained without augmentation techniques. Both of the methods studied in this work, YOLOv4 and YOLACT, outperform the models proposed in [19] by at least 9.01% and 3.47% in terms of mAP_{25} and mAP_{50}, respectively.

6   Conclusions

In this study we presented a comparison between two real-time deep learning frameworks used for detecting artefacts in endoscopic video frames, YOLOv4 and YOLACT. Both methods were trained with three different types of data augmentations techniques - *photometric, geometric,* and *geophotometric-* to evaluate the effect of increasing the variability of the input training data. The models were trained on the single frames dataset of the EAD2020 sub-challenge and tested on the sequential frames dataset of the same sub-challenge. Evaluating both models and the selected data augmentation techniques give us an insight of how the pre-processing of the training data leads to an improvement in its own performance even when tested on a dataset coming from a different distribution. Based on our experiments, the YOLOv4 architecture achieves a higher performance in terms of mAP_{25}, mAP_{50}, and mAP_{75}, than YOLACT and also outperforms the EfficientDet methods presented in [19] considering mAP_{25} and mAP_{50}. The data augmentation techniques that achieves a higher improvement was the *geometric* augmentation, which applies flips and rotation transformations to the training data. As part of our future work, we will explore the implementation of another state-of-the-art real-time method for artefact detection and we will work on the implementation of an ensemble approach with all three methods.

Acknowledgments. The authors wish to thank the AI Hub and the CIIOT at ITESM for their support for carrying the experiments reported in this paper in their NVIDIA's DGX computer.

References

1. Ali, S., et al.: Deep learning for detection and segmentation of artefact and disease instances in gastrointestinal endoscopy. Medical Image Anal. **70**, 102002 (2021). https://doi.org/10.1016/j.media.2021.102002arXiv:2010.06034
2. Bochkovskiy, A., Wang, C.Y., Liao, H.Y.M.: YOLOv4: optimal speed and accuracy of object detection (2020). https://doi.org/10.48550/ARXIV.2004. 10934arxiv:2004.10934
3. Bodenstedt, S., et al.: Comparative evaluation of instrument segmentation and tracking methods in minimally invasive surgery (2018)
4. Bolya, D., Zhou, C., Xiao, F., Lee, Y.J.: YOLACT: real-time instance segmentation. In: 2019 IEEE/CVF International Conference on Computer Vision (ICCV), pp. 9156–9165. IEEE, Seoul, Korea (South), October 2019. https://doi.org/10. 1109/ICCV.2019.00925, https://ieeexplore.ieee.org/document/9010373/
5. Casado-García, Á., Heras, J.: Ensemble methods for object detection. In: ECAI (2020)
6. Chen, H., Lian, C., Wang, L.: Endoscopy artefact detection and segmentation using deep convolutional neural network (2020)
7. Elgendy, M.: Deep Learning for Vision Systems. Manning Publications Co, Shelter Island, NY (2020)
8. Howard, A.G., et al.: MobileNets: efficient convolutional neural networks for mobile vision applications (2017). https://doi.org/10.48550/ARXIV.1704.04861, arxiv:1704.04861

9. Jadhav, S., Bamba, U., Chavan, A., Tiwari, R., Raj, A.: Multi-plateau ensemble for endoscopic artefact segmentation and detection, March 2020
10. Kirthika, N., Sargunam, B.: YOLOV4 for multi-class artefact detection in endoscopic images, pp. 73–77, May 2021. https://doi.org/10.1109/ICSPC51351.2021. 9451761, https://ieeexplore.ieee.org/document/9451761/
11. Kohli, D.R., Baillie, J.: How Endoscopes Work (2019)
12. Maier-Hein, L., et al.: Heidelberg colorectal data set for surgical data science in the sensor operating room. Sci. Data **8**, 101 (2021). https://doi.org/10.1038/s41597-021-00882-2
13. Münzer, B., Schoeffmann, K., Böszörmenyi, L.: Content-based processing and analysis of endoscopic images and videos: a survey. Multimedia Tools Appl. **77**(1), 1323–1362 (2017). https://doi.org/10.1007/s11042-016-4219-z
14. Polat G., Sen D., Inci, A., Temizel, A.: Endoscopic artefact detection with ensemble of deep neural networks and false positive elimination. In: CEUR Workshop (2020)
15. Redmon, J., Divvala, S., Girshick, R., Farhadi, A.: You only look once: unified, real-time object detection. arXiv:1506.02640 [cs], May 2016
16. Tang, Y., Anandasabapathy, S., Richards-Kortum, R.: Advances in optical gastrointestinal endoscopy: a technical review. Mol. Oncol. 1878–0261.12792 (2020). https://doi.org/10.1002/1878-0261.12792
17. Ward, T.M., et al.: Computer vision in surgery. Surgery **169**(5), 1253–1256 (2021). https://doi.org/10.1016/j.surg.2020.10.039
18. WHO: https://gco.iarc.fr/
19. Xu, Z., Ali, S., Gupta, S., Celik, N., Rittscher, J.: Improved artifact detection in endoscopy imaging through profile pruning. In: Papież, B.W., Yaqub, M., Jiao, J., Namburete, A.I.L., Noble, J.A. (eds.) Medical Image Understanding and Analysis. p. 87–97. Lecture Notes in Computer Science, Springer International Publishing, Cham (2021). DOI: https://doi.org/10.1007/978-3-030-80432-9_7
20. Zhang, Y., Xie, D.: J. Zhejiang Univ.-Sci. B **20**(12), 1014–1020 (2019). https://doi.org/10.1631/jzus.B1900340

White Blood Cell Detection and Classification in Blood Smear Images Using a One-Stage Object Detector and Similarity Learning

Atoany Nazareth Fierro-Radilla[1]([✉])[iD], Monica Larre Bolaños Cacho[1][iD],
Karina Ruby Perez-Daniel[2][iD], Armando Arredondo Valle[1][iD],
Carlos Alberto López Figueroa[2][iD], and Gibran Benitez-Garcia[3][iD]

[1] Tecnológico de Monterrey, Xochitepec Morelos 62790, Mexico
{afierror,monica.larre}@tec.mx
[2] Universidad Panamericana, Mexico City 03920, Mexico
kperezd@up.edu.mx
[3] The University of Electrocommunications, Tokyo, Japan
gibran@ieee.org

Abstract. White blood cells are a fundamental part of the immune system which protect human body against infections and diseases. The complete blood count is a routine analysis that provides doctors information about the patients. Monitoring the immune system allows doctor to select preventive treatments against several diseases. The complete blood count relies in a rigorous observation of a blood sample through a microscope; the accuracy of the result depends on the expertise and time of the analyst. In this paper, a novel vision-based method using convolutional neural networks for white blood cell detection and classification is presented. The results show the proposed method is robust against the huge number of easy negatives in object detection, as well, the high inter-class similarity among images can be reduced for a better white blood cell classification.

Keywords: WBC · CNN · Siamese network · Object detection · Image classification

1 Introduction

The blood is composed by red blood cells (RBC), white blood cells (WBC), platelets and plasma. The 45% of the peripheral blood is composed by cells and 55% of plasma [1]. The function of RBCs is to carry oxygen to body tissues, platelets help with blood clotting and WBCs are responsible for the immune system [2]. WBCs are divided into five subclasses: eosinophil, lymphocyte, monocyte, basophil and neutrophil [3]. The information about counts and percentages of each type of WBC in blood is invaluable for doctors to diagnose illness in

O. Pichardo Lagunas et al. (Eds.): MICAI 2022, LNAI 13612, pp. 339–351, 2022.
https://doi.org/10.1007/978-3-031-19493-1_27

patients [5] such as anemia, leukemia, infectious diseases, liver diseases, bone marrow deficiency diseases, etc. In order to evaluate the health condition of patients, medical professional often request the Complete Blood Count (CBC). The manual WBC count in CBC is a time consuming task which is based on the microscopic observation of the blood smear by the analyst who can differentiate the subtypes mainly based on the morphological features of the cell nucleus and cytoplasmic matrix [2,7]; the result depends highly on the time and experience of the analyst. This manual counting is a very challenging task due WBC datasets present a high inter class similarities, which means that types of WBC are very similar, for example, eosinophils and neutrophils; in Fig. 1 one sample of these two classes is presented. Automated hematology analyzer devices such as impedance-based or flow cytometry counters have been available since the past three decades, however, the classification of RBCs and WBCs is restricted to a few classes, and, in addition, these machines require the use of expensive chemicals [8], making them very expensive, especially for low-income countries [9].

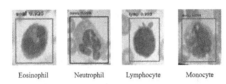

Eosinophil   Neutrophil   Lymphocyte   Monocyte

Fig. 1. Four classes of WBC are presented. Eosinophils and neutrophils are very similar; eosinophil is a bi-lobed cell, while neutrophil is a multi-lobed one.

Researchers have proposed several approaches to for WBC classification using computer vision (CV), machine learning (ML) and deep learning (DL). There are two manners to classify WBC in blood smear; it can be by extracting information from the whole image (image classification) or from image region using bounding boxes (object detection). In this paper, a novel method for white blood cell detection and classification is proposed. Retinanet is used for WBC detection and siamese VGG16 architecture for classification. The proposed approach is divided into two stages, the first one is to detect WBCs from blood smear images (object detection); in the second stage, a WBC stratification task is performed using a siamese VGG16 architecture (image classification). The performance evaluation of the proposed method considers precision (P), recall (R) and F1 score. The main contributions of this paper are the following:

- Comparison between handcrafted and CNN-based methods for white blood cell detection and classification.
- Evaluation of the proposed method using commonly used metrics such as Accuracy, Precision, Recall and F1-score.
- Experimentation of a novel method which combines image classification and object detection for WBC stratification.
- Implementation of an statistical analysis in order to demonstrate siamese networks reduce the high inter-class similarity among WBC images.

2   Related Works

There are many studies that propose vision-based methods for white blood cell classification. Ramesh et al. in [3] proposed to use color information and morphology to classify 1930 WBCs images using linear discriminant analysis (LDA) obtaining an overall acccuracy of 93.9%. On the other hand, Barrero et al. in [4] developed a system to identify and classify blood cells using networks of Gaussian Radial Base Functions (RBFN), achieving an average accuracy of 85.83%, where the accuracy values for each class were of 93.4% for lymphocytes, 79.5% for neutrophils, 97.37% for monocytes, and 73.07% for eosinophils. Huang et al. in [13] proposed to use Otsu threshold to segment cell nuclei and texture and to extract shape features followed by PCA in order to recognize leukocytes, achieving 81.6% of accuracy. Another approach is proposed by Gautam et al. in [14]. They proposed to extract morpholical features such as area, eccentricity, perimeter and circularity and use Naïve Bayes classifier; authors achieved 80.88% accuracy. In another work, Rosyadi et al. in [5] concluded in their paper that upon implementation of k-means algorithm, the most significant geometry feature is its circularity, generating an accuracy of 67%. The methods mentioned above are handcrafted-based approaches, which means that the features are manually engineered. Some other works are focused on CNN-based techniques, for example, Macawile et al. in [15] proposed a method to classify the 5 WBC classes using HSV (Hue, Saturation and Value) microscopic images. On the other hand, Sahlol et al. in [16] extracted deep features using VGGNet and using the Salp Swarm Algorithm, these features were filtered in order to classify WBCs for leukemia classification. Another authors, such as Liang et al. in [17] in proposed to combine CNN and Recurrent Neural Networks (RNN) such as Inception V3, Xception and Resnet, obtaining 90.79% accuracy.

3   Retinanet

Retinanet is a one-stage object detector which uses focal loss to address class imbalance [10]. Negative samples contribute to achieve lower loss in training. The main contribution of focal loss is that it is concentrated in hard samples [18]. Retinanet relies on three main tasks: feature extraction which is done by Resnet50 [19] and Feature Pyramid Network (FPN) [20]; classification of the detected object; and, bounding box regression. In Fig. 2 the three tasks of Retinanet are presented. Resnet50 (Residual Neural Network) is a type of CNN composed by 50 stacked residual blocks on top of each other to form a network. A residual block allows layers to feed into the next layer and directly into the layers about two or three hops forward; this helps to reduce the vanishing gradient problem during propagation. The architecture of Resnet50 used as backbone is presented in Table 1

The FPN augments a standard convolutional network with a top-down pathway and lateral connections in order to obtain a rich multi-scale feature pyramid from a single resolution input image, see Fig. 2. This allows the network to detect

Table 1. Resnet50 architecture.

Layer name	Output size	Configuration
Conv1	112×112	7×7, 64, stride 2
Conv2_x	56×56	3×3 $\max_{p}ool$, stride 2
Conv2_x	56×56	$3x([1 \times 1, 64][3 \times 3, 64][1 \times 1,256])$
Conv3_x	28×28	$4x([1 \times 1, 128][3 \times 3, 128][1 \times 1,512])$
Conv4_x	14×14	$6x([1 \times 1, 256][3 \times 3, 256][1 \times 1,1024])$
Conv5_x	7×7	$3x([1 \times 1, 512][3 \times 3, 512][1 \times 1,2048])$
FC	1×1	Average pool, 1000-D FC, Softmax

objects at a different scale [18]. This classification subnet predicts the probability of object presence at each spatial position for each of the A anchors and k object classes. The architecture is a fully convolutional network (FCN) attached to each FPN level which receives a feature map of C channels from a specific FPN level. The regression subnet is another FCN which is attached in parallel to the Classification Subnet. Each pyramid level is connected to his regression model in order to compute the offset from each anchor box to a nearby ground-truth object. Focal loss is proposed in [18] and it was designed to address the problem of extreme imbalance between foreground and background classes during training. Focal loss is a variation of cross entropy loss function, which is defined as:

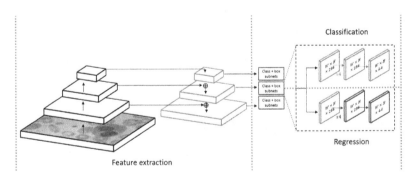

Fig. 2. Retinanet is composed by three main tasks, i) feature extraction is done using the feature pyramid network backbone, ii) the classification of the detected object and iii) the coordinates of the bounding box.

$$CE(p,y) = \begin{cases} -log(p) & if\, y = 1 \\ -log(1-p) & otherwise \end{cases} \tag{1}$$

where $y\epsilon\{\pm1\}$ specifies the ground-truth class and $p\epsilon[0,1]$ is the predicted probability for the class with label $y = 1$. Let p_t be defined as:

$$p_t = \begin{cases} p & if y = 1 \\ 1 - p & otherwise \end{cases} \tag{2}$$

Equation 1 can be rewritten as:

$$CE(p, y) = CE(p_t) = -log(p_t) \tag{3}$$

In order to address the class imbalance, a weighting factor $\alpha\epsilon[0,1]$ is introduced. The weighted equation (3) can be written as:

$$CE(p_t) = -\alpha_t log(p_t) \tag{4}$$

In most of the object detectors, the easy negatives samples comprise the majority of the loss. Easy negatives samples are those that is very easy to classify as negative due to the huge amount of examples presented in the image, usually these samples correspond to the background. On the other hand, hard positives samples are those samples that it is very difficult to detect and classify because the amount of these examples is too low compared to easy negatives, In Fig. 3. Thus, in object detector a class imbalance is presented.

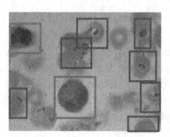

Fig. 3. The samples inside red squares are easy negatives, from them, any useful information is extracted. Samples inside green squares are the hard positives and provide information about the detected object. (Color figure online)

To address this problem, a modulating factor is introduced to the loss function in order to focus on hard negatives only. The final focal loss function proposed in [18] is defined as:

$$FL(p_t) = -\alpha_t(1 - p_t)^\gamma log(p_t) \tag{5}$$

According to experiments, α and γ should be set 0.25 and 2, respectively [18].

4   Siamese Network

A siamese convolutional neural network is a type of architecture that contains two identical networks sharing their parameters (as shown in Fig. 4) and are used to find similarities of the outputs by comparing the embedding each network generate, in other words, siamese CNN focuses on learning semantic similarity. It is expected that using semantic similarity learning can reduce the high inter-class similarity among white blood cell images [11]. Specifically, the siamese architecture relies on an image pair as inputs; this pair of images can be positive (images of the same class) or negative (images of different classes). Each image is processed through its corresponding branch, where each branch will generate an image embedding, which is then fed into the contrastive loss, responsible for similarity learning. Let be f(A) the embedding of image A and f(B) the embedding of image B, then:

$$D(A, B) = \sqrt{\sum_{i=1}^{n} (f(A)_i - f(B)_i)^2} \tag{6}$$

where D(.) is the euclidean distance between the n-dimensional f(A) and f(B) image embedding. If (6) is small, it means that image A and image B are similar and vice versa. The contrastive loss is defined as:

$$L = \frac{1}{2} l D^2 + \frac{1}{2} (max(0, m - D))^2 \tag{7}$$

where l is a binary label indicating if A and B belong to the same class (l=1) or not (l=0); m is a margin selected for dissimilarity images (m must be greater than zero). As seen from (7), the distance between the embeddings of the same class images must be small, and the distance between the ones obtained from different class images must be large.

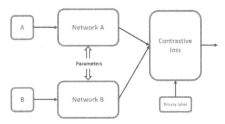

Fig. 4. Siamese network relies on two identical networks which share their parameters. The contrastive loss function is the responsible of generate image embeddings according to the similarity of the input image pair.

5   Proposed Method

In this paper, a detection-classification method is proposed in order to detect and classify white blood cells in smear images. To do so, the proposed method (shown in Fig. 5) is divided into two stages, object detection and image classification. The experiments were done using an artificially augmented BCCD dataset [12].

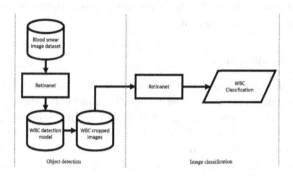

Fig. 5. The proposed method uses a one-stage object detector to determine in which region of the image there is a WBC; the siamese architecture is the responsible for WBC stratification.

5.1   Dataset

The dataset used was sub dataset of a variation of the BCCD dataset. The BCDD dataset is composed by 364 images across three classes: WBC, RBC and Platelets. The staining used in the blood cells was Gismo-right and the images were obtained using a regular light microscope with zoom 100x. The variation dataset is published in [12]. This dataset was generated by artificially augmentation applying random rotations, scalings, reflections and shearings; in addition, the white blood cells were labeled according to the corresponding class. More specifically, this dataset contains 12,500 augmented images of blood cells, approximately 3,000 images for each of four different white blood cells types. The types are eosinophil, lymphocyte, monocyte and neutrophil; the ground-truth bounding boxes were manually labeled. In this paper it was used only the 33% randomly selected of the entire dataset in order to reduce the computational cost.

5.2   Object Detection

Retinanet was trained to extract features using Resnet50 and FPN, and then, using two specific subnets, the coordinates and the class of the detected white blood cell were used. The dataset used for experiments is composed by 3,865 images of dimension 416 × 416 × 3 divided into four classes, eosinophil, neutrophil, monocyte and lymphocyte. The dataset was divided into three subsets, training, validation and test, which 2,700, 778 and 387 images respectively. It was implemented a transfer learning using the COCO weights [21] for 20 epochs and an IoU (Intersection over Union) value of 0.5. The values of training mAP and validation mAP were 0.9769 and 0.9743, respectively. From here, it can be seen that the network is not overfitted. In Fig. 7, the predictions for 9 random samples from testing set are presented; it is worth noting that Retinanet is invariant to different geometric transformation.

5.3   Image Classification

For image classification stage, the Retinanet model was used for WBC image cropping; these cropped images were used for similarity learning. Randomly, positive and negative pairs were generated for feeding siamese network. The architecture used in image classification in a siamese version is VGG16. VGG16 is a CNN considered to be one of excellent vision model architecture. This network instead of having a large number of hyper parameter, they focused on having convolutional layers of 3 × 3 filter with stride 1, same padding and max pooling layer of 2 × 2 filter with stride 2. In Table 2 it is presented the different architecture for VGG16; in this paper the type D was used.

Each VGG16 network were fine-tuned by freezing the first convolutional layer and replacing the default dense layers by two new fully connected layer. The siamese VGG16 was trained for 20 epochs and the results are the following: 0.0311 training loss, 0.9630 training accuracy, 0.0611 validation loss and 0.9229 validation accuracy.

5.4   Experimental Results

The result for WBC classification is shown in Table 3. The average accuracy of the proposed network is 95%. As can be observed, the proposed method performs well the WBC classification. It is important to note that there still exists a certain level of inter-class similarity between eusonohils and neutrophils. Monocytes and lymphocytes have different morphological features, that is why the proposed method can classify them well. In order to understand this, t-SNE (t-distributed stochastic neighbor embedding) was implemented, which is a nonlinear dimensionality reduction method well-suited for embedding high-dimensional data for visualization in a low-dimensional space that allows to observe the image embedding the siamese VGG16 is generating. In Fig. 6a can be observed the distribution of each image embedding. The size of each image embedding generated by the siamese VGG16 is four, however, using t-SNE technique, is possible to represent them in two dimensions only. Monocytes and lymphocytes are separated by a large distance, representing the morphological similarity. However, for eusinophils and neutrophil, the distance is small, in addition, it can be observed some overlapping between this two classes. This is because the morphological similarity in these two classes. In order to compare the proposed method with

Table 2. VGG architecture.

A	A-LRN	B	C	D	E
11	11	13	16	16	19
Weight	Weight	Weight	Weight	Weight	Weight
Layers	Layers	Layers	Layers	Layers	Layers
input (224 × 224 RGB image					
conv64	conv64	conv64	conv64	conv64	conv64
	LRN	conv64	conv64	conv64	conv64
Maxpool					
conv128	conv128	conv128	conv128	conv128	conv128
		conv128	conv128	conv128	conv128
maxpool					
conv256	conv256	conv256	conv256	conv256	conv256
conv256	conv256	conv256	conv256	conv256	conv256
			conv1-256	conv256	conv256
conv512	conv512	conv512	conv512	conv512	conv512
conv512	conv512	conv512	conv512	conv512	conv512
			conv1-512	conv512	conv512
maxpool					
conv512	conv512	conv512	conv512	conv512	conv512
conv512	conv512	conv3	conv512	conv512	conv512
			conv1-512	conv512	conv512
					conv512
maxpool					
FC-4096					
FC-4096					
FC-1000					
Softmax					

standalone Retinanet, t-SNE was applied as well to the last layer of the network. This layer has four neurons which contain the class probability of each bounding box. The result of t-SNE is shown in Fig. 6b. It can be observed that Retinanet is trying to classify in four classes, however, the samples are overlapped, which makes the classification a difficult task. In Fig. 7 can be observed the classification results of nine random samples using the proposed method. As it was mentioned before, the object detection stage detects the location of the WBC, while the image classification stage determines the class of the detected WBC. As it can be seen from the results, the proposed method is capable to detect the WBC in a blood smear image, and, using similarity learning, the classification becomes an easier task due to the image embeddings are generated according to the similarity of the image pair. In spite siamese network reduces the inter-class similarity, there are still some level in eosinophil and neutrophil classes.

Table 3. Classification results.

WBC class	Precision	Recall	F1-Score
Eosinophil	0.88	0.93	0.91
Lymphocyte	1.00	1.00	1.00
Monocyte	1.00	1.00	1.00
Neutrophil	093	0.88	0.91

A research was performed in order to find published works that used the same dataset in order to compare the proposed method. In the literature the work of Liang et al. [17] was found, which is based on CNN. In that paper, authors proposed to use a combination of CNN and RNN to classify BCCD images of white blood cell; this comparison is presented in Table 4

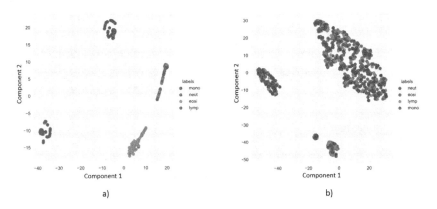

Fig. 6. t-SNE visualization. a) Visualization of the distribution of each image embedding generated by the Siamese VGG16. The distance between monocytes and lymphocytes is large, meaning this classes are not similar. Eosinophil and neutrophil are very similar, the distance between them is small. b) Distribution of the last layer of Retinanet for each bounding box detection. The image embedding are overlapped, which makes classification a hard task.

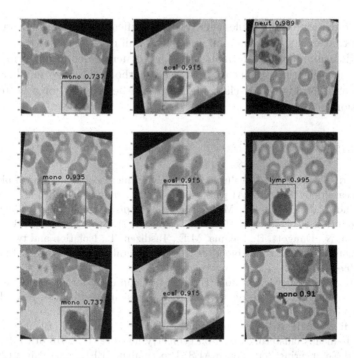

Fig. 7. Predictions of the proposed method on nine randomly selected images from testing set. The bounding box coordinates is predicted by the object detection stage and the class probability (class name and confidence appear above the bounding box) by the image classification.

Table 4. Comparison.

Reference	Method	Accuracy
Gautam et al. [14]	Morpholical features and Naıve Bayes classifier	88.8%
Liang et al. [17]	CNN and RNN combination	90.7%
Proposed	Semantic similarity learning	95%

6   Conclusions

WBCs are the responsible of the human immune system. The number of WBCs can increase or decrease over time, however, if it exceeds the normal range, it can provide information about several diseases. The constant monitoring of WBC count can prevent many diseases, as well, it is possible to generate a medical profile for each patient. In this paper it is proposed a method to detect and classify white blood cell in order to play the role of an intelligent assistant to medical staff. One of the main problems in object detection is the huge amount of easy negatives examples; this overwhelms the loss function and leads to a false convergence state of the network. Focal loss can address this problem focusing on hard examples only. Another problem in WBC classification, is the high inter-class similarity that exists in eusonophil and neutrophil classes. It was demonstrated with t-SNE technique that Retinanet does not generate good image embeddings for image classification. Using the proposed method, the huge number of easy negatives and the high inter-class similarity can be reduced for a better WBC classification.

References

1. Mukund, N., Gite, S., Aluvalu, R.: A review of microscopic analysis of blood cells for disease detection with AI perspective. PeerJ Comput. Sci. **7**, 1–27 (2021)
2. Mahmudul, M., Tariqul, M.: Machine learning approach of automatic identification and counting of blood cells. Healthc. Technol. Lett. **6**(4), 103–108 (2019)
3. Ramesh, N., Dangott, B., Salama, M.E., Tasdizen, T.: Isolation and two-step classification of normal white blood cells in peripheral blood smears. J. Pathol. Inf. **3**(1), 99–110 (2012)
4. Barrero, C., Romero, L., Roa, E.: A novel approach for objective assessment of white blood cells using computational vision algorithms. Adv. Hematol. **2018**(4716370) (2018)
5. Rosyadi, T., Arif, A., Nopriadi, Achmad, B.F.: Classification of leukocyte images using K-means clustering based on geometry features. In: 2016 6th International Annual Engineering Seminar (InAES) Proceedings. IEEE, Yogyakarta (2016)
6. Cruz, D., et al.: Determination of blood components (WBCs, RBCs, and Platelets) count in microscopic images using image processing and analysis. In: 2017IEEE 9th International Conference on Humanoid, Nanotechnology, Information Technology, Communication and Control, Environment and Management (HNICEM) Proceedings. IEEE, Philippines (2017)
7. Cheuque, C., Querales, M., Leon, R., Salas, R., Torres, R.: An efficient multilevel convolutional neural network approach for white blood cells classification. Diagnostics **12**(248), 1–15 (2022)
8. Habibzadeh, M., Krzyżak, A., Fevens, T.: White blood cell differential counts using convolutional neural networks for low resolution images. In: Rutkowski, L., Korytkowski, M., Scherer, R., Tadeusiewicz, R., Zadeh, L.A., Zurada, J.M. (eds.) ICAISC 2013. LNCS (LNAI), vol. 7895, pp. 263–274. Springer, Heidelberg (2013). https://doi.org/10.1007/978-3-642-38610-7_25
9. Tavakoli, S., Ghaffari, A., Kouzehkanan, Z.M., et al.: New segmentation and feature extraction algorithm for classification of white blood cells in peripheral smear images. Sci. Rep. **11**(19428), 1–13 (2021)
10. Perez-Daniel, K., Fierro-Radilla, A., Peñaloza-Cobos, J.P.: Rotten fruit detection using a one stage object detector. In: Martínez-Villaseñor, L., Herrera-Alcántara, O., Ponce, H., Castro-Espinoza, F.A. (eds.) MICAI 2020. LNCS (LNAI), vol. 12469, pp. 325–336. Springer, Cham (2020). https://doi.org/10.1007/978-3-030-60887-3_29
11. Fierro, A., Perez, K., Benitez, G., Najera, P., Fuentes, R.: Similarity learning for CNN-based ASL alphabet recognition. In: Frontiers in Artificial Intelligence and Applications. Proceedings of the 20th Interational Conference on New Trends in Intelligent Software Methodologies, Tools and Techniques (SoMeT 2021). IOS Press. (2021)

12. Blood Cell Kaggle Dataset. https://www.kaggle.com/datasets/paultimothymooney/blood-cells. Accessed 29 June 2022
13. Huang, D., Hung, K., Chan, Y.: A computer assisted method for leukocyte nucleus segmentation and recognition in blood smear images. J. Syst. Softw. **85**(9), 2104–2118 (2012)
14. Gautam, A., Singh, P., Raman, B., Bhadauria, H.: Automatic classification of leukocytes using morphological features and Naïve Bayes classifier. In: 2016 IEEE Region 10 Conference (TENCON) Proceedings. IEEE, Singapore (2016)
15. Macawile, M., Quiñones, V., Ballado, A., Dela Cruz, J., Caya, V.: White blood cell classification and counting using convolutional neural network. In: 2018 3rd International Conference on Control and Robotics Engineering Proceedings, pp. 259–263. IEEE, Nagoya (2018)
16. Sahlol, A., Kollmannsberger, P., Ewees, A.: Blood cell leukemia with improved swarm optimization of deep features. Sci. Rep. **10**(2536), 1–11 (2020)
17. Liang, G., Hong, H., Xie, W., Zheng, L.: Combining convolutional neural network with recursive neural network for blood cell image classification. IEEE Access **6**, 36188–36197 (2018)
18. Li, T., Goyal, P., Girshick, R., He, K., Dollár, P.: Focal loss for dense object detection. IEEE Trans. Pattern Anal. Mach. Intell. **42**(2), 318–327 (2018)
19. He, K., Zhang, X., Ren, S., Sun, J.: Deep residual learning for image recognition. In: IEEE Conference on Computer Vision and Pattern Recognition (CVPR2016) Proceedings. IEEE, Las Vegas (2016)
20. Lin, T., Dollár, P., Girshick, R., He, K., Hariharan, B., Belogie, S.: Feature pyramid networks for object detection. In: IEEE Conference on Computer Vision and Pattern Recognition (CVPR2017) Proceedings. IEEE, Honolulu (2017)
21. Common Object Context Weights Repository. https://github.com/fizyr/keras-retinanet/releases/download/0.5.1/resnet50_coco_best_v2.1.0.h5. Accessed 29 June 2022

Evolutionary and Metaheuristic Algorithms

Towards a Complete Multi-agent Pathfinding Algorithm for Large Agents

Stepan Dergachev[1,2]([⊠]) [iD] and Konstantin Yakovlev[1,2] [iD]

[1] National Research University Higher School of Economics, Moscow, Russia
sadergachev@edu.hse.ru
[2] Federal Research Center for Computer Science and Control of Russian
Academy of Sciences, Moscow, Russia
yakovlev@isa.ru

Abstract. Multi-agent pathfinding (MAPF) is a challenging problem which is hard to solve optimally even when simplifying assumptions are adopted, e.g. planar graphs (typically – grids), discretized time, uniform duration of move and wait actions etc. On the other hand, MAPF under such restrictive assumptions (also known as the Classical MAPF) is equivalent to the so-called pebble motion problem for which non-optimal polynomial time algorithms do exist. Recently, a body of works emerged that investigated MAPF beyond the basic setting and, in particular, considered agents of arbitrary size and shape. Still, to the best of our knowledge no complete algorithms for such MAPF variant exists. In this work we attempt to narrow this gap by considering MAPF for large agents and suggesting how this problem can be reduced to pebble motion on (general) graphs. The crux of this reduction is the procedure that moves away the agents away from the edge which is needed to perform a move action of the current agent. We consider different variants of how this procedure can be implemented and present a variant of the pebble motion algorithm which incorporates this procedure. Unfortunately, the algorithm is still incomplete, but empirically we show that it is able to solve much more MAPF instances (under the strict time limit) with large agents on arbitrary non-planar graphs (roadmaps) compared to the state-of-the-art MAPF solver – Continous Conflict-Based Search (CCBS).

Keywords: Multi-agent systems · Coordination of multiple vehicle systems · Multi-agent path finding · Pebble motion · Large agents

1 Introduction

Multi-agent pathfinding (MAPF) is a challenging problem with topical applications in robotics, video games etc. There exist different ways to define the MAPF problem [8] and approaches to solve it. On the one hand, optimal and bounded sub-potimal solvers exist for what is known as Classical MAPF, like

O. Pichardo Lagunas et al. (Eds.): MICAI 2022, LNAI 13612, pp. 355–367, 2022.
https://doi.org/10.1007/978-3-031-19493-1_28

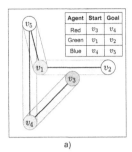 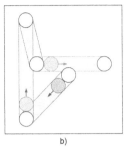

a)   b)

Fig. 1. An example of the multi-agent path finding for large agents (MAPF-LA) problem instance. It can only be solved if the synchronous moves of the agents are allowed (as shown on the right).

the ones presented in [2,3,6,7]. On the other hand fast prioritized planners without any completeness/optimality guarantees are widespread [4,11]. Finally, complete, non-optimal algorithms exist, such as the ones described in [5,9], which borrow the solving techniques from the so-called Pebble Motion on Graph (PMG) problem. Sill, all these algorithms do no consider the size/shape of the agents. Indeed, attempts to lift this restricting assumption are known [1,10], however the algorithms known so-far do not guarantee completeness. This works aims at drawing an attention to this gap and try narrowing it by adopting the PMG algorithms to the setting with the large agents, dubbed as MAPF-LA futher on.

More specifically, we focus on one of the routines, regularly needed, in solving MAPF-LA instances – the one that makes it possible for one agent to traverse an edge without colliding to the other agents that prevent the transition due to their large bodies. We elaborate on how these agents can be safely moved away so the transition becomes valid. The suggested procedure was implemented and incorporated to the well-known PUSH AND ROTATE algorithm [5]. Unfortunately, the current variant of this algorithm is still incomplete for MAPF-LA. However, as we show in our empirical evaluation, it outperforms the stat-of-the-art competitors, i.e. CCBS algorithms [1], in terms of number of solved MAPF-LA instances under the strict time limit.

The rest of this paper is organized as follows. We considere the definitions of MAPF-LA in Sect. 2. Section 3 describes a possible implementation of the procedure for moving away interfering agents, and also discuss cases when the proposed procedure is not sufficient to solve the planning problem. We report the results of of an experimental evaluation in Sect. 4 and conclude in Sect. 5.

2   Problem Statement

Consider a tuple $(\mathcal{W}, G, r, K, start, goal)$, where $\mathcal{W} \subset \mathcal{R}^2$ is a metric workspace where K agents are operating. Each agent is modeled as a disk of radius $r > 0$. $G = (V, E)$ is a graph embedded in the workspace, i.e. each vertex $v \in V$ is associated with a point in $\mathcal{W}$. Edges correspond to the transitions between the

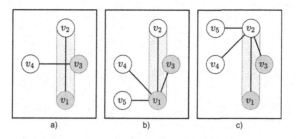

Fig. 2. An illustration of three cases that can occur when agents should be moved away from the edge along which the current agent needs to transit

locations. It is assumed that when moving along the edge the agent follows a straight-line segment connecting the corresponding vertices. $start : K \to V$ is a function that specifies the initial locations of the agents, $goal$ is the similar function specifying the target locations.

A set of K distinct graph vertices $S = (s_1, ..., s_K)$, $s_i \in V$, $\forall i, j : s_i \neq s_j$ forms a *state*. Here s_i is a position of the ith agent. A state is valid *iff* $dist(s_i, s_j) \geq 2r$, where $dist$ stands for the Euclidean distance. In other words the state is valid if the bodies of the agents do not overlap. In this work we adopt an assumption that the distance between any two vertices of G is greater than $2r$. This infers that any state, as defined above, is valid.

A *transition* is formally a function $\pi(S, S') \to \{0, 1\}$, where $\pi = 1$ stands for the valid transition and $\pi = 0$ for the invalid one. Informally, transition corresponds to the movement of (some) agents between the locations in the workspace via the edges of the given graph. Conceptually, two possible assumptions regarding the transitions can be made:

- general: synchronous moves of the agents are allowed, i.e. more than one agent can change its location as a result of the transition
- restrictive: only one agent can change its location, while the rest stay at the same vertices

In this work we follow the second assumption. In such case for a transition $\pi(S, S')$ to be valid the following conditions should be met. First, the moving agent i may move only using one of the outgoing edges, i.e. $(s_i, s_i') \in E$. Second, the move should be collision-free, i.e. $\forall j \neq i : segdist(e, s_j) > 2r$, where $segdist$ is the distance between the segment, defined by the edge e, and the vertex s_j.

The problem of multi-agent pathfing for large agents (MAPF-LA) is now formulated as follows. Given $(\mathcal{W}, G, r, K, start, goal)$ find the sequence of states $(S_0, S_1, ..., S_n)$ s.t. $\forall s_i \in S_0 : s_i = start(i)$, $\forall s_i \in S_n : s_i = goal(i)$, $\forall i = 0, ...n-1$ a valid transition $\pi(S_i, S_{i+1})$ exists. In other words, the problem is to find the sequence of moves for the agents that transfer them from their start locations to their goal locations, while avoiding the collisions.

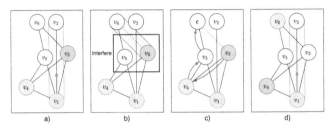

Fig. 3. Illustration of execution of PUSHTOEMPTY procedure. (a) The green agent must move along the edge (v_1, v_2), but the red agent interferes with it. (b) First of all, we mark all edges that are interfered with by the vertex v_2 as untraversable and find all interfering with (v_1, v_2) vertices. (c) Single empty and non-interfering with (v_1, v_2) vertex v_6 to which there is a path not through v_1 or v_2 remain on the graph. (d) After all, pushing the red and blue agents along the path between v_3 and v_6. Thus, the green agent can move along the edge (v_1, v_2) (Color figure online)

Example. An illustrative example of the considered problem is depicted in Fig. 1. Here the graph G consists of 5 vertices and 4 edges. The start and goal locations of the 3 agents are specified on the left part of the figure. Basically, each agent has to transfer to the adjacent vertex. However, under the considered assumption that only one agent moves at a time, the instance is not solvable. Meanwhile, if synchronous moves are allowed the problem is trivially solved via a single transition in which the agents simultaneously move to the adjacent vertices (as shown on the right). This highlights how defining the transition influence the possibility to find a solution. This is similar to the pebble motion on graphs problem, in which different assumptions regarding cycle-moves and chains-moves can be adopted, see [12] for details.

3   Suggested Approach

3.1   Preliminaries

The problem considered in this work, multi-agent pathfinding for large agents (MAPF-LA), is similar to the pebble motion on graphs (PMG) problem [12]. However the crucial differences exist, that prevent the straightforward applica- tion of the known methods to solve PMG for the considered formulation. Gener- ally, two core differences between the MAPF-LA and PMG are as follows. First, in PMG every placement of pebbles (agents) on distinct graph vertices by defi- nition form a valid state. In MAPF-LA this is not the case, however we adopted a (restrictive) assumption that the vertices of the given graph are located $2r$ distance units away from each other. Thus every placement of (large) agents on disjoint vertices also result in the valid state.

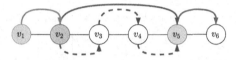

Fig. 4. Illustration of execution of PUSHALONGPATH procedure

Second, in PMG for a transition of one agent to be valid it is only required that the source vertex is free. In MAPF-LA this is not enough as the target vertex of the move can be free, but the moving agent, say a, may collide with the other agents while traversing an edge, as these agents stay too close to the edge itself. Such agents can be referred to as the *interfering* agents w.r.t. to the given edge $e = (v_{from}, v_{to})$. Thus, in order to reduce (our formulation of) MAPF-LA to PMG the following problem should be solved. Given a valid state S and an agent a that needs to traverse the edge $e = (v_{from}, v_{to})$ find a sequence of the valid transitions $(\pi_0, ..., \pi_k, ..., \pi_m)$ that results in the state S', where the agent a is located at v_{to} and all other agents occupy the same vertices as in S. Here the transition π_k corresponds to the move of the agent a, while the other transitions are moves of the other agents which are made, first, in order to remove the interfiring agents so the move through e is possible, and, second, move all agents (except a) back their vertices.

Lets denote the procedure that solves the described problem as MOVE-LA. Next we elaborate on how this procedure can be constructed. Generally, after MOVE-LA is defined, one can use one of the PMG algorithms to solve MAPF-LA. E.g., in this work we use PUSH AND ROTATE ALGORITHM [5], however other choices are possible.

3.2 Moving Along an Edge

A possible implementation of the MOVE-LA procedure consist of the three following steps. The first step is the sequential removal of every agent a' from every vertex v' that interfere with the move along e. This can be done via finding a path (for each interfering agent) to an unoccupied vertex and, then, sequentially moving the agent along this path (PUSH operation). The second step is to move the a along the e. The third step is to return every a' to its initial vertex. However, this should be done in such a way that agent a remains at v_{to}. We identify three different cases that may arise while removing an interfering agent a' (Fig. 2).

In the first case, a path to some empty vertex can be found for agent a' that does not go through the vertices v_{from} and v_{to}, as well as through the edges for which vertices v_{to} are interfering. Thus, agent a' can be pushed along such a path, and the resulting sequence of moves can be reversed at the end of the MOVE-LA operation to return agent a' to the initial position. An example of such a case is shown in Fig. 2a, where the green agent needs to move along the (v_1, v_2). To do this, it is enough to move the blue agent to vertex v_5, and after passing the green agent, return the blue one to v_3

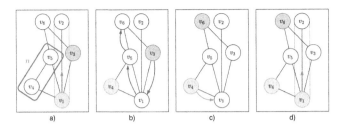

Fig. 5. Illustration of execution of PUSHTHROUGHVFROM procedure. (a) The green agent must move along the edge (v_1, v_2), but the red agent on the v_5 vertex interferes with it. There are no paths between v_5 and non-interfering vertices, that do not pass through v_1. So, it is necessary to move the green agent at one of the neighboring vertices so that the red agent can pass (b) After that, it is necessary to move the interfering agent from its position using the PUSHALONGPATH procedure (c) Next, the green agent can return to its original position v_1 (d) Thus, the green agent can move along the edge (v_1, v_2) (Color figure online)

In the second case, the path of a' can go through the vertex v_{from}, but not through the edges for which vertices v_{to} are interfering. However, for this, it is necessary to first push agent a from vertex v_{from}.Then we need to push a' to some non-interfering vertex. After the pushing of agent a' completes, agent a must be returned. The sequence of moves obtained in this way can be also reversed to return all agents to their positions, except for some actions that must be ignored when carrying out the reverse operation.

For the green agent on Fig. 2b, which illustrates the second case, to make the required move, it must first go to vertex v_5. After that, the blue agent will be able to go to vertex v_4, and the green agent can return to v_1 and move to v_2. Finally, the resulting solution can be reversed after deleting the moves of the green agent.

In the third case, to remove the agent from the interfering vertex, it is necessary to find a path through v_{to} (and optional through v_{from}, but not through the edge e itself), or through the edges, for which vertices v_{to} (and optional v_{from}) are interfering. In this case, it is impossible to return the agents by a reversal, since by the time this operation is performed, the vertex v_{to} will be occupied by agent a, which will lead to a collision.

In the case on Fig. 2c, the blue agent can be moved to a non-interfering vertex only when passing through v_2. Thus, after the green agent moves to v_2, the blue agent can return to its original position v_3 only if the green agent misses it (e.g., when the blue agent leaves to v_4, the green agent must go to v_5 for the blue one to return to v_3).

We propose PUSHTOEMPTY and PUSHTHROUGHVFROM procedures that can be used to solve the first and the second case respectively. Let's consider these procedures in more detail.

Algorithm 1 REVERSABLEEDGECLEANING procedure
___
Input: G – graph, S – current state, $e = (v_{from}, v_{to})$ – edge to clear,
U – blocked vertices, r – agents radius
Output:
π – resulting solution, π_{rev} – the sequence of valid moves, which returns interfering
agents back

1: $\pi \leftarrow [\,]$, $a \leftarrow$ agent, that need to move by edge e, $NotCleared \leftarrow \{\}$
2: $I \leftarrow$ interfere vertices of e, $I_f \leftarrow$ unoccupied interfere vertices of e
3: **for all** $v' \in I \backslash I_{free}$ **do**
4:     $\pi' \leftarrow [\,]$, $S' \leftarrow S$
5:     **if** PushToEmpty(G, S', π', v', $U \cup \{v_{to}\}$, e, I_f, r) **then**
6:        $\pi \leftarrow \pi + \pi'$, $\pi_{rev} \leftarrow \pi_{rev} + \pi'$ except moves of a
7:        $S \leftarrow S'$, $I_f \leftarrow I_f \cup \{v'\}$
8:     **else**
9:        $NotCleared \leftarrow NotCleared \cup \{v'\}$
10: **for all** $v' \in NotCleared$ **do**
11:    $a_e \leftarrow \{\}$, $\pi' \leftarrow [\,]$, $S' \leftarrow S$
12:    $\pi'' \leftarrow$ PushThroughVfrom(G, S', π', v', U, e, I_f, r)
13:    **if** $\pi'' \neq false$ **then**
14:       $\pi \leftarrow \pi + \pi'$, $\pi_{rev} \leftarrow \pi_{rev} + \pi''$ except moves of a
15:       $S \leftarrow S'$, $I_f \leftarrow I_f \cup \{v'\}$, $NotCleared \leftarrow NotCleared \backslash \{v'\}$
16: $U \leftarrow U \backslash \{v_{to}\}$, $\pi_{rev} \leftarrow$ Reverse(π_{rev})
17: **if** $NotCleared$ not empty **then**
18:    **return** false
19: **return** π, π_{rev}
___

3.3 PushToEmpty

The procedure PUSHTOEMPTY is designed to remove interfering agent a' without affecting the vertex v_{to} and without pushing agent a' through v_{from} (Fig. 3a). First of all, mark all edges that are interfered by the vertex v_{to} as untraversable (Fig. 3b). This is necessary so that when the obtained solution is reversed, there are no conflicts with agent a who passed using the considered edge e. After that, all possible options are considered to move agent a' from the interfering vertex v'. For this, a set of empty, non-interfering with e vertices is formed. For each selected empty vertex ϵ, an attempt is made to find a path, avoiding using v_{from} and v_{to} (Fig. 3c) and pushing the agent a' along this path (using PUSHALONG-PATH procedure). As a result, the agent a' from the interfering vertex is moved so that agent a can move along the edge e (Fig. 3d).

If the path to the vertex was found, but the PUSHALONGPATH operation failed, then the edge, through which the operation MOVE-LA inside PUSHALONGPATH could not be performed, is temporarily marked as untraversable and the path to ϵ has searched again. If the path to ϵ cannot be found, then the next empty vertex from the list is taken. A more detailed description of the procedure is provided in pseudocode in Appendix A.

PushAlongPath. Lets consider PUSHALONGPATH procedure. It consists of the sequential moving of agents along path to empty vertex starting from the last agent in the path. An important feature of this operation is that when passing a path through empty vertices, they will remain free after the end of the operation.

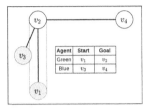

Fig. 6. An example of a case where it is necessary to correctly determine the planning order, even if there is a complete procedure for moving an agent along an edge (Color figure online)

An illustration of this operation is shown in Fig. 4. Agents (green, red and blue circles) must be pushed along path $v_1 - v_6$. In addition to the last vertex v_6, the path also contains intermediate empty vertices v_3 and v_4. The operation starts by moving the blue agent. He goes to vertex v_6. All subsequent agents move to those vertices that were occupied by the previous ones (the red agent moves to the vertex v_5 passing through empty vertices, and the green agent moves to the vertex v_2). At the end of the operation, the first vertex of the path is freed because the last vertex of the path becomes occupied.

3.4   PushThroughVFrom

To solve the second case of removing agent a' from interfering vertex v' we suggest the PUSHTHROUGHVFROM procedure. It consists of two stages. At the first stage, agent a moves away to one of the neighbouring vertices n. If n is occupied, the operation of clearing the vertex is performed, similar to PUSHTOEMPTY.

If the operation of clearing of n was performed successfully, or if n was initially not occupied, then the operation MOVE-LA from v_{from} to n is performed. Note that if the edge e is marked as untraversable in the MOVE-LA operation, vertex v_{to} can be involved in it, since the obtained actions π'' will not be included in the REVERSE operation when the interfering agents return to their vertices. In the case when at least one of the operations described above fails, then an attempt is made to move agent a to another vertex n.

After the passage through v_{from} is cleared, an attempt is made to move agent a' away from v' also similarly to PUSHTOEMPTY. It is important to note that when creating the path of agent a', it is necessary to block the vertices that are the current positions of the π'' participants. This is necessary to guarantee the return of agent a to the vertex v_{from} using the REVERSE operation.

If it was possible to find a path to an empty vertex for agent a', after which the PUSHALONGPATH was successful, then the obtained solution is saved and

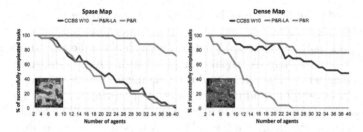

Fig. 7. Success rates of the suboptimal version of CCBS (CCBS W10), the suggested approach (P&R-LA) and "naive" version of the PUSH AND ROTATE for large agents (P&R) on two different roadmaps with varied number of agents

supplemented with reverses actions π'' to return agent a to vertex v_{from}. In addition, the solution is saved with the exclusion of action π'', which is necessary for the further return of agent a' to vertex v'. A more detailed description of the procedure is also provided in pseudocode in Appendix A.

3.5   ReversableEdgeCleaning

The sequential resolving algorithm of the first two cases can be combined into a single REVERSABLEEDGECLEANING procedure (Algorithm 1), the result of which is the removal of interfering agents possible for considered cases, as well as a sequence of moves that will return all pushed agents to their positions after agent a passes along edge e.

The proposed algorithm consists of two stages. At the first stage, the procedure PUSHTOEMPTY is launched for each occupied vertex that interferes with the edge e (lines 6–12). If any of these vertices cannot be freed using procedure PUSHTOEMPTY, then they are stored in the *NotCleared* set (lines 12). After that, the procedure PUSHTHROUGHVFROM is executed for each element of the *NotCleared* set (lines 13–19).

3.6   Discussion

It should be noted that at the moment the proposed algorithm is not complete for MAPF for large agents problem, since it does not take into account two significant points.

The first point refers to the third case inside MOVE-LA procedure previously mentioned in the text. In this case, the path from interfering to the non-interfering vertex lies through the vertex v_{to} or the edges that this vertex is interfering with. Then there is no possibility of returning the interfering agent to its original position by reversing its actions. Thus, agent a must let agent a' go to its initial position v', or another path must be found that leads agent a' to v'.

The second point is that may be the case that the interfering agent a' cannot return to the vertex v' at the end of MOVE-LA procedure (and MOVE-LA procedure fails), but still there exists a solution in which a' can be moved from vertex v' and not returned there. A trivial example of such a case is shown in Fig. 6. If the green agent has a higher priority during planning, then the blue agent cannot be pushed from vertex v_3 and returned there after moving the green agent. However, if planning starts with a blue agent, then a solution will be found. Thus, to construct a complete algorithm for MAPF-LA it is not enough to obtain a complete procedure for moving an agent along an edge. One of the possible solution to this problem is the choice of the correct planning order, as it is done in the PUSH AND ROTATE algorithm for solving not bi-connected instances.

4 Experimental Evaluation

We incorporated the suggested procedures to the well-known MAPF algorithm PUSH AND ROTATE, so it can be used to solve MAPF-LA instances. We denote it as P&R-LA. As one of the baselines we have also implemented a "naive" version of the PUSH AND ROTATE for large agents that simply halts when trying to move an agent along an edge with other interfering agents present. This version is denoted as, simply, P&R. Finally, the main baseline we were comparing with was the well-known CCBS algorithm [1] (we used the official implementation available on Github).

We evaluated planners on two different graphs (roadmaps) which were used in the CCBS paper: sparse and dense. The sparse roadmap contains 158 vertices and 349 edges, while the dense one – 878 vertices and 7341 edges. Originally, these roadmaps were automatically generated based on the **den520d** map from the MovingAI MAPF benchmark set [8]. An illustration of the roadmaps is shown in Fig. 7.

For each roadmap 25 scenarios were created, each one involving with 40 non-overlapping start and goal vertices. In each scenario, the first n start-goal pairs were selected, and then the evaluated algorithm was launched with a time limit of 30 s. In the experiment, the value of n varied from 2 to 40. We also set the sub-otimality factor for CCBS to 10, which notably speeds up the search (this feature is not described in the original paper, however is supported in the authors' code).

The resultant success rates, i.e. the fractions of the solved instances per fixed number of agents, are presented in Fig. 7 (the higher - the better). As one can see, our modification of PUSH AND ROTATE outperforms the competitors, especially when the number of agents goes up. E.g. our algorithm managed to solve 80% of tasks with 40 agents on the sparse roadmap, while the success rate of both competitors was close to zero. The reason why CCBS failed almost always is that the density of the agents, i.e. the ratio of agents' number to the number of graph vertices/edges is high and no easy solution is possible. This explains why CCBS copes better with the same number of agents on the dense roadmap – here there are much more graph vertices/edges that the algorithm can use to find non-conflicting plans. Notably, the reasons why our algorithm failed to solve instances invovling large number of agents differ for different maps. In sparse roadmap it terminated without providing a solution, while in the dense one it was not able to finish within the time limit. Thus, we infer, that a more efficient implementation of our method can actually provide a better success rate on the dense map.

5   Conclusion

In this work, we have considered the problem of designing a complete algorithm for a challenging variant of the multi-agent pathfinding problem when the size of the agents has to be taken into account (MAPF-LA). We elaborate on one of the core procedures such algorithm should incorporate, i.e. the procedure that clears an edge to allow for one agent to use this edge for a safe transition. We embed our implementation of this procedure to the well-known MAPF algorithm PUSH AND ROTATE enabling it to solve MAPF-LA problems. The results of the empirical evaluation provided us with the clear evidence that the resultant algorithm is able to find solutions for non-trivial MAPF-LA instances involving dozens of agents under the strict time limits (while its competitors often fail to do so).

Indeed, the main direction of future research is to develop a provably complete algorithm for solving MAPF-LA, as the method proposed in this work is only a step towards this goal (as it does not guarantee completeness).

A   PushToEmpty and PushThroughVfrom procedures

Algorithm 2 PUSHTOEMPTY procedure

Input: G – roadmap, S – current state, π – solution, U – blocked vertices,
v' – interfering vertex, $e = (v_{from}, v_{to})$ – edge to clear, r – agents radius, I_f – unoccupied vertices interfering to e.

1: $E \leftarrow$ edges for which vertex v_{to} is interfering, $G' \leftarrow$ remove E from G
2: **for all** ϵ in EmptyVertices$(G, S) \setminus I_f$ **do**
3:    **while** true **do**
4:       $p \leftarrow$ path from v' to ϵ in $G' \setminus U \cup \{v_{from}\}$)
5:       **if** $p =$ false **then**
6:          **break while**
7:       $\pi' \leftarrow [], S' \leftarrow S, e_f \leftarrow$ PushAlongPath(G', S', π', p, U)
8:       **if** $e_f =$ false **then**
9:          $\pi \leftarrow \pi + \pi', S \leftarrow S'$, **return** true
10:      **else**
11:         Remove edge e_f from G'
12: **return** false

Algorithm 3 PushThroughVfrom procedure

Input: G – roadmap, S – current state, π – solution, U – blocked vertices, v' – interfering vertex, a' – agent from v', $e = (v_{from}, v_{to})$ – edge to clear, r – agents radius, I_f – unoccupied vertices interfering to e.

```
 1: E ← edges for which vertex v_to is interfering
 2: for all n ∈ Neighbours(G, v_from) \U ∪ {v'} do
 3:     G' ← remove edges E from G, e_f ← false, p ← true
 4:     if n is occupied then
 5:         for all ϵ ∈ EmptyVertices(S) \(I_f ∪ {v_to}) do
 6:             e_f ← false
 7:             while true do
 8:                 S' ← S, π' ← [], p ← path from n to ϵ in G' \U ∪ {v_from, v_to, v'}
 9:                 if p = false then
10:                     break while
11:                 e_f ← PushAlongPath(G', S', π', p, U ∪ {v_to})
12:                 if e_f = false then
13:                     break for
14:                 Remove edge e_f from G'
15:         if p =false or e_f ≠false then
16:             continue with next n
17:         G'' ← remove edge e from G, π'' ← []
18:         if not move-la(G'', S', π'', v_from, n, U, r) then
19:             continue with next n
20:         P ← I_f∪ vertices of π'' ∪ interfere vertices of (v_from, n)
21:         U' ← U ∪ {v_to}∪ current positions in S' of agents from π''
22:         for all ε ∈ EmptyVertices(S) \P do
23:             e_f ← false
24:             while True do
25:                 S'' ← S', π''' ← [], p ← path from v' to ε in G' \U'
26:                 if p = false then
27:                     break while
28:                 e_f ← PushAlongPath(G', S'', π''', p, U ∪ {v_to})
29:                 if e_f = false then
30:                     π ← π + π' + π'' + π''', remove all moves of a' from π''
31:                     π ← π + reverse(π''), return π' + π'''
32:                 else
33:                     Remove edge e_f from G'
34: return false
```

References

1. Andreychuk, A., Yakovlev, K., Boyarski, E., Stern, R.: Improving continuous-time conflict based search. In: AAAI Conference on Artificial Intelligence, vol. 35, pp. 11220–11227 (2021)

2. Barer, M., Sharon, G., Stern, R., Felner, A.: Suboptimal variants of the conflict-based search algorithm for the multi-agent pathfinding problem. In: SoCS 2014, vol. 2014-January, pp. 19–27 (2014)

3. Boyarski, E., et al.: ICBS: Improved Conflict-Based Search Algorithm for Multi-Agent Pathfinding. In: IJCAI 2015, pp. 740–746 (2015)

4. Čáp, M., Novák, P., Kleiner, A., Selecký, M.: Prioritized planning algorithms for trajectory coordination of multiple mobile robots. IEEE Trans. Autom. Sci. Eng. **12**(3), 835–849 (2015)

5. De Wilde, B., Ter Mors, A.W., Witteveen, C.: Push and rotate: Cooperative multi-agent path planning. In: AAMAS 2013, vol. 1, pp. 87–94 (2013)

6. Sharon, G., Stern, R., Felner, A., Sturtevant., N.R.: Conflict-based search for optimal multiagent path finding. Artif. Intell. **218**, 40–66 (2015)

7. Sharon, G., Stern, R., Felner, A., Sturtevant, N.R.: Meta-agent conflict-based search for optimal multi-agent path finding. SoCS **2012**(1), 97–104 (2012)

8. Stern, R., et al.: Multi-agent pathfinding: definitions, variants, and benchmarks. In: SoCS 2019, pp. 151–158 (2019)

9. Surynek, P.: A novel approach to path planning for multiple robots in bi-connected graphs. In: ICRA 2009, pp. 3613–3619 (2009)

10. Walker, T.T., Sturtevant, N.R., Felner, A.: Extended increasing cost tree search for non-unit cost domains. In: IJCAI 2018, vol. 2018-July, pp. 534–540 (2018)

11. Yakovlev, K., Andreychuk, A., Vorobyev, V.: Prioritized multi-agent path finding for differential drive robots. In: ECMR 2019, pp. 1–6 (2019)

12. Yu, J., Rus, D.: Pebble motion on graphs with rotations: efficient feasibility tests and planning algorithms. In: Akin, H.L., Amato, N.M., Isler, V., van der Stappen, A.F. (eds.) Algorithmic Foundations of Robotics XI. STAR, vol. 107, pp. 729–746. Springer, Cham (2015). https://doi.org/10.1007/978-3-319-16595-0_42

Analysis of the Anytime MAPF Solvers Based on the Combination of Conflict-Based Search (CBS) and Focal Search (FS)

Ilya Ivanashev[1]([✉]), Anton Andreychuk[2], and Konstantin Yakovlev[1,2,3]

[1] HSE University, Moscow, Russia
ivanashevi@yandex.ru
[2] AIRI, Moscow, Russia
andreychuk@airi.net
[3] Federal Research Center for Computer Science and Control of Russian Academy of Sciences, Moscow, Russia
yakovlev@isa.ru

Abstract. Conflict-Based Search (CBS) is a widely used algorithm for solving multi-agent pathfinding (MAPF) problems optimally. The core idea of CBS is to run hierarchical search, when, on the high level the tree of solutions candidates is explored, and on the low-level an individual planning for a specific agent (subject to certain constraints) is carried out. To trade-off optimality for running time different variants of bounded sub-optimal CBS were designed, which alter both high- and low-level search routines of CBS. Moreover, anytime variant of CBS does exist that applies Focal Search (FS) to the high-level of CBS – Anytime BCBS. However, no comprehensive analysis of how well this algorithm performs compared to the naive one, when we simply re-invoke CBS with the decreased sub-optimality bound, was present. This work aims at filling this gap. Moreover, we present and evaluate another anytime version of CBS that uses FS on both levels of CBS. Empirically, we show that its behavior is principally different from the one demonstrated by Anytime BCBS. Finally, we compare both algorithms head-to-head and show that using Focal Search on both levels of CBS can be beneficial in a wide range of setups.

Keywords: MAPF · CBS · Anytime · Focal search · Bounded sub-optimal search

1 Introduction

Multi-agent pathfinding (MAPF) is a non-trivial problem that asks to find a set on collision-free paths for a set of mobile agents operating in the shared workspace. It naturally arises in robotics [22], video-games [20], automated warehouses [23], aircraft-towing [16], etc. One of the prominent MAPF solvers that is getting a lot of attention in the recent years is Conflict Based Search (CBS) [19]. It is a two-level algorithm, which on the high level explores different solutions candidates and runs an individual planning for a specific agent on the low level.

CBS is a provably optimal MAPF solver that is highly modular in a sense that it allows modifications of its different algorithmic parts to either tweak its performance or adapt it to different MAPF problem statements. Indeed numerous enhanced modifications of CBS exists [1,7,12,14]. Still, the scalability of CBS is limited as it is tailored to find optimal MAPF solutions. On the other hand, practically-wise it is reasonable to trade-off optimality for lower runtime. This led the community to developing the bounded suboptimal versions of CBS [2,15], i.e. such modifications of CBS that given a suboptimality factor $\varepsilon > 1$ return a solution whose cost does not exceed the cost of an optimal solution by a factor of ε (the so-called ε-suboptimal solutions). While these algorithms are able to find a solution much faster than regular CBS, it might be difficult to choose the ε value suitable for a particular MAPF problem. This problem is known to the community and one of the ways of solving it is designing *anytime* versions of the algorithms, that gradually converge to an optimal solution via the series of bounded-suboptimal searches while keeping track of the found solutions (so the best available solution can be reported any time the algorithm is stopped).

We are aware of only one anytime bounded-suboptimal variant of CBS, that was recently proposed in [5]. It combines CBS with the Focal Search [17] that is run on the high-level of CBS, while keeping the low-level search of CBS unchanged. In this work we will refer to this algorithm as Anytime BCBS, where BCBS stands for the bounded-suboptimal variant of CBS that keeps the low-level search unmodified as proposed in [2]. Anytime BCBS starts the search provided with the user-defined initial suboptimality factor (usually set rather high, e.g. $\varepsilon = 10$) and iteratively decreases it while reusing the search efforts between the iterations. It was shown in the original paper [5] that Anytime BCBS, indeed, converges to the very-close-to-optimal solutions under the strict time limits. However, it was not clear how Anytime BCBS compares to the naive sequential invocation of BCBS with the decreasing suboptimality factor without search re-use. This is the first research question we answer in this work, and the answer is that search re-use in Anytime BCBS is, indeed, beneficial.

Moreover, we suggest another variant of anytime MAPF solver based on Conflict Based Search and Focal Search – the one that utilize Focal Search on both levels of CBS. We call it Anytime ECBS, following the notation from [2]. Surprisingly, naive version of Anytime ECBS, i.e. the one that starts the search from scratch each time when the suboptimality factor is decreased, outperforms the version that reuses the search effort in many cases.

Finally, we compare the best version of Anytime BCBS, i.e. the one that relies on the search re-use, to the best version of Anytime ECBS, i.e. the one that runs the search from scratch on each iteration. Evidently, Anytime ECBS often obtains the first solution faster and converges to the better quality solutions.

Thus, one might infer that Anytime ECBS is a promising algorithm for the practical applications when the bounded-suboptimal solutions for challenging MAPF problems are sought under the strict time limits.

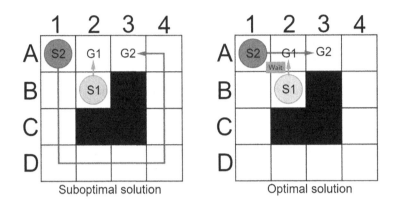

Fig. 1. Examples of the suboptimal and optimal MAPF solutions.

2   Problem Statement

In classical MAPF [21] one needs to find the set of collision-free paths for n agents moving along the same graph $G = (V, E)$ from the specified start vertices to the goal ones. The time is discretized and at each time step an agent is allowed to perform one of the following actions: move to the neighboring vertex or wait in its current vertex. The duration of both actions are considered to be of the uniform (1 time step). The individual plan for each agent is defined as the sequence of actions that moves this agent from its start to goal. The cost of the plan is defined by the time step the agent reaches the goal. Plans for two agents are said to be conflict-free if the agents do not occupy any vertex and the same time step and do not traverse the same edge in the same time step. In other words they do not have any vertex or edge conflicts.

MAPF solution is the set of individual plans for n agents s.t. any pair of them is conflict-free. Cost of the MAPF solution is the sum-of-costs (SOC) of the individual plans comprising this solution. In this work we are interested in designing anytime bounded-suboptimal MAPF algorithm. I.e. the algorithm which is provided with i) the MAPF instance, ii) the time limit, iii) the initial suboptimality bound ε, as an input, and is expected to initially find the ε-suboptimal solution very fast and use the remaining time for improving this solution, providing (when the time is up) the solution whose suboptimality bound is less than ε.

Figure 1 provides the example of MAPF instance with two possible solutions. Initially, if the ε value is set high, an anytime algorithm can find a suboptimal solution, shown at the left part of the figure. In that solution the first agent immediately moves towards its goal node, blocking the way for the second agent, which then has to go around the obstacle. Then an algorithm can improve the obtained solution, finding an optimal one (shown in the right part of the figure), where the first agent waits during one time step, allowing the second agent to path by.

3   Background and Related Work

Conflict Based Search. Conflict-Based search (CBS) [19] is an optimal MAPF solver which operates on two levels. The high level of the algorithm builds the Constraints Tree (CT). Each node in this tree (CT-node) is characterized by the set of constraints (that tell which vertices/edges particular agents should not occupy in which time steps), the set of individual plans (consistent with the constraints), and the cost (the sum of costs of individual plans). The root node contains an empty set of constrains and the set of individual plans that are likely to contain conflicts. On each step the algorithm chooses a CT-node with the least cost and checks it for conflicts. If the chosen node has no conflicts, CBS reports finding the optimal solution. Otherwise, the algorithm picks a conflict and creates two successor CT-nodes whose constraints sets are extended by one constraint in the following way. If the picked conflict was between the agents i and j which visited the vertex (edge) v (e) at time t, then the first successor is provided with the constraint, prohibiting i from being at v (e) at time t, and the similar constraint but for the agent j is added to the second successor. The individual plans of the constrained agents are then rebuilt with a low-level search algorithm (to be discussed later) and the CT-nodes are added to the CT-tree. CBS now proceeds to picking the next best CT-node.

Numerous extensions of CBS exist nowadays that boost its performance while not violating the optimality guarantees. Among the most widespread techniques are: prioritizing conflicts [19], by-passing conflicts [3], adding heuristics to high-level [6], disjoint splitting [13] and many others. As in this work we are not targeting optimal solutions (but rather bounded sub-optimal), these improvements are not within the scope of the paper.

Low-Level Planning for CBS. The basic version of CBS uses A* [8] as the low level planner. The search is performed in the space where each state is characterized by a pair (v, t) where v is a graph vertex and t is a time step. When expanding a search node (v, t) the successors corresponding to moving to the adjacent vertices are added to the search tree (if transitions to them are not prohibited by the CBS constraints). Moreover, the successor corresponding to the wait action, i.e. $(v, t + 1)$, is also added as well (if not prohibited by CBS constraints).

A technique that is frequently used for the A* search operating at the low-level of CBS is breaking ties in accordance with the *Conflict avoidance table* (CAT). This structure stores the information about the number of agents which visit every vertex and move through every edge at any time step. Thus, when similarly perspective nodes are encountered by A* (i.e. the ones that have the same f-value) the algorithm picks the one that have the lowest number of conflicts in CAT.

Another popular low-level planner for CBS is Safe Interval Path Planning (SIPP) [18]. It operates with the time intervals as opposed to distinct time steps and is notably faster than A*. Recently, even more advanced variants of low-level planning for CBS were proposed [9]. However, in our work we mainly focus on the basic variant of the low-level search for CBS, i.e. A* with CAT, as it is more straightforward (and widespread) to integrate it with the bounded-suboptimal variants of CBS.

Focal Search. Focal search [17] is a variant of the A* algorithm that is tailored to produce ε-suboptimal solutions. Besides conventional OPEN and CLOSED lists used in A*, Focal Search uses an additional FOCAL list that contains a subset of nodes from OPEN with f-values that differ from the minimal f-value no more than by a factor of ε. All the nodes in FOCAL list are ordered in accordance with a heuristic h_{focal}, which is not needed to be monotone or consistent. Focal Search can be utilized within the CBS framework to obtain a bounded-suboptimal MAPF solver as described below.

Bounded-Suboptimal Variants of CBS. Different variants of bounded-suboptimal CBS exist. The most relevant to this work are the ones introduced in [2], i.e. Bounded CBS (BCBS) and Enhanced CBS (ECBS).

The first variant uses the Focal Search both on high and low levels of CBS with two separate bounds (ε_H, ε_L). On the low level BCBS uses h_{focal} which is defined as the number of conflicts accumulated by the path from the start node to the current one, which is obtained from CAT. For the the high level h_{focal} is defined as the total number of conflicts in CT-nodes (other variants also possible). Contrary to BCBS, Enhanced CBS allows to specify a single suboptimality bound ε and distribute it between high and low levels automatically. It was shown empirically that ECBS(ε) outperforms BCBS with different combinations of ε_H and ε_L, s.t. $\varepsilon_H \cdot \varepsilon_L = \varepsilon$, and in particular BCBS(ε, 1).

More advanced variants of bounded-suboptimal CBS appeared recently [4, 15]. In this work, however, we focus on BCBS and ECBS and use them as building blocks for Anytime CBS. Implementing Anytime CBS using the advanced variants of bounded-suboptimal CBS is an appealing direction for future research.

Anytime Variants of CBS. The easiest way of creating an anytime version for a ε-suboptimal algorithm consists in the following naive approach. During the first iteration a regular version of the algorithm is being run, with an initial value of ε. After the solution is encountered, ε is decreased in such a way that this solution does not meet it. Thus the new solution that meets the bound has to be found, and the algorithm is restarted from scratch with this decreased value of ε. The algorithm continues to perform such iterations with a decreasing sequence of ε values, until it has some time left for execution or until it is able to find an optimal solution.

More advanced anytime variant of CBS, which is able to re-use the results of previous iterations, was presented in [5]. It builds on the anytime modification of Focal Search (AFS) and applies this technique to the high level of the BCBS(ε, 1) algorithm, while keeping its low-level (A* + CAT) unchanged. We call this algorithm Anytime BCBS. As in the naive approach, in Anytime BCBS algorithm BCBS(ε, 1) is being run iteratively with the decreasing suboptimality bound ε, where the new value for ε is always chosen in such a way that it is not being met by the old solution. The difference, however is that the algorithm does not start growing the new CT-tree from scratch but rather continues to grow the CT-tree constructed in the previous iteration. In order to achieve that, all nodes in the high-level FOCAL list that no longer satisfy the ε-suboptimality condition are removed from it, after which the search process resumed. Intuitively, this saves computational effort, however the original paper on Anytime BCBS lacks comparison with the naive approach, described above. In this work we fill this gap and empirically show that, indeed, re-using the CT-tree for Anytime BCBS is beneficial.

It should be noted here that numerous other (non CBS-based) anytime MAPF planners exist nowadays. The most prominent are: MAPF-LNS [10] and MAPF-LNS2 [11] etc. These planners, however, do not provide any theoretical guarantees on the cost of the returned solution, while we in this work are interested in getting bounded-suboptimal solutions.

4   Anytime ECBS

As with the BCBS algorithm, one can construct the anytime version for ECBS using the naive approach. However, we have also developed a version of the algorithm, referred to as Anytime ECBS, which is able to reuse the results of the previous iterations. It works as follows. The first iteration of the algorithm invokes ECBS and obtains a ε-suboptimal solution. The only difference is that $OPEN_N$, $FOCAL_N$ and $CLOSE_N$ lists of the low level planner are saved for every CT-node N. Further these lists will be used to efficiently rebuild the individual agents' trajectories between the iterations with respect to the new value of ε. This have to be done, because, in contrast with BCBS(ε, 1), these trajectories are also suboptimal and depend on the current value of suboptimality factor.

After decreasing the value of ε to the lower value ε', a new search iteration is performed. For each CT node N including already expanded CT nodes, we update the trajectories with respect to the new value of ε' (if necessary) using the saved $OPEN_N$, $FOCAL_N$ and $CLOSE_N$ lists. To do that, for every high-level node N a new AFS iteration is performed: all low-level nodes which don't meet the new suboptimality factor, are removed from $FOCAL_N$, and the low level FS is resumed and continued until an ε'-optimal solution is found. This procedure is applied to CT nodes downward from the root to the leafs of CT tree. Thus, when any CT node is updated, agents' paths in its predecessors are already rebuilt and added into CAT, so the new path can be constructed with minimal amount of conflicts with other trajectories. However, it should be mentioned, that the values of h_{focal} heuristic aren't recalculated for the nodes, which were already added into the $OPEN_N$, $FOCAL_N$ and $CLOSE_N$ lists at the end of previous iteration, as it would require to traverse the whole low level search tree again. Because of that some conflicts may be created, which could be otherwise avoided, if the trajectory was constructed from scratch. That can have negative effect on the performance of Anytime ECBS and may be one of the potential reasons, why it would expand more high level nodes, than the naive algorithm for some problems. However, it is hard to tell how much influence this issue had in the experiments, conducted in our study, as well as to fully explain the differences in behavior between Anytime ECBS and its naive version. The reason for this is that the sequences of CT nodes expanded by the algorithms can diverge at the very beginning of the search and become completely different, after which it is hard to determine, why a particular algorithm was able to find a better solution, or finish the execution earlier.

The constraints sets in all the nodes remain the same and have to be satisfied in the updated trajectories. It is possible that some constraints in constraint set will become irrelevant, i.e. applying them will not help to prevent any conflicts, because trajectories of the agents, which were involved in the conflict previously, have already been changed.

We consider two possible strategies of dealing with such situations. Firstly, one can remove the whole subtree of this node from the CT, and reinsert it into the OPEN list in order to find a new conflict in the solution, which corresponds to it. Alternatively, all nodes can be left in the CT with the same constraints. The initial hypothesis, prompting us to apply the second strategy, was that even irrelevant constraints can still be useful, because they are often applied for the positions with high probability of conflict appearance and therefore they may help to prevent some future conflicts (this hypothesis however wasn't actually confirmed by the experiments, and it was seen that keeping irrelevant constraints in the constraints set, usually only worsens algorithms performance). We denote the parameter, defining what strategy to use, as CIC (cut irrelevant conflicts): if CIC = True the first strategy is used and if CIC = False, the second.

After all CT nodes are updated, every node contains a ε'−suboptimal solution satisfying all of the constraints in the node's constraint set. Then the nodes with the solution costs that do not meet the new threshold are removed from the high-level FOCAL list. After that the search is continued until a new solution without conflicts is found.

Example. This section shows how the CT is updated between the stages of anytime ECBS algorithm. In the MAPF problem, shown on the Fig. 2 there are two agents with starting nodes $S_1 = A2$, $S_2 = B1$ and goal nodes $G_1 = E4$, $G_2 = D5$. Their initial individual trajectories, shown with dotted lines, have cost 6 and have a conflict in the node $B2$ at the moment 1. If the intial value of ε is not less than $\frac{7}{6}$, the first iteration of Anytime ECBS will be able to find a valid solution in both successors of the root node, by adding one waiting action into the agents trajectories. The whole CT, which will be constructed by the

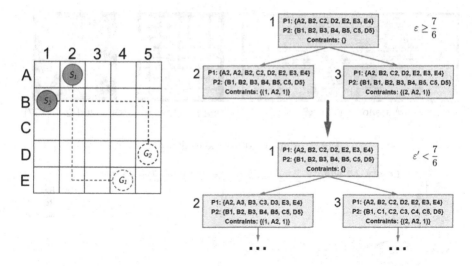

Fig. 2. Running example of Anytime ECBS on a simple MAPF problem.

algorithm in this case, is shown at the right top of the figure (constraints are presented as (a, n, t) triples, meaning that agent a is prohibited from being in node n at time t). In contrast, Anytime BCBS algorithm would have to create more high-level nodes in the first iteration, because updated agents trajectories would still be optimal and a new conflict would appear (e.g. the first agent would satisfy the constraint by firstly moving to A3 and then moving down, but it would create a conflict in the node B3).

After the end of the first iteration, ε will be replaced with new suboptimality factor $\varepsilon' < \frac{7}{6}$. Then the trajectories of agents 1 and 2 in the CT nodes 1 and 2 will be rebuild in order to satisfy the new suboptimality factor, which means, that they will have to become optimal trajectories of length 6 (see the right bottom of the figure). Then, similarly to the first iteration of Anytime BCBS, algorithm would have to add new constraints to rediscover a valid solution again.

5 Empirical Evaluation

The algorithms were implemented in C++ (the code can be found at[1]) and evaluated on 4 different maps taken from the well-known in the MAPF community MovingAI benchmark [21]: empty-16-16, room-32-32-4, warehouse-10-20-10-2-2 and den520d (for the sake of simplicity later in the article we refer to them as Empty, Warehouse, Rooms and Den520d). These maps are widely used to evaluate MAPF algorithms as they represent different types of the environments as shown on Fig. 3 (empty map is not shown, obviously).

For every map the benchmark provides 25 distinct scenarios. Each scenario is a list of (non-overlapping) start-goal locations. To obtain a MAPF instance

---

[1] https://github.com/PathPlanning/Push-and-Rotate--CBS--PrioritizedPlanning.

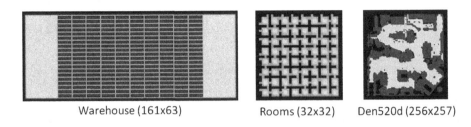

Warehouse (161x63)   Rooms (32x32)   Den520d (256x257)

Fig. 3. Maps used for the evaluation.

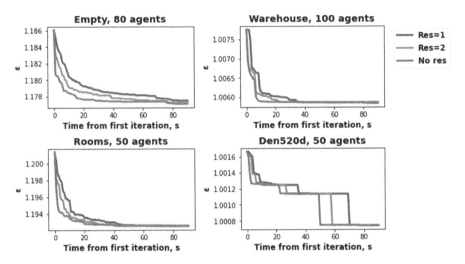

Fig. 4. Changes of ε over time for different versions of Anytime BCBS algorithm.

for k agents first k start-goal pairs form the scenario are used. While evaluating we incrementally increase the number of agents to obtain the instances of the variable difficulty.

The experiments were run on Intel Core i5-1135G7 CPU, 2.40 GHz, 4 cores running Windows 10 Home OS. We imposed a time limit of 90 s for solving each instance, i.e. if an algorithm was not able to find a solution it was interrupted and this run was counted as failure.

Evaluating Anytime BCBS. In the first series of experiments we compared three versions of the Anytime BCBS algorithm (dubbed as ABCBS):

- ABCBS, res $= 1$ – the algorithm that always starts a new search from scratch, i.e. never re-uses the previously built CT-tree;
- ABCBS, res $= 2$ – the algorithm that starts the search from scratch on odd iterations, and on even iterations re-uses the previously build CT-tree;
- ABCBS, No res – the algorithm that always continues to use the previously built CT-tree.

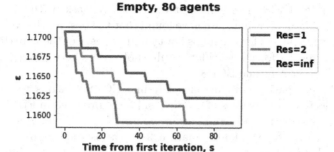

Fig. 5. Comparison of different versions of Anytime BCBS on particular scenario.

The initial value of ε was set to 10 to increase the chance of finding the first (possibly highly suboptimal) solution quickly. At each following iteration ε was decreased in the way described in Sect. 3. Figure 4 shows how ε was changing for certain setups (map + number of agents).

Each point corresponds to the suboptimality factor ε, for which the solution was already found, averaged over all of the scenarios for which the algorithm was able to find at least one solution within the given time limit. It also should be noted that for different scenarios the completion time of the first iteration could be different, so the x axis shows the relative time starting from that moment.

As one can see, the version of the algorithm, which is never restarted, shows the best results out of all of the versions. This can be explained by the fact, that the sequences of ε values are approximately the same for all versions of the algorithm, as can be seen, for example, on Fig. 5, that shows how the value of ε changes over time on one particular scenario. As result of that, the sizes of CT trees at the end of every iteration are also close for different versions, and version without restarts is able to finish every new iteration faster, compared to the naive algorithm, since it doesn't need to rebuild the first part of constraint tree.

Similar comparison was also performed for Anytime ECBS algorithm. However, it turned out, that setting initial value of ε too high can actually slow the ECBS algorithm down, because it would have to expand more nodes on the low level. For example, the following situation can be considered. Let's say that in some intermediate solution in ECBS algorithm, agent i stops in its goal node n at the moment t. Also let's say that agent j has to go through the node n at the moment $t' > t$. Then there will always be a conflict with an agent i in its trajectory in the node n. If the value of ε is set too high, the algorithm will spend a lot of time, trying to avoid this conflict, and expanding a lot of low level nodes. That makes the low level search very time consuming, which negates the possible time saving from expanding less nodes on the high level.

Considering the observations, described above, it was decided to specifically select a preferable initial value of ε for Anytime ECBS for every map.

After running ECBS using different values of ε on tasks with different numbers of agents for all four maps, we have found that the best results were obtained when using the ε value 2 for the maps Empty and Rooms. For the maps Warehouse and Den520d results for all considered values of ε were very close, so the value 10 was used, as in Anytime BCBS.

Then the comparison of different Anytime ECBS versions was performed using the selected initial values of ε. The results are provided in Fig. 6. For every map the results for two different agent numbers are shown. It's also should be mentioned that for the Rooms map in 2 scenarios there were less than 110 agents provided in the data set, thus these scenarios weren't considered for the corresponding plot.

In addition to the Res parameter, previously described parameter CIC was considered. That gives us 5 possible configurations of parameters (for the naive version of the algorithm only CIC=True is possible, because all CT is removed after every iteration). The results depicted in Fig. 6 indicate that in many cases the naive version of Anytime ECBS algorithm allows to obtain solutions with approximately the same or even better quality as the advanced versions. This can be explained by the fact, that the decreasing sequences of ε values in that algorithm can vary significantly between different versions, and the advanced version may have to expand more high level nodes than the naive one. Alternatively, for some scenarios the number of nodes, expanded by the advanced version, could be approximately the same, or even less, but the value of ε would decrease slower.

As was mentioned above, the naive version of Anytime ECBS can potentially get an advantage over advanced version, because in the latter algorithm values of h_{focal} heuristic aren't updated between iterations. Moreover, the performance of Anytime ECBS can be negatively affected by keeping the irrelevant constraints in the versions of the algorithm with CIC=False. In particular, the version of the algorithm that never restarts (and therefore can have the least relevant values of h_{focal} heuristic) and keeps the irrelevant constraints shows considerably worse results for the maps Rooms and Empty in the tasks with high number of agents. Although, as it was previously mentioned, it is not clear, how much influence each of these points had, and the difference between the versions on the instances with lower number of agents was even less noticeable.

Chart for a particular scenario on Empty map, shown on Fig. 7, indicates that in contrast to Anytime BCBS there is almost no correlation between the decreasing sequences of ε values for different versions of Anytime ECBS algorithm.

However, for two other maps – Warehouse and Den520d, advanced versions of the algorithm show a noticeable improvement over the naive one for some of the tasks with the higher number of agents, although there was no clear leader between them. Nevertheless, the fact that the naive version doesn't require additional memory consumption and is easier to implement, means that it probably can be preferred over the other versions.

Finally, the version of Anytime BCBS algorithm without restarts was compared to the naive version of Anytime ECBS algorithm. Additionally, for the

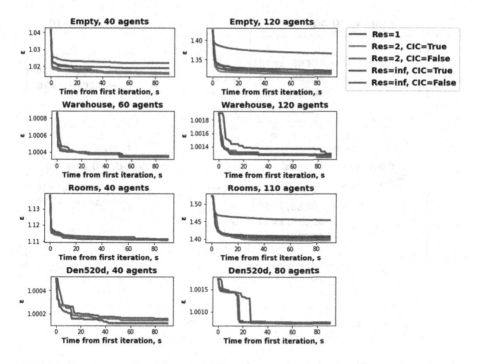

Fig. 6. Changes of ε over time for different versions of Anytime ECBS algorithm.

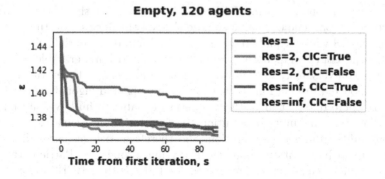

Fig. 7. Comparison of different versions of Anytime EBCBS on particular scenario.

maps Empty and Rooms, where a specifically chosen value of ε was used, a version with initial value of ε equal 10 was added to the comparison. The results of this experiment are shown in Fig. 8. As one can see, Anytime ECBS often finds better solutions than Anytime BCBS. This can be a result of higher flexibility of ECBS algorithm: it is able to build slightly worse trajectory for one agent, in order to avoid the creation of new conflicts, which would then allow to make better trajectories for the other agents (although, as in the previous cases it might be not the full explanation and might be not relevant for some

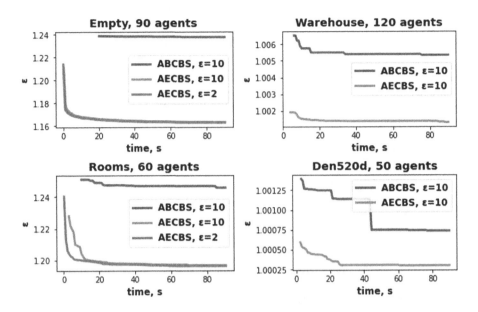

Fig. 8. Comparison between anytime BCBS and Anytime ECBS.

of the problems). Considering that and the fact that ECBS algorithm is usually faster than BCBS(ε, 1), i.e. the first iteration in Anytime ECBS can be finished faster, naive version of Anytime ECBS can be preferred to the advanced version of Anytime BCBS. The one can also note that on the Rooms map the version of Anytime ECBS with ε equal 10 was slower, and found the initial solution later, while for the Empty map both versions of the algorithm were able to find an initial solution very fast, so there wasn't much difference between them.

It should be also mentioned, that for some maps and algorithms there were scenarios where different algorithms were not capable to find even initial solution within the timelimit. In addition to that, for some scenarios algorithms were only able to finish one iteration, and therefore such scenarios didn't give any additional information about their anytime properties. Particularly, large number of such scenarios was presented for the Anytime BCBS algorithm on the Warehouse and Den520d maps. For example, there were only 8 scenarios for the Warehouse map with 100 agents and only 11 for the Den520d map with 50 agents, where Anytime BCBS was able to finish more than one iteration.

6   Conclusion and Future Work

In this work we have presented a novel bounded-suboptimal anytime MAPF solver, based on the prominent ECBS algorithm - Anytime ECBS. We empirically compared it with previously existing bounded-suboptimal anytime MAPF solver – Anytime BCBS. Both algorithms were also compared with their naive versions, in which the search is restarted from scratch at the beginning of every iteration. It was shown, that while Anytime BCBS always outperforms its naive version, for Anytime ECBS the naive algorithm can often be preferred. However, even the naive version of Anytime ECBS had some advantages over the Anytime BCBS algorithm, as the former was usually able to finish the first iteration faster, and the solutions obtained by it typically had lower costs compared to the ones found by Anytime BCBS.

Avenues for future work may include developing novel techniques aimed at decreasing the number of low level nodes which have to be stored in Anytime ECBS, or investigation of how the stored information can be used to efficiently rebuild agents paths after addition of the new constraints not only during the process of repairing the constraint tree between the iterations of anytime algorithm but also during its building (analogously to incremental search techniques).

References

1. Andreychuk, A., Yakovlev, K., Atzmon, D., Stern, R.: Multi-agent pathfinding with continuous time. In: Proceedings of the 28th International Joint Conference on Artificial Intelligence (IJCAI 2019), pp. 39–45 (2019)
2. Barer, M., Sharon, G., Stern, R., Felner, A.: Suboptimal variants of the conflict-based search algorithm for the multi-agent pathfinding problem. In: Seventh Annual Symposium on Combinatorial Search (2014)
3. Boyrasky, E., Felner, A., Sharon, G., Stern, R.: Don't split, try to work it out: bypassing conflicts in multi-agent pathfinding. In: Proceedings of the International Conference on Automated Planning and Scheduling, vol. 25, pp. 47–51 (2015)
4. Chan, S.H., Li, J., Gange, G., Harabor, D., Stuckey, P.J., Koenig, S.: ECBS with flex distribution for bounded-suboptimal multi-agent path finding. In: Proceedings of the International Symposium on Combinatorial Search, vol. 12, pp. 159–161 (2021)
5. Cohen, L., et al.: Anytime focal search with applications. In: IJCAI, pp. 1434–1441 (2018)
6. Felner, A., et al.: Adding heuristics to conflict-based search for multi-agent path finding. In: Proceedings of the International Conference on Automated Planning and Scheduling, vol. 28, pp. 83–87 (2018)
7. Gange, G., Harabor, D., Stuckey, P.J.: Lazy CBS: implicit conflict-based search using lazy clause generation. In: The International Conference on Automated Planning and Scheduling (ICAPS), pp. 155–162 (2019)
8. Hart, P.E., Nilsson, N.J., Raphael, B.: A formal basis for the heuristic determination of minimum cost paths. IEEE Trans. Syst. Sci. Cybern. 4(2), 100–107 (1968)
9. Hu, S., Harabor, D.D., Gange, G., Stuckey, P.J., Sturtevant, N.R.: Multi-agent path finding with temporal jump point search. In: Proceedings of the International Conference on Automated Planning and Scheduling, vol. 32, pp. 169–173 (2022)
10. Li, J., Chen, Z., Harabor, D., Stuckey, P., Koenig, S.: Anytime multi-agent path finding via large neighborhood search. In: International Joint Conference on Artificial Intelligence (IJCAI) (2021)
11. Li, J., Chen, Z., Harabor, D., Stuckey, P.J., Koenig, S.: MAPF-LNS2: fast repairing for multi-agent path finding via large neighborhood search. In: Proceedings of the AAAI Conference on Artificial Intelligence (2022)

12. Li, J., Felner, A., Boyarski, E., Ma, H., Koenig, S.: Improved heuristics for multi-agent path finding with conflict-based search. In: Proceedings of the International Joint Conference on Artificial Intelligence (IJCAI-2019), pp. 442–449 (2019). https://doi.org/10.24963/ijcai.2019/63

13. Li, J., Gange, G., Harabor, D., Stuckey, P.J., Ma, H., Koenig, S.: New techniques for pairwise symmetry breaking in multi-agent path finding. In: Proceedings of the International Conference on Automated Planning and Scheduling, vol. 30, pp. 193–201 (2020)

14. Li, J., Harabor, D., Stuckey, P.J., Felner, A., Ma, H., Koenig, S.: Disjoint splitting for multi-agent path finding with conflict-based search. In: Proceedings of the International Conference on Automated Planning and Scheduling, vol. 29, pp. 279–283 (2019)

15. Li, J., Ruml, W., Koenig, S.: EECBS: a bounded-suboptimal search for multi-agent path finding. In: Proceedings of the AAAI Conference on Artificial Intelligence (AAAI) (2021)

16. Morris, R., et al.: Planning, scheduling and monitoring for airport surface operations. In: Planning for Hybrid Systems, Papers from the 2016 AAAI Workshop (2016)

17. Pearl, J., Kim, J.H.: Studies in semi-admissible heuristics. IEEE Trans. Pattern Anal. Mach. Intell. **PAMI-4**(4), 392–399 (1982)

18. Phillips, M., Likhachev, M.: Sipp: safe interval path planning for dynamic environments. In: 2011 IEEE International Conference on Robotics and Automation, pp. 5628–5635. IEEE (2011)

19. Sharon, G., Stern, R., Felner, A., Sturtevant, N.R.: Conflict-based search for optimal multi-agent pathfinding. Artif. Intell. **219**, 40–66 (2015)

20. Silver, D.: Cooperative pathfinding. In: The First Artificial Intelligence and Interactive Digital Entertainment Conference, pp. 117–122 (2005)

21. Stern, R., et al.: Multi-agent pathfinding: definitions, variants, and benchmarks. In: Twelfth Annual Symposium on Combinatorial Search (2019)

22. Veloso, M.M., Biswas, J., Coltin, B., Rosenthal, S.: CoBots: robust symbiotic autonomous mobile service robots. In: the International Joint Conference on Artificial Intelligence (IJCAI), pp. 4423–4429 (2015)

23. Wurman, P.R., D'Andrea, R., Mountz, M.: Coordinating hundreds of cooperative, autonomous vehicles in warehouses. In: the AAAI Conference on Artificial Intelligence (AAAI), pp. 1752–1760 (2007)

Studying Special Operators for the Application of Evolutionary Algorithms in the Seek of Optimal Boolean Functions for Cryptography

Sara Mandujano[1] , Juan Carlos Ku Cauich[2] , and Adriana Lara[1](✉)

[1] Instituto Politécnico Nacional, ESFM Edificio 9 Unidad Profesional Adolfo López M., Zacatenco, 07738 Ciudad de México, Mexico
`smandujanov2000@alumno.ipn.mx`, `alaral@ipn.mx`
[2] Computer Science, CINVESTAV-IPN, Av. IPN 2508, San Pedro Zacatenco, 07300 Mexico, Mexico
`jcku@cs.cinvestav.mx`
`http://www.ipn.mx`

Abstract. The role of Boolean functions in modern cryptography has triggered the necessity of developing methods to construct them with adequate properties, such as balancedness and high non-linearity—making them more resistant to a variety of cryptanalytic attacks. Research into the construction of *weight-wise perfectly balanced* Boolean functions using Evolutionary Algorithms is scarce but encouraging (e.g., [1]). In this work, we first investigate the effect on an evolutionary algorithm's performance when relying solely on the penalty function, as opposed to the solution repairment method. Second, we focus on the effect of problem-specific crossover operators (e.g., those used on [2]), and particularly proposing a novel one free of solution repairs to preserve balancedness. The results obtained suggest that an adequate penalty factor and the use of specifically designed evolutionary operators is sufficient to find Boolean functions with weight-wise perfect balancedness and high non-linearity, as desired.

Keywords: Boolean functions · Genetic algorithms · Cryptography

1 Introduction

Boolean functions are widely used for cryptographic purposes. In order to achieve resistance to the different cryptanalytic attacks, it is desired to find in them a high algebraic degree, high non-linearity, differentiability and high immunity correlation, among other characteristics. The most common attacks are to block ciphers and stream ciphers [5]. The combination of the cryptographic properties of these functions may be in conflict. Thus, finding cryptographically strong functions involves making a trade-off when optimising the properties. There are

O. Pichardo Lagunas et al. (Eds.): MICAI 2022, LNAI 13612, pp. 383–396, 2022.
https://doi.org/10.1007/978-3-031-19493-1_30

several methods to build Boolean functions, such as random searches, algebraic constructions, heuristics, and combinations of these methods [17]. Within the heuristic methods, evolutionary algorithms stand out, given the extensiveness of the search space (for Boolean functions with n inputs, the search space contains 2^{2^n} functions). Moreover, heuristic constructions are more accessible to design than algebraic methods, and lately, results of similar quality to algebraic methods have been obtained [6]. Also, there exist several variants within evolutionary algorithms. For example, Picek et al. [16] used genetic algorithms (GA), genetic programming (GP), and Cartesian genetic programming. In addition, they experimented with both single-objective algorithms and multi-objective approaches.

This work will focus on the use of GA for constructing weight-wise perfectly balanced (WPB) Boolean functions with high non-linearity. The work by Millan et al. [12] is the first GA known to find highly nonlinear functions. Moreover, they obtained faster and better non-linearity values as compared to a random search. Since then, some GAs [3,13–15] have been developed to obtain balanced functions with high non-linearity and low autocorrelation, using simulated annealing and hill climbing, among other techniques. Recently, I. López-López et al. [6] created the first memetic algorithm to generate 10-variable Boolean functions of similar quality to those obtained with algebraic methods used to find high non-linearity.

WPB are a new class of Boolean functions, which are used in the family of stream ciphers known as FLIP [2,9,10]. These are globally balanced functions and, additionally, they preserve the balance for each specific weight between 1 and $n - 1$, where the Boolean function has domain $\mathbb{F}_2^n$. To find WPB functions, two fitness functions are suggested [9] described in terms of the constrained linearity and a penalty factor. In this work, we aim to obtain WPB Boolean functions with a high non-linearity, starting from unbalanced Boolean functions, using the above fitness functions with a slight modification.

Our GAs are based on those proposed in [9]; however, the fitness evaluation is carried out using *fitness 2* only. Moreover, within the fitness function, the non-linearity is evaluated as in the general case. In addition to the cases evaluated in [9], we also consider the cases in which the search is carried out in the entirety of the 2^{2^n}-search-space. Consequently, we propose alternatives to the variation operators which allow for non-balanced Boolean functions, namely, the classic swap mutation operator is used in conjunction with the counter-based crossover and the one-point crossover operators. Our results suggest that allowing the GAs to explore the entirety of the search space rather than a constrained region is an effective method to find WPB Boolean functions with high non-linearity. As predicted, when allowing the population to include non-feasible individuals, the penalty is sufficient to gear the population towards the feasible space while allowing sufficient diversity for an adequate evolution of the population. In fact, the highest non-linearity of 112 was achieved more frequently when exploring within the unrestricted search space using the WPB representation.

2   Background

Let $\mathbb{F}_2$ be the finite field with two elements. These can be represented by $\{0, 1\}$ with addition modulo two. Also, we denote by $\mathbb{F}_2^n$ the n-dimensional vector space over $\mathbb{F}_2$, $n \in \mathbb{N}$. The following definitions and theorems come from [1,7].

Definition 1. *Every function with domain $\mathbb{F}_2^n$ and codomain $\mathbb{F}_2$ is called a Boolean function. The set of all Boolean functions is denoted as $\mathcal{B}_n$.*

Thus $\mathcal{B}_n := \{f \mid f : \mathbb{F}_2^n \to \mathbb{F}_2\}$ and has dimension 2^n as a vector space structure, and its cardinality is 2^{2^n}.

A horizontal truth table can represent the set of images of a function $f \in \mathcal{B}_n$ as a vector of length 2^n denoted $ev(f) := \left(f(v)_{v \in \mathbb{F}_2^n}\right)$ or vertically as in Table 1. The inputs must always be arranged in the same order, most typically ordered lexicographically.

The function $f(x) \in \mathcal{B}_2$ defined by

$$f(x_1, x_2) = x_1 \oplus x_2$$

is an example of a Boolean function; here $\oplus$ represents addition modulo two.

The set of images of f determines the vector

$$[0, 1, 1, 0].$$

Table 1. Truth table for the Boolean function $f(x_1, x_2) = x_1 \oplus x_2$.

x_1	x_2	ev(f)
0	0	0
0	1	1
1	0	1
1	1	0

Definition 2. *The support of a vector $x \in \mathcal{B}_n$, denoted $supp(x)$, is the set containing the non-zero positions in the vector. The Hamming weight of a vector $x \in \mathbb{F}_2^n$, denoted $w_H(x)$, is the number of non-zero positions in the vector.*

Definition 3. *The support of a Boolean function $f \in \mathcal{B}_n$, denoted $supp(f)$, is the set containing the non-zero positions in its truth table. The Hamming weight of a Boolean function $f \in \mathcal{B}_n$, denoted $w_H(f)$, is the number of non-zero positions in its truth table.*

Definition 4. *The Hamming distance between two vectors x, y, denoted $d_H(x, y)$, is the number of positions in which their values are different. The Hamming distance between two functions f, g, denoted $d_H(f, g)$, is the number of positions in their truth tables in which their values are different.*

We can see that
$$w_H(x) = |supp(x)|, \quad d_H(x,y) = w_H(x \oplus y), \quad w_H(f) = |supp(f)|, \text{ and}$$
$$d_H(f,g) = w_H(f \oplus g).$$

Definition 5. *A Boolean function $f \in \mathcal{B}_n$ is balanced if its truth table has an equal number of zeros and ones.*

Hence, a Boolean function is balanced if $w_H(f) = 2^{n-1}$.

Taking it a step further, a Boolean function is said to be weight-wise perfectly balanced when the truth table corresponding to inputs of a specific weight, k, is balanced for $1 \leq k \leq n-1$, [9].

One way to represent Boolean functions is the Algebraic Normal Form (A.N.F.).

Definition 6. *A Boolean function f has a A.N.F. if it can be expressed as*

$$f(x_1, \ldots, x_n) := \sum_{u \in \mathbb{F}_2^n} a_u \left(\prod_{i=1}^{n} x_i^{u_i} \right); \quad u = (u_1, \ldots, u_n), \quad a_u \in \mathbb{F}_2.$$

Note that in the previous example the function f is expressed in its A.N.F.

Definition 7. *The basic Boolean functions are the affine functions defined by the set*

$$\mathcal{A} := \{ f | f(x_1, \ldots, x_n) = a_1 x_1 + \cdots + a_n x_n + a_0 = a \cdot x + a_0 \},$$

$a = (a_1, \ldots, a_n) \in \mathbb{F}_2^n$ *and* $a_0 \in \mathbb{F}_2$.

It is possible to define the non-linearity of a Boolean function, which indicates how far a Boolean function is from the Boolean functions of algebraic degree equal to 1.

Definition 8. *The non-linearity, denoted N_f, of the Boolean function f is the Hamming distance between f and the set of all affine functions.*

It can be written in Hamming distance notation:

$$N_f := \min_{g \in \mathcal{A}} d_H(f, g).$$

Definition 9. *Let $f \in \mathcal{B}_n, a \in \mathbb{F}_2^n$. The Walsh-Hadamard transform of f, denoted W_f, is defined as follows:*

$$W_f : \mathbb{F}_2^n \to \mathbb{F}_2, \quad W_f(a) := \sum_{x \in \mathbb{F}_2^n} (-1)^{f(x) + a \cdot x},$$

where $a \cdot x$ is the usual dot product on $\mathbb{F}_2^n$.

It is possible to express the non-linearity in terms of the Fourier transform:

Theorem 10. *The non-linearity of the Boolean function f is*

$$N_f = 2^{n-1} - \frac{1}{2} \max_{a \in \mathbb{F}_2^n} |W_f(a)|.$$

Theorem 11 *(Parseval's equality). Let f be a boolean function. Then*

$$\sum_{a \in \mathbb{F}_2^n} [W_f(a)]^2 = 2^{2n}.$$

Definition 12. *A Boolean function is a Bent function if it achieves maximum non-linearity.*

By the Parseval equality, we know that $\max_{a \in \mathbb{F}_2^n} |W_f(a)| (\geq 2^{n/2})$. Then the non-linearity of a Boolean function has an upper bound, $N_f \leq 2^{n-1} - 2^{\frac{n}{2}-1}$.

The only functions that achieve the equality are Bent functions because $W_f(a) = \pm 2^{n/2}$ for all $a \in \mathbb{F}_2^n$.

In particular, if f is a balanced function, then $N_f \leq 2^{n-1} - 2^{\frac{n}{2}-1} - 2$, n is an even number [18].

If f is a balanced function, then $W_f(0) = 0$. Hence, f can't obtain maximum non-linearity, conversely, Bent functions can't be balanced. Thus, if we seek balanced Boolean functions, these will always have a non-linearity below the maximum.

3 Methodology

This Section discusses the details of the genetic algorithms used in the search for WPB Boolean functions with high non-linearity, contrasting them with those used in [9]. Firstly, the search space is considered for each instance, alongside the corresponding encoding. Next, the variation operators are analysed, with a particular focus on the crossover operators. Then, the fitness functions initially proposed in [9] are revisited and the modifications proposed in this work are explored. Finally, the Section concludes by taking a look at the experimental settings employed for each of the experiments carried out.

3.1 Search Space

The naive way to search for the required WPB Boolean functions is to explore the entire space of n-variable Boolean functions $\mathcal{B}_n = \{f : \mathbb{F}_2^n \to \mathbb{F}_2\}$. However, it is easy to show that the size of $\mathcal{B}_n$ is super-exponential in n, its cardinality given by 2^{2^n}. Moreover, we recall that WPB Boolean functions only exist for $n = 2^m$ [11]. Thus, the size of such spaces grows rapidly, meaning an exhaustive search is only feasible for $n = 2$ or $n = 4$, which are too small for any applicability in cryptography. Therefore, the case to tackled for this work, as in [9], is $n = 8$, with a search space containing $2^{2^8} \approx 1.16 \times 10^{77}$ candidate functions, which is too large for an exhaustive approach to be considered.

In [9], two refinements are proposed to reduce the search space. In the first instance, $\mathcal{H}_n$ is defined as the set of all globally balanced Boolean functions in $\mathbb{F}_2^n$, which has a cardinality of $\binom{2^n}{2^{n-1}}$, in the case of $n = 8$ equating to $\binom{256}{128} \approx 5.77 \times 10^{76}$. Next, $\mathcal{W}_n$ is defined as the set of all WPB Boolean functions in $\mathbb{F}_2^n$, with a cardinality of 5.1×10^{70} for $n = 8$, calculated using Eq. 1.

$$|\mathcal{W}_n| = \prod_{k=1}^{n-1} \binom{\binom{n}{k}}{\frac{1}{2} \cdot \binom{n}{k}} \tag{1}$$

Initially, it seems advantageous to reduce the search space in order to focus on other qualities of the Boolean functions, namely their non-linearity in this case. However, extensive investigation [19] has shown that it is beneficial to use infeasible candidates in the search during a constrained evolutionary search, in this case suggesting that it is beneficial to have non-balanced candidates as part of the population. Therefore, in our experiments, we consider two of the aforementioned search spaces, $\mathcal{B}_n$ and $\mathcal{W}_n$, to analyse how each reflects on the performance of the genetic algorithms.

3.2   Encoding and Variation Operators

As in [9], we contemplate two encodings: the *truth table representation* and the *WPB representation*. However, in addition to the variation operators described in [8], we suggest an additional variation operator without repairment, thus allowing an adequate consideration of non-feasible candidates throughout our search. Table 2 offers a summary of the different encodings and variation operators considered as part of this work.

In the *truth table representation*, each individual is encoded as a vector of 2^n elements, corresponding to the truth table vector of the corresponding n-variable Boolean function, see Table 1. With this representation, we explore within the entire $\mathcal{B}_n$ search space, using classic variation operators: one-point crossover alongside flip mutation.

On the other hand, the *WPB representation* consists of a list of vectors, each vector corresponding to the truth table resulting from inputs of a given weight. An example of an individual is given by 2. This representation allows us to search uniquely within $\mathcal{W}_n$, which can be achieved by generating vectors with Hamming weight of half their length. Moreover, specific variation operators are applied to maintain each vector's balancednes, specifically those described in [8]. As crossover operators, the *map of ones* and *counter-based* [8] operators are used, both in conjunction with the *swap-based* mutation operator. In all cases, the operators are applied independently to each vector within the list.

$$I = [[1, 0, 1, 0], [0, 0, 0, 1, 1, 1], [1, 1, 0, 0]] \tag{2}$$

However, we also consider the case in which the *WPB representation* is used, but allowing for candidate solutions to be unbalanced. This alternative requires different variation operators. The mutation operator used in this case is now the classic *swap* operator, while the crossover is carried out using the *counter-based*, as before, and the traditional *one-point crossover*, but applied to the list of vectors rather than the vectors themselves.

Table 2. Summary of the encodings and variation operators used in this work, indicating the name which identifies each combination considered.

	Initial Pop	Representation	Crossover	Mutation
GA-TT	Unbalanced	Truth table	One point	Flip
GA-CBC	Balanced	WPB	Counter-based	Swap-based
GA-MOOC	Balanced	WPB	Map of ones	Swap-based
GA-UB-CBC	Unbalanced	WPB	Counter-based	Swap
GA-UB-OP	Unbalanced	WPB	One point variation	Swap

3.3   Fitness Functions

The fitness function used in this paper is based on those suggested in [9]. However, the main difference is that the calculation of the non-linearity is done using the unrestricted Walsh-Hadamard Transform. We explore this alternative as, if successful, it would allow us to use the *Fast Walsh-Hadamard Transform* in future work, making the calculation more efficient and thus allowing for its application to larger cases.

$$fit(f) = \delta_{pen} \cdot \left(\min_{2 \leq k \leq 2/n} \{N_f\} \right) - pen(f) \qquad (3)$$

As can be seen in Eq. 3, the fitness function has two main components, the penalty, based on the balancedness of the function, and the non-linearity, which is what we are trying to maximise.

The non-linearity is calculated as described in Sect. 2; thus, we focus on the penalty component, which is directly linked to the delta coefficient of the first component. The penalty factor evaluates whether a given function is WPB, applying a penalty if it is not, and is calculated in the following way:

$$pen(f) = \sum_{k=1}^{n-1} unb_k(f) \qquad (4)$$

In essence, $pen(f)$ evaluates how far the truth table for each subset corresponding to inputs of a given Hamming weight, k, is from being balanced. This evaluation must be done in subsets, for we must recall that a function may be globally balanced without being WPB. Likewise, it is essential to note that the cases from $k = 0$ and $k = n$ are not considered as those subsets always have a single value. In fact, when evaluating the non-linearity, the former is forced to take a value of zero, while the latter is forced to take a value of one.

The unbalancedness of each restricted truth table, $unb_k(f)$, is given by:

$$unb_k(f) = \left| \frac{\#E_{n,k}}{2} - w_H(f_{(k)}) \right| \tag{5}$$

where $\#E_{n,k}$ is the cardinality of the truth table corresponding to the inputs of Hamming weight k, given by

$$\binom{n}{k}$$

and $w_H(f_{(k)})$ is the Hamming weight of the restriction $f_{(k)}$, given by:

$$w_H(f_{(k)}) = \frac{\#E_{n,k} - W_{f_{(k)}}(0)}{2}. \tag{6}$$

It is important to note that when calculating the penalty, we do, in fact, calculate the restricted Walsh-Hadamard Transform, this is done in the same way as stated in Sect. 2, with the sole difference that now we have $a \in E_{n,k}$, rather than $a \in \mathbb{F}_2^n$, as in the usual case.

Finally, we consider the delta coefficient of the first component in Eq. 3, which takes a value of one when the penalty component is equal to zero and a value of zero otherwise.

3.4 Experimental Settings

All the programs used for experimentation were programmed by the authors in Python. The programs were executed using an *Ubuntu Server* with an *Intel Xeon Bronze 3204* and RAM of 93 GB. The overall processing of the experiments took three weeks.

Table 3. Outline of the configuration set up used for the GAs considered.

Pop. size	Generations	Tournament size	p_{cross}	p_{mut}
200	10,000	3	1	0.1
				0.3
				0.5
				0.7
				0.9

All experiments were run for Boolean functions with $n = 8$, using their truth table values to uniquely represent them, as described in Sect. 3.2. A population of 200 individuals was used in all cases, considering the case in which the population was constrained to WPB individuals and the case in which unbalanced individuals were also considered as part of the population. In all cases, parent selection was done using 3-tournament elimination, as in [9]. The variation operators described in Sect. 3.2 were applied with crossover probability, $p_{cross} = 1$ and with mutation probability $p_{mut} \in \{0.1, 0.3, 0.5, 0.7, 0.9\}$.

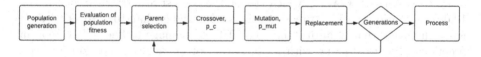

Fig. 1. Flowchart illustrating the stages of a GA. It can be seen that for the configuration of each GA specific parameters need to be defined for the crossover and mutation probabilities.

In the first three scenarios where the results for the GAs from [9] were being reproduced, all parameters were kept the same, with the sole difference being the alteration in the fitness function. That is to say, that the parameters for the crossover and mutation stages, as seen in Fig. 1, are set according the specifications given in [9].

In the two instances proposed in this work, in which the WPB representation was used, but allowing for unbalanced individuals as part of the initial population, the operators used varied slightly, but the parameter values remained the same as before. The population size was kept the same at 200 individuals. Likewise, the 3-tournament elimination for parent selection was considered in the same way; three individuals are randomly chosen from the population, of which the two with highest fitness will be selected to be the parents, and the third will be replaced with the offspring. For the crossover we considered the two crossover operators as described in Sect. 3.2: one-point crossover at list level, and counter-based crossover at vector level, as before. In both cases the crossover probability was kept at $p_{cross} = 1$. Regarding the mutation, we now considered the classic swap mutation operator rather than the swap-based, meaning that the bits being swapped need not have different values. However, as in the previous cases, we considered a mutation probability of $p_{mut} \in \{0.1, 0.3, 0.5, 0.7, 0.9\}$. Table 3 summarises the parameters used for all the experiments carried out as part of this work.

Additionally, it should be noted that each variation of the experiment was run 30 times, evaluating 10,000 generations in each case. Moreover, the generations taken to reach the best individual were measured, recording how many generations were needed to reach fitness values of 110 and 112, as these were the highest fitness values reached.

4   Results

In this Section we present the results obtained from our various experiments. In order to facilitate the understanding the GAs are denoted as GA-TT, GA-CBC, GA-MOOC, GA-UB-CBC and GA-UB-OP, according to the specifications given in Table 2. Throughout this Section we make reference to the number of generations taken to arrive to a given fitness value. However, this is equivalent to referring to the number of evaluations carried out as in this case we only carry out one evaluation in each generation, see Sect. 3.4.

Firstly, we consider the fitness values obtained from our experiments. In first instance we consider GA-TT, which yielded the poorest results; when considering 10,000 generations it did not reach a fitness value higher than 108. Nonetheless, it is worth noting that in all instances GA-TT did manage to find WPB Boolean functions, despite starting with a population of unbalanced individuals. Now, we consider the GAs with a search space restricted to $\mathcal{W}_n$. The highest fitness reached in the majority of the executions, regardless of the mutation probability, was 110. This fitness value was typically reached more rapidly by GA-MOOC. Moreover, both GAs reached a fitness value of 112 on a few occasions, as seen in Table 4. These results are interesting, suggesting a better performance of GA-MOOC, when using a restricted search-space.

Next, we consider the GAs using the WPB representation with an unrestricted search space. GA-UB-OP consistently reached a fitness of 110, only failing to reach it within the 10,000 generations being considered on six occasions, in which cases it reached a fitness of 108. On the other hand, it also managed to reach a fitness value of 112 on five occasions, for different mutation probabilities. Overall this GA's results had the biggest variation, although the results remain of better quality than those of GA-TT, in general. On the other hand, GA-UB-CBC stands out as it was able to reach the highest fitness value of 112 within 10,000 generations more frequently than the other GAs explored in this paper, as observed in Table 4, arriving at a fitness of 110 in all other runs. The high performance of GA-UB-CBC is not surprising, as in [9] it was also found that the *counter-based crossover* operator yielded the best results.

Given the poor results obtained from GA-TT, this case will not be considered in the ensuing analysis. We will now focus only on the cases using the *WPB representation*. This result is congruous with the findings of Mariot et al. [9].

We now explore the issue of diversity within the population in more depth. The diversity of a population is a measure of how many different individuals are present in the population; this can be measured with respect to the fitness values, the genotype or the phenotype, [4]. In this case we will be referring to diversity with respect to the variety of fitness values in the population. It is known that diversity is crucial in order to achieve an adequate evolution of the population, else the GA is more likely to arrive at a premature convergence, in which case the GA might get trapped in a local optimum [4].

In the experiments where the search space was restricted to $\mathcal{W}_n$ we found that in the majority of runs an individual with the best fitness was already within the population in the first generation. For this analysis 110 was taken to be the best fitness, as this was the case in the vast majority of runs. In Table 4 we can clearly see that in both GA-CBC and GA-MOOC we obtain a value of one generation for the median, meaning that in at least half of the runs the best fitness was already in the population from the start. The only exception to this was GA-

CBC with $p_{mut} = 0.1$, which had a median of 174 generations. Additionally, Fig. 2b graphically illustrates the fast convergence towards the best individual in the vast majority of cases, most converging within the first 600 generations, leading to a rapid loss of diversity in the population.

Table 4. Number of generations taken for the GAs to reach fitness values of 110 and 112. *Count* indicates the number of executions out of 150 which successfully arrived at a fitness value of 110 or 112—the 150 runs consider 30 runs for each mutation probability considered. We also provide statistical values for the number of generations taken to reach the desired fitness values to illustrate the general behaviour of each algorithm.

Algorithm	110						112					
	Count	Mean	Std	Median	Min	Max	Count	Mean	Std	Median	Min	Max
GA-TT	0	–	–	–	–	–	0	–	–	–	–	–
GA-CBC	150	167.6	272.0	1	1	1639	5	3717.0	3250.1	1719	1039	9439
GA-MOOC	150	157.3	249.9	1	1	1429	7	6529.0	2789.4	7449	1939	9939
GA-UB-CBC	150	362.9	282.2	299	9	1079	11	5169.0	3688.9	7939	229	9939
GA-UB-OP	144	1443.3	434.5	1399	559	3549	5	4441.0	1782.9	5389	1269	6269

In contrast, when the entirety of $\mathcal{B}_n$ was considered for the search space a minimum of 9 generations, when using the *counter-based crossover*, were required to find the best individual, though it was usually a value surpassing 200, as seen in Table 4. Figure 2a clearly illustrates that in most cases diversity was retained for a longer period when exploring $\mathcal{B}_n$ fully, thus allowing a better balance between exploration and exploitation in the GA. It is interesting to see that, while diversity is retained longer, all instances consistently reached a fitness of 110 within 1,200 generations, showing greater robustness in comparison with GA-CBC, as seen in Fig. 2b. Although this was also more time consuming, the advantage of retaining greater diversity is evidenced by the high fitness value of 112 being reached by GA-UB-CBC with greater frequency than the other GAs.

This result is of great importance as it highlights the key role that diversity plays in order to allow the GA to adequately explore the search space. One must recall that a GA will usually find a good solution, however it is not guaranteed that it is the best. In Fig. 2b we see that all instances reach a good solution in few generations, regardless of the mutation probability used. However, upon comparing with the fitness values obtained by other GAs we realise that better solutions may be achieved, albeit more slowly. This understanding will allow for a more efficient exploration of the search space when larger cases are explored, such as the case for $n = 16$, which, to the best of our knowledge, has not yet been tackled.

At this time, we were unable to explore a larger problem size due to the complexity of the problem. A quick experiment was run using GA-CBC with a mutation probability of 0.7 to illustrate why it is not currently feasible to consider the case $n = 16$. The GA was run for $n \in \{2, 4, 8\}$, and in each run the time taken to complete the run was recorded. Table 5 reflects the results obtained from this experiment, clearly illustrating the exponential growth in the

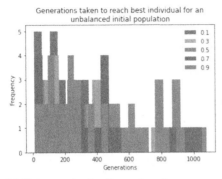

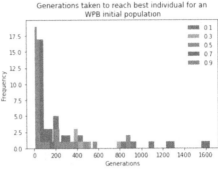

(a) Histogram showing the number of generations taken to reach the best individual over 30 runs when starting with an unbalanced population, using GA-UB-CBC with $p_{mut} \in \{0.1, 0.3, 0.5, 0.7, 0.9\}$.

(b) Histogram showing the number of generations taken to reach the best individual over 30 runs when starting with an WPB population, using GA-CBC with $p_{mut} \in \{0.1, 0.3, 0.5, 0.7, 0.9\}$.

Fig. 2. Histograms contrasting the generations taken to reach the best fitness when exploring with different search spaces, $\mathcal{B}_n$ and W_n.

time required to execute the GA as the value of n grows. Using these values we estimate that a single run for the case $n = 16$ would take several weeks with the current setup.

Table 5. Time taken to run one iteration of GA-CBC for problem sizes $n \in \{2, 4, 8\}$.

n	Mean time (s)	Std
2	1.405	0.016
4	13.781	0.166
8	7982.469	766.559

5   Conclusion and Further Work

In this work we sought to further investigate the construction of WPB Boolean functions by means of GAs, particularly focusing on the constraints of the search space and variation operators. The interest in these functions arises due to their role in the design of stream ciphers, such as FLIP [10]. Though the size of the Boolean functions developed in this work is too small for real application, the results seek to help in achieving a greater understanding of WPB Boolean functions in general, thus allowing for suitable techniques to be developed for functions with more variables. In this paper we focused on Boolean functions with $n = 8$ as a continuation to the work done by Mariot et al. [9]. For these functions we considered two distinct representations, namely the classical *truth table representation* and the *WPB representation*. While the latter representation allows us to restrict the search-space to explore solely within $\mathcal{W}_n$, we analyse the results upon using this representation to explore $\mathcal{B}_n$ in its entirety, as was originally done with the *truth table representation*. Moreover, we focused on a single fitness function, which now evaluated the non-linearity of the functions without restrictions, to test whether attempting to use the *Fast Walsh-Hadamard Transform* on this problem is something we could aspire towards.

Our results show that it is in fact feasible to use the WPB representation to explore the whole of $\mathcal{B}_n$. In all iterations of our experiments, the increased size of the search space did not prevent the GAs from finding adequate WPB Boolean functions with high non-linearity. What's more, our results yielded higher fitness-values with more frequency when searching throughout the entirety of $\mathcal{B}_n$, as opposed to the restricted search space, thus evidencing the importance of preserving diversity within the population when working with GAs. Additionally, the successful change in the fitness function to evaluate non-linearity without restriction is a very promising result as the implementation of the *Fast Walsh-Hadamard Transform* could allow this approach to be applied to larger Boolean functions.

However, there remains much work to be done going forward. As mentioned, we hope that our findings will allow us to scale up this approach to bigger problems, starting with $n = 16$. But, in order to explore the applicability of this technique to bigger cases, we must first explore alternatives in order to generate the initial population efficiently. An interesting path to be explored is the possibility of exploiting the WPB representation itself during the creation of the initial population, as it allows us to break each individual into smaller parts. Additionally, we consider that other aspects of the WPB representation can be further taken advantage off during the application of crossover operators at different levels and in allowing for a more in depth understanding of the distinct subsets within each WPB Boolean function.

Acknowledgement. The first author acknowledges the CONACYT scholarship to pursue graduate studies. The third author acknowledges support from project IPN-SIP 20221938. We thank Manzoni et al., authors of [9] for their support in this investigation.

References

1. Carlet, C., Guillot, P.: A new representation of Boolean functions. In: Fossorier, M., Imai, H., Lin, S., Poli, A. (eds.) AAECC 1999. LNCS, vol. 1719, pp. 94–103. Springer, Heidelberg (1999). https://doi.org/10.1007/3-540-46796-3_10
2. Carlet, C., Méaux, P., Rotella, Y.: Boolean functions with restricted input and their robustness; application to the flip cipher. Cryptology ePrint Archive (2017)
3. Clark, J.A., Jacob, J.L.: Two-stage optimisation in the design of Boolean functions. In: Dawson, E.P., Clark, A., Boyd, C. (eds.) ACISP 2000. LNCS, vol. 1841, pp. 242–254. Springer, Heidelberg (2000). https://doi.org/10.1007/10718964_20
4. Eiben, A.E., Smith, J.E., et al.: Introduction to Evolutionary Computing, vol. 53. Springer, Heidelberg (2003). https://doi.org/10.1007/978-3-662-05094-1

5. Katz, J., Lindell, Y.: Introduction to Modern Cryptography. CRC Press, Boca Raton (2020)
6. López-López, I., Sosa-Gómez, G., Segura, C., Oliva, D., Rojas, O.: Metaheuristics in the optimization of cryptographic Boolean functions. Entropy **22**(9), 1052 (2020)
7. MacWilliams, F.J., Sloane, N.J.A.: The Theory of Error Correcting Codes, vol. 16. Elsevier, Amsterdam (1977)
8. Manzoni, L., Mariot, L., Tuba, E.: Balanced crossover operators in genetic algorithms. Swarm Evol. Comput. **54**, 100646 (2020)
9. Mariot, L., Picek, S., Jakobovic, D., Djurasevic, M., Leporati, A.: Evolutionary construction of perfectly balanced boolean functions. arXiv preprint arXiv:2202.08221 (2022)
10. Méaux, P., Journault, A., Standaert, F.-X., Carlet, C.: Towards stream ciphers for efficient FHE with low-noise ciphertexts. In: Fischlin, M., Coron, J.-S. (eds.) EUROCRYPT 2016. LNCS, vol. 9665, pp. 311–343. Springer, Heidelberg (2016). https://doi.org/10.1007/978-3-662-49890-3_13
11. Mesnager, S., Su, S.: On constructions of weightwise perfectly balanced Boolean functions. Cryptogr. Commun. **13**(6), 951–979 (2021)
12. Millan, W., Clark, A., Dawson, E.: An effective genetic algorithm for finding highly nonlinear Boolean functions. In: Han, Y., Okamoto, T., Qing, S. (eds.) ICICS 1997. LNCS, vol. 1334, pp. 149–158. Springer, Heidelberg (1997). https://doi.org/10.1007/BFb0028471
13. Millan, W., Clark, A., Dawson, E.: Heuristic design of cryptographically strong balanced Boolean functions. In: Nyberg, K. (ed.) EUROCRYPT 1998. LNCS, vol. 1403, pp. 489–499. Springer, Heidelberg (1998). https://doi.org/10.1007/BFb0054148
14. Millan, W., Clark, A., Dawson, E.: Boolean function design using hill climbing methods. In: Pieprzyk, J., Safavi-Naini, R., Seberry, J. (eds.) ACISP 1999. LNCS, vol. 1587, pp. 1–11. Springer, Heidelberg (1999). https://doi.org/10.1007/3-540-48970-3_1
15. Millan, W., Fuller, J., Dawson, E.: New concepts in evolutionary search for Boolean functions in cryptology. Comput. Intell. **20**(3), 463–474 (2004)
16. Picek, S., Carlet, C., Guilley, S., Miller, J.F., Jakobovic, D.: Evolutionary algorithms for Boolean functions in diverse domains of cryptography. Evol. Comput. **24**(4), 667–694 (2016)
17. Picek, S., Jakobovic, D., Miller, J.F., Marchiori, E., Batina, L.: Evolutionary methods for the construction of cryptographic Boolean functions. In: Machado, P., et al. (eds.) EuroGP 2015. LNCS, vol. 9025, pp. 192–204. Springer, Cham (2015). https://doi.org/10.1007/978-3-319-16501-1_16
18. Seberry, J., Zhang, X.-M., Zheng, Y.: Nonlinearly balanced Boolean functions and their propagation characteristics. In: Stinson, D.R. (ed.) CRYPTO 1993. LNCS, vol. 773, pp. 49–60. Springer, Heidelberg (1994). https://doi.org/10.1007/3-540-48329-2_5
19. Singh, H.K., Alam, K., Ray, T.: Use of infeasible solutions during constrained evolutionary search: a short survey. In: Ray, T., Sarker, R., Li, X. (eds.) ACALCI 2016. LNCS (LNAI), vol. 9592, pp. 193–205. Springer, Cham (2016). https://doi.org/10.1007/978-3-319-28270-1_17

Unification of Source-Code Re-Use Similarity Measures

René Arnulfo García-Hernández[1]([⊠])[ID], Yulia Ledeneva[1][ID],
Ángel Hernández-Castañeda[1,2][ID], and Gabriela Villada[1]

[1] Autonomous University of the State of Mexico, Instituto Literario 100, Col.
Centro., 50000 Toluca, Mexico State, Mexico
renearnulfo@hotmail.com
[2] Cátedras CONACyT, Av. Insurgentes Sur 1582, Col. Crédito Constructor,
03940 Mexico City, Mexico

Abstract. Computer programs and their source code are commonly available online, making it relatively easy to create new programs from the resource available. Simple stated, methods for detecting the source code reuse apply individual similarity measures between two source codes (the original and the suspect) to identify a case of reuse based on a manually determined threshold; however, the relevance of each similarity measure and the selection of the correct threshold in this task has been little explored. In this study, we propose an evolutionary approach to automatically obtain the relevance of each individual similarity measure and its threshold. Furthermore, we propose a unified method to combine the strengths of individual similarity measures to increase retrieval accuracy. Our experimental results provided three individual similarity systems that outperform the original ones and a unified system that obtains the best result.

Keywords: Source code reuse · Similarity measures · Optimization · Genetic algorithm

1 Introduction

Nowadays, the internet allows the dissemination and access to the knowledge that various authors generate through their original works and products; this knowledge is, in turn, a creative engine to produce new works. It worth noting that reuse is a fundamental part of the creative process of any original work. However, the reuse of works or knowledge without the author's consent could lead to illegal acts such as plagiarism [3]. Plagiarism can be defined as the reuse of original works presenting them as their own without acknowledging the original author [6].

Software development is a creative process in which authors encode their key knowledge in source code to produce computer programs that provide services to users. There are different reuse schemes in software development, such as: analysis models, design and source code; specifically, these schemes may involve the reuse of algorithms, parameter settings, libraries, code compilation, and source code, among others [21,23]. In this sense, Davey et al. [5] claim that between 25% and 30% of source code is copied and adapted in software development. Therefore, the reuse of the source code stand for the object of greatest interest when performing software plagiarism.

Formally, a code fragment $CF1$ is a copy of another $CF2$ if the similarity between them is greater than or equal to a threshold μ, that is: Similarity(CF1, CF2) $\geq \mu$ [18]. A Similarity Measure (SM) is a mathematical expression that denotes the degree of relationship between two elements in which their similarity depends on the attributes considered. In current standards, the similarity between source code fragments is obtained by representing the latter as vectors by using some mapping method [20]. The representation of source code fragments can be defined according to their textual or functional characteristics. Copies of fragments with textual features can be classified as follows: Type 1-(exact copy) identical codes with formatting variations and comments, Type 2-(renamed copy) with renamed identifiers, Type 3-(near copy) with modifications and reordering of instructions; and Type 4-(functional copy) with functional equivalence without direct evidence [5,18].

Detecting source code reuse requires determining the identity of a suspicious source code to discover if it shares the same functionality with other source codes, considering that "given a suspicious element Cs within a reference collection C, the goal is find if there is a code $c \in C$ used as a copy of the Cs element" [2].

The early stages of a source code reuse system depend on the number of similarity measures used, but in practice, a system only uses one SM.

In this study we analyze the relevance of each Individual Similarity Measure (ISM) used in the source code reuse detection task. For this, the framework proposed in the SOCO 2014 source code detection task is used. In addition, an automatic search of the similarity threshold is performed.

2   Related Works

Several approaches have been proposed for the reuse source code detection that, in general, consist of five stages: 1) split the source code in small parts, 2) then remove or replace all unnecessary information, next 3) use some representing method (for example, use latent semantic analysis (LSA) for representing source codes as a vector or see the parts of the source code as strings), 4) comparing representations with a proximity measure, and finally 5) make a decision whether it is a case of source code reuse.

Konecki et al. [15] compare source codes as simply strings considering various preprocessing steps, for example: source codes are splitted into functions; the authors removed declaration of variables and function, input and output commands, blank lines and spaces; the variable and function names are replaced by a constant. The resultant lines, represented as strings, are compared to identify reuses cases with proximity measures such as: Hamming, Levenshtein, Damerau-Levenshtein and Jaro-Winkler distance.

In more recently studies, the problem of cross-language codes is addressed. For instance, Flores et al. [7] attempt to avoid using external resources to perform a reuse detection system that do not depend of the source code language. The claims outperform corpora-dependent models, by proposing a combination of character 3-grams and pseudo-cognateness, when a large corpus is not available.

In the study of Flores et al. [9], they include several models to mapping source codes into vectors and then consider them as a classifier input. These mapping methods can extract features at different language levels. For example, Latent Semantic Analysis (LSA) examines the similarity between word contexts and creates a vector space that taking into account words that appear in similar contexts. Another method that consider semantic information is Explicit Semantic Analysis (ESA) in which source code vectors are generated based on a reference corpus that represents the world knowledge. ESA compare a source code against each one from the comparable collection to generate a vector of similarities that stand for the source code. Another useful information is obtained from cognates (COG). COG are defined as tokens of different languages that shares common phonological or orthographic properties. This information may detect some variations of a reused source code when the variation is not necessarily the translation of the terms to another language.

Another approaches attempt to capture the writing style of the programmers in order to determine plagiarism, that is, the way to write of programmers may determine whether someone else make use of their codes. Therefore, the authors considers two type of features: stylistic and comment-based. On the one hand, stylistic features includes the number of lines, the number of upper and lower case letters, vocabulary size, and lexical richness among others. On the other hand, the comment-based features consider the explanations given by the authors on their own source codes to create a vector based on character 3-grams. Similarity between obtained vectors is evaluated by the cosine similarity. Finally, the authors measure the performance of each representation by establishing a manual threshold for detecting plagiarism.

Some automatic tools have been developed to assist with the problematic of the reuse detection of source code. JPLAG and MOSS are examples of free tools. JPLAG [17] was developed by Guido Malpohl in 1996 which supports Java, C#, C++, Scheme and natural language text; this system uses a variation of the Karp-Rabin comparison algorithm developed by Wise [22]. MOSS [1] (Measure Of Software Similarity) was developed by Alex Aiken in 1994. MOSS works with different languages: C, C++, Java, Pascal, Ada, Lisp and Scheme; this system is based on getting fingerprints which identifying a source code in particular way.

Most methods turn source codes into vector representations and, in turn, a similarity measure determine a reuse source code case based on a manual determined threshold. However, although several representation methods have been analyzed, performance and relevance of similarity measures and the threshold selection have little explored. Therefore, this work goal is to analyze and optimize different proximity measures and, in addition, automatically determine an optimal threshold to detect reuse source code cases.

3 Individual Similarity Measures

This section briefly describes the individual similarity measures used by source code reuse detection systems.

3.1 Longest Common Substring (LCS) Similarity

Given a pair of source codes represented as strings of tokens (reserved words, logical operators, identifiers, etc.), LCS similarity aligns identical tokens between strings to obtain the longest common substring. The similarity calculation can be performed using the length of the common string or it can be normalized using the length of the longest original string. To find the LCS of the strings p and q, it is necessary to find the longest common suffix for all string prefixes, as shown in Eqs. 1 and 2.

$$LCSuff(p_{1...i}, q_{i...j}) = \begin{cases} LCSuff(p_{1...i-1}, q_{1...j-1}) \ , p(i) = q(j) \\ 0 \qquad\qquad\qquad\qquad , p(i) \neq q(j) \end{cases} \tag{1}$$

$$LCS = MaxLCSuff(p_{1...i}, q_{i...j}) \tag{2}$$

LCS similarity works well when a string is identified with a single order among its elements, so it works well for Type 1 and 2 source code copy detection. However, when two different strings represent the same object, as in the case of Type 3 copies, where there is reordering of instructions or methods, the LCS only recovers a part of the copy. To identify Type 3 copies, the sum of the longer common substrings lengths [11,12] have been used.

3.2 Cosine Similarity

The representation of a source code is given by vectors where each token (t) used is weighted (w) to give a relevance of the token according to the task, like the presence or absence of the token in a source code (Boolean weighting), or the token frequency in the source code. Cosine similarity is a measure used to calculate the angle that is formed between two sets of terms expressed as vectors [20]. Given two source codes p and q, to calculate the cosine distance it is necessary to weight the terms expressed as vectors by applying Eq. 3.

$$cos_t^w(p,q) = \frac{\sum_{i=1}^{|t_p \cup t_q|}(w_{t_i,p} * w_{t_i,q})}{\sqrt{\sum_{i=1}^{|t_p \cup t_q|}(w_{t_i,p})^2}\sqrt{\sum_{i=1}^{|t_p \cup t_q|}(w_{t_i,q})^2}} \tag{3}$$

3.3 KR-Greedy String-Tiling (KRG-ST) Similarity

KRG-ST similarity is an algorithm proposed by Wise in 1995 [22], which consists of finding the maximum tiling of the strings p and q, where a tiling is a set of tiles (T) representing a substring of p that corresponds to a substring of q. The JPlag system proposes to calculate the similarity by the coincidences obtained from the KRG-ST algorithm with Eqs. 4 and 5 [17].

$$KRG - ST(p, q) = \frac{2 * coverage(T)}{|P| + |Q|} \qquad (4)$$

$$coverage(T) = \sum_{match(p,q,length \in T)} length \qquad (5)$$

4   Proposed Method

Our proposed method unifies ISMs into a combined measure and the decision is made with a similarity threshold and a ranking threshold. Therefore, our method performs an evolutionary setting that involves both the unified measure (named *Mixmetric*) and similarity and ranking thresholds to make the decision on source code reuse, see Fig. 1.

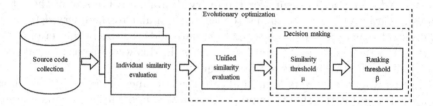

Fig. 1. Proposed assembled system for detection of source code reuse with the unification of multiple individual measures

The unification of n ISMs into a combined measure (Mixmetric) is done through a linear function where the similarity is expressed as a weighted sum (Eq. 6). In Mixmetric, each individual similarity measure is assigned a weight that indicates its relevance; therefore, the sum of all weights is 1. Given a pair of source codes p and q, the evaluation of each ISM is performed, both (p, q) and (q, p) within the training collection. Therefore, under an evolutionary approach is determined the set of: weights (w) associated with measurements, similarity threshold μ and ranking threshold β. The similarity threshold μ has the function of recovering all the pairs that reach or exceed its value, while the ranking threshold is responsible of selecting the β most similar pairs among the pairs recovered by the threshold μ.

$$Mixmetric(p, q) = \sum_{i=1}^{n} w_i * s_i(p, q), where \sum_{i=1}^{n} w_i = 1 \qquad (6)$$

A reuse case is confirmed if the optimized similarity value is greater than or equal to the similarity threshold μ (Eq. 7).

$$Reuse(p, q, \mu) = \begin{cases} true \ , & Mixmetric(p, q, w_{1...n}) \geq \mu \\ false \ , & in - other - case \end{cases} \tag{7}$$

$$Reuse \ Cases = last \ \beta \ elements \ \in \{x | Reuse(p, q, \mu) = true\} \tag{8}$$

Simply stated, the proposed method searches, under an evolutionary approach, for the similarity threshold μ that maximizes the accuracy of the source code reuse cases (Eq. 8). Thus, the adjustment of these parameters depends on a training set.

For the search of parameters, we propose to use a genetic algorithm with the following representation. In the chromosome coding process, the weights $W = w_1, w_2, ..., w_n$ associated to each measure are represented by a binary chromosome with five decimal places of precision, where each weight has a value between 0 and 1. Then, to form the initial population, all chromosomes are created randomly. To evaluate the GA population, a key step of a GA is the fitness function. In this study, this function is defined as follows: given a pair of codes (d_i, d_j), the f-measure for the query d_i evaluates the size of the set of codes retrieved in the first ranking (codes more similar to the query d_i), but if d_j does not appear in the last set, the f-measure adds the size of the set of codes retrieved in the next ranking, until d_j appears. In this way, f-measure evaluates the ability to find relevant codes from a query.

In this way, the weights found indicate the relevance of similarity measures as a whole and the thresholds found provide clear support for a decision-making on source code reuse.

5   Experimentation

In this section, the experimental results on optimizing similarity measures are shown. First, the description of the data set used for training and testing the proposed method and its classification by scenarios is shown (Sect. 5.1. Then, the individual similarity measures optimization is shown in Sect. 5.2. Next, the unification of similarity measures to build the Mixmetric measure is described in Sect. 5.3. Finally, a discussion of the results and their comparison with the state of art is achieved.

5.1   Dataset and Related Systems Description

Due to the high frequency of cases of source code reuse, either for plagiarism detection purposes or to search for source code in repositories, the SOCO (Detection of SOurce COde Reuse) forum arises as part of the event held at FIRE (Forum for Information Retrieval Evaluation). In this task, it is not necessary to show the fragments with reuse or the direction in which the reuse occurs in pairs [10].

The training and testing experiments were performed with the SOCO forum corpus, which has source codes in the C and C++ (SOCO-C) languages. The SOCO-C training set has 79 source codes, so it produces 6,241 suspiciously viewed pairs, however, only 26 pairs are confirmed as reuse cases, which is equivalent to 0.416% of all possible pairs (Table 1). Detection of reuse cases, in the corpus, was carried out manually by three reviewers to establish reliable relevance judgments.

Table 1. Characteristics of the SOCO-C training and testing set for the C/C++ language

Set	Source codes	Suspicious pairs (100%)	Confirmed reused pairs
Train	79	6,240	26 (0.416%)
Test	19,895	395,811,024	322 (8.1×10^{-5}%)

The test corpus was built from the set of 19,895 codes selected in the 2012 Google Code Jam Contest, generating 395,811,024 suspects pairs. However, only 322 pairs are confirmed to be instances of reused source code, which is equivalent to 8.1×10^{-5}%. The test collection is divided by scenarios where each one represents a level of complexity to identify a code (see Table 2).

The systems participating in the SOCO-C corpus are briefly described as follows:

- UAEM [11]: This system only uses the LCS as ISM (described in Sect. 3.1) with two decision thresholds and decision rules that must be met in both directions.
- UAM-C [4]: This system uses 2 stages, the first one is responsible for the extraction of three representative features of the source code through eight ISMs. The second stage of this system is the decision making using the Tree Forest classification algorithm.
- Baseline-1 [13]: This baseline is based on the Kalsruhe University's JPlag system.
- Baseline-2 [8]: Baseline based on tokens of trigrams (3-grams), where each trigram is weighed with frequency (f) to represent the source code. The similarity calculation is performed by measuring $cos^f_{trigram}$ (described in Eq. 3). The reuse decision is made through a similarity threshold of $\mu = 0.95$%.
- Apoorv and Rajat: SOCO-C original systems without a description of the method used.

The same evaluation metric used in the SOCO task based on the f-measure is used to evaluate all experiments. Table 3 shows the results of the systems participating in the SOCO-C test set, divided by scenarios, for the C programming language corpus.

Table 2. SOCO-C testing set divided by scenarios

Scenarios of the testing set					
A1	A2	B1	B2	C1	C2
5,408	5,195	4,939	3,873	335	145

Table 3. Evaluation of the original systems with the whole collection and by scenarios of the testing set of SOCO-C

System	A1	A2	B1	B2	C1	Whole
UAEM	**0.382**	**0.372**	**0.587**	**0.531**	0.485	**0.440**
Baseline-2	0.294	0.255	0.326	0.323	0.429	0.295
Baseline-1	0.101	0.113	0.245	0.349	0.762	0.190
Rajat	0.110	0.106	0.236	0.146	0.066	0.129
Apoorv	0.035	0.023	0.022	0.014	0.029	0.022
UAM-C	0.010	0.009	0.024	0.019	**0.800**	0.013

5.2 Optimization of Individual Similarity Measures

In the first experiment, the ISMs used by the original systems (LCS, KRG-ST, $Cos_{trigram}^{tf}$ and Lexical) are optimized separately. In this case, the best similarity threshold is searched with a genetic algorithm based on the training corpus. Table 4 shows that the proposed system based on the LCS obtain the best performance using a threshold of 0.620.

Table 4. Evaluation of the training set of our proposed system for 4 ISMs (threshold μ)

Optimized ISM (μ)	Precision	Recall	F-measure
LCS (0.620)	0.933	0.538	**0.683**
Léxica (0.800)	0.667	0.538	0.596
$Cos_{trigram}^{tf}$ (0.800)	0.667	0.538	0.596
KRG-ST (0.550)	0.778	0.269	0.400

Table 5 shows the comparison of the proposed ISM-based systems with the original participating systems in the test set. The first column shows the name of the original system and in parentheses the name of the ISM used. In this case, our proposed system based on LCS similarity obtained the best performance. It is important to mention that the proposed system based on the LCS measure outperforms the UAEM system that uses the same individual measure. Furthermore, our proposed systems based on the KRG-ST and Lexicon ISM outperform the original systems using the same measures. It is worth noting that the proposed system based on the KRG-ST measure exceed both baselines. In addition, the proposed ISM-based systems of $Cos^{tf}_{trigram}$ and Lexical outperform the Baseline-1. Only the system with the $Cos^{tf}_{trigram}$ measure does not outperform the original system.

Table 5. Comparison of the proposed systems with the original systems for the testing set of SOCO-C

System	Precision	Recall	F-measure
LCS (Proposed)	0.799	0.668	**0.728**
UAEM (LCS)	0.282	1.000	0.440
KRG-ST (Proposed)	0.202	0.578	0.299
Baseline-2 ($Cos^{tf}_{trigram}$)	0.258	0.345	0.295
$Cos^{tf}_{trigram}$ (Proposed)	0.167	0.658	0.267
Léxica (Proposed)	0.147	0.578	0.234
Baseline-1 (KRG-ST)	0.350	0.130	0.190
Rajat	0.077	0.404	0.129
Apoorv	0.011	0.543	0.022
UAM-C (Léxica)	0.006	1.000	0.013

5.3   Unified System of Individual Similarity Measures

The ISMs are unified to build the Mixmetrix measure and are optimized with the proposed method. Table 6 shows that the LCS measure obtained the highest relevance with 69.3%, followed by the KRG-ST measure with 16.5%, followed by the Lexica measure with 8.7% and, finally, the $Cos^{tf}_{trigram}$ measure with 5%. It is important to point out that, to the best of the authors' knowledge, the relevance of similarity measures to the source code reuse task had not been obtained before. The obtained weights work with the similarity threshold of 0.490 and the ranking threshold of 2.

Table 6. Weighting, cut-off threshold and similarity threshold found by the proposed method for Mixme-tric with the training set

System	Weighting	Similarity Threshold μ	Cut-off Threshold β
LCS	0.693	0.490	2
Léxica	0.087		
KRG-ST	0.165		
$Cos^{tf}_{trigram}$	0.050		

Table 7 shows the comparison of the proposed systems for the training set. It can be seen that Mixmetric obtains the best results. This is consistent with the hypothesis that a combined measure exceeds the individual measures on the same data set. It is worth mentioning that the SOCO forum does not present results for the training set.

Table 7. Evaluation of Mixmetric with the training set

System	Precision	Recall	F-measure
Mixmetric	0.917	0.846	**0.880**
LCS	0.933	0.538	0.683
Léxica	0.667	0.538	0.596
$Cos^{tf}_{trigram}$	0.667	0.538	0.596
KRG-ST	0.778	0.269	0.400

Table 8 shows the results of the evaluation of the test set divided by scenarios. Each scenario shows a reuse case with a different level of complexity. The results of the proposed system Mixmetric exceeds to the original SOCO systems in all scenarios on the test set.

Table 8. Evaluation of the proposed systems and the original systems divided by scenarios for the testing set of SOCO-C

System	Scenario				
	A1	A2	B1	B2	C1
Mixmetric	**0.830**	**0.792**	**0.862**	**0.845**	**0.933**
LCS	0.739	0.704	0.752	0.692	0.769
UAEM	0.382	0.372	0.587	0.531	0.552
KRG-ST	0.273	0.189	0.595	0.442	0.667
Baseline-2	0.294	0.255	0.326	0.323	0.333
$Cos^{tf}_{trigram}$	0.193	0.200	0.260	0.520	0.400
Léxica	0.265	0.240	0.251	0.368	0.571
Baseline-1	0.101	0.113	0.245	0.349	0.429
Rajat	0.110	0.106	0.236	0.146	0.066
Apoorv	0.035	0.023	0.022	0.014	0.029
UAM	0.010	0.009	0.024	0.019	0.737

Finally, all the fits (ISM weights, similarity μ and ranking β threshold) found by the genetic algorithm, based on the training set, are evaluated on the test set. These results can be seen in Table 9, where our proposed Mixmetric and LCS systems take first and second place, respectively.

Table 9. Evaluation of the proposed systems and the original systems with the SOCO-C test set

System	Precision	Recall	F-measure
Mixmetric	**0.832**	**0.929**	**0.832**
LCS	0.799	0.668	0.728
UAEM (LCS)	0.282	1.000	0.440
KRG-ST	0.202	0.578	0.299
Baseline-2 ($Cos^{tf}_{trigram}$)	0.258	0.345	0.295
$Cos^{tf}_{trigram}$	0.167	0.658	0.267
Léxica	0.147	0.578	0.234
Baseline-1 (KRG-ST)	0.350	0.130	0.190
Rajat	0.077	0.404	0.129
Apoorv	0.011	0.543	0.022
UAM-C (Léxica)	0.006	1.000	0.013

6   Conclusions

The reuse of source code is an activity that is frequently carried out in the academic and professional sector. The relevance of improving reuse detection systems is twofold: either to detect plagiarism or to recover code to build systems quickly. That is why the detection of source code reuse is also seen as an information retrieval problem, since when faced with a query (a suspicious source), the system must retrieve cases similar to the request made.

In this study, a method was proposed to determine the optimized parameters of a source code reuse system based on one or multiple individual similarity measures for source code reuse. In specific, four systems were proposed based on the LCS, $Cos^{tf}_{trigram}$, KRG-ST and Lexicon individual measures. According to the experimentation, it is verified that the system based on the LCS measure exceeds the results obtained in the previous works for SOCO-C, either by scenario or globally.

It is worth mentioning that the proposed systems based on the LCS, KRG-St and Lexicon similarity measure outperformed the system that used the same measure. Additionally, all systems exceeded Baseline-1. In this sense, it is important to remember that an individual similarity measure considers a particular aspect to determine the similarity value between two source codes, whether focusing on lexical, syntactic or semantic aspects; making it have strengths and weaknesses in the face of various scenarios and types of reuse. Our proposed system unifies individual measures with the advantage that the weights and thresholds found provide simple and clear support for decision-making in a reuse case.

In future work, it is considered to enrich Mixmetric with other measures not used by the original systems, as well as other configurations to find coincidences and to calculate similarities.

References

1. Aiken, A.: MOSS (measure of software similarity) plagiarism detection system (2000). http://www.cs.berkeley.edu/moss/
2. Cedeño, L.A.B.: Detección automática de plagio en texto. Master's thesis, Universidad Politécnica de Valencia (2008)
3. Cosma, G., Joy, M.: Towards a definition of source-code plagiarism. IEEE Trans. Educ. **51**(2), 195–200 (2008)
4. Ramırez-de-la Cruz, A., Ramırez-de-la Rosa, G., Sánchez-Sánchez, C., Luna-Ramırez, W., Jiménez-Salazar, H., Rodrıguez-Lucatero, C.: UAM@ SOCO 2014: detection of source code reuse by means of combining different types of representations. FIRE [4] (2014)
5. Davey, N., Barson, P., Field, S., Frank, R., Tansley, D.: The development of a software clone detector. Int. J. Appl. Softw. Technol. (1995)
6. Española, R.A.: Rae. Diccionario de la lengua española **22** (2018)
7. Flores, E., Barrón-Cedeno, A., Moreno, L., Rosso, P.: Cross-language source code re-use detection. In: Proceedings of the 3rd Spanish Conference on Information Retrieval (CERI), pp. 145–156 (2014)
8. Flores, E., Barrón-Cedeño, A., Rosso, P., Moreno, L.: Towards the detection of cross-language source code reuse. In: Muñoz, R., Montoyo, A., Métais, E. (eds.) NLDB 2011. LNCS, vol. 6716, pp. 250–253. Springer, Heidelberg (2011). https://doi.org/10.1007/978-3-642-22327-3_31
9. Flores, E., Moreno, L., Rosso, P.: Detecting source code re-use with ensemble models. In: Proceedings of the 4th Spanish Conference on Information Retrieval, pp. 1–7 (2016)
10. Flores, E., Rosso, P., Moreno, L., Villatoro-Tello, E.: PAN@ FIRE: overview of SOCO track on the detection of source code re-use. Notebook papers of FIRE 2014 (2014)
11. Garcia-Hernández, R., Lendeneva, Y.: Identification of similar source codes based on longest common substrings. FIRE [4] (2014)
12. García-Hernández, R.A., Martínez-Trinidad, J.F., Carrasco-Ochoa, J.A.: A new algorithm for fast discovery of maximal sequential patterns in a document collection. In: Gelbukh, A. (ed.) CICLing 2006. LNCS, vol. 3878, pp. 514–523. Springer, Heidelberg (2006). https://doi.org/10.1007/11671299_53
13. Hage, J., Rademaker, P., van Vugt, N.: Plagiarism detection for Java: a tool comparison. In: Computer Science Education Research Conference, pp. 33–46 (2011)
14. Kamiya, T., Kusumoto, S., Inoue, K.: CCFinder: a multilinguistic token-based code clone detection system for large scale source code. IEEE Trans. Software Eng. **28**(7), 654–670 (2002)
15. Konecki, M., Orehovački, T., Lovrenčić, A.: Detecting code re-use potential. In: Proceedings of the 19th Central European Conference on Information and Intelligent Systems, pp. 627–631 (2008)
16. Muddu, B., Asadullah, A., Bhat, V.: CPDP: a robust technique for plagiarism detection in source code. In: 2013 7th International Workshop on Software Clones (IWSC), pp. 39–45. IEEE (2013)
17. Prechelt, L., Malpohl, G., Philippsen, M., et al.: Finding plagiarisms among a set of programs with JPlag. J. Univers. Comput. Sci. **8**(11), 1016 (2002)
18. Roy, C.K., Cordy, J.R., Koschke, R.: Comparison and evaluation of code clone detection techniques and tools: a qualitative approach. Sci. Comput. Program. **74**(7), 470–495 (2009)

19. Roy, C.K., Cordy, J.R.: A survey on software clone detection research. Queen's School Comput. TR **541**(115), 64–68 (2007)
20. Sidorov, G., Gelbukh, A., Gómez-Adorno, H., Pinto, D.: Soft similarity and soft cosine measure: similarity of features in vector space model. Computación y Sistemas **18**(3), 491–504 (2014)
21. Sommerville, I.: Ingeniería del software. Pearson educación (2005)
22. Wise, M.J.: Neweyes: a system for comparing biological sequences using the running Karp-Rabin greedy string-tiling algorithm. In: ISMB, pp. 393–401 (1995)
23. Yang, F.P., Jiau, H.C., Ssu, K.F.: Beyond plagiarism: an active learning method to analyze causes behind code-similarity. Comput. Educ. **70**, 161–172 (2014)

Considerations in the Incremental Hypervolume Algorithm of the WFG

Raquel Hernández Gómez[1], Jesús Guillermo Falcón-Cardona[2] ,
and Carlos A. Coello Coello[1]([⊠])

[1] CINVESTAV-IPN, Department of Computer Science, Evolutionary Computation
Group, Av. IPN No. 2508, Col. San Pedro Zacatenco, 07360 Mexico City, Mexico
`ccoello@cs.cinvestav.mx`
[2] Tecnologico de Monterrey, School of Engineering and Sciences,
Ave. Eugenio Garza Sada 2501, 64849 Monterrey, Nuevo León, México
`jfalcon@tec.mx`

Abstract. The hypervolume indicator (HV) has been subject of a lot
of research in the last few years, mainly because its maximization yields
near-optimal approximations of the Pareto optimal front of a multi-
objective optimization problem. This feature has been exploited by several evolutionary optimizers, in spite of the considerable growth in computational cost that it is involved in the computation of HV as we
increase the number of objectives. Some years ago, the Walking Fish
Group (WFG) implemented a new version of the incremental hypervolume algorithm, named IWFG 1.01. This implementation is the fastest
reported to date for determining the solution that contributes the least
to the HV of a non-dominated set. Nevertheless, this new version has
gone mostly unnoticed by the research community. We believe that this
is due to an error in the source code provided by the authors of this
algorithm, which appears when coupling it to a multi-objective evolutionary algorithm. In this paper, we describe this error, and we propose
a solution to fix it. Moreover, we illustrate the significant gains in performance produced by IWFG 1.01 in many-objective optimization problems
(i.e., problems having three or more objectives), when integrated into
the S-Metric Selection Evolutionary Multi-Objective Algorithm (SMS-
EMOA).

Keywords: Hypervolume indicator · Multi-objective optimization ·
Selection mechanism

1 Introduction

The hypervolume indicator (HV) [15], also known as the *Lebesgue measure* or
S-metric, is one of the most preferred quality indicators (QIs) for comparing

The third author acknowledges support from CONACyT project no. 2016-01-1920
(*Investigación en Fronteras de la Ciencia 2016*).

O. Pichardo Lagunas et al. (Eds.): MICAI 2022, LNAI 13612, pp. 410–422, 2022.
https://doi.org/10.1007/978-3-031-19493-1_32

multi-objective optimizers. In a single value, HV captures convergence to the Pareto optimal front as well as spread along the objective space. HV and its variants are the only unary QIs that are known to be Pareto compliant [16] and it has been proved that maximizing HV is equivalent to reaching the Pareto optimal set [10]. For these reasons, several multi-objective evolutionary algorithms (MOEAs) have incorporated HV in their survival selection mechanism [9].

Although the computational cost of calculating the exact HV is exponential with the scaling of the objectives [13], the Walking Fish Group (WFG) (http://www.wfg.csse.uwa.edu.au/hypervolume) has proposed clever implementations where, in practice, the real performance is unrelated to this worst case complexity [5,13,14]. Of our particular interest is the Incremental Hypervolume Algorithm (IWFG) [5,14], designed for determining which point in a set contributes least to HV. This algorithm uses several ideas to provide a substantial speed up. The most recent implementation is the IWFG 1.01 [5], which was released in November 2015. This version reported outstanding performance for even large fronts, being significantly faster than previous approaches in many-objective optimization problems [3]. However, this important version has gone unnoticed by the research community. Popular frameworks of evolutionary multi-objective optimization, such as jMetal (http://jmetal.github.io/jMetal) and MOEA Framework (http://moeaframework.org) do not have this update. We believe that this omission is because of the occurrence of an error, which is triggered when integrating IWFG 1.01 into an MOEA.

The main contributions of this paper are the isolation, replication and description of this error, as well as an easy-to-implement solution to it. Furthermore, we show the potential gains in speed up of IWFG 1.01 when coupled to the S-Metric Selection Evolutionary Multi-Objective Algorithm (SMS-EMOA) [1] (a hypervolume-based algorithm) on some test problems of the Deb-Thiele-Laumanns-Zitzler (DTLZ) test suite [8]. The rest of this paper is organized as follows. Section 2 defines the concepts and notation used in multi-objective optimization. Section 3 outlines the IWFG 1.01 algorithm. Section 4 provides our contribution. Section 5 presents the validation of our proposed solution. Section 6 contains our conclusions.

2 Background

We are interested in solving Multi-Objective Optimization Problems (MOPs) of the form:

$$\text{Minimize} \quad \mathbf{f}(\mathbf{x}) := (f_1(\mathbf{x}), f_2(\mathbf{x}), \dots, f_m(\mathbf{x})) \tag{1}$$

$$\text{subject to} \quad \mathbf{x} \in X, \tag{2}$$

where $X \subset \mathbb{R}^n$ is the feasible region in decision space, and $Z \subset \mathbb{R}^m$ is in the objective space. Each decision vector $\mathbf{x} \in X$ is related to an objective vector $\mathbf{f}(\mathbf{x}) \in Z$. Since objectives might be in conflict with one another, it is not possible to compare two solutions $\mathbf{x}, \mathbf{y} \in X$ in a straightforward manner as in single-objective optimization. As an alternative, the *Pareto dominance relation* must be applied. It is said that $\mathbf{x}$ "dominates" $\mathbf{y}$, if it stands:

$$\mathbf{x} \prec \mathbf{y} \Leftrightarrow (\forall i \in \{1, \ldots, m\}, f_i(\mathbf{x}) \leq f_i(\mathbf{y})) \wedge$$
$$(\exists j \in \{1, \ldots, m\}, f_j(\mathbf{x}) < f_j(\mathbf{y})).$$

The non-dominated solutions of a set $A \subseteq X$ are defined as:

$$\mathrm{NDS}(A) := \{\mathbf{a} \in A \colon \nexists \mathbf{a}' \in A, \mathbf{a}' \prec \mathbf{a}\}. \tag{3}$$

The solution to an MOP consists of finding the optimal set of non-dominated decision vectors in all X, which cannot be improved in any objective without worsening at least another objective. This set is known as the *Pareto Optimal Set*, and its image is named the *Pareto Optimal Front*.

The hypervolume indicator [15] determines the size of the portion of the objective space that is dominated by a set A of non-dominated solutions, collectively and bounded by a reference point $\mathbf{z} \in \mathbb{R}^m$, defined as:

$$HV(A; \mathbf{z}) = \Lambda \left(\bigcup_{\mathbf{a} \in A} \{\mathbf{x} \mid \mathbf{a} \prec \mathbf{x} \prec \mathbf{z}\} \right), \tag{4}$$

where Λ denotes the Lebesgue measure in $\mathbb{R}^m$, and $\mathbf{z}$ should be dominated by all members of A.

Another concept is the *inclusive hypervolume* of a solution $\mathbf{p}$ which is used to denote the size of the part of the objective space dominated by $\mathbf{p}$ alone, that is:

$$IncHV(\mathbf{p}; \mathbf{z}) := HV(\{\mathbf{p}\}; \mathbf{z}). \tag{5}$$

The *hypervolume contribution* or *exclusive hypervolume* of a solution $\mathbf{p}$ relative to a set A (denoted as $ExcHV(\mathbf{p}, A; \mathbf{z})$) is the size of the part of the objective space that is dominated by $\mathbf{p}$ but is not dominated by any element of A. Hence, $ExcHV(\mathbf{p}, A; \mathbf{z}) < IncHV(\mathbf{p}; \mathbf{z})$. The exclusive hypervolume is defined as:

$$ExcHV(\mathbf{p}, A; \mathbf{z}) := HV(A \cup \{\mathbf{p}\}; \mathbf{z}) - HV(A; \mathbf{z}). \tag{6}$$

In this work, we focus on SMS-EMOA since it is one of the most important HV-based MOEAs [9]. SMS-EMOA is a steady-state MOEA that employs the Pareto dominance relation as its main selection criterion and a density estimator based on the exclusive hypervolume. At each iteration, a single solution is created and added to a temporary population which is divided into layers, using the non-dominated sorting algorithm [7]. If the last layer (the worst one according to the Pareto dominance) has more than one solution, the one having the minimum exclusive hypervolume is deleted. The identification of the minimum exclusive hypervolume value is the core idea behind SMS-EMOA. Software frameworks for evolutionary multi-objective optimization, such as jMetal and MOEA framework implement this step using a naïve approach that iteratively calculates the hypervolume indicator of $|P| - 1$ individuals, as shown in Algorithm 1.

Algorithm 1. Naive method to determine the solution with the lowest exclusive hypervolume.

Input: $A \subset Z$ set of solutions, reference point $\mathbf{z}$
Output: Solution $\mathbf{s}$ that contributes the least to $HV(A; \mathbf{z})$
1: $t \leftarrow HV(A; \mathbf{z})$
2: $m \leftarrow \infty$
3: **for all** $\mathbf{a} \in A$ **do**
4:    $c \leftarrow t - HV(A \setminus \{\mathbf{a}\}; \mathbf{z})$
5:    **if** $c < m$ **then**
6:       $m \leftarrow c$
7:       $\mathbf{s} \leftarrow \mathbf{a}$
8:    **end if**
9: **end for**
10: **return** $\mathbf{s}$

3   IWFG 1.01 Algorithm

In Algorithm 2, we reproduce the pseudocode of IWFG 1.01 [5]. This improved version of Algorithm 1 consists of two phases: the slicing process (lines 1 to 8), and the full computation of the exclusive hypervolume of the least-contributing solution (lines 9 to 14). Here, *head* and *tail* are list functions.[1] In the first phase, *Rank heuristic* imposes the order in which objectives will be processed (in a worsening sequence). The overall HV is then processed in "slices" made by cuts along the corresponding objective. Those slices related to a solution $\mathbf{a}$ are stored in the list $S[\mathbf{a}]$ (line 3). The elements of this list are assumed to be ordered by size from the largest to the smallest. In lines 4 and 5, the biggest slice of a solution $\mathbf{a}$ is successively divided by making $k - 1$ cuts along the remaining objectives. These sub-slices are reinserted into the list $S[\mathbf{a}]$. In line 7, for each solution, the partial exclusive hypervolume relative to the biggest slice is determined. In the second phase, a greedy approach is adopted, named "best-first" queuing mechanism. The idea is to process at each iteration the solution $\mathbf{s}$ with the smallest partial HV until its list of slices has been completely processed. Moreover, instead of using the expression (6) for calculating the exclusive hypervolume, IWFG 1.01 uses a more efficient mechanism [2]:

$$ExcHV(\mathbf{p}, A; \mathbf{z}) := HV(\{\mathbf{p}\}; \mathbf{z}) - HV(\text{NDS}(B); \mathbf{z}), \tag{7}$$

where

$$B := \{\text{limit}(\mathbf{p}, \mathbf{a}) \mid \mathbf{a} \in A\}, \tag{8}$$

$$\text{limit}(< p_1, \ldots, p_m >, < a_1, \ldots, a_m >)$$
$$:= < \text{worse}(p_1, a_1), \ldots, \text{worse}(p_m, a_m) > .$$

In Fig. 1, we illustrate the two different ways to compute the exclusive hypervolume. In this case, expression (7) calculates the HV of only two solutions,

---

[1] For instance, head($[a, b, c, d]$) := a and tail($[a, b, c, d]$) := $[b, c, d]$.

Algorithm 2. Incremental Hypervolume IWFG 1.01

Input: $A \subset Z$ set of solutions, reference point $\mathbf{z}$, depth $k \in \mathbb{N}$
Output: Solution $\mathbf{s}$ that contributes the least to $HV(A; \mathbf{z})$
 1: **for all a** in A **do**
 2: Sort the objectives of **a** according to Rank heuristic, using the binary search
 3: $S[\mathbf{a}] \leftarrow$ the slices for **a** at the top level m
 4: **for** $d = 1$ **to** $k - 1$ **do**
 5: $S[\mathbf{a}] \leftarrow \text{slice}(\text{head}(S[\mathbf{a}]), m - d) \cup \text{tail}(S[\mathbf{a}])$
 6: **end for**
 7: $p[\mathbf{a}] \leftarrow ExcHV(\mathbf{a}, \text{head}(S[\mathbf{a}]); \mathbf{z})$
 8: **end for**
 9: $\mathbf{s} \leftarrow \arg\min_{\mathbf{a} \in A} p[\mathbf{a}]$
10: **while** $S[\mathbf{s}] \neq [\,]$ **do**
11: $p[\mathbf{s}] \leftarrow p[\mathbf{s}] + ExcHV(\mathbf{s}, \text{head}(S[\mathbf{s}]); \mathbf{z})$
12: $S[\mathbf{s}] \leftarrow \text{tail}(S[\mathbf{s}])$
13: $\mathbf{s} \leftarrow \arg\min_{\mathbf{a} \in A} p[\mathbf{a}]$
14: **end while**
15: **return s**

---

whereas expression (6) considers six solutions. This computational effort reduction is because of the filtering of non-dominated solutions. With these ideas, the IWFG 1.01 algorithm determines the exclusive hypervolume in a fraction of the time needed to process the total HV [5].

4   Contribution

In Fig. 2(a), we reproduce a common error of Algorithm IWFG 1.01 using data produced by an MOEA. The program receives as input the file "sample.dat", which contains one front delimited by #, and a reference point with five objectives. As can be noticed, the component throws a fatal error causing an abnormal termination. In this case, the segmentation fault is raised by hardware, which has memory protection, notifying the operating system that the program iwfg attempts to access a memory location that is not allowed.

In order to track the source of this error, we relied on the debugging tools Valgrind (http://valgrind.org) and gdb (https://www.gnu.org/software/gdb). We found that the problem lies in the binarySearch function of Fig. 3 since it does not contemplate the situation of identical solutions, as it is the case for the objective vector $(0.51, 0.46, 0.73, 0.00, 0.00)$ from our example in Fig. 2(a). In evolutionary multi-objective optimization, these copies are known as *indifferent solutions* [4, p. 244], and are occasionally present in a population when variation operators are not applied, so the offspring become clones of the parents. According to expression (3), indifferent solutions are considered non-dominated to each other, so the requirement of the IWFG 1.0 to accept only fronts with non-dominated solutions is still fulfilled. The purpose of the function int binarySearch(POINT p,int d) is to locate the index i at which

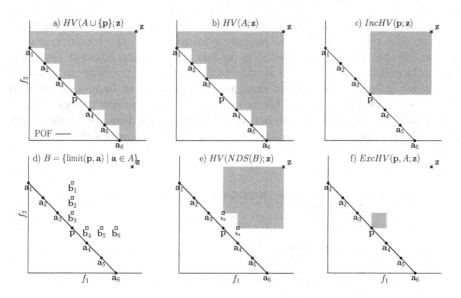

Fig. 1. Steps for the calculation of the exclusive hypervolume of a solution **p** using the naive way $HV(A \cup \{\mathbf{p}\}; \mathbf{z}) - HV(A; \mathbf{z})$ and the efficient way $IncHV(\mathbf{p}; \mathbf{z}) - HV(NDS(B); \mathbf{z})$, where $A = \{\mathbf{a}_1, \mathbf{a}_2, \mathbf{a}_3, \mathbf{a}_4, \mathbf{a}_5, \mathbf{a}_6\}$ and $B = \{\mathbf{b}_1, \mathbf{b}_2, \mathbf{b}_3, \mathbf{b}_4, \mathbf{b}_5, \mathbf{b}_6\}$.

(a)

```
> cat sample.dat
#
0.00  0.00  0.00  0.00  1.00
0.51  0.46  0.73  0.00  0.00
0.47  0.43  0.46  0.45  0.42
0.00  0.47  0.54  0.70  0.00
0.51  0.46  0.73  0.00  0.00
0.00  0.81  0.00  0.58  0.00
0.93  0.00  0.36  0.00  0.00
#
> ./iwfg sample.dat 1.1 1.1
     1.1  1.1  1.1
Segmentation fault (core
     dumped)
```

(b)

```
> ./iwfg sample.dat 1.1 1.1
     1.1  1.1  1.1
mehv(1) = 0.00
Smallest: 0.51  0.46  0.73  0.00
     0.00
Total time = 0.00 (s)
```

Fig. 2. Output of the IWFG 1.01 component using the functions (a) BinarySearch and (b) ourBinarySearch.

the solution p resides in the array of memory addresses `fsorted[d].points[i]`, assuming that elements are already sorted by the given objective d from the highest to the lowest value. The ordering relation is achieved by the function `int greaterorder(&p,&q)`, which numerically compares two solutions. This function returns -1 if the dth objective of p is greater than the dth objective of q. In the opposite case, it returns 1, and if they have the same value, the remainder objectives are inspected in the same way using the order imposed by the Rank heuristic. In the case of indifferent solutions, `greaterorder` returns 0.

During the search, the error originates when the first occurrence of a repeated solution does not match with the memory address of **p**. Thus, the binary search focuses on the upper half of the array in lieu of examining adjacent elements. So, if the solution is not found in this half, the function returns **-1**, which is an invalid index. It is important to mention that the error happens only from three objectives onwards since for two objectives the exclusive hypervolume is computed. The **binarySearch** function is invoked by the Rank heuristic, which stores the returned misinformation. The slicing process accesses the indices, at which point the fault occurs.

```
1  int binarySearch (POINT p, int d) {
2      int min = 0;
3      int max = fsorted [d]. nPoints - 1;
4      gorder = torder [d];
5
6      while (min <= max) {
7          int mid = (max+min) /2;
8          if (p. objectives ==
9              fsorted [d]. points [mid]. objectives )
10             return mid;
11         else if ( greaterorder (&p,
12                 &fsorted [d]. points [mid]) ==-1)
13             max = mid - 1;
14         else
15             min = mid + 1;
16     }
17     return - 1;
18 }
```

Fig. 3. Source code (in ANSI C) of the original binarySearch function.

One possible solution to this issue is to include the case when **greaterorder** recognizes two identical solutions. In Fig. 4, we present the source code of our proposed correction, named **ourBinarySearch**. Once a duplicated objective vector is found, in lines 17 to 32, adjacent memory locations are inspected until there is a match with the address of **p**. In Fig. 2(b), we show the right output of our previous example using the proposed function. It is worth noticing that one of the duplicated solutions is suggested for removal.

The computational complexity of **binarySearch** is $O(m \lg |P|)$, where m represents the number of objectives and $|P|$ is the number of non-dominated solutions in the front. For **ourBinarySearch** is $O(m(\lg |P| + k))$, where k denotes the number of indifferent solutions. Here, the worst case occurs when all elements are repeated, so the computational complexity is $O(m|P|)$. However, this is very unlikely, and in the average case $k << |P|$. Thus, the complexity of our proposed function remains the same as the original one.

```
1 int ourBinarySearch(POINT p, int d) {
2    int i, r;
3    int min = 0;
4    int max = fsorted[d].nPoints-1;
5    gorder = torder[d];
6
7    while(min <= max) {
8       int mid = (max+min)/2;
9
10      if(p.objectives ==
11          fsorted[d].points[mid].objectives)
12         return mid;
13      else if((r = greaterorder(&p, &fsorted[d].points[mid])) == -1)
14         max = mid-1;
15      else if(r == 1)
16         min = mid+1;
17      else { /* (r = 0) duplicated solutions */
18         /* check solutions on the left of mid */
19         i = mid - 1;
20         while(i >= min && greaterorder(&p, &fsorted[d].points[i]) == 0) {
21            if(p.objectives == fsorted[d].points[i].objectives)
22               return i;
23            i--;
24         }
25         /* check solutions on the right of mid */
26         i = mid + 1;
27         while(i <= max && greaterorder(&p, &fsorted[d].points[i]) == 0) {
28            if(p.objectives == fsorted[d].points[i].objectives)
29               return i;
30            i++;
31         }
32      }
33   }
34   return -1;
35 }
```

Fig. 4. Source code (in ANSI C) of our proposed binarySearch function.

The source code of the IWFG 1.0 algorithm, as well as other algorithms, is available at http://computacion.cs.cinvestav.mx/~rhernandez, being the IWFG modules thread-safe. EMO Project runs on Unix-based systems, and it is implemented in ANSI C, MPI (Message Passing Interface) and Gnuplot (http://www.gnuplot.info). As shown in Fig. 5, EMO Project is constituted by three main parts: the applications, the EMO library, and the parallelization layer. In addition, there are two special actors: the common user and the developer. The former can invoke predefined applications, while the second can define new problems, implement algorithms and create more applications. The applications consist of a set of command-line programs, which start with the prefix "emo_", and their purpose is to perform essential operations in evolutionary multi-objective optimization. The EMO library is composed of a set of built-in functions and structured data types, whereas the parallelization layer allows, among other functionalities, the simultaneous execution of different MOEA calls over a set of available processors using a Round-robin scheme. Interested readers are referred to [11] for further details.

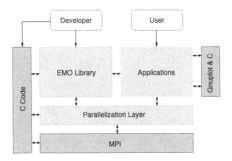

Fig. 5. Architecture of the evolutionary multi-objective optimization project (EMO Project).

5 Experimental Study

We compared the performance of IWFG 1.01 versus the variant that calculates the HV using the method described in [13], and determines the contributions with Algorithm 1. This latter version, commonly applied in most frameworks, is denoted here as IWFG 1.00. Both versions were coupled to SMS-EMOA. Additionally, we considered in our experiments NSGA-III [6], which was designed to deal with many-objective optimization problems. In the survival selection mechanism of this optimizer, the non-dominated sorting procedure [7] is combined with a niching strategy that requires a set of well-spread reference points in such a way that the population is normalized and associated with the lines passing through the reference points and the origin. Those individuals having the closest perpendicular distance to isolated lines are chosen for the next generation.

As test problems, we adopted the DTLZ1, DTLZ2, and DTLZ7 instances [8] with the number of decision variables of $m + 4$, $m + 9$, and $m + 19$, respectively. The variation operators were Polynomial-based mutation and Simulated Binary Crossover (SBX). For the mutation operator, its probability and distribution index were set to $1/n$ and 20, respectively. For the crossover operator, these parameters varied according to the number of objectives: for two objectives we adopted 0.9 and 20, whereas for higher dimensionality we adopted 1.0 and 30. In all cases, the population size was set to 100 individuals. The set of reference points for NSGA-III was generated using the Uniform Design method [12] having the same cardinality as the population. The maximum number of evaluations (1×10^3) was set to 40, 60, 70, 80, 80, 90 for 2 to 7 objectives, respectively.

For the performance assessment, we relied on the hypervolume indicator using the reference point $(2, 2, \ldots)$ for DTLZ1,2 and $(2, 2, \ldots, 2m + 1)$ for DTLZ7. In all experiments, we performed ten independent runs. Besides, we applied two Wilcoxon rank sum tests to the mean hypervolume indicator values in order to determine: A) if the distributions of both variants of SMS-EMOA were identical or different (two-tailed test), and B) if SMS-EMOA IWFG 1.01 performed better than NSGA-III (one-tailed test). Both statistical tests were contemplated at the confidence interval of 99%. Finally, executions have been done over the

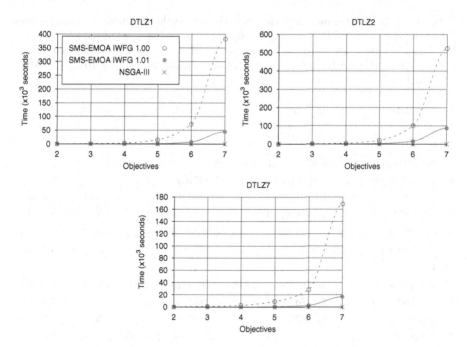

Fig. 6. Average execution time of the MOEAs on some instances of the DTLZ benchmark.

GNU/Linux Xiuhcoatl Cluster of 72 nodes with 252 GB of RAM and InfiniBand interconnection network. Each node is a 32-core AMD Opteron(TM) Processor 6274 1.36 GHz. Algorithms were implemented in the C language, compiled with gcc 4.4.7 -O3 and parallelized with Open MPI version 3.0.0 using the command emo_task [11].

In Fig. 6, we show the average execution time of all optimizers. As expected, the fastest algorithm was NSGA-III since its computational complexity of $\mathcal{O}(|P|^2 m + m^3)$ is much lower than that of HV-based MOEAs. In the second place was SMS-EMOA IWFG 1.01, which spent much less computational time than SMS-EMOA IWFG 1.00. Here, it is worth mentioning that time reduction becomes more significant as the number of objectives increases. Regarding the quality of the solutions in terms of the hypervolume indicator (see Table 1) both versions of SMS-EMOA produced slightly different Pareto-front approximations even though we used the same random seeds. This occurs because, during the survival selection process, several individuals may have the same HV contribution. Thus, the choice of the methods depends on the way in which the population is sorted. In spite of this, there is no significant difference in quality.

Although SMS-EMOA IWFG 1.01 is not the fastest state-of-the-art algorithm, it achieved results which are significantly better than those generated by NSGA-III, in all cases (see Table 1). The only exception is DTLZ7 with four objectives in which there was a tie.

Table 1. Median and standard deviation of the hypervolume indicator. If the p-value of test A is greater than 0.01, then it means that the two samples of SMS-EMOA are equivalent (denoted by $=$). If the p-value of test B is less or equal than 0.01, then it means that SMS-EMOA IWFG 1.01 performs significantly better than NSGA-III (indicated by $\uparrow$).

m	SMS-EMOA IWFG 1.00		SMS-EMOA IWFG 1.01		NSGA-III		p-value Test A	Test B
DTLZ1								
2	3.873652e+0	1.8e-4	3.873610e+0	1.5e-4	3.865911e+0	3.2e-4	9.1e-1 =	9.1e-5 ↑
3	7.974010e+0	4.8e-5	7.974043e+0	8.3e-5	7.937169e+0	1.0e-3	7.1e-1 =	9.1e-5 ↑
4	1.599436e+1	3.1e-5	1.599437e+1	1.2e-5	1.590821e+1	2.9e-3	2.4e-1 =	8.0e-5 ↑
5	3.199857e+1	6.1e-5	3.199859e+1	5.1e-5	3.184074e+1	8.5e-3	4.9e-1 =	9.0e-5 ↑
6	6.399957e+1	2.1e-5	6.399956e+1	2.5e-5	6.368232e+1	4.4e-2	5.2e-1 =	9.0e-5 ↑
7	1.279999e+2	4.2e-5	1.279999e+2	4.8e-5	1.273449e+2	7.5e-2	6.5e-1 =	6.4e-5 ↑
DTLZ2								
2	3.211015e+0	1.9e-5	3.211003e+0	2.6e-5	3.200341e+0	2.4e-4	6.5e-1 =	9.1e-5 ↑
3	7.427029e+0	5.4e-5	7.427018e+0	5.8e-5	7.317104e+0	5.8e-3	8.5e-1 =	9.1e-5 ↑
4	1.558050e+1	7.7e-5	1.558050e+1	7.7e-5	1.518218e+1	1.8e-2	1.0e+0 =	9.0e-5 ↑
5	3.168567e+1	7.6e-5	3.168567e+1	7.6e-5	3.067499e+1	3.5e-2	1.0e+0 =	9.0e-5 ↑
6	6.375871e+1	1.1e-4	6.375871e+1	1.1e-4	6.145779e+1	9.7e-2	1.0e+0 =	9.1e-5 ↑
7	1.278103e+2	1.4e-4	1.278103e+2	1.4e-4	1.215988e+2	9.0e-1	1.0e+0 =	8.4e-5 ↑
DTLZ7								
2	4.418220e+0	6.5e-6	4.418217e+0	4.4e-6	4.403340e+0	2.6e-3	1.9e-1 =	8.9e-5 ↑
3	1.357868e+1	1.4e-4	1.357868e+1	1.4e-4	1.312882e+1	6.2e-2	5.2e-1 =	9.1e-5 ↑
4	3.014482e+1	4.2e+0	3.014535e+1	4.2e+0	3.194008e+1	1.4e+0	6.9e-1 =	2.9e-1
5	7.769183e+1	5.8e+0	7.769183e+1	5.8e+0	6.765668e+1	2.2e+0	5.2e-1 =	9.1e-5 ↑
6	2.057445e+2	1.0e+1	1.867199e+2	1.0e+1	1.374160e+2	6.3e+0	2.7e-1 =	9.1e-5 ↑
7	4.257511e+2	3.3e+1	4.264531e+2	2.7e+1	2.601411e+2	1.6e+1	7.2e-1 =	9.1e-5 ↑

6   Conclusions

Recently, an optimized version of the incremental hypervolume algorithm of the Walking Fish Group (IWFG) was proposed. This algorithm determines the solution that contributes the least to the HV of a non-dominated set. However, its use has been limited due to a bug in its implementation. We observed that this error occurs during the slicing process, specifically in the function `binarySearch`, where duplicated solutions are not considered for problems with more than two objectives. In this paper, we have proposed a corrected version of such function, which has an average-case complexity of $O(m \lg |P|)$, where m denotes the number of objectives and $|P|$ the population size. Clearly, there are other possible solutions to this issue, such as to remove duplicated solutions before calculating the incremental hypervolume. However, we have presented the one that we believe is the easiest to update in the component while keeping a low computational cost. The potential performance of the IWFG component should be exploited by the many-objective community since it can achieve high-quality solutions at an affordable computational cost.

References

1. Beume, N., Naujoks, B., Emmerich, M.: SMS-EMOA: multiobjective selection based on dominated hypervolume. Eur. J. Oper. Res. **181**(3), 1653–1669 (2007)
2. Bradstreet, L., While, L., Barone, L.: A new way of calculating exact exclusive hypervolumes. Technical report, UWA-CSSE-09-002, The University of Western Australia, School of Computer Science and Software Engineering (2009)
3. Bradstreet, L., While, L., Barone, L.: A fast incremental hypervolume algorithm. IEEE Trans. Evol. Comput. **12**(6), 714–723 (2008)
4. Coello Coello, C.A., Lamont, G.B., Van Veldhuizen, D.A.: Evolutionary Algorithms for Solving Multi-Objective Problems, 2nd edn. Springer, New York (2007). https://doi.org/10.1007/978-0-387-36797-2. ISBN 978-0-387-33254-3
5. Cox, W., While, L.: Improving the IWFG algorithm for calculating incremental hypervolume. In: 2016 IEEE Congress on Evolutionary Computation (CEC), pp. 3969–3976, July 2016
6. Deb, K., Jain, H.: An evolutionary many-objective optimization algorithm using reference-point-based nondominated sorting approach, part I: solving problems with box constraints. IEEE Trans. Evol. Comput. **18**(4), 577–601 (2014)
7. Deb, K., Pratap, A., Agarwal, S., Meyarivan, T.: A fast and elitist multiobjective genetic algorithm: NSGA-II. IEEE Trans. Evol. Comput. **6**(2), 182–197 (2002)
8. Deb, K., Thiele, L., Laumanns, M., Zitzler, E.: Scalable test problems for evolutionary multiobjective optimization. In: Abraham, A., Jain, L., Goldberg, R. (eds.) Evolutionary Multiobjective Optimization, pp. 105–145. Advanced Information and Knowledge Processing, Springer (2005). https://doi.org/10.1007/1-84628-137-7_6
9. Falcón-Cardona, J.G., Coello, C.A.C.: Indicator-based multi-objective evolutionary algorithms: a comprehensive survey. ACM Comput. Surv. **53**(2) (2020). https://doi.org/10.1145/3376916
10. Fleischer, M.: The measure of pareto optima applications to multi-objective metaheuristics. In: Fonseca, C.M., Fleming, P.J., Zitzler, E., Thiele, L., Deb, K. (eds.) EMO 2003. LNCS, vol. 2632, pp. 519–533. Springer, Heidelberg (2003). https://doi.org/10.1007/3-540-36970-8_37
11. Hernández Gómez, R.: Parallel hyper-heuristics for multi-objective optimization. Ph.D. thesis, CINVESTAV-IPN, Mexico City, Mexico, March 2018
12. Tan, Y., Jiao, Y., Li, H., Wang, X.: MOEA/D plus uniform design: a new version of MOEA/D for optimization problems with many objectives. Comput. Oper. Res. **40**(6), 1648–1660 (2013)
13. While, L., Bradstreet, L., Barone, L.: A fast way of calculating exact hypervolumes. IEEE Trans. Evol. Comput. **16**(1), 86–95 (2012)

14. While, L., Bradstreet, L.: Applying the WFG algorithm to calculate incremental hypervolumes. In: 2012 IEEE Congress on Evolutionary Computation (CEC 2012), Brisbane, Australia, 10–15 June 2012, pp. 489–496. IEEE Press (2012)
15. Zitzler, E.: Evolutionary algorithms for multiobjective optimization: methods and applications. Ph.D. thesis, Swiss Federal Institute of Technology (ETH), Zurich, Switzerland, November 1999
16. Zitzler, E., Thiele, L., Laumanns, M., Fonseca, C.M., da Fonseca, V.G.: Performance assessment of multiobjective optimizers: an analysis and review. IEEE Trans. Evol. Comput. **7**(2), 117–132 (2003)

A Hybrid Hyperheuristic Approach for the Containership Stowage Problem Considering the Ship Stability

Paula Hernández-Hernández[1]($^{\boxtimes}$) [iD], Laura Cruz-Reyes[1] [iD], Patricia Melin[2] [iD],
Norberto Castillo-García[3] [iD], and Claudia Guadalupe Gómez-Santillán[1] [iD]

[1] Tecnológico Nacional de México/I.T. Ciudad Madero, Ciudad Madero, Mexico
paulahdz314@hotmail.com, {laura.cr,claudia.gs}@cdmadero.tecnm.mx
[2] Tecnológico Nacional de México/I.T. Tijuana, Tijuana, Mexico
pmelin@tectijuana.mx
[3] Tecnológico Nacional de México/I.T. Altamira, Altamira, Mexico

Abstract. In this work we face the Containership Stowage Problem, also referred to as Master Bay Planning Problem (MBPP) in the literature. MBPP is an NP-hard combinatorial optimization problem that consists in finding the best plan to load a set of containers into a set of available locations in the containership, subject to several structural and operational constraints. This problem is really difficult to solve and very import in the context of maritime port logistics. Since it is a practical decision-making problem with high complexity and challenging instances, a hybrid hierarchical approach is developed in this paper. Our algorithmic proposal couples a heuristic procedure with a perturbative hyperheuristic. The validation of the proposed approach is performed by solving pseudo-randomly instances available in the literature. The computational results show the efficiency of the proposed hybrid hierarchical algorithm when comparing with the reference results from the literature.

Keywords: Containership Stowage Problem · Hybrid Approach · Ship Stability

1 Introduction

In this paper we tackle the containership stowage problem, also known as the Master Bay Planning Problem (MBPP) in the literature. In general, combinatorial optimization problems commonly arise in the context of maritime terminals and MBPP is one example of them. In fact, MBPP is a highly important problem involved in the efficiency of port operations. This is so because subsequent problems such as quay crane scheduling and yard allocation directly depends on the containership stowage plan [1, 2].

MBPP is an NP-hard combinatorial optimization problem that is defined as follows. Let C be the set of n containers of different types to be loaded on the ship and S be the set of m available locations on the containership. The problem is to assign each container to an available location such that all the structural and operational constraints are satisfied, and the total stowage time is minimized.

O. Pichardo Lagunas et al. (Eds.): MICAI 2022, LNAI 13612, pp. 423–433, 2022.
https://doi.org/10.1007/978-3-031-19493-1_33

In the case of optimizing the stowage plan for a single port, the main constraints considered are related to the ship structure. Specifically, they are focused on the size, type, weight, destination, and distribution of the containers to be loaded. We refer the reader to [3] for a more detailed description of these constraints and complete definition of the problem.

As mentioned previously, MBPP is an important problem with many constraints. In the literature, some approaches have been investigated methods to tackle these constraints by means of exact and approximate optimization [1, 3–6]. Recent studies have approached complex problems such as MBPP in a hierarchical way [6–8]. Therefore, in this paper, we investigate an extension of a previously proposed hierarchical method in [8], which has demonstrated finding feasible solutions considering the global ship stability of the overall stowage plan. Nevertheless, this initial experiment used in the first phase a relaxed solution, that is, the constraints of stability were removed. This initial solution was obtained by solving the relaxed mathematical formulation in a commercial optimization software; and the second phase was intended to generate that solution feasible through simple heuristics handled by the hyperheuristic designed with online learning [9].

Clearly, the use of an exact method to obtain an initial solution in real-world complex problems is unpractical since it is a time-consuming process, especially in large test cases. To improve the performance of the algorithm of the literature, we hybridize a deterministic heuristic procedure with the perturbative hyperheuristic. In this contribution a comparative study of these two hybrid hierarchical approaches on the containership stowage problem is presented. In order to demonstrate their efficiency and performance, a computational experiment with pseudo-randomly instances available in the literature has been performed. Computational results demonstrate that both algorithms manage to reach good solutions. However, the hybrid procedure with a deterministic heuristic in the first phase is better in terms of efficiency.

This paper is organized into four parts. Section 2 describes our proposed hybrid approach. Section 3 presents the computational experiment and results. Finally, the last section shows the conclusions.

2   Proposed Hybrid Approach

In this section we describe our hybrid hierarchical approach on the containership stowage problem. This procedure consists of two phases (see Fig. 1). In the first phase a heuristic procedure is executed to generate an initial solution. This procedure is based on the computation of an upper bound from the MBPP literature. The upper bound used in this study was the one with the best performance reported by Cruz-Reyes et al. in [10]. The first phase is fully described in Sect. 2.1. In Sect. 2.2 we present the second phase of our proposed approach, which consist in the perturbative hyperheuristic proposed in [8].

2.1   Initial Solution

In this section, we describe a deterministic heuristic (DH) for MBPP. This heuristic procedure considers the balanced distribution of the containers to find feasible partial

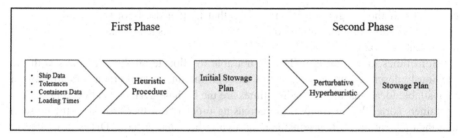

Fig. 1. Hybrid hierarchical approach proposed on the containership stowage problem.

plans. This Algorithm has three main stages: preprocessing (Lines 1–4), feasible assignations (Lines 5–10) and stowage of unassigned containers (Line 11). In the initial stage the preprocessing consists of splitting both the set of locations S and set of containers C. The goal of splitting the locations is to assign the containers into the containership locations considering the stability of the vessel (see Fig. 2). The splitting of containers is performed taking into account their destination and type. The purpose is to minimize the number of unsatisfied constraints. In order to satisfy the *weight constraint*, the containers of each subset are sorted by weight in decreasing order (Line 4), since the heaviest containers must be loaded first.

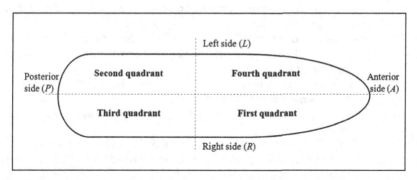

Fig. 2. Distribution of the locations of the containership according to the quadrants [10].

The second stage of the algorithm consists in stowing containers into the containership. More precisely, the procedure tries to load first the 40-feet containers and then the 20-feet containers. In both cases, the loading sequence starts with the containers whose destinations are farther and ends with those whose destinations are closer.

When the algorithm tries to load a container, it must firstly select a quadrant. If it is the first assignation for any type of containers (20-feet or 40-feet), the procedure selects the first quadrant. Otherwise, it orderly searches for the next quadrant with an available location. The 40-feet containers will be assigned to locations in even bays whereas the 20-feet containers will be assigned to locations in odd bays. Once the location has been selected, the algorithm verifies its partial feasibility, that is, without considering the stability. Specifically, it verifies all the constraints excluding those related to the stability conditions. If the assignation is unfeasible, that is, if it does not satisfy all the other constraints apart from the stability ones, the algorithm tries to allocate the container into a different quadrant.

Sometimes, our algorithm (DH) is not able to allocate all the containers with the previously described procedure. In this case, all the unassigned containers are stowed in available locations whose loading times are the highest. DH starts allocating 40-feet containers sorted by destination in decreasing order (from the farthest to the closest) and then allocating 20-feet containers applying the same criteria. DH is described in Algorithm 1.

Algorithm 1: DH Algorithm (S, C).

1. Split S, the locations of the containership, in four subsets according to the stablished quadrants.
2. Split C, according to the destinations of containers. Thus, obtaining set $C' = \{C_1, C_2, ..., C_D\}$, where each C_d denotes the set of containers having as destination port d and D stands for the number of destination ports.
3. Split each C_d according to the type of containers, that is 20' and 40'. Thus, obtaining sets C_{dT} (Twenty) and C_{dF} (Forty), respectively.
4. Sort each C_{dX} in decreasing weight order, where $X \in \{T, F\}$.
5. For each type of container $X \in \{F, T\}$ do:
6.   For each destination d, starting from the last one (D) back to 1, assign first containers belonging to C_{dX} as follows:
7.   Select an unexplored quadrant according to established conditions.
8.   Select a location of the quadrant previously chosen.
9.   If the selected location $l \in S$ is available, verify the feasibility of stowing container $c \in C_{dX}$ into the aforementioned location. If it is feasible, stow c into l.
10.   If the container was not assigned, then go to step 7 to try to assign it in another quadrant.
11. If there are unassigned containers, stow first all the containers in C_{dF} into the available locations whose loading times are the highest. Then, stow all the containers in C_{dT} into the remaining locations with the largest loading times.

2.2 Perturbative Hyperheuristic

The perturbative hyperheuristic (HH) approach proposed in this study uses an ant colony optimization (ACO) algorithm as a high-level metaheuristic [11] and seven low level heuristics, which are completely described in [8], that interact directly with the solutions of the problem. HH minimizes the containers loading time on the ship and optimizes the global ship stability of the overall stowage plan. Since the initial solution generated by DH does not consider the stability conditions, the hyperheuristic makes it feasible by performing perturbative moves.

We consider the objective function $Z(x) = M(\sigma_1(x) + \sigma_2(x)) + L(x)$ to evaluate the hyperheuristic performance. The traditional objective function is expressed in terms of the sum of the time t_{lc} required for loading a container c in location l, such that $L = \sum_{lc} t_{lc}, \forall c \in C, l \in S$. However, in this paper, like in [7], the objective function considers the ship stability but also the total loading time $L(x)$. In this function $\sigma_1(x)$ and $\sigma_2(x)$ are the horizontal and cross equilibrium stability violation functions, respectively. M is a coefficient, such that $M \gg 0$, to strongly penalize, the stability violation functions, in such a way that we give a high priority to the generation of feasible solutions.

The ant hyperheuristic process is showed in Algorithms 2–4, which is performed by the *hyperheuristic agents* supplied with an initial solution S_0 obtained by DH. These agents travel through the graph G traing to improvement its solution. The set of vertices of the graph contains the seven low level heuristics while the set of directed edges joins to every heuristic to each other. Once obtained the initial solution, HH applies to it a heuristic, which generates a new candidate solution. This solution is feasible if satisfies the weight, assignment, and destination constraints of MBPP [1]. This process is performed until a maximal number of cycles is reached. In this approach, a *cycle* is the period of time between all ants beginning their paths and all ants completing their paths. The algorithm can be divided into three stages.

In the first stage (see Algorithm 2), so-called *initialization*, visibility table does not have information and all pheromone table is initialized with a low value named τ_0. First, the ants are located uniformly among the vertices of the network (line 4). After that, they are provided with an initial solution $S = S_0$ (line 7) and each ant applies to its copy of S, the heuristic i (corresponding to its location) to provide an initial visibility value (line 12). Each ant adds its first heuristic i to its respective path (line 9).

Algorithm 2: Initialization ($G = (V, E), S_0$)

```
 1. Initialize: S ← S₀, S_bc ← S₀, S_g ← S₀, h_bc ← 0
 2. For each vertex i set an initial value η_i ← 0
 3. For each edge (i,j) set an initial value τ_ij ← τ₀
 4. Scatter the ants uniformly on the |H| vertices
 5. For each ant k do
 6.    Initialize the path P_k ← {∅}
 7.    Provide a copy of initial solution S_k ← S
 8.    Apply heuristic i to solution S_k to produce S'_k
 9.    Add to path P_k ← P_k ∪ i
10.    Update S_bc and h_bc
11.       if S'_k is better than S_bc, then   S_bc ← S'_k and h_bc ← i
12.    Update η_i visibility value
13. End for
```

Subsequently (see Algorithm 3), the next stage is the *construction process*. The ants then construct a path (sequence of heuristics) by traversing the hyperheuristic network. The choice of the next vertex (heuristic) to be added is done probabilistically at each construction step (line 4). Later, each ant traverses the arc to the selected vertex, and applies the heuristic represented by that vertex to its current solution (line 5). Visibility table is updated when all ants have completed one construction step of the path. This updating process is done until all ants construct their paths completely.

Algorithm 3: ConstructionProcess ($G = (V, E)$, S, S_{bc}, S_g, h_{bc})

```
 1.  For each cycle c do
 2.    For each step s do
 3.      For each ant k do
 4.        Apply the selection rule: j = f({p_{k,i,j}|j ∈ H})
 5.        Apply heuristic j to solution S_k to produce S'_k
 6.        Add to path P_k ← P_k ∪ j
 7.        Update S_bc and h_bc
 8.          if S'_k is better than S_bc, then  S_bc ← S'_k and h_bc ← j
 9.      End for
10.      Update η_j visibility value
11.    End for
12.    UpdateProcess (G = (V,E), S, S_bc, S_g, h_bc)
13.  End for
```

In the *update process*, final stage of the algorithm HH (see Algorithm 4) the ants evaluate their generated solution. Additionally, each ant deposits the pheromone trail on the traveled path (line 1), that is, the sequence of low level heuristics selected for it. A further description of the selection and update rules used in HH can be found in [8]. At the end of each cycle all of the ants are relocated in region of the solution space where the best solution of that cycle was found. Then, in the next cycle the ants start their paths at the vertex of the network whose associated heuristic discovered the best solution of the previous cycle (lines 2–7). Finally, HH returns the best solution S_g found during all cycles.

Algorithm 4: UpdateProcess ($G = (V, E)$, S, S_{bc}, S_g, h_{bc})

```
 1.  Update τ_{i,j} pheromone trail
 2.    For each ant k do
 3.      S ← S_bc
 4.      Provide a copy of best solution of the cycle S_k ← S
 5.      i ← h_bc
 6.      i_k ← i
 7.    End for
 8.    Update S_g   //S_g is the output of the algorithm
 9.      if S_bc is better than S_g, then  S_g ← S_bc
```

3 Computational Experiment

In the following sections we report the conditions under the computational experiment was conducted. Specifically, in Sect. 3.1 we describe the test cases used to assess the performance of our hybrid hierarchical hyperheuristic approach. Section 3.2 reports the hardware and software conditions of the experiment. Finally, in Sects. 3.3, 3.4 and 3.5 we analyze the performance of our proposed solution method against the one proposed in the literature.

3.1 Test Cases

In order to validate our hybrid hierarchical approach, we used the dataset formed by small-sized instances [3, 8]. Table 1 reports the containers characteristics of the considered 10 instances, showing the total number of containers, in TEU and absolute number (n), the number of containers of types 20' (T) and 40' (F), the number of containers for three classes of weight (L: low, M: medium, H: : high) and the partition of containers for each destination.

These instances concern a small size containership, with a maximum capacity of 240 TEU, composed of 12 odd bays, 4 rows and 5 tiers (3 in the hold and 2 in the upper deck, respectively). Table 2 shows the loading times for the small containership. The maximum horizontal weight tolerance (Q_1) was fixed to 18% of the total weight of all containers to load. While the maximum cross weight tolerance (Q_2) was fixed to 9% of the total weight, expressed in tons. Respecting MT, that is, the maximum stack weight tolerance of three containers of 20', was fixed to 45 tons and MF (the maximum stack weight tolerance of three containers of 40') was fixed to 66 tons.

Table 1. Containers for the set of small-sized instances.

Instance	TEU	n	Type (n)		Weight (n)			Destination (n)		
			T	F	L	M	H	D_1	D_2	D_3
1	69	50	31	19	23	25	2	23	27	0
2	83	60	37	23	26	32	2	27	33	0
3	85	65	45	20	30	33	2	31	34	0
4	88	65	42	23	29	34	2	31	34	0
5	90	70	50	20	31	37	2	30	40	0
6	90	75	60	15	35	38	2	32	43	0
7	93	65	37	28	30	33	2	31	34	0
8	93	70	47	23	29	39	2	32	38	0
9	93	70	47	23	31	36	3	25	20	25
10	94	74	54	20	34	38	2	25	25	24

Table 2. Loading times for the set of small-sized instances, the times are expressed in 1/100 ofminute, taken from [7].

	Tier 02	Tier 04	Tier 06	Tier 82	Tier 84
Row 04	270	260	250	240	230
Row 02	260	250	240	230	220
Row 01	250	240	230	220	210
Row 03	240	230	220	210	200

3.2 Infrastructure

The computational experiment was carried out under the Microsoft Windows 7 Home Premium Operating System. The solution method was implemented in Java (JDK 1.6) and NetBeans 7.2 Integrated Development Environment. Solver Gurobi 5.0.1. Regarding the hardware, the proposed approach was executed on a computer with an Intel Core i5 CPU M430 at 2.27 GHz and 4 GB of RAM. Both algorithms were implemented and executed under the same conditions to compare them fairly.

3.3 EHA Performance Measurement

EHA is a two-phase algorithm. In the first phase a partial solution, named Relaxed 0/1 LP formulation, is obtained by means of an exact method. Specifically, the solution is generated by solving a relaxed binary linear programming formulation until the first feasible solution is found. In this phase EHA uses the well-established commercial optimization engine GUROBI. Moreover, the relaxed formulation is the complete binary linear programming model proposed in [1] without considering the horizontal and cross equilibrium constraints. In the second phase the hyperheuristic algorithm presented in Sect. 2.2 is executed.

3.4 HHA Performance Measurement

HHA is a hybrid hierarchical algorithm consisting of two phases. Unlike the previous procedure EHA, HHA generates the initial solution by means of the deterministic heuristic DH described in Sect. 2.1. DH has empirically demonstrated a good performance on the set of tested instances in terms of the loading percentage and computational time [10]. Like EHA, the second phase of HHA consists in executing the hyperheuristic detailed in Sect. 2.2.

3.5 Experimental Results and Discussion

Table 3 shows the computational results obtained by EHA and HHA for the set of instances described in Sect. 3.1. The results are presented in two main columns: one for EHA and the other for HHA. For each algorithmic procedure, we report the objective value of the initial solution (*Obj*) and the execution time spent to generate the initial solution (*CPU Time*). Additionally, we report the average objective value reported by HH (*Avg Obj*), the average executing time of the second phase (*Avg Time*), and the average CPU time of both phases (*Tot Time*). The objective values are the total loading time and are expressed in 1/100 of a minute. Furthermore, the CPU time measured in this research is given in seconds.

Table 3. Comparison of the performance of HHA with respect to EHA.

Inst.	EHA					HHA				
	Relaxed 0/1 LP formulation*		HH			DH		HH		
	Obj	CPU Time	Avg Obj	Avg Time	Tot Time	Obj	CPU Time	Avg Obj	Avg Time	Tot Time
1	11970	4.081	11996.666	7.359	11.440	12040	0.032	11961	0.392	0.424
2	14590	23.975	14363	8.733	32.708	14340	0.000	14301	0.499	0.499
3	15610	14.723	15544.666	9.852	24.576	15650	0.000	15578	0.514	0.514
4	15650	19.874	15523.666	10.374	30.248	15670	0.000	15571.666	0.294	0.294
5	16790	29.659	16743.666	9.554	39.213	16870	0.000	16746.333	0.479	0.479
6	18000	31.245	17949.333	11.112	42.358	17930	0.000	17874.666	0.430	0.430
7	15200	8.505	15389	10.441	18.946	15560	0.000	15469.666	0.300	0.300
8	16760	25.651	16712	11.165	36.817	16780	0.016	16716.666	0.666	0.682
9	16820	36.064	16746.666	14.205	50.269	16810	0.000	16745	0.696	0.696
10	17980	40.735	17758.666	11.565	52.301	17810	0.000	17740.333	0.655	0.655
Avg	15937	23.451	15872.733	10.436	33.888	15946	0.004	15870.433	0.492	0.497

*It was stopped when the first feasible solution is reached by the commercial software GUROBI.

In this research, EHA and HHA were executed 30 times for each instance. Both approaches used the following configuration for HH (second phase). The number of ants, the number of low-level heuristics, and the path length were set to 7. The number of ant generations was set to 1000, $\tau_0 = 0.009$, $\alpha = 1.0$, $\beta = 2.0$ and $\gamma = \rho = 0.5$.

From Table 3, we can observe that HHA and EHA have similar performances. More precisely, EHA reached an average total loading time (*Avg Obj*) of 158.727 min and a total CPU time (*Tot Time*) of 33.888 s. Likewise, HHA obtained an *Avg Obj*-value of 158.704 min and a *Tot Time*-value of 0.497 s. It is clear that no algorithm is better than the other in terms of effectiveness (objective value). Nevertheless, HHA outperforms EHA in 98.53% in efficiency (execution time).

In order to statistically validate the computational results, we conducted the well-known Wilcoxon Rank Sum Test through the statistical computing software R. The Wilcoxon test found a p-value of 0.002961. This means that the null hypothesis is rejected, and hence, the differences in efficiency between EHA and HHA are statistically significant with a confidence level of 99.99%.

As can be observed, by swapping the method to generate the initial solution in the first phase, the effectiveness is similar, but the execution time is smaller. Therefore, HHA is more suitable to solve instances arising in the context of the real-world.

4 Conclusions

In this paper we faced the Containership Stowage Problem, also called the Master Bay Planning Problem (MBPP). This is an NP-hard combinatorial optimization problem in the context of maritime ports. In order to solve the problem, we proposed a hybrid hierarchical approach (HHA) based on a deterministic heuristic with a perturbative hyperheuristic. We empirically assess our proposal by comparing its performance against a previous work documented in the literature (EHA). The computational results showed that HHA outperforms EHA by 98.53% in efficiency preserving the quality of the solutions found. This fact was confirmed by the Wilcoxon Rank Sum Test with a confidence level of 99.99%. Taking into account the obtained experimental results, we conclude that our proposal is a good alternative to solve real-world instances for the tackled problem.

Acknowledgments. The authors would like to thank *Tecnológico Nacional de México* for their support in this research. The authors thank the Mexican Council for Science and Technology (CONACYT) for its support through the Mexican National System of Researchers (SNI). Besides, the first author also thanks the CONACYT postdoctoral program for the grant to develop this research.

References

1. Ambrosino, D., Sciomachen, A., Tanfani, E.: Stowing a containership: the master bay plan problem. Transp. Res. Part A: Policy Pract. **38**, 81–99 (2004)
2. Steenken, D., Voß, S., Stahlbock, R.: Container terminal operation and operations research-a classification and literature review. OR Spectrum **26**(1), 3–49 (2004)
3. Cruz-Reyes, L., et al.: Constructive algorithm for a benchmark in ship stowage planning. In: Castillo, O., Melin, P., Kacprzyk, J. (eds.) Recent Advances on Hybrid Intelligent Systems. Studies in Computational Intelligence, vol. 451, pp. 393–408. Springer, Heidelberg (2013). https://doi.org/10.1007/978-3-642-33021-6_31
4. Cruz-Reyes, L., et al.: A loading procedure for the containership stowage problem. In: Castillo, O., Melin, P., Pedrycz, W., Kacprzyk, J. (eds.) Recent Advances on Hybrid Approaches for Designing Intelligent Systems. SCI, vol. 547, pp. 543–554. Springer, Cham (2014). https://doi.org/10.1007/978-3-319-05170-3_38
5. Hernández, P.H., et al.: An efficient representation scheme of candidate solutions for the master bay planning problem. In: Melin, P., Castillo, O., Kacprzyk, J. (eds.) Design of Intelligent Systems Based on Fuzzy Logic, Neural Networks and Nature-Inspired Optimization. SCI, vol. 601, pp. 441–453. Springer, Cham (2015). https://doi.org/10.1007/978-3-319-17747-2_33
6. Delgado, A., Jensen, R.M., Janstrup, K., Rose, T.H., Andersen, K.H.: A constraint programming model for fast optimal stowage of container vessel bays. Eur. J. Oper. Res. **220**, 251–261 (2012)
7. Ambrosino, D., Anghinolfi, D., Paolucci, M., Sciomachen, A.: A new three-step heuristic for the master bay plan problem. Maritime Econ. Logist. **11**, 98–120 (2009)
8. Hernández, P., et al.: An ant colony algorithm for improving ship stability in the containership stowage problem. In: Castro, F., Gelbukh, A., González, M. (eds.) Advances in Soft Computing and Its Applications. LNCS (LNAI), vol. 8266, pp. 93–104. Springer, Heidelberg (2013). https://doi.org/10.1007/978-3-642-45111-9_8

9. Burke, E.K., Hyde, M.R., Kendall, G., Ochoa, G., Ozcan, E., Woodward, J.R.: Exploring hyper-heuristic methodologies with genetic programming. In: Mumford, C.L., Jain, L.C. (eds.) Computational Intelligence. ISRL, vol. 1, pp. 177–201. Springer, Heidelberg (2009). https://doi.org/10.1007/978-3-642-01799-5_6

10. Cruz-Reyes, L., et al.: Lower and upper bounds for the master bay planning problem. Int. J. Combin. Optim. Probl. Inform. 6(1), 42–52 (2015)

11. Maniezzo, V., Carbonaro, A.: Ant Colony Optimization: An Overview. In: Essays and Surveys in Metaheuristics. Operations Research/Computer Science Interfaces Series, vol. 15, pp. 469–492. Springer, Boston, MA (2002). https://doi.org/10.1007/978-1-4615-1507-4_21

Mathematical Optimization Model for Raw Sugar Unloading Delay from Harbor to Storage Silos

Sidi Mohamed Douiri[✉]

Laboratory of the Mathematics, Computing and Applications,
Mohammed V University in Rabat, Rabat, Morocco
douirisidimohamed@gmail.com

Abstract. In this paper, we are introducing a mathematical model to describe the process of unloading the whole bulk carrier ship's raw sugar cargo, imported by a company, to be stored in storage silos at the refinery. The main point is to optimize the duration of the bulk carrier ship's stay at the harbor deck. First of all a mathematical formula is elaborated to describe the real life process of unloading the whole bulk carrier ship's cargo using a set of inequalities. An algorithm is then proposed to optimize the duration of the bulk carrier ship's stay at the harbor deck which is combining "branch and bound" and "tabu search" methods. The results found are very encouraging since it was possible to minimize the unloading delay from 10 days currently observed to 5 days as well as the scenarios found using the mathematical model were actually applicable in reality.

Keywords: Raw sugar unloading · Mathematical model · Branch and bound · Tabu search

1 Introduction

This paper will summarize the study, analyzes and modeling conducted, in an internship at a Company refinery. The subject of this internship turned about studying and minimizing the delay of unloading the bulk carrier ship's raw sugar cargo at the harbor which will be transported by a fleet of trucks from the deck to the storage silos. The analyses of the studied problem fixed as an additional goal to suggest an optimal manner to guaranty the unloading of the whole of the bulk carrier ship's cargo in less than 5 days in order to avoid any penalty or additional cost to ship charters.

The problem studied in this paper is a logistic one, and more specifically a transport problem. This category of problem consists on organizing and optimizing the tours of a fleet of vehicles. To resolve this kind of problem we can use either an "exact method" witch allows us to find the optimal solution of the problem, or an "approximate method" or "metaheuristic" providing us an approximate solution in a reasonable calculation time [8,9].

O. Pichardo Lagunas et al. (Eds.): MICAI 2022, LNAI 13612, pp. 434–445, 2022.
https://doi.org/10.1007/978-3-031-19493-1_34

In the maritime sector, closely impacting our study case, it is essential to respect delivery times and reduce the costs of various container handling and transfer operations, taking into account the productivity of the harbor. Improving the performance of a harbor is often a very important issue, in particular because of the considerable costs involved in managing it.

Following all these stakes several works has been elaborated in the field of scheduling and optimization problems in a maritime terminal as for example, optimization problem for loading operations of outbound containers. In this work the scheduling problem for loading operations is formulated as a mixed linear program model. The objective function is to minimize the make span of loading operations by yard cranes. The mathematical model is based on various assumptions and it includes the potential interferences and rehandle. A heuristic method is developed for solving this problem, namely adaptive large neighborhood search [7]. Another problem consists to study a combination between two knowns problems, the first is the storage location assignment problem, and the second is the straddle carrier scheduling problem. This approach leads to the use of multi-objective optimization. The objective is to minimize the operating cost. To solve the problem an adapted multi-objective tabu search algorithm is proposed.

2 Problem Description and the Mathematical Model

2.1 Problem Description

The process of unloading raw sugar imported by the company is divided into three crucial steps. The first one is the loading of the trucks. At this stage, the company uses a feets of 54 to 104 trucks, with a capacity of 28 Tons each, rented near several carriers to load in the bulk carrier ship's cargo.

The bulk carrier ship accosts generally in a first time at deck T3/T4 where only one crane is assigned to unload it. This phase is called "Relief Phase" and it can last one or two days. The objective of this phase is to reduce the weight of the vessel in order to be able to move it towards quay 36 where two cranes can be assigned to unload it.

The crane assigned to the ship carries out the unloading of the cargo according to the instructions of the bulk carrier vessel's captain who makes sure that the unloading operation will not destabilize the vessel.

The second phase consists on trucking the raw sugar from the deck to the storage silos. In the beginning of this phase, the truck driver covers his truck filled with raw sugar then moves towards the custom office for the control of exit. After that, the charged truck goes towards company refinery taking a path predefined by contract.

The last step is the unloading of the truck's cargo into the storage silos at the refinery. In this phase, a controller at the entrance of refinery checks the papers provided at customs office. The truck is weighed then moves to one of the two hoppers or directly in one of the three storage silos to discharge its cargo. The truck must once again carry out the weighing of its tare before going back to the harbor to start proceeding again. This process is repeated as much as the schift is not finished.

The analysis of the studied process shows that the company can act only on the number of trucks assigned to the process of unloading the bulk carrier ship's cargo. This consideration reduces significantly complexity of the problem in a mathematical modeling and optimization point of view. In front of these considerations, and in order to deal with the problem in a broader horizon, it was decided to consider the problem within a more general framework which remains adaptable to the particular case raised by the company. It is a problem of logistics very running for the industrialists as well for the large accounts having great means as for the small and medium-size companies forced to manage their expenditure as well as possible in order to guarantee good performances and comfortable margins of benefits. The work schedule at the port follows a particular operating mode, working by schift. The day is therefore divided into three schifts, first schift starts from 7:00 until 14:30, second schift starts from 15:00 until 22:30 and third schift starts from 23:00 until 06:30.

2.2   Mathematical Model

There are two categories of trucks with two different capacities that constitute the fleet used for trucking the raw sugar from the deck to the storage silos. The objective is know how much truck is needed from each category to minimize the time of unloading the ship's cargo. This minimization of the unloading's time passes by the maximization of raw sugar's amount discharged in a schift. First of all, we will present the model, then we will define the variables, the parameters and the constants of the problem.

The problem can then be modeled as follows:

Minimize

$$\sum_{k=1}^{15}\sum_{i=1}^{m}\sum_{j=1}^{2} y_i^k x_{ij}^k (n_i^k + 1) T_j^{charg} \tag{1}$$

subject to

$$y_i^k \otimes (\sum_{i=1}^{m} y_{i-1}^k \otimes y_i^k) = 0 \quad (k = 1, 2, ..., 15) \tag{2}$$

$$\overline{x_{ij}^k} n_i^k = 0 \quad (k = 1, 2, ..., 15) \tag{3}$$

$$\sum_{k=1}^{15}\sum_{i=1}^{m}(\sum_{j=1}^{2} x_{ij}^k Q_j)(n_i^k + 1) \geq C_T \tag{4}$$

$$\sum_{p=1}^{i-1}\sum_{j=1}^{2} T_j^{charg} y_i^k x_{ij}^k + \sum_{j=1}^{2} T_j^{charg} x_{ij}^k + \sum_{j=1}^{2} (T_j^{charg} + T_j^{rot}) y_i^k x_{ij}^k n_i^k \leq \sum_{i=1}^{m}\sum_{j=1}^{2} y_i^k x_{ij}^k (n_i^k + 1) T_j^{charg} \tag{5}$$

$$\sum_{j=1}^{2}\sum_{i=1}^{m} y_i^k T_j^{charg} (n_i^k + 1) \leq 420 \quad (k = 1, 2, ..., 15) \tag{6}$$

Where

- y_i^k: binary variable which is worth 1 if the number of trucks in the solution is equal to i or higher than i during the schift k and 0 if not.
- x_{ij}^k: binary variable which is worth 1 if the truck i in the schift k be longs to the category j.
- n_i^k: rotation's number of the trucks i during the schift k.
- T_j^{charg}: loading's time truck of the category j during the schift k.
- T_{jk}^{rot}: rotation's time truck of the category j during the schift k.
- Q_j: capacity's truck of the category j.
- C_T: total capacity of the cargo to be discharged.

Let $m = 420/T_{min}^{charg}$, with T_{min}^{charg} is the time of loading of a truck with smallest capacity (420min=7h = duration of the schift). The objective function minimizes the time required for the unloading of the cargo. Indeed, the minimization of the time for the unloading a cargo effect automatically the duration of the stay of the bulk carrier ship. Constraint (2) ensures the exit of a vector full with 1 and 0 starting from a certain row, the operator used in this constraint is defined as follows: $a \otimes b = \overline{a}b + a\overline{b}$.

Constraint (3) binds the existence of a truck in the solution to the possibility of making rotations. In the other words, if the truck isn't present in solution its number of rotations must be null for not confuse the solution. Constraint (4) constitute not only a stop condition of the process but is also a condition for sizing of the fleet. Constraint (5) represents the working time of a truck that must be less than the total time worked. The last constraint reflects the fact that the total time worked by a schift must not exceed the time of the schift.

3   Branch and Bound and Tabu Search

To solve the problem we use two methods: the first one is the exact method "branch and bound", the second one is "tabu search". In this section we will represent this two methods and some of their applications.

3.1   Branch and Bound

The branch and bound method was first proposed by A. H. Land and A. G. Doig in 1960 [1] for discrete programming, and has become the most commonly used tool for solving NP-hard optimization problems [2]. The name "branch and bound" first occurred in the work of Little et al. On the traveling salesman problem [3,4]. A branch-and-bound algorithm consists of a systematic enumeration of candidate solutions by means of state space search: the set of candidate solutions is thought of as forming a rooted tree with the full set at the root. The algorithm explores branches of this tree, which represent subsets of the solution set. Before enumerating the candidate solutions of a branch, the branch is checked against upper and lower estimated bounds on the optimal solution, and is discarded if it cannot produce a better solution than the best one found so far by the algorithm. This approach is used for a number of NP-hard problems like: integer programming, nonlinear programming, travelling salesman problem, Maximum satisfiability problem and many other problems.

3.2 Tabu Search

Tabu search method, created by Fred W. Glover in 1986 [5] and formalized in 1989, [6] is a metaheuristic search method employing local search methods used for mathematical optimization. Local searches take a potential solution to a problem and check its immediate neighbors (that is, solutions that are similar except for one or two minor details) in the hope of finding an improved solution. Local search methods have a tendency to become stuck in suboptimal regions or on plateaus where many solutions are equally fit.

Tabu search enhances the performance of local search by relaxing its basic rule. First, at each step worsening moves can be accepted if no improving move is available. In addition, prohibitions are introduced to discourage the search from coming back to previously-visited solutions. The implementation of tabu search uses memory structures that describe the visited solutions or user-provided sets of rules [6]. If a potential solution has been previously visited within a certain short-term period or if it has violated a rule, it is marked as "tabu" (forbidden) so that the algorithm does not consider that possibility repeatedly.

4   Proposed Idea

The objective of this work is to find the number of trucks and the number of schifts necessary we need to unload the content of the bulk carrier ship within a period which doesn't exceed 5 days. In order to achieve this objective it has been decided to program the studied real life process of only one schift since all the schifts are identical. At the end of the simulation, the program gives us as output the number of schifts required to discharge the cargo in a minimum possible time and that does not exceed 5 days as well as the number of trucks necessary to ensure unloading. The basic idea was to use the branch and bound method in order to have an initial solution for the tabu search algorithm, this initial solution is the number of trucks that can be used to ensure a maximum unloaded quantity. The tabu search gives thus the best scenario which proposes the number of trucks of each category, their order of passage and the quantity discharged in each schift using the consideration before. The major difficulty we were confronted to when solving the problem was the large number of variables involved. It was necessary to find a way to reduce the number of variables.

This reduction was made possible by the introduction of intermediate variables:

C_j: The number of trucks of the j category required to ensure unloading.
N_j: The total number of rotations made by C_j.

The introduction of these intermediate variables make it possible to rewrite the constraints in the form $AY \leq b$ with Y is a variable vector. To code the constraints in the algorithm we have decided to construct the A_s matrix for schift and the two vectors b_s second member and c_s the objective, these matrix and vectors which serve as input of the branch and bound algorithm, represent the constraints and the objective of the problem which are modeled under the equations. In this work, the branch and bound method was used to solve the reduced model. First, we introduce the adapted branch and bound algorithm used in this paper. The input of the branch and bound algorithm, which we have developed, are A_s, b_s and c_s constructed by a function appointed "MatrixForSchift".

After application of its algorithm, the branch and bound provides a solution consisting of two vectors:

- V_{sol} vector containing the required number of trucks and the number of rotation of each category.
- Q_{sol} is the unloaded quantity by the achieved fleets in the schift.

The tabu search method is used in this work to improve and supplement the results given by the branch and bound algorithm. The algorithm adapted to this method allowed us to have the best scenario to unload the cargo while respecting the constraints and realizing the objective, to be able to arrive at these results one opted for an improvement of the tabu search this improvement is based on the strategy of the "Best fit" that explores the entire neighborhood in order to give the best solution. The algorithm keeps at each iteration the best solution and no solution can be repeated. In order to construct a solution, the algorithm calculates the time made by each combination and the quantity discharged by this combination and retains the best distribution characterized by a maximum unloaded capacity, number of trucks and a minimum unloading time during the schift. It should be noted that it is not always the same distribution since in each schift there are factors that can influence the number of trucks, the unloading time as well as the capacity discharged. This will be seen with more details in the results section.

Algorithm 1:
Input: V_{sol}, Q_{sol}, R, T_r, T_c, T_{schift};
Ensure: V_{max}, Q_{max}, R_{max};
While there are solutions and the number tested is less than N_{max};
$Q_{max} = \text{GetValue}(V_{sol}, Q_{sol}, R, T_r, T_c, T_{schift})$;
if($Q_{max} > Q_{sol}$);
$V_{sol} = V_{max}$;
End if;
$V_{max} = \text{GetNext}(V_{max})$;
End while.

Algorithm 2:
Input: C_t, Q_1, Q_2, T_{1charg}, T_{2charg}, T_{1rot}, T_{2rot}, V_{sol}, Q_{sol}, R, T_r, T_c, T_{schift};
Ensure: V_{max}, Q_{max}, R_{max};
$A_s, b_s, c_s \leftarrow MatrixSchift(C_t, T_{1charg}, T_{2charg}, T_{1rot}, T_{2rot}, Q_1, Q_2)$;

$Q_{sol}, V_{sol} \leftarrow BB(c_s, A_s, b_s)$ % Branch and bound algorithm;
$Q_{max}, V_{max}, R_{max} \leftarrow TabuSearch(V_{sol}, Q_{sol}, R, T_r, T_c, T_{schift})$;

5   Results

In this paper we have treated different situations. In the first one, we have considered that the time of works is continuous and there is no pause in the schift no traffic jam in the path. As shown in the previous model, we consider that the unloading process begins with a first trip, which is considered as a half rotation, then we start calculating the rotations. According to this reconciliation and to know the unloaded quantity, we multiply the number of truck of the fleet by the capacity of the trucks, in order to know the unloaded quantity in the first trip then it is added to the multiplication of the rotation's number by the capacity of the trucks in the fleet.

5.1   Uniform Fleet

Situation 1: No Break No Delay
In this situation, the algorithm shows that 11 trucks can do the mission. Indeed, the company can use just 11 trucks making 79 rotations, so 79 rotations plus the first trip of the 11 trucks allows to unload 2520 Tons in the first schift. Its the same situation for the second schift. For the third schift, the company can use just 7 truck which must make 83 rotations plus the first trip of the whole fleet to ensure 2520 Tons of sugar unloaded. **Situation 2: Break** In this situation we considered that there is a break in each schift. The aim of this consideration is to restore the more realistic results. The break considered causes a decrease in the unloaded quantity in schift which leads to an augmentation of the total unloading duration of the bulk carrier ship. The Table 3 shows that if the 11 trucks make 73 rotations plus the first trip of the whole fleet, the quantity unloaded will be 2352 Tons in the two first schifts. For the third schift, the company can use just 7 truck which must make 77 rotations plus the first trip of the whole fleet to ensure 2352 Tons of sugar unloaded. The Table 4 shows that the number of schift increases from 12 to 13 schifts thus from 4 to 5 days (Tables 1 and 2).

Table 1. Results of simulation without delay and without break

Schifts	Number of trucks	Number of rotations	Unloaded quantity in Tons
Schift 1	11	79	2520
Schift 2	11	79	2520
Schift 3	7	83	2520

Table 2. Required number of schift

Time limit to unload the total quantity	4 days
Total number of schift	12

Table 3. Results of simulation with break

Schifts	Number of trucks	Number of rotations	Unloaded quantity in Tons
Schift 1	11	73	2352
Schift 2	11	73	2352
Schift 3	7	77	2352

Situation 3: Break and Delay

In this part, we introduce a new factor which affects the process of unloading the bulk carrier ship's cargo, it is the delay due to the traffic's problem between the harbor and refinery specially in peak hours to talk into account of the delay's problems, we considered 4 peak hours distributed over day as follows: 8:30, 12:15, 13:45 et 18:00. The delay in each peak hours is simulated using the normal low.

The Table 5 shows the effect of the delay due to traffic to the performance of unload especially in the two first schifts. The result of the last schift is unchanged because there is no peak hour in this schift. So, the introduction of the delay effects the duration of unloading the cargo of the bulk carrier ship. Instead of 13 schifts the operation of unloading in this situation needs 14 schifts, with 11 trucks in the two first schifts and 7 trucks in the last schift. The quantity unloaded will be 2100 Tons in the two first schifts if the 11 trucks make 64 rotations plus the first trip of the whole fleet. For the third schift, the company can use just 7 truck which must make 77 rotations plus the first trip of the whole fleet to ensure 2352 Tons of sugar unloaded. The capacity discharged during the first and the second schifts can be improved as shown in the Table 7 below.

The Table 7 shows that if the 11 trucks make 67 rotations plus one trip of the whole fleet, the quantity unloaded will become 2352 Tons in the two first schifts. For the third schift, the company can use just 7 truck which must make 77 rotations plus one trip of the whole fleet to ensure 2352 Tons of sugar unloaded. These results show that the improvement in unloading performance during the schifts 1 and 2 is possible by increasing the number of trucks from 11 to 17. This improvement means that the effect of the delay caused by peak traffic is offset by the number of trucks. Improvement of the performances of unloading by increasing the number of trucks, has been the subject of study. The

Table 4. Required number of schift

Time limit to unload the total quantity	5 days
Total number of schift	13

Table 5. Results of simulation with break and delay

Schifts	Number of trucks	Number of rotations	Unloaded quantity in Tons
Schift 1	11	64	2100
Schift 2	11	64	2100
Schift 3	7	77	2352

Table 6. Required number of schift

Time limit to unload the total quantity	5 days
Total number of schift	14

Table 7. Improved simulation results with pause and delay

Schifts	Number of trucks	Number of rotations	Unloaded quantity in Tons
Schift 1	17	67	2352
Schift 2	17	67	2352
Schift 3	7	77	2352

Table 8. Required number of schift

Time limit to unload the total quantity	5 days
Total number of schift	13

graph identify the influence of the number of trucks on the unloaded quantity, it represents the results which considered the delay as well as the break. We remark that the unloaded quantity is stagnated from a certain number of trucks. This conclusion is valid for all schifts. Indeed, unnecessary to increase the number of trucks. The saturation threshold for the schift 3 is lower than those of the schift 1 and the schift 2. This finding is logical because the performances of the schift 3 isn't impacted by the delay due to the traffic contrary to the schift 1 and 2, for which an increase in the number of trucks can offset the effect of delay until the stagnation threshold. The Table 9 shows that the company uses 71 trucks during the first schift to unload a quantity of 1988 Tons, in the second schift the company uses 63 trucks to unload 1764 Tons, the unloaded quantity in the last schift is 1344 Tons with 48 truck. We note that in our simulation a number of 11 trucks allows to unload a quantity of 2100 Tons in front of a number of 71 trucks for the unloading of a quantity of 1988 Tons in reality (Fig. 1 and Tables 6, 8).

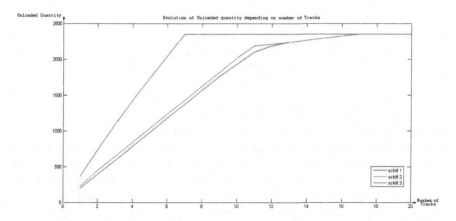

Fig. 1. Evolution of the unloaded quantity according to the number of trucks

Table 9. Results of a working day at the company

Schifts	Number of trucks	Unloaded quantity in Tons
Schift 1	71	1988
Schift 2	63	1764
Schift 3	48	1344

5.2 Diversified Fleet

In this part, we bring out the interest to use a diversified fleet of trucks with two categories, the first with a capacity of 28 Tons and the second with 32 Tons.

Table 10. Simulation of diversified fleet

Schifts	Number of trucks	Order of passage	Number of rotations	Unloaded quantity in Tons
Schift 1	10	1 1 0 1 1 1 1 0 1 0	19 | 44	2248
Schift 2	10	1 1 0 1 1 1 1 0 1 0	19 | 44	2248
Schift 3	7	0 0 0 0 0 0 0	77 | 00	2352

It should be noted that the trucks in category 1 are represented by zeros and those in category 2 by ones. The first number in the box "number of rotation" represents the total number of turns made by the fleet of category one as well as the second is that of category 2. According to the Table 10, if the company use a diversified fleet with 10 trucks, 3 trucks from the first category must do 19 rotations and 7 trucks from the second category must do 44 rotations, plus one trip of the fleet the unload quantity is 2248 Tons in the two first schifts. For the third schift, the algorithm shows that there is no need to use a diversified fleet, just uniform fleet with 7 trucks, with capacity is 28 Tons each, must doing 77 rotations plus one trip of the fleet and the unloaded quantity will be 2352 (Table 11).

Table 11. Required number of schift

Time limit to unload the total quantity	5 days
Number total of schift	14

A comparison of the results in Tables 10 and 5 demonstrates the value of using a diversified fleet as defined above. The fleet used in the simulation of Table 10 allows better unloading performance than the one obtained by the results in Table 5, either in terms of the quantity discharged by schift or in terms of the overall time of unloading of the vessel. It should be noted that the improvement of the results of Table 5 carried out at the level of the simulation of Table 7 allows performance comparable but less than that of the diversified fleet, except that it requires 17 trucks for schifts 1 and 2 against 10 trucks only in the latter case.

6   Conclusion

The conclusions we can draw from the work carried out are the following:

Unloading the whole bulk carrier ship's raw sugar cargo is possible within a period of 5 days from berthing and the operation during the 3 schifts of the day is a necessary condition for unloading the cargo of the bulk carrier within 5 days. A fleet consisting of 11 trucks for the first and the second schift, 7 trucks for the schift 3 is sufficient to unload the bulk carrier within the time limit allowing to the company to avoid additional costs to shippers. The results obtained make it possible to envisage the assignment of a different truck group for each schift according to the dimensions proposed by the solutions. Implementation of this provision could make systematic night schift operation on the one hand and improve the performance and working conditions of the fleet on the other hand. The results obtained in this paper are much better then what actually happens. Indeed, the company unloads the entire cargo of the ship within a period that varies between 8 and 10 days at a fleet of 64 trucks or more. Adding to this, these results are not just numbers that are compared but they are also strategies of controlling several factors in order to obtain the same results existing in this paper. Finally, it is necessary to mention that the model and the resolution developed are not only valid for the company, but also can be perfectly adapted to the context of different companies having an activity similar to the problem of unloading a cargo, from point A to point B via a fleet of trucks.

References

1. Land, A.H., Doig, A.G.: An automatic method of solving discrete programming problems. Econometrica **28**(3), 497–520 (1960)
2. Watermeyer, K., Zimmermann, J.: A partition-based branch-and-bound algorithm for the project duration problem with partially renewable resources and general temporal constraints. OR Spectr. **44**(2), 575–602 (2022)
3. Dey, S.S., Shah, P.: Lower bound on size of branch-and-bound trees for solving lot-sizing problem. Oper. Res. Lett. **50**(5), 430–433 (2022)
4. Egon, B., Paolo, T.: Branch and bound methods for the traveling salesman problem. Carnegie Mellon University Graduate School of Industrial Administration (1983)
5. Glover, F.: Tabu search - Part 1. ORSA J. Comput. **1**(2), 190–206 (1989)
6. Glover, F.: Future paths for integer programming and links to artificial intelligence. Comput. Oper. Res. **13**(5), 533–549 (1986)
7. Chebli, K.: Optimisation des mouvements des conteneurs dans un terminal maritime. Department of mathematics and industrial engineering, polytechnic school of Montreal, Montreal University (2011)
8. Douiri, S.M., Medeni, M.B.O., Elbernoussi, S.: New steganography scheme using graphs product. In: Proceedings of 2014 International Conference on Interactive Collaborative Learning, pp. 525–528, 7017827 (2014)
9. Douiri, S.M., El Bernoussi, S.: An ant algorithm for the sum coloring problem. Int. J. Appl. Math. Stat. **27**(3), 102–110 (2012)

Author Index

Printed in the United States
by Baker & Taylor Publisher Services